seventh
edition

Fundamentals of Early Childhood Education

GEORGE S. MORRISON

University of North Texas

PEARSON

Boston   Columbus   Indianapolis   New York   San Francisco   Upper Saddle River
Amsterdam   Cape Town   Dubai   London   Madrid   Milan   Munich   Paris   Montreal   Toronto
Delhi   Mexico City   São Paulo   Sydney   Hong Kong   Seoul   Singapore   Taipei Tokyo

Vice President and Editorial Director: Jeffery W. Johnston
Senior Acquisitions Editor: Julie Peters
Development Editor: Bryce Bell
Editorial Assistant: Andrea Hall
Director of Marketing: Margaret Waples
Senior Marketing Manager: Chris Barry
Senior Managing Editor: Pamela D. Bennett
Production Project Manager: Carrie Mollette
Senior Operations Supervisor: Matt Ottenweller

Senior Art Director: Laura Gardner
Cover Art: JGI/Jamie Grill/Getty Images
Full-Service Project Management: Thistle Hill Publishing Services, LLC
Composition: S4Carlisle Publishing Services
Printer/Binder: R.R. Donnelley/Willard
Cover Printer: Lehigh Phoenix Color/Hagerstown
Text Font: Garamond

Credits and acknowledgments for material borrowed from other sources and reproduced, with permission, in this textbook appear on the appropriate page within the text.

Every effort has been made to provide accurate and current Internet information in this book. However, the Internet and information posted on it are constantly changing, so it is inevitable that some of the Internet addresses listed in this textbook will change.

Photo Credits: Angie Passons, p. iv; Ariel Skelley/Getty Images, p. 4; Michael Newman/PhotoEdit, pp. 9, 168; Contributed by Jodi Lee Conrad, p. 11; Keturah Collins, pp. 15, 125, 126; bst2012/Fotolia, p. 25; matka_Wariatka/Fotolia, p. 43; darko64/Fotolia, p. 49 (left); Andres Rodriguez/Fotolia, p. 49 (right); Laura Lee Reed, p. 51; David L. Moore/Alamy, p. 54; ZUMA Press, Inc./Alamy, p. 62; Pearson Learning Studio, p. 78; David Bacon/Alamy, p. 84; Bob Ebbesen/Alamy, p. 87; Krista Greco/Merrill, pp. 89 (top), 102, 215; kilukilu/Fotolia, p. 89 (center); Anyka/Fotolia, p. 89 (bottom); BananaStock Ltd., pp. 93, 211 (2nd from right); Monkey Business/Fotolia, pp. 101 (top), 200 (left), 351 (2nd from left); Darren Baker/Fotolia, p. 101 (2nd from top); EyeWire Collection/Getty Images, p. 101 (2nd from bottom); Patrick White/Merrill, p. 101 (bottom); Montessorium, LLC, p. 128 (all); Corbis Bridge/Alamy, p. 129; Lynn B. Rhodes, p. 159; Laura Bolesta/Merrill, p. 166 (top, 2nd from bottom); Comstock Images/Jupiter Unlimited, p. 166 (2nd from top); Annie Pickert/Merrill, p. 166 (center); endostock/Fotolia, p. 166 (bottom); Annie Fuller/Merrill, pp. 170, 372; Patrick White/Merrill, p. 175; Michal Kowalski/Shutterstock, p. 176; Mona Makela/Shutterstock, p. 200 (2nd from left); Felix Mizioznikov/Fotolia, p. 200 (2nd from right); Kenishirotie/Fotolia, p. 200 (right); auremar/Fotolia, p. 211 (right); Ruth Jenkinson/Dorling Kindersley, p. 211 (center left); Karen Ilagan/iStockphoto, p. 211 (center right); George Dodson/Lightworks Studio/PH College, p. 211 (left); Arkady Chubykin/Fotolia, p. 211 (2nd from left); Sean Locke/iStockphoto, p. 213; Used with permission from Darren Murtha Design, p. 224 (all); Stockbyte/Getty Images, p. 235; Felicia Sprayberry, p. 236; SW Productions/Getty Images, pp. 256, 398; AISPIX by Image Source/Shutterstock, p. 262; Lynn Rhodes, pp. 270 (all), 291 (all); Monkey Business Images/Shutterstock, p. 272 (top); Jim West/Alamy, p. 272 (bottom); David Mager/Pearson Learning Photo Studio, p. 284; Celeste E. Hanvey and Kathy Stroud, pp. 304, 306 (all), 309 (all); Rayna Freedman, p. 310 (all); Katelyn Metzger/Merrill, pp. 312, 373; Tetra Images/Alamy, p. 325; Jeff Greenberg/Alamy, p. 326; Anthony Magnacca/Merrill, p. 341; Greystone Digital, p. 342 (top); Ablenet, Inc., p. 342 (2nd from top, 3rd from top, 2nd from bottom, bottom); Touch Screens Inc., p. 342 (3rd from bottom); Janine Wiedel Photolibrary/Alamy, p. 344; Krivosheev Vitaly/Shutterstock, p. 351 (bottom left); iofoto/Fotolia, p. 351 (2nd from right); Goodluz/Fotolia, p. 351 (top right); Scott Foresman/Pearson Education, pp. 356, 371; Kerstin Dautenhahn, p. 375; ZUMA Wire Service/Alamy, p. 377; Bonnie Jacobs/iStockphoto, p. 380; Jim Arbogast/Getty Images, p. 390; Brand X Pictures/Thinkstock, p. 391; Exactostock/SuperStock, p. 408

Library of Congress Cataloging-in-Publication Data

Morrison, George S.
  Fundamentals of early childhood education / George S. Morrison, University of North Texas. — Seventh edition.
    pages cm
  Includes bibliographical references and index.
  ISBN-13: 978-0-13-285337-8 (pbk.)
  ISBN-10: 0-13-285337-X (pbk.)
  1. Early childhood education—United States. I. Title.
  LB1139.25.M67 2014
  372.21—dc23

                                          2012033562

10 9 8 7 6 5 4 3 2 1

ISBN 10:   0-13-285337-X
ISBN 13: 978-0-13-285337-8

For Betty Jane—Whose life is full of grace and whose heart is full of love.

GEORGE S. MORRISON is professor of early childhood education in the Department of Teacher Education and Administration, College of Education, at the University of North Texas. He teaches courses in early childhood education and teacher education to undergraduate and graduate students. He is an experienced public school teacher and principal and has supervised student teachers. In addition to his affiliation with the University of North Texas, Dr. Morrison has been a professor at Edinboro University of Pennsylvania, the University of Tennessee at Martin, and Florida International University.

Professor Morrison's accomplishments include a Distinguished Academic Service Award from the Pennsylvania Department of Education and an Outstanding Service and Teaching Award from Florida International University. His books include *Early Childhood Education Today* (also translated into Spanish and Mandarin Chinese), *Fundamentals of Early Childhood Education* (also translated into Mandarin Chinese and Malay), and *Teaching in America*.

Dr. Morrison is a popular author, speaker, and presenter. He serves on the editorial boards of *Annual Editions: Early Childhood* and the *International Journal of Early Childhood Education* and is senior contributing editor for the *Public School Montessorian*. He also contributes his opinions and ideas to a wide range of publications. His speaking engagements and presentations focus on the future of early childhood education, the globalization of early childhood education, the changing roles of teachers, the influence of contemporary educational reforms on education, and the application of best practices to early childhood education. Professor Morrison also lectures, conducts seminars, and gives keynote addresses on topics of early childhood education in Thailand, Taiwan, South Korea, China, and the Philippines.

Professor Morrison with third graders at the "Science Extravaganza" at Blanton Elementary, Denton, Texas. Professor Morrison regularly judges science fairs, participates in school-based STEM activities, and talks with K–3 children about STEM subjects and careers in STEM.

PREFACE

When I ask my colleagues in early childhood education how I can help them be better professionals, their answers are always the same: They want an early childhood textbook that is user-friendly and applies theory to practice. *Fundamentals of Early Childhood Education,* Seventh Edition, is a textbook that is practical, is based on current research and thinking about how young children learn, and provides concrete classroom examples for how to teach children from birth to age eight.

As you, other early childhood professionals, and the public respond to the changing field of early childhood education, more opportunities arise for new programs, curricula, and appropriate practices to meet the ever-changing needs of children and families. This textbook is designed to develop competent and confident early childhood education professionals, prepared to assume their professional roles in the ever-changing world of early childhood education.

WHAT'S NEW IN THIS EDITION?

Students and professors will benefit from new content and features in this seventh edition:

- Videos embedded in the Pearson eText link you directly to illustrations of children's development and learning, teaching strategies, views of early childhood classrooms, and many more insights into high-quality teaching practices. Look for the play button in the margins to link directly from your Pearson eText to a video that exemplifies, models, or expands upon chapter concepts. Some of these videos also appear in the exercises in MyEducationLab™ for *Introduction to Early Childhood Education,* but many do not.

- A new feature, *Applying Research to Teaching,* examines research to inform specific teaching practices.

- *Teaching and Learning in the Inclusive Classroom,* a new section in each chapter, addresses teaching practices in inclusive environments.

- Fifty percent of the book's content is new to reflect the following important changes occurring in early childhood education today:

  - Teaching with and to the Common Core Standards (CCS)

  - Recent changes in the field influencing the care and education of young children, including new research about children's development and supporting their learning and the changing roles and responsibilities of early childhood professionals

  - The politicization of the field, reflected in the use of early childhood education by politicians to implement national policies regarding the importance of a highly trained and educated workforce of the future, and the accountability surrounding it

  - A growing emphasis on accommodating children with diverse needs, reflecting the increasingly diverse early childhood population and the growing number of children with disabilities

  - The increasing integration of technology in instructional processes

  - Programs and curricula that are increasingly environmentally friendly

- Seventy-five percent of the research is new or updated.
- In response to reviewers' comments, core content examples and illustrations have been increased and extended to make this seventh edition more practical and applied.
- An updated and redesigned Study Plan on MyEducationLab™ provides a practice multiple-choice quiz, enrichment exercises to scaffold learning and increase achievement, and a posttest multiple-choice quiz. See the MyEducationLab™ section for more details about the Study Plan.

FEATURES AND THEIR PURPOSES

The many features in this text were developed with a pedagogical purpose and content focus. They include:

- ***Learning Outcomes.*** These are written to organize the chapter content in advance of reading it and to provide an overview of what you will be expected to know and be able to do after reading the chapter. Review these carefully before you read the chapter, and review them again after you've read the chapter. Also, look over and try to answer or complete the *Activities for Professional Development* at the end of the chapter, which are written to reinforce what you learned in each section of the chapter and are aligned with the *Learning Outcomes.*
- ***Professionalism in Practice.*** Written by experienced teachers and administrators of early childhood programs, these features give you insight into their professional philosophies and behaviors. Many of these are labeled as *Competency Builders*, which include step-by-step strategies, guidelines, or steps to walk students through the details of key tasks expected of them, such as observation, lesson planning, and creating a multicultural classroom. They help students begin building professional competencies in their work with children and families.
- ***Diversity Tie-In.*** Includes a variety of topics to create an awareness of the uniqueness and diversity of all children and families.
- ***Technology Tie-In.*** Includes specific examples of technology use linked to chapter content. Helps future teachers become technologically literate, understand the options available, and use them to their fullest extent to teach, communicate with parents, and manage a classroom.

- ***Portraits of Children.*** To familiarize students with developmental capabilities of children in each age group in the early childhood age range and to become sensitive to universality and diversity in child development, these features put a spotlight on several children in an age range in the Infant and Toddler chapter, the Preschool chapter, the Kindergarten chapter, and the Primary Grades chapter. Photos of children, a list of their capabilities and interests by domain, and questions about developmentally appropriate practice get students thinking about individual needs and approaches and applications to address those needs.
- ***Ethical Dilemmas.*** Scenarios help readers learn to make important professional decisions based on NAEYC's Code of Ethical Conduct.

- **NAEYC Code of Ethical Conduct.** Included in the appendix, this document introduces students to the profession's recommendations and expectations.
- **Correlation to NAEYC Standards for Early Childhood Professional Practice.** The inside cover of the book includes a helpful matrix linking the text's content to the NAEYC Standards. In addition, every chapter-opening page includes the standard or standards relevant to that chapter's topic and what they mean for teachers. This reinforces for students what is expected of them in their work with children, families, and communities.

MyEducationLab™

MyEducationLab™ is an online homework, tutorial, and assessment product designed to improve results by helping students quickly master concepts and by providing educators with a robust set of tools for easily gauging and addressing the performance of individuals and classrooms.

MyEducationLab™ engages students with high-quality multimedia learning experiences that help them build critical teaching skills and prepare them for real-world practice. In practice exercises, students receive immediate feedback so they see mistakes right away, learn precisely which concepts are holding them back, and master concepts through targeted practice.

For educators, MyEducationLab™ provides highly visual data and performance analysis to help them quickly identify gaps in student learning and make a clear connection between coursework, concept mastery, and national teaching standards. And because MyEducationLab™ comes from Pearson, it's developed by an experienced partner committed to providing content, resources, and expertise for the best digital learning experiences.

In *Preparing Teachers for a Changing World,* Linda Darling-Hammond and her colleagues point out that grounding teacher education in real classrooms—among real teachers and students and among actual examples of students' and teachers' work—is an important and perhaps even an essential part of training teachers for the complexities of teaching in today's classrooms.

In the MyEducationLab™ for this course, educators will find the following features and resources.

> **MyEducationLab**
>
> Go to Topic 12 (Professionalism/Ethics) in the MyEducationLab (www.myeducationlab.com) for your course, where you can:
>
> - Find learning outcomes for Professionalism/Ethics along with the national standards that connect to these outcomes.
> - Complete Assignments and Activities that can help you more deeply understand the chapter content.
> - Apply and practice your understanding of the core teaching skills identified in the chapter with the Building Teaching Skills and Dispositions learning units.
> - Access video clips of CCSSO National Teachers of the Year award winners responding to the question, "Why Do I Teach?" in the Teacher Talk section.
> - Hear viewpoints of experts in the field in Professional Perspectives.
> - Check your comprehension on the content covered in the chapter by going to the Study Plan in the Book Resources for your text. Here you will be able to take a chapter quiz, receive feedback on your answers, and then access Review, Practice, and Enrichment activities to enhance your understanding of chapter content.

Advanced Data and Performance Reporting Aligned to National Standards

Advanced data and performance reporting helps educators quickly identify gaps in student learning and gauge and address individual and classroom performance. Educators easily see the connection between coursework, concept mastery, and national teaching standards with highly visual views of performance reports. Data and assessments align directly to national teaching standards, including NAEYC Standards for Early Childhood Professional Preparation Programs, and support reporting for state and accreditation requirements.

Study Plan Specific to Your Text

MyEducationLab™ gives students the opportunity to test themselves on key concepts and skills, track their own progress through the course, and access personalized Study Plan activities.

The customized Study Plan is generated based on students' pretest results. Incorrect questions from the pretest indicate specific textbook learning outcomes the student is struggling with. The customized Study Plan suggests specific enriching activities for particular learning outcomes, helping students focus. Personalized Study Plan activities may include eBook reading assignments and review, practice, and enrichment activities.

After students complete the enrichment activities, they take a posttest to see the concepts they've mastered or areas where they still may need extra help.

MyEducationLab then reports the Study Plan results to the instructor. Based on these reports, the instructor can adapt course material to suit the needs of individual students or the entire class.

Assignments and Activities

Designed to enhance students' understanding of concepts covered in class, these assignable exercises show concepts in action (through videos, cases, and/or student and teacher artifacts). They help students deepen content knowledge and synthesize and apply concepts and strategies they have read about in the book. (Correct answers for these assignments are available to the instructor only.)

Building Teaching Skills and Dispositions

These unique learning units help students practice and strengthen skills that are essential to effective teaching. After examining the steps involved in a core teaching process, students are given an opportunity to practice applying this skill via videos, student and teacher artifacts, and/or case studies of authentic classrooms. Providing multiple opportunities to practice a single teaching concept, each activity encourages a deeper understanding and application of concepts, as well as the use of critical thinking skills. After practice, students take a quiz that is reported to the instructor gradebook and performance reporting.

IRIS Center Resources

The IRIS Center at Vanderbilt University (http://iris.peabody.vanderbilt.edu), funded by the U.S. Department of Education's Office of Special Education Programs (OSEP), develops training enhancement materials for preservice and practicing teachers. The Center works with experts from across the country to create challenge-based interactive modules, case study units, and podcasts that provide research-validated information about working with students in inclusive settings. In your MyEducationLab™ course we have integrated this content where appropriate.

Teacher Talk

This feature emphasizes the power of teaching through videos of master teachers, who tell their compelling stories of why they teach. Each of these featured teachers has been awarded the Council of Chief State School Officers Teacher of the Year award, the oldest and most prestigious award for teachers.

CONNECT Modules

Learn about practices to solve dilemmas in early childhood settings. Videos, activities, and narratives will guide you through a process to learn about serving children with disabilities effectively. These modules are created by the Frank Porter Graham Child Development Institute at the University of North Carolina, Chapel Hill, which has partnered with Pearson in providing these modules for student use.

Course Resources

The Course Resources section of MyEducationLab™ is designed to help students put together an effective lesson plan, prepare for and begin a career, navigate the first year of teaching, and understand key educational standards, policies, and laws.

The Course Resources section includes the following:

- The **Lesson Plan Builder** is an effective and easy-to-use tool that students can use to create, update, and share quality lesson plans. The software also makes it easy to integrate state content standards into any lesson plan.

- The **Certification and Licensure** section is designed to help students pass licensure exams by giving them access to state test requirements, overviews of what tests cover, and sample test items.

  The Certification and Licensure section includes the following:

  - **State Certification Test Requirements:** Here, students can click on a state and be taken to a list of state certification tests.

  - Students can click on the **Licensure Exams** they need to take to find:
    - Basic information about each test
    - Descriptions of what is covered on each test
    - Sample test questions with explanations of correct answers

  - **National Evaluation Series**™ by Pearson: Here, students can see the tests in the NES, learn what is covered on each exam, and access sample test items with descriptions and rationales of correct answers. Students can also purchase interactive online tutorials developed by Pearson Evaluation Systems and the Pearson Teacher Education and Development group.

  - **ETS Online Praxis Tutorials:** Here, students can purchase interactive online tutorials developed by ETS and by the Pearson Teacher Education and Development group. Tutorials are available for the Praxis I exams and for select Praxis II exams.

- The **Licensure and Standards** section provides access to current state and national standards.

- The **Preparing a Portfolio** section provides guidelines for creating a high-quality teaching portfolio.

- **Beginning Your Career** offers tips, advice, and other valuable information:

  - *Resume Writing and Interviewing*: Includes expert advice on how to write impressive resumes and prepare for job interviews.

  - *Your First Year of Teaching*: Provides practical tips to set up a first classroom, manage student behavior, and more easily organize for instruction and assessment.

  - *Law and Public Policies:* Details specific directives and requirements needed to understand the No Child Left Behind Act and the Individuals with Disabilities Education Improvement Act of 2004.

- The **Multimedia Index** aggregates resources in MyEducationLab™ by asset type (e.g., video or artifact) for easy location and retrieval.

Visit** www.myeducationlab.com **for a demonstration of this exciting new online teaching resource.

ACKNOWLEDGMENTS

In the course of my teaching, service, consulting, and writing, I meet and talk with many early childhood professionals who are deeply dedicated to doing their best for young children and their families. I am always touched, heartened, and encouraged by the openness, honesty, and unselfish sharing of ideas that characterize my professional colleagues. I thank all the individuals who contributed to the *Professionalism in Practice, Diversity Tie-In,* and *Technology Tie-In* features, as well as other program descriptions. They are all credited for sharing their personal accounts of their lives, their children's lives, and their programs.

I value, respect, and use the feedback and sound advice provided by the following reviewers: Linda Bufkin, Saint Louis University; Benita Flores, Del Mar College; Michele Herrera, Post University; Linda M. Mitchell, Wichita State University; and Kevin J. Swick, University of South Carolina.

I am blessed to work with my colleagues at Pearson. My editor, Julie Peters, is always thinking of ways to make *Fundamentals* an even better book. Julie is a constant source of bright and exciting ideas and is continually opening new doors and possibilities. I can always count on her for wise counsel about how to make *Fundamentals* more engaging and relevant for students and professors. Development Editor Bryce Bell is a pleasure to work with. Bryce is attentive to details, conscientious, and provides many insightful suggestions for making *Fundamentals* better. Because of Bryce's devotion to excellence, *Fundamentals* is a much better book. Andrea Hall, Editorial Assistant, is an expediter *par excellence*. Andrea is always pleasant and efficient and gets the job done. Project Managers Carrie Mollette and Angela Williams Urquhart (Thistle Hill Publishing Services) are very attentive to detail and always make sure every part of the production process is done right.

Finally, I want to thank my wonderful team of student assistants: Cassie Blake, Dylan Lee, and Amanda Bower. Thank you for your hard work! Cassie is positive, focused, dedicated, and smart. She gets the job done! Thank you, Cassie, for working late nights and weekends to help meet all the deadlines and last-minute requests! Dylan is dependable and helpful. I can always depend on Dylan to move our project along. Amanda is resourceful, dedicated, and an expert at researching and finding materials.

SUPPLEMENTS TO THE TEXT

All supplements are available online. To download and print supplement files, go to www.pearsonhighered.com and select "Catalog & Instructor Resources" from the "Educators" menu.

Online Instructor's Manual (0-13-336416-X) This manual contains chapter overviews and activity ideas to enhance chapter concepts, as well as instructions for assignable MyEducationLab™ material.

Online Test Bank (0-13-285403-1) The Test Bank includes a variety of test items, including multiple-choice, true/false, matching, and short-answer items.

TestGen (0-13-285406-6) This powerful test generator is for use in conjunction with the TestGen testbank file for your text. Assessments may be created for print or online testing. You install TestGen on your personal computer (Windows or Macintosh) and create your own tests for classroom testing and for other specialized delivery options, such as over a local area network or on the Web.

The tests can be downloaded in the following formats:

TestGen—PC

TestGen—MAC

TestGen—Blackboard 9

TestGen—Blackboard CE/Vista (WebCT)

Angel

D2L

Moodle

Sakai

Online PowerPoint™ Slides (0-13-285402-3) PowerPoint slides highlight key concepts and strategies in each chapter and enhance lectures and discussions.

BRIEF CONTENTS

CONTENTS

chapter 6

Observing and Assessing Young Children
Guiding, Teaching, and Learning 164

chapter 7

Infants and Toddlers
Critical Years for Learning 198

chapter 8

The Preschool Years
Getting Ready for School and Life 230

chapter 9

Kindergarten Today
Meeting Academic and
Developmental Needs 266

chapter 10

The Early Elementary Grades:
One Through Three
Preparation for Life 300

chapter 11

Educating Children with Diverse Backgrounds and Special Needs
Ensuring Each Child Learns 334

chapter 12

Guiding Children's Behavior
Helping Children Be Their Best 362

SPECIAL FEATURES

applying research to practice

applying research to practice

Supportive Teachers Play Critical Roles in Children's Academic Success

In a longitudinal study involving academically at-risk children, researchers examined factors that contribute to children's ongoing success. Here is one of their findings:

Children who have a supportive relationship with their teacher, in an environment where they feel accepted and secure, are more likely to work hard and perceive themselves as academically capable.[37]

So, what does this mean for you?

- Any efforts to close or eliminate achievement gaps have to begin with instructional practices that focus on helping each child gain the confidence and ability to do better. Only in this way will children break out of the predictable

pattern of only achieving at the same level from one year to the next.
- Children need teachers such as you to create a positive social and emotional relationship with them so they are motivated and engaged in classroom learning.
- Nurturing teacher–student relationships have their greatest impact on children with existing behavioral problems and those who have trouble regulating their behavior. Often these children don't get the nurturing teacher–child relationships that they need in order to succeed. Going above and beyond to provide love, affection, and nurturing to problem children is essential for their ongoing academic achievement. For some children, you are their main source of love, affection, and attention.

professionalism in practice

professionalism in practice

Teaching as a Passion

Daniel Leija, known as "Dan the science man," a third grade teacher at Esparza Elementary School, is the 2011 Texas Teacher of the Year. Every Monday, Daniel conducts televised science experiments to the whole campus as one way to help bridge the gap between concepts and real-world application. As a ten-year veteran of early childhood education, Leija has written an essay about what it means to be a teacher and to be passionate about early childhood education. Here are his ideals, which can guide your teaching, too!

I am a teacher. I have answered my nation's call to redefine the future. I have been entrusted to nurture and develop our country's most precious resource . . . our children.
I am a coach, mentor, counselor and friend, fully prepared

many seek and relatively few realize. My classroom door is always open for my students and all who wish to catch a glimpse of how tomorrow's leaders are being prepared.
I am a shepherd. I openly reach out to and guide each student who passes through my door; rich, poor, privileged, or disadvantaged. I nurture and encourage each student to achieve their full potential. My students will overcome life's obstacles to become successful.
I am an advocate. I encourage my students to take risks, think outside the box, and always dream big. I help my students learn to be humble winners, gracious losers, and work together as a team to achieve their goals.
I am a confidant. I offer counsel to students who have nowhere else to turn in times of personal crisis. I offer the support, guidance,

diversity tie-in

technology tie-in

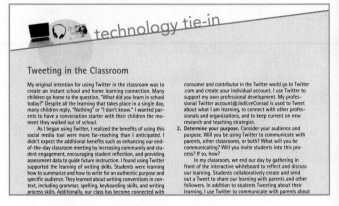

portraits of children

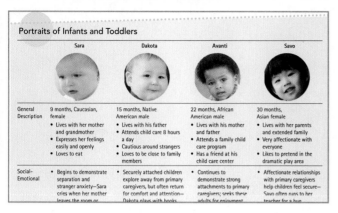

competency builder

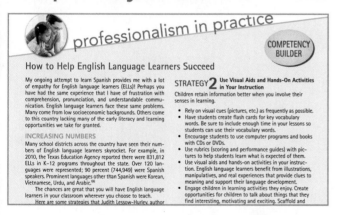

Fundamentals of Early Childhood Education

chapter 1

YOU AND EARLY CHILDHOOD EDUCATION

Becoming a Professional

NAEYC Standards for Early Childhood Professional Preparation

Standard 1. Promoting Child Development and Learning

I am grounded in a child development knowledge base. I use my understanding of young children's characteristics and needs, and of multiple interacting influences on children's development and learning, to create environments that are healthy, respectful, supportive, and challenging for each child.[1]

Standard 2. Building Family and Community Relationships

I understand that successful early childhood education depends upon partnerships with children's families and communities. I know about, understand, and value the importance and complex characteristics of children's families and communities. I use this understanding to create respectful, reciprocal relationships that support and empower families, and to involve all families in their children's development and learning.[2]

Standard 3. Observing, Documenting, and Assessing to Support Young Children and Families

I understand that child observation, documentation, and other forms of assessment are central to the practice of all early childhood professionals. I know about and understand the goals, benefits, and uses of assessment. I know about and use systematic observations, documentation, and other effective assessment strategies in a responsible way, in partnership with families and other professionals, to positively influence the development of each child.[3]

Standard 4. Using Developmentally Effective Approaches to Connect with Children and Families

I understand that teaching and learning with young children is a complex enterprise, and its details vary depending on children's ages, characteristics, and the settings within which teaching and learning occur. I understand and use positive relationships and supportive interactions as the foundation for my work with young children and families. I know, understand, and use a wide array of developmentally appropriate approaches, instructional strategies, and tools to connect with children and families and positively influence each child's development and learning.[4]

Standard 5. Using Content Knowledge to Build Meaningful Curriculum

I use my knowledge of academic disciplines to design, implement, and evaluate experiences that promote positive development and learning for each and every young child. I understand the importance of developmental domains and academic (or content) disciplines in an early childhood curriculum. I know the essential concepts, inquiry tools, and structure of content areas, including academic subjects, and can identify resources to deepen my understanding. I use my own knowledge and other resources to design, implement, and evaluate meaningful, challenging curricula that promote comprehensive developmental and learning outcomes for every young child.[5]

Standard 6. Becoming a Professional

I identify and conduct myself as a member of the early childhood profession. I know and use ethical guidelines and other professional standards related to early childhood practice. I am a continuous, collaborative learner who demonstrates knowledgeable, reflective, and critical perspectives on my work, making informed decisions that integrate knowledge from a variety of sources. I am an informed advocate for sound educational practices and policies.[6]

MARIA CARDENAS is excited about her new assignment as a pre-kindergarten teacher. After years of study and serving as an assistant teacher, Maria now has her own classroom of three- and four-year-old children. "I can't believe this day has finally come! I've worked so hard, and now my dream has come true! I can't wait to get started! I want my children to learn and be all they can be!"

Maria did not become a teacher overnight. She spent two years at a local community college and three at my university, learning the content, pedagogical, and professional knowledge and dispositions necessary to be a highly qualified early childhood teacher. There was never any doubt in Maria's mind or mine that she would achieve her goals! I first met Maria as her faculty advisor when she entered my university teacher education program. From the beginning, Maria was enthusiastic about her career choice and determined that she would be a high-quality professional. In addition to all of her coursework, Maria volunteered in many community and school-based programs to get the experiences she needed to help her prepare for the day when she would have her "own" classroom. After five years of going to school part-time, Maria is ready to make a difference in the lives of "her" children. I hope you are as excited as Maria about your opportunity to teach young children!

Today, more than ever, the public and politicians all over the world are creating a lot of excitement by seeking ways to improve the quality of early childhood education and teaching.[7] As a result, you have a wonderful opportunity to work with young children and their families, develop new and better programs, and advocate for better practices and high-quality programs. Like Maria, you can be a leader in helping the early childhood profession make high-quality education a reality for all children.

WHO IS AN EARLY CHILDHOOD PROFESSIONAL?

Early childhood professionals promote child development and learning; build family and community relationships; observe, document, and assess to support young children and families; promote positive teaching and learning for young children; and identify with and conduct themselves as members of the early childhood profession.

You are preparing to be an early childhood professional; a person who successfully teaches all children (birth to age eight), promotes high personal standards, and continually expands his or her skills and knowledge. You will teach all children and develop supportive relationships with them to help assure that each child can achieve and be successful. For example, National Teacher of the Year Michelle Shearer promotes high-quality teaching based on her belief that an educator's strong positive connection with students is essential to their academic success.[8]

Professionals promote high standards for themselves, their colleagues, and their students. They are multidimensional people who use their many talents to enrich the lives of children and families.

Early childhood professionals constantly change in response to new jobs created by the expanding field of early childhood education. They continually improve their skills and knowledge. You can expect that you will participate in many professional development activities, will be constantly involved in new programs and practices, and will have opportunities to engage in new and different roles as a professional.

THE SIX STANDARDS OF PROFESSIONALISM

Being a professional goes beyond academic degrees and experiences. Professionalism in early childhood education is based on the six NAEYC Standards for professional development. All six of the standards are important for your professional development, as shown in Figure 1.1. These are:

1. Promoting child development and learning
2. Building family and community relationships

MyEducationLab

Visit the MyEducationLab for *Fundamentals of Early Childhood Education* to enhance your understanding of chapter concepts with a personalized Study Plan. You'll also have the opportunity to hone your teaching skills through video-based Assignments and Activities as well as Building Teaching Skills and Dispositions lessons.

FOCUS QUESTIONS

1. Who is an early childhood professional?

2. What are the six standards for becoming an early childhood education (ECE) professional?

3. What is developmentally appropriate practice?

4. What are pathways to professional development for early childhood educators?

5. Why is developing a philosophy of education important?

6. What are the new roles for early childhood professionals?

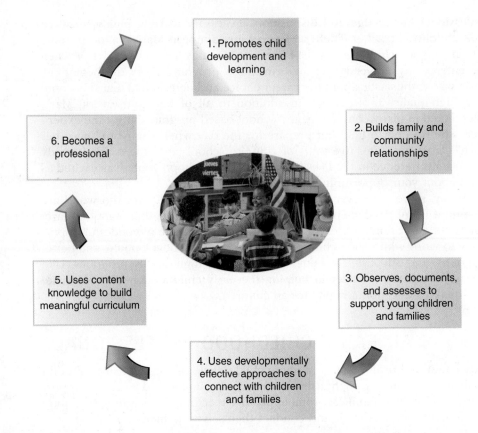

FIGURE 1.1 Six Standards of Early Childhood Professional Development

These standards of professional preparation provide guidelines for what you should know and be able to do in your lifelong career as an early childhood professional.

Source: National Association for the Education of Young Children, NAEYC Standards for Early Childhood Professional Preparation: July 2009.

early childhood professional
A person who successfully teaches all children (birth to age eight), promotes high personal standards, and continually expands his or her skills and knowledge.

3. Observing, documenting, and assessing to support young children and families
4. Using developmentally effective approaches to connect with children and families
5. Using content knowledge to build meaningful curriculum
6. Becoming a professional

Each of these standards plays a powerful role in determining who and what a professional is and how professionals implement practice in early childhood classrooms. Let's examine each of these standards and see how you can apply them to your professional practice.

Standard 1: Child Development and Learning

child development The stages of physical, social, mental, and linguistic growth that occur from birth through age eight.

As an early childhood professional, you will need to know about **child development**, the stages of physical, social, mental, and linguistic growth that occur from birth through age eight. Knowledge of child development is fundamental for all early childhood educators regardless of their roles or the ages of the children they teach. It enables you to confidently implement developmentally appropriate practices with all children. All early childhood professionals "use their understanding of young children's characteristics and needs, and of multiple interacting influences on children's development and learning, to create environments that are healthy, respectful, supportive, and challenging."[9]

Multiple Influences and Child Development. Young children are shaped by multiple influences that determine their life outcomes:

- *Children's culture.* Culture is a group's or an individual's way of life including basic values, beliefs, religion, language, clothing, food, and various practices. Culture determines the foods children eat, the kind of care they receive or do not receive from their parents, and helps determine how they view and react to the world.

- *Language.* Quite often in immigrant families, the burden of helping the non-English speaking family members communicate falls on the child. Children often act as interpreters for their families and have to learn to communicate as a survival skill.

- *Social relationships.* Getting along with one's peers and significant adults, such as teachers, is as important a skill as learning to read and write. Unfortunately, many young children don't have the parental guidance and support they need in order to learn the social skills necessary for peaceful and harmonious living.

- *Children's and families' socioeconomic conditions.* Children in poverty represent 24 percent of the total population.[10] Research clearly shows that children in poverty do not do well in school and life. This means that you will teach children in poverty and as a professional are responsible for their learning, growth, and development.

- *Children with disabilities.* It is estimated that 5.2 percent of all children in public schools have a disability of some kind.[11] There is every reason to believe that this number will increase as diagnostic methods increase. Children come to child care, preschool, and grades K–3 with many physical, behavioral, and learning disabilities. As an early childhood professional, you will care for and educate children with physical, behavioral, and learning disabilities.

Early Childhood Special Education Standards and You. Just as NAEYC has standards for professional development, so does the Division of Early Childhood of the Council for Exceptional Children. These professional standards guide the preparation of teachers who are preparing to be early childhood special education teachers. These standards apply to you for two reasons: First, you will be teaching in an inclusive classroom, a classroom in which children with disabilities are included in the regular classroom. The inclusive classroom is the "new normal" for teachers today. Second, you must know about typical and atypical child growth and development and how to provide developmentally appropriate teaching and learning for children with disabilities in your classroom. You can access DEC's professional standards in the Linking to Learning section at the end of the chapter.

Standard 2: Building Family and Community Relationships

Families are an important part of children's lives. In fact, the family and its environment are the single most important factor in a child's life. It makes sense for you to involve, work with, and advocate for parents and families. To do this, you need to know and understand the characteristics of children's families and the communities in which they live. Your collaboration with families will also involve supporting and empowering them. In addition, you will want and need to know how to involve families and communities in all aspects of children's development and learning. It is very important to be respectful of children and their families in order to build strong relationships. Saying that you are respectful of children and families is one thing; putting it

culture A group's or an individual's way of life including basic values, beliefs, religion, language, clothing, food, and various practices.

inclusive classroom A classroom in which children with disabilities are included in the regular classroom.

professionalism in practice

Teaching as a Passion

Daniel Leija, known as "Dan the science man," a third grade teacher at Esparza Elementary School, is the 2011 Texas Teacher of the Year. Every Monday, Daniel conducts televised science experiments to the whole campus as one way to help bridge the gap between concepts and real-world application. As a ten-year veteran of early childhood education, Leija has written an essay about what it means to be a teacher and to be passionate about early childhood education. Here are his ideals, which can guide your teaching, too!

I am a teacher. I have answered my nation's call to redefine the future. I have been entrusted to nurture and develop our country's most precious resource . . . our children.

I am a coach, mentor, counselor and friend, fully prepared to take the necessary steps to make each student's dream become a reality. I will never waver from my course.

I am a professional, the descendant of a proud and honorable heritage. I hold myself to a higher standard because I am accountable to our nation, my community, the students, and myself. I will always conduct myself in a manner that will bring credit to my field. I actively seek ways to sharpen my skills through continuing education and collaboration with my colleagues.

I am a partner. I work together with the community, business organizations, support agencies, administration, and parents to ensure each student receives the quality education that many seek and relatively few realize. My classroom door is always open for my students and all who wish to catch a glimpse of how tomorrow's leaders are being prepared.

I am a shepherd. I openly reach out to and guide each student who passes through my door; rich, poor, privileged, or disadvantaged. I nurture and encourage each student to achieve their full potential. My students will overcome life's obstacles to become successful.

I am an advocate. I encourage my students to take risks, think outside the box, and always dream big. I help my students learn to be humble winners, gracious losers, and work together as a team to achieve their goals.

I am a confidant. I offer counsel to students who have nowhere else to turn in times of personal crisis. I offer the support, guidance, and encouragement my students need to pilot them through their hour of darkness. I will never jeopardize that bond of trust. I gladly take on each of these roles to ensure my students have the tools they need to be successful in an ever-changing world.

I am a teacher. I have answered the call. I cannot and will not fail.[12]

Daniel Leija's determination and passion for education serve as a model for you and all educators.

....

Source: Contributed by Daniel Leija, Teacher of the Year at Esparza Elementary School.

into practice means you will use your knowledge and skills of child development and family involvement to make respectfulness a reality. Here are a few examples of things you can do to demonstrate your respectfulness for children and families:

- Talk with parents whose children have restricted diets to determine acceptable foods and recipes so all children can participate in classroom nutrition activities such as cooking.
- Validate children's home languages by learning some words and teaching them to the other children. For example, when counting the days on the calendar, you can count in English, Spanish, Vietnamese, and so on.
- Learn and find out about families' child-rearing practices and how they handle routines relating to toileting, behavioral problems, and so on.

Learning how to build family relationships is an important part of your professional development. Respectful and reciprocal relationships with parents and families empower them to be involved in their children's education.

Standard 3: Observing, Documenting, and Assessing to Support Children and Families

One of your most important responsibilities as an early childhood professional is to observe, document, and assess children's learning. **Assessment** is the process of collecting information about children's development, learning, behavior, academic progress, need for special services, and achievement to make decisions. The outcomes of your assessment guide you in making decisions about what and how to teach young children, and they will also provide you with abundant information to share with parents and families. Consider assessment a three-way process: you the professional gathering data; using that data to make instructional decisions; and sharing assessment data with parents to get their comments, opinions, feedback, and advice about how best to teach their young children.

Observation and documentation are just two forms of assessment that you will use in ongoing systematic ways. In fact, observation is one of your main means for gathering information about young children.

assessment The process of collecting information about children's development, learning, behavior, academic progress, need for special services, and achievement to make decisions.

Standard 4: Using Developmentally Effective Approaches to Connect with Children and Families

Selecting and using developmentally effective approaches is an essential part of your professional responsibility. In Standard 1, we discussed how to promote child development and learning. The use of developmentally appropriate practices and approaches supports Standard 4. Throughout this text, in each chapter, we discuss how to use and apply developmentally appropriate practice. In fact, one of the hallmarks of this book is the integration of developmentally appropriate practices in all dimensions of providing high-quality learning environments for young children.

Using Developmentally Effective Approaches.   Developmentally effective approaches and methods include fostering language development and communication; making the most of the environment and routines; capitalizing on incidental teaching, focusing on children's characteristics, needs, and interests; linking children's language and culture to the early childhood program; teaching through social interactions; creating support for play; addressing children's challenging behaviors; supporting learning through technology; and using integrative approaches to curriculum.[13]

In addition, as an early childhood professional, you will integrate your understanding of and relationships with children and families, your understanding of developmentally effective approaches to teaching and learning, and your knowledge of academic disciplines to design, implement, and evaluate experiences that promote positive developmentally appropriate learning for all children.[14] To be a professional in this area, you will demonstrate positive relationships with children and families. In the final analysis, all education is about relationships: how you relate to your colleagues, how you relate to parents and other family members, and how you relate to children. In **responsive relationships** you are responsive to the needs and interests of all children and their families.

responsive relationships You, the teacher, are responsive to the needs and interests of children and their families.

Standard 5: Using Content Knowledge to Build Meaningful Curriculum

Content areas are important to children's learning. Content areas form the basis for children's learning to read, write, do mathematics and science, be creative, and be successful in school and in life. Consequently, early childhood professionals understand the importance of each content area in children's development and learning, demonstrate the essential knowledge and skills needed to provide appropriate environments that support learning in each content area, and demonstrate basic knowledge of the research base underlying each content area.[15]

Content Areas.   The content areas in early childhood are the following:

- Language and literacy, which consists of listening, speaking, reading, and writing
- Reading, which includes the learning skills necessary for beginning to read and being able to read fluently for meaning. The national goal for reading is for all children to read on grade level by grade three.
- The arts, including music, creative movement, dance, drama, and various forms of art
- Mathematics, the study of numbers, patterns, space, and change
- Science, the use of observation and experimentation to describe and explain things
- Technology, the application of tools and information to change and modify the natural environment in order to solve problems and make products
- Engineering, the process of utilizing materials and forces of nature for the benefit of mankind
- Social studies, which involves geography, history, economics, and social relations/civics
- Physical activity and physical education, which includes dance, sports, health, and nutrition

Science, Technology, Engineering, and Mathematics (STEM).   Today there is a growing emphasis on incorporating engineering and technology content in the school curriculum beginning in preschool. You will hear a lot about STEM throughout your teaching preparation and career. For example, Michelle Shearer, 2011 National Teacher of the Year, is an advocate for STEM education for all K–12 students and successfully reaches those who have been traditionally underrepresented in scientific fields, including students with special needs and those from diverse racial and socioeconomic backgrounds. Her teaching methods rely heavily on real-life applications of scientific concepts.[16]

Much of the content knowledge in pre-K through third grade programs is integrated in state, national, and the Common Core national standards adopted by the states. However, not all of the curriculum is specified by or through standards. What is taught in early childhood programs is also based on children's interests and on the "teachable moment," when classroom, school, and communities lend themselves to teaching ideas, concepts, and skills. How you teach with standards is a result of your professional background and training. This is where Professional Standard 4, Using Developmentally Effective Approaches to Connect with Children and Families, applies to your teaching in each of the content areas and your use of instructional processes to teach each area.

The knowledge of the content areas is known as **content knowledge**. Teachers must understand the subjects they teach, for example, math, science, social studies. In addition to learning and knowing content knowledge, teachers also must know *how* to teach students so that they learn content knowledge. **Pedagogical knowledge** involves learning how to teach and how to facilitate children's learning and achievements. Pedagogical knowledge includes instructional practices and how to use them to help children learn. For example, you take your knowledge of mathematics and the standards and use appropriate instructional practices. Finally, high-quality teachers must also know about and understand the children they teach. This is called *knowledge of learners and learning* and involves applying developmentally appropriate practices (DAP) to your teaching.

content knowledge The knowledge that comes from content areas.

pedagogical knowledge Facilitating learning, including knowledge of how students develop and learn; school, family, and community contexts; and children's prior experiences, to develop meaningful learning experiences.

Modeling and Using Technology for Teaching and Learning. **Technology** is the application of tools and information to make products and solve problems and the use of electronic and digital applications. In your classroom, you and your children will use technology for word processing, sending and receiving messages, publishing, and Web research. Brandi Ousley, Technology Teacher of the Year at McAllen ISD in Texas, believes:

> Reaching my kids, that's my job. In this fast-paced world I have to compete with hand-held systems, Internet, YouTube, and every other piece of technology out there. In order for me to be an effective teacher, I have to meet my students in their world. Simply put, I must use technology to educate them. Using technology allows me to be a part of my students' world. By using educational videos, PowerPoint presentations, iPod Touches, document readers, projectors and the Internet I am able to effectively teach the Texas Essential Knowledge and Skills in an enjoyable way.[17]

Like Brandi, today's teacher is a technological teacher. Today's students are technological students. One reality of society and education today is that technology permeates all facets of our life: working, teaching, and learning. You will use technology of all kinds in order to:

- Create meaningful learning activities for children.
- Teach children how to use technology and technological applications to enhance their own learning.
- Assess children's achievement.
- Connect children to learning experiences outside the classroom and around the world.
- Teach children the technological skills they will need in the workforce of the future.
- Keep your own records and communicate with families.

You can learn more about technology and your role as a teacher by accessing the *ISTE National Educational Technology Standards (NETS-T) and Performance Indicator for Teachers* at the website of the International Society for Technology in Education in the Linking to Learning section at the end of this chapter.

Standard 6: Becoming a Professional

Early childhood professionals conduct themselves as professionals and identify themselves as members of their chosen profession. Your identification and involvement in your profession enables you to say proudly that you are a teacher of young children. Being a professional means that you (1) know about and engage in ethical practice; (2) engage in continuous lifelong learning and professional development; (3) collaborate with colleagues, parents, families, and community partners; (4) engage in reflective practice; and (5) advocate on behalf of children, families, and the profession. These competencies represent the heart and soul of professional practice. You should include in your professional development plan steps to increase your knowledge in each of these areas.

technology The application of tools and information to make products and solve problems.

The role of technology is increasing in today's classrooms. As you watch this **video**, notice how the teacher uses technology in a developmentally appropriate way with her students and incorporates the use of technology across the curriculum.

Early childhood educators are professionals who, in addition to teaching and caring for children, are ethical, engage in lifelong learning, collaborate with colleagues and families, are reflective practitioners, and advocate for children and families.

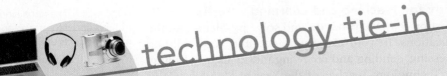

Tweeting in the Classroom

My original intention for using Twitter in the classroom was to create an instant school and home learning connection. Many children go home to the question, "What did you learn in school today?" Despite all the learning that takes place in a single day, many children reply, "Nothing" or "I don't know." I wanted parents to have a conversation starter with their children the moment they walked out of school.

As I began using Twitter, I realized the benefits of using this social media tool were more far-reaching than I anticipated. I didn't expect the additional benefits such as enhancing our end-of-the-day classroom meeting by increasing community and student engagement, encouraging student reflection, and providing assessment data to guide future instruction. I found using Twitter supported the learning of writing skills. Students were learning how to summarize and how to write for an authentic purpose and specific audience. They learned about writing conventions in context, including grammar, spelling, keyboarding skills, and writing process skills. Additionally, our class has become connected with other classes in and out of our school district, and around the country. My students are learning essential twenty-first century skills, including digital citizenship and how to use technology to collaborate and communicate with others in our global society.

GETTING STARTED

1. **Use Twitter.** The best way to experience the potential of using Twitter in the classroom is to Tweet. To be a

consumer and contributor in the Twitter world go to Twitter.com and create your individual account. I use Twitter to support my own professional development. My professional Twitter account@JodiLeeConrad is used to Tweet about what I am learning, to connect with other professionals and organizations, and to keep current on new research and teaching strategies.

2. **Determine your purpose.** Consider your audience and purpose. Will you be using Twitter to communicate with parents, other classrooms, or both? What will you be communicating? Will you invite students into this process? If so, how?

In my classroom, we end our day by gathering in front of the interactive whiteboard to reflect and discuss our learning. Students collaboratively create and send out a Tweet to share our learning with parents and other followers. In addition to students Tweeting about their learning, I use Twitter to communicate with parents about upcoming events, provide important reminders, and make parents aware of online learning resources.

3. **Set up a Twitter account for your classroom.** Create a Twitter account for your classroom at Twitter.com. You may want to use your class name. For example, MsConradAL1 is my classroom Twitter name. I used my name, school abbreviation (Abraham Lincoln), and 1 for first grade. Create a sense of ownership by getting students involved

ethical conduct The exercise of responsible behavior with children, families, colleagues, and community members.

Engaging in Ethical Practice.   **Ethical conduct**—your exercise of responsible behavior with children, families, colleagues, and community members—enables you to confidently engage in exemplary professional practice. The profession of early childhood education has a set of ethical standards to guide your thinking and behavior. NAEYC has developed a Code of Ethical Conduct and Statement of Commitment, which states in part:

As an individual who works with young children, I commit myself to furthering the values of early childhood education as they are reflected in the NAEYC Code of Ethical Conduct. To the best of my ability I will

- Never harm children.
- Ensure that programs for young children are based on current knowledge of child development and early childhood education.
- Respect and support families in their task of nurturing children.
- Respect colleagues in early childhood education and support them in maintaining the NAEYC Code of Ethical Conduct.

from the beginning and creating your Twitter name as a class.

4. **Share your Twitter account with students.** Explain to the class what Twitter is and how it will be used in the classroom. Twitter is a micro-blog. This means that you only have 140 characters to communicate your message. Twitter is a tool that is used to share ideas with others on the Internet. Let students know that parents will be invited to follow the class on Twitter.

5. **Consider privacy settings and options.** Twitter offers a variety of privacy settings. You will find many options in account settings. When selecting the settings to meet the needs of your classroom, consider your own comfort level with sharing information in this type of social media outlet as well as checking with your district's technology department. They will be able to help you select the privacy settings that your district is comfortable with.

6. **Share your Twitter name with parents and invite them to follow you.** Explain to parents what Twitter is, your purpose for using it in the classroom, and the security measures you have in place to ensure the safety of the students. Share your Twitter name and invite parents to follow the class.

Using Twitter in the classroom is a learning experience for my students and me! Twitter authentically engages students and makes them reflect on their learning, summarize the most important parts of their day, and share their learning with a real audience. My students created a Tweet to share their learning about a reading and writing unit: "We are reading & writing series books. We are adding dialogue to our books to show what the characters are saying & how they are saying it." To share their learning about a new reading strategy we learned about, students Tweeted, "We read

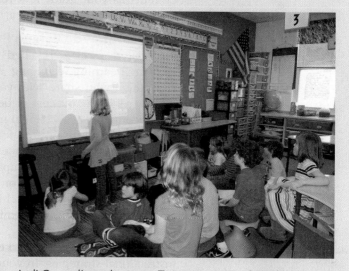

Jodi Conrad's students use Twitter to review their day.

Long Night Moon by Cynthia Rylant. We talked about how Cynthia Rylant uses descriptive language to help us visualize the story." I am surprised by the extensive instructional benefits of Twitter. Using Twitter provides me the daily opportunity to quickly assess student learning, engagement, and understanding before students leave for the day. Gathering this data at the end of each day in a meeting format supports and enhances classroom community and collaboration, and it provides invaluable information that I use to plan future instructional strategies.

....

Source: Contributed by Jodi Conrad, first grade teacher at Abraham Lincoln Elementary School in Glen Ellyn, Illinois.

- Serve as an advocate for children, their families, and their teachers in community and society.
- Stay informed of and maintain high standards of professional conduct.
- Engage in an ongoing process of self-reflection, realizing that personal characteristics, biases, and beliefs have an impact on children and families.
- Be open to new ideas and be willing to learn from the suggestions of others.
- Continue to learn, grow, and contribute as a professional.
- Honor the ideals and principles of the NAEYC Code of Ethical Conduct.[18]

You can begin now to incorporate professional ethical practices into your interactions with children and colleagues. To stimulate your thinking, the Activities for Professional Development at the end of each chapter include an **ethical dilemma**, a situation an individual encounters in the workplace for which there is more than one possible solution, each carrying a strong moral justification. A dilemma requires a person to choose between two alternatives; each has some benefits but also some costs. Typically, one stakeholder's legitimate needs and interest will give way to those of another.[19]

ethical dilemma A situation an individual encounters in the workplace for which there is more than one possible solution, each carrying a strong moral justification.

As you reflect on and respond to each dilemma, use the NAEYC Code of Ethical Conduct as your guide and resource. You can access it at the NAEYC website in the Linking to Learning section at the end of the chapter.

Continuous and Lifelong Professional Development Opportunities.
A professional is never a "finished" product; you will always be involved in a process of studying, learning, changing, and becoming more professional. Teachers of the Year and others who share with you their philosophies and beliefs throughout this book are always in the process of becoming more professional.

Becoming a professional means you will participate in training and education beyond the minimum needed for your current position. You will also want to consider your career objectives and the qualifications you might need for positions of increasing responsibility. For example, Lauren Gonzalez, a former kindergarten and third grade teacher, has certification in English as a Second Language (ESL) and special education. Lauren now teaches children with disabilities in a special education classroom.

Part of your lifelong learning will involve collaborative planning. You will engage in **collaborative planning**, meeting collaboratively in grade-level teams or across grade-level teams in order to examine student data together and to plan and develop instructional strategies. In your planning, you will incorporate and align your curriculum with local, Common Core, and state standards.

collaborative planning Meeting collaboratively in grade-level teams or across grade-level teams in order to examine student data together and to plan and develop instructional strategies.

Collaborating with Parents, Families, and Community Partners.
Parents, families, and the community are essential partners in the process of schooling. Knowing how to effectively collaborate with these key partners will serve you well throughout your career.

Family education and support are important responsibilities of the early childhood professional. Children's learning begins and continues within the context of the family unit, whatever that unit may be. Learning how to comfortably and confidently work with parents and families is an essential part of teaching children.

Reflective Practice.
Reflective practice is a process that helps you think about how children learn and enables you to make decisions about how to best support their development and learning. Thinking about learning and understanding how children learn makes it easier for you to improve your teaching effectiveness, student learning, and professional satisfaction. Reflective practice involves deliberate and careful consideration about the children you teach, the theories on which you base your teaching, how you teach, what children learn, and how you will teach in the future. Although solitary reflection is useful, the power of reflective practice is more fully realized when you engage in such practice with your mentor teacher and colleagues. In a word, the reflective teacher is a thoughtful teacher. Reflective practice involves the three integrated steps shown in Figure 1.2.

reflective practice A process that helps you think about how children learn and enables you to make decisions about how best to support their development and learning.

Advocacy.
Advocacy is the act of pleading the causes of children and families to the profession and the public and engaging in strategies designed to improve the circumstances of those children and families. Advocates move beyond their day-to-day professional responsibilities and work collaboratively to help others. Children and families today need adults who understand their needs and who will work to improve the health, education, and well-being of all young children. You and other early childhood professionals are in a unique position to know and understand children and their needs and to make a difference in their lives. For example, Connecticut Teacher of the Year Kristi Luetjen is praised for integrating students with special needs into her classroom. She dedicates herself to improving the services for kindergartners with special needs. She blends the lines of regular and special education. She collaborates with other teachers and incorporates yoga practice into the curriculum to create a

advocacy The act of pleading the causes of children and families to the profession and public and engaging in strategies designed to improve the circumstances of those children and families.

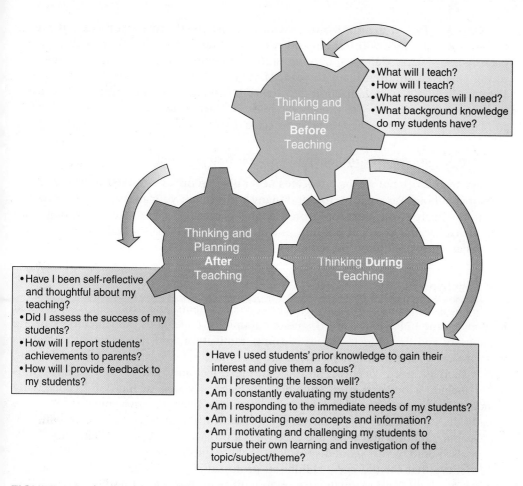

FIGURE 1.2 The Cycle of Reflective Practice: Thinking, Planning, and Deciding

Your role as an early childhood professional means you will continually engage in the reflective practice of thinking before, during, and after any activity.

yoga program for kindergartners. Luetjen says, "I am grateful for the opportunity to advocate for our youngest students, our students with disabilities, and the general importance of a kindergarten education."[20]

Like Kristi Luetjen, you can be a voice for children. These four steps will empower you as an advocate for children and their families:

Step 1. ***Pick a topic you are passionate about!*** Advocates are passionate about issues for which they advocate. Some issues that need passionate advocates are better pay for child care workers, universal preschool for all children, increased quality of child care, early literacy programs for all children, equal rights and opportunities for children with disabilities, and better dental health for young children.

Step 2. ***Do something about it!*** Advocate the way you communicate—network! Use Facebook, Twitter, Google +, and other social media to connect with others. Alternatively, you could make a presentation and volunteer to speak to groups. For example, one of my students, Nicki, advocates for the use of therapy dogs for children with autism. Nicki has developed a presentation using Prezi (a type of presentation software and storytelling tool for exploring and sharing ideas on a virtual canvas) to tell her story about therapy dogs and their power to help children with disabilities. Nicki uses this presentation to speak to children, parents, and teachers.

Step 3. *Join a group!* Solitary advocates can be effective, but there is power in numbers! Collaborate with others and use social media to connect and advocate for your cause. Martha Gallegos, another student of mine, is passionate about helping young Hispanic children learn to read. Martha has teamed up with Success for Life Through Reading, an organization devoted to involving university students in reading to and giving books away to preschool children. Martha says "I found Success for Life so I could make a difference on a larger scale. Last year we read to over 500 Hispanic children!"

Step 4. *Never give up!* Keep focused on your passion!

It's easy to give up, but strong advocates never give up on advocating for what they are passionate about. Be creative and find many ways to get your message out. Advocacy gets to the heart of our next topic, professional dispositions, because it is through and with advocacy that you will put into practice many of the values and beliefs that you hold as an early childhood professional.

Professional Dispositions

professional dispositions
The values, commitments, and professional ethics that influence behaviors toward students, families, colleagues, and members of the community and affect student learning, motivation, and development as well as the educator's own professional growth.

Professional dispositions are the values, commitments, and professional ethics that influence your behaviors toward students, families, colleagues, and members of the community and that affect student learning, motivation, and development as well as your professional growth. Dispositions are grounded in beliefs and attitudes related to values such as caring, fairness, honesty, and responsibility. For example, dispositions might include a belief that all students can learn, a vision of high and challenging standards, or a commitment to a safe and supportive learning environment.[21] We have already discussed other dispositions, such as ethical conduct, collaborating with colleagues and families, and reflective practice. All programs that prepare childhood professionals should have a set of dispositions that are important for professional practice.

I believe that for the early childhood professional, *caring* is the most important disposition of all. Professionals care about children; they accept and respect all children and their cultural and socioeconomic backgrounds. As a professional, you will work in classrooms, programs, and other settings where things do not always go smoothly—for example, children will not always learn ably and well, and they will not always be clean and free from illness and hunger. Children's and their parents' backgrounds and ways of life will not always be the same as yours. Caring means you will lose sleep trying to find a way to help a child learn to read, and you will spend long hours planning and gathering materials. Caring also means you will not leave your intelligence, enthusiasm, and other talents at home but will bring them into the center, the classroom, administration offices, board of directors meetings, and wherever else you can make a difference in the lives of children and their families.

The Professionalism in Practice feature about caring and kindness illustrates this important point with many examples that you can use in your program or classroom.

DEVELOPMENTALLY APPROPRIATE PRACTICE

developmentally appropriate practice (DAP) A framework of principles and guidelines for best practice in the care and education of young children, birth through age eight.

Knowledge of child development provides the foundation for conducting **developmentally appropriate practice (DAP)**, which is a framework of principles and guidelines for best practice in the care and education of young children, birth through age eight. With your understanding of child development you will be able to select essential curricula and instructional approaches with confidence. All early childhood professionals use their understanding of child development as the foundation for their work with young children.

Knowing Children.   It is essential for you to have and demonstrate an understanding of child development for both regularly developing children and children with disabilities. Child development knowledge enables you to understand how children grow and develop across all developmental domains—cognitive, linguistic, social, emotional, physical, language, and aesthetic domains as well as play, activity, learning processes, and motivation to learn.[22] Knowledge of individual children, combined with knowledge of child growth and development, enables you to provide care and education that is developmentally appropriate for each child. Today's early childhood professionals teach in inclusive classrooms. Inclusive classrooms are classrooms in which students with disabilities are supported in chronologically age-appropriate general education classes in their home schools and receive the specialized instruction they need to be successful within the context of the core curriculum and general class activities. Developmentally appropriate practice (DAP) means basing your teaching on how children grow and develop. DAP is the recommended teaching practice of the early childhood profession. The following Teaching and Learning in the Inclusive Classroom section provides you with eight professional practices for teaching in the inclusive classroom.

TEACHING AND LEARNING IN THE INCLUSIVE CLASSROOM: PROFESSIONAL PRACTICES

It is essential to treat all children fairly regardless of their needs. Refer to all students as people first and offer the support they need to be successful. When you explain to someone that you teach students with special needs, say, "I teach children with autism." Don't say: "I teach autistic students." Put the child first, the disability second.

State and federal laws are forever changing and opening more and more opportunities for all children with disabilities to be included in the classroom and across the school campus. Inclusion may already be in place in your school or it may still be in the planning stages. Here are some helpful ways you can embrace it:

1. Accept all children for who they are as a person, not how they will perform on grade-level tests.

2. Include all children with disabilities in the same activities, events, and opportunities all children have in the same grade and age level.

3. Understand the age and grade level that you teach. Offer books, posters, and classroom materials that are safe and fun for all students. These are in addition to the required materials for lessons and the assigned curriculum.

4. Encourage and support peer collaboration. Peers can help children with special needs by modeling appropriate learning behaviors and promoting developmentally appropriate socialization.

5. Develop individual visual schedules and make work and behavioral expectations throughout the school day clear to each child. Allowing a student with disabilities

Golden Apple Teacher of the Year Laura Lee Reed teaches children with autism how to read.

professionalism in practice

A Garden of Kindness and Caring

"Kind hearts, the garden; kind thoughts, the root; kind words, the blossoms; kind deeds, the fruit." If we think of our classrooms as gardens, then teachers are the master gardeners. Not only do we need to plant academic seeds of many varieties; we need to plant the seeds of kindness and caring, as well. Our actions and our attitudes define who we are. Kindness and caring are not skills; they are attitudes. As teachers, we need to be the essence of kindness and caring. We must cultivate our students to bloom into the loveliest of flowers, and it starts with the attitude and the actions of the teacher. We believe that students who can express kindness are happier and more productive in the classroom.

We are instructors in a team classroom: forty students and two teachers. Every student in our classroom knows that he/she is loved and accepted and every student in our classroom knows that he/she is accountable for his/her attitudes and actions. We promote a simple, yet positive behavior plan for our classroom: be safe, be respectful, be responsible. We also believe in task-oriented consequences, rather than time-oriented consequences. For example, if a child says something unkind to another student, resulting in hurt feelings, a letter/ picture of apology is a better choice than missing five minutes of playtime.

Elizabeth

to look at a visual schedule and the rules of the classroom promotes independence and creates a safe learning environment for all children.

6. Provide rewards and incentives to all children. Rewards and incentives go beyond candy and toys. They can be fun and educational activities. For example, allowing the class to participate in an active song or opportunity to follow directions through music allows for legitimate movement and creates happy and involved children.

7. Know and use your resources on campus and in the district. For example, use district resource teachers to help you plan for how to transition your children from one grade to another.

8. Collaborate with parents. Parents can provide you with critical information about how their children learn and about what motivates them, etc. This process also enables parents to feel included and a part of their children's education. Remember, parents have information you need to help you and their children be successful!

Contributed by Laura Lee Reed, Pre-K Special Needs Teacher, Lee County (Florida), Golden Apple Teacher of the Year.

At the beginning of the school year, we read the book *Have You Filled a Bucket Today? A Guide to Happiness for Kids* by Carol McCloud. This book encourages positive behavior through love, kindness, and appreciation. The premise of the book is that everyone in the world carries an invisible bucket. The bucket has only one purpose, and it is to hold good thoughts and feelings about yourself; but you need other people to fill your bucket. So when you smile, show love to someone, say or do a kind deed, you are being a bucket filler. But you can also dip into someone's bucket and take out some happiness when your words and actions are inappropriate. Every morning, during our morning meeting, we encourage our students to be bucket fillers, not bucket dippers. We encourage our students to say, "Thank you for filling my bucket!" when an act of kindness is shown, or "You dipped into my bucket." when hurtful words or actions are not acceptable.

To promote our action plan of kindness, each student decorates his/her own bucket, including a self-portrait to be displayed yearlong in our classroom. (See photo.) We often refer to our bulletin board when issues arise in our classroom. Our "visible buckets" remind us of the importance of being kind at school, on the playground, in the cafeteria, on the bus. Our "invisible buckets" travel everywhere with us, reminding us that we can make a difference, through kindness and caring, wherever we are!

We can also promote kindness and caring though community service. Each month, we "fill the buckets of others" in our school or community with acts of kindness. Recently, we made an American flag from chain-links and presented it to our local firefighters and policemen as a way of saying thank you for keeping our school safe. (See photo.) There are so many ways that "wee hands can do big deeds."

Most important, we need to teach our students to be kind and caring through example. Our students learn from our actions and our attitudes. Every teacher has a garden and your garden will have a variety of plants. How you choose to cultivate your garden will determine its beauty. Choose to cultivate kindness and caring in your classroom.

Source: Contributed by Christa Pehrson and Vicki Sheffler, 2002 USA TODAY All-USA First Team Teachers, Amos K. Hutchinson Elementary School, Greensburg, Pennsylvania.

Core Considerations in Developmentally Appropriate Practice

Every day, as an early childhood practitioner, you will make a great many decisions, both long-term and short-term. As you do so, plan with your state, local, and Common Core standards for children's learning and development and be intentional in helping children achieve these outcomes. The core of developmentally appropriate practice lies in this intentionality, the knowledge that you as a practitioner consider when you make decisions, and that you always aim for goals that are both challenging and achievable for all children.

Making Developmentally Appropriate Decisions

In all aspects of their work with young children, early childhood professionals consider three areas that are essential to the implementation of developmentally appropriate practice, as shown in Figure 1.3.

Child Development and Learning.   This refers to knowledge of age-related characteristics that permits general predictions about what experiences are likely to best promote children's learning and development.

Core Considerations in Developmentally Appropriate Practice		
Knowledge of Child Development	Knowledge of the Child as an Individual	Knowledge of Social and Cultural Contexts in Which Children Live
Knowledge of age-related characteristics that permit general predictions about what experiences are likely to best promote childeren's learning and development.	Referring to what practitioners learn about each child that has implications for how best to adapt and be responsive to that individual variation.	Referring to the values, expectations, and behavioral and linguistic conventions that shape children's lives at home and in their communities that practitioners must strive to understand in order to ensure that learning experiences in the program or school are meaningful, relevant, and respectful for each child and family.

FIGURE 1.3 Core Considerations in Developmentally Appropriate Practice

Teachers who are knowledgeable about child development and learning are able to make broad predictions about what children of a particular age group typically will be like, what they typically will and won't be capable of, and what strategies and approaches will most likely promote their optimal learning and development. With this knowledge, teachers can make preliminary decisions with some confidence about environment, materials, interactions, and activities.[23]

Each Child as an Individual.   This refers to what teachers learn about each child and has implications for how best to adapt for and be responsive to that individual variation. To be effective, you must get to know each child in the group well. You do this using a variety of methods—such as observation, interactions, examination of children's work, and talking with families. From this information, you make plans and adjustments to promote each child's individual development and learning as fully as possible. Developmental variation among children is the norm; but any one child's progress also will vary across domains and disciplines, contexts, and time. Children differ in many other respects, too—in their strengths, interests, preferences, personalities, approaches to learning, knowledge and skills based on prior experiences, and more. Children may also have special learning needs; sometimes these have been diagnosed and sometimes they have not. Responding to each child individually is fundamental to developmentally appropriate practice.[24]

Social and Cultural Contexts.   This refers to the values, expectations, and behaviors that teachers must strive to understand in order to ensure that learning experiences are meaningful, relevant, and respectful for each child and family. For example, growing poverty in the United States places more children at risk for learning than ever before. This socioeconomic context has many implications for your teaching. It means you will have to help children overcome family conditions that may put them at risk for learning. Language is influenced by cultural context. Another example involves many immigrant families who come to the United States illiterate in both English and their native language. You will work with such families as you endeavor to create literacy programs that will help them and their children.

As children grow up in families and in cultural communities, they come to certain understandings about what their group considers appropriate—what it values, expects, and admires. They learn this through direct teaching from parents and other important people in their lives, and by observing the behavior of those around them. Children learn to show respect, how to interact with people they know well and those they have just met, how to regard time and personal space, how to dress, and countless other attitudes and actions. Children typically absorb these rules very early and very deeply, so they live by them with little conscious thought. When young children are in a group setting outside the home, what makes sense to them and how they experience their world depend on the social and cultural contexts to which they are accustomed. Teachers take such contextual factors into account, along with the children's age and their individual differences, in shaping all aspects of the learning environment.[25]

Ideas for how to conduct DAP are found throughout this book. These ideas and specific strategies for implementing DAP serve as your road map of teaching. As you read about DAP suggestions, consider how you can begin to apply them in your professional practice.

Developmentally and culturally responsive practice (DCRP) includes being sensitive to and responding to children's cultural and ethnic backgrounds and needs. The United States is a nation of diverse people, and this diversity will increase. Children in every early childhood program represent this diversity. When children enter schools and programs, they do not leave their uniqueness, gender, culture, socioeconomic status, and race at the classroom door. As part of your professional practice you will embrace, value, and incorporate **multiculturalism** into your teaching. Learning how to teach children of all cultures is an important part of your professional role. In addition, the antibias curriculum information that follows offers guidelines that will help you teach children from diverse backgrounds. The following list shows some popular and informative books that can help you achieve this goal. As you read these books, make a list of key ideas and how you can incorporate them into your teaching.

developmentally and culturally responsive practice (DCRP) Includes being sensitive to and responding to children's cultural and ethnic backgrounds and needs.

multiculturalism An approach to education based on the premise that all peoples in the United States should receive proportional attention in the curriculum.

- ***Delpit, L. (2006). Other People's Children: Conflict in the Classroom. New York: New Press.*** In an interesting analysis of what is going on in American classrooms today, Lisa Delpit suggests that many of the academic problems attributed to children of color are actually the result of miscommunication as schools and "other people's children" struggle with the imbalance of power and the dynamics of inequality plaguing our system.

- ***Derman-Sparks, L., and Ramsey, P. (2006). What If All the Kids Are White? Anti-Bias Multicultural Education with Young Children and Families. New York: Teachers College Press.*** How do educators teach about racial and cultural diversity if all their students are Caucasian? The authors propose seven learning themes to help young Caucasian children resist messages of racism and build identity and skills for thriving in a multicultural country and world.

- ***Espinosa, L. M. (2010). Getting It Right for Young Children from Diverse Backgrounds: Applying Research to Improve Practice. Upper Saddle River, NJ: Pearson.*** This book reflects the current state of the field in terms of best practice and research. It provides a rich and comprehensive look at the needs of young children from diverse backgrounds. Espinosa also emphasizes the importance of collaboration among teachers and families to best serve students.

- *Gonzalez-Mena, J. (2007). Diversity in Early Care and Education: Honoring Differences, 5th ed. Chicago: McGraw-Hill.* This book explores the rich diversity encountered in programs and environments for children ages birth to eight, including those serving children with special needs. The emphasis is on the practical and immediate concerns of the early childhood professional and family service worker, through all information has strong theoretical support.

- *March, M. M., and Turner-Vorbeck, T. (2007). Other Kinds of Families: Embracing Diversity in Schools. New York: Teachers College Press.* The authors contend that the vast diversity found in schools and society today suggests an urgent need to reconsider the ways in which families are currently represented and addressed in school curriculum and culture. They address such issues as multigenerational views of the schooling experiences of immigrant families, the educational needs of gay and lesbian families, and the experiences of homeless students and their families with the educational system.

In this video, a third grade teacher talks about the diversity in her classroom. Watch and listen closely as she explains her beliefs and strategies for handling individual differences in the classroom. How do they compare with your own beliefs and experiences?

Teaching Diverse Children.   Think for a moment about all of the classrooms of children across the United States. What do you think their cultural, ethnic, and linguistic makeup is? More than likely, the demographics of these children are different from those of the children you went to school with in kindergarten or first grade. Consider this data about America's children:

- In 2009, 55 percent of U.S. children were white, non-Hispanic; 23 percent were Hispanic; 15 percent were black; and 4 percent were Asian.[26]

- The percentage of children who are Hispanic has increased faster than that of any other racial or ethnic group. Hispanics accounted for 16.3 percent of the U.S. population in 2010.[27]

The increase in racial, ethnic, and cultural diversity in America is reflected in early childhood classrooms, which are also receiving increased numbers of children with disabilities and developmental delays. Consider the current student population at two elementary schools in different parts of the country. At Susan B. Anthony Elementary School in Sacramento, California: 22 percent are Hispanic, 60 percent are Asian, 13 percent are African American, and 1 percent are white. Moreover, 97 percent of the children receive discounted/free lunches.[28] In San Angelo, Texas, at Alta Loma Elementary: 69 percent are Hispanic, less than 1 percent are Asian, 7 percent are African American, and 20 percent are white; 84 percent of the children receive discounted/free lunches.[29] The chances are that you will teach in a school in which the majority of students are minority students! The accompanying Diversity Tie-In provides you with ideas to help you be a successful teacher of diverse children.

Antibias Curriculum.   Conducting a developmentally and culturally appropriate program also means that you will include in your curriculum activities and materials that help challenge and change all biases of any kind that seek to diminish and portray as inferior all children based on their gender, race, culture, disability, language, or socioeconomic status. You can accomplish this standard by implementing an **antibias curriculum**. Antibias curriculum is an approach that seeks to provide children with an understanding of social and behavioral problems related to prejudice and seeks to provide them with the knowledge, attitude and skills needed to combat prejudice. The book *Anti-Bias Curriculum: Tools for Empowering Young Children*[30] is the profession's primary resource for understanding and implementing an antibias curriculum. If you have not read this book, you should put it at the top of your list of professional books to read. An antibias curriculum:

antibias curriculum An approach that seeks to provide children with an understanding of social and behavioral problems related to prejudice and seeks to provide them with the knowledge, attitude, and skills needed to combat prejudice.

> embraces an educational philosophy as well as specific techniques and content. It is value based: Differences are good; oppressive ideas and behaviors are not. It sets up

diversity tie-in

Meeting the Challenge: Teaching with Respect and Equity

The diverse composition of early childhood classrooms challenges you to make your classroom responsive to the various needs of all your children, which is part of your professional responsibility. Developmentally appropriate practice also means that you will take into consideration the diverse nature of each child. In classrooms today, early childhood teachers work with children of varying cultural and socioeconomic backgrounds and needs.

Let's look at some of the things you can do to be a responsible professional who is culturally aware and who teaches with respect and equity:

STRATEGY 1 Be Aware of Your Own Multicultural Development

- Honestly examine your attitudes and views as they relate to people of other cultures. You may be carrying baggage that you have to get rid of to authentically and honestly educate all of your children to their fullest capacity.
- Read widely about your cultural role as a professional.
- Learn about the habits, customs, beliefs, and religious practices of the cultures represented by your children.
- Ask some of your students' parents to tutor you in their language so you can learn basic phrases for greeting and questioning, the meaning of nonverbal gestures, and the way to appropriately and respectfully address parents and children.

STRATEGY 2 Make Every Child Welcome

- Make your classroom a place where diversity is encouraged and everyone is treated fairly. Create a classroom environment that is vibrant and alive with the cultures of your children. You can do this with pictures, artifacts, and objects provided by parents.
- Support and use children's home language and culture. Create a safe environment in which children feel free to talk about and share their culture and language. Encourage children to discuss, draw, paint, and write about what their culture means to them.

STRATEGY 3 Make Every Parent Welcome

- Invite parents and families to share their languages and cultures in your classroom. Music, stories, and customs provide a rich background for learning about and respecting other cultures.
- Communicate with parents in their home languages.
- Work with parents to help them (and you) bridge the differences between the way schools operate and the norms of their homes and cultures.

STRATEGY 4 Collaborate with Your Colleagues

- Ask colleagues to share ideas with you about how to respond to questions, requests, and concerns of children and parents.
- Volunteer to form a faculty study group to read, discuss, and learn how to meet the cultural and linguistic needs of all children.

STRATEGY 5 Become Active in Your Community

- Learn as much as you can about your community and the cultural resources it can provide. Communities are very multicultural places!
- Collaborate with community and state organizations that work with culturally and linguistically diverse families and populations. Ask them for volunteers who can help you meet the diverse needs of your children. Children need to interact with and value role models from all cultures.
- Volunteer to act as a community outreach coordinator to provide families with services such as family literacy and school readiness information.

You can't be a complete early childhood professional without a cultural dimension. As you become more culturally aware, you will increase your capacity for caring and understanding—and you and your students will learn and grow together.

a creative tension between respecting differences and not accepting unfair beliefs and acts. It asks teachers and children to confront troublesome issues rather than covering them up. An anti-bias perspective is integral to all aspects of daily classroom life.[31]

Here are some antibias strategies you should follow in your classroom:

- ***Evaluate your classroom environment and instructional materials to determine if they are appropriate for an antibias curriculum.*** Get rid of materials that are obstacles to your antibias goals, such as books that include children of only one race. In my visits to early childhood classrooms, I observe many that are "cluttered," meaning they contain too many materials that do not contribute much to a multicultural learning environment. Include photos and representations from all cultures in your classroom and community.

- ***Develop a plan for redesigning your classroom.*** For example, you may decide to add a literacy center that encourages children to "read" and "write" about cultural themes. Remember that children need the time, opportunity, and materials required to read and write about a wide range of antibias topics. In addition, since most classrooms don't have enough books on topics relating to gender or with cultural and ethnic themes, make sure you provide them.

- ***Evaluate your current curriculum and approaches to diversity.*** This will help you understand how your curriculum is or is not supporting antibias approaches. Learning experiences should be relevant to your students, their community, and their families' cultures.

- ***Observe children's play and social interactions to determine what you have to do to make sure that all children are accepted and valued.*** For example, some children of different cultural backgrounds may not be included in particular play groups. This information allows you to develop plans for ensuring that children of all cultures and genders are included in play groups and activities.

- ***Evaluate how you interact with children.*** You can reflect on your teaching, videotape your teaching, and/or have a colleague observe your teaching. Such valuable professional material provides you with invaluable insight into how you interact with all children so you can make appropriate changes if necessary. For example, you may unknowingly give more attention to boys than to girls. Or you may be overlooking some important environmental accommodations that can support the learning of children with disabilities.

- ***Include antibias activities in your daily and weekly classroom plans.*** Intentional planning helps ensure that you are including a full range of antibias activities in your program. Intentional antibias planning also helps you integrate antibias activities into your curriculum for meeting national, state, and local learning standards.

- ***Work with parents to incorporate your antibias curriculum.*** Remember, parents are valuable resources in helping you achieve your standards.[32]

Implementing an antibias curriculum will not be easy and it will require a lot of hard work and effort on your part. However, this is what teaching and being a professional is all about. You owe it to yourself, your children, and the profession to conduct programs that enable all children to live and learn in bias-free programs.

Creating Healthy, Respectful, Supportive, and Challenging Learning Environments.   Research consistently shows that children cared for and taught in enriched environments are healthier, happier, and more achievement-oriented.[33] To achieve this standard for all children, you must provide them with environments that are healthy, respectful, supportive, and challenging. There are many school-wide efforts that provide for high-quality learning and social environments for young children. These include providing breakfast for children, supporting school-wide healthy living campaigns, and implementing anti-bullying programs. At the classroom level you can involve children in healthy eating lessons and activities such as having them conduct an environmental survey of the school to examine health and safety issues.

Healthy Environments. Provide for children's physical and psychological health, safety, and sense of security. For example, the Austin Eco School in Austin, Texas, creates an environment for its students where they can learn and play in an environment that is free from chemical toxins typically found in cleansers, paint, and flooring. Increasingly, child care programs across the country are using eco-friendly diapers, nontoxic methods to control pests, and organic baby foods.

Respectful Environments. Show respect for each individual child and for his or her culture, home language, individual abilities or disabilities, family context, and community. Marcy Henniger, author of *Setting the Stage for Learning,* encourages parents and teachers to promote learning through cooking. Teachers can have an "exploration center" filled with learning activities and materials from different cultures such as foods and recipe books, where children can experiment and interact with cooking.[34]

Santos Ramirez, a first grader at Jay Shideler Elementary School in Topeka, Kansas, has ataxic cerebral palsy. He uses a DynaVox Vmax, an augmentative and alternative communication device that helps him communicate. Santos is in a regular, inclusive classroom with other first graders and enjoys physical education and recess along with his friends. Santos's teacher, Lisa Hamilton, was initially nervous about having Santos in her class; however, "He won everyone over. He's a regular kid trapped in a body that won't work the way he wants it to. He is capable of the first grade curriculum. He is very intelligent."[35]

Supportive Environments. Believe each child can learn and help children understand and make meaning of their experiences. Some schools and classrooms encourage and support their students by pairing students who have autism with typically developing children. This approach helps children with autism become familiar with the traditional classroom and brings the regular school experience to students who may spend most of their day in a classroom for autistic children.

Challenging Environments. Provide achievable and "stretching" experiences for all children. In challenging environments, children are encouraged to be their best and do their best. For example, one of Teacher of the Year Tracie Gossett's second graders says of her, "She makes learning fun and makes us work hard so we can meet our standards." But at the same time, Gossett's children have fun learning! Another of her students says, "She makes everything a fun game and just fun by itself." So, encouraging children to meet high standards while having fun learning is one of the hallmarks of a challenging environment.[36]

Teaching the Whole Child

Children are not one- or two-dimensional persons. Children are a unified whole across all developmental domains! There is much discussion today about teaching the whole child—physically, socially, emotionally, cognitively, linguistically, and spiritually. This renewed interest in teaching the whole child reflects the profession's ongoing dedication to developmentally appropriate practice. The Association for Supervision and Curriculum Development (ASCD) leads the Whole Child Initiative, a national effort to include the whole child in all instructional programs and practices.

The Whole Child Initiative is straightforward. If students are to master world-class academics, they need to be physically and emotionally healthy. They need to be well

applying research to practice

Supportive Teachers Play Critical Roles in Children's Academic Success

In a longitudinal study involving academically at-risk children, researchers examined factors that contribute to children's ongoing success. Here is one of their findings:

Children who have a supportive relationship with their teacher, in an environment where they feel accepted and secure, are more likely to work hard and perceive themselves as academically capable.[37]

So, what does this mean for you?

- Any efforts to close or eliminate achievement gaps have to begin with instructional practices that focus on helping each child gain the confidence and ability to do better. Only in this way will children break out of the predictable pattern of only achieving at the same level from one year to the next.
- Children need teachers such as you to create a positive social and emotional relationship with them so they are motivated and engaged in classroom learning.
- Nurturing teacher–student relationships have their greatest impact on children with existing behavioral problems and those who have trouble regulating their behavior. Often these children don't get the nurturing teacher–child relationships that they need in order to succeed. Going above and beyond to provide love, affection, and nurturing to problem children is essential for their ongoing academic achievement. For some children, you are their main source of love, affection, and attention.

fed and safe. They need to be intellectually challenged and have supportive adults who know them well and care about their success. And they need to be interested and engaged in what they are learning. It is common sense—a hungry student can't learn, a scared student can't think, and a student who is bored or intimidated by schoolwork will just slip through the cracks.[38]

Figure 1.4 shows the various dimensions involved in guiding children in and across all domains. As you work with your children, reflect on how you can promote their positive development in all dimensions. In addition, another facet of the whole child—spiritual development—has not received enough attention. A recent trend in this area is a greater emphasis on supporting children's spiritual development through moral and character education.[39]

PATHWAYS TO PROFESSIONAL DEVELOPMENT

The educational dimension of professionalism involves knowing about and demonstrating essential knowledge of the profession and professional practice. This knowledge includes the history and ethics of the profession, understanding how children develop and learn, and keeping up-to-date on public issues that influence early childhood and the profession.

Training and certification issues are a major challenge facing all areas of the early childhood profession and those who care for and teach young children. Training and certification requirements vary from state to state, and more states are tightening personnel standards for child care, preschool, kindergarten, and primary-grade professionals.

Many states have career ladders that specify the requirements for progressing from one level of professionalism to the next. As an example, Figure 1.5 outlines the early childhood practitioner's professional pathway for Oklahoma, which is fairly typical of

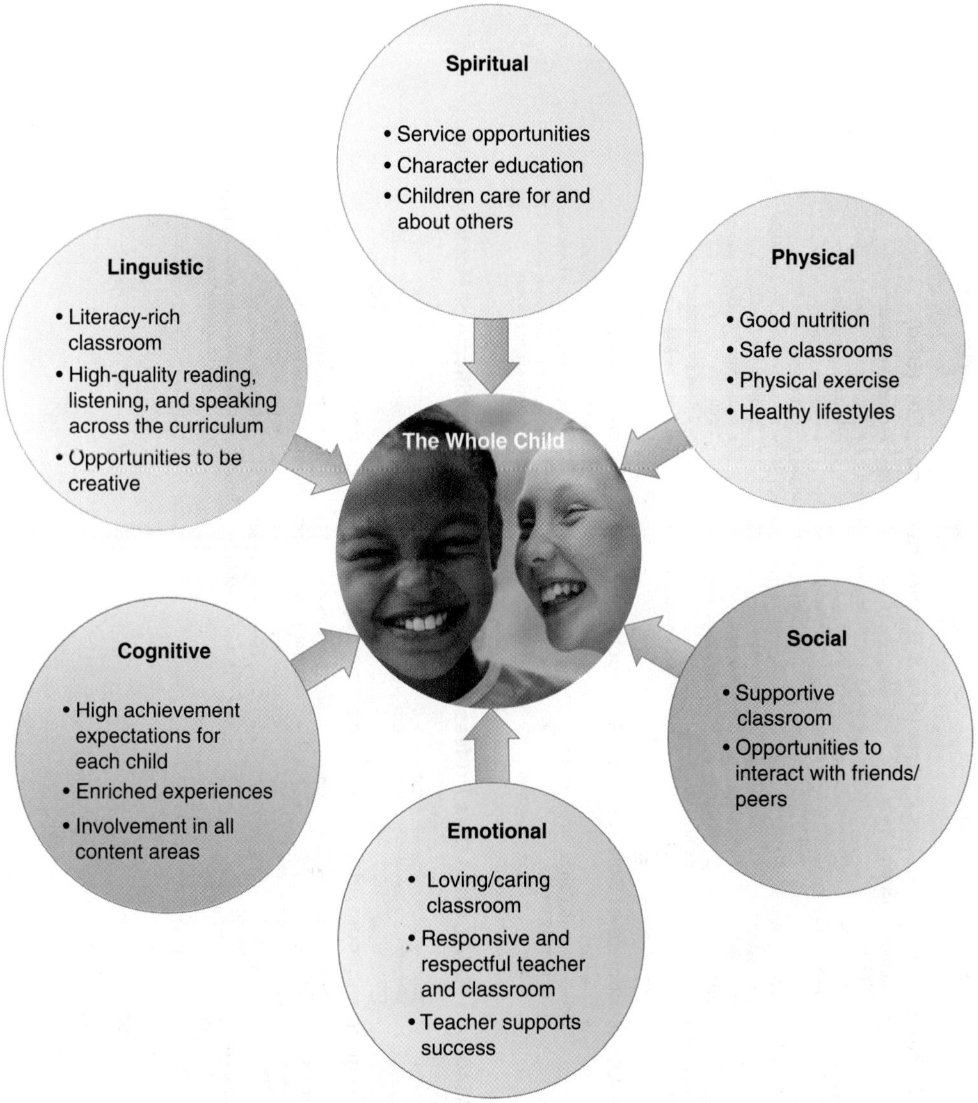

FIGURE 1.4 Guiding the Whole Child

A key to guiding children's behavior is to guide their behavior across all developmental domains as shown here.

career pathways across the United States. What two things do you find most informative about this career pathway? How can you use the Oklahoma pathway to enhance your own professional development?

Just as there are many ways to enter any profession, the same is true of early childhood education. There is not just one way to enter the field. Some teachers enter the teaching profession after military service; others work in business or industry for several years and then decide that their true calling is to teach; and many others, perhaps like you, have always wanted to be a teacher because of the influence your teachers had on you.

The CDA Program

The **Child Development Associate (CDA)** National Credentialing Program is a competency-based assessment system that offers early childhood professionals the

Child Development
Associate (CDA) A National
Credentialing Program is a
competency-based assessment system that offers early
childhood professionals the
opportunity to develop and
demonstrate competence in
their work with children ages
five and younger.

Early Education Professional Development Career Pyramid

Advanced Level and Degrees — MS, MA, PhD, EdD, JD, MD, RN

Traditional:
- Early care and education Instructor at technology centers
- Teacher educator at a two year college or four year university
- Instructor/curriculum specialist
- Child development specialist
- Child guidance specialist
- Research/writer
- Early intervention
- Director/specialist in a child care resource and referral
- Family support and education

Related with further education/training/certifications:
- Social worker
- Teacher/administrator/special educator in a public or private elementary school – certification required
- Child advocate/lobbyist
- Librarian
- Pediatric therapist – occupational and physical
- Human resources personnel in industry
- Child life specialist in a hospital
- Speech and hearing pathologist – health department, public/private school, private practice, university teaching
- Early childhood consultant
- Entertainer/musician/song writer for children
- Career coach
- Agency administrator/director
- Author and illustrator of children's books
- Physician/Pediatrician
- Pedodontist (works only with children)
- Dietitian for children
- Counselor
- Child psychologist
- Psychiatrist
- Dietetic assistant
- Recreation supervisor
- Children's policy specialist
- Dental hygienist
- Scouting director
- Hospice care
- Domestic violence counselor
- Positions in elder care
- Child care center or playground/recreation center designer
- Probation officer
- County extension educator with 4-H
- Adoption specialist
- "Friend of the Court" counselor
- Psychometrist
- Attorney with primary focus on children/elderly
- Faith-based community coordinator and educator
- Family mediator
- Marriage and family therapy
- Infant/Child mental health specialist

Baccalaureate Level—Bachelors of Science (BS), Bachelors of Arts (BA) & Bachelors of Education (BEd)

Traditional:
- Early childhood teacher in public school, Head Start or child care settings-certification required
- Special education teacher
- Family child care home provider
- Nanny
- Administrator in a Head Start program
- Child care center director/owner/coordinator
- Child care center director in the armed services

Related with some positions requiring additional coursework at the baccalaureate level which will be in a field other than early childhood:
- Parent/family educator
- Family advocate
- Case manager in a state agency/recourse coordinator
- Parents as teachers coordinator
- Director of school-age (out of school time) program
- Mentor/coach
- Child advocate/lobbyist
- Recreation director/worker/leader
- Web master
- Adult educator
- Journalist/author/publisher/illustrator of children's books
- Children's librarian
- Retail manager of children's toy or book stores
- Licensing worker
- Human resource personnel in industry
- Music teacher, musician/entertainer for children
- Recreation camp director
- Camp counselor/scouts camp ranger
- Domestic violence prevention and education
- Sex education and prevention
- Resource and referral trainer/data analyst
- Referral specialist/child care food program consultant
- Childbirth educator
- Gymnastic or dance teacher
- Pediatric nurse aide
- Child and parenting practitioner certification
- Producer of children's television shows and commercials
- Faith community coordinator and educator
- Substance abuse educator
- Foster care services

Associate Level—Associate of Arts (AA), Associate of Science (AS), & Associate of Applied Science (AAS)

Traditional:
- Child care center director
- School-age provider
- Early intervention/special needs program
- Para-professional assistant

Related in addition to those listed at the core level:
- Parent educator
- Family and human services worker
- LPN – specialized nurse training
- Entertainer for children at theme restaurants, parks or parties
- Social service aide
- Youth services
- Playground monitor
- Physical therapy assistant
- Nursing home aide/worker/technician
- Faith community coordinators for families and children

National Credential Level—Child Development Associate (CDA), Child Care Professional (CCP), & Oklahoma Certificate of Mastery (CoM)

Traditional:
- Head Start teacher (CDA required)
- Child care teacher – master teacher
- Family childhood care home provider
- Teacher assistant in public school classroom (additional college hours required)
- Child care center director
- Home visitor
- Nursing home aide/worker
- Nanny

Core Level—these positions require minimum education and training depending on the position

Traditional:
- Child care teaching assistant
- Family child care home provider
- Head Start teacher assistant
- Nanny
- Foster parent
- Church nursery attendant

Related positions which involve working with children in settings other than a child care center, family child care home, Head Start, or public school program may require specialized pre-service training:
- Children's storyteller, art instructor or puppeteer
- Recreation center assistant
- Salesperson in children's toys, clothing or bookstore
- School crossing guard
- Children's party caterer
- Restaurant helper for birthday parties
- Van or transportation driver
- Children's art museum guide
- Receptionist in pediatrician's office
- Camp counselor
- Special needs child care assistant
- Live-in caregiver
- Respite caregiver
- Cook's aide, camp cook, Head Start or child care center cook

FIGURE 1.5 Early Childhood Practitioner's Professional Pathway for Oklahoma

Source: © 2008 Center for Early Childhood Professional Development, University of Oklahoma Board of Regents.

opportunity to develop and demonstrate competence in their work with children ages five and younger. Since its inception in 1975, the CDA program has provided a nationally recognized system that has stimulated early childhood training and education opportunities for teachers of young children in every state in the country and on military bases worldwide. The credential is recognized nationwide in state regulations for licensed centers as a qualification for teachers, directors, and/or family child care providers. The standards for performance that this program has established are used as a basis for professional development in the field.

The CDA program offers credentials to caregivers in four types of settings: (1) center-based programs for preschoolers, (2) center-based programs for infants/toddlers, (3) family child care homes, and (4) **home visitor programs**. Regardless of setting, all CDA candidates must demonstrate their ability to provide competent care and early educational practice in thirteen skill areas organized into six competency areas. Evidence of ability is collected from a variety of sources including firsthand observational evidence of the CDA candidate's performance with children and families. This evidence is weighed against national standards. The CDA national office sets the standards for competent performance and monitors this assessment process so that it is uniform throughout the country.

home visitor program A program that involves visitation of children, parents, and other family members in their homes by trained personnel who provide information, training, and support.

Associate Degree Programs

Many community colleges provide associate degrees in *early childhood education*, which qualifies recipients to be **child care** aides, primary child care providers, and assistant teachers. For example, the Associate in Early Childhood Education program at St. Philips College in San Antonio, Texas, is designed to prepare students for a career working with children and families in a variety of work settings. The degree offers students early childhood opportunities in administration, staff training, social service, child advocacy, classroom instruction, as well as other child-related jobs. This AAS degree may transfer credits toward a bachelor's degree in early childhood, child development, or human sciences. The AAS qualifies an individual for, but does not limit him or her to, positions as a lead teacher or director in an Early Head Start program, program coordinator, public school early childhood teacher, and assistant or staff development specialist.[40]

child care The comprehensive care and education of young children outside their homes.

Baccalaureate Programs

Four-year colleges provide programs that result in early childhood teacher certification. The ages and grades to which the certification applies vary from state to state. Some states have separate certification for **pre-kindergarten** programs and nursery schools; in other states, these certifications are "add-ons" to elementary (K–6, 1–6, 1–4) certification. At the University of South Florida, the age three through grade three teacher certification program includes coursework and extensive field experiences in early childhood settings to enable students to integrate theory with teaching practice.

pre-kindergarten A class or program preceding kindergarten for children usually from three to four years old.

Alternative Certification Programs

Many professionals enter the teaching profession after they have a baccalaureate degree in another field, such as finance, psychology, biology, or English. These individuals don't need another bachelor's degree. What they need is the pedagogical knowledge and skills necessary to be a highly effective teacher. To fulfill this need for a different pathway to the teaching profession, many states, school districts, and private agencies offer alternative certification programs. **Alternative certification** programs are routes to teacher certification through which an individual who already has at least

alternative certification Programs that are routes to teacher certification through which an individual who already has at least a bachelor's degree can obtain certification to teach without necessarily having to go back to college and complete a college-based teacher education program. These alternative teacher training programs are sponsored by colleges of education, state departments of education, and for-profit agencies.

a bachelor's degree can obtain certification to teach without necessarily having to go back to college and complete a college-based teacher education program. These alternative teacher training programs are sponsored by colleges of education, state departments of education, and for-profit agencies.

Master's Degree Programs

Depending on the state, individuals may advance their learning and/or gain initial early childhood certification at the master's level. Many colleges and universities offer master's programs for professionals who want to qualify as program directors or assistant program directors or who want to pursue a career in teaching. In addition, others may use the master's degree to pursue their lifelong dream of teaching after spending several years in another profession. For example, Mary Ladd graduated with a bachelor's degree in business and worked for five years in a high-tech company. However, she kept feeling a call to teach and satisfy her desire to work with young children. Mary earned a master's degree and teacher certification and now teaches first grade in an urban setting, where she enjoys helping young children learn to read.

Your Ongoing Professional Development

You will find throughout your career that the majority of your professional development will occur through other pathways than formal education. For example, the teachers at Bunnell Elementary at Daytona Beach, Florida, participate in a program called Teachers Teaching Teachers. In this program, teachers visit other teachers' classrooms and observe, up close and personal, other teachers' techniques and teaching practices. Topics teachers are involved in range from dealing with behavior issues and preventing bullying to teaching inductive and deductive reasoning. Abra Seay, a second grade teacher who developed the Teachers Teaching Teachers program, says, "Professional development is absolutely critical!" More than likely you will be involved in similar kinds of teacher-led programs designed to introduce new ideas and sharpen teaching skills.[41]

Academic Coaching.   The chances are good too that when you take your first job or move from one school to another, an **academic coach**, an experienced teacher with a strong knowledge of providing instruction in a specific area such as math, science, reading, or technology, will help you improve your instructional skills by advising and supporting you with instructional materials and offer guidance on planning and assessment. For example, new teachers at Northwest (Texas) Independent School District work with technology academic coaches Cathy Faris and Carla Burkholder who help them integrate technology into their instructional practices.

DEVELOPING A PHILOSOPHY OF EDUCATION

Professional practice entails teaching with and from a philosophy of education, which acts as a guidepost to help you base your teaching on what you believe about children.

A **philosophy of education** is a set of beliefs about how children develop and learn and what and how they should be taught. Your philosophy of education is based in part on your philosophy of life. What you believe about yourself, about others, and about life determines your philosophy of education. For example, we previously talked about optimism. If you are optimistic about life, chances are you will be optimistic for your children, and we know that when teachers have high expectations for their children, they achieve at higher levels. Core beliefs and values about education and teaching include what you believe about children, what you think are the purposes of education, how you view the teacher's role, and what you think you should know and be able to do.

academic coach An experienced teacher with a strong knowledge of providing instruction in a specific area such as math, science, reading, or technology.

philosophy of education A set of beliefs about how children develop and learn and what and how they should be taught.

In summary, your philosophy of education guides and directs your daily teaching. The following guidelines will help you develop your philosophy of education.

Read

Read widely in textbooks, journals, and on the Web to get ideas for your philosophy. For example, these are some of the short philosophies of education from teachers of the year in Lee County, North Carolina:

Lisa Howard, second grade teacher: "It is my belief that the goal of education is to provide students with the tools necessary to achieve success. Through guidance and nurturing, teachers can empower students to become positive contributors to our society."

Candace Bloedorn, third grade teacher: "I believe that every child has the ability to learn. As an educator, I hope to create an environment where children are able to take risks, make mistakes, and learn from them. I hope to inspire and motivate our twenty-first century learners by incorporating technology and providing instruction that is meaningful and hands-on."

Donna Thomas, first grade teacher: "Every child is unique and special. My role is to facilitate learning while guiding students toward self-discovery in an environment that is conducive to positive physical, social, cognitive, and emotional growth in an accepting, caring, supportive, and safe environment that encourages every child to reach his/her fullest potential."[42]

Reflect

As you read through and study this book, make notes and reflect about your philosophy of education. The following prompts will help you get started:

- I believe the purposes of education are . . .
- I believe that children learn best when they are taught under certain conditions and in certain ways. Some of these are . . .
- The curriculum, all of the activities and experiences of my classroom, should include certain "basics" that contribute to children's social, emotional, intellectual, and physical development. These basics include . . .
- Children learn best in an enriched environment that is healthy, respectful and challenging. Features of a good learning environment are . . .
- Children live and breathe in a technological age. My feelings about integrating technology in my teaching include . . .
- All children have certain needs that must be met if they are to grow and learn at their best. Some of these basic needs are . . .
- Some ways I can meet children's needs are . . .
- All teachers should have certain qualities and behave in certain ways. Qualities I think important for teaching are . . .

Discuss

Discuss with successful teachers and other educators their philosophies and practices. The personal accounts in the Professionalism in Practice boxes in each chapter of this text are evidence that a philosophy can help you be a successful, effective teacher. They also serve as an opportunity to "talk" with successful professionals and understand how they translate theory into practice.

Write

Once you have thought about your philosophy of education, write a draft and have other people read it. Share your ideas through Facebook, Twitter, and blogs. In fact, creating a class blog about philosophies of education is a good way to get you and your classmates involved. Writing and sharing your philosophy will help you clarify your ideas and redefine your thoughts, because your philosophy should be understandable to others (although they do not necessarily have to agree with you!).

Evaluate

Finally, evaluate your philosophy using this checklist:

- Does my philosophy accurately relate my beliefs about teaching? Have I been honest with myself?
- Is it understandable to me and others?
- Does it provide practical guidance for my teaching?
- Are my ideas consistent with one another?
- Does what I believe make good sense to me and others?

Now finalize your draft into a polished copy. A well-thought-out philosophy will be like a compass throughout your career. Keep in mind that your philosophy of education will change and evolve as you grow as a professional. My philosophy of education constantly changes as I think about and reflect on classroom teaching, as I read and review new research, and as I engage in professional activities with my colleagues. The same will be true for you. Ongoing, continuous professional and personal development is expected as you constantly reflect on and engage in teaching young children and collaborating with their families and your colleagues. You will have many twists and turns in your career, but your philosophy will point you in the right direction and keep you focused on doing your best for all children.

NEW ROLES FOR EARLY CHILDHOOD PROFESSIONALS

The role of the early childhood professional today is radically different from what it was even five years ago. Although the standards of professionalism and the characteristics of the high-quality professional remain the same, responsibilities, expectations, and roles have changed. Let's examine some of these new roles of the contemporary early childhood professional.

- ***Teacher as instructional leader.*** Teachers have always been responsible for classroom and program instruction, but this role is now reemphasized and given a much more prominent place in what early childhood teachers do, such as planning for what children will learn, guiding and teaching so that children learn, assessing what children learn, and arranging the classroom environment so that children learn. Today, the instructional emphasis is on each child's learning and achievement.
- ***Intentional teaching of district and Common Core State (CCS) standards.*** Intentional teaching occurs when instructors teach for a purpose, are clear about what they teach, and teach so that children learn specific knowledge and skills. In this context, teachers spend more time during the day actually teaching and make a conscious effort to be more involved in each child's learning process. Intentional

teaching can and should occur in a child-centered approach for specified times and purposes throughout the school day.

- *Performance-based accountability for learning.* Teachers today are far more accountable for children's learning than at any other time in American history. Previously, the emphasis was on the process of schooling. Teachers were able to explain their role as "I taught Mario how to. . . ." Today the emphasis is on the learning that takes place, such as "What did Mario learn?" and "Did Mario learn what he needs to know and do to perform at or above grade level?"

- *Teaching of reading, math, science, and technology.* Although the teaching of reading has always been a responsibility of early childhood professionals, the instructional role of today's teachers has been expanded and includes an emphasis on math, science, and technology.

- *Increased emphasis on linking assessment and instruction.* Today, all teachers use the results of assessment to plan for teaching and learning. Assessment and planning are an essential part of the teaching-learning process.

- *New meaning of child-centered education.* Early childhood professionals have always advocated child-centered education and approaches. However, today there is a rebirth of child-centered education processes. Essential to the child-centered approach are the ideas that each child can reach high levels of achievement, that each child is eager to learn, and that children are capable of learning more than many people previously thought they could learn. A new concept of child-centeredness embraces the whole child in all dimensions: social, emotional, physical, linguistic, and cognitive.

Integration of Early Childhood and Special Education

The ongoing integration of early childhood education and early childhood special education is a seismic shift in the profession. This integration will continue to occur and I predict will be complete by 2015. I anticipate that future teachers will receive more special education training and that you, as a practicing professional, will undergo considerable professional development to help you be a more effective teacher in your inclusive classroom. Today, teaching in the inclusive classroom is the new normal.

The number of children with disabilities being identified is growing rapidly. It is estimated that 2.8 million children in public schools have a disability of some kind.[43] Your role as an early childhood professional includes using instructional strategies and ideas integrated from the field of special education. Another of your roles, regardless of the grade you teach, is to ensure that all children receive all the benefits of federal and state laws designed to ensure that all children, regardless of ability or disability, receive educational services according to their needs.

TWENTY–FIRST CENTURY TEACHERS

Twenty-first century teachers are knowledgeable about a wide range of subjects, collaborate with their colleagues, teach so children learn, and engage in continuing their professional development. Figure 1.6 identifies other skills of the twenty-first century teacher.

Highly Effective Teachers

There are many qualities that make up highly effective teachers. Some of these are included in the Applying Research to Practice feature.

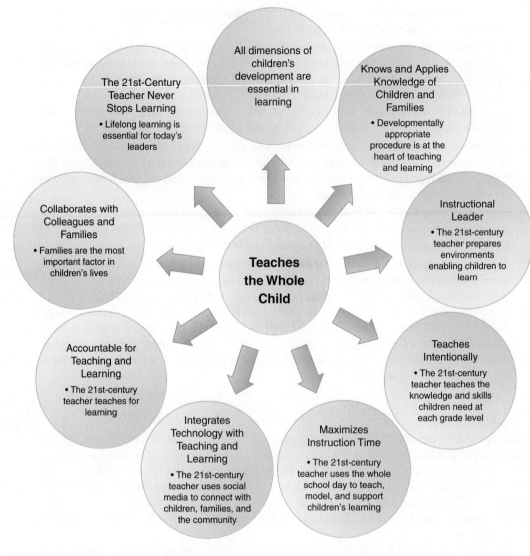

FIGURE 1.6 Twenty-First Century Teacher

The twenty-first century teacher is a multitalented and multiskilled individual who is dedicated to ensuring that each child will learn to his or her fullest capacity. Read and reflect on these skills that are required of you as a twenty-first century teacher. Plan now for how you will incorporate all of these skills into your professional development, in order for you to be a highly effective twenty-first century teacher.

Teaching in Early Childhood Today

As the field of early childhood continues to change, the details of your role as an early childhood professional will continue to be refined. You will want to devote the time and energy necessary to keep yourself in the forefront of your field.

My purpose in writing this book is to support your professional development from the stage where you are—novice or midlevel to highly skilled expert. The professional development checklist in Figure 1.7 is a powerful tool you can begin to use now to achieve this goal. The Desired Professional Competencies come from a number of sources: the Professional Standards of the National Association for the Education of Young Children, the initial certification standards for early childhood certification of the National Council for Accreditation of Teacher Education (NCATE), National Teachers of the Year, National Board Certified teachers, and professors of early childhood education.

applying research to practice

Highly Effective Teachers

According to the National Commission on Teaching and America's Future, teacher expertise has a direct correlation to high student achievement. "Students who have highly effective teachers three years in a row score as much as 50 percentile points higher on achievement tests than those who have ineffective teachers for three years in a row," states Linda Darling-Hammond. Effective teachers "know the content they are teaching, engage students in learning, and challenge them to greater accomplishments."[44]

Today, in many cases, students' knowledge is summarized as a test score, and teachers' effectiveness is perceived as their contribution to that test score. Although student scores on standardized tests can be useful gauges of a teacher's effect, they should not be the sole criteria. Test scores do not give a full picture of teacher contributions and student circumstances, not to mention which students get tested and on what content.

Defining teacher effectiveness is not about creating a simplistic, single view of effective teaching. "It is a dramatic conceptual shift," says ASCD executive director Gene Carter, "from focusing exclusively on the teacher to focusing on the act of learning." The National Comprehensive Center for Teacher Quality (NCCTQ) suggests extending the definition of teacher effectiveness "beyond teachers' contribution to student achievement gains to include how teachers impact classrooms, schools, and their colleagues as well as how they contribute to other important outcomes for students."

So what does this mean to you?
Teacher effectiveness consists of five dimensions:

- Effective teachers have high expectations for all students and help them learn, as demonstrated on tests, teacher assessments, and self-assessments.
- Effective teachers contribute to positive academic, attitudinal, and social outcomes for students such as regular attendance, on-time promotion to the next grade, self-efficacy, and cooperative behavior.
- Effective teachers use diverse resources to plan and structure engaging learning opportunities, monitor student progress, adapt instruction as needed, and evaluate learning using multiple sources of evidence.
- Effective teachers contribute to the development of classrooms and schools that value diversity and civic-mindedness.
- Effective teachers collaborate with other teachers, administrators, parents, and education professionals to ensure students' success, particularly the success of students with special needs and those at high risk of failure.

Defining teacher effectiveness as the sum of multiple parts means education communities will need to employ multiple measures to evaluate different aspects of teacher effectiveness.[45]

FIGURE 1.7

Seventeen Competencies for Becoming a Professional: A Professional Development Checklist

NAEYC Standard	Desired Professional Goals
Standard 1	**Promoting Child Development and Learning** I use my understanding of young children's characteristics and needs, and of multiple interacting influences on children's development and learning, to create environments that are healthy, respectful, supportive, and challenging for each child.
Standard 1	**Delivering Education and Child Care** I am familiar with a variety of models and approaches for delivering education and child care, and I use this knowledge to deliver education and child care in a safe, healthy learning environment.
Standard 1	**Guiding Behavior** I understand the principles and importance of behavior guidance. I guide children to be peaceful, cooperative, and in control of their behavior.
Standard 1	**Theories of Early Childhood Education** I understand the principles of each major theory of educating young children. The approach I use is consistent with my beliefs about how children learn.
Standard 2	**Building Family and Community Relationships** I know about, understand, and value the importance and complex characteristics of children's families and communities. I use this understanding to create respectful, reciprocal relationships that support and empower families, and to involve all families in their children's development and learning.
Standard 3	**Observing, Documenting, and Assessing to Support Young Children and Families** I know about and understand the goals, benefits, and uses of assessment. I know about and use systematic observations, documentation, and other effective assessment strategies in a responsible way, in partnership with families and other professionals, to positively influence the development of each child.
Standard 4	**Using Developmentally Effective Approaches to Connect with Children and Families** I use my knowledge of children and families, developmentally effective approaches, and academic disciplines to design, implement, and evaluate learning experiences for all children.
Standard 4	**Educating Diverse Students** I understand that all children are individuals with unique strengths and challenges. embrace these differences, work to fulfill special needs, and promote tolerance and inclusion in my classroom. I value and respect the dignity of all children.
Standard 4	**Developmentally Appropriate Practice** I understand children's developmental stages and growth from birth through age 8, and use this knowledge to implement developmentally appropriate practice. I do all I can to advance the physical, intellectual, social, and emotional development of the children in my care to their full potential.
Standard 4	**Technology** I am technologically literate and integrate technology into my classroom to help all children learn.
Standard 5	**Using Content Knowledge to Build Meaningful Curriculum** I understand the importance of developmental domains and academic (or content) disciplines in early childhood curriculum. I know the essential concepts, inquiry tools, and structure of content areas, including academic subjects, and can identify resources to deepen my understanding. I use my own knowledge and other resources to design, implement, and evaluate meaningful, challenging curricula that promote comprehensive developmental and learning outcomes for every young child.
Standard 6	**Becoming a Professional** I identify and conduct myself as a member of the early childhood profession. I know and use ethical guidelines and other professional standards related to early childhood practice. I am a continuous, collaborative learner who demonstrates knowledgeable, reflective, and critical perspectives on my work, making informed decisions that integrate knowledge from a variety of sources. I am an informed advocate for sound educational practices and policies.
Standard 6	**Ongoing Professional Development** I have a professional career plan for the next year. I engage in study and training programs to improve my knowledge and competence, belong to a professional organization, and have worked or am working on a degree or credential (CDA, AA, BS, or BA). I strive for positive, collaborative relationships with my colleagues and employer.

FIGURE 1.7 Continued

Level of Accomplishment? (Circle One)	If High, Provide Evidence of Accomplishment	If Needs Improvement, Specify Action Plan for Accomplishment	Target Date of Completion of Accomplishment	See the following for more information on how to meet the Desired Professional Outcomes
High Needs Improvement				Chapters 1, 4, 5, 6, 7, 8, 9, 10, 11, 12, and 13
High Needs Improvement				Chapters 3, 4, 7, 8, 9, 10, 11, and 12 and all chapters' Technology Tie-In features
High Needs Improvement				Chapter 12
High Needs Improvement				Chapters 3 and 4
High Needs Improvement				Chapters 2, 11, and 13 and all chapters' Diversity Tie-In features
High Needs Improvement				Chapters 1 and 6
High Needs Improvement				Chapters 1, 2, 3, 4, 5, 6, 7, 8, 9, 10, 11, 12, and 13
High Needs Improvement				Chapters 1, 2, 4, 6, 7, 8, 9, 10, 11, 12, and 13 and all chapters' Diversity Tie-In features
High Needs Improvement				Chapters 1, 2, 3, 4, 5, 6, 7, 8, 9, 10, 11, 12, and 13
High Needs Improvement				Chapters 7 and 9 and all chapters' Technology Tie-In features
High Needs Improvement				Chapters 1, 2, 3, 4, 6, 7, 8, 9, 10, and 11 and all chapters' Diversity Tie-In and Technology Tie-In features
High Needs Improvement				Chapters 1, 5, 6, and 13 and all chapters' Ethical Dilemma and Professionalism in Practice features
High Needs Improvement				Chapters 1 and 7 and all chapters' Activities for Professional Development and Ethical Dilemma features

(continued)

FIGURE 1.7 Continued

NAEYC Standard	Desired Professional Goals
Standard 6	**Philosophy of Teaching** I have thought about and written my philosophy of teaching and caring for young children. My actions are consistent with this philosophy.
Standard 6	**Keeping Current in an Age of Change** I am familiar with the profession's contemporary development, and I understand current issues in society and trends in the field. I am willing to change my ideas, thinking, and practices based on study, new information, and the advice of colleagues and professionals.
Standard 6	**Professional Dispositions** I work with students, families, and communities in ways that reflect the dispositions expected of professional educators as delineated in professional, state, and institutional standards. I recognize when my own dispositions may need to be adjusted and am able to develop plans to do so.
Standard 6	**Historical Knowledge** I am familiar with my profession's history, and I use my knowledge of the past to inform my practice.

ACTIVITIES FOR PROFESSIONAL DEVELOPMENT

ethical dilemma

"It isn't fair; she got a bigger raise than I did!"

Emily Johnson is a kindergarten teacher in Madison Hills School District. Last year, the district adopted a performance-based salary system based in part on student achievement scores and on criteria assessed through the principal's classroom observations. Emily just received her notification of her salary increase for next year. When she compared her salary increase to her friend Kim's salary increase, Emily was flabbergasted and shocked. Kim's raise was twice as much as Emily's raise, despite the fact that Emily's children scored higher on the state achievement test. When Emily talked with her principal about her pay raise compared to Kim's, the principal responded, "My classroom observation scores in Kim's classroom were much higher than yours. I thought she did an outstanding job, so I rewarded her for it."

What should Emily do? Should she ask for a specific written explanation as to why the principal gave higher scores to Kim and not to her? Should Emily remain quiet and try to do better next year? Or should Emily pursue another course of action? What would you do?

FIGURE 1.7 Continued

Level of Accomplishment? (Circle One)	If High, Provide Evidence of Accomplishment	If Needs Improvement, Specify Action Plan for Accomplishment	Target Date of Completion of Accomplishment	See the following for more information on how to meet the Desired Professional Outcomes
High Needs Improvement				All chapters' Activities for Professional Development and Ethical Dilemma features
High Needs Improvement				Chapters 1, 2, 3, 4, 5, 6, 7, 8, 9, 10, 11, 12, and 13
High Needs Improvement				Chapters 1, 2, 5, 11, and 12 and all chapters' Professionalism in Practice, Activities for Professional Development, and Ethical Dilemma features
High Needs Improvement				Chapters 3 and 6

Note: These professional development outcomes are consistent with the core values of the NAEYC and the competencies of the CDA.

Source: Adapted from Morrison, George S., *Early Childhood Development Today,* 12th ed., © 2012. Reprinted and Electronically reproduced by permission of Pearson Education, Inc., Upper Saddle River, New Jersey.

Application Activities

1. You can learn a great deal about what is involved in being a high-quality early childhood educator by reading the biographies of National Teachers of the Year. Go to the website of the Council of Chief State School Officers (www.ccsso.org) and read the biographies of National and State Teachers of the Year. Make a list of the characteristics and dispositions that you think make them effective teachers. From your list, choose three characteristics/dispositions and tell how you will incorporate them into your professional development plan. Post your ideas on your class discussion board or blog and ask for your classmates' comments and feedback.

2. One thing is for certain: All of the six standards for becoming an early childhood education professional are extremely important. Rank the six standards in the order that you think is most important for you and your professional development. For example, which do you think is the most important standard? Write a short paragraph about why you rank-ordered the six professional standards in the order you chose. Post your rank ordering and your paragraph on your class discussion board and ask your colleagues for feedback.

3. Access the NAEYC website (www.naeyc.org/about/positions.asp) and review the *Developmentally Appropriate Practice* position statement. Give three specific examples of how you will apply DAP to your teaching so that children learn at high levels. Use the professional development checklist and a daily/monthly planner to develop your professional development plan for the next year. First, list your career development goals and then, on a monthly basis, specify activities, events, and other ways that you will achieve these goals. For example, in addition to attending classes at a local community college, Rosa Vaquerio plans to read a book a month on a topic related to teaching (see books for suggested reading in the chapters of this book).

4. Return to the website for the Council of Chief State School Officers (www.ccsso .org) and review philosophies of education for national and state teachers of the year. Follow the steps outlined in the chapter for developing your own philosophy of education. Develop a "rough draft" of your philosophy of education and post it online for your classmates to review and provide feedback.

5. The roles of early childhood professionals are constantly changing. Review the nine characteristics of the twenty-first century teacher, as shown in Figure 1.6. For each characteristic, tell what you will do to prepare yourself so that you can be a twenty-first century teacher. Develop a presentation in Prezi (www.prezi.com) and volunteer to present your Prezi to your class.

Linking to Learning

Council for Exceptional Children Professional Standards

www.cec.sped.org

International Society for Technology in Education National Educational Technology Standards for Teachers

www.iste.org

Code of Ethical Conduct Position Statement

www.naeyc.org

MyEducationLab

Go to Topic 12 (Professionalism/Ethics) in the MyEducationLab (www.myeducationlab.com) for your course, where you can:

- Find learning outcomes for Professionalism/Ethics along with the national standards that connect to these outcomes.

- Complete Assignments and Activities that can help you more deeply understand the chapter content.

- Apply and practice your understanding of the core teaching skills identified in the chapter with the Building Teaching Skills and Dispositions learning units.

- Access video clips of CCSSO National Teachers of the Year award winners responding to the question, "Why Do I Teach?" in the Teacher Talk section.

- Hear viewpoints of experts in the field in Professional Perspectives.

- Check your comprehension on the content covered in the chapter by going to the Study Plan in the Book Resources for your text. Here you will be able to take a chapter quiz, receive feedback on your answers, and then access Review, Practice, and Enrichment activities to enhance your understanding of chapter content.

EARLY CHILDHOOD EDUCATION TODAY

Understanding and Responding to Current Issues

NAEYC Standards for Early Childhood Professional Preparation

Standard 1. Promoting Child Development and Learning

I use my understanding of young children's characteristics and needs, and of multiple interacting influences on children's development and learning, to create environments that are healthy, respectful, supportive, and challenging for each child.[1]

Standard 6. Becoming a Professional

I identify and conduct myself as a member of the early childhood profession. I know and use ethical guidelines and other professional standards related to early childhood practice. I am a continuous, collaborative learner who demonstrates a knowledgeable, reflective, and critical perspective on my work, making informed decisions that integrate knowledge from a variety of sources. I am an informed advocate for sound educational practices and policies.[2]

ISSUES INFLUENCING THE PRACTICE OF EARLY CHILDHOOD EDUCATION

We hear a lot about change. America wants change from its elected officials. America also wants change in its schools and in the way children are educated. This national demand for change is based on the many economic and social problems facing our nation such as poverty, low school achievement rates, and how to implement the latest research in educational practice. The call for educational change is a result of the many problems facing children and schools.

Child abuse; childhood diseases such as obesity, asthma, and lead poisoning; low-quality child care and education; and society's inability to meet the needs of all children are perennial sources of controversy and concern. New ideas and issues relating to the education and care of young children keep the field of early childhood education in a state of constant change. In fact, change is one constant in the field of early childhood education. As a result, you will be continuously challenged to determine what is best for young children and their families as you meet the demands of society today as an early childhood professional.

You are part of the solution, making it possible for all children to achieve their full potential. Politicians and the public look to you and your colleagues to help develop educational solutions to social and political problems. Teacher of the Year Tina Repetti Renzullo says, "I view teaching as a form of activism in support of our country. It is with great pride of purpose that I approach each school day. My efforts in developing the knowledge and talents of the children in my community provide economic and social benefits of enduring value. I am grateful for and humbled by the trust my country and my community places in me. I honor that confidence in my resolve to ensure that my students learn not only the foundations of reading, writing, and arithmetic, but also the value and promise their education holds for the future."[3]

And as Anthony Mullen, Connecticut Teacher of the Year, notes, ". . . the greatest institution for social change is the school and the greatest instrument of change is the teacher. No other democracy created by man to promote the welfare of all people has ever existed. Schools and teachers have always been *the* catalyst for human progress because knowledge and learning have created the world in which we live."[4]

So, in the spirit of creating change in response to social and educational issues, let's examine some issues in early childhood and consider how you can respond to them.

Children of the Great Recession

Throughout the course of their in-school and out-of-school lives, children's successes and achievement are greatly influenced by their family's socioeconomic status (SES). SES consists of three broad but interrelated measures: parents' education levels, parents' employment status, and family income. These three measures, acting individually and as an integrated whole, influence (1) how children are reared; (2) family–child interactions; (3) home environments and the extent to which they do or do not support language development and learning; (4) the kind and amount of discipline used; and (5) the kind and extent of future plans involving children's education and employment.

The Current SES Status of Children and Families.
The headline says it all: "Poverty Rate Hits 18-year High as Median Income Falls."[5] Forty-six million people live in poverty—that's 15.1 percent of the population! Twenty-one percent of young children live in poor families.[6] Currently the federal poverty level is $23,050 for a family of four.[7] This gives you some idea of the circumstances that poor children and their families face. When I ask my university students to consider whether or not they could—or would want to—live in a family of four whose income is less than $23,050, not one student answers affirmatively. No one wants to be poor, but we have so many children and families who are. We should not bestow the label of *poor* or the conditions that go with being poor on any of our nation's children.

MyEducationLab

Visit the MyEducationLab for *Fundamentals of Early Childhood Education* to enhance your understanding of chapter concepts with a personalized Study Plan. You'll also have the opportunity to hone your teaching skills through video-based Assignments and Activities as well as Building Teaching Skills and Dispositions lessons.

FOCUS QUESTIONS

1. What are critical, contemporary issues that influence the practice of early childhood education?

2. What can I do to promote cultural diversity in my classroom?

3. How can I prevent violence, bullying, and abuse in my classroom?

4. How can I be politically aware and keep current in the rapidly changing field of early childhood education?

poverty The state of a person who lacks a usual or socially acceptable amount of money or material possessions.

As we examine in closer detail the numbers behind the stark poverty statistics, we find that the number of children who live in poverty in America is on the increase:

- Since 2000, the number of children living in poverty has increased by 3.8 million.[8]
- The number of children who fell into poverty between 2008 and 2009 was the largest single-year increase ever recorded.[9]
- One out of nine American children, or 8.1 million children, are living with an unemployed parent.[10] Children whose parents are unemployed are at increased risk for experiencing poverty, homelessness, and child abuse.[11]

Children Living with Grandparents.   Another consequence of the Great Recession is that the devastating effects of poverty cascade through children's and families' lives with intergenerational consequences. One child in ten in the United States lives with a grandparent.[12] Several conditions confound the ability of grandparents to raise their grandchildren. Many grandparents have limited resources, with one in five—20 percent—living in poverty![13] In addition, many grandparents are unfamiliar with how to parent a new generation of children. The demands of the contemporary curriculum and the behavioral challenges of contemporary schooling frequently overwhelm them. It is important to connect grandparents with the resources to help raise their grandchildren.

Latinos and Blacks.   Increasing poverty in the United States is especially hard on historically impoverished cultural groups. The number of Hispanic children in poverty jumped by 36 percent from 2007 to 2011.[14] Hispanics suffered in the Great Recession in part because they were heavily employed in industries like housing that experienced sharp declines. Poverty is especially hard on black and Latino males and adversely affects their life outcomes, leading to higher rates of delinquency and poorer health.[15]

Decreasing Support for Schools.   Unfortunately, as poverty increases, support for America's schools, especially inner-city and low-income neighborhood schools, decreases. Because of the nature of school finance systems in the United States, schools in poor neighborhoods tend to have far less money per pupil than do schools in wealthier districts. Unfortunately, and to children's detriment, school districts in the United States systematically assign less experienced, less qualified, and less effective teachers to schools with poor students.[16]

Neglecting America's children is not the answer. John Dewey said, "What the best and wisest parent wants for his own child . . . that must be what the community wants for all of its children. Any other ideal for our schools is narrow and unlovely."[17]

Solutions to the Great Recession.   So what can we—you and I—do? Here are some programs and solutions that you and other early childhood professionals can embrace and advocate for:

- *Community and neighborhood-based parenting education programs* help assure that all children are ready and eager to learn at their entrance to preschool and kindergarten. Such programs should include home visiting, activities, parenting education classes, and linking families to safety-net programs such as health care benefits, food-based programs such as food stamps, vouchers and coupons, and rent and utility subsidies.
- *High-quality, universal (available for all children), full-day preschool* paid for by tax dollars. I have long argued that we should provide public-supported, high-quality preschool programs through public schools and community-based agencies as a means of helping all children succeed and learn.

- *The development of a pre-K–12 continuum of education.* Historically and unfortunately, preschool is often left out of any discussion of the K–12 continuum of education services and programs. One of the best things that could happen to pre-K is to be included in discussions of and funding for the K–12 continuum on education.

- *Full-day, full-year services.* Parents want full-day, full-year services for their children because such programs fit with parents' work schedules and lifestyles. Working parents in particular find it difficult to patch together child care and other arrangements when their children are not in school. Parents also believe that full-day, full-year services support and enhance their children's learning.

Parents want their children to do well academically. Hopefully, we will see more full-day, full-year early childhood programs of all kinds in the years to come!

- *School readiness.* There is and will continue to be an increase in programs designed to provide families, grandparents, and others with child development information, parenting skills, and learning activities that will help them get every child ready for school. Working with parents to help them get their children ready for learning and school is an important and growing part of early childhood services and your responsibility as an early childhood professional.

- *Early literacy learning.* There is a growing awareness of the critical role literacy plays in school and life success. Consequently, today there is a great emphasis in all early childhood programs on teaching literacy skills and reading.

The challenges of the Great Recession are monumental both domestically and internationally. We as professionals cannot bypass or ignore the children of the Great Recession. We must seek every opportunity to make sure that the children of the Great Recession are not neglected, left out, or left behind.

As we are bombarded by such data about the severity of the Great Recession on children and families, you, other early childhood professionals, and I must maintain an optimistic spirit and attitude regarding how best to serve the nation's young children even in tough times. We must conduct advocacy for young children and their families to ensure they have the services and the programs necessary to help each child reach his or her potential.

> One of the major roles of early childhood programs today is to ensure that all children are ready to achieve at high levels as they enter kindergarten programs. Keep in mind also that readiness involves providing for the needs of the whole child—academic, social, linguistic, and physical and mental health.

The Achievement Gaps

Perhaps the most devastating of all achievement gaps are those related to pervasive poverty. The achievement gaps among students of different income levels are severe. Compared to their peers from higher-income families, infants and toddlers from low-income families score lower on cognitive assessments, are less likely to be in excellent or very good health, and are less likely to receive positive behavior ratings at both nine and twenty-four months old. Impoverished students are roughly two years of learning behind the average better-off students of the same age. The **income achievement gap** appears early and persists over a student's lifetime.[18]

Achievement gaps are the difference in performance between low-income and minority students, students of different genders, and students with different levels of

income achievement gap The achievement gap among students of different income levels.

achievement gaps The difference in performance between low-income and minority students, students of different genders, and students with different levels of maternal education, compared to that of their peers.

diversity tie-in

The Ongoing Decline of Child Well-Being in the United States

As we have discussed, the Great Recession has had a serious impact on children in the United States. Projections are that tough times are still ahead for children of the Great Recession. More children will have two parents who are unemployed. Fewer children will enroll in pre-kindergarten programs, and fewer teenagers will find jobs. More children are likely to commit suicide, be overweight, and be victimized by crime.[19] Unfortunately, researchers believe these dire consequences of the Great Recession for children will persist well into the future. The long-term effects of the Great Recession on children mean that:

- As more families fall below the poverty line, increasing numbers of children will be left behind at the schoolhouse door. These children's preparedness for school will be well below that of their more advantaged peers from wealthier families. For many children of the Great Recession, inequality begins at birth.
- As states scramble for ways to fund entitlement programs such as Social Security, Medicare, public sector health benefits, and so on, more states will underfund or fail to fund existing preschool programs and will delay or indefinitely postpone funding for new preschool programs. This means more preschool-age children will not have the chance to attend preschool, thus denying them opportunities to participate in early literacy and reading programs that can help ensure their individual success and their ability to read on grade level by grade three.
- When children enter school already behind their peers, they will continue to do less well, and the potential for their ongoing failure and eventual dropping out of school increases.
- For the United States, the effects of the Great Recession on children may jeopardize efforts to make America's children more globally competitive and keep the country economically competitive in a global society.
- The number of children experiencing food insecurity is on the increase as more families sink into poverty. Food insecurity occurs when all family members do not have access at all times to safe and nutritious food to maintain an active and healthy lifestyle.[20]

food insecurity Occurs when all family members do not have access, at all times, to safe and nutritious food to maintain an active and healthy lifestyle.

maternal education, compared to that of their peers. Traditionally, low-income and minority children have not performed as well as their peers on tests.[21] Therefore, lower test scores for Latinos, blacks, and low-income students equals less funding, which equals the perpetuation of the achievement gap.[22]

The achievement gap also influences individual outcomes. There is a demonstrable link between early performance in school and subsequent rates of high school graduation, college attendance and completion, and ultimately earnings. The less education children have, the more likely they are as adults to be incarcerated, a smoker, obese, uninsured, and not vote.[23]

maternal education achievement gap The achievement gap between children of higher educated mothers and children of lesser educated mothers.

Maternal Education Achievement Gap. The maternal education achievement gap describes the differences in achievement of children with mothers of higher education compared to children of mothers with lesser education. For example, compared to infants whose mothers have a BA or higher, infants and toddlers whose mothers have less than a high school diploma score lower on both cognitive and behavioral measures. They are also less likely to be in excellent or very good health and less likely to have a secure attachment to their mother. The disparities are usually small at nine months of age, but grow to be moderate or large disparities by twenty-four months of age.[24]

Gender Achievement Gap. There has long been a prevailing idea that science, math, and athletic-based classes are considered to be "masculine" subjects. Teachers, parents, and students all hold this belief. The idea that when girls excel at math, it is due to hard work, and that when boys excel at math, it is due to natural talent, still persists. Teachers are reported to show preferential treatment of boys in math classes.[25] As a result, there is a high participation gap in math and science subjects between genders. The math achievement gap between girls and boys remains. This has created a shortage of girls in science, technology, engineering, and math, or STEM-related classes and later on in scientific career fields (which produce more income than female-dominated fields).[26] In addition, for black boys, the **gender achievement gap** is severe. By grade four, only 11 percent of black males in large city schools are proficient in reading.[27]

Research informs us that teacher expertise has a direct correlation to high student performance and eliminating achievement gaps. Students who have highly effective teachers three years in a row score as much as 50 percent higher on achievement tests than those who have ineffective teachers for three years in a row.[28] Effective teachers "know the content they are teaching, engage students in learning, and challenge them to greater accomplishments."[29] As a highly effective teacher, here are some things you could do to help close the achievement gaps:

- Teach for achievement. Today's teachers are intentional teachers who have high expectations for their students and want them to achieve high standards.
- **Differentiate** (teach in response to the diverse needs of students so that all students within a classroom can learn effectively regardless of differences in ability) instruction so all children learn. Angelica L. Jordan, Department of Defense Education Activity (DoDEA's) Teacher of the Year, believes that "effective teachers spend time building relationships with students, parents, colleagues, and administrators. When I know a student's likes, dislikes, and interests, I can differentiate lessons."
- Assess each student's academic strengths and weaknesses.
- Incorporate the learning style of each student in your lesson plans and teaching.
- Communicate with parents as partners in the education process.[30]

gender achievement gap A prevailing idea that science, math, and athletic-based classes are considered to be "masculine" subjects. The idea that when girls excel at math, it is due to hard work; and that when boys excel at math, it is due to natural talent.

differentiate To teach in response to the diverse needs of students so that all students within a classroom can learn effectively, regardless of differences in ability.

BRAIN DEVELOPMENT

The brain plays a powerful and important role in growth and development. It is no wonder, then, that brain research and the implementation of that research have focused a great deal of interest on the first three years of life. Research on the brain has enormous implications for early childhood education and public policy. Brain research provides a strong basis for making decisions about what programs to provide for young children, as well as what environmental conditions promote optimal child development. Brain research also underscores the importance of early experiences and the benefits of early intervention services, thus pointing toward a positive economic return on investments in young children.

Public interest in the application of brain research to early childhood education has intensified. In many cases that research affirms what early childhood educators have always intuitively known: good parental care, warm and loving attachments, and positive age-appropriate stimulation from birth onward make a tremendous difference in children's cognitive development for a lifetime. Let's review some interesting facts about infant and toddler brain development and consider the implications they have for your practice as a professional.

The Brain

The brain is a fascinating and complex organ. Anatomically, the young brain is like the adult brain, except it is smaller. The average adult brain weighs approximately 3 pounds. At birth, the infant's brain weighs 14 ounces; at six months, 1.31 pounds;

and at three years, 2.4 pounds. So you can see that during the first two years of life the brain undergoes tremendous physical growth. The brain finishes developing at about age ten, when it reaches its full adult size.

neurons Nerve cells.

At birth, the brain has one hundred billion **neurons**, or nerve cells, which is the total amount it will ever have! It is important for parents, you, and other caregivers to play with, respond to, interact with, and talk to young children because this is the way brain connections develop and learning takes place. As they are used repeatedly, brain connections become permanent. However, brain connections that are not used or used only a little may wither away. This withering away is known as *neural shearing* or *pruning*. This helps explain why children who are reared in language-rich environments do well in school, while children who are not reared in such environments may be academically at risk.

synaptogenesis The proliferation of neural connections.

Also, by the time of birth, these billions of neurons have formed over fifty trillion connections, or *synapses,* through a process called **synaptogenesis**, the proliferation of neural connections. This process will continue to occur until the age of ten. The experiences that children have help form these neural connections. Experiences count. If children don't have the experiences they need to form neural connections, they may be at risk for poor developmental and behavioral outcomes. In this regard, remember that while experiences count, not all experiences are equal. Children need high-quality experiences that contribute to their education and development. Such high-quality experiences can include talking, reading and singing to and with children, helping children to develop good peer relationships, and helping children talk with an increasingly larger vocabulary.

critical period A period when children need the right experiences at the right times.

In addition, children need the right experiences at the right times. These "right times" are known as **critical periods**. Critical periods represent a narrow window of time during which a specific part of the body is most vulnerable to the absence of stimulation or to environmental influences.[31] For example, the critical period for language development is the first year of life. It is during this time that the auditory pathways for language learning are formed. Beginning at birth, an infant can distinguish the sounds of all the languages of the world. But at about six months, through the process of neural shearing or pruning, infants lose the ability to distinguish the sounds of languages they have not heard. By twelve months, their auditory maps are pretty well in place.[32] It is literally a case of "use it or lose it." An infant whose mother or other caregiver talks to her is more likely to have a larger vocabulary than an infant whose mother doesn't talk to her.

sensitive periods A time during which it is easier to learn something than it is at another time.

Having the right experiences at the right time also relates to broad, developmental "windows of opportunity" or **sensitive periods** during which it is easier to learn something than it is at another time. Sensitive periods represent a less precise and often longer period of time when skills, such as acquiring a second language, are influenced. However, if the opportunity for learning does not arise, these potential new skills may be lost forever. They may be harder to learn or they may not be learned fully.[33] During the last decade, scientists and educators have spent considerable time and energy exploring the links between brain development and classroom learning. Brain research provides many implications for how to develop enriched classrooms for children and for how to engage them in activities that will help them learn and develop to their optimal levels. Most importantly, brain research has made educators aware of the importance of providing young children stimulating activities early in life.

Applying Brain Research to Your Teaching

Brain research also tells us a great deal regarding stimulation and the development of specific areas of the brain. For example, brain research suggests that listening to music and learning to play musical instruments at very early ages stimulate the brain areas associated with mathematics and spatial reasoning.[34] In addition, brain research suggests that gross-motor activities and physical education should be included in a child's daily schedule throughout the elementary years.[35] Regrettably, school systems often cut programs such as physical education and music in times of budget crisis, even though research shows that these programs are essential to a child's complete cognitive development. Physical activities and exercise are essential for good physical health just as mental activities are essential for cognitive growth.

Brain-Based Guidelines for Teaching.   Reflect on the following conclusions about children's development and consider the brain-based implications they have for your teaching:

1. Child development is shaped by a dynamic and continuous interaction between biology and experience. For example, the years from birth to age eight are extremely important environmentally, especially for nutrition, stimulation of the brain, affectionate relationships with parents and others, and opportunities to learn. Think for a moment about how other kinds of environmental influences—such as family, school, and friends—affect development.

2. Culture influences every aspect of human development and is reflected in child-rearing beliefs and practices designed to promote healthy adaptations. For example, the kinds of foods parents feed their children, the ways they discipline, and their beliefs about the importance of education are based on cultural beliefs and customs.

3. The growth of self-regulation is a cornerstone of early childhood development that cuts across all domains of behavior. For example, children learn to regulate their behaviors with the help of parents and teachers who provide help in controlling their behavior and who guide them in making good choices.

4. Children are active participants in their own development, reflecting the intrinsic human drive to explore and master one's environment. This drive to explore is especially evident in toddlers' constant exploring and "getting into things."

5. Child–adult relationships and the effects of these relationships on children are the building blocks of healthy development. For example, children whose parents read to them develop positive attitudes toward and happy memories of reading.[36]

6. The timing of early childhood experiences is important. However, children remain vulnerable to risks throughout the early years of life and into adulthood. For example, much of what represents a threat to healthy brain development involves what we call *toxic stress,* resulting from chronic negative stressors such as child abuse, neglect, and lack of love and affection. We know that the presence of these stressors can change brain chemistry and affect behavior.[37] This is why you and other professionals must help protect children from stress and harm.

Wellness and Healthy Living

As you know, when you feel good, life goes much better. The same is true for children and their families. One major goal of all early childhood programs is to provide for the safety and well-being of children. A second goal is to help parents and other family members provide for the well-being of themselves and their children. Poor health and unhealthy living conditions are major contributors to poor school achievement and life outcomes. A number of health issues facing children today put their chances for learning and success at risk. Figure 2.1 shows ways that early childhood professionals work with children and their families to improve their overall health, well-being, and school achievement.

technology tie-in

Music, the Arts, and the Brain

Since the beginning of the recorded history of early childhood education, music and the arts have had an important place in the education of young children. Educators have supported children's involvement in music and the arts in three ways: appreciation, performance, and creation. You and I may not agree on the kind of music and art we like, but one thing is certain: We all like music and the arts of some kind, and they all affect us in some way. The same is true for children. I have not met a child who does not like to sing, dance, paint, and create.

Aristotle believed that art and drama were good for people because through them they were able to work out their emotions vicariously and as a result be calmer and better persons. Maria Montessori believed that children should be involved in learning. Art appreciation is part of the Montessori curriculum, and many Montessori classrooms have paintings by famous artists on display. Abraham Maslow places a high value on creativity and the importance of creating aesthetically pleasing classrooms for young children. Some early childhood programs provide keyboard lessons and experiences for all children based on the link some research shows between learning music and high academic achievement. You can involve your children in music and the arts in many ways as appreciators, performers, and creators. All early childhood programs should involve all children in music education.

The values of integrating music are many:

- Young children who take music lessons show different brain development and improved memory over the course of a year, compared to children who do not receive musical training. Musically trained children perform better in a memory test that is correlated with general intelligence skills such as literacy, verbal memory, visual-spatial processing, mathematics, and IQ.[38]
- Playing a musical instrument significantly enhances the brainstem's sensitivity to speech sounds. This relates to encoding skills involved with music and languages. Experience with music at a young age can "fine-tune" the brain's auditory system.[39]
- Children who received music instruction excel above their peers in memory skills as well as nonmusical abilities such as literacy, mathematics, and even IQ.[40]

Some ways to integrate music in your classroom and instruction with technology are the following:

- Music notation programs such as Noteflight.com or Sibelius 7, which are designed to assist all levels of learners in writing, composing and sharing music
- Music apps for iPads, iMacs, and smartphones such as *Itsy Bitsy Spider* by Duck Duck Moose and *DJ Mix Kids Pro*
- Music CDs such as *Tune Your Brain with Mozart* and *Bach for Book Lovers,* which purport to stimulate the brain

When you think of children's illnesses, you probably think of measles, rubella, and mumps. Actually, dental cavities (caries), asthma, lead poisoning, diabetes, and obesity are the leading childhood diseases.

dental caries Tooth decay.

Dental Caries. **Dental caries** (tooth decay) remains the most prevalent chronic disease in both children and adults, even though it is largely preventable.[41] Forty-two percent of children two to eleven have had dental caries in their primary teeth and 23 percent have untreated dental caries. Black and Hispanic children and those living in families with lower incomes have more untreated decay.[42] Providing children the dental health they need should be a huge priority for society and the early childhood profession. Some things you can do to promote children's dental health include the following:

- Provide parents with information about the importance of tooth brushing and flossing. Some of my university students are surprised to learn that tooth brushing begins with the first tooth!

Early Childhood Professional:	Family and Child Outcomes:
• Parent/family education to help parents learn basic child-rearing knowledge and skills • Literacy programs to support children's literacy development • Readiness activities and programs designed to get children ready for school • Family referrals to community agencies that can provide help (e.g., the Special Supplement Nutrition Program for Women, Infants, and Children (WIC), a health and nutrition program that promotes optimal growth and development) • Teaching and promoting good nutrition and health habits	• Less family and child stress • Healthier families and children • More involvement of families in their children's education • Increased school achievement and success • Reduced child abuse and neglect • A better quality of life for children and families • Enhanced child and family health and educational outcomes

FIGURE 2.1 How Early Childhood Professionals Support Families' and Children's Overall Health and Well-Being

An important role is for you to meet the health and educational needs of children and families. Today, the emphasis on working with young children and their families is to improve their overall physical and mental health, both of which play an important role in learning.

- Remind children of the importance of brushing and flossing by reading stories, dramatic play, and other activities.
- Encourage parents to cut back on and reduce the amount of carbonated beverages and candy that their children consume.
- Provide time in the daily schedule for children to brush and floss their teeth, especially after meals and snacks.
- Invite dental hygenists to present programs on the dos and don'ts of good dental health.

Asthma. Asthma, a chronic inflammatory disorder of the airways, is also one of the most prevalent childhood illnesses in the United States. An estimated 7.1 million children under the age of eighteen suffer from asthma; 4.1 million children suffer from an asthma attack or episode every year.[43] Asthma is caused in part by poor air quality, dust, mold, animal fur and dander, allergens from cockroaches and rodent feces, and strong fumes. Many of these causes are found in poor and low-quality housing. You will want to reduce asthma-causing conditions in your early childhood programs and work with parents to reduce the causes of asthma in their homes. Here are some things you can do to reduce the causes of asthma: (1) Reduce or remove as many asthma and

asthma A chronic inflammatory disorder of the airways.

allergy triggers (such as smoke, mold, pet dander, cockroaches, and strong fumes or odors) as possible from homes and programs. And speaking of pet dander, 90 percent of U.S. homes have pet dander even though only 50 percent have a pet. This can be a problem for asthmatic children.[44] (2) Use air filters and air conditioners—and properly maintain them. (3) Keep in mind that vacuum cleaners with poor filtration and design characteristics release and stir up dust and allergens.[45]

Lead Poisoning.   Lead poisoning is also a serious childhood disease. The Centers for Disease Control and Prevention (CDC) estimate that approximately 250,000 U.S. children between birth and age five have dangerous blood lead levels.[46] Lead enters the body through inhalation and ingestion. These children are at risk for low IQs, short attention spans, reading and learning disabilities, hyperactivity, and behavioral problems. A major source of lead poisoning is from old lead-based paint in many older homes and apartments; most homes built before 1978 have lead-based paint in them. The federal government banned the use of lead in paint in 1978, but paint with lead has a sweet taste that children like, so it is not uncommon for them to eat chips of paint and to scratch a tooth on window sills.[47] Across the United States many homes are near the sites of former lead factories. The soil in these areas is so contaminated with lead that it poses grave risks to the children who play in it—yet many do. You can access information and maps about lead contamination from old factories in the Linking to Learning section at the end of this chapter. Young children are especially vulnerable since they put many things in their mouths and crawl on floors.

Childhood Diabetes.   Diabetes is fast becoming one of the most common childhood diseases.[48] There are two types of diabetes in children. Type 1 diabetes, usually diagnosed in children and young adults, was previously known as juvenile diabetes. In Type 1 diabetes the body does not produce insulin.[49] In Type 2 diabetes the body produces insufficient amounts of insulin or does not adequately use the insulin that is produced. What is so alarming about the increased incidences of Type 2 diabetes in children is that it is usually an adult disease, more frequently diagnosed beginning in middle adulthood. Reasons for the increase in Type 2 diabetes include increasing childhood obesity, poor eating habits, and an emphasis on high-calorie and sugary foods and drinks. Preventive measures for Type 2 diabetes go hand in hand with efforts to reduce childhood obesity, mainly healthy diets and regular (daily) exercise.[50]

Obesity.   Today's generation of young children is often referred to as the "Supersize Generation," due to their obesity. In fact, the Supersize Generation is getting younger! The American Heart Association reports that more than nine million children between the ages of six and nineteen are considered overweight; 11.5 percent of children between the ages of six months and twenty-three months are overweight; and nearly 14 percent of preschool children between the ages of two and five are overweight. Among American children two to nineteen, 17.6 percent are overweight.[51] Additionally, the tipping point for early childhood obesity begins in infancy. More and more obesity prevention programs are geared toward infants and toddlers.[52]

In addition, new waves of research report the relationship of obesity to other diseases and health problems, especially later in life. Excess weight in childhood and adolescence predicts weight problems in adults. Overweight children, ages ten to fourteen, with at least one overweight or obese parent, are reported to have an 80 percent likelihood of being overweight into adulthood.[53] Obesity can also cause heart problems. Research reveals that children who are substantially overweight throughout much of their childhood and adolescence have a higher incidence of depression than those who aren't overweight. There were several significant findings related to this research. First, a link was shown between obesity and psychiatric disorders. Second, researchers found that boys were at greater risk than girls for weight-related depression.[54]

obesity A condition characterized by excessive accumulation and storage of fat in the body.

 Healthy eating can be fun. Watch this **video** to see how a teacher uses a story read in class to incorporate a lesson on nutrition and a healthy snack.

The dramatic rise in obesity is due to a combination of factors, including less physical activity and more fat and calorie intake. More children spend more time in front of televisions and computer screens, and fewer schools mandate physical education. Also, restaurant promotions to "supersize" meals encourage high-fat and high-calorie diets. Studies suggest that a ban on fast-food advertisements on television, especially those targeting young children, could reduce the number of overweight children by as much as 18 percent. Although it is unlikely that such a ban will ever materialize, the study does demonstrate how advertising food and childhood obesity are linked.[55]

As the rate of obesity in American children continues to rise, it is especially important for you to keep yourself healthy and to model healthy habits for the children you teach to ensure that they have a good role model as encouragement to develop healthy nutritional habits.

Here are some ways you can help children and parents win the obesity war:

FIGURE 2.2 Good Nutrition for Young Children

The MyPlate icon is intended to prompt consumers to think about how to build a healthy plate at mealtimes. It also provides a means to combat childhood obesity.

Source: U.S. Department of Agriculture, accessed June 21, 2012, from www.choosemyplate.gov.

- *Provide parents with information about nutrition.* What children eat—or don't eat—plays a major role in how they grow, develop, and learn. Diet also plays a powerful role in whether or not children engage in classroom activities with energy and enthusiasm. For example, send home copies of MyPlate for Kids (see Figure 2.2). You can log on to MyPlate for Kids using the Web address in the Linking to Learning section at the end of this chapter and individualize a food "plate" for each of your children.

  You can also send this information home to parents and share with them how to access and use the MyPlate nutrition guide in order to serve healthy meals to their families.

- *Encourage your children to eat breakfast and for parents to provide breakfast for their children.* Also, investigate your school's lunch and breakfast programs. If your program does not serve breakfast to children, you can advocate for a breakfast program for children whose families' incomes make them eligible for federal- and state-supported nutrition programs. Research is very clear that serving breakfast to children who do not get it elsewhere significantly improves their cognitive abilities; this enables them to be more alert, pay better attention, and do better in terms of reading, math, and on standardized test scores.[56]

- *Counsel parents to pull the plug on the television.* TV watching at mealtime is associated with obesity because children are more likely to eat fast foods such as pizza and salty snack foods while they watch TV. Also, children who watch a lot of television tend to be less physically active, and inactivity tends to promote weight gain.[57]

- *Cook with children and talk about foods and their nutritional values.* Cooking activities are also a good way to eat and talk about new foods. Cooking and other nutrition-related activities are ideal ways to integrate math, science, literacy, art, music, and other content areas.

- *Integrate literacy and nutritional activities.* Reading and discussing labels is a good way to encourage children to be aware of and think about nutritional information. For example, calories provide energy; too much fat and sugar are not good for us; and protein is important, especially in the morning.[58]

- *Provide opportunities for physical exercise and physical activities every day.*

  For their part, schools are fighting the obesity war in the following ways:

- Banning the sale of sodas and candy bars in school vending machines during lunch hours[59]

Involving children in nutritional and cooking activities is an excellent way to promote literacy development and build a strong foundation for good nutritional habits.

- Banning bake sales and other fundraising activities involving non-nutritious foods.
- Teaching about and encouraging healthier lifestyles in and out of school
- Including salad bars as part of their cafeterias (e.g., in California, the Riverside Unified School District Farm to School Program is designed to promote healthy eating in children by increasing the availability of fruits and vegetables in school lunches and providing nutrition education to increase knowledge of and improve attitudes toward eating a variety of locally grown produce).[60]
- Banning cupcakes and other sweets at class birthday parties and being urged to consider healthier snack choices for homeroom celebrations[61]
- Restoring recess and physical education to the elementary school curriculum
- Working with parents to help them get their children to be more active and to eat healthier foods at home

The First Lady's Let's Move! Project is a federal program that encourages healthy living. Let's Move! is a comprehensive initiative launched by First Lady Michelle Obama, dedicated to solving the challenge of childhood obesity within a generation, so that children born today will grow up healthier and able to pursue their dreams. Combining comprehensive strategies with common sense, Let's Move! is about putting children on the path to a healthy future during their earliest months and years by giving parents helpful information and:

- Fostering environments that support healthy choices
- Providing healthier foods in our schools
- Ensuring that every family has access to healthy, affordable food
- Helping kids become more physically active

The goal of this program is to reduce childhood obesity from 20 percent to 5 percent by 2030. In order to achieve this, Let's Move! also includes recommendations for fighting early childhood obesity, including the following:

- Educate and help women conceive at a healthy weight and have a healthy weight gain during pregnancy.
- Encourage and support breastfeeding.
- Educate and support parents in efforts to reduce kids' screen time (i.e., less time watching television and using digital media and more time being physically active).
- Improve federal early childhood programs' child nutrition and physical activity practices.[62]

You can access Let's Move! with the Web address found in the Linking to Learning section at the end of this chapter.

PROVIDING FOR DIVERSE CHILDREN AND CULTURES

There are many words such as *standards, testing*, and *accountability* that highlight education today. Add *diversity* of children to your list! Nowhere is America's diversity more apparent than in Census data.

Shifting Demographics

Across the United States, seismic demographic changes herald how diverse populations are transforming regional geographic areas, states, school districts, and schools. In several states, non-Hispanic white children account for less than half of the general population of children. The nine states (and Washington, DC) with a "minority majority" child population are Hawaii (87 percent); Washington, DC (83 percent); New Mexico (74 percent); California (73 percent); Texas (66 percent); Arizona (58 percent); Florida (54 percent); Maryland (54 percent); Georgia (53 percent); and Mississippi (51 percent). Eight of these states are Sun Belt states. As a result, the South is the first region in the country where more than half of public school students are poor and where more than half are members of minorities. This shift is fueled by an influx of Latinos and other ethnic groups; the return of African Americans to the South; and higher birthrates among African American and Latino families.[63]

In addition, the Census Bureau reports that for the first time in U.S. history, minority babies are now the majority. The census also reveals that 50.4 percent of children under age one are Hispanic, black, Asian, or some other minority group. This means that for many of you, by the time you graduate, these children will be in your preschool or kindergarten. The numbers also herald the future of the United States as a whole, as minority students are expected to exceed 50 percent of all public school enrollment by 2020, and the share of students poor enough to qualify for free or reduced price lunches will continue to rise.[64]

The changing demographics of the United States means more students will require special education, bilingual education, and other special services. Issues of culture and diversity shape instruction and curriculum. These demographics also have tremendous implications for how you teach and how your children learn.

Culturally Responsive Teaching

Multicultural awareness is the appreciation for and understanding of people's cultures, socioeconomic status, and gender. It also includes understanding one's own culture. Cultural awareness programs and activities focus on other cultures while making children aware of the content, nature, and richness of their own. Learning about other cultures while children are learning about their own culture enables them to integrate commonalities and appreciate differences without inferring inferiority or superiority of one or the other. Promoting multiculturalism in an early childhood program has implications far beyond your school, classroom, and program. Multiculturalism influences and affects work habits, interpersonal relations, and a child's general outlook on life. Early childhood teachers take these cultural influences into consideration when designing curriculum and instructional processes. One way to accomplish the primary goal of multicultural education—to positively change the lives of children and their families—is to infuse multiculturalism into early childhood activities and practices.

multicultural awareness Appreciation for and understanding of people's culture, socioeconomic status, and gender.

The teacher in this **video** shares the importance of being aware of the cultural differences within the classroom.

Multicultural Infusion

Multicultural infusion means that culturally aware and sensitive education permeates the curriculum to alter or affect the way young children and you think about diversity issues. In a larger perspective, infusion strategies are used to ensure that multiculturalism becomes a part of the entire center, school, and home. Infusion processes foster cultural awareness; use appropriate instructional materials, themes, and activities; teach to children's learning styles; and promote family and community involvement.

multicultural infusion A situation in which multicultural education permeates the curriculum to influence the way young children and teachers think about diversity issues.

Fostering Cultural Awareness.   Keep in mind that you are the key to a cultural classroom. These guidelines will help you foster cultural awareness:

- *Recognize that all children are unique.* Children have special talents, abilities, and styles of learning and relating to others. Make your classroom a place in which children are comfortable being who they are. Always value uniqueness and diversity.

- *Get to know, appreciate, and respect the cultural background of each child.* Visit families and community neighborhoods to learn more about cultures, religions, and the ways of life they engender. For example, Teacher of the Year María Márquez says, "In today's diverse society, a teacher must be aware and sensitive to the multicultural differences in order to better understand and encourage the individual child to achieve to his/her highest potential. In the teaching of citizenship and character traits, I strive to help each child learn to share the concern for the well-being and dignity of others. They must learn to demonstrate loyalty and pride toward our country. They must also be responsible, courteous and honest toward others with whom we share our values."[65]

- *Use authentic situations to provide for cultural learning and understanding.* For example, a field trip to a culturally diverse neighborhood of your city or town provides children an opportunity for understanding firsthand many of the details about how people live. Such an experience provides wonderful opportunities for involving children in writing, cooking, reading, and dramatic play activities. What about setting up a replica of a local market in your classroom?

- *Use authentic assessment activities to asses fully children's learning and growth.* Portfolios are ideal for assessing children's learning in nonbiased and culturally sensitive ways.

- *Infuse culture into your lesson planning, teaching, and caregiving and make it a foundation for learning.* Use all subject areas—math, science, language arts, literacy, music, art, and social studies—to relate culture to children's lives and cultural backgrounds. This approach makes students feel good about their backgrounds, cultures, families, and experiences.

- *Be a role model by accepting, appreciating, and respecting other languages and cultures.* In other words, infuse multiculturalism into your personal and professional lives.

- *Be knowledgeable about, proud of, and secure in your own culture.* Children will ask about you, and you should be prepared to share your cultural background with them.

Using Appropriate Instructional Materials. Carefully consider and select appropriate instructional materials to support the infusion of cultural education in your classroom. Here are some suggestions for achieving this goal.

- *Multicultural literature.* Choose literature that embraces similarities and welcomes differences regarding how children and families live their *whole lives.*

- *Themes.* Select and teach thematic units that help strengthen children's understanding

As the United States becomes more diverse and multicultural, it is important for you to integrate multicultural information, practices, and activities in your classroom.

of themselves, their culture, and the cultures of others. Here are some appropriate theme topics, all of which are appropriate for meeting Common Core standards and the standards of the National Council for the Social Studies (NCSS):

- Getting to know myself, getting to know others
- What is special about you and me?

- Growing up in the city
- How is my state similar to and different from other states?
- Tell me about Africa (or South America, China, etc.)

- *Personal accomplishments.* Add to classroom activities, as appropriate, the accomplishments of people from different cultural groups, women of all cultures, and individuals with disabilities.

When you select materials for use in a cultural curriculum for early childhood programs, make sure you do the following:

- Represent people of all cultures fairly and accurately.
- Include people of color, many cultural groups, and people with exceptionalities.
- Verify that historical information is accurate and nondiscriminatory.
- Ensure gender equity—that is, boys and girls are represented equally and in non-stereotypic roles.

Promoting Family and Community Involvement. You will work with children and families of diverse cultural backgrounds. As such, you will need to learn about the cultural background of children and families so that you can respond appropriately to their needs.

It is important for you to understand that each family and child is unique. Don't assume families hold particular values and beliefs just because they speak a particular language or are from a different country of origin. Take time to discover the actual values, beliefs, and practices of the families in your community.

You will teach children from different cultures whose first language is not English. Educating students with diverse backgrounds and special needs makes for a challenging and rewarding career. Learning how to constantly improve your responses to students' special needs and improve learning environments and curricula will be one of your ongoing professional responsibilities. Society, families, and children change as diversity increases, and as more students with special needs come to school, you will have to change how and what you teach. The accompanying Professionalism in Practice Competency Builder provides seven strategies for becoming a successful teacher of linguistically and culturally diverse children. Your students are waiting for you to make a difference in their lives!

TEACHING AND LEARNING IN THE INCLUSIVE CLASSROOM

Now that you have read about public policy and current issues affecting children who are typically developing in early childhood today, let's look at one issue that conjures many policy implications as well as an issue about which many early childhood teachers have questions: *inclusion*, typically defined as educating children with and without disabilities in the same classroom. While the Division for Early Childhood (DEC) of the Council for Exceptional Children (CEC) and the National Association for the Education of Young Children (NAEYC) have identified inclusion as the preferred service delivery option for young children with special needs, there is no agreement on a model for developing and delivering these services. A classroom template for inclusion is not available, but it is essential that teachers believe that preparing all children to function in society is best achieved by creating environments that include children whose diversity includes varying abilities, disabilities, and backgrounds.

professionalism in practice

How to Help English Language Learners Succeed

My ongoing attempt to learn Spanish provides me with a lot of empathy for English language learners (ELLs)! Perhaps you have had the same experience that I have of frustration with comprehension, pronunciation, and understandable communication. English language learners face these same problems. Many come from low socioeconomic backgrounds. Others come to this country lacking many of the early literacy and learning opportunities we take for granted.

INCREASING NUMBERS

Many school districts across the country have seen their numbers of English language learners skyrocket. For example, in 2010, the Texas Education Agency reported there were 831,812 ELLs in K–12 programs throughout the state. Over 120 languages were represented; 90 percent (744,949) were Spanish speakers. Prominent languages other than Spanish were Korean, Vietnamese, Urdu, and Arabic.[66]

The chances are great that you will have English language learners in your classroom wherever you choose to teach.

Here are some strategies that Judith Lessow-Hurley, author of *Foundations of Dual Language Instruction* (5th ed.), suggests you use for helping your English language learners be successful:

STRATEGY 1 Develop Content Around a Theme

The repetition of vocabulary and concepts reinforces language and ideas and gives English language learners better access to content.

- Provide a word wall or word bank for students to display the vocabulary associated with the theme being studied. Use pictures to explain vocabulary whenever possible.
- Provide a variety of reading, writing, listening, and speaking experiences around the theme.
- Include higher-order thinking skills, such as evaluating, synthesizing, and application for children to think about and problem-solve.

STRATEGY 2 Use Visual Aids and Hands-On Activities in Your Instruction

Children retain information better when you involve their senses in learning.

- Rely on visual cues (pictures, etc.) as frequently as possible.
- Have students create flash cards for key vocabulary words. Be sure to include enough time in your lessons so students can use their vocabulary words.
- Encourage students to use computer programs and books with CDs or DVDs.
- Use rubrics (scoring and performance guides) with pictures to help students learn what is expected of them.
- Use visual aids and hands-on activities in your instruction. English language learners benefit from illustrations, manipulatives, and real experiences that provide clues to meaning and support their language development.
- Engage children in learning activities they enjoy. Create opportunities for children to talk about things that they find interesting, motivating and exciting. Scaffold and build their academic language and they will learn English and grow academically, too.

STRATEGY 3 Use Routines to Reinforce Language

Use routines in your classroom. Repetition allows students to tie language to what's happening around them. Routines also increase children's comfort level of learning a new language because they can know what to expect. Language acquisition is easier in low stress environments. For example, start your school day with a morning routine that includes counting the children present, noting the day of the month, and talking about the weather, etc.

- Use daily reading with pictures, gestures, and a dramatic voice to help convey meaning.

Once teachers support the philosophy of inclusion, they must be able to plan for and provide for the needs of the diverse children in their classroom. Creating a successful inclusive environment requires a well-planned and well-organized classroom. Teachers who plan and evaluate the different aspects of the classroom setting can construct classrooms that meet the needs of all students. You will gradually gain the skills, awareness, and dispositions to do this. The following list provides some examples of ways to create, implement, evaluate, and modify classrooms so optimal learning conditions are created for all students:

- Provide "scripts," instructions for a set of actions, by tying language to content, instead of simply trying to teach language in isolation. For example, engage children in role plays where they act out common activities such as lining up, going to the cafeteria, recess, or going to the zoo. Teach useful language frames like, "Can you help me find the bathroom?"
- Remember that there is a distinction between the language children use on the playground and academic language—the language they need to succeed with tasks they encounter in school. Teachers need to consciously and carefully scaffold academic language. For example, before you ask children to retell a story, teach words like "first," "then," and "after."

STRATEGY 4 Engage English Language Learners with English Speakers

Cooperative learning groups, composed of children with mixed language abilities, give students a meaningful content for using English.

- Use cooperative learning. Cooperative learning groups usually assist your children of different achievement levels—in this case language ELLs need English role models to help them learn English. Language learning requires interaction. You want to get your students talking. Cooperative learning creates a context for students to converse about meaningful ideas. Pairs work, too—pair ELLs with English speakers in a variety of activities. Small groups (four or less) and pairs promote interaction. Remember, learning is social and good language learning environments are not quiet and involve student interaction!
- Make language learning fun. Children don't learn language because they think they want a career in international marketing. They learn language because they want to talk, make friends, and do the things that children do.

STRATEGY 5 Allow Students to Use Nonverbal Responses

Permit students to demonstrate their knowledge and comprehension in alternative ways. For example, one teacher asks her children to hold up cardboard "lollipops" (green or red side forward) to indicate a yes or no answer to a question.

- Allow students to draw pictures to demonstrate their understanding. They can explain about their picture to a small group. Remember, a picture is worth 1,000 words!
- Don't correct all nonstandard responses. It's better to get students talking; they acquire accepted forms of language usage and communication through regular use and practice. You can always paraphrase a student's answer to model Standard English.

STRATEGY 6 Use Technology

You can use technology to scaffold language development of ELLs. Technology is student centered and gives students some control over their own learning. Focus on technological tools and activities. For example:

- Use iPods as voice recorders so children can hear themselves read and talk. When students are able to record and hear themselves read and talk, they become more engaged and motivated to learn English.
- English Language Development teacher Amy Wegener Taganashi says, "An array of technology helps engage students and provides the structured one-on-one English practice they need. . . . Software, online tools, and other technologies help students hone basic language skills they can later apply in authentic social settings. The kids spend most of their day listening and not interacting with the language as much. But technology mixes things up, captures students' attention, and engages them in a way traditional classroom instruction doesn't."[67]

STRATEGY 7 Respect, Preserve, and Honor Children's Culture

Encourage students to preserve their cultural identity as they are learning English.

- Have children show their countries of origin on a world map, then talk and write about it.

....

Source: Contributed by Judith Lessow-Hurley, Professor, Elementary Education, San José State University.

- *Classroom schedule.* A consistent schedule helps students feel secure and adds to the predictability of the environment. A visual schedule that is reviewed orally every day benefits all children. In addition, some students will need their own individual schedules, particularly if their day includes therapists to assist them.
- *Routines.* Routines for different times of the day and scheduling a particular activity at the same time every day or on the same day every week is beneficial for students who need the stability of knowing what their day will entail.

cooperative learning Learning that creates a context for students to converse about meaningful ideas.

- *Classroom curriculum.* Classroom curriculum that is appropriate for all children does not mean each child will do the same things every day. The curriculum must include activities that can be modified and adapted to meet the needs of each child.

- *Classroom management.* Teachers must support and encourage appropriate behavior, prevent inappropriate behavior, and guide or redirect misbehavior when it does occur. In the inclusive classroom, you can achieve this goal by creating a positive management plan that addresses skill deficits. A **skill deficit** is the inability to perform a skill because the child does not possess the skill. For example, a child with a disability may have a social skill deficit associated with making friends and gaining popularity. Motivational deficits involve the unwillingness or lack of cooperation of children to perform a skill they possess, either entirely or at an appropriate level. For example, some children may be reluctant or hesitant to engage in an activity because of their disability. In contrast, some children may lack motivational self-control and may be aggressive and intrusive in their behavior.

- *Grouping.* The inclusive classroom can include heterogeneous and homogeneous grouping, depending on the activity. Teachers must have explicit individual behavioral and academic expectations for each child depending on his or her needs.

- *Physical arrangement.* In the early childhood classroom, the four-desk cluster provides the most opportunities for students with disabilities to be included in the classroom. Teachers can move efficiently from child to child, and socialization, cooperation, and group work are optimized.

- *Rules.* Rules should be stated positively, limited in number, observable, measurable, and applied to behavior only. Rules should not address academic or homework issues that could unfairly impact students with disabilities or who are linguistically diverse.

- *Transitions.* Strategies that support smooth transitions between activities include verbal cues (e.g., 5 minutes before cleanup), visual cues (e.g., picture schedules), auditory cues (e.g., timers), and praise after successful transitions.

Teachers who actively prepare for all students are better able to provide accommodations, supports, and instruction where needed.

PREVENTING VIOLENCE, BULLYING, AND ABUSE

Every day news reports are full of graphic accounts of how children are abused, abandoned, neglected, bullied, and treated inhumanely.

Violence

Violence seems to pervade American society. From television to video games to domestic violence, children are exposed to high doses of undesirable behavior. Children experience violence, both directly and indirectly, in these ways:

- Every day in the United States, ten young children are murdered, sixteen killed in firearm accidents, and 8,042 are reported as physically abused.[68]
- Over three million children per year witness domestic violence in their homes.[69]
- Children in poverty are twenty-two times more likely to be physically abused and sixty times more likely to die from the abuse than those in the middle class.[70]

skill deficit The inability to perform a skill because the child does not possess the skill.

applying research to practice

Does *SpongeBob SquarePants* Impair Kids' Thinking?

A recent research study raises the issue of whether fast-paced cartoons such as *SpongeBob SquarePants* are good for young children. The study differentiates between naturally paced children's programs, such as *Sesame Street*, slow-paced programs, such as *Mister Rogers' Neighborhood*, and fast-paced programs, such as *SpongeBob SquarePants*.[71] Fast-paced programing is associated with the "overstimulation hypothesis" that is based on the theory that fast pacing and sequencing of programs may tax children's brains (or parts of the brain). In this study, the researchers examined the effects of *SpongeBob SquarePants* on children's executive functions (EF), a collection of skills and behaviors including attention, working memory, inhibitory control, problem solving, self-regulation, and delay of gratification.[72]

The researchers found that children who watched nine minutes of *SpongeBob* had executive function impairment immediately after viewing the cartoon, compared with children who were assigned a drawing task and those who watched educational television.[73] The researchers advised that "it is important that parents are alert to the possibility of lower levels of EF in your children at least immediately after watching such shows."[74]

WHAT DOES ALL OF THIS MEAN FOR YOU?

Not everyone agrees that cartoons are necessarily detrimental to children or that fast-paced cartoons affect children's executive function. However, you can do the following:

- Advise parents that the American Academy of Pediatrics recommends that children under the age of two should not watch any television and that they recommend only one to two hours of educational, nonviolent television for older children.[75] Although the research study discussed above was conducted with four-year-old children, your advice to parents could include the recommendation that they limit the television viewing of their preschool children as well.
- Communicate with parents about the nature and kind of television cartoons children watch and alert parents to the fact that fast-paced cartoons may have an immediate influence (after watching the shows) on children's ability to demonstrate the behaviors included in executive function.
- Advise parents about age-appropriate content. Not all children's programs are made for all children. For example, the producers of *SpongeBob* say the program is designed for children ages six to eleven, not four-year-olds. Parents have to be vigilant in monitoring their children's television viewing behavior.[76] Advise parents that they cannot assume that all cartoons are equal and not all are of high quality.

- By the time they reach middle school, children will have watched 100,000 acts of violence through television, including 8,000 depictions of murder.[77]
- On average, school-age children play video games fifty-three minutes per day; 49 percent of video games feature serious violence, and 40 percent show violence in a comic way.[78]

Research shows that violent behavior is learned and that it is learned early.[79] Your students' brains are remarkably **plastic**, or capable of being molded or adapted to conditions; the neurons are still arranging and rearranging connections. Brain plasticity usually works to children's advantage, because it enables them to learn and develop in spite of poor influences, allowing us to redirect neural pathways away from violence and toward amiable and peaceful conflict resolution. However, when children are routinely and repeatedly exposed to violence, their emotions, cognition, and behavior become centered on themes of aggression and violence.

plastic Capable of adapting to conditions, such as the neurons in a child's brain, which are constantly arranging and rearranging connections to form neural pathways.

Increasing acts of violence lead to proposals for how to provide violence-free homes and educational environments; how to teach children to get along nonviolently with others, such as by using puppets to discuss feelings with younger children or by role-playing and discussing appropriate ways to behave on the playground with older children; and how to reduce violence on television, in the movies, and in video games.[80] Advocating for reducing violence on television, for example, in turn leads to discussions for ways to limit children's television viewing. Such proposals include "pulling the plug" on television; using the V-chip, included in every TV, which enables parents to block programs with violent content; boycotting companies whose advertisements support programs with violent content; and limiting violence shown during prime-time viewing hours for children. Here are some other steps you can take to prevent or reduce violence in children's lives:

- Show children photographs and have children identify various emotions; discuss appropriate responses to these emotions.
- Have children role-play how to respond appropriately to various emotions.
- Discuss with your students their behavior and the clear logical consequences of that behavior.
- Have children involved in disagreements discuss with one another the feelings that caused their actions and think about how they could have done things differently.
- Discuss violence openly in your classroom. Be honest about the repercussions of violence. Focus on the pain and humiliation it causes. For example, if you are reading a book in class in which the characters engage in violence, discuss how the victim felt, what the character could have done differently, and what they themselves would have done in the same situation.
- Send home information about media violence and encourage parents to monitor and limit screen time.

Bullying

All across the country, state legislatures have passed laws requiring schools to implement anti-bullying programs. In response, school activists have developed proactive programs such as that at Kate Schenck Elementary School in San Antonio, Texas. Each morning the children take an anti-bullying pledge and each Thursday the children wear anti-bullying T-shirts, both shown in Figure 2.3. The student council of Kate Schenck was instrumental in developing the pledge and designing the T-shirt.

Programs to prevent and curb bullying are another example of how educators are combating the effects of violence on children. Although in the past bullying has been dismissed as "normal" or "kids' play," this is no longer the case, because bullying is related to personal and school violence. Bullying includes teasing, slapping, hitting, pushing, unwanted touching, taking personal belongings, name-calling, and making sexual comments and insults about looks, behavior, or culture.

Here are some things you can do to help prevent bullying in your classroom:

- Talk to children individually and in groups when you see them engage in hurtful behavior. For instance: "Chad, how do you think Brad felt when you pushed him out of the way?"
- Be constantly alert to any signs of bullying behavior in your classroom and intervene immediately.
- Teach cooperative and helpful behavior, courtesy, and respect. Much of what children do, they model from others' behaviors. When you provide examples of courteous and respectful behavior in your classroom it sets a good example for children.

bullying To treat abusively or affect by means of force or coercion.

In this video, a young girl shares her thoughts on bullies and her experience with being bullied. Notice what she has to say about the motivation of bullies, the effect of bullying, and the role of adults in stopping this behavior.

Kate Schenck Elementary Bully Pledge

As a Kate Schenck Owl I promise to stomp out bullying of all kinds; verbal, emotional and physical. I promise to do my part to help our school be safe and be a happy place. I promise to treat everyone equal no matter the language spoken, the athletic ability, the level of education or the physical appearance of others. I promise to stop it, control it, and report it. I know that Kate Schenck will be a better place because of me! Remember: *Our school is too Cool to be Cruel!* Bully-Free IT STARTS WITH ME!!

FIGURE 2.3 Kate Schenck Elementary School, San Antonio, Texas, Bully Pledge and Bully T-Shirt

Source: Kate Schenck E.S. (SAISD) 2010 Student Council under the direction of Mary Martinez (4th grade teacher); revised by Assistant Principal Nora Mozingo.

- Have children work together on a project. Then, have the students talk about how they got along and worked together.
- Make children and others in your classroom feel welcome and important.
- Talk to parents and help them understand your desire to stop bullying and to have a bully-free classroom.
- Conduct a workshop for parents on anti-bullying behavior and for signs of bullying.
- Report bullying to your principal! Remember that if you are aware of bullying behavior and do nothing about it, then you have not done your job of protecting and advocating for every child.

- Teach your students the "talk, walk, and squawk" method (or some other method your school uses) in response to bullying. Role-play and practice this technique in class:
  - *Talk.* Encourage your students to stand up for themselves verbally: "Leave me alone" or "You don't scare me" are some choices. Have children practice these responses in a calm and assertive voice.
  - *Walk.* Teach your students to walk away, but not to run away. If students run away, it is likely to increase the intensity of the bullying.
  - *Squawk.* The last step is to tell a teacher. Teachers can then take steps to halt the bullying behavior.[81]
- Keep parents informed of their child's interactions with violence in school. If a child is a bully or is being bullied, tell the parents so that you and they can collaborate to remediate the situation.
- Read books about bullying. You can read books about bullying to and with your children during story time, group reading lessons, guided reading, and shared reading. You can also send books home for parents to read with their children. Some books you might want to read are the following:
  - *The Juice Box Bully* by Bob Sornson, Maria Dismondy, and Kim Shaw. Have you ever seen a bully in action and done nothing about it? The kids at Pete's new school get involved instead of being bystanders. When Pete begins to behave badly, his classmates teach him about "The Promise." Will Pete decide to shed his bullying ways and make "The Promise"?
  - *The Savvy Cyber Kids: Defeat of the Cyber Bully* by Ben Halpert and Taylor Southerland. While playing an online game, CyberPrincess and CyberThunder encounter a cyber bully. Throughout the book, Tony and Emma learn strategies on how to appropriately respond to a bully online.
  - *Confessions of a Former Bully* by Trudy Ludwig and Beth Adams. After Katie gets caught teasing a schoolmate, she's told to meet with Mrs. Petrowski, the school counselor, so she can make right her wrong and learn to be a better friend. Bothered at first, it doesn't take long before Katie realizes that bullying has hurt not only the people around her, but hurt her, too.
  - *Jungle Bullies* by Steven Kroll and Vincent Nguyen. No one in the jungle will share. Elephant orders Hippo out of the pond and as Elephant is much bigger than Hippo, in turn Hippo orders Lion out of the path; Lion orders Leopard out of the grass; and Leopard orders Monkey off the branch of the tree. But Monkey's mama has some very good advice about standing up for himself and teaching others how to share.
  - *Bullies Never Win* by Margery Cuyler and Arthur Howard. When the class bully, Brenda Baily, makes fun of Jessica's skinny legs and her boyish lunch box, Jessica doesn't know what to do. She doesn't want to be a tattletale, but she also wants the bullying to stop. Can Jessica find the courage to stand up for herself?

Cyber bullying is fast becoming a serious issue and poses a threat to many children. It is important for you to educate yourself and your students about the dangers and consequences of cyber bullying.

Cyber Bullying. The widespread use of the Internet, iPhones, texting devices, and social networking sites has led to the development of a new type of bullying: cyber bullying. **Cyber bullying** is the threatening, stalking, harassment, tormenting, and humiliation of one child by another through cell phones, MySpace, Facebook, Twitter, chat rooms, blogs, texting, and picture messaging. Cyber bullying is often anonymous and sometimes occurs between cliques and a single victim. Cyber bullying occurs in females more frequently than males.[82]

Here are some examples of cyber bullying:

- Sydney sent Emily an e-mail that said she was fat, stupid, and ugly.
- Mia Photoshopped a naked picture with Gina's face and posted it on MySpace.
- Kiera posted a note in a popular after-school study group chat room that Shawna was the biggest _____ in the third grade.
- Jonathon sent Matt an e-mail calling him a nerd and a pointy head.
- Rebecca stole Ashton's password and pretended to be Ashton, while saying derogatory remarks about another student in a chat room.

How to Prevent Cyber Bullying.   Here are some ways to help prevent cyber bullying:

- Tell children the consequences of forwarding any type of electronic message.
- Discuss with children the dangers involved in posting and sharing their personal information online and through social media.
- Advise students that if they think they are being cyber bullied, they should log off; report the incident to their teachers and parents; and change their privacy settings on social networking sites.

Because most cyber bullying takes place outside the classroom, parents must take time to educate children about cyber bullying. Here are more steps that parents can take to prevent cyber bullying in their own homes:

- Understand what cyber bullying is and how technology can be used to bully others.
- Contact the Internet service provider to see what parental controls are offered.
- Monitor what children are doing.
- Talk to children about the online activity in which they are engaging.
- Notify school officials if there is an incident that involves the school.
- Save all harassing messages so they can be reported.
- Keep computers in a common area.
- Look for signs that a child may be a victim of cyber bullying.[83]

Being aware of the different ways that you can prevent cyber bullying will help you become more knowledgeable about how to avoid this type of behavior in your classrooms. By learning about cyber bullying, you can provide children with different ways to appropriately use technology.

Childhood Abuse and Neglect

Many of our views of childhood are highly romanticized. We tend to believe that parents always love their children and enjoy caring for them. We also envision family settings full of joy, happiness, and harmony. Unfortunately for children, their parents, and society, these assumptions are not always true. In fact, the extent of child abuse is far greater than we might imagine. Annually there are 2 million referrals to child protective services (CPS) agencies involving the alleged maltreatment of about 5 million children.[84]

Child abuse is not new; abuse—in the form of abandonment, infanticide, and neglect—has been documented throughout history. The attitude that children are the property of the parents partly accounts for this record. Parents have believed, and some still do, that they own their children and can do with them as they please.

cyber bullying The threat, stalking, harassment, torment, and humiliation of one child by another through cell phones, MySpace, Facebook, Twitter, chat rooms, blogs, texting, and picture messaging.

Valid statistics are difficult to come by because definitions of child abuse and neglect differ from state to state and reports are categorized differently. Because of the increasing concern over child abuse, social agencies, hospitals, child care centers, and schools are becoming more involved in identification, treatment, and prevention of this national problem.

Public Law 93-247, the Child Abuse Prevention and Treatment Act, defines *child abuse and neglect* as follows:

> Physical or mental injury, sexual abuse, negligent treatment or maltreatment of a child under the age of eighteen by a person who is responsible for the child's welfare under circumstances which indicate that the child's health or welfare is harmed or threatened thereby as determined in accordance with regulations prescribed by the secretary.[85]

In addition, all states have some kind of legal or statutory definition of child abuse and mistreatment, and many define penalties for child abuse.

Just as debilitating as physical abuse and neglect is *emotional abuse,* which occurs when parents, teachers, and others strip children of their self-esteem. Adults take away children's self-esteem by continually criticizing, belittling, screaming and nagging, creating fear, and intentionally and severely limiting opportunities. Because emotional abuse is difficult to define legally and difficult to document, the unfortunate consequence for emotionally abused children is that they are often left in a debilitating environment.

Figure 2.4 will help you identify abuse and neglect, both of which adversely affect children's growth and development.

Remember that the presence of a single abuse symptom or sign does not necessarily indicate abuse. You should observe a child's behavior and appearance over a period of time and generally be willing to give parents the benefit of the doubt about a child's condition. Moreover, we also want to make sure we are practicing and upholding the best interest and welfare of each child.

Reporting Child Abuse.   As a teacher you are a mandatory reporter of child abuse. Other mandatory reporters include physicians, nurses, social workers, counselors, and psychologists. Each state has its own procedure and set of policies for reporting child abuse. You need to be familiar with your state and district policies about how to identify child abuse and how to report it.

The following guidelines should govern your response to a child with suspected abuse or neglect:

- Remain calm. A child may retract information or stop talking if he or she senses a strong reaction.
- Believe the child. Children rarely make up stories about abuse.
- Listen without passing judgment. Most children know their abusers and often have conflicted feelings.
- Tell the child you are glad that he or she told someone.
- Assure the child that abuse is not his or her fault.
- Do what you can to make certain that the child is safe from further abuse.
- Do not investigate the case yourself. Report your suspicions to your principal or program administrator or to the child and family services agency.

How child abuse is reported varies from state to state. In Washington, DC, for example, if child abuse or neglect is suspected, you are to call the reporting hotline immediately at 202-671-SAFE. To make a report, you would need to provide the following information:

- Name, age, sex, and address of the child who is the subject of the report; also the names of any siblings and of the parent, guardian, or caregiver

Physical Abuse

Physical Indicators

- Unexplained bruises and welts
  - On torso, back, buttocks, thighs, or face
  - Identifiable shape of object used to inflect injury (belt, electrical cord, etc.)
  - Appear with regularity after absence, weekend, or vacation
- Unexplained burns
  - On soles of feet, palms, back, buttocks, or head
  - Hot water, immersion burns (glove-like, sock-like, or doughnut-shaped burn on buttocks or genitals
- Unexplained fractures or dislocations
- Bald patches on scalp

Behavioral Indicators

- Child states s/he "deserves" punishment
- Fearful when others cry
- Behavioral extremes (aggressive, withdrawn)
- Frightened of parents or caretakers
- Afraid to go home
- Child reports injury by parents or caretakers
- Inappropriate/immature acting out
- Needy for affection
- Manipulative behaviors to get attention
- Tendency toward superficial relationships
- Unable to focus—daydreaming
- Self-abusive behavior or lack of concern for personal safety
- Wary of adult contact

Sexual Abuse

Physical Indicators

- Difficulty walking or sitting
- Torn, stained, or bloody undergarments
- Pain, swelling, or itching in genital area
- Pain when urinating
- Bruises, bleeding, or tears around the genital area
- Vaginal or penile discharge
- Sexually transmitted diseases
  - Herpes, crabs, vaginal warts
  - Gonorrhea, syphilis
  - HIV, AIDs
- Excessive masturbation

Behavioral Indicators

- Unwilling to change for gym or participate in physical education activities
- Sexual behavior or knowledge inappropriate to child's age
- Sexual acting out on younger children
- Poor peer relations
- Delinquent or runaway behavior
- Report of sexual assault
- Drastic change in school performance
- Sleep disorders/nightmares
- Eating disorders
- Aggression; withdrawal; fantasy; infantile behavior
- Self-abusive behavior or lack of concern for personal safety
- Substance abuse
- Repetitive behaviors (hand-washing, pacing, rocking)

Neglect

Physical Indicators

- Not meeting basic needs (food, shelter, clothing)
- Failure to thrive (underweight, small for age)
- Persistent hunger
- Poor hygiene
- Inappropriate dress for season or weather
- Consistent lack of supervision and emotional care
- Unattended physical problems or medical needs
- Abandonment

Behavioral Indicators

- Begging or stealing food
- Early arrival at or late departure from school
- Frequent visits to the school nurse
- Difficulty with vision or hearing
- Poor coordination
- Often tired or falling asleep in class
- Takes on adult roles and responsibilities
- Substance abuse
- Acting out behavior
- Educational failure
- Child verbalizes lack of care-taking

Emotional Abuse

Physical Indicators

- Speech disorders
  - Stuttering
  - Baby talk
  - Unresponsiveness
- Failure to thrive (underweight, small for age)
- Hyperactivity

Behavioral Indicators

- Learning disabilities
- Habits of sucking, biting, rocking
- Sleep disorders
- Poor social skills
- Extreme reactions to common events
- Unusually fearful
- Overly compliant behaviors (unable to set limits)
- Suicidal thoughts or actions
- Self-abuse
- Difficulty following rules or directions
- Child expects to fail so does not try

FIGURE 2.4 Indicators of Abuse and Neglect

Familiarize yourself with these signs of abuse and neglect. As an early childhood professional, it is your responsibility to be aware of and sensitive to children's physical and emotional conditions and to report signs of child abuse and neglect.

- Nature and extent of the abuse or neglect, as you know it (and any previous abuse or neglect)
- Any additional information that may help establish the cause and identity of persons responsible
- Your name, occupation, contact information, and a statement of any actions taken concerning the child

Seeking Help.   What can be done about child abuse? There must be a conscious effort to educate, treat, and help abusers and potential abusers. The school is a good place to begin. Federal agencies are another source of help. For information, contact any of the organizations listed in the Linking to Learning section at the end of the chapter.

POLITICS AND REFORM IN EARLY CHILDHOOD EDUCATION

The more early childhood is in the news, the more it generates public interest and attention; this is part of the political context of early childhood education. Whatever else can be said about education, it is political. Politicians and politics exert a powerful influence in determining what is taught, how it is taught, to whom it is taught, and by whom it is taught. Early childhood education is no exception. As a result, federal, state, and local policy makers are constantly counseling reforms and programs that will improve teaching and learning.

Federal and State Involvement in Early Childhood Programs

Federal and state funding of early childhood programs has greatly increased during the past decade.[86] This trend will continue for several reasons. First, politicians and the public recognize that the early years are the foundation for future learning. Second, spending money on children in the early years is more cost effective than trying to solve problems in the teenage years. For example, the Federal Reserve Bank estimates that the returns on public investment in quality early childhood development programs for low-income children, in terms of reduced spending on public programs and increased tax payments, is 16 percent. Children who attend quality early childhood programs do better in school, are less likely to become involved in the juvenile justice system, and are more likely to own homes and have jobs as adults.[87]

Expanded Federal Support for Early Childhood Education

Another reason for increased federal involvement in early childhood politics and programs relates to America's stature and leadership on the global stage. The United States is a world leader in politics and education and wants to stay that way. Our country wants and needs highly educated citizens to remain competitive in the world. This is what President Obama believes about the role of education in keeping our nation internationally competitive:

> A world-class education is the single most important factor in determining not just whether our kids can compete for the best jobs but whether America can out-compete countries around the world. America's business leaders understand that when it comes to education, we need to up our game. That's why we're working together to put an outstanding education within reach for every child.[88]

This effort to have a highly trained and highly skilled citizenry begins in the early years.

One of the most dramatic changes occurring in U.S. education today is the expanded role of the federal government in the funding for public education. More federal dollars are currently allocated for education than ever before.

Race to the Top (RTT).   Race to the Top is a U.S. Department of Education competition among the 50 states for $4.35 billion in federal funding and is designed to spur systemic reform and embrace innovative approaches to teaching and learning in America's schools. The reforms contained in the Race to the Top will help prepare America's students to graduate ready for college and career and enable them to out-compete any worker, anywhere in the world.[89]

Race to the Top emphasizes the following reform areas:

- Designing and implementing rigorous standards and high-quality assessments, by encouraging states to work jointly toward a system of common academic standards that builds toward college and career readiness, and that includes improved assessments designed to measure critical knowledge and higher-order thinking skills

- Attracting and keeping great teachers and leaders in America's classrooms, by expanding effective support to teachers and principals; reforming and improving teacher preparation; revising teacher evaluation, compensation, and retention policies to encourage and reward effectiveness; and working to ensure that our most talented teachers are placed in the schools and subjects where they are needed the most.

- Supporting data systems that inform decisions and improve instruction, by fully implementing a statewide longitudinal data system, assessing and using data to drive instruction, and making data more accessible to key stakeholders.

- Using innovation and effective approaches to turn around struggling schools, by asking states to prioritize and transform persistently low-performing schools.

- Demonstrating and sustaining education reform, by promoting collaborations between business leaders, educators, and other stakeholders to raise student achievement and close achievement gaps, and by expanding support for high-performing public charter schools, reinvigorating math and science education, and promoting other conditions favorable to innovation and reform.[90]

All of the above reforms are currently affecting early childhood programs and will continue to do so for a long time to come. For example, forty-four states and their local school districts and teachers are implementing the Common Core Standards, beginning in kindergarten. Every day, teachers use student assessment data to drive or guide their instructional processes.

The Race to the Top–Early Learning Challenge Grants (RTT–ELCG) are part of the federal government's efforts to reform early childhood education. The U.S. Department of Education has provided a $500 million grant to states in a competition to reform preschool programs.

The Race to the Top–Early Learning Challenge supports the development of new approaches to raise the bar across early learning centers and to close the school readiness gap. States are working to build statewide systems of high-quality early learning and development for all early learning programs, including Head Start, public pre-K, child care, and private preschools. Key reforms include aligning and raising standards for existing early learning and development programs; improving training and support for the early learning workforce through evidence-based practices; and building evaluation systems that promote effective practices and programs to help parents make informed decisions.[91]

Twenty-First Century Learning Skills

Twenty-first century learning skills represent student outcomes necessary for the twenty-first century. Business leaders have identified skills and knowledge they think are essential for success in the workplace. Four components that describe twenty-first century skills and knowledge are the following:

- Core subjects and the twenty-first century themes (such as language arts, mathematics, science, global awareness, and financial literacy)
- Learning and innovation skills (such as creativity, innovation, critical thinking, and problem solving)
- Information, media, and technology skills
- Life and career skills (such as initiative and self-direction)[92]

Essentially, these skills are ones necessary for living in a technological world and for living and working in a rapidly changing global society.

Changes in society constantly cause changes in the field of early childhood education. One of your major challenges as an early childhood teacher is to keep current in terms of new directions in your field. In this way you will be able to judge what is best for young children and implement the best practices that will enable young children to succeed in school and life.

This is a great time for early childhood education and a wonderful time to be a teacher of young children. The federal government and the U.S. Department of Education continue to press for more legislation, funding, and increased awareness for early childhood education and programs. This context of constant change and progress provides you many opportunities to become more professional, and to ensure that all children learn the knowledge and skills necessary for success in school and life.

ethical dilemma

"Our children need recess!"

Third grade teacher Allison Renfo can't believe the text message she received from her friend Courtney telling her their school board members are preparing to vote on a proposal to eliminate recess in the elementary grades next year. Allison agitatedly whips out her cell phone and calls Courtney: "You've got to be kidding me; how can the board be so short-sighted? The board doesn't have all the information they need to make such a decision! I just read a research report today that said that there is a clear link between obesity in early childhood and cardiovascular risk later in life. We were just talking the other day about how our children seem to be more obese than in previous years. Exercise is one way we can prevent obesity!" exclaims Allison. "Taking away recess in light of the national obesity epidemic just doesn't make a lot of sense to me. We should do something about it."

What should Allison do? Should Allison organize a flash mob through Twitter and Facebook to raise awareness about the board's proposal? Should she organize a group to "Occupy the School Board" the night of the meeting? Or should Allison do nothing and hope the board votes against the proposal? What should Allison do? What would you do?

Application Activities

1. Think about problems that young children and their families face in education (e.g., children who have problems with reading or children with autism). Search the Internet and identify three agencies in your community that are available to intervene and assist families. List three ways that you as a teacher could work with these agencies to help your children and families. Post your ideas on your class discussion board.

2. Many young children live in diverse families. Conduct online research about the challenges of providing for different types of families. Think about diverse families, the challenges families face, and what you can do as an early childhood professional to support contemporary families. Log on to Twitter and share with a small group of classmates your findings through Twitter's online website. To do this, go to www.twitter.com and type "diverse families" in the search box.

3. Think about and list five ways you can create a healthy and safe classroom for the grade level you plan to teach. Log on to Facebook and share your ideas with other classmates by creating an online blog. Take a look at the number of people that have viewed your blog and their comments. What do their comments tell you?

4. Reading online news is one way to keep up to date in a changing society and in a changing early childhood educational environment. In my early childhood classes, I electronically post (Twitter, class discussions, blogs, etc.) items that I refer to as "Early Childhood in the News." My students respond by also posting articles they find interesting. Over a two-week period, blog, Tweet, and electronically post with

your classmates some "Early Childhood in the News" items that relate to a topic you are studying in class.

5. Over the next three or four months, keep an electronic journal about changes you notice in the field of early childhood. Include these topics:

   a. What changes intrigue you the most?

   b. Not all changes are for the better. Make a list of changes that you think have a negative effect on children (e.g., rising poverty).

   c. Document or identify three things you personally and professionally can do in response to changes in society and education.

Linking to Learning

USA Today—Ghost Factories

www.ghostfactories.usatoday.com
Collection of comprehensive investigative reports on contaminated soil and the effects of children's play in these contaminated areas

Child Welfare Information Gateway

www.childwelfare.gov
A service of the Administration for Children and Families, U.S. Department of Health and Human Services, which helps coordinate and develop programs and policies concerning child abuse and neglect

Childhelp USA

www.childhelp.org
Handles crisis calls and provides information and referrals to every county in the United States; hotline 1-800-422-4453 or 4-A-CHILD

Let's Move!

www.letsmove.gov
A national initiative founded and run by First Lady Michelle Obama to bring awareness of obesity and dramatic change in obesity rates within one generation

U.S. Department of Agriculture—MyPlate

www.choosemyplate.org
Provides useful information on current nutrition guidelines, illustrating the five essential food groups for a healthy diet using the image of a dinner plate

MyEducationLab

Go to Topic 3 (Family/Community) in the MyEducationLab (www.myeducationlab.com) for your course, where you can:

- Find learning outcomes for Family/Community along with the national standards that connect to these outcomes.

- Complete Assignments and Activities that can help you more deeply understand the chapter content.

- Apply and practice your understanding of the core teaching skills identified in the chapter with the Building Teaching Skills and Dispositions learning units.

- Check your comprehension on the content covered in the chapter by going to the Study Plan in the Book Resources for your text. Here you will be able to take a chapter quiz, receive feedback on your answers, and then access Review, Practice, and Enrichment activities to enhance your understanding of chapter content.

chapter 3

HISTORY
AND THEORIES
Foundations for
Teaching and Learning

NAEYC Standards for Early Childhood Professional Preparation

Standard 4. Using Developmentally Effective Approaches to Connect with Children and Families

I understand and use positive relationships and supportive interactions as the foundation for my work with young children and families. I know, understand, and use a wide array of developmentally appropriate approaches, instructional strategies, and tools to connect with children and families and positively influence each child's development and learning.[1]

Standard 6. Becoming a Professional

I identify and conduct myself as a member of the early childhood profession. I know and use ethical guidelines and other professional standards related to early childhood practice. I am a continuous, collaborative learner who demonstrates knowledgeable, reflective, and critical perspectives on my work, making informed decisions that integrate knowledge from a variety of sources. I am an informed advocate for sound educational practices and policies.[2]

 ## THE HISTORY OF EARLY CHILDHOOD EDUCATION: WHY IS IT IMPORTANT?

There is a history of just about everything: a history of teaching, a history of schools, and a history of early childhood education. While you don't need to know the history of comic books to read and enjoy one, if you are a comic book collector, knowing the history of comic books is essential! The same applies to you as an early childhood educator. You will be a much more informed professional and effective teacher if you know the history of your profession.

When we know the beliefs, ideas, and accomplishments of people who have devoted their lives to young children, we realize that many of today's early childhood programs are built on enduring beliefs about how children learn, grow, and develop. There are at least three reasons why it is essential for you to know about ideas and theories that have and are influencing early childhood education.

Rebirth of Great Ideas

Great ideas and practices persist over time and tend to be reintroduced in educational thought and practices in ten- to twenty-year cycles. For example, many practices popular in the past—such as the emphasis on early literacy, the education of the whole child, and teacher-initiated instruction—are now popular once again. I hope you will always be as amazed as I am about the way early childhood professionals recycle enduring ideas and practices and use them in their teaching.

Build the Dream—Again

Many ideas of famous educators are still dreams because of our inability to translate dreams into reality due to politics and lack of funding. For example, the idea of universal preschool in the United States has been around since 1830, when the Infant School Society of Boston submitted a petition to incorporate infant schools into the Boston Public Schools.[3] We are *still* trying to implement universal preschool education. Horace Mann, a nineteenth-century education reformer, often referred to as "the father of American public education," stressed the importance and necessity of educating all children.

This goal of educating all children remains elusive, but nonetheless the goal remains. As Secretary of Education Arne Duncan says:

> President Obama and I believe that every child deserves a world-class education. When the President says every child, it is not just rhetoric—he means every child, regardless of his or her skin color, nationality, ethnicity, or ability.
>
> And we know, more than ever before, that in a global economy, a country's economic security depends on the skills and knowledge of its workers. The country that out-educates us today will out-compete us tomorrow. America does not have expendable students.[4]

The dream of educating all children to their full potential is a worthy one, and we can and should use it as a base to build meaningful teaching careers and lives for children and their families. We have an obligation to make the bright visions that others have had for children *our visions* as well. After all, if we don't have bright visions for children, who will?

Implement Current Practice

Beliefs of famous educators will help you better understand how to implement current teaching strategies, whatever they might be. For instance, Rousseau, Froebel, and Montessori all believed children should be taught with dignity and respect. Dignity and respect for all children are essential foundations of all good teaching and quality programs, and those traits apply today, just as they did hundreds of years ago. In addition, great educators always believed in educating the whole child, which is something that we always need to be reminded of. For example, Teacher of the Year Laura Cynthia Murr Watkins says:

> My teaching philosophy is based on a holistic approach to teaching and learning. This philosophy encompasses a child-centered approach, which promotes the child's individuality, creative exploration, and active involvement in his/her education. I teach to the whole child, thereby addressing the intellectual, emotional, physical, and social factors that influence children's learning and development and respecting the complexity of children's lives.[5]

THE IMPORTANCE OF THEORIES OF LEARNING

When you work with young children to help them discover and learn how plants grow, you talk about soil, sun, water, and the need for fertilizer. Perhaps you even use the word *photosynthesis* as part of your theory of plant growth.

MyEducationLab

Visit the MyEducationLab for *Fundamentals of Early Childhood Education* to enhance your understanding of chapter concepts with a personalized Study Plan. You'll also have the opportunity to hone your teaching skills through video-based Assignments and Activities as well as Building Teaching Skills and Dispositions lessons.

FOCUS QUESTIONS

1. Why is it important to know the history of early childhood education?

2. Why is it important to know theories of learning?

3. Who were the famous individuals who have influenced early childhood education and what were their contributions?

4. What are basic beliefs essential for high-quality programs?

5. How have instructional practices to accommodate disabilities changed over time?

Describing the processes of the mental and physical growth of children, however, is not as straightforward. How do children develop? How do children learn? I'm sure you have ideas and explanations based on your experiences to help answer these questions. We also have the theories of others to help us explain these questions.

A **theory** is a statement of principles and ideas that attempts to explain events and how things happen; in our case, it is learning more about children's early childhood. We will learn about theories that attempt to explain how children grow, develop, and learn.

Learning is the process of acquiring knowledge, behaviors, skills, and attitudes. As a result of experiences, children change in each of these areas. So, we can also consider learning to be changes that occur in behavior over a period of time. The children who enter your kindergarten class in September are not the same children who exit your kindergarten class in May. Learning is a complex process, and many educators have developed theories to explain how and why learning occurs in children. We use **child development**, which is the study of how children change over time from birth to age eight, to examine changes in children's lives.

Theories about how children learn and develop are an important part of your professional practice for several reasons. Let's look at the role of educational theories.

> **theory** A statement of principles and ideas that attempts to explain events and how things happen.
>
> **learning** The acquisition of knowledge, behaviors, skills, and attitudes.
>
> **child development** The study of how children change over time from birth to age eight.

Communicate

Theories enable you to explain to others, especially families, how the complex process of learning occurs and what you and they can expect of children. Communicating with clarity and understanding to parents and others about how children learn is one of the most important jobs for all early childhood professionals. To do this, you need to know the theories that explain how children develop and learn.

Evaluate Learning

Theories also enable you to evaluate children's learning. Theories describe behaviors and identify what children are able to do at certain ages. You can use this information to evaluate learning and plan for teaching. Evaluation of children's learning is another important job for all teachers.

Provide Guidance

Theories help us understand how, why, where, and when learning occurs. As a result, they can guide you in developing programs for children that support and enhance their learning. For example, as we will see shortly, what Piaget believed about how children learn directly influences classroom arrangement, what is taught, and how it is taught. Developing programs and curriculum is an important part of your professional practice. Thus, the history of early childhood and theories about how children learn enable you to fulfill essential dimensions of your professional role. Table 3.1 summarizes the contributions of famous educators to the early childhood field. Those educators are profiled in the following section.

FAMOUS HISTORICAL FIGURES AND THEIR INFLUENCE ON EARLY CHILDHOOD EDUCATION

Throughout history many people have contributed to our understanding of what children are like and how to best teach them. The following accounts will help you understand the history of early childhood and theories about how to best teach children. Table 3.1 will help you trace how historical figures and important moments in education have influenced education up to the present.

TABLE 3.1 Contributions of Famous Individuals to Early Childhood Education

Individual and Dates	Major Contributions	Influences on Modern Theorists
Martin Luther (1483–1546)	• Translated the Bible from Latin to vernacular language, allowing people to be educated in their own language. • Advocated establishing schools to teach children how to read.	• Universal education. • Public support of education. • Teaching of reading to all children. • Adult literacy.
John Comenius (1592–1670)	• Wrote *Orbis Pictus*, the first picture book for children. • Thought early experiences formed what a child would be like. • Said education should occur through the senses.	• Early learning helps determine school and life success. • Sensory experiences support and promote learning. • Believed teaching/learning should progress from easy to difficult.
John Locke (1632–1704)	• Said children are born as blank tablets, or *tabula rasa*. • Believed children's experiences determine who they are. Experiences are the basis of all learning.	• Learning should begin early. • Children learn what they are taught—teachers literally make children. • It is possible to rear children to think and act as society wants them to.
Jean-Jacques Rousseau (1712–1778)	• Advocated natural approaches to child rearing. • Felt that children's natures unfold as a result of maturation according to an innate timetable.	• Natural approaches to education work best (e.g., family grouping, authentic testing, and environmental literacy).
Johann Pestalozzi (1746–1827)	• Advocated that education should follow the course of nature. • Believed all education is based on sensory impressions. • Promoted the idea that the mother could best teach children.	• Family-centered approaches to early childhood education. • Home schooling. • Education through the senses. • Laid the basis for discovery learning. • Believed in the idea that when children can represent their experiences through drawing, writing, etc., then learning really occurs.
Robert Owen (1771–1858)	• Held that environment determines children's beliefs, behaviors, and achievements. • Believed society can shape children's character. • Taught that education can help build a new society.	• Importance of infant programs. • Education can counteract children's poor environment. • Early childhood education can reform society.
Friedrich Froebel (1782–1852)	• Believed children develop through "unfolding." • Compared children to growing plants. • Founded the kindergarten, or the "Garden of Children." • Developed "gifts" and "occupations" to help young children learn. • Believed children can and should learn through play.	• Teacher's role is similar to a gardener's. • Children should have specific materials to learn concepts and skills. • Learning occurs through play.

(continued)

TABLE 3.1 Contributions of Famous Individuals to Early Childhood Education *Continued*

Individual and Dates	Major Contributions	Influences on Modern Theorists
Maria Montessori (1870–1952)	• The Montessori method for educating young children. • All knowledge comes intrinsically from sensory experiences. • Learning materials to meet the needs of young children. • Sensory-based materials that are self-correcting. • Prepared environments are essential for learning. • Respect for children is the foundation of teaching.	• Large number of public and private Montessori schools that emphasize her approach, methods, and materials. • Renewed emphasis on preparing environment to support and promote children's learning. • Teacher training programs to train Montessori teachers.
John Dewey (1859–1952)	• Progressive education movement. • Children's interests form the basis of the curriculum. • Educate children for today—not tomorrow.	• Child-centered education. • Curriculum based on children's interests. • Discovery learning.
Jean Piaget (1896–1980)	• Theory of cognitive development based on ages and stages. • Children are "little scientists" and literally develop their own intelligence. • Mental and physical activities are important for cognitive development. • Project approach to learning.	• Constructivist approaches to early childhood education. • Matching education to children's stages of cognitive development. • Active involvement of children in learning activities.
Lev Vygotsky (1896–1934)	• Sociocultural theory, which emphasizes importance of interpersonal relationships in social and cognitive development. • Concept of zone of proximal development—children can learn more with the help of a more competent person. • Communication between teachers and children can act as a means of scaffolding to higher levels of learning.	• Use of scaffolding techniques to help children learn. • Use of cooperative learning and other forms of social learning.
Abraham Maslow (1908–1970)	• Theory of self-actualization based on needs motivation. • Human development is a process of meeting basic needs throughout life. • Humanistic psychology.	• Importance of meeting basic needs before cognitive learning can occur. • Teachers develop programs to meet children's basic needs. • Growth of the self-esteem movement. • Emphasis on providing safety, security, love, and affection for all children.
Erik Erikson (1902–1994)	• Theory of psychosocial development—cognitive development occurs in conjunction with social development. • Life is a series of eight stages with each stage representing a critical period in social development. • How parents and teachers interact with and care for children helps determine their emotional and cognitive development.	• Play supports children's social and cognitive development. • The emotional plays as great a role as the cognitive in development. • All children need predictable, consistent love, care, and education.

TABLE 3.1 Contributions of Famous Individuals to Early Childhood Education *Continued*

Individual and Dates	Major Contributions	Influences on Modern Theorists
Urie Bronfenbrenner (1917–2005)	• Ecological systems theory views the child as developing within a system of relationships. • Five interrelating systems—microsystem, mesosystem, exosystem, macrosystem, and chronosystem—have a powerful impact on development. • Each system influences and is influenced by the other. • Development is influenced by children and their environments.	• Teachers are more aware of how different environments shape children's lives in different ways. • Parents and educators strive to provide positive influences in each system and minimize or eliminate negative influences. • Teachers and parents recognize that children's development depends on children's natures and their environments.
Howard Gardner (b. 1943)	• Theory of multiple intelligences. • Intelligence consists of nine abilities. • Intelligence is not a single broad ability, but rather a set of abilities.	• Teachers develop programs and curricula to match children's particular intelligences. • Teachers individualize curricula and approaches to children's intelligences. • More awareness and attention to multiple ways in which children learn and think.

1500–1700: The Foundation

The contributors to the American education system are many and distinguished. In the following paragraphs, you will read about some of the most notable contributors to education as we know it today. As you read, consider how the contributions of the past play a part in the work you will do in early childhood education. Reflect on how historical figures and important moments in education have influenced one another and how events from the past influence us even today. Also, ask yourself these questions: "How will I contribute to the field? How will I continue or influence or modify the ideas of the founders of the field?"

Martin Luther

Martin Luther (1483–1546) emphasized the necessity of establishing schools to teach children to read. Luther replaced the authority of the Catholic Church with the authority of the Bible. Luther believed that individuals were free to work out their own salvation through the scriptures. This meant that people had to learn to read the Bible in their native tongue.

Luther translated the Bible into German, marking the real beginning of teaching and learning in people's native language. In these ways, the Protestant Reformation encouraged and supported popular universal education and the importance of learning to read.

Today, literacy for all continues to be a national priority. As you can see by the accompanying Diversity Tie-In feature, ensuring that all children can read and learn in their native language, as Luther suggested, are issues we still deal with today.

John Amos Comenius

John Amos Comenius (1592–1670) spent his life teaching school and writing textbooks. Two of his famous books are *The Great Didactic* and *Orbis Pictus* ("The World in Pictures"), considered the first picture book for children.

Comenius believed education should begin in the early years because "a young plant can be planted, transplanted, pruned, and bent this way or that. When it has become a tree these processes are impossible."[6] Today, new brain research reminds us again that learning should begin early and that many "windows of opportunity" for learning occur early in life.

Comenius also thought that sensory education forms the basis for all learning and that insofar as possible, everything should be taught through the senses. This approach to education was endorsed by Montessori and forms the basis for much of early childhood practice to this day.

John Locke

John Locke (1632–1704) is best known for his theory of the mind as a blank tablet, or *tabula rasa*. By this, Locke meant that environment and experience literally form the mind. According to Locke, development comes from the stimulation children receive from parents and caregivers and through experiences they have in their environment.

The implications of this belief are clearly reflected in modern educational practice. The notion of the importance of environmental influences is particularly evident in programs that encourage and promote early education as a means of helping children get a good foundation for learning early in life. These programs assume that differences in learning, achievement, and behavior are attributable to environmental factors such as home and family conditions, socioeconomic background, and early education and experiences. The current move toward universal schooling for three- and four-year-olds is based on the premise that getting children's education right from the beginning can help overcome negative effects of poverty and neglect and can help erase differences in children's achievement due to difference in socioeconomic levels.

Throughout this book, I consistently and persistently stress the importance of educating all of America's children. We cannot and must not neglect any children regardless of who or where they are, in urban, suburban, rural, or in Indian country territory. The United States has not always done all that it can or should do for First Citizen children. As Secretary of Education Arne Duncan says,

> We all know that far too many Native students drop out of high school. Far too few go on to college. Together, we must do more to nurture the next generation. The status quo is unacceptable, and we have to improve faster than ever before. We must work with urgency, for dramatically better outcomes. We must prepare these students to preserve the proud heritage and vibrant cultures that have shaped America's history for centuries. We must be their champions now, so they can lead in the future.

1700–1850: From Naturalism to Kindergarten

The foundation laid by philosophers like Luther and Locke paved the way for others to focus on education as a humanistic imperative. With this foundation, the world of education was able to evolve with the sometimes revolutionary ideas of Rousseau, Wollstonecraft, Owen, and Froebel.

Jean-Jacques Rousseau

Jean-Jacques Rousseau (1712–1778) is best remembered for his book *Émile,* the opening lines of which set the tone for his education and political views: "God makes all things good; man meddles with them and they become evil."[7] Because of this belief, Rousseau advocated the "natural" education of young children, encouraging growth without undue interference or restrictions.

Rousseau also believed in the idea of **unfolding**, in which the nature of children—who and what they will be—unfolds as a result of development according to their innate timetables. Such an approach is at the heart of developmentally appropriate

unfolding Rousseau's belief that the nature of children—who and what they will be—unfolds as a result of development according to their innate timetables.

diversity tie-in

Preserving Proud Heritages and Vibrant Cultures in American Indian and Alaskan Native Communities

Head Start and Early Head Start programs operate within communities that typically are deprived socially and economically, more so than any other grouping of peoples in the United States. The most current data indicates that Indian reservations suffer from Depression-era economics, with terrible crime and health statistics to match. Extraordinary measures are needed to address the ongoing crisis in much of Indian country, but more resources are needed, including strong leadership within Tribal communities, efficient and effective preschool programs, and coordinated child care programs.

Early Head Start (EHS) programs across the country incorporate the cultures and languages, the strengths and challenges of the families and communities they serve. Many programs are also committed to restoring the traditional practices of their families. Language, customs, values, and beliefs can survive only if they are passed on to the next generation, who in turn practice and pass on these traditions to their children. Because of decades of assimilation and poverty, only the tribal elders still hold the language and traditions. The American Indian and Alaska Native communities are using EHS programs as one way of bringing these cultures to very young children and their families in meaningful ways.

Today, educators recognize how child development and early learning are enhanced by cultural diversity, and they design curricula and educational materials that are culturally sensitive and inclusive.

EHS programs use a variety of strategies for bringing the native language and traditions to life within the American Indian and Alaska Native programs. Some programs are creating immersion classrooms where the teachers use only the native language with babies and toddlers all day. Many programs invite tribal elders to visit the classrooms regularly to speak their native language and sing traditional songs with the babies. The Blackfeet Tribal Business Council EHS program uses native language as well as flute and drum music in their work with expectant families, exposing the babies in the womb to traditional sounds and rhythms. When the baby is born, the prenatal instructor arranges a ceremony that honors the generations and welcomes the new baby into the tribe. Elders talk about the family's background, the child's name, and the importance of being a member of the tribe.

Indian Head Start and Early Head Start programs span the continental United States and Alaska. The service area of programs varies in size from expansive, spanning many counties and multiple states, to small areas.

....

Source: Contributed by the National Indian Head Start Directors Association.

---

practice, in which childhood educators match their educational practices to children's developmental levels and abilities. Every day you will make decisions about how to make sure what you teach and how you teach it is appropriate for each child based on his or her developmental level.

Johann Heinrich Pestalozzi

Johann Heinrich Pestalozzi (1746–1827) was influenced by both Comenius and Rousseau. Pestalozzi believed that all education is based on sensory impressions and that through the proper sensory experiences, children can achieve their natural potential. To achieve this goal, Pestalozzi developed "object lessons," manipulatives that encouraged activities such as counting, measuring, feeling, and touching. Pestalozzi also wrote two books—*How Gertrude Teaches Her Children* and *Book for Mothers*—to help parents teach their young children in the home. Today, enter any major bookstore (either online or in the shopping mall) and you will see shelves jammed with books on how to parent, how to teach young children, how to guide children's behavior, and many similar topics. You will be able to help families by providing them with books and/or suggestions for books to read that will help them enhance their guidance skills.

Robert Owen

Robert Owen (1771–1858) believed children's environments contribute to their beliefs, behavior, and achievement just as we believe today. He maintained that individuals and society can use environments to shape children's character. Owen was also a *utopian,* believing that by controlling the circumstances and consequent outcomes of child rearing, it was possible to build a new and perhaps more perfect society. Such a view of child rearing makes environmental conditions the dominant force in directing and determining human behavior.

To implement his beliefs, Owen opened an infant school in 1816 in New Lanark, Scotland, designed to provide care for about a hundred children, ages eighteen months to ten years, while their parents worked in the cotton mills he owned. This emphasis on early education eventually led to the opening of the first infant school in London in 1818.

Several things about Owen's efforts and accomplishments are noteworthy. First, his infant school preceded Froebel's kindergarten by about a quarter century. Second, Owen's ideas and practices influenced educators concerning the importance of early education and the relationship between educational and societal improvements, an idea much in vogue in current educational practice. In addition, early childhood professionals also seek to use education as a means of reforming society and as a way of making a better world for everyone.

Froebel believed, as early childhood professionals believe today, that play is a process through which children learn. Learning flows from play. These children are engaged in play that supports their growth and development. Froebel urged early childhood educators to support the idea that play is the cornerstone of children's learning.

Friedrich Wilhelm Froebel

Friedrich Wilhelm Froebel (1782–1852) is known as the "father of the kindergarten." Froebel's concept of children and learning is based in part on the idea of unfolding, also held by Comenius and Pestalozzi. According to this view, the teacher's role is to observe children's natural unfolding and provide activities that enable them to learn what they are ready to learn when they are ready to learn it.

Froebel compared the child to a seed that is planted, germinates, brings forth a new shoot, and grows from a young, tender plant to a mature, fruit-producing one. He likened the role of teacher to a gardener. Think for a moment how we still use the teacher-as-gardener metaphor to explain our role as teachers of young children. For example, I view myself as a planter of seeds in my work with young children. Froebel wanted his *kindergarten,* or "garden of children," to be a place where children unfolded like flowers. Froebel believed development occurred primarily through self-activity and play. The concepts of unfolding and learning through play are two of Froebel's greatest contributions to early childhood education.

To promote self-activity, Froebel developed a systematic, planned curriculum for the education of children based on "gifts," "occupations," songs, and educational games. Think of these as similar to the materials and toys we have today to promote children's learning. For example, we teach the alphabet and other concepts with songs,

Gift 1:
Six colored balls of soft yarn or wool

Gift 2:
Wooden sphere, cylinder, and cube

Gift 3:
Eight cubes, presented together as a cube

Gift 4:
Eight rectangular pieces,
presented as a cube

Gift 5:
Twenty-one cubes, six half-cubes, and
twelve quarter-cubes

Gift 6:
Twenty-four rectangular pieces, six
columns, and twelve caps

Gift 7:
Parquetry tablets derived from the
surfaces of the gifts, including
squares, equilateral triangles, right
triangles, and obtuse triangles

Gift 8:
Straight sticks of wood, plastic, or metal
in various lengths, plus rings and half-
rings of various diameters made from
wood, plastic, or metal

Gift 9:
Small points in various colors made of
plastic, paper, or wood

Gift 10:
Materials that utilize rods and
connectors, similar to Tinker Toys

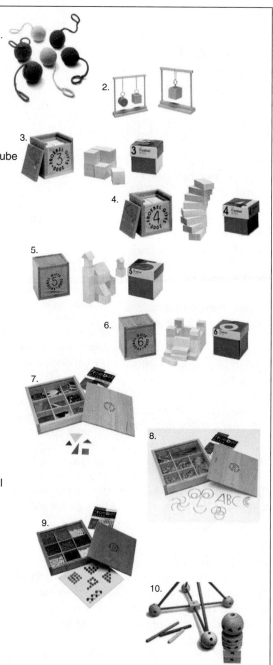

FIGURE 3.1 Froebel's Gifts

Froebel's concept of learning through play remains one of the basic principles of early childhood practice.

Source: Used by permission of Scott Bultman, FroebelUSA.com.

use blocks to teach size and shape, and use colored rods to teach concepts of length and serration.

Gifts were objects for children to handle and use in accordance with teachers' instructions so they could learn shape, size, color, and concepts involved in counting, measuring, contrasting, and comparison. Figure 3.1 describes Froebel's gifts. Think of some specific examples of how they relate to educational toys and materials today.

Occupations were materials designed for developing various skills through activities such as sewing with a sewing board, drawing pictures by following the dots,

professionalism in practice

How to Teach in a Child-Centered Program

The City and Country School believes an educator's greatest challenge isn't to teach children, but rather to create an environment that keeps their inherent curiosity intact. The C&C classroom serves as an ideal place for children to explore, experiment, learn and grow, both as individuals and as a group.

In the partnership of learning among children and teachers, community is lived through purposeful experiences that foster responsibility, cooperation, active participation, care and respect—qualities necessary to the life of a democratic society.

Lower School classrooms are equipped with ample space and an abundant supply of carefully chosen, open-ended materials, including blocks, paint, clay, paper, wood, sand and water. These materials, along with teachers who expertly guide their use, promote children's active involvement and independence while also inspiring creativity and cooperation. Children use the materials to explore, experiment, and in the process, build a foundation in the academic disciplines of social studies, reading, writing, math and science. As the children move through the Lower School, academic skills are taught more formally. Systematic teaching of reading begins in Kindergarten.

GUIDELINE 1 Arrange the classroom to support child-centered learning.

Example: C&C teachers, rather than filling the room with teacher-driven materials, display the work and current interests of the children, such as child-created murals that may depict their social studies. Furthermore, the design of the room provides materials and space that allow children to experiment with sand and water; research their interests with books; and recreate their learning through blocks, clay, woodshop materials, artwork, writing and dramatic play.

GUIDELINE 2 Provide easily accessible materials and supplies.

Example: The classrooms at C&C are simple in design, with child-accessible shelves filled with clearly labeled and organized open-ended materials and tools. The children keep their spaces orderly, and are responsible for classroom tasks, such as distributing snack and cleaning tables. In this and other ways, the children have ownership of their space.

GUIDELINE 3 Provide opportunities for children to move around and engage in active learning.

Example: Woodworking, block and dramatic play offer children opportunities to use their bodies and minds. For example, starting in the 4s, children start working with real woodworking tools in their classroom. If they want a boat or a car to use in their play, they can create one. By trusting children to achieve their visions in such a substantial way, they gain a tremendous sense of autonomy, accomplishment,

modeling with clay, cutting, stringing beads, weaving, drawing, pasting, and folding paper. All of these activities are part of early childhood programs today.

Froebel devoted his life to developing both a program for young children and a system of training for kindergarten teachers. Many of his ideas and activities form the basis for activities in preschools and kindergartens today.

1850–1950: From a Garden of Children to the Children's House

Contemporary education programs have their roots in the past and continue to be influenced by John Dewey and Maria Montessori.

John Dewey and Progressive Education Theory

John Dewey (1859–1952) did more than any other person to redirect the course of education in the United States, and his influence is ongoing.

Dewey's theory of schooling, usually called *progressivism,* emphasizes children and their interests rather than subject matter. From this child-centered emphasis come the terms *child-centered curriculum* and *child-centered school,* two topics very much in the forefront of educational practice today. Dewey believed that education "is a process of

and respect. Furthermore, children at C&C are not restricted to sitting at a desk or table as they find a comfortable way to work.

GUIDELINE 4 Provide materials and space for focused hands-on activities.

Example: As social studies topics are explored in depth, children engage in active learning by first exploring their ideas through research, such as trips, and then reconstruct their knowledge in many number of ways. For example, as the 6s learn about transportation, they may visit Grand Central Station where they use research logs to take notes of their observations (in pictures or writing), they later might create books based on their research, and then plan, build and accessorize a large-scale Grand Central Station and railroads with blocks and art materials.

GUIDELINE 5 Arrange furniture so that children can work and play together.

Example: Tables and workspaces are provided so children can work together, side by side, and across from one another, rather than in desks and rows. C&C classrooms also provide ample open space for children to work with blocks and on large-scale group work, such as murals.

GUIDELINE 6 Support cooperative learning.

Example: Our youngest children share materials, space, and group responsibilities. When children ages four and older recreate their research and interests in blocks or plays, they share and discuss what they've learned as a group, then plan the layout and design, or scripts and sets, together as a whole group, and work on smaller, discrete tasks in small groups.

In this way, the goals of the whole group are achieved in a variety of social configurations and contexts for democratic decision-making.

GUIDELINE 7 Provide for individual differences and individualized instruction.

Example: After studying the operations of a restaurant, the 6-year-old children plan the opening of a real restaurant in the classroom. They can work on areas of specific interest to them, such as cooking, menu creation, organizing the space, practicing communicating with their customers, and writing down orders, thus allowing each child to take ownership of his or her learning. Teachers work alongside the child and challenge each child to explore their strengths, and take time to work on areas where they are less experienced.

GUIDELINE 8 Provide ample time for children to engage in cooperative activities.

Example: As the 8s learn multiplication tables, they are also working on opening the school post office. In order to quickly tally orders, they must know their multiplication tables. This real-world need for a rote skill solidifies the knowledge in a concrete activity, while group-mates are relying on them to keep the post office running smoothly. The motivation to learn the math facts is intrinsic to the group's need and to the job at hand.

City and Country School remains committed to its founding principles and continues to promote and exemplify progressive education.

Source: Contributed by Jennifer Moran, Director of Publications and Archives, City and Country School.

living and not a preparation for future living" and that daily life should be a source of activities through which children learn about life and the skills necessary for living.[8] He also believed that "the child is more important than the subject" and that "schools should be based on democratic, not authoritarian principles."[9] For example, read the Professionalism in Practice feature, "How to Teach in a Child-Centered Program."

Classroom work in Dewey's school was a carefully designed extension of children's familiar life in the home. Rote exercises were minimized. Projects resembling those of a traditional household—crafts and cooking, for example—were used as ways to teach practical lessons of reading and arithmetic.[10]

Dewey's school was based on five basic principles, all of which are very contemporary and applicable to early childhood practice today:

- The child's early school experiences reflect the home life (cooking, sewing, construction); academic skills would be an outgrowth of these activities/occupations.[11]
- Children are part of a human community in school that focuses on cooperation.
- Learning is focused on problems that children solve (e.g., numbers would be learned through understanding relationships rather than memorizing multiplication tables).

- Motivation is internal to the experiences and the child.
- The teacher's role is to know the children and to choose stimulating problems for them.

In a classroom based on Dewey's ideas, children are actively involved in activities, making and using things, solving problems, and learning through social interactions. Dewey felt that an ideal way for children to express their interests was through daily life-skills activities such as cooking and through occupations such as carpentry.

John Dewey represents a dividing line between the educational past and the educational present. This would be a good time for you to review and reflect on the "Time Line of the History of Early Childhood Education" in Appendix A.

John Dewey is important to the field of early childhood education in another way. His progressive education movement, based on children learning by doing, forms the foundation for, and is a transition to, constructivist education, which is the foundational theory for the practice of early childhood education. Dewey's ideas form a framework for contemporary constructivist ideas and practices.

Maria Montessori and the Montessori Method

Maria Montessori (1870–1952) developed a system for educating young children that has greatly influenced early childhood education. The first woman in Italy to earn a medical degree, she became interested in educational solutions for problems such as deafness, paralysis, and mental retardation.

At that time she said, "I differed from my colleagues in that I instinctively felt that mental deficiency was more of an educational than medical problem."[12]

While preparing herself for educating children, Montessori was invited to organize schools for young children of families who occupied tenement houses in Rome. In the first school, named the *Casa dei Bambini,* or "Children's House," she tested her ideas and gained insights into children and teaching that led to the perfection of her system. The Montessori method is currently used in over four thousand early childhood programs.[13]

1950–1962: From Politics to the Classroom

Education always occurs within a social and political context and is often a direct outgrowth of social and political trends. The purposes of education, how we view children, and how we teach them are all influenced by what is going on in the world around us. Social and political trends of the last fifty years have created an educational culture that influenced your education and will influence you as a teacher.

Education as National Defense.　After the end of World War II in 1945, the United States and the Soviet Union became embroiled in a heated competion consisting of a nuclear arms race, a race to be first in space, and a race for world dominance. Out of this "cold war" came *Sputnik.*

Sputnik.　In 1957, The Soviet Union launched *Sputnik,* the world's first satellite. *Sputnik* sparked a nationwide fear of Soviet dominion, the spread of communism, and the fall of the United States as a world power. In response to this national fear, Congress passed the *National Defense Education Act* (NDEA) of 1958. NDEA's founding idea was that the best defense is a good (educational) offense. NDEA provided federal funding for science, technology, engineering, math (STEM), and foreign language education and is considered by many to be the beginning of federal standards in education.

The launch of *Sputnik* is important to you today because the current emphasis on science, math, and technology was born out of the race for world superiority.

applying research to practice

Linking Pre-K, Half-Day, Full-Day Kindergarten to Third Grade Reading: How to Spend the Funds

STUDY WEIGHS OPTIONS FOR EARLY EDUCATION

Over the centuries, all of the great educators have advocated that the education of young children should begin early. Generally, the public and politicians have been willing to support early education as long as the necessary funds are available. How to get the funds to support early education is an ongoing issue confronting the advocates and supporters of early childhood education. The Great Recession of 2008–2012 has greatly diminished the funds available for early childhood education. Given the diminishing amounts of federal and state dollars to spend on early childhood programs, states and local politicians continually weigh the evidence, pros and cons, for funding new and existing programs. Specifically, they have to make decisions between preschool and half-day and full-day kindergarten. A recent study provides some new data school districts can use about how to invest their scarce funds. The research says that if schools have to make choices, and most do, then the best use of scarce funds to achieve higher reading skills by third

grade is to invest in preschool and half-day kindergarten rather than to invest all their funds only in full-day kindergarten. The research also shows that the impact of pre-K and half-day kindergarten was the greatest for Hispanic children, black children, English Language Learners (ELLs), and children from low-income families.[14]

So, what does this mean for you?

- This research helps you and others make decisions about how best to spread resources so that they provide the most benefits for young children.
- In your role as advocate for young children, you can use research such as this to help persuade policy makers, school board members, and program directors to spend their money wisely.
- Research is quite clear about the benefits of preschool and kindergarten programs. What is important is that you should be a strong advocate for universal, full-day preschool and kindergarten programs.

It resulted in amazing scientific discoveries that impact how we think about education and how we teach children.

Today, the worldwide race for science, technology, engineering, and mathematic superiority continues. The idea that education is a nationalistic imperative also continues. The race for superiority is also evident today in the emphasis on teaching the Common Core standards and encouraging all children to achieve at high levels.

1962 to the Present: From Civil Rights to the Education of Today

In the 1960s the civil rights movement permanently altered the course of education as we know it today. With the civil rights movement, the federal government became more involved in ensuring education for all and in altering the environments of education as a whole.

Education as Equalizer. In the 1960s, society began to stress civil rights, and the education system played, and continues to play, a large part in assuring equality to everyone. The *Civil Rights Act* of 1964 included a provision that protects the constitutional rights of individuals in public facilities, including public education. Congress amended the Civil Rights Act in 1972. The most famous of these amendments is Title IX, which provides for equal opportunity in sports for all women. The education amendments of the Civil Rights Act are now called the Equal Opportunity in Education Act.

These Head Start children are busily involved in activities that enable them to gain the literacy skills they need to be ready for kindergarten. Head Start is designed to provide comprehensive services for children and families that contribute to their success in school and life.

The Economic Opportunity Act.   Part of President Lyndon B. Johnson's war on poverty was the *Economic Opportunity Act* (EOA) of 1964. The EOA implemented several social programs to promote the health, education, and general welfare of people with low socioeconomic status and was designed to put them to work. The EOA provided for the beginning of Head Start in 1965. The EOA was later updated as the Head Start Act of 1981. *Head Start* is one of the longest-running programs to address systemic poverty in the United States. Its programs include Early Head Start, Head Start, Family and Community Partnerships, Migrant and Seasonal Head Start, and American Indian–Alaska Native Head Start.

Elementary and Secondary Education Act.   In 1965, Congress passed the *Elementary and Secondary Education Act* (ESEA), which serves to more fully fund primary and secondary education. The ESEA provides monies to help educate children from low-income families. This portion of the ESEA is known as *Title I*. Eligibility for Title I funds is based on children's eligibility for free or reduced-price school lunches. Funds are used to provide additional academic support and learning opportunities so that children can master challenging curricula and meet state standards in core academic subjects. For example, funds support extra instruction in reading and mathematics, as well as special preschool, after-school, and summer programs to extend and reinforce the regular school curriculum. More than 30,000 schools use the Title I funds for the whole school, and at last count, Title I served more than 17 million children.[15] Of these students, approximately 60 percent were in kindergarten through fifth grade. Therefore, it is almost certain that you will teach children served by Title I funds.[16]

No Child Left Behind.   The current reauthorization of ESEA is the No Child Left Behind Act (NCLB) of 2001. The *No Child Left Behind Act* continues the the standards movement established by the National Defense Education Act and emphasizes accountability through testing. Currently, all 50 states have standards that specify what children should know and do. NCLB provides federal funding for schools that accrue high test scores and meet adequate yearly progress (AYP) standards, an accountability measurement. Opponents of NCLB and the accountability movement argue that it relies too heavily on standardized testing rather than authentic means of assessment. There is an ongoing discussion in the country right now concerning the reauthorization of NCLB. Currently, however, there is no sign that Congress will engage in a new reauthorization of NCLB. In the meantime, while some states continue to abide by NCLB regulations, others request and are granted waivers from testing and accountability.

The Education of All Handicapped Children Act.   In 1975, Congress passed Public Law 94-142: *The Education of All Handicapped Children Act* (EAHC). The EAHC mandated that in order to receive federal funds, states must develop and implement policies that ensure a free appropriate public education (FAPE) for all children with disabilities.

The Individuals with Disabilities Education Act.   In 1990, the Education of All Handicapped Children Act was reauthorized and renamed the Individuals with Disabilities Education Act (IDEA). IDEA was reauthorized again in 1997 and 2004, and it is still in effect today. IDEA provides for inclusion, *universal design* (UD) (the process of making classroom environments and the curriculum accessible to all children); *Response to Instruction* (RTI) (a multitiered approach to the early identification and support of students with learning and behavior needs); and *differentiated instruction* (DI) (an approach that enables teachers to plan strategically to meet the needs of every student in order to teach to the needs of each child and allow for diversity in the classroom). IDEA was the foundation for the integration and blending of early childhood education and early childhood special education. Today, every early childhood teacher is a special education teacher.

Providing equality education for all of the country's children continues to be one of the larger purposes of federally funded education. However, as the following discussion on the views of children shows, we are still fighting the battle of equality in the education system.

Integrating History and Theories

The history of early childhood and the theories of early childhood go together. They are integrated in the sense that you really can't understand one without the other. This is why we study them together. Let's turn our attention now to how theories influence what and how you teach.

Jean Piaget and Constructivist Learning Theory

Jean Piaget (1896–1980) was interested in how children learn and develop intellectually. He devoted his life to conducting experiments, observing children (including his own), and developing and writing about his cognitive theory approach to learning. Piaget's theory is a constructivist theory.

Constructivism. Constructivism is a cognitive theory of development and learning based on the ideas of John Dewey, Jean Piaget, and Lev Vygotsky. The *constructivist approach* supports the belief that children actively seek knowledge; it explains children's cognitive development, provides guidance for how and what to teach, and provides direction for how to arrange learning environments.

Constructivism is defined in terms of the individual's organizing, structuring, and restructuring of experience—an ongoing lifelong process—in accordance with existing schemes of thought. In turn, these very schemes become modified and enriched in the course of interaction with the physical and social world.[17]

Constructivism and Cognitive Development. The constructivist process involves organization, structure, and restructure of children's experiences.[18] Constructivism rests on the notion that instead of absorbing or passively receiving knowledge, children should gain through experimental learning—personal involvement and self-initiated deep thinking during which they can actively construct knowledge by integrating new information and experiences into what was taught. Pedagogy based on constructivist theory—such as class discussion, group presentation, and project work—is supportive in stimulating students' creativity and fostering their learning.[19]

Children, through activity and interaction with others, continuously organize, structure, and restructure experiences in relation to existing *schemes,* or mental images of thought. As a result, children build their own intelligence.

How Do Children Construct Knowledge? Even though children have parents, teachers, and others to provide for them, to take care of them, and to create learning environments for them, nonetheless it is children who are constructing their cognitive and social development for themselves. Lev Vygotsky, a leading proponent and developer of constructivist ideas, says that learning nudges development, and this is true. But learning comes with the assistance of more competent others and the children

cognitive theory Jean Piaget's proposition that children develop intelligence through direct experiences with the physical world. In this sense, learning is an internal (mental) process involving children's adapting new knowledge to what they already know.

constructivism Theory that emphasizes the active role of children in developing their understanding and learning.

constructivist process The continuous mental organizing, structuring, and restructuring of experiences, in relation to schemes of thought, or mental images, that result in cognitive growth.

themselves as they construct their world. How do children construct knowledge? Here are some processes they engage in, which make possible the "construction" of knowledge schemes and their understanding of the world:

- *Organization.* Children are self-organizing systems who gather information by experiencing the world around them through **active involvement** with people, places, and things. This self-organization occurs through the cognitive processes of assimilation, accommodation, and equilibrium, which are discussed below.

- *Repetition.* Much of children's learning is characterized by repetition. When children continually bounce a ball, they are creating a relationship between the ball and themselves, their motor functions. So by bouncing the ball, they are developing and creating the muscle memory necessary to make ball bouncing possible. For example, Colton, my seven-year-old neighbor, repeatedly bounces, throws, and catches a tennis ball off the side of his home. As a result, he has excellent hand-eye coordination and is adept at throwing and catching. Children love to repeat poems and nursery rhymes over and over again. They sing a favorite song repeatedly. Such repetition is essential for the construction of knowledge and schemes.

- *Social interactions.* Lev Vygotsky repeatedly reminds us that learning is social and that cognitive development occurs in social contexts. Put another way, socialization is essential for construction of knowledge and learning. Children seek others to establish relationships, to engage in experiences, and to test out their ideas. Socializing with others creates dynamic interactions in which children share their thoughts, ideas, and artifacts. Such interactions are the crucible for the construction of knowledge. Reciprocally, socialization provides children access to others' ideas, thoughts, and points of view. This reciprocal socialization is an essential ingredient whereby children are able to construct knowledge.

- *Problem solving.* Children are great problem solvers. They are willing to repeat experiences and to keep working on a project in order to problem-solve. Environments, well-designed activities, and materials (concrete objects, props, etc.) support children's experimenting and problem solving, which contribute to the construction of knowledge.

Notice, in this **video**, how the teacher facilitates play and then intentionally withdraws. Watch how the girls' play evolves and their roles change as they continue to play.

Constructivism and Play.   Play is one primary way in which children are actively involved in their environments and by which they think and learn. Play provides hands-on and "minds-on" opportunities so children can experience and learn through all kinds of materials—water, sand, clay, indoor and outdoor equipment, puzzles, blocks, real-life toys, housekeeping furniture, dolls, dress-up clothes, carpentry equipment, musical instruments, and so forth. The physical activity involved in play supports children's natural ways of learning by enabling them to touch, explore, feel, test, experiment, talk, and think. It is through these processes that children gain meaning of their world and learn how things work. As a result, children learn to make sense of the world.

The Constructivist Classroom.   The constructivist classroom is child centered and learning centered. Here are some essential features of constructivism applied to teaching and learning:

- Children are physically and mentally active.
- Children are encouraged to initiate learning activities.
- Children carry on dialogues and conversations with peers, teachers, and other adults.
- Teachers create and support children's social interactions with peers, teachers, and other adults to provide a context for cognitive development and learning.

- Teachers provide rich social environments characterized by children's collaboration, projects, problem solving, and cooperative learning.
- Teachers arrange classroom desks, tables, and learning centers to support student collaboration and social interaction.
- Teachers create a classroom climate of mutual respect and cooperation.
- Teachers and children are partners in learning.
- Teachers provide guided assistance.
- Teachers can promote the construction of knowledge by observing individual children and asking questions or making suggestions that will further their thinking.
- Teachers link children's prior knowledge and experiences with current classroom activities and experiences.

In a constructivist classroom, children are physically and mentally active in activities that are designed to help them discover ideas and solve problems. The role of the teacher in a constructivist classroom is to provide guided assistance.

Piaget's Cognitive Development Theory. Piaget's theory explains how individuals think, understand, and learn. Piaget believed that intelligence is the cognitive, or mental, process by which children acquire knowledge. *Intelligence* is "to know" and involves the use of *mental operations* developed as a result of acting mentally and physically in and on the environment. Active involvement is basic to Piaget's theory that children develop intelligence through direct hands-on experiences with the physical world. These hands-on experiences provide the foundations for a "minds-on" ability to think and learn.

Piaget also thought intelligence helped children adapt to their environments. For example, in the process of physical adaptation, children react and adjust to their environments. Piaget applied the concept of adaptation to the mental level, using it to explain how children change their thinking and grow cognitively as a result of encounters with parents, teachers, siblings, peers, and the environment.

Cognitive Development and Adaptation. According to Piaget, the adaptive process at the intellectual level operates much the same as at the physical level. The newborn's intelligence is expressed through reflexive motor actions such as sucking, grasping, head turning, and swallowing. Early in life, reflexive actions enable children to adapt to the environment, and their intelligence develops from these adaptations.

Through interaction with the environment, children organize sensations and experiences and grow mentally. Obviously, therefore, the quality of the environment and the nature of children's experiences play a major role in the development of intelligence. For example, Jason, with various and differing objects available to grasp and suck, and many opportunities for this behavior, will develop differentiated sucking organizations (and therefore an intelligence) quite different from those of Amber, who has nothing to suck but a pacifier. Consequently, one of your roles is to provide enriched environments for young children and to work with parents to provide rich home learning environments.

Learning as the Adaptation of Mental Constructs. Piaget believed that adaptation is composed of two interrelated processes: assimilation and accommodation.

assimilation The taking in of sensory data through experiences and impressions and incorporating them into existing knowledge.

Assimilation. Assimilation is the taking in of sensory data through experiences and impressions and incorporating the data into existing knowledge. Through assimilation, children use old methods or experiences to understand and make sense of new information and experiences. In other words, children use their experiences and what they have learned from them as a basis for learning more. This is why quality learning experiences are so important. All experiences are not equal. Out of all the possible learning experiences you could provide, make sure the ones you select have the highest potential to promote learning.

accommodation The process of changing old methods and adjusting to new situations.

Accommodation. Accommodation is the process of changing old methods and adjusting to new situations. Robbie has several cats at home. When he sees a dog for the first time, he may call it a kitty. He has assimilated *dog* into his organization of *kitty*. However, Robbie must change (accommodate) his model of what constitutes "kittyness" to exclude dogs. He does this by starting to construct or build a scheme for dogs and thus for what "dogness" represents.[20]

The processes of assimilation and accommodation, functioning together, constitute *adaptation.*

equilibrium A state of balance between the cognitive processes of assimilation and accommodation, allowing children to successfully understand new data.

Equilibrium. If adaptation is the functioning together of assimilation and accommodation, then equilibrium is the balance between the two processes. According to Piaget's theory of intelligence, as assimilation and accommodation function with each other, there must be balance between the two in order to allow children to successfully understand new data.

When they receive new sensory and experiential data, children assimilate, or fit, these data into their already existing knowledge (scheme) of reality and the world. If the new data can be immediately assimilated, then equilibrium occurs. If unable to assimilate the data, children try to accommodate and change their way of thinking, acting, and perceiving to account for the new data and restore the equilibrium to the intellectual system. It may well be that Robbie can neither assimilate nor accommodate the new data; if so, he rejects the data entirely.

Rejection of new information is common if experiences and ideas children are trying to assimilate and accommodate are too different from their past experiences and their level of knowledge and understanding. This partially accounts for Piaget's insistence that new experiences must have some connection or relationship to previous experiences. Child care and classroom experiences should build on previous life and school experiences.

scheme A unit of knowledge that a child develops through experience that defines how things should be.

Schemes. Piaget used the term scheme to refer to units of knowledge that children develop through adaptation. Piaget believed that in the process of developing new schemes, physical activity is very important. Physical activity leads to mental stimulus, which in turn leads to mental activity—our hands-on, minds-on concept. Thus, it is not possible to draw a clear line between physical activity and mental activity in infancy and early childhood. Teachers and parents should provide classrooms and homes that support active learning by enabling all children to explore and interact with people and objects in meaningful ways.

Stages of Intellectual Development. Figure 3.2 summarizes Piaget's developmental stages and provides examples of stage-related characteristics. As you review these now, keep in mind that Piaget contended that developmental stages are the same for all children and that all children progress through each stage in the same order. The ages identified with each stage are only approximate and are not fixed. The sequence of growth through the developmental stages does *not* vary; the ages at which progression occurs *do* vary.

I. The Sensorimotor Stage

Appropriate Age:
Birth to about 2 years

Characteristics:
Children use their innate sensorimotor systems of sucking, grasping, and gross-body activities to build schemes. They begin to develop object permanency and "think" with their senses and their innate reflexive actions. In addition, children "solve" problems by playing with toys and using everyday "tools" such as a spoon to learn to feed themselves.

Teachers' Role:
• Provide interactive toys, such as rattles, mobiles, and pound-a-peg
• Provide many and varied multisensory toys to promote investigation and sensory involvement; include household items such as pots, pans, and spoons
• Provide environments in which infants and toddlers can crawl and explore, keeping infants out of their cribs as much as possible
• Play hide-and-seek games that involve looking for hidden objects
• Provide rich language environments to encourage interaction with people and objects

II. The Preoperational Stage

Appropriate Age:
2 to 7 years

Characteristics:
Children depend on concrete representations and "think" with concrete materials. They use the world of here and now as frame of reference. Children in this stage enjoy accelerated language development. They are very egocentric in thought and action and therefore tend to internalize events. Children think everything has a reason or purpose. Children are perceptually bound and therefore make judgments based primarily on how things look.

Teachers' Role:
• Provide toys and materials for pretend play
• Provide building blocks of many kinds
• Provide materials for arts and crafts
• Provide many and varied kinds of manipulative materials, such as puzzles, counters, and clay
• Provide many concrete learning materials and activities
• Provide many developmentally appropriate language opportunities involving speaking, listening, reading, and writing

III. The Concrete Operations Stage

Appropriate Age:
7 to 17 years

Characteristics:
Children are able to reverse their thought processes and conserve and understand numbers. Children depend on how things look for decision making, but are less egocentric. They begin to structure time and space and to think logically. In this stage, children can apply logic to concrete situations.

Teachers' Role:
• Use props and visual aids, especially when dealing with sophisticated material
• Give students a chance to manipulate and test objects
• Make sure presentations and readings are brief and well organized
• Use familiar examples to explain more complex ideas
• Give opportunities to classify and group objects and ideas on increasingly complex levels
• Present problems that require logical, analytical thinking
• Provide opportunities for role taking, problem solving, and self-reflection

FIGURE 3.2 Piaget's Stages of Cognitive Development

Sensorimotor Stage. The sensorimotor stage is the first of Piaget's stages of cognitive development. When children use their primarily reflexive actions to develop intellectually, they are in the **sensorimotor stage**. During this period from birth to about two years, children use their senses and motor reflexes to build knowledge of the world. They use their eyes to see, mouths to suck, and hands to grasp. These reflexive actions help children construct a mental scheme of what is suckable and what is not (what can fit into the mouth and what cannot) and what sensations (warm and cold) occur by sucking. Children also use the grasping reflex in much the same way to build schemes of what can and cannot be grasped. Through these innate sensory and reflexive actions, they continue to develop an increasingly complex, unique, and individualized hierarchy of schemes about their world. What children are to become

sensorimotor stage The first of Piaget's stages of cognitive development, when children primarily use their senses and motor reflexes to develop intellectually.

physically and intellectually is related to these sensorimotor functions and interactions. This is why it is important for teachers and others to provide quality experiences and environments for young children.

Children in the sensorimotor stage:

- Exhibit dependence on and use of innate reflexive actions, which are the basic building blocks of intelligence.
- Begin to develop *object permanency*—the understanding or awareness that objects exist even when they are not seen, heard, or touched.
- Exhibit egocentric behavior. They see themselves as the center of the world. They believe what they see, feel, and think is true of everyone. Egocentric children are unable to see life and events from other people's perspectives. Cognitively, they are unable to "put themselves in someone else's shoes."
- Depend on concrete representations (things) rather than symbols (words, pictures) for information.
- Are less reliant on sensorimotor reflexive actions and, by the end of the second year, begin to use symbols for things that are not present.

Preoperational Stage. The second stage of cognitive development, the preoperational stage, begins at age two and ends at approximately seven years. Preoperational children are cognitively different from sensorimotor children in these ways:

- Rapidly accelerating language development
- Less dependence on sensorimotor actions
- Increased ability to internalize events and think by using symbols such as words to represent things

Preoperational children express their ideas mainly on how they see things. How things look to preoperational children is the foundation for several other stage-related characteristics. First, when children look at an object that has multiple characteristics, such as a long, round, yellow pencil, they will "see" whichever of those qualities first catches their eye. Preoperational children's knowledge is based mainly on what they are able to see, simply because they do not yet have operational intelligence or the ability to think using mental images.

Second, the inability to perform operations makes it impossible for preoperational children to *conserve,* or understand that the quantity of an object does not change simply because some transformation occurs in its physical appearance. For example, as shown in Figure 3.3, place two identical rows of pennies in front of preoperational children. Ask whether each row has the same number of pennies. The children should answer affirmatively. Next, space out the pennies in one of the rows, and ask whether the two rows still have the same number of pennies. They may insist that more pennies

egocentric Centered on the self; an inability to see events from other people's perspectives.

preoperational stage The stage of cognitive development in which young children are not capable of mental representations.

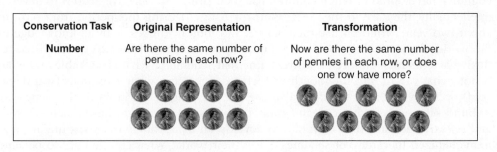

FIGURE 3.3 Conservation of Numbers

are in one row "because it's longer." Children base their judgment on what they can see—namely, the spatial extension of one row beyond the other row. This example also illustrates that preoperational children are not able to mentally reverse thoughts or actions, which in this case would require mentally putting the "longer" row back to its original length.

Furthermore, preoperational children believe and act as though everything happens for a specific reason or purpose. This explains their constant and recurring questions about why things happen and how things work.

Preoperational children believe everyone thinks as they think and acts as they do for the same reasons, and for this reason preoperational children have a hard time putting themselves in another's place. This egocentrism helps explain why it is difficult for them to be sympathetic and empathetic. The children tend to talk *at* each other rather than *with* each other. This dialogue between two children playing at a child care center illustrates one example of egocentrism:

Carmen: My mommy's going to take me shopping.

Mia: I'm going to dress this doll.

Carmen: If I'm good, I'm going to get an ice cream cone.

Mia: I'm going to put this dress on her.

The point is that egocentrism is a fact of cognitive development in the early childhood years. Developmentally appropriate practice means you will take this into account as you teach.

Another important characteristic of children in the preoperational stage is activity. As we previously discussed, activity is a critical developmental force in children's physical, social, emotional, linguistic, and cognitive development. Activity in the form of play provides children with opportunities to be active in early childhood classrooms.

During the preoperational stage, *make-believe play* (also called *dramatic play* or *pretend play*) is one of children's favorite types of play. They engage in it with seriousness and purposefulness. For young children, the world of make-believe play is their world.

Make-believe play helps children learn about their world, helps them deal with their feelings and emotions, enables them to try out roles (mommy, daddy, doctor, nurse, community helper, etc.), and helps them relate to others. Through make-believe play children also learn:

- About themselves, their families, and the world around them
- To talk to, get along with, and work with others—how others act, think, and feel
- To plan and decide what they want to do
- To be creative and solve problems
- To develop physical skills by using large and small muscles
- To stick with a task until it's finished

You can be supportive of children's make-believe play by providing:

- Time and opportunity for children to engage in make-believe play
- Props and materials (clothing and equipment) with which children can play
- A housekeeping area as a learning center where children can play
- A theater-drama area for puppets, costumes, and other props

Concrete Operations Stage. **Concrete operations** is the third stage of operational or logical thought. Piaget defined an **operation** as an action that can be carried out in thought and in direct experiences and that is mentally and physically reversible.

concrete operations Piaget's third stage of operational or logical thought, often referred to as the "hands-on" period of cognitive development because the ability to reason is based on tangible objects and real experiences.

operation A reversible mental action.

This **video** shows children of different ages engaged in reasoning tasks involving conservation. Notice the differences in reasoning between the preoperational stage child and the child at the concrete operations stage.

reversibility The notion that actions can be reversed. Awareness of reversibility develops during the concrete operations stage of development.

The concrete operations stage is often referred to as the "hands-on" period of cognitive development because children's ability to reason is based on tangible objects and real experiences.

Children in the concrete operations stage, from about age seven to about age twelve, begin to develop the understanding that change involving physical appearances does not necessarily change quality or quantity. They can reverse mental operations. For example, operational children know that the amount of water in a container does not change when it is poured into a different-shaped container. They can mentally reverse the operation by going back over and "undoing" the mental action just accomplished—a mental process that preoperational children cannot accomplish, known as **reversibility**. Awareness of reversibility allows the child to see physical transformations and then imagine reversing them so that the change is canceled out. Without being able to imagine, say, pouring liquid from a tall, narrow container back into a wider container, the preoperational child cannot "see" that the amount of liquid has not changed.

You can encourage the development of mental processes during this stage through the use of concrete or real objects when talking about and explaining concepts. For example, instead of just giving the children a basket of beads to play with, ask them to sort the beads into a red group, a blue group, a yellow group, and a green group.

The process of development from one cognitive stage to another is gradual and continual and occurs over a period of time as a result of maturation and experiences. No simple set of exercises will cause children to move up the developmental ladder. Rather, ongoing developmentally appropriate activities lead to conceptual understanding.

Other mental operations typical of this stage are:

- ***One-to-one correspondence.*** This is the basis for counting and matching objects. Concrete operational children have mastered the ability, for example, to give one cookie to each classmate and a pencil to each member of their work group.

- ***Classification of objects, events, and time according to certain characteristics.*** Classifying is a way of comparing.

    classification The ability, developed during the concrete operations stage of cognitive development, to group things together according to their similar characteristics.

    Classification refers to putting like things together and naming the group, such as big bears, little bears; shiny shells, dull shells; round buttons, square buttons; or smooth rocks, rough rocks. Classification schemes are important for young children to construct, as they are central to scientific thinking. Rocks, sea shells, birds, seeds, and just about everything in nature has a classification system.[21]

    For example, a child in the concrete operations stage can classify events as occurring before or after lunch.

- ***Classification involving multiple properties.*** Multiple classification occurs when a child can classify objects on the basis of more than one property, such as color and size, shape and size, or shape and color.

- ***Class inclusive operations.*** Class inclusion also involves classification. For example, if children in this stage are shown five apples, five oranges, and five lemons and asked whether there are more apples or more fruit, they are able to respond with "fruit."

The popularity of Piaget's theory with early childhood education is testimony to the power of the theory to explain how children develop intellectually. It is a theory you can use with confidence throughout your teaching career.

Lev Vygotsky and Sociocultural Theory

This **video** features two scenarios that demonstrate the zone of proximal development. Notice how each teacher, through her interactions, helps the children to accomplish the task.

Lev Vygotsky (1896–1934), a contemporary of Piaget, increasingly inspires the practices of early childhood professionals. Vygotsky's theory of development is particularly useful in describing children's mental, language, and social development.

Social Interaction. Vygotsky believed that children's mental, language, and social development is supported and enhanced by others through social interaction. This view is opposite to the Piagetian perspective, in which children are much more solitary developers of their own intelligence and language. For Vygotsky, development is supported by social interaction: "Learning awakens a variety of developmental processes that are able to operate only when the child is interacting with people in his environment and in collaboration with his peers. Once these processes are internalized, they become part of the child's independent developmental achievement."[22] Vygotsky further believed that children seek adults for social interaction beginning at birth; development occurs through these interactions.

Zone of Proximal Development. For early childhood professionals, one of Vygotsky's most important concepts is that of the **zone of proximal development (ZPD)**, which he defines as follows:

> The area of development into which a child can be led in the course of interaction with a more competent partner, either adult or peer. [It] is not some clear-cut space that exists independently of joint activity itself. Rather, it is the difference between what the child can accomplish independently and what he or she can achieve in conjunction with another, more competent person. The zone is thus created in the course of social interaction.[23]

As Figure 3.4 illustrates, the ZPD represents the potential space between the child's level of independent performance and the child's level of maximally assisted performance.[24] Thus, the ZPD is the range of tasks a child can perform when helped by a more competent person—for example, the teacher, a parent, a teenager, another child. Tasks below the ZPD are those that children can learn independently. Tasks, concepts, ideas, and information above the ZPD are those that children are not yet able to learn, even with help.

Experience and Development. Vygotsky believed that learning drives development. In this regard, the experiences children have influence their development. This is why it is important for you and others to provide high-quality learning experiences for all children.

Vygotsky also believed communication or dialogue between teacher and child is very important and literally becomes a means for helping children to *scaffold,* or develop new concepts and thus think their way to higher level concepts. **Scaffolding** is assistance in the ZPD that enables children to complete tasks they cannot complete independently. When adults "assist" toddlers in learning to walk, they are scaffolding from not being able to walk to being able to walk. Technology provides another useful means for helping scaffold children's learning.[25] For example, KidPix is a popular software program designed to reinforce basic skills such as language arts and math through technology. Figure 3.4 shows this relationship while the accompanying Professionalism in Practice feature, "How to Scaffold Children's Learning," will help you learn how to put into practice the Vygotskian teaching skill of scaffolding.

Vygotsky believed that as a result of teacher–child collaboration, the child uses concepts learned in the collaborative process to solve problems when the teacher is not present. As Vygotsky said, the child "continues to act in collaboration even though

The zone of proximal development is the mental and social state of concept development and learning in which children are about to "go beyond" and achieve at higher levels with the assistance of more competent "others." In this way, learning and development are very social.

zone of proximal development (ZPD) The range of tasks that children can perform with help from a more competent partner. Children can perform tasks below their ZPD on their own, but they are not yet able to learn tasks or concepts above their ZPD, even with help.

scaffolding Assistance or support of some kind from a teacher, parent, caregiver, or peer to help children complete tasks they cannot complete independently.

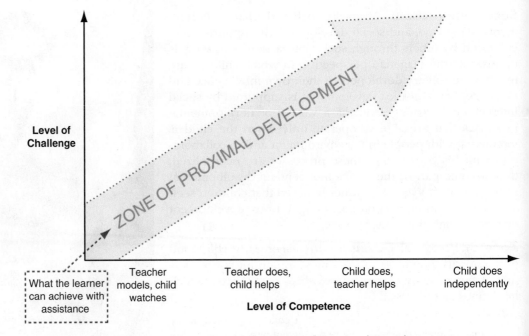

FIGURE 3.4 Teaching and Learning in the Zone of Proximal Development

the teacher is not standing near him. . . . This help—this aspect of collaboration—is invisibly present. It is continued in what looks from the outside like the child's independent solution of the problem."[26] According to Vygotsky, social interactions and collaboration are essential ingredients in the processes of learning and development.

Features of a Vygotskian Classroom. Many current practices such as cooperative learning, joint problem solving, coaching, collaboration, mentoring, and other forms of assisted learning are based on Vygotsky's theory of development and learning. Vygotsky believed that social and cultural features of the classroom play an important role in children's learning. The following suggestions will help you apply Vygotsky's theories and enable children to learn to their fullest. A Vygotskian classroom has the following features:

- Children are grouped by differing abilities.
- There is ample opportunity for all kinds of play with peers and adults.
- Activities, materials, and learning centers support independent discovery.
- Teachers guide each child's learning in his or her zone of proximal development. Vygotsky believed that challenging tasks promote maximum cognitive growth.
- Diversity is valued, respected, and expected. Vygotsky believed children of different cultural backgrounds will develop somewhat different knowledge, skills, and ways of thinking.
- There is ample opportunity for peer collaboration and cooperation on classroom projects.
- Children are encouraged to help each other.
- Children are provided with the opportunity, time, and materials necessary to explore, experiment, and learn.
- There is collaboration among adults, "expert" peers, and other more competent students (elementary, middle, and high school students, and other adults).
- "Assisted discovery" is supported and encouraged as children help each other and as the teacher guides the children through scaffolding.

professionalism in practice

How to Scaffold Children's Learning

Vygotsky believed that cognitive development occurs through children's interactions with more competent others—teachers, peers, parents—who act as guides, facilitators, and coaches to provide the support children need to grow intellectually. Much of that support is provided through conversation, examples, and encouragement. When children learn a new skill, they need that competent other to provide a scaffold, or framework, to help them—to show them the overall task, break it into doable parts, and support and reinforce their efforts.

THE SCAFFOLDING PROCESS

Here are the basic steps involved in effective scaffolding. Study them carefully and then look for them in the ... example that follow[s]:

STEP 1 Observe and Listen
You can learn a great deal about what kind of assistance is needed.

STEP 2 Approach the Child
Ask what he or she wants to do, and ask for permission to help.

STEP 3 Talk About the Task
Describe each step in detail—what is being used, what is being done, what is seen or touched. Ask the child questions about the activity.

STEP 4 Remain Engaged in the Activity
Adjust your support, allowing the child to take over and do the talking.

STEP 5 Gradually Withdraw Support
See how the child is able to perform with less help.

STEP 6 Observe the Child Performing Independently
After you have withdrawn all support, check to be sure the child continues to perform the task successfully.

STEP 7 Introduce a New Task
Present the child with a slightly more challenging task, and repeat the entire sequence.

EXAMPLE—WORKING A PUZZLE

Celeste has chosen a puzzle to work and dumps the pieces out. She randomly picks up a piece and moves it around inside the frame. She tries another. Look at her face: Is she smiling or showing signs of stress? Is she talking to herself?

Perhaps Celeste needs a puzzle with fewer pieces. If so, you can offer her one. But from prior observation, you may know she just needs a little assistance. Try sitting with Celeste and suggesting that you will help. Start by turning all the pieces right side up. As you do this, talk about the pieces you see: This one is red with a little green, this one has a straight edge, this one is curved. Move your finger along the edge.

Ask Celeste whether she can find a straight edge on the side of the puzzle and then whether she can find a piece with a straight edge that matches the color. Ask what hints the pieces give her. Repeat with several other pieces. Then pause to give Celeste the opportunity to try one on her own. As she does, describe what she is doing and the position, shape, and color of the piece. Demonstrate turning a piece in different directions while saying, "I'll try turning it another way." (If you just say "Turn the piece," she will most likely turn it upside down.)

By listening to you verbalize and by repeating the verbalizing, Celeste is learning to self-talk—that is, to talk herself through a task. By practicing this private speech, children realize they can answer their own questions and regulate their own behavior. When the puzzle is complete, offer Celeste another of similar difficulty and encourage her to try it on her own while you stay nearby to offer assistance as needed, allowing her to take the lead.

Source: Contributed by Elena Bodrova, principal researcher at Mid-Continent Research for Education and Learning, Denver, Colorado; and Deborah Leong, professor emerita of psychology and director of Tools of the Mind program.

self-actualization Abraham Maslow's theory of motivation based on the satisfaction of needs; Maslow maintained that children cannot achieve self-actualization until certain basic needs—including food, shelter, safety, and love—are met.

- Teachers guide learning with explanations, verbal prompts, demonstrations, and modeling of behavior.
- There is ample opportunity for child–children, teacher–child, and child–teacher conversations.

Abraham Maslow and Self-Actualization Theory

Abraham Maslow (1908–1970) developed a theory of motivation called **self-actualization** based on the satisfaction of human needs illustrated in Figure 3.5.

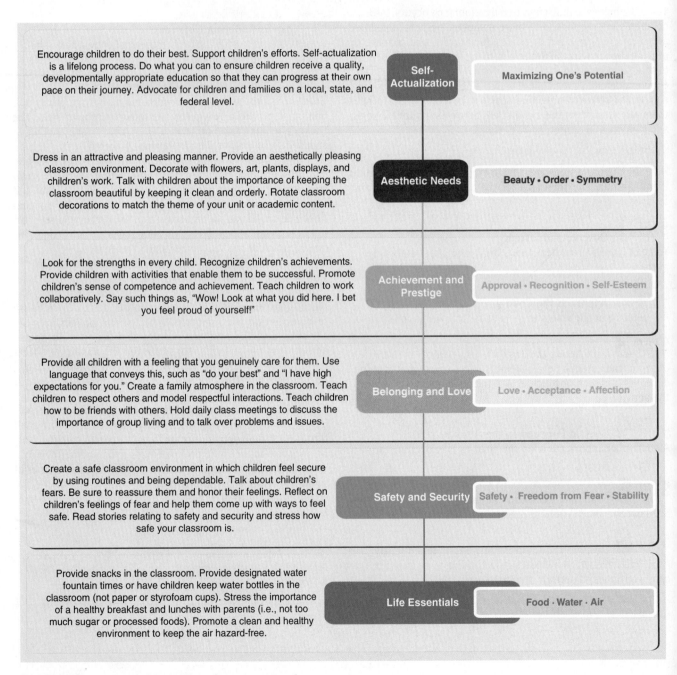

FIGURE 3.5 Maslow's Hierarchy of Human Needs

Maslow identified self-actualization, or self-fulfillment, as the highest human need. However, Maslow maintains that people don't achieve self-actualization until the needs for life essentials, safety and security, belongingness and love, achievement and prestige, and aesthetics are met. Helping children meet their basic needs is an important role for you, parents, and others.

Life Essentials. The most basic of human needs that must be met before self-actualization can be achieved are the life essentials. Life essentials are basic survival necessities such as food, water, and air. Everyone has these basic needs regardless of sexual orientation, race, gender, socioeconomic status, or age. Satisfaction of basic needs is essential for children to function well and to achieve all they are capable of achieving.

Nutrition. When children are hungry they perform poorly in school. Children who begin school without eating breakfast don't achieve as well as they should and experience difficulty concentrating on their school activities. Research shows far-ranging benefits of breakfast consumption affecting children's health and learning through increased attendance, higher standardized test scores and grades, decreased classroom disruptions, and fewer trips to the nurse.[27] This explains why many early childhood programs provide children with breakfast, lunch, and snacks throughout the day.

Safety and Security. The next step to self-achievement is safety and security. Safety and security needs play an important role in children's lives. When children think that their teachers do not like them or are fearful of what their teachers say and how they treat them, they are deprived of a basic need. As a consequence, they do not do well in school and become fearful in their relationships with others. Here are some things you can do to provide for children's safety needs:

- Develop routines and predictability to provide children with a sense of safety and security.
- Provide consistent behavioral rules and guidelines for how children are to act and behave. For example, here are the classroom policies for Ms. Kelly Barker's kindergarten in Arlington, South Dakota:[28]
  1. Be Polite
     - Use an "inside" voice
     - Say please and thank you
     - Wait your turn/Share with others
  2. Be Respectful
     - Look at the person who is speaking
     - Raise your hand
     - Keep hands and feet to yourself
  3. Be Responsible
     - Remember planner/materials needed for class
     - Put away your things
     - Follow directions
- Provide a warm, loving, and comfortable classroom. Some teachers use plants to make the classroom attractive and have reading corners with pillows to provide comfort and security.

Belonging and Love. After safety and security, needs for belonging and love must be met. Children need to be loved and feel that they "belong" within their home and school in order to thrive and develop. All children have affectional needs that teachers can satisfy through smiles, hugs, eye contact, and nearness. For example, in my work with three- and four-year-old children, many want to sit close to me and want me to put my arms around them especially when we are reading stories. To satisfy this basic need, they seek love and look to their teachers and me.

Achievement and Prestige.   Also, before self-actualization can occur, children need to gain achievement and prestige. Recognition and approval are self-esteem needs that relate to success and accomplishment. Children who are independent and responsible, and who achieve well, have high self-esteem. Today, many educators are concerned about how to enhance children's self-esteem.

Friendship is a key to self-esteem. Teach children how to socialize and get along with others. Some children need help making friends. Teach cooperation and helpfulness. Instill new skills. Learning new skills forms the basis for achievement, and achievement is another cornerstone of high self-esteem. Have high and individually appropriate expectations for all of your children. Nothing diminishes self-esteem more than low or no expectations for a child. Provide many opportunities for children to be recognized for their achievement. Once children have their basic needs met, they can become self-actualized. They have a sense of satisfaction, are enthusiastic, and are eager to learn. They want to engage in activities that will lead to higher levels of learning.

Praise Children's Successes.   Praising children's successes does wonders to boost their abilities to do good work and keep on doing it. Give love and affection to every child every day. Feeling loved and wanted is a cornerstone of self-esteem. Pay attention to children. Show children that you are interested in them. Build a foundation on which children can succeed. This foundation is built on this four-step process:

1. Tell children what you want them to do.
2. Show/model for children what to do.
3. Have children practice and demonstrate.
4. Have children work independently.

Here are some examples to follow on praising your students:

- Give a particular student your attention:

  "Jason, I really like the way you got right to work on your journaling; you must have some interesting things to share today."

- Help students to understand the value of their accomplishments:

  "Josh, your explanation of how you answered that word problem helped your classmates to see a new way that they might want to use to try to solve a similar problem."

- Credit the student's effort to succeed:

  "Mason, I see that you are working hard to improve your spelling; you spelled more words correctly this week than you did last week."

- Show students you focused on their work because you could see that they were enjoying their learning process:

  "Emma, I admire how you added some amazing details to your illustration. You looked like you were really enjoying what you were doing"[29]

Aesthetic Needs.   Finally, children need their aesthetic needs met before they can self-actualize. Children like and appreciate beauty. They like to be in classrooms and homes that are physically attractive and pleasant. As an early childhood professional, you can help satisfy aesthetic needs by being well dressed and providing a classroom that is pleasant to be in, one that includes plants and flowers, art, and music. Many teachers meet children's safety and security needs and aesthetic needs by creating a home-like atmosphere in the classroom.

Refer to the accompanying Technology Tie-In to learn more about Maslow's hierarchy of needs.

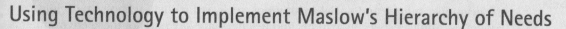

technology tie-in

Using Technology to Implement Maslow's Hierarchy of Needs

Early childhood theories are supportive of technology. The theories ECE professionals use to guide their practice of developing pedagogy for children K–age 8 lend themselves to implementation with technology. Teachers use technology to develop curriculum and instructional activities and children use technology to play and learn the knowledge and skills outlined in program, state, and national Common Core Standards. Here are some ways technology can support your implementation of Maslow's Hierarchy of Needs.

Self-Actualization: Maximum Potential
- A self-actualized child is working to fulfill her potential and become all she is capable of becoming.
- Helping children learn from their inner natures, according to their learning styles, helps them be self-actualized. For example, for kinesthetic learners, Singing Fingers HD allows children to fingerpaint with sound.

Aesthetic Needs: Beauty • Order • Symmetry
- Children like beauty in their homes and classrooms. They want to create beauty and appreciate beauty.
- Microsoft Paint, Drawing Pad, and Interactive Act for Kids can encourage children to create beauty.
- Use a digital camera to have children take pictures of what they think is beautiful and then use the photos to illustrate a booklet about beauty and order in their classroom, school, and community.

Achievement and Prestige: Approval • Recognition • Self-Esteem
- Every child wants to be successful. You can use the following apps to help them achieve their goals:
  - Montessori Words
  - Book Creator for iPad
- Young children need to develop "technology-handling" skills associated with early "digital literacy." This is especially important for poor children who are less likely to have access to such technologies in their homes. These technology-handling skills are similar to the "book-handling" skills associated with early literacy development.

Belonging and Love: Love • Acceptance • Affection Being members of a loving, caring family and classroom community
- Digital cameras provide an excellent way for you to help children feel important, wanted, and members of the classroom community. Have children use pictures of themselves in a biography that they write and share with their classmates.

Safety and Security: Safety • Freedom from Fear • Stability in Home and Classroom
- Childcare programs and schools are increasing measures to protect children. Some programs have parents sign in on a computer, enter their own PIN, and specify the time they check their children in and out of the child care center.
- Increasing numbers of child care programs make it possible for parents to "check on" their children by providing video streaming of classroom activities throughout the day.

Life Essentials: Food • Water • Air • Clothing and Shelter
- Childhood obesity and nutrition are huge national issues.
- Use www.choosemyplate.gov to teach children good nutritional habits and wise food choices; use it with families to help them practice good nutritional skills at home.

Erik Erikson and Psychosocial Theory

psychosocial development Erik Erikson's theory that cognitive and social development occur simultaneously and cannot be separated.

Erik H. Erikson (1902–1994) developed his theory of **psychosocial development**, based on the idea that cognitive and social development occur hand in hand and cannot be separated. According to Erikson, children's personalities and social skills grow and develop within the context of society and in response to society's demands, expectations, values, and social institutions such as families, schools, and child care programs. Adults, especially parents and teachers, are key parts of these environments and therefore play a powerful role in helping or hindering children in their personality and cognitive development. For example, school-age children must deal with demands to learn new skills or risk a sense of incompetence, or a crisis of "industry"—the ability to do, be involved, be competent, and achieve—versus "inferiority"—marked by failure and feelings of incompetence. Many of the cases of school violence in the news today are caused in part by children who feel inferior and unappreciated and who lack the social skills for getting along with their classmates. Figure 3.6 outlines the stages of psychosocial development according to Erikson.

Urie Bronfenbrenner and Ecological Theory

Urie Bronfenbrenner's (1917–2005) *ecological theory* looks at children's development within the context of the systems of relationships that form their environment. There are five interrelating environmental systems: the microsystem, the mesosystem, the exosystem, the macrosystem, and the chronosystem. Figure 3.7 shows a model of these environmental systems and the ways each influences development. Each system influences and is influenced by the other.

microsystem The various environmental settings in which children spend their time (e.g., children in child care spend about thirty-three hours a week in the microsystem of child care).

The **microsystem** encompasses the environments of parents, family, peers, child care, schools, neighborhood, religious groups, parks, and so forth. The child acts on and influences each of these and is influenced by them. For example, four-year-old April might have a physical disability that her child care program accommodates by making the classroom more accessible. Five-year-old Mack's aggressive behavior might prompt his teacher to initiate a program of bibliotherapy.

mesosystem The links or interactions between microsystems that influence children's development.

The **mesosystem** includes linkages or interactions between microsystems. Interactions and influences there relate to all of the environmental influences in the microsystem. For example, the family's support of or lack of attention to literacy may have a major influence on the child's performance in school. Likewise, school support for family literacy will influence the extent to which families value literacy.

exosystem The environments or settings in which children do not play an active role but which nonetheless influence their development.

The **exosystem** is the environmental system that encompasses those events with which children do not have direct interaction but which nonetheless influence them. For example, when school boards enact policies that end social promotion or when a parent's workplace mandates increased work time (e.g., a ten-hour workday), this action influences children's development with the parent and the school.

macrosystem The broader culture in which children live (absence or presence of democracy, societal violence, religious freedom, etc.), which influences their development.

The **macrosystem** includes the culture, customs, and values of society in general. For example, contemporary societal violence and media violence influence children's development. Many children are becoming more violent, and many children are fearful of and threatened by violence.

chronosystem The environmental influences and events that influence children over their lifetimes, such as living in a technological age.

The **chronosystem** includes environmental influences over time and the ways they impact development and behavior. For example, today's children are technologically adept and are comfortable using technology for education and entertainment. In addition, the large-scale entry of mothers into the workforce has changed family life.

Clearly, there are many influences on children's development. Currently there is a lot of interest in how these influences shape children's lives and what parents and educators can do to enhance positive influences and minimize or eliminate negative environmental influences as well as negative social interactions.

Stage I: Basic Trust versus Mistrust

During this stage, children learn to trust or mistrust their environment and their caregivers. Trust develops when children's needs are met consistently, predictably, and lovingly. Children then view the world as safe and dependable.

Appropriate Age:
Birth to 18 months

Characteristics:
Infants learn to trust or mistrust that others will care for their basic needs, including nourishment, warmth, cleanliness, and physical contact. Children begin to learn how to get their needs met (smiling, laughing, crying, etc.) and develop attachments that are either secure and based on trust or insecure and based on mistrust.

Teachers' Role:
- Meet children's needs with consistency and continuity.
- Identify and take care of basic needs such as diapering and feeding.
- Hold babies when feeding them—this promotes attachment and develops trust.
- Socialize through smiling, talking, and singing.
- Be attentive—respond to infants' cues and comfort infants when in distress.

Autonomy versus Shame and Doubt

This is the stage when children want to do things for themselves. Given adequate opportunities, they learn independence and competence. Inadequate opportunities and professional overprotection result in self-doubt and poor achivement; children come to feel ashamed of their abilities.

Appropriate Age:
18 months to 3 years

Characteristics:
Toddlers learn to be self-sufficient or to doubt their abilities in activities such as toileting, feeding, walking, and talking. At this stage, children explore their environments and relationships. Children either learn to trust themselves and their relationships or learn to doubt others and themselves.

Teachers' Role:
- Encourage children to do what they are capable of doing.
- Do not shame children for any behavior.
- Do not use harsh punishment or discipline.
- Provide for safe exploration of classrooms and outdoor areas.

Initiative versus Guilt:

During the preschool years children need opportunities to respond with initiative to activities and tasks, which gives them a sense of purposefulness and accomplishment. Children can feel guilty if they are discouraged or prohibited from initiating activities and are overly restricted in attempts to do things on their own.

Appropriate Age:
3 to 5 years

Characteristics:
Children are learning and want to undertake many adultlike activities, sometimes overstepping the limits set by parents and feeling guilty. Children seek and respond to opportunities to explore, learn, experiment, and experience new things. Children begin to gain a sense of a success and failure and others' preference for success, which can lead to guilty feelings when children perceive they have failed.

Teachers' Role:
- Observe children and follow their interests.
- Encourage children to engage in many activities.
- Provide environments in which children can explore.
- Promote language development. Allow each child the opportunity to succeed.

Industry versus Inferiority

Children display an industrious attitude and want to be productive. They want to build things, manipulate objects, and find out how things work. They also want recognition for their productivity, and adult response to their efforts and accomplishments helps develop a sense of self-worth. Feelings of inferiority result when children are criticized or belittled or have few opportunities for productivity.

Appropriate Age:
5 to 8 years

Characteristics:
Children actively and busily learn to be competent and productive or feel inferior and unable to do things well. Children who feel they are unable to do things well feel they are inferior in comparison to others. Children need to feel they are capable and equal to peers to avoid inferiority.

Teachers' Role:
- Help children win recognition by making things.
- Help assure children are successful in literacy skills and learning to read.
- Provide support for students who seem confused or discouraged.
- Scaffold classroom "jobs"/tasks.

FIGURE 3.6 Erik Erikson and Psychosocial Theory

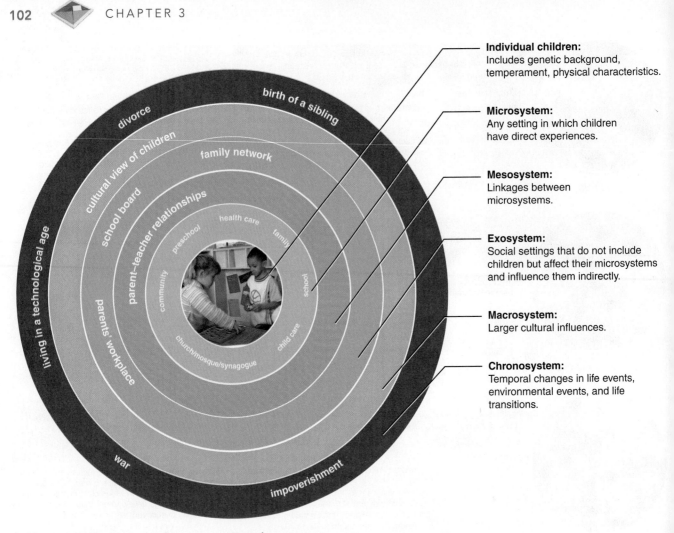

Individual children:
Includes genetic background, temperament, physical characteristics.

Microsystem:
Any setting in which children have direct experiences.

Mesosystem:
Linkages between microsystems.

Exosystem:
Social settings that do not include children but affect their microsystems and influence them indirectly.

Macrosystem:
Larger cultural influences.

Chronosystem:
Temporal changes in life events, environmental events, and life transitions.

FIGURE 3.7 Ecological Influences on Development

Howard Gardner and Multiple Intelligence Theory

Howard Gardner (b. 1943) has played an important role in helping educators rethink the concept of intelligence. Rather than relying on a single definition of intelligence, Gardner's philosophy of **multiple intelligences** suggests that people can be "smart" in many different ways.

Gardner has identified nine intelligences: visual/spatial, verbal/linguistic, mathematical/logical, bodily/kinesthetic, musical/rhythmic, intrapersonal, interpersonal, naturalist, and existentialist. Gardner's view of intelligence and its multiple components has and will undoubtedly continue to influence educational thought and practice. Review Figure 3.8 to learn more about these nine intelligences and how to apply them to your teaching.

multiple intelligences
Howard Gardner's concept that people can be "smart" in many different ways; those intelligences include verbal/linguistic, musical/rhythmic, mathematical/logical, visual/spatial, bodily/kinesthetic, interpersonal, intrapersonal, naturalist, and existentialist.

FROM LUTHER TO TODAY: BASIC BELIEFS ESSENTIAL FOR HIGH-QUALITY EARLY CHILDHOOD PROGRAMS

Throughout this chapter we have considered the basic beliefs that are essential for developing high-quality programs and for teaching young children. As you read the following beliefs, reflect on how you can embrace them and make them a part of your

- **Characteristics:** Learning visually and organizing ideas spatially. Seeing concepts in action in order to understand them. The ability to "see" things in one's mind in planning to create a product or solve a problem.
- **Teachers' Role:** Provide a visually stimulating environment; work with manipulatives; ultilize technologies such as KidPix or Smart Boards.

Visual/Spatial

- **Characteristics:** Learning through the spoken and written word. This intelligence was always valued in traditional classrooms and in traditional assessments of intelligence and achievement.
- **Teachers' Role:** Introduce new vocabulary; provide opportunities for speaking in front of class; incorporate drama in classroom.

Verbal/ Linguistic

- **Characteristics:** Learning through reasoning and problem solving. Also highly valued in the traditional classroom, where students are asked to adapt to logically sequenced delivery of instruction.
- **Teachers' Role:** Present objectives at the beginning of an activity to provide structure; encourage debates; incorporate puzzles into learning centers.

Mathematical/ Logical

- **Characteristics:** Learning through interaction with one's environment. This intelligence is not only the domain of "overly active" learners. It promotes understanding through concrete experiences.
- **Teachers' Role:** Provide hands-on learning centers; offer experiences in movement to rhythm and music; allow opportunities for building and taking apart.

Bodily/ Kinesthetic

- **Characteristics:** Learning through patterns, rhythms, and music. This includes not only auditory, but the indentification of patterns through all the senses.
- **Teachers' Role:** Work with pattern blocks; have students move to rhythm; have students listen to music while working.

Musical/ Rhythmic

- **Characteristics:** Learning through feelings, values, and attitudes. This is a decidedly affective component of learning through which students place value on what they learn and take ownership for their learning.
- **Teachers' Role:** Differentiate instruction; provide activities that offer learner choices; have students set goals for themselves in the classroom; include daily journal writing.

Intrapersonal

- **Characteristics:** Learning through interaction with others. Not the domain of children who are simply "talkative" or "overly social." This intelligence promotes collaboration and working cooperatively with others.
- **Teachers' Role:** Allow interaction among students during learning tasks; include group work tasks; form cooperative groups so each member has an assigned role.

Interpersonal

- **Characteristics:** Learning through classification, categories, and hierarchies. The naturalist intelligence picks up on subtle differences in meaning. It is not simply the study of nature; it can be used in all areas of study.
- **Teachers' Role:** Use graphic organizers; provide sorting and grouping tasks; build portfolios of student work.

Naturalistic

- **Characteristics:** Children who learn in the context of where humankind stands in the "big" picture of existence. They ask, "Why are we here?" and "What is my role in my family, school, and community?" This intelligence is seen in the discipline of philosophy.
- **Teachers' Role:** Offer an overview before starting new instruction; discuss how topics are important to the classroom, school, and community; bring in resource people or offer additional perspectives on a topic.

Existential

FIGURE 3.8 Gardner's Nine Intelligences

Source: Reprinted with permission from Walter McKenzie, "Multiple Intelligences Overview," 1999; available online at http://surfaquarium.com/MI/overview.htm. "Howard Gardner's Theory of Multiple Intelligences"; available online at http://surfaquarium.com/MI/overview.ht.

philosophy of education and how you can apply them to your teaching. Many people have influenced and changed the course of early childhood education. That process continues today. Part of your role as an early childhood professional is to stay up to date, be open to ideas and practices, and inspire children.

Basic Beliefs About Teaching Children

- Everyone needs to learn how to read and write.
- Children learn best when they use all their senses.
- All children are capable of being educated.
- All children should be educated to the fullest extent of their abilities.
- Education should begin early in life. Today especially there is an increased emphasis on beginning education at birth.
- Children should be appropriately taught what they are ready to learn when they are ready to learn it and should be prepared for the next stage of learning.
- Learning activities should be interesting and meaningful.
- Social interactions with teachers and peers are a necessary part of development and learning.
- All children have many ways of knowing, learning, and relating to the world.

Basic Beliefs About Teachers and Teaching

- Teachers should love and respect all children, have high expectations for them, and teach them to their highest capacities.
- Teachers should be dedicated to the teaching profession.
- Good teaching is based on a theory, a philosophy, goals, and objectives.
- Children's learning is enhanced through the use of concrete materials.
- Teaching should move from the concrete to the abstract.
- Observation is a key way to determine children's needs.
- Teaching should be a planned, systematic process.
- Teaching should be centered on children rather than adults or subjects.
- Teaching should be based on children's interests.
- Teachers should collaborate with children as a means of promoting development.
- Teachers should plan so they incorporate all types of intelligence in their planning and activities.

Basic Beliefs About Collaborating with Parents and Families

- The family is the most important institution in children's education and development. The family lays the foundation for all future education and learning.
- Parents are their children's primary educators; they are their children's first teachers. However, parents need help, education, and support to achieve this goal.
- Parents must guide and direct young children's learning.
- Parents should be involved in every educational program their children are involved in.
- Everyone should have knowledge of and training for child rearing.
- Parents and other family members are collaborators in children's learning.
- Parents must encourage and support their children's many interests and their unique ways of learning.

TEACHING AND LEARNING IN THE INCLUSIVE CLASSROOM: THEN AND NOW

As an early childhood professional, it is important for you to know about and understand the nature of disabilities. It has not always been an American priority to accommodate differences. People with **epilepsy** (a neurological disorder in which electrical discharges in the brain cause a seizure) or **Tourette's syndrome** (a genetic neuropsychiatric disorder characterized by multiple physical and/or vocal tics) were once thought to be possessed by the devil. People with mental impairments were put in group homes, out of the public eye, and often abused. Deaf and mute children were often considered "idiots" and not worth teaching.

Because people with various disabilities were often hidden from the public eye or considered unable to contribute to society, our recent awareness of and attention to children with diverse backgrounds and abilities may seem to exist in a contemporary vacuum. However, children and adults have always had learning differences, physical disabilities, and mental health deficits. Alexander the Great had epilepsy, Vincent Van Gogh had **bipolar disorder** (a mood disorder involving cycles of depression and mania that are severe and often lead to impaired functioning), Woodrow Wilson had **dyslexia** (a learning disability that is characterized by difficulties in reading, spelling, writing, speaking, or listening), Alexander Graham Bell had **mathematics disorder** (a learning disability characterized by decided lack of ability to calculate or comprehend mathematical problems), and Thomas Edison had **attention deficit hyperactivity disorder (ADHD)** (the inability to maintain attention and constrain impulsivity, accompanied by the presence of hyperactivity).

While individual differences have existed throughout human history, treating them, working with them, and attempting to improve the lives of those with differences is relatively new in the United States and other countries. It was not until 1790 in Paris that iron shackles no longer bound mental patients. Thereafter, professionals began to make more gains in attempts to accurately identify and address differences. *Rush's Medical Inquires and Observations,* published in 1805, is one of the first known attempts to explain mental disorders. Later, in 1845, Heinrich Hoffman wrote a book about his son who simply could not stop "fidgeting" or focus on tasks. In the 1890s, Maria Montessori worked with children labeled by society as "uneducable" or "defective" and tailored her teaching methods to meet their needs, enabling them to excel in state board examinations. In the 1920s, researchers advanced the movement to accommodate children with disabilities by identifying specific interventions for reading disabilities. By the late 1970s, the U.S. federal government began to outline strategies for educational models, assistance, and teacher training to address the needs of students with learning differences.

Today, inclusionary classroom practices, medication, and various therapies attempt to address and accommodate the different needs of children. To accommodate differences in your classroom:

- Be well versed in differences you will see in your classroom such as ADD/ADHD, autism, and learning disabilities. Discover what treatments are available such as the DIR/Floortime model, assistive technologies (e.g., DynaMyte, alternative keyboards, and text-to-speech software), and listening therapy.

- Be available to parents to discuss their children's needs. Respond to their requests, questions, and concerns in a sensitive and timely manner in order to develop and maintain a close working relationship with them.

epilepsy A neurological disorder in which electrical discharges in the brain cause a seizure.

Tourette's syndrome A genetic neuropsychiatric disorder characterized by multiple physical and/or vocal tics.

bipolar disorder A mood disorder involving cycles of depression and mania that are severe and often lead to impaired functioning.

dyslexia A learning disability characterized by difficulties in reading, spelling, writing, speaking, or listening, despite at least average intelligence.

mathematics disorder A learning disability characterized by decided lack of ability to calculate or comprehend mathematical problems.

attention deficit hyperactivity disorder (ADHD) The inability to maintain attention and constrain impulsivity, accompanied by the presence of hyperactivity.

- Contact and collaborate with various professionals who specialize in working with and teaching children with disabilities. These professionals include occupational therapists, physical therapists, speech pathologists, counselors, and classroom tutors. As a member of a team, you can help your children more than if you worked alone.

ACTIVITIES FOR PROFESSIONAL DEVELOPMENT

ethical dilemma

"Why don't my kids get their fair share?"

Latisha is a novice first grade teacher in Rocky Springs School District. Her class of twenty-eight children includes fifteen Hispanic students, nine African American students, and four Vietnamese students. Latisha's room is sparsely furnished, many of the tables and chairs need repair, and the classroom library of thirty-seven books is old and worn. Last week, at an orientation for pre-K–3 teachers held across town at the new Valley View Ranch elementary school, Latisha learned that the students there are 90 percent white and class size averages nineteen. A tour of the classrooms revealed the latest in furniture, learning materials, and technology with well-stocked classroom libraries. Latisha has read the latest research about how school districts invest fewer resources in poorer neighborhoods. She is very concerned about the unequal distribution of resources in the school district, and she knows her children are not getting their fair share.

What should Latisha do? Should she just keep quiet and hope things get better? Should she advocate for her students by using Facebook to organize a group of her colleagues who share her concerns? Should Latisha start a blog about the unequal distribution of resources in the district to raise support for her views? Or should Latisha take some other course of action? What should Latisha do? What would you do?

Application Activities

1. From John Dewey to the present, early childhood professionals have used children's interests as a basis for developing learning activities. Talk with three young children about what they like to do, their favorite activities, favorite television programs, and so on. Select three of their interests and plan three learning experiences related to literacy, math, and science. Share your ideas online with your classmates and ask for their comments.

2. Throughout the history of education, great educators have been concerned with what they believed was best for children, how best to teach them, and what is worthwhile for children to know and be able to do.

   a. Based on the ideas and practices discussed in this chapter, identify three teaching practices with which you most agree. State the learning outcomes you think are appropriate for all children.

   b. Review the curriculum goals and standards for the pre-K–3 grades in your state/local school district. Identify three examples of what contemporary educators identify as important knowledge and skills that are substantiated by the beliefs of great educators.

3. Think for a minute what would happen if you gave six-month-old Emily some blocks. What would she try to do with them? More than likely she would put them

in her mouth. She wants to eat the blocks. However, if you gave blocks to Emily's three-year-old sister Madeline, she would try to stack them. Both Emily and Madeline want to be actively involved with things and people as active learners. This active involvement comes naturally for them. Observe two or three children in a number of early childhood programs and identify five ways they learn through active learning. Use your data to develop a Prezi presentation on active learning. Post your Prezi link to your class discussion board and ask for feedback.

4. Your professor assigned you to write a brief historical summary of the major ideas of five educational pioneers you read about in this chapter. You are limited to fifty words for each person and are to write as though you were the person. For example:

> Locke: "At birth the mind is a blank slate and experiences are important for making impressions on the mind. I believe learning occurs best through the senses. A proper education begins early in life, and hands-on experiences are an important part of education."

Use Prezi to post your summaries to your class discussion board.

5. Everyday learning theories play an important role in your teaching. They also form the basis for your philosophy of education. Brainstorm ways to develop your philosophy. Write a short paragraph—three to five sentences—about two of the theories.

Linking to Learning

Maria Montessori

www.webster.edu
Search "Montessori" for an historical perspective of her life and teaching methods.

Jean-Jacques Rousseau

www.infed.org
Search "Rousseau" for brief statements on education by Rousseau.

MyEducationLab

Go to Topics 1 (History) and 2 (Child Development/Theories) in the MyEducationLab (www.myeducationlab.com) for your course, where you can:

- Find learning outcomes for History and Child Development/Theories along with the national standards that connect to these outcomes.

- Complete Assignments and Activities that can help you more deeply understand the chapter content.

- Apply and practice your understanding of the core teaching skills identified in the chapter with the Building Teaching Skills and Dispositions learning units.

- Explore interactive CONNECT Modules to practice classroom skills and enhance professional development.

- Check your comprehension on the content covered in the chapter by going to the Study Plan in the Book Resources for your text. Here you will be able to take a chapter quiz, receive feedback on your answers, and then access Review, Practice, and Enrichment activities to enhance your understanding of chapter content.

chapter 4

IMPLEMENTING EARLY CHILDHOOD PROGRAMS

Applying Theories to Practice

NAEYC Standards for Early Childhood Professional Preparation

Standard 1. Promoting Child Development and Learning

I use my understanding of young children's characteristics and needs, and of multiple interacting influences on children's development and learning, to create environments that are healthy, respectful, supportive, and challenging for each child.[1]

Standard 4. Using Developmentally Effective Approaches to Connect with Children and Families

I understand and use positive relationships and supportive interactions as the foundation for my work with young children and families. I know, understand, and use a wide array of developmentally appropriate approaches, instructional strategies, and tools to connect with children and families and positively influence each child's development and learning.[2]

THE GROWING POPULARITY OF QUALITY EARLY CHILDHOOD PROGRAMS

Currently the National Association for the Education of Young Children accredits over 6,500 high-quality programs serving over a million children.[3] These programs are only a fraction of the total number of early childhood programs in the United States. Think for a minute about what goes on in these and other programs from day to day. For some children, teachers and staff have developed well-thought-out and articulated programs that provide for their growth and development across all the developmental domains—cognitive, linguistic, emotional, social, and physical. This should be the goal of all programs that serve young children.

Early Childhood Programs

In the United States, early childhood programs come in many different varieties and are sponsored and supported by many different agencies. Unlike other countries with more centralized governments, the United States operates a more decentralized educational system, which accounts for the variety of programs for young children.

The federal government is a huge supporter of early childhood programs, including Head Start and Early Head Start. The public schools are the largest provider of early childhood programs. These include preschool (for three- and four-year-old children), kindergarten, and grades one through three. Public schools also provide before- and after-school care for children in the form of organized activities, including help with schoolwork and enrichment activities such as music, art, and drama. Faith-based programs are providers of school options including mothers' day out (MDO) programs, preschools, kindergarten, and primary grade (one through three) programs.

Individuals and for-profit agencies are also providers of child care, preschool, and other programs. Individual proprietary school owners provide the vast majority of the Montessori programs and provide individuals and for-profit programs for the majority of infant/toddler child care. In addition, many preschool programs adopt and use the Montessori, HighScope, and Reggio Emilia models as a basis for their program approaches.

Regardless of the kind of programs they offer, parents, politicians, and the public want early childhood professionals to provide programs that:

- Ensure children's early school success, which enables them to succeed in school and life. The public believes that pre-kindergarten services are a wise and sound investment.[4]
- Provide high-quality education for all children. The public is concerned about the growing achievement gap between African American and Hispanic American children and their white counterparts.

The following are goals these programs aim to meet:

- Include language and reading readiness activities in programs and curricula that enable children to learn and read well.[5]
- Help children develop the social and behavioral skills necessary for them to lead civilized, peaceful lives. In response to daily headlines about violence and abuse, the public wants early childhood programs to assume an ever-growing responsibility for helping get children off to a nonviolent start in life. In addition, they want schools and other programs to keep their children safe.[6]
- Prepare children for a world shaped by global competition. Early childhood programs play a vital role in preparing the children of today for the world of tomorrow.[7] This is one reason why early childhood programs are placing more emphasis on science, math, technology, engineering, and learning a second language.
- Meet the work and lifestyle needs of parents for child care around the clock, 24/7.

As you read about and reflect on the programs in this chapter, think about the ways each tries to best meet the needs of children and families and the goals above. Pause for a minute and review Table 4.1, which outlines the programs of early childhood education discussed in this chapter.

CHILD CARE: SERVING CHILDREN AND FAMILIES

Child care is assuming an increasingly prominent role in the American education system. It is part of the seamless system of providing for the nation's children and youth that begins at birth and continues through high school and

MyEducationLab

Visit the MyEducationLab for *Fundamentals of Early Childhood Education* to enhance your understanding of chapter concepts with a personalized Study Plan. You'll also have the opportunity to hone your teaching skills through video-based Assignments and Activities as well as Building Teaching Skills and Dispositions lessons.

FOCUS QUESTIONS

1. Why is there a growing demand for quality early childhood programs?

2. How does child care serve children and families?

3. What are the characteristics of quality education and care?

4. What are program models such as High-Scope, Montessori, and Reggio Emilia, and what are their basic features?

5. What early childhood programs does the federal government sponsor and fund?

6. Why is it important for you to know and understand early childhood programs?

TABLE 4.1 Comparing Early Childhood Programs

Program	Main Features	Teacher's Role
Child Care	• Comprehensive health, social, and education services are provided. • Program quality is determined by each program. • Each program has its own curriculum.	• Provides care and education for the whole child. • Provides a safe and secure environment. • Collaborates with and involves families.
HighScope	• Theory is based on Piaget, constructivism, Dewey, and Vygotsky. • Plan-do-review is the teaching–learning cycle. • Emergent curriculum is not planned in advance. • Children help determine curriculum. • Key experiences guide the curriculum in promoting children's active learning.	• Plans activities based on children's interests. • Facilitates learning through encouragement. • Engages in positive adult–child interaction strategies.
Montessori	• Theoretical basis is the philosophy and beliefs of Maria Montessori. • A prepared environment supports, invites, and enables learning. • Children educate themselves—self-directed learning is a cornerstone. • Sensory materials invite and promote learning. • A set curriculum regarding what children should learn is offered. Montessorians try to stay as close to Montessori's ideas as possible. • Children are grouped in multiage environments. • Children learn by manipulating materials and working with others. • Learning takes place through the senses.	• Follows the child's interests and needs. • Prepares an environment that is educationally interesting and safe. • Directs unobtrusively as children individually or in small groups engage in self-directed activity. • Observes, analyzes, and provides materials and activities appropriate for the child's sensitive periods of learning. • Maintains regular communications with the parent.
Reggio Emilia	• Theory is based on Piaget, constructivism, Vygotsky, and Dewey. • Emergent curriculum is not planned in advance. • Curriculum is based on children's interests and experiences. • Curriculum is project oriented. • *The Hundred Languages of Children* represents the symbolic representation of children's work and learning. • Learning is active. • A special teacher—the atelierista—is trained in the arts. • An art/design studio—the atelier—is used by children and teachers.	• Works collaboratively with other teachers. • Organizes environments rich in possibilities and provocations. • Acts as recorder for the children, helping them reflect on and revisit their words and actions.

TABLE 4.1 Comparing Early Childhood Programs *Continued*

Program	Main Features	Teacher's Role
Head Start	• The program is federally sponsored and funded. • Programs must comply with federal performance standards and standards of learning. • The arts are integrated into all curriculum areas. • There is a comprehensive approach to educating the whole child. • Head Start offers comprehensive services, including health and nutrition. • The comprehensive program is designed to strengthen families. • Families and the community are involved in delivery of program services.	• Teaches to and provides for all children's developmental areas—social, emotional, physical, and cognitive. • Provides programs for children that support their socioeconomic, cultural, and individual needs in developmentally appropriate ways. • Involves families and the community in all parts.
Project Approach	• Enables a small group of children to be involved in an investigation or project. • Is an authentic approach to discovery learning. • Can be used by all children including children with disabilities (see the accompanying Professionalism in Practice: Tips for Implementing the Project Approach in Inclusive Classrooms). • Provides a means for integrating concepts and ideas across the curriculum. For example, children use math to measure, conduct research on their topic, and read all kinds of literature (fiction and informational) about their project. • Puts constructivist ideas into action.	• Facilitates projects and investigations that come from children's thinking and ideas. • Enables and supports children's behavior and work as they assume responsibility for project activities. • Encourages and supports children to make choices and decisions about their project. • Values children's intrinsic motivation to be independent and do good work. • Provides a supportive classroom environment with the necessary and appropriate learning materials including technology. • Provides children with appropriate experiences that extend and enrich their project learning such as selecting and providing appropriate reading materials, taking children on field trips, inviting outside parents and community members to talk with children about their project, etc.

beyond. For this important reason, it is included in this chapter on early childhood programs.

Child care is a comprehensive service to children and families that supplements the care and education children receive from their families. Comprehensive child care includes high-quality care and education along with activities and experiences appropriate to support children's social, emotional, linguistic, physical, and academic development.

Child care is educational. It provides for children's cognitive development, helps engage them in the process of learning that begins at birth, and incorporates learning activities as part of the curriculum. Furthermore, child care staff work with parents to help them learn how to support children's learning in the home. A comprehensive view of child care considers the child to be a whole person; therefore, the major purpose of child care is to facilitate optimal development of the whole child and support efforts to achieve this goal.

The Importance of Child Care

Child care is popular and important for a number of reasons. First, recent demographic changes have created a high demand for care outside the home. There are more dual-income families and more working single parents than ever before. For example, about 64 percent of mothers with children under age six are employed, and it is not uncommon for mothers to return to work as early as six weeks after giving birth.[8]

Second, child care is viewed as a critical early intervention program for all children and families. High-quality early child care promotes pre-academic skills and school readiness, enhanced language performance, and increased positive developmental outcomes. Thus, child care plays a vital role in the health, welfare, and general social and academic well-being of all of the nation's children.

Third, for low-income families, quality child care is critical. High-quality child care provides safe places for children to be and grow. These programs provide good nutrition and environments for socialization, physical development, and learning.[9]

In addition, especially as demand for child care increases, you and your colleagues must participate in advocating for and creating high-quality child care programs that meet the needs of children and families.

Types of Child Care

Child care is offered in many places by many persons and agencies that provide a variety of care and services as shown in Table 4.2. While the options for child care are almost endless, the following are some of the most popular.

Care by Family Members, Relatives, and Friends. Grandparents, aunts, uncles, other relatives, or friends provide both continuity and stability of care for children. According to the Child Care Bureau, in 2010 the average percentage of children served by relatives was about 50 percent of all children receiving some kind of care while their parents worked.[10]

Family Child Care. When an individual caregiver provides care and education for a small group of children in his or her home, we call this family child care. As you read, consider if you would want your child placed in a program of family child care.

TABLE 4.2 Children in Different Types of Child Care Arrangements

Type of Care	Percent of Children
Center-based care	24%
Mother/father care	23%
Grandparent care	20%
Other relative care	13%
Other care arrangements	20%

Source: Forum on Child and Family Statistics, "Child Care," 2010; accessed January 25, 2012, at www.childstats.gov.

Intergenerational Programs.   Intergenerational programs integrate children and the elderly in an early childhood and adult care facility. For example, the Mount Kisco Day Care Center in Mount Kisco, New York, is a dynamic interactive community for young children and older adults under one roof. Mount Kisco Day Care Center provides early care and education for 160 infants, toddlers, preschool, and school-age children.[11] The facility has been specially designed around the needs of older adults and children, providing optimal space for both structured programs and spontaneous interaction.[12]

Center-Based Care.   Center-based child care is conducted in many types of facilities. Some of these facilities are newly constructed, while others are refurbished homes and buildings. Some operate in churches and other such facilities. For example, KIDCO Child Care Centers in Miami, Florida, operate four centers with enrollment of over 450 children in renovated churches, public schools, and community buildings.

Employer-Sponsored Care.   To meet the needs of working parents, some employers provide child care at the work site. Some employers may also provide for care in off-site facilities. For example, Bright Horizons Family Solutions is the world's leading provider of employer-sponsored child care and education. Through its full-service programs, children six weeks to six years experience a world rich with discovery, guided by skilled professionals who celebrate each child's individuality.[13]

Proprietary Child Care.   Some child care centers are run by corporations, businesses, or individual proprietors for the purpose of making a profit. For-profit child care is very profitable for those centers that are well run and managed. In addition, they are usually very comprehensive and provide a full range of care and educational services.

Before- and After-School Care.   In many respects, public schools are logical places for before-school and after-school care; they have the administrative organization, facilities, and staff to provide such care. In addition, many taxpayers and professionals have always believed that schools should not sit empty in the afternoons, evenings, holidays, and summers. Thus, using resources already in place for child care makes good sense.

The before-and after-school child care programs of Broward County, Florida, provide students with:

- An inclusive child care program that is safe and nurturing in a comfortable environment.
- A cultural enriching program that promotes the physical, intellectual, emotional, and social development of each child.
- A program that meets the highest quality of child care standards.

Currently more than 20,000 children are being served in 180 before-and after-school child care programs. Programs at elementary schools and centers are either school board operated or operated by a private provider.[14]

Nadine Rudk-Kelly leads a kindergarten before-and-after-school program in Raynham, Massachusetts, offering a variety of activities such as academics, arts, crafts, stories, and physical activites. The student-to-teacher ratio for this program is 10:1. In the before-school program, children engage in quiet activities and eat a light breakfast before the start of the school day. In the after-school program, the children do homework; participate in games, science projects, and outdoor play; and receive homework help.[15]

Military Child Care.   The Department of Defense (DoD) military child development system (CDS) provides daily services for the largest number of children of any employer in the United States. Military child care is provided in nine hundred centers in more than three hundred geographic locations, both within and outside the continental United States.[16]

Four main components make up the DoD CDS: child development centers, family child care, school-age care, and resource and referral programs. Through these four areas, the DoD serves more than 200,000 children (ages six weeks to twelve years) daily. The system offers full-day, part-day, and hourly (i.e., drop-in) child care; part-day preschool programs; before-and after-school programs for school-age children; and extended-hour care, including nights and weekends.[17]

Military families face challenges that are not found in other work environments. Shifting work schedules that are often longer than the typical eight-hour day and the requirement to be ready to deploy anywhere in the world on a moment's notice requires a child development system that is flexible in nature yet maintains high standards. Frequent family separations and the need to move, on average, every three years place military families in situations not often experienced in the civilian world. For this population, affordable, high-quality child care is paramount if they are to be ready to perform their missions and their jobs. It is also important to military personnel that child care services be consistent at installations throughout the military.

However, regardless of the kinds of child care provided, the three key essentials of *quality, affordability,* and *accessibility* should always be part of child care services.

WHAT IS QUALITY EDUCATION AND CARE?

Although there is much debate about the quality of child care and what it involves, we can nonetheless identify the main characteristics of quality programs. The dimensions and indicators of quality child care include a healthy, respectful, supportive, challenging, and safe and pleasant environment, as outlined below. Let's consider each of these child care environmental dimensions. Then we'll explore other factors that a quality early childhood program should consider.

A Healthy Environment

A healthy environment supports children's physical and mental health. A healthy environment is clean, well maintained, and has separate areas for toileting (and for changing diapers), eating, and sleeping. Caregivers teach infants and toddlers healthy habits, such as hand washing after toileting, before and after mealtime, and after other appropriate activities. A healthy environment also provides a relaxed and happy eating environment. Substantial research clearly indicates that a healthy diet and environment contribute to children's overall health and well-being.[18]

Mental Health.   A healthy environment supports children's mental health. Caregivers support children's mental health when they provide responsive and loving care and create environments that have a balance of small and large open areas. Small areas provide the opportunity for infants and toddlers to be alone or in small groups and older children to play and engage in cooperative activities. The open areas encourage active involvement with larger numbers of children. In addition, child care staffs collaborate with and involve parents to help them know about and understand the importance of children's mental health. Caregivers also provide children with environments that are clean and pesticide and mold free. They attempt to reduce children's risks for exposure to lead and other toxic materials.

For infants and children, a major source of chemical pesticide exposure is through their food. Research shows children's levels of chemical pesticide exposure drop quickly and significantly when they are switched from a normal diet to an organic one.[19] The Little Dreamers, Big Believers Daycare in Columbus, Ohio, uses ingredients that are 70 percent organic. Children eat meals such as rigatoni with tomato sauce, garlic bread, and broccoli, all designed to provide healthy habits in accord with the MyPlate nutritional guide.[20]

Nontoxic Pesticides.   Exposure to pesticides at schools is associated with illnesses among employees and students. Rates of illness from pesticide exposure at schools are higher in school staff than in children because staff members are more likely to handle pesticides. However, children may be particularly susceptible to pesticide toxicity because their organ systems have not reached developmental maturity. Exposure to pesticides can produce coughs, shortness of breath, nausea, vomiting, headaches, and eye irritation.[21]

In child care programs, keep all surfaces free of food and water, and reduce opportunities for pests to enter the building. Sanitary food habits, properly handling garbage, and sealing food in airtight containers help prevent problems with pests. Also, periodically vacuuming furniture and draperies can reduce dust mites and other pests.[22]

The more that you can do to promote high-quality, healthy programs, the better it will be for you, children, and families.

A Respectful Environment

A respectful environment is one in which caregivers deeply care about children and families. Caregivers create a respectful environment by listening, observing, and being aware of children's verbal and nonverbal communications. Caregivers interpret or "read" children's behavior by asking themselves: "What does the child's behavior say to me?" A respectful environment is also one in which children's unique individualities are honored and provided for. Each child's unique individuality is a product of such dimensions as temperament, gender, race, language, culture, and socioeconomic status.

Culturally Appropriate Practice.   Respectful environments include culturally appropriate practices. Here are some things you can do to create a culturally respectful environment for your children.

- Greet families in a culturally sensitive manner; for example, some Hispanic families prefer the father to be greeted first, then the mother, and the children last.
- Provide inclusive artwork; for example, murals include children with different skin and hair colors.
- Use linguistically appropriate materials and provide books in English and Spanish.
- Adjust teacher-infant interaction style according to culture; although most infants who are Hispanic are calmed with quick, repetitive, choppy phrases and back patting, infants who are Laotian, for example, are calmed through soft, smooth talking, cradling, and gentle rocking.
- Apply limits to cultural accommodation when necessary. Discuss compromises with parents. For example, some cultures allow infants to eat items they could choke on, such as hot dogs. In this case, explain the dangers of certain foods and ask parents to bring alternative snacks.
- Communicate with parents and other family members in your program. Place a high priority on daily communication about children's progress. In addition, share with parents how your program and community agencies provide information in such critical areas as child development and nutrition.[23]

A Safe Environment

Caregivers provide safe environments through responsive relationships and by developing close and nurturing bonds with the children they care for. Responsive and close relationships enable infants and toddlers to experience trust and feel safe with you and in your program. Research assures us that healthy development depends on safe experiences during the first few years of life.[24]

Safe child care centers supervise children at all times.[25] Safe centers enforce strict security measures. Some centers install security cameras so that staff can monitor traffic. For example, Kiddie Academy buildings are equipped with secure entries and exits that require a pass or identification card for entry. Some buildings also utilize fingerprint verification and video monitoring. All child care programs should conduct background checks on every employee.[26] Keeping children physically safe contributes to their feeling safe and trusting emotionally.

A Supportive Environment

A supportive environment means that you will spend time with children, pleasantly interact with them, and encourage and help them. Supportive environments encourage and promote children's routine social interactions. A supportive environment accommodates children's individual differences and provides for active play. It also offers a wide range of learning materials. This type of environment promotes children's mental health and encourages child-centered activities. In a supportive environment, you respond to children's physical, social, emotional, and cognitive needs.

A Challenging Environment

A challenging environment provides opportunities for all children to be actively involved with other children, staff, and parents. These interactions are extremely important as children learn about their world and themselves. An environment that supports social interaction lays the foundation for children's school readiness and other life outcomes. A challenging environment provides materials and activities that are matched to the needs, interests, and abilities of children and which provide for many hands-on activities that support seeing, touching, feeling, and moving. Supportive and challenging environments complement each other.

A Pleasant Environment

At all age levels, a pleasant physical and social setting is important. The rooms, home, or center should be clean, well lit, well ventilated, and cheerful. A pleasant and attractive environment supports Maslow's theory, which states that we must address and meet children's aesthetic needs. Here are some things you can do to create a pleasant environment:

- Be attentive to students' needs. Let your children know that you love them and care for them. Every child wants to feel important, valued, and loved.
- Create a pleasant, home-like environment. Display children's photographs and family pictures. Provide comfortable areas where children can read, rest, relax, and feel safe and secure.
- Involve children in helping keep their classroom/child care space clean and orderly. Ask children for their ideas on how together you can create a pleasant environment.

Other Considerations for a Quality Child Care Program

In addition to the environmental dimensions of quality care we just discussed, early childhood professionals also recognize other components that contribute to a good early childhood education for all children such as optimal caregiver-to-child ratio, developmentally appropriate programs, meeting individual needs, and appropriately managing children's behavior.

TABLE 4.3 Teacher-to-Child Ratio According to NAEYC Guidelines

Age	Maximum Teacher-to-Child Ratio	Maximum Group Size
Birth to 15 month	1:4	8
12 to 28 month	1:4	10
21 to 36 month	1:6	12
2½-year-olds to 3-year-olds (30–48 month)	1:9	18
4-year-olds	1:10	20
5-year-olds	1:10	20
Kindergarten	1:12	24

Caregiver-to-Child Ratio.   The ratio of adults to children in child care programs should be sufficient to give children the individual care and attention they need. NAEYC guidelines for the ratio of caregivers to children are 1:3 or 1:4 for infants and toddlers and 1:8 to 1:10 for preschoolers, depending on group size.[27]

Table 4.3 shows the NAEYC's recommendations for ratios and standards.

Research shows that when programs meet these recommended child-to-staff ratios and recommended levels of caregiver training and education, children have better outcomes.[28]

Developmentally Appropriate Programs.   Programs should have written, developmentally based curricula for meeting children's needs. A program's curriculum should specify activities for children of all ages, which caregivers can use to stimulate infants, provide for the growing independence of toddlers, and address the readiness and literacy skills of four- and five-year-olds. All programs should include curricula and activities that meet the physical, social, emotional, and cognitive needs of all children. Quality programs use developmentally appropriate practices to implement the curriculum and achieve their goals. You can develop a good understanding of developmentally appropriate practice by reading *Developmentally Appropriate Practice in Early Childhood Programs Serving Children from Birth Through Age 8.*[29]

Individual Needs.   Good care and education provide for children's needs and interests at each developmental stage. For example, infants respond to good physical care and to continuity of care, love and affection, and **cognitive sensory stimulation**. Cognitive sensory stimulation is the process of providing appropriate sensory stimulation, which in turn supports cognitive development. The way infants and toddlers learn is through their senses. Providing children appropriate sensory stimulation through toys of different colors, shapes, and textures, such as foam balls and blocks, enables them to learn through their senses and develop cognitive schemes. Toddlers need safe surroundings and opportunities to explore. They need caregivers who support and encourage active involvement. However, within these broad categories of development, individual children have unique styles of interacting and learning that you must accommodate. Each child must feel valued and respected.

cognitive sensory stimulation The process of providing appropriate sensory stimulation, which in turn supports cognitive development.

Managing Behavior.   Learning how to adapt your teaching to children's individual needs and learning styles and how to manage their behavior are two important teacher skills. Sometimes children's behavior can be difficult to manage. For example, a preschooler might demonstrate challenging behavior that makes it difficult for the teacher to help the child learn and be involved with others. A skillful teacher can redirect that behavior in order to help the child stay engaged and learn.

Accommodating Individual Needs. Providing for individual children's needs also means that you will accommodate their individual disabilities and developmental delays. For example, in your child care program, two-and-a-half-year-old Bobby has not learned to use the toilet. His parents have noticed that he shows interest in using the toilet, tells them after he urinates or defecates in his diaper, and does not say "no" as often as he did—all indications that Bobby is ready to start learning to use the toilet. Bobby, however, is not able to say when he needs to use the toilet. Here are some things you can do to accommodate Bobby, other children, and their parents:

- Discuss toilet-learning procedures with Bobby's parents. Discuss their wishes and views about toilet learning. (Is Bobby using training pants or big boy underwear? What words do they use at home for urination and defecation?) Consistency and continuity are the keys to success in toilet learning, so discuss with his parents what they are doing at home. Remember, different cultures have different approaches to toilet learning. However, you cannot use harsh, punitive methods under any circumstances.

- Always keep the door open when you help children with toileting. Children are not yet concerned with privacy. In fact, some child care centers and schools mandate that doors remain open when adults are in the restroom with children.

- Start a schedule. To begin, take Bobby to the restroom every hour. Once you have an idea of his body rhythms, you can take him less or more often. Use the words that his family wants you to use (e.g., "pee" or "poop"), so that Bobby learns to tell you when he needs to use the toilet.

- Have Bobby help take off his own training pants or underwear and then sit on the toilet. Read him a short developmentally appropriate book about potty learning or sing several songs. If he has not done anything in the toilet by the end of the book or songs, then have him help put his clothes back on and try again in an hour.

- Encourage Bobby by saying, "You are so big. You are using the toilet (potty) just like Mommy and Daddy do."

- If Bobby has an accident, tell him the words he can use next time before he pees or poops. Be positive and encouraging at all times. Never scold Bobby for having an accident. Some children learn quickly and others slowly. Bobby's parents may want you to use a reward, such as a sticker, when he is successful.

If you take these steps to accommodate Bobby's individual needs, you will help him become more independent and developmentally on track.

The Effects of Care and Education on Children

Research reveals that high-quality early care and education have influences that last a lifetime. A valuable source of research about child care comes from the Study of Early Child Care and Youth Development (SECCYD) by the National Institute of Child Health and Human Development (NICHD).[30] The SECCYD is a comprehensive longitudinal study initiated by NICHD, designed to answer questions about the relationship between child care experiences and characteristics and children's developmental outcomes. Listed below are some of the study's findings on the use of child care and its effects on children and families. The study results make it clear that professionals must provide high-quality programs and must advocate for high quality with the public and state legislators. Reflect on what surprises you most as you review the study results.

Child Care Arrangements

- During the first year of life the majority of children in nonparental care experienced more than two different child care arrangements.
- More than one-third experienced three or more arrangements.

Hours in Child Care

- At their first entry into nonmaternal care, children averaged 29 hours of care per week.
- By twelve months, children averaged 33.9 hours a week of care.

Child Care and Income

- Families with the lowest nonmaternal income were the most likely to place infants in care before the age of three months, probably because they were the most dependent on the mother's income.
- The higher their mothers' earnings, the more hours infants spent in nonmaternal care; however, the higher the *nonmaternal* earnings in the family, the *fewer* hours they spent in care.

Maternal Attitudes and Child Care

- Mothers who believed their children benefited from their employment tended to place their infants in care earlier, and for more hours, in nonauthoritarian, nonmaternal care.
- In contrast, mothers who believed maternal employment carried high risks for their children tended to put their infants in care for fewer hours and were especially likely to rely on the infant's father for child care.

Quality of Nonmaternal Care

- Observations at six months indicated that more positive caregiving occurred when children were in smaller groups, child–adult ratios were lower, caregivers held less authoritarian beliefs about child rearing, and physical environments were safe, clean, and stimulating.

Social, Emotional, Cognitive, and Health-Related Child Outcomes

- Observed quality of caregivers' behavior—particularly the amount of language stimulation provided—was positively related to children's performance on measures of cognitive and linguistic abilities at ages fifteen, twenty-four, and thirty-six months.
- Quality of care was also related to measures of social and emotional development. At twenty-four months, children who had experienced higher quality care were reported by both their mothers and their caregivers to have fewer behavior problems and were rated higher on social competence by their mothers. At thirty-six months, higher quality care was associated with greater compliance and less negative behavior during mother–child interactions and fewer caregiver-reported behavior problems.
- Quality of care is associated with developmental outcomes throughout the preschool years.

It is clear that high-quality child care has beneficial outcomes for children and families. You will be involved in advising parents about child care. The research data above helps you be informed and knowledgeable so you and parents can make wise and informed decisions.[31]

PROGRAM MODELS

Models are guides that provide us with instructions, ideas, and examples. We use models to guide a lot of what we do in life. We model our lives after others we respect and admire. We adopt the fashions of models in advertisements—and in early childhood education, we model our programs after highly respected models such as HighScope, Montessori, and Reggio Emilia. While none of these individual models are intended for all children, they nonetheless are widely used in the United States and around the world, especially in preschool programs. The HighScope model, the first model we examine, is widely used in Head Start, corporate-sponsored preschool programs, and public preschool programs.

HighScope: A Constructivist Model

The **HighScope educational model** uses curriculum that is geared to children's stages of development, promotes constructive processes of learning, and broadens the child's emerging intellectual and social skills.[32] The HighScope model is based on Piaget's cognitive development theory. Here are three principles of the HighScope model:

> **HighScope educational model** A constructivist educational model based on Piaget's cognitive development theory, providing realistic experiences geared to children's current stages of development.

- Active participation of children in choosing, organizing, and evaluating learning activities, which are undertaken with careful teacher observation and guidance in a learning environment that has a rich variety of materials located in various classroom learning centers
- Regular daily planning by the teaching staff in accord with a developmentally based curriculum model and careful child observations
- Developmentally sequenced goals and materials for children based on the HighScope "key developmental indicators"[33]

Basic Principles and Goals of the HighScope Model.   The HighScope program strives to develop in children a broad range of skills, including the problem-solving, interpersonal, and communication skills that are essential for successful living in a rapidly changing society. The curriculum encourages student initiative by providing children with materials, equipment, and time to pursue activities they choose. At the same time, it provides teachers with a framework for guiding children's independent activities toward sequenced learning goals. The teacher plays a key role in instructional activities by selecting appropriate, developmentally sequenced material and by encouraging children to adopt an active, problem-solving approach to learning. This teacher–student interaction—teachers helping students achieve developmentally sequenced goals while also encouraging them to set many of their own goals—uniquely distinguishes the HighScope curriculum from direct-instruction and teacher-centered curricula.[34]

Five Elements of the HighScope Model.   Professionals who use the HighScope curriculum are fully committed to providing settings in which children actively learn and construct their own knowledge. Teachers create the context for learning by implementing and supporting five essential elements: active learning, classroom arrangement, the daily schedule, assessment, and the curriculum (content).

   Active Learning.   Teachers support children's active learning by providing a variety of materials, making plans and reviewing activities with children, interacting with and carefully observing individual children, and leading small- and large-group active learning activities.

   Classroom Arrangement.   The classroom contains five or more interest centers that encourage choice. The classroom organization of materials and equipment supports the daily routine. Children know where to find materials and what materials they can use. This encourages development of self-direction and independence.

The teacher selects the centers and activities to use in the classroom based on several considerations:

- Interests of the children (e.g., preschool children are interested in blocks, house-keeping, and art)
- Opportunities for facilitating active involvement in seriation (e.g., big, bigger, big-gest), numbers (e.g., counting), time relations (e.g., before–after), classification (e.g., likenesses and differences), spatial relations (e.g., over–under), and language development
- Opportunities for reinforcing needed skills and concepts and functional (real-life) use of these skills and concepts

Classroom arrangement is an essential part of professional practice in order to appropriately implement a program's philosophy. This is true for HighScope, as well as Montessori and every other program with which you may be involved.

Daily Schedule.   The schedule considers developmental levels of children, incorporates a sixty- to seventy-minute plan-do-review process, provides for content areas, is as consistent throughout the day as possible, and contains a minimum number of transitions.

Assessment.   Teachers keep notes about significant behaviors, changes, statements, and things that help them better understand a child's way of thinking and learning. Teachers use two mechanisms to help them collect data: the Key Developmental Indicators note form and a portfolio. In addition, teachers use the Child Observation Record (COR) to identify and record children's progress in key behavioral and content areas.

Curriculum.   The educational content of HighScope preschool programs is built around forty-two Key Developmental Indicators (KDIs) in five curriculum content areas. The curriculum content areas are as follows: (1) approaches to learning; (2) language, literacy, and communication; (3) social and emotional development; (4) physical development, health, and well-being; and (5) arts and sciences (math, science and technology, social studies, and arts).

The KDIs are early childhood milestones that guide teachers as they plan and assess learning experiences and interact with children to support learning.[35] For instance, the KDIs for language, literacy, and communication are: (1) talking with others about personally meaningful experiences; (2) describing objects, events, and relations; (3) having fun with language (e.g., listening to stories and poems, making up stories and rhymes); (4) writing in various ways (e.g., drawing, scribbling, letter-like forms, invented spelling, conventional forms); (5) reading in various ways (reading storybooks, signs and symbols, one's own writing); and (6) dictating stories.[36]

These developmental indicators are representative of the many that are available for teachers to choose from when identifying learning activities for children. In many ways, the KDIs are similar to standards that specify what children should know and do.

A Daily Routine That Supports Active Learning.

The HighScope curriculum's daily routine is made up of a plan-do-review sequence that gives children opportunities to express intentions about their activities while keeping the teacher intimately involved in the whole process. The following five processes support the daily routine and contribute to its successful functioning.

Planning Time.   Planning time gives children a structured, consistent chance to express their ideas to adults and to see themselves as individuals who can act on decisions.

The teacher talks with children about the plans they have made before the children carry them out. This helps children clarify their ideas and think about how to proceed. Talking with children about their plans provides an opportunity for the teacher to encourage and respond to each child's ideas, to suggest ways to strengthen the plans so they will be successful, and to understand and gauge each child's level of development and thinking style. Children and teachers benefit from these conversations and reflections. Children feel reinforced and ready to start their work, while teachers have ideas of what opportunities for extension might arise, what difficulties children might have, and where problem solving may be needed.

Key Developmental Indicators. Teachers continually encourage and support children's interests and involvement in activities, which occur within an organized environment and a consistent routine. Teachers plan from Key Developmental Indicators (KDIs) that broaden and strengthen children's emerging abilities. Children generate many of these experiences on their own; others require teacher guidance. Many KDIs are natural extensions of children's projects and interests.

Work Time. This part of the plan-do-review sequence is generally the longest time period in the daily routine. The teacher's role during work time is to observe children to see how they gather information, interact with peers, and solve problems. When appropriate, teachers enter into the children's activities to encourage, extend, and set up problem-solving situations.

Cleanup Time. During cleanup time, children return materials and equipment to their labeled places and store their incomplete projects, restoring order to the classroom. All children's materials in the classroom are within reach and on open shelves. Clear labeling enables children to return all work materials to their appropriate places.

Recall Time. Recall time, the final phase of the plan-do-review sequence, is the time when children represent their work time experience in a variety of developmentally appropriate ways. They might recall the names of the children they involved in their plan, draw a picture of the building they made, or describe the problems they encountered. Recall strategies also include drawing pictures, making models, physically demonstrating how a plan was carried out, or verbally recalling the events of work time. The teacher supports children's linking of the actual work to their original plan.

This review permits children to reflect on what they did and how it was done. It brings closure to children's planning and work time activities. Putting their ideas and experiences into words also facilitates children's language development. Most important, it enables children to represent their mental schemes to others.

Advantages of HighScope. Implementing the HighScope approach has several advantages. First, it offers you a method for employing a constructivist-based program that has its roots in Piagetian cognitive theory. Second, it is widely popular and has been extensively researched and tested. Third, the HighScope Foundation provides a rather extensive network of training and support. Fourth, HighScope teachers emphasize the broad cognitive, social, and physical abilities that are important for all children, instead of focusing on a child's deficits. HighScope teachers identify where a child is developmentally and then provide a rich range of experiences appropriate for that level. For example, they would encourage a four-year-old who is functioning at a two-year-old level to express his or her plans by pointing, gesturing, and saying single words, and they would immerse the child in a conversational environment that provided many natural opportunities for using and hearing language.[37] Reviewing the organization's website will help you decide if HighScope is a program you would consider implementing in your classroom.

The Montessori Method

The Montessori method is attractive to parents and teachers for a number of reasons. First, Montessori education has always been identified as a quality program for

Montessori method A system of early childhood education founded on the philosophy, procedures, and materials developed by Maria Montessori. Respect for the child is the cornerstone on which all other Montessori principles rest.

young children. Second, parents who observe a good Montessori program like what they see: orderliness, independent children, self-directed learning, a calm environment, and children at the center of the learning process.

During the past decade, the implementation of Montessori education has increased in both private and public school early childhood programs. Maria Montessori would probably smilingly approve of the contemporary use of her method once again to help change the nature and character of early childhood education.

Role of the Montessori Teacher.   The Montessori teacher demonstrates certain behaviors to implement the principles of this child-centered approach. The teacher's six essential roles in a Montessori program are as follows: (1) respect children and their learning; (2) make children the center of learning; (3) encourage children's learning; (4) observe children; (5) prepare learning environments; and (6) introduce learning materials and demonstrate lessons.

Maria Montessori contended, "It is necessary for the teacher to *guide* the child without letting him feel her presence too much, so that she may be always ready to supply the desired help, but may never be the obstacle between the child and his experience."[38] The teacher as a guide is a pillar of Montessori practice.

The Montessori Method in Action.   In a prepared environment, certain materials and activities provide for three basic areas of child involvement: *practical life* for motor education, *sensory materials* for training the senses, and *academic materials* for teaching writing, reading, and mathematics. All of these activities are taught according to prescribed procedures.

Practical Life.   The prepared environment emphasizes basic, practical, everyday motor activities, such as walking from place to place in an orderly manner, carrying objects such as trays and chairs, greeting a visitor, learning self-care skills, and doing other practical activities. For example, the "dressing frames" are designed to perfect the motor skills involved in buttoning, zipping, lacing, buckling, and tying. The philosophy for activities such as these is to make children independent of the adult and develop concentration. Water-based activities play a large role in Montessori methods, and children are taught to scrub, wash, and pour as a means of developing coordination. Practical life exercises also include polishing mirrors, shoes, and plant leaves; sweeping the floor; dusting furniture; and peeling vegetables.

Montessorians believe that as children become absorbed in an activity, they gradually lengthen their span of concentration. As they follow a regular sequence of actions, they learn to pay attention to details. Montessori educators also believe that concentration and involvement through the senses enable learning to take place. Teacher verbal instructions are minimal; the emphasis in the instruction process is on *showing how*—modeling and practice.

Practical life activities are taught through four different types of exercises. *Care of the person* involves activities such as using the dressing frames, polishing shoes, and washing hands. *Care of the environment* includes dusting, polishing a table, and raking leaves. *Social relations* include lessons in grace and courtesy. The fourth type of exercise involves *analysis and control of movement* and includes locomotor activities such as walking and balancing.

Sensory Materials.   For many early childhood educators the core of the Montessori program is the specialized set of learning materials that help children learn and that support Montessori's ideas about how to best facilitate children's learning. Many of these materials are designed to train and use the senses to support learning. Figure 4.1 shows basic Montessori sensory materials. Montessori sensory materials are popular, attractive, and support children's cognitive development. Authentic Montessori materials are very well made and durable.

Material	Illustration	Descriptions and Learning Purposes
Pink tower		Ten wooden cubes of the same shape and texture, all pink, the largest of which is ten centimeters. Each succeeding block is one centimeter smaller. Children build a tower beginning with the largest block. (Visual discrimination of dimension)
Brown stairs		Ten wooden blocks, all brown, differing in height and width. Children arrange the blocks next to each other from thickest to thinnest so the blocks resemble a staircase. (Visual discrimination of width and height)
Red rods		Ten rod-shaped pieces of wood, all red, of identical thickness but differing in length from ten centimeters to one meter. The child arranges the rods next to each other from largest to smallest. (Visual discrimination of length)
Cylinder blocks		Four individual wooden blocks that have holes of various sizes and matching cylinders; one block deals with height, one with diameter, and two with the relationship of both variables. Children remove the cylinders in random order, then match each cylinder to the correct hole. (Visual discrimination of size)
Smelling jars		Two identical sets of white opaque glass jars with removable tops through which the child cannot see but through which odors can pass. The teacher places various substances, such as herbs, in the jars, and the child matches the jars according to the smells. (Olfactory discrimination)
Baric tablets		Sets of rectangular pieces of wood that vary according to weight. There are three sets—light, medium, and heavy—that children match according to the weight of the tablets. (Discrimination of weight)
Color tablets		Two identical sets of small rectangular pieces of wood used for matching color or shading. (Discrimination of color and education of the chromatic sense)
Cloth swatches		Two identical swatches of cloth. Children identify them according to touch, first without a blindfold but later using a blindfold. (Sense of touch)
Tonal bells		Two sets of eight bells, alike in shape and size but different in color; one set is white, the other brown. The child matches the bells by tone. (Sound and pitch)
Sound boxes		Two identical sets of cylinders filled with various materials, such as salt and rice. Children match the cylinders according to the sounds the fillings make. (Auditory discrimination)
Temperature jugs or thermic bottles		Small metal jugs filled with water of varying temperatures. Children match jugs of the same temperature. (Thermic sense and ability to distinguish between temperatures)

FIGURE 4.1 Montessori Sensory Materials

As you review these materials, think about their purposes and how they act as facilitators of children's learning. Sensory materials include brightly colored rods and cubes and sandpaper letters. One purpose of these sensory materials is to train children's senses to focus on some obvious, particular quality. For example, with red rods, it is the quality of length; with pink tower cubes, size; and with bells, musical pitch. Montessori felt that children need help discriminating among the many stimuli they receive. Accordingly, the sensory materials help children become more aware of the capacity of their bodies to receive, interpret, and make use of stimuli. In this sense, the Montessori sensory materials are labeled *didactic;* they are designed to instruct and help children learn.

Second, the sensory materials help sharpen children's powers of observation and visual discrimination. These skills serve as a basis for general beginning reading readiness. Readiness for learning is highly emphasized in early childhood programs.

Third, the sensory materials increase children's ability to think, a process that depends on the ability to distinguish, classify, and organize. Children constantly face decisions about sensory materials: which block comes next, which color matches the other, which shape goes where? These are not decisions the teacher makes, nor are they decisions children arrive at by guessing; rather, they are decisions made by the sensory and cognitive processes of observation and selection based on knowledge gathered through the senses.

Finally, the sensory activities are not ends in themselves. Their purpose is to prepare children for the onset of the sensitive periods for writing and reading. In this sense, all activities are preliminary steps in the writing–reading process.

Materials for training and developing the senses have these characteristics:

- *Control of error.* Materials are designed so children, through observation, can see whether or not they have made a mistake while completing an activity. For example, if a child does not use the blocks of the pink tower in their proper order while building the tower, she does not achieve a tower effect.

- *Isolation of a single quality.* Materials are designed so that other variables are held constant except for the isolated quality or qualities. Therefore, all blocks of the pink tower are pink because size, not color, is the isolated quality.

- *Active involvement.* Materials encourage active involvement rather than the more passive process of looking. Montessori materials are "hands-on" in the truest sense of hands-on active learning.

- *Attractiveness.* Materials are attractive, with colors and proportions that appeal to children. In this sense, they help satisfy aesthetic needs for beauty and attractiveness.

As you watch this video of a teacher pointing out and explaining Montessori materials, think and reflect on how they promote the Montessori curriculum and how they support children's sensory learning.

Academic Materials for Writing, Reading, and Mathematics. The third type of Montessori materials is academic, designed specifically to promote writing, reading, and mathematics.

Exercises using these materials are presented in a sequence that supports writing as a basis for learning to read. Reading, therefore, emerges from writing. Both processes, however, are introduced so gradually that children are never aware they are learning to write and read until one day they realize they are writing and reading. Describing this phenomenon, Montessori said that children "burst spontaneously" into writing and reading. She anticipated contemporary practices such as the whole-language approach in integrating writing and reading and in maintaining that children learn to read through writing.

Montessori believed many children were ready for writing at four years of age. Consequently, children who enter a Montessori program at age three have done most of the sensory exercises by the time they are four. It is not uncommon to see four- and

Here a child at Children's House Montessori School works on a moveable alphabet lesson. Notice the child has one set of alphabet letters in red and one set in blue. This enables her to distinguish between beginning and ending sounds and to form the words she is sounding out.

Here a child at Children's House Montessori School works on a lesson with the cylinder blocks. Notice his use of the pincer grip and notice the different depths of the cylinder inserts.

five-year-olds in a Montessori classroom writing and reading. In fact, children's success with early academic skills and abilities serves as a magnet to attract public and parental attention.

Additional Features. Other features of the Montessori system are *mixed-age grouping* and *self-pacing*. A Montessori classroom always contains children of different ages, usually from two and a half to six years. This strategy is becoming more popular in many early childhood classrooms. Advantages of mixed-age groups are that children learn from one another and help each other, a wide range of materials is available for all ages of children, and older children become role models and collaborators for younger children. Contemporary instructional practices of student mentoring, scaffolding, and cooperative learning all have their roots in and are supported by multiage grouping.

In a Montessori classroom, children are free to learn at their own rates and levels of achievement. They decide which activities to participate in and work at their own pace. Through observation, the teacher determines when children have perfected one exercise and are ready to move to a higher level or different exercise. If a child is not able to correctly complete an activity, the teacher gives him or her additional help and instruction. Table 4.4 shows the instructional practices used in a Montessori program and how they apply to teacher roles and the curriculum. Review these practices now

TABLE 4.4 Montessori Instructional Practices

These instructional practices, combined with the roles of the Montessori teacher and the sensory materials, serve as the essential core of Montessori programs.

Integrated curriculum	Montessori provides an integrated curriculum in which children are actively involved in manipulating concrete materials across the curriculum—writing, reading, science, math, geography, and the arts. The Montessori curriculum is integrated by age and developmental level.
Active learning	In Montessori classrooms, children are actively involved in their own learning. Manipulative materials provide for active and concrete learning.
Individualized instruction	Curriculum and activities should be individualized for children. Individualization occurs through children's interactions with the materials as they proceed at their own rates of mastery.
Independence	The Montessori environment emphasizes respect for children and promotes success—both of which encourage children to be independent
Appropriate assessment	Observation is the primary means of assessing children's progress, achievement, and behavior in a Montessori classroom. Well trained Montessori teachers are skilled observers of children and adept at translating their observation into appropriate ways for guiding, directing, facilitating, and channeling children's learning.
Developmentally appropriate practice	What is specified in developmentally appropriate practice is included in Montessori practice. It is more likely that quality Montessori practitioners understand, as Maria Montessori did, that children are much more capable than some early childhood practitioners think.

diversity tie-in

Providing for Diversity and Disability

Montessori education is ideally suited to meet the needs of children from diverse backgrounds, those with disabilities, and those with other special needs such as giftedness. Montessori believed that all children are intrinsically motivated to learn and that they absorb knowledge when they are provided appropriate environments at appropriate times of development. Thus Montessorians believe in providing for individual differences in enriched environments.

By following children's growth and interests teachers are able to provide children with the care and education they need. Montessori programs and materials are suited to providing for the needs of children's with disabilities.

- **In the multiage classroom.** In many Montessori classrooms the children and teachers are on a three-year cycle, which allows the teachers to have an ongoing relationship with children, to authentically learn their needs and interests, and to provide for differentiation and accommodation in learning activities. In a Montessori program there is no "failure" from one grade to another. Children are working at the level that is developmentally appropriate for them. In addition, Montessori encouraged all

teachers to "follow" the child. Following the child means the children will work at their own pace and that children are developing their own education and are not competing with other children to complete projects or for grades.

- **Montessori materials.** Montessori materials are ideally suited to children with disabilities. The materials are hands-on and appeal to the interests and learning needs of children. In addition, the materials are of various shapes, sizes, and textures, which satisfies the learning styles of children with disabilities.
- **Respect for the child.** Since respect for the child lies at the heart of Montessori programs, children with disabilities will receive that respect from teachers who respect and honor their unique disabilities and needs.

All in all, Montessori can be ideally suited for children with disabilities. However, simply because a program is a Montessori program does not mean that it can or will meet the needs of children with disabilities. You will have to work with and council families with children of disabilities to observe programs and do their homework to ensure that their child with a disability is a good fit for a particular Montessori program.

---

and think how they are similar to or different from instructional practices you have observed in other early childhood programs.

The accompanying Diversity Tie-In feature explains how a Montessori education can encourage the personal growth of children.

Reggio Emilia

Reggio Emilia, a city in northern Italy, is widely known for its approach to educating young children founded by Loris Malaguzzi (1920–1994). Reggio Emilia sponsors programs for children from three months to six years of age. Certain essential beliefs and practices underlie the **Reggio Emilia approach**. These basic features are what define it, make it a constructivist program, and identify it as a model that attracts worldwide attention. The Reggio approach has been adapted and implemented in a number of U.S. early childhood programs.

Beliefs About Children and How They Learn. As we have discussed, your beliefs about young children determine how you teach them, what kind of programs you provide for them, and your expectations for their learning and development. This is the case with Reggio. Their beliefs drive their program practices.

Relationships. Reggio education focuses on each child and is conducted in relation with the family, other children, the teachers, the school environment, the

Reggio Emilia approach An early childhood educational program named for the town in Italy where it originated. The method emphasizes a child's relationships with family, peers, teachers, and the wider community; small-group interaction; schedules set by the child's personal rhythms; and visual arts programs coordinated by a specially trained atelierista.

technology tie-in

Maria at the Apple Store

Sandpaper letters and number rods on iPhone/iPad apps? Yes, technology is integrating with the 105-year-old Montessori method! Montessorium is one of the companies that has developed Montessori apps for both the iPad and iPhone. Here are images from the company's Intro to Math and Intro to Letters apps.

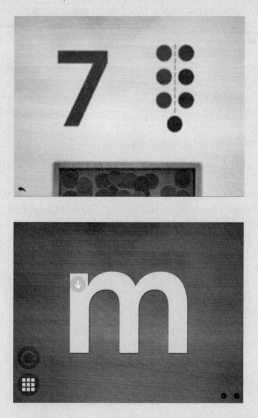

As you might expect, there are pros and cons to the use of apps in a Montessori setting.

1. Apps may help spark a renewed interest in Montessori education by introducing Montessorians to the technological age.
2. The children of today are technologically oriented and want to learn with technology, regardless of the program they are in; children should have access to technology and should use technology to learn.

At stake is the future of Montessori to change and to use technology to drive that change! I for one believe that apps will play an important role in the future of Montessori education and if Montessori were alive today, she would be shopping at the Apple Store!

Cons:

1. Apps of a concrete material are not the same as hands-on experience with the material itself. For example, with an app students cannot feel the kinesthetic roughness of the sandpaper letters, and an app for the number rods does not allow children to feel the weight of the rods. Montessori said, "The hand is the tool of the mind."
2. Those who advocate staying "true" to Montessori's ideas and methods believe that deviations from what Montessori taught violate an authentic implementation of her method. Consequently, a virtual representation and application of Montessori's materials would be no substitute for the real thing.

Keturah Collins, director of the Children's House Montessori Program in Reston, Virginia, offers the following opinions:

Introduction to Letters Pros:

This is basically a good app to teach the sounds.

There is a good correction of error when your finger leaves the shape of the letter.

I like "you did it" instead of "good job" as a more authentic encouragement.

Introduction to Letters Cons:

Some of the sounds aren't quite as clear as they could be; there is an extra syllable on the end of some of the sounds such as *b* and *d*. The sound needs to be shortened and crisper.

The capital letters should not be given the name of the letter. There should be a separate section of the app to teach the name of the letters, with a clear explanation of this.

Introduction to Math Pros:

This app is entertaining and fun.
I liked dragging the red rods into order.
I like "you did it" instead of "good job" as a more authentic encouragement.
Great that the 3-period lesson is used; "this is . . ." "show me . . ." "what is this?"

Introduction to Math Cons:

Sometimes the correct drag of the numbers in the last game is rejected; it seems a little too sensitive.

· · · · · · · · · · · · · · · · · · · ·

Source: Montessorium.

community, and the wider society. Each school is viewed as a system in which all of these interconnected relationships are essential for educating children. In other words, as Vygotsky believed, children learn through social interactions, and, as Montessori maintained, the environment supports and is important for learning.

Teachers are always aware, however, that children learn a great deal in exchanges with their peers, especially when they interact in small groups. Such small groups of two, three, four, or five children provide possibilities for paying attention, hearing, and listening to each other; developing curiosity and interest; asking questions; and responding.

Time.   Reggio Emilia teachers believe that time is not set by a clock and that learning continuity should not be interrupted by the calendar. Children's own sense of time and their personal rhythm are considered in planning and carrying out activities and projects. The full-day schedule provides sufficient time for being together among peers in an environment that is conducive to getting things done with satisfaction.

Teachers get to know the personal rhythms and learning styles of each child. This intensive getting to know children is possible in part because children stay with the same teachers and the same peer group for three-year cycles (infancy to three years and three years to six years).

In the Reggio program, children are encouraged and supported to document their experiences of learning. The documentation helps children know that their efforts and acheivements are valued by their peers, teachers, and parents.

Adults' Roles.   Adults play a powerful role in children's lives. Children's well-being is connected with the well-being of parents and teachers. The well-being of all is supported by recognizing and supporting basic rights. Children have a right to high-quality care and education that supports the development of their potential. Adults and communities who provide these educational necessities honor this right. Parents have a right to be involved in the life of the school. As one parent remarked, "I'm not a visitor at school; this is my school!" Teachers have the right to grow professionally through collaboration with other teachers and parents.

The Teacher.   Teachers observe and listen closely to children to know how to plan or proceed with their work. They ask questions and discover children's ideas, hypotheses, and theories. They collaboratively discuss what they have observed and recorded, and they make flexible plans and preparations. Teachers then enter into dialogues with the children and offer them opportunities for discovering, revisiting, and reflecting on experiences. In this sense, teachers support learning as an ongoing process. Teachers are partners and collaborators with children in a continual process of research and learning.

The Atelierista.   An atelierista is a teacher trained in the visual arts, who works closely with other teachers and children in every Reggio preprimary school and makes visits to the infant/toddler centers. The atelierista's specific training in the visual arts opens up another kind of dialogue, helping children use materials to create projects that reflect their involvement in and efforts to solve problems.

atelierista A Reggio Emilia teacher trained in visual arts who works with teachers and children.

Families.   Families are an essential component of Reggio, and they are included in the advisory committee that runs each school. Family participation is expected and supported and takes many forms: day-to-day interaction, work in the schools, discussion of educational and psychological issues, special events, excursions, and celebrations.

The Environment.   The infant/toddler centers and school programs are the most visible aspect of the work done by teachers and families in Reggio Emilia. They convey many messages, of which the most immediate is that they are environments where adults have thought about the quality and the instructive power of space.

The Physical Space.   In addition to welcoming whoever enters, the layout of physical space fosters encounters, communication, and relationships. The arrangement of structures, objects, and activities encourages children's choices, supports problem solving, and promotes discoveries in the process of learning.

Reggio centers and schools are beautiful. There is attention to detail everywhere: in the color of the walls, the shape of the furniture, the arrangement of objects on shelves and tables. Light from the windows and doors shines through transparent collages and weavings made by children. Healthy, green plants are everywhere.

The environment is highly personal and full of children's own work. Everywhere there are paintings, drawings, paper sculptures, wire constructions, transparent collages coloring the light, and mobiles moving gently overhead. Such things turn up even in unexpected spaces such as stairways and bathrooms.

atelier A special area or studio in a Reggio Emilia school for creating projects.

The Atelier.   The atelier is a special workshop or studio, set aside and used by all the children and teachers in the school. It contains a great variety of tools and resource materials, along with records of past projects and experiences. In the view of Reggio educators, the children's use of many media is not art or a separate part of the curriculum but an inseparable, integral part of the whole cognitive/symbolic expression involved in the learning process.

Program Practices.   Cooperation is the powerful mode of working that makes possible the achievement of the goals Reggio educators set for themselves. Teachers work in pairs in each classroom. They see themselves as researchers gathering information about their work with children by means of continual documentation. The strong collegial relationships that are maintained with teachers and staff enable them to engage in collaborative discussion and interpretation of both teachers' and children's work.

Documentation.   Transcriptions of children's remarks and discussions, photographs of their activity, and representations of their thinking and learning using many media are carefully arranged by the atelierista and other teachers. These document children's work and the process of learning. This documentation has five functions:

1. To make parents aware of children's experiences and maintain their involvement
2. To allow teachers to understand children and to evaluate their own work, thus promoting professional growth
3. To facilitate communication and exchange of ideas among educators
4. To make children aware that their effort is valued
5. To create an archive that traces the history of the school and the pleasure of learning by children and their teachers

Curriculum and Practices.   The Reggio curriculum is not established in advance. In this sense, Reggio is a process approach, not a set curriculum for teachers to implement. Teachers express general goals and make hypotheses about what direction activities and projects might take. After observing children in action, teachers compare, discuss, and interpret together their observations and make choices that they share with the children about what to offer and how to sustain the children in their exploration and learning. In fact, the curriculum emerges in the process of each activity or project and is flexibly adjusted accordingly through this continuous dialogue among teachers and with children.

Projects provide the backbone of the children's and teachers' learning experiences. These projects are based on the conviction that learning by doing is of great importance and that to discuss in groups and to revisit ideas and experiences is the premier way of gaining understanding and learning.

Ideas for projects originate in the experiences of children and teachers as they construct knowledge together. Projects can last from a few days to several months. They may start from a chance event, an idea or a problem posed by one or more children, or an experience initiated directly by teachers.

Considerations. As you consider the Reggio Emilia approach, keep in mind that its theoretical base rests within constructivism and shares ideas compatible with those of Piaget, Vygotsky, Dewey, and Gardner, and the process of learning by doing. In addition, like the Montessori approach, Reggio places a high value on respect for each child. In a Reggio program everyone has rights—children, teachers, and parents. Children with disabilities have special rights and are routinely included in programs for all children.

This video allows you to see inside a Reggio Emilia Program. Note the important role documentation and teacher collaboration play in the effectiveness of the program.

Review the following Teaching and Learning for the Inclusive Classroom section to learn more about how to use different approaches to make your teaching more appropriate for children's different learning styles.

TEACHING AND LEARNING IN THE INCLUSIVE CLASSROOM: LEARNING MODALITIES

Regardless of the program you use in your classroom, such as child care, Montessori, Head Start, HighScope, or Reggio Emilia, you should be aware that every child learns differently and thus experiences the world differently. Third grader Kate, for example, is a very physical child and comprehends material best when she can touch, feel, or move the information herself. Her classmate Tenisha, a linguistic learner, learns best if she can write or read information. Eli, on the other hand, is very visual; he learns best if information is presented in pictures or diagrams. Unlike Eli, Juan learns best when material is presented to him in a musical manner. Combining visual, tactile, and auditory components is helpful for all of your students. When you teach in a multisensory way, you increase children's understanding, memory, and mastery of content, knowledge, and skills.

To accommodate diverse learners like Kate, Tenisha, Eli, and Juan in your inclusive classroom, follow these tips.

Tip 1. *Teach face-to-face with your students.* Give directions and discuss subjects so all children can see and hear you. Children who are visual learners need to see your mouth moving and look at your facial expressions to completely hear your words. Ask children to "find my face" or to "give me your eyes and ears" when you give instructions so they understand you are telling them something important.

Tip 2. *Allow movement in your classroom.* Children want and need to be active. Activity is the basis for active learning! Tactile, linguistic, and auditory learners like Kate, Tenisha, and Juan often tap their feet or pencils or scribble on paper while learning. Physical movement or scribbling helps them to internalize and concentrate. Movement is a self-help tool that helps students learn.

Tip 3. *Present information in a variety of ways.* For example:

- When you discuss the day's schedule, in addition to talking about it, have pictorial representations of the schedule for visual learners like Eli (snack time can be represented by a picture of crackers, math represented by a picture of an addition problem, etc.). Your visual schedule can be arranged vertically or horizontally to encourage the left-to-right, top-to-bottom reading process.
- Attach pictures to the daily schedule with Velcro strips. Have tactile learners like Kate peel an activity off as it is finished. Kate can then put the picture of the activity in an "all done" or "finished" box.
- Accompany the schedule with a song such as, "Our snack time is finished, our snack time is done," for auditory learners like Juan.

Tip 4. *Include multisensory approaches in all your teaching.* For example:

- Discuss new words in a singsong fashion or set them to a popular children's tune such as "Baa Baa Black Sheep" for auditory learners like Juan.
- Make learning letters and words a tactile experience. Children can mold words out of play dough, make letters 3-D by twisting them out of colorful pipe cleaners, trace words in shaving cream, or cut them out of sandpaper. Many letters—like "B," "D," "I," "V," and "L"—can be made with the hands and fingers. Encourage children to use their hands to help them remember which way letters orient and to demonstrate how they can be combined to form words. For example, to spell "bed," show students how to make their left hand in the shape of a "b" and their right hand into a letter "d." Use a written letter "e" to go in the middle.

Tip 5. *Form learning groups based on children's learning modalities.* For example:

- Pair Eli, a visual learner, with Tenisha, a linguistic learner. Have them write and illustrate their own story. Eli can be the illustrator and Tenisha the writer. This allows them both to be co-authors.

The more senses you incorporate into your teaching, the more your students will learn and the more fun they will have.

The Project Approach

Project Approach An educational approach that encourages in-depth investigation by an individual student or small group of students, or even by the whole class, of a topic the students want to learn more about.

The Project Approach is not new! For as long as children have been building things—and this is a long time—they have been involved in projects. The **Project Approach** is popular in early childhood education today, traces its roots back to John Dewey's use of projects, and is based on constructivist ideas and practices. John Dewey and his wife developed the approach over a number of years at Dewey's laboratory school at the University of Chicago. Dewey's friend and colleague William Kilpatrick popularized the approach and made it more accessible to teachers of the time.

In this video, a teacher interacts with young children to teach them about birds. Notice how the teachers in this video capture children's interest and plan an in-depth unit around a theme.

With the Project Approach, an investigation is undertaken by a small group of children within a class, sometimes by a whole class, and occasionally by an individual child. The key feature of a project is that it is a search for answers to questions about a topic worth learning more about, something the children are interested in.[39] The Project Approach can be used in any kind of early childhood program regardless of its name and provides opportunities for children to be meaningfully and actively involved. The Professionalism in Practice: Tips for Implementing the Project Approach in Inclusive Classrooms feature gives you insight into how you can implement the Project Approach.

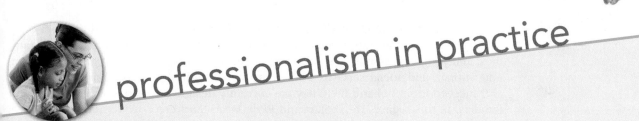

professionalism in practice

Tips for Implementing the Project Approach in Inclusive Classrooms

The Project Approach (PA) allows children to deeply explore a topic of interest over time while meaningfully integrating curriculum areas. Projects progress in phases from selection of a topic, to investigation of that topic, and end with a culminating activity representing learning. Children are actively engaged as they seek the answers to collaboratively generated questions. Consistent with universal design for learning, which makes the classroom and instruction available to all children, children are able to access information, become engaged, and demonstrate what they know in a variety of ways. The Project Approach is uniquely suited for implementation in inclusive settings. You can successfully implement the Project Approach in your inclusive classroom by following these simple steps:

TIP 1 Select a topic of interest to a child(ren) with disabilities

Select a topic of particular interest to one or more of the children with a disability. Beginning with an interest of a child with a disability affords an opportunity for taking a leadership role and for being meaningfully involved. When children are interested in materials, this enhances engagement, which increases learning and builds further interests. Use a planning web so you can help teachers to consider inclusion of standards, Individual Education Plan (IEP) goals, and connections to interests of other children in the class. The topic selection phase must consider the individual interests and needs of children with disabilities, while also taking into account the importance of a sense of community to the collaborative explorations of the Project Approach. All children should have an opportunity to share what they already know and what they want to know about the topic.

TIP 2 Provide resources

During the investigation phase keep in mind the principles of universal design for learning. Provide varied resources for research including visiting experts, books, online resources, podcasts, interactive books/games on tablets, and accessible field site visits. Provide a range of materials for children to document questions and represent their learning in a variety of ways.

TIP 3 Document the project

Maintain detailed documentation to make learning visible and use data to make instructional decisions. Project documentation can and should be a form of authentic ongoing assessment showing children's current level of understanding as well as progress over time.

TIP 4 Engage and inform families

When parents are involved in meaningful ways, the education of children with disabilities is more effective. Projects can allow for developing positive strengths based on relationships with families who may serve as visiting experts, connections to community experts, and facilitators of research at home. The project becomes a context not only for learning, but also for relationship building.

TIP 5 Involve the community

Community members may serve as a resource during investigation as well as an audience during culminating activities. Participation with the classroom community as well as observations of the strengths and contributions of all children may serve a role in facilitating inclusivity in larger community settings.

....

Source: Contributed by Helene Arbouet Harte, EdD, Assistant Professor of Education, University of Cincinnati, Blue Ash College.

FEDERAL PROGRAMS FOR YOUNG CHILDREN

The federal government exerts tremendous influence on early childhood education. Every dimension of almost every educational program—public, private, and faith based—is touched in some way by the federal government.

Head Start (children ages three to five) and Early Head Start (children from birth to age three) are comprehensive child development programs that serve children, families, and pregnant women. These programs provide comprehensive health, nutrition, educational, and social services in order to help children achieve their full potential and succeed in school and life. They are currently designed to serve poor children and families. In this regard, Head Start and Early Head Start are **entitlement programs**. This means that children and families who qualify, in this case by low income, are entitled to the services simply by meeting the qualifying criteria. However, only about one-third of eligible children and families receive these services because of the lack of funding to support full implementation.

entitlement programs
Programs and services that children and families are entitled to because they meet the eligibility criteria.

Head Start Programs

Head Start, America's premier preschool program, was implemented during the summer of 1965. The first programs were designed for children entering first grade who had not attended kindergarten. The purpose of Head Start was literally to give children from low-income families a "head start" on their kindergarten experience and, ideally, on life itself. As public schools have provided more kindergarten and preschool programs, Head Start now serves younger children. It is administered by the Administration for Children and Families (ACF) in the Department of Health and Human Services. In 2007, Congress passed the Improving Head Start for School Readiness Act of 2007, which reauthorized Head Start through September 2012. Since then, Congress has increased Head Start funding, but it has not passed new legislation to officially reauthorize it. In addition, the American Recovery and Reinvestment Act (ARRA) of 2009 earmarked $1.1 billion additional funding for the expansion of Head Start and $1.1 billion in funding for Early Head Start.

As of 2011, the National Head Start program has an annual budget of $7 billion and serves 904,153 low-income families. There are 1,604 Head Start programs nationwide, with a total of 18,275 centers and 49,400 classrooms. The average cost per child of the Head Start program is $7,600 annually. Head Start has a paid staff of 220,000 and 1,384,000 volunteers.[40]

The accompanying Applying Research to Practice feature shows how Head Start can increase parents' participation in their children's lives.

Head Start Child Development and Early Learning Framework. The Head Start Child Development and Early Learning Framework in Figure 4.2 shows the domains of school readiness and identifies essential areas of learning and development that shape the Head Start curriculum. This child development and early learning framework is important for you for several reasons.

- It specifies learning outcomes that are essential to children's success in school and life.
- It ensures that all children in Head Start programs work toward the same learning outcomes.
- It impacts what children learn in all preschool programs, not just Head Start.

Eligibility for Head Start Services. To be eligible for Head Start services, children must meet age and family income criteria. Head Start enrolls children ages three to five from low-income families. Income eligibility is determined by whether or not family incomes fall below the official poverty line, which is set annually by the U.S. Department of Health and Human Services.

Ninety percent of Head Start enrollment has to meet the income eligibility criteria. The other 10 percent of enrollment can include children from families that exceed the

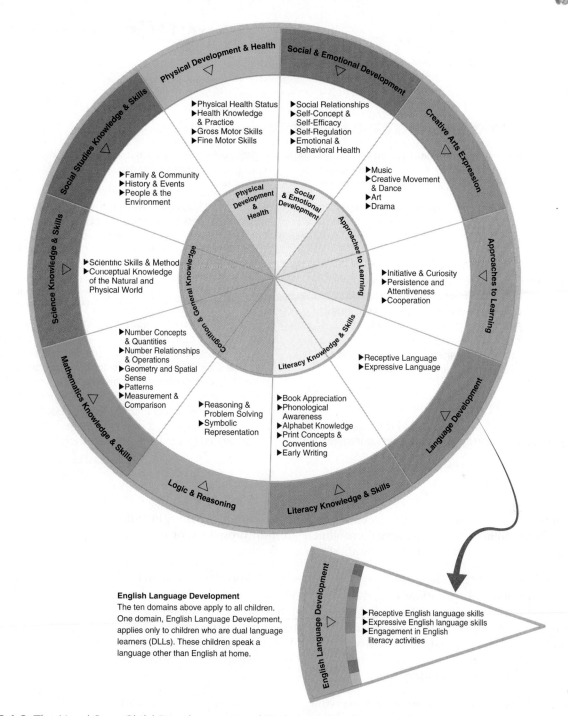

FIGURE 4.2 The Head Start Child Development and Early Learning Framework

The framework represents the foundation of the Head Start Approach to School Readiness. It aligns with and builds from the five essential domains of school readiness identified by the National Education Goals Panel (see inner circle) and lays out essential areas of learning and development. The framework can be used to guide curriculum, implementation, and assessment to plan teaching and learning experiences that align to school readiness goals and track children's progress across developmental domains. The domains and domain elements apply to all three- to five-year-olds in Head Start and other early childhood programs, including dual language learners and children with disabilities.

Source: Department of Health and Human Services www.eclkc.ohs.acf.hhs.gov.

applying research to practice

Head Start Programs Increase Parent Involvement

Researchers gathered information about parents' involvement with their Head Start children. The findings of the study are interesting and revealing. The researchers concluded that:

- Head Start parents read more often and for longer periods of time at each sitting to their children compared to children and parents who are not in Head Start.
- Even after children are no longer attending Head Start, parents appear to "invest" more in their children. This is particularly true for fathers who were not living in the homes of their children. They spent more days visiting their children when their children were enrolled in Head Start as well as after they were no longer enrolled.
- Head Start programs that raised children's cognitive test scores also tended to raise parents' involvement with their children.[41]

SO WHAT DOES THIS MEAN FOR YOU?

What is interesting about this study is that it indicates that as their children do well, parents respond by encouraging their children to do well and spending more time with them. Here are some specific things you can do:

- Encourage your students' parents to volunteer in your program and classroom. As you involve parents in your program, suggest more ways for them to be more involved in their children's lives at home. As parents are more involved with their children, children's achievement increases.
- Share children's achievements with parents and thank and praise parents for their involvement and encouragement of their children's achievements. Parents, in turn, will invest more time, effort, and energy in helping their children succeed.
- The researchers speculate that one of the reasons Head Start parents spent more time with (invested in) their children is because their children were more pleasant to be with. You should consider how you can make your children more pleasant to be with. Some strategies: teach children behavioral control, teach manners, and get children involved in community service acts. Remember, every parent wants a child who is a "winner." As children do better, parents tend to like them more!

low-income guidelines. In addition, 10 percent of a program's enrollment must include children with disabilities. Often, the actual enrollment in local programs for children with disabilities surpasses the 10 percent requirement.

Improving Head Start. The Improving Head Start for School Readiness Act of 2007 increased teacher qualifications by requiring that 50 percent of Head Start teachers nationwide have a minimum of a baccalaureate degree in early childhood education or a related field by 2013. It also requires Head Start programs to develop career ladders and annual professional development plans for full-time staff. Also, it requires that all Head Start programs use research-based practices to support the growth of children's preliteracy and vocabulary skills.

Head Start Research. A question that everyone always asks is, "Do Head Start and Early Head Start programs work?" By *work*, people generally mean, "Do these programs deliver the services they are authorized and funded to deliver, and do these services make a difference in the lives of children and families?"

Over the last decade, the federal government has been aggressive in attempting to ensure that the programs it funds provide results. Consequently, we have seen a tremendous increase in federal monies allocated for research of federally funded programs and a corresponding increase in the number of research studies designed to measure the effectiveness of those programs.

The 2010 Head Start Impact Study reveals these results:

- **_Head Start access._** Access to Head Start has positive impacts on children's preschool experiences and school readiness:
  - For the four-year-old group, progress by the end of the Head Start year concentrates on language and literacy, including positive improvements in vocabulary, letter-word identification, spelling, pre-academic skills, color identification, letter naming, and parent-reported emergent literacy.
  - For the three-year-old group, benefits include improvements in vocabulary, letter-word identification, pre-academic skills, letter naming, elision (phonological processing or understanding letter and word sound), parent-reported emergent literacy, perceptual motor skills and prewriting, and applied problem-solving (math).
  - Children attending Head Start show greater cognitive progress than the control group children. Three-year-old children who had attended Head Start demonstrated modest gains in language, literacy, prewriting, and math skills. Four-year-old children demonstrated modest gains in language and literacy skills.[42]
- **_Cognitive impacts._** By the end of first grade, only a single cognitive impact was found for each group. Children who attended Head Start as three- and four-year-old children do significantly better on vocabulary.[43]

While the overall results of the Head Start Impact Study are generally positive, the big issue is the "fade-out" effect of Head Start benefits to children at the end of first grade. The fade-out effect refers to the fact that for some early childhood programs the benefits children receive in a particular program tend to decrease or "fade out" over time, generally after a year or two. So, positive outcomes for children such as enhanced vocabulary, increased reading and math readiness, and increased school readiness skills tend to fade out as children progress through kindergarten and first grade. Many early childhood professionals believe that the causes of the fade out include a lack of continuity of program services from preschool to kindergarten to first grade; a lack of high-quality teachers who have high achievement standards for all children in kindergarten and first grade; and poor-quality schools. We will hear much about the pros and cons of the long-term benefits of Head Start in the years to come.

New Guidelines for Renewal of Head Start and Early Head Start Grants.
Beginning in November 2011, all of the nation's 1,600 Head Start and Early Head Start programs had to meet new performance criteria in order to have their grants renewed. Each Head Start program had to develop school readiness goals, including the expectations of children's status across the domains of language and literacy, cognition and general knowledge, approaches to learning, physical well-being, motor development, and social and emotional development, that will improve their readiness for kindergarten.[44] Each Head Start's program's classroom quality is measured by the Classroom Assessment Scoring System™ (CLASS™), an observational tool that provides a common lens and language focused on what matters—the classroom interactions that boost student learning.[45]

Head Start programs that do not measure up the standards as measured by CLASS will not have their grants renewed. This is a historic event in the more than forty-seven-year history of the Head Start program. This is the first time that Head Start programs have had to prove that they prepare their children for kindergarten in order to keep and/or have their grants renewed.

Head Start has always been and remains a program for children of poverty. Although it currently reaches a significant number of poor children, increasing federal support for Head Start will likely increase the number of poor children served. However, we must keep in mind that the federal government is using Head Start to reform all of early childhood education. Federal officials believe that the changes they make in the Head Start curriculum—what and how teachers teach and how Head Start operates—will serve as a model for other programs as well.

Early Head Start

Early Head Start (EHS), created in 1995, is designed to promote healthy prenatal outcomes for pregnant women, enhance the development of very young children (birth through age three), and promote healthy family functioning. Early Head Start enrolls pregnant women. When the child is born, the mother is provided family services. As with Head Start, EHS is a program for low-income families who meet federal poverty guidelines. Currently, 10 percent of the overall Head Start budget is used to serve low-income families with infants and toddlers through the Early Head Start program. EHS serves about 64,000 infants and toddlers.[46] In addition, the American Recovery and Reinvestment Act of 2009 allocated $1.1 billion for Early Head Start. EHS program services include quality early education both in and out of the home; parenting education; comprehensive health and mental health services, including services to women before, during, and after pregnancy; nutrition education; and family support services.

Head Start's entry into the field of infant/toddler care and education has achieved several things. It has given Head Start an opportunity to work with a long-neglected age and socioeconomic population. As the public schools have enrolled preschoolers at an accelerated rate, the infant/toddler field gives Head Start a new group to serve. It has enabled Early Head Start to be a leader in the field of infant/toddler education. Without a doubt, EHS has been a pioneer and catalyst in providing high-quality programs for infants and toddlers.

EARLY CHILDHOOD PROGRAMS AND YOU

As an early childhood teacher, it is important for you to know about various programs for young children. Knowing about programs will enable you to talk knowledgably with colleagues and parents and will enable you to critically compare and contrast features of one program with another. As you engage in this critical analysis you will be able to identify what you think are the strengths and weaknesses of each program and what features of each program you like the best. Knowing about early childhood programs enables you to always be clear about what you believe is best for children and families and to think, talk, and act as a confident professional.

The Politics of Early Childhood Education

As you learn more about early childhood education, you will learn that early childhood and its programs are very politicized. The politics of early childhood programs revolve around issues of which programs are most effective for which children, and which programs are capable of supporting children's learning so that they are ready for school and life. Today, the purposes of early childhood programs go far beyond merely educating young children. The purposes of early childhood programs also include developing curricula for closing the achievement gaps between African American and Hispanic American children and their white counterparts, getting children ready for school, and laying the foundation for a well-prepared workforce. During the Great Recession beginning in 2008, the United States went through a very difficult economic time. Early childhood programs became more essential to the politicians and the public. Early childhood programs were then and are seen today as a way of enabling the United States to recover economically and to play a major role on the world's economic stage.

ACTIVITIES FOR PROFESSIONAL DEVELOPMENT

ethical dilemma

"Why can't Wally come to class?"

Kindergarten teacher Alisha Seymour was excited to learn that six-year-old Stevie Kiflinger and his service dog, Wally, would join her class at the beginning of the week. However, Alisha's excitement turned to outrage several days later when her principal told her that Stevie would be coming to her classroom without Wally. When Alisha asked why Wally wouldn't be accompanying Stevie, the principal said that Wally was not a certified dog through Assistance Dogs International. The principal explained that school policy specifically stated that all assistance dogs must be certified by Assistance Dogs International. However, Wally is certified through Assistance Dogs for Life. "I don't believe this!" exclaimed Alisha. "I just read a research study about how service dogs lower stress in children, especially children like Stevie who has epilepsy. The findings also show that the use of therapy dogs for epileptic children may be an effective way to decrease their anxiety."[47]

What should Alisha do? Should she accept the school policy and do nothing? Should she defy school board policy and let Wally come to school with Stevie? Or should she organize her friends and co-workers through Facebook and other social media to try to change the policy? What should Alisha do? What would you do?

Application Activities

1. As an early childhood professional, you will need to make decisions about what to teach and how to teach it. Choose one of the programs you read about in this chapter and explain how you would implement it in your classroom. Blog on your class discussion board and give five examples of how you would implement the program in the classroom. Post your views and ask for comments.

2. In your profession, you will need to be able to find ways to work with children and families with different lifestyles and work schedules. As a childcare provider, think of three ways you can meet the needs of families who begin work early and families who work after the traditional 5 p.m. closing time of many businesses. Discuss three ideas with your classmates.

3. Think back to your own experiences in child care and/or elementary school classrooms. What were three characteristics that made them high or below-average in quality? Based on what you read in your textbook and on your research on the Internet, identify three ways that you would recommend to make any child care or elementary school classroom more pleasant, safe, supportive, and healthy. Share these ideas with your classmates.

4. Review in the chapter the HighScope, Montessori, and Reggio Emilia models of teaching. Go online and find an example of each progam. Determine how the programs that you selected do or don't implement the basic features of each model. Discuss this with your classmates.

5. Federal programs play an important part in funding, maintaining, and regulating early childhood education. Go back in the chapter and review the Applying Research to Practice: Head Start Programs Increase Parent Involvement feature. How can you use federal programs like Head Start to increase parents' involvement with their children's learning? Share your opinions with friends and classmates on Facebook and on your online class discussion board and see what your friends and classmates think.

6. There are many different kinds of early childhood programs, and it will be your job to be familiar with them. Look online for three different kinds of early childhood programs other than those discussed in this chapter. Assess the strengths and weaknesses of each one. Share your results with your classmates and ask for comments and opinions.

Linking to Learning

The Project Approach

www.projectapproach.org
Provides information about Project Approach and how you can implement its practices in your classroom. Offers an array of project examples to use for inclusion in the classroom, according to grade level.

Reggio Emilia Approach—The Preschool Child's Languages of Learning

www.reggioemiliaapproach.net
Contains information and resources related to the Reggio Emilia approach, history, and learning environment.

HighScope Educational Research Foundation

www.highscope.org
Official site for the HighScope Educational Research Foundation. Provides information on HighScope curriculum, assessment, and research as well as e-tools, lists of trainings and conferences, and an online store for purchasing HighScope classroom materials.

MyEducationLab

Go to Topic 5 (Program Models) in the MyEducationLab (www.myeducationlab.com) for your course, where you can:

- Find learning outcomes for Program Models along with the national standards that connect to these outcomes.

- Complete Assignments and Activities that can help you more deeply understand the chapter content.

- Apply and practice your understanding of the core teaching skills identified in the chapter with the Building Teaching Skills and Dispositions learning units.

- Check your comprehension on the content covered in the chapter by going to the Study Plan in the Book Resources for your text. Here you will be able to take a chapter quiz, receive feedback on your answers, and then access Review, Practice, and Enrichment activities to enhance your understanding of chapter content.

chapter 5

TEACHING WITH STANDARDS

Supporting Children's Learning

NAEYC Standards for Early Childhood Professional Preparation

Standard 4: Using Developmentally Effective Approaches to Connect with Children and Families

I understand and use positive relationships and supportive interactions as the foundations for my work with young children. I know, understand, and use a wide array of developmentally appropriate approaches, instructional strategies, and tools to connect with children and families and positively influence each child's development and learning.[1]

Standard 5: Using Content Knowledge to Build Meaningful Curriculum

I understand the importance of developmental domains and academic (or content) disciplines in early childhood curriculum. I know the essential concepts, inquiry tools, and structure of content areas, including academic subjects, and can identify resources to deepen their understanding. I use my own knowledge and other resources to design, implement, and evaluate meaningful, challenging curriculum that promotes comprehensive development and learning outcomes for every young child.[2]

WHEN I VISIT early childhood classrooms and ask teachers, "What are you teaching?" I get a lot of different responses. Some teachers reply that they teach about "animals" or "holidays." Others respond that they are teaching "themes," "social skills," and "beginning reading." But what are these teachers really teaching their children? And more importantly, what are the children learning?

Have you asked yourself, "What should I teach?" How do *you* answer this question? Perhaps you reply that you will teach your children reading, writing, and mathematics. But let's look at your answer for a minute. What reading skills will you teach? Will you teach phonics? Word meaning? Vocabulary development? In what order will you teach these skills? To what achievement level will you teach them? These questions are not easily answered, and not all teachers answer them the same way. These are some of the many reasons we have standards.

standards Statements of what pre-K–12 students should know and be able to do.

Standards, statements of what students should know and be able to do, help answer questions about what to teach children and what they should learn. Local, state, and national standards help to answer the questions, "What should students learn?" and "What should I teach?" Chapter 8, "The Preschool Years," discusses *early learning guidelines,* which influence what teachers of children younger than age 5 need to consider as they create environments and curriculum plans for young children. This chapter focuses primarily on the Common Core Standards for children in grades K–3.

FOUNDATIONS OF THE STANDARDS MOVEMENT

The standards movement is a little over thirty years old. Not long in the time-line of major events in the history of education, but tremendously influential in its impact on the future of education in the twenty-first century. Three federal initiatives have played a tremendous role in the development and implementation of the current standards movement:

- ***A Nation at Risk: The Imperative for Educational Reform, National Commission on Excellence in Education (1983).*** The U.S. Department of Education created the National Commission on Excellence in Education to provide a report about the quality of education in America. The commission recommended, among other things, curriculum reform, more rigorous and measurable standards, and higher expectations for the nation's students.[3]

- ***Goals 2000: Educate America Act (2000).*** This act was designed to ensure that all students reached high levels of achievement. Goals 2000 established eight national education goals. Goal three specified that by the year 2000, "All students will leave grades 4, 8, and 12 having demonstrated competency over challenging subject matter including English, mathematics, science, foreign languages, civics and government, economics, the arts, history, and geography, and every school in America will ensure that all students learn to use their minds well, so they may be prepared for responsible citizenship, further learning, and productive employment in our nation's modern economy."[4] Goal four of this act stated that by the year 2000, U.S. students would be first in the world in science and mathematics achievements.

- ***No Child Left Behind Act (2001).*** The former Elementary and Secondary Education Act of 1965 was rechristened the No Child Left Behind Act (NCLB), and it is currently the main federal law affecting education from kindergarten through high school. NCLB is built on four principles: accountability for results, more choices for parents, greater local control and flexibility, and an emphasis on doing what works based on scientific research.[5] NCLB mandates goals for improving education in elementary, middle, and high schools by setting high expectations for students, teachers, and administrators of each state with the result of greater educational achievement for all students.[6]

No Child Left Behind

The No Child Left Behind Act of 2001 is intended to significantly reform K–12 education. It changes the federal government's role in K–12 education by asking America's schools to base their success on what children learn. Since its passage, it has radically and rapidly changed how America conducts its educational business. NCLB emphasizes state and district accountability, mandates state standards for what children should know and be able to do, puts in place a comprehensive program of testing in grades three to twelve, and encourages schools to use teaching methods that have research evidence demonstrating their ability to help children learn.

NCLB stresses that school districts must use federal dollars on "programs that work," also referred to as scientifically based or research-based programs that demonstrate that they can increase student achievement.

MyEducationLab

Visit the MyEducationLab for *Fundamentals of Early Childhood Education* to enhance your understanding of chapter concepts with a personalized Study Plan. You'll also have the opportunity to hone your teaching skills through video-based Assignments and Activities as well as Building Teaching Skills and Dispositions lessons.

FOCUS QUESTIONS

1. What are the foundations for the standards movement?

2. What are the Common Core Standards (CCS)?

3. Why are the Common Core Standards important?

4. How are Common Core Standards changing teaching and learning?

5. How are Common Core Standards and curriculum materials related?

6. What are issues associated with Common Core Standards?

scientifically based programs *or* research-based programs Programs based on scientific research that demonstrates they can increase student achievement.

NCLB targets six fundamental areas:

- Stronger accountability for results
- An emphasis on academics, especially literacy and reading
- An emphasis on teaching methods and curriculum programs that work, based on scientific research
- Ongoing professional development to provide behavior, knowledge, and instructional strategies necessary to help each child learn
- The implementation of technology into the teaching–learning process
- Expanded options for parental involvement[7]

NCLB will continue to influence what and how you teach for many years to come. The act has influenced pre-kindergarten education because of its major emphasis on getting children ready for school. Many federally funded programs now use guidelines and mandates in the No Child Left Behind Act to develop goals and objectives for their own programs. In other words, all facets of programs that serve young children have been and will continue to be influenced by NCLB.

It is fair to say that NCLB is a law that the majority of education professionals love to hate. Many educators and the public oppose some of the provisions of NCLB, especially those that relate to testing. Critics of NCLB argue that the focus on assessment encourages teachers to teach a narrow range of skills. In addition, they argue that students are subjected to too much testing. Table 5.1 shows some pros and cons for NCLB as it now exists. NCLB was due to be reauthorized seven different times (in 2002, 2004, 2006, 2007, 2008, 2009, and 2010).[8] However, because of political differences regarding how much testing is too much testing, how to appropriately evaluate and reward teachers, and the basic purposes of school reform, Congress has been unwilling to arrive at the compromises necessary to pass a new NCLB act.

What Is the Future of NCLB?

It is likely that Congress will eventually reauthorize NCLB in some form, most likely with a new name. The federal Department of Education supports the law's focus on high standards and school and state accountability for student achievement. However, it wants to make the testing provision of the law less punitive and will push for a new version of the law.[9] Draft revisions of NCLB reveal that a new revision of NCLB would eliminate the provisions of the law that use standardized test scores in reading and math to label tens of thousands of public schools as failing.[10] Keep in mind that draft revisions of NCLB are just that and that we will not know the provisions of the law until it is finished several years from now. Whatever happens, it seems certain that federal initiatives on standards and accountability will continue to have a powerful influence on early childhood programs.

NCLB Waiver Plans. In the meantime, while the public schools wait for Congress to act, the U.S. Department of Education is granting waivers to states in exchange for promises to improve how they prepare and evaluate students. These waivers give flexibility with federal funds and NCLB's one-size-fits-all mandate. As a result, districts are able to tailor solutions to meet their unique educational needs.

Common Core Standards (CCS)

All fifty states have state standards for what their students should know and do. Educators, politicians, and the public, however, realize that what students learn depends on where they live. State standards are not uniform across states. What students learn in California is not necessarily what children learn in New York. The public's

TABLE 5.1 Pros and Cons of NCLB

Pros	Cons
NCLB sets accountability standards, which are measured annually by each state to guide educational growth and achievement. Results about how well students and schools perform are reported to parents and the public.	The federal government underfunds NCLB, but states have to comply with all provisions of NCLB in order to receive federal funding. NCLB rewards schools that score well on standardized tests; therefore, teachers are forced to teach a narrow set of test-taking skills and test a limited range of knowledge.
	In efforts to ensure that children do well on tests, too much time is spent on testing, teaching to the test, and teaching children how to take tests, frequently referred to as "test beating."
NCLB emphasizes math and reading achievement.	Focus on reading and math "narrows" the curriculum. Other subjects such as the arts don't get the attention they need and deserve.
	Schools whose students don't make "adequate yearly progress" can be shut down.
	NCLB sets impossibly high standards for many children to meet.
NCLB links state academic content with student educational outcomes and requires school improvement to be implemented using "scientifically based research."	Emphasis on "scientifically based" curriculum takes away from teachers' creativity and using other curriculum materials.
NCLB measures education status and growth by ethnicity and helps close the achievement gap between white and minority students.	
All children including children with disabilities are held to high standards and achievement.	Not all children, especially ones with disabilities and ELLs, are able to meet the same standards.
NCLB sets standards for qualifications and certification. All teachers are to be highly qualified.	

desire for uniformity among state standards laid the foundation for Common Core State Standards.

Additional reasons for the development and implementation of national standards include the following:

- The Great Recession of 2008–2012 further documented the need for a well-trained workforce. Leaders of businesses and industry have complained that they cannot find the highly skilled and educated workers they need to compete nationally and internationally. Business leaders look to the public schools for well-educated workers. They want the schools to beef up their standards and teaching and provide highly educated students for the workforce of today and tomorrow.

- The United States has consistently ranked behind other nations in test scores of reading and mathematics, as shown in Figure 5.1.[11] Politicians believe the lack of U.S. student achievement is a threat to national security and is eroding U.S. global economic and political influence.

All of the above set the stage for the development of national Common Core Standards.

Implementing Common Core Standards. The National Governors Association (NGA) and the Chief Council of State School Officers (CCSSO) launched the Common Core State Standards initiative (also known as the Common Core Standards), a state-led effort to construct national academic standards that would

FIGURE 5.1 International Comparison Rankings in Test Scores of Reading and Mathematics

prepare students for success in higher education and future careers. In 2014 and 2015, two assessment agencies will begin administering tests, replacing old state exams to review whether teachers and students are meeting the goals of the Common Core Standards.[12]

WHAT ARE COMMON CORE STANDARDS (CCS)?

Common Core Standards
The Common Core State Standards provide a consistent, clear understanding of what students are expected to learn, so teachers and parents know what they need to do to help them.

The **Common Core Standards** are national benchmarks in math and English created to have uniformity no matter where students attend public schools. They are part of a state-led effort to give all students the skills and knowledge they need to succeed. The federal government was not involved in the development of the standards. Individual states choose whether or not to participate in and adopt these standards. In 2010, the final version of the CCS was released to the public and the Validation Committee published its final report. This report stated:

> The Common Core State Standards are based on best practices in national and international education, as well as research and input from numerous sources. . . . The Common Core State Standards represent what American students need to know and do to be successful in college and careers. Once the standards are adopted and implemented, states will determine how best to measure and hold students accountable for meeting these standards.[13]

There are many good arguments for adopting the CCS. In particular, they:

- Provide clarity about what students are expected to learn in mathematics and English language arts.
- Help teachers zero in on the most important knowledge and skills.
- Establish shared goals among students, parents, and teachers.
- Help states and districts assess the effectiveness of schools and classrooms and give all students an equal opportunity for high achievement.[14]

The CCS focus heavily on the skills needed to be prepared for careers and for college. That's the perspective teacher Christie Neise has about the new curriculum, as well. "We've been doing this already," says the kindergarten teacher at Northmore Elementary in West Palm Beach, Florida, during training on the new curriculum. "The focus will just have to be a little sharper."[15]

CCS Mission Statement

The Common Core Standards mission statement clearly states their intended purposes. They are to provide a consistent, clear understanding of what students are expected to learn, so teachers and parents know what they need to do to help them. The standards are designed to be robust and relevant to the real world, reflecting the knowledge and skills that young people need for success in college and careers. With American students fully prepared for the future, our communities will be best positioned to compete successfully in the global economy.[16]

The CCS define the knowledge and skills students should have in their K–12 education careers so that they will graduate from high school able to succeeed in entry-level, credit-bearing academic college courses and in workforce training programs. The standards:

- Are aligned with college and work expectations.
- Are clear, understandable, and consistent.
- Include rigorous content and application of knowledge through higher-order skills.
- Build upon strengths and lessons of current state standards.
- Are informed by other top-performing countries, so that all students are prepared to succeed in our global economy and society.
- Are evidence based.[17]

As we discuss standards, keep in mind that constitutionally, the responsibility of education rests with the states. So this explains why states have taken the lead in developing national standards for what students should know and do.

WHY ARE COMMON CORE STANDARDS IMPORTANT?

By now, you have gained a pretty good idea that standards are playing an important role in the lives of children, teachers, families, and administrators. Let's examine some of the reasons for the prominent and important role standards have in education today.

Identify What Children Should Know

The Common Core Standards identify what every child in every state and in every school district should know and be able to do. This is significant in that, with CCS, the expectations are the same for all children, regardless of their socioeconomic backgrounds, their culture, their race or ethnicity, their abilities and disabilities, or where they go to school. In this sense, standards level the educational playing field and help ensure that all students learn the same content and will achieve at a high level. Implementing standards is one way to help close the achievement gap. Read the accompanying Diversity Tie-In feature for steps on what you can do to help close the achievement gap.

diversity tie-in

Closing the Achievement Gap with Standards

There's a lot of discussion today about the education achievement gap. The achievement gap is the difference between what certain groups of children know and are able to do as opposed to what other social and ethnic groups of children know and are able to do. The achievement gap is wide between white children and black and Latino children. Consider this example:

> The 26-point reading achievement gap between white and Hispanic fourth-graders in 2007 was not significantly different from the 25-point gap in 2009. The reading achievement gap between Black and White 4th-grade students in 2009 (–26 points) was not measurably different from the gap in 2007.[18]

CCS are often cited as one way that teachers and schools can help all children learn what they need to know, and as a result close the achievement gap. Certainly CCS do play a role in helping close achievement gaps; however, standards by themselves cannot close achievement gaps. A number of other things are required, including the following:

- **Programs for young children at an early age** that will help them gain the knowledge, skills, and behaviors necessary for them to enter school and be successful.

- **A highly effective teacher** who is well prepared to teach all children regardless of diversity and socioeconomic background and who can help all children achieve at least one grade level at the end of the school year.[19]
- **Parent education programs** designed to help parents gain the knowledge and skills that will help them help their children get ready to learn before they come to school. Parents are the most important part of a child's education and are essential to a child's well-being and school achievement.[20]

In addition, here are some things you can do to make sure that you help all young children learn, and as a result, eliminate achievement gaps:

- **Be familiar with the Common Core Standards.** These standards are important because they outline what each and every child should know and be able to do, not just some children.
- **Develop your lesson plans and teaching activities so that they incorporate the CCS**, and focus on the essential knowledge, skills, and behaviors that all children need to know. The 5-E lesson plan, an instructional model based on the constructivist theory in which teachers involve children in five phases of learning—engage, explore,

Provide a Basis for Reform and Accountability

Standards help the public and politicians hold teachers and schools accountable for ensuring that children learn. As pointed out earlier, using standards as a basis for accountability, teachers can no longer say, "I taught Maria reading." Now the question is: "Did Maria learn to read?" Even more important from an accountability point of view is the question: "Did Maria achieve the benchmark of being able to read at or above her grade level?"

Allow Federal and State Control of Education

Primarily, education is a state function. Historically, states have delegated the responsibility for education to local districts and programs. However, beginning in about 1995, states have increasingly taken more control for educating children, monitoring teaching, and holding schools accountable for student achievement. CCS are one way to achieve this goal. Not everyone is happy or satisfied with this state and federal control of education, for a number of reasons. First, they claim that it takes away from the ability of local programs to develop their own curriculum based on what they think is best for their children. Essentially this is a local control of schools idea and is

explain, elaborate and evaluate—is my lesson plan of choice for my students and me, and I encourage you to learn to plan using the 5-E model.

- **In your planning, focus on what your children will be tested on** at the end of the year. You and other teachers should not "teach to the test"; however, you need to be aware of what your children will be tested on.
- **Differentiate your instruction** so that you can provide for the diverse learning needs of all your students. One instructional approach does not fit all, and in today's educational environment increasing numbers of teachers differentiate their instruction to help ensure that all students learn. Here are some ways to differentiate instruction:

  - **Use reading buddies.** Reading buddies don't have to be at the same reading level. What is important is that children are reading away from the teacher and are having opportunities to read.
  - **Group children for instructional purposes** based on the skills they know and need to learn.
  - **Provide children with different levels of instructional materials.**
  - **Provide individual instruction to children who need help,** such as struggling readers.
  - **Use peer teaching.** Children learn from each other and they love to help others. Remember what Vygotsky said about "competent others" providing assistance in the zone of proximal development.

- **Make the best use of your classroom time for instructional purposes.** When children are meaningfully engaged in learning activities, there is a better chance for them to learn what they need to know and do. Remember that you have a limited amount of time with children, so strive to make the best use of it. At the same time, your teaching should be developmentally appropriate and children should be involved in activities they find interesting and worthwhile. Keep in mind that children need opportunities to play and interact with each other.
- Integrate technology into your teaching and learning. Children enjoy technology, and technology adds interest to their learning. At the same time, it can help children learn what the standards specify.
- **Work with families and parents** to help them understand what you are teaching their children and why. Seek family members' cooperation so they can help support and encourage in the home what you are teaching in the classroom. Sending simple lessons home, such as a packet of learning activities that children and family members can do together, helps involve parents in the teaching–learning process and impresses on them and their children the importance of school achievement. One first grade teacher sends home each night a book bag containing books for children to read with their parents. Also included in the book bag is an evaluation sheet for the parents and students to fill out regarding the time they spent reading together and what parents believe are areas in which their children might need help.

Closing the achievement gap between cultures, races, and socioeconomic groups is an ongoing process, but it is one to which you must dedicate yourself. After all, helping all children succeed is why we teach and is what we dedicate our lives to.

embedded in the belief that local communities know what is best for their children. Second, some early childhood educators believe that state and federal control leads to the implementation of programs that are developmentally inappropriate for young children, especially preschool and kindergarten children. However, standards are now a part of the political and educational landscape.

differentiate Teaching so that you can provide for the diverse learning needs of your students.

Meet the Educational Needs of Low-Achieving Students

CCS are considered to be the minimum necessary for grade-level achievement. In this way, they help ensure that all children will be taught what they need to know to accomplish the skills appropriate for their grade level. There has always been a concern that low-socioeconomic-status children are not being taught or challenged to achieve. Teaching to the CCS addresses this issue and hopefully helps to prevent failure and school dropout.

Integrate Use of Technology

Integrating technology into the curriculum is another way to align CCS, teaching, and learning. Technology is also a developmentally appropriate way to assess young children and measure their achievement. The accompanying Technology Tie-In feature helps you get a feeling for how one elementary school integrates technology across the curriculum to help children meet all state standards.

Provide Clarity and Focus

CCS enables you to know what schools expect of their children and teachers. In this regard, they bring clarity and focus to the program curriculum and teaching. In order to know what skills need to be aligned with each other to produce the best learning experience for the child, CCS identify the knowledge that needs to be taught. For example, Table 5.2 demonstrates the reading standards for kindergarten and second

TABLE 5.2 Common Core Standards for English Language Arts, Reading, and Literature in Kindergarten and Second Grade

	Key Ideas and Details	Craft and Structure	Integration of Knowledge and Ideas	Range of Reading and Level of Text Complexity
Kindergarten	• With prompting and support, ask and answer questions about key details in a text. • With prompting and support, retell familiar stories, including key details. • With prompting and support, identify characters, settings, and major events in a story	• Ask and answer questions about unknown words in a text. • Recognize common types of texts (e.g., storybooks, poems). • With prompting and support, name the author and illustrator of a story and define the role of each in telling the story.	• With prompting and support, describe the relationship between illustrations and the story in which they appear (e.g., what moment in a story an illustration depicts). • With prompting and support, compare and contrast the adventures and experiences of characters in familiar stories.	• Actively engage in group reading activities with purpose and understanding.
Grade 2	• Ask and answer such questions as *who, what, where, when, why,* and *how* to demonstrate understanding of key details in a text. • Recount stories, including fables and folktales from diverse cultures, and determine their central message, lesson, or moral. • Describe how characters in a story respond to major events and challenges.	• Describe how words and phrases (e.g., regular beats, alliteration, rhymes, repeated lines) supply rhythm and meaning in a story, poem, or song. • Describe the overall structure of a story, including describing how the beginning introduces the story and the ending concludes the action. • Acknowledge differences in the points of view of characters, including by speaking in a different voice for each character when reading dialogue aloud.	• Use information gained from the illustration and words in a print or digital text to demonstrate understanding of its characters, setting, or plot. • Compare and contrast two or more versions of the same story (e.g., Cinderella stories) by different authors or from different cultures.	• By the end of the year, read and comprehend literature, including stories and poetry, in the grades 2–3 text complexity band proficiently, with scaffolding as needed at the high end of the range.

Source: Common Core Standards for English Language Arts, Reading, and Literature in Kindergarten and Second Grade, © Copyright 2010. National Governors Association, Center for Best Practices, and Council of Chief State School Officers. All rights reserved.

grade and Table 5.3 shows the mathematics standards for grades one and three. They show that students need to know how to ask and answer questions like *who, what, when, where, why,* and *how*. Teacher Wendy Loeb in Buffalo Grove, Illinois, takes the results from her daily assessment tests and uses these data to see which students are having difficulty in the five "W" questions (Who? What? When? Where? Why?). This enables her to plan the level and kinds of intervention individual students need.[21]

TABLE 5.3 Common Core Standard for Mathematics Grades 1 and 3

	Operations and Algebraic Thinking	Number and Operations in Base Ten	Measurement and Data	Geometry	Mathematical Practices
Grade 1	• Represent and solve problems involving addition and subtraction. • Understand properties of multiplication and the relationship between addition and subtraction. • Add and subtract within 100. • Work with addition and subtraction equations.	• Use place value understanding and properties to add and subtract. • Understand place value. • Extend the counting sequence	• Measure lengths indirectly and by iterating length units. • Tell and write time. • Represent and interpret data.	• Reason with shapes and their attributes.	• Make sense of problems and persevere in solving them. • Reason abstractly and quantitatively. • Construct viable arguments and critique the reasoning of others. • Model with mathematics. • Use appropriate tools strategically. • Attend to precision.
Grade 3	• Represent and solve problems involving multiplication and division. • Understand properties of multiplication and the relationship between multiplication and division. • Multiply and divide within 100. • Solve problems involving the four operations, and identify and explain patterns in arithmetic.	• Use place value understanding and properties to perform multidigit arithmetic.	• Solve problems involving measurement and estimation of intervals of time, liquid volumes, and masses of objects. • Geometric Measurement: Understand concepts of area and relate area to multiplication and to addition. • Geometric Measurement: Recognize perimeter as an attribute of plane figures and distinguish between linear and area measures.	• Reason with shapes and their attributes.	• Look for and make use of structure. • Look for and express regularity in repeated reasoning.

Source: Common Core Standard for Mathematics in Grades 1 and 3, © Copyright 2010. National Governors Association, Center for Best Practices, and Council of Chief State School Officers. All rights reserved.

Integrate Concepts

By knowing the CCS, you can integrate concepts, ideas, and skills into your teaching. For example, if you are a preschool teacher, knowing about kindergarten standards enables you to provide your preschoolers with the language, literacy, and math skills they must have for a successful transition to kindergarten. It is important for you and other professionals to know what is expected of children at each grade level, pre-K–3, so that you can ensure your children are well prepared for learning in the next grade.

Provide Accountability

Standards serve as one means by which states and local programs can be accountable for teaching and learning. Accountability implies that all students will achieve what the standards specify, leading to greater focus on student achievement. At the same time, advocates of greater accountability believe that more focus on student achievement for all students will narrow and hopefully eliminate the achievement gaps between races and socioeconomic classes.

All of the above reasons point to the fact that standards are an essential part of early childhood today. Hardly a teacher or classroom in the country is not impacted in some way by standards.

HOW ARE COMMON CORE STANDARDS CHANGING TEACHING AND LEARNING?

As indicators of what children should know and be able to do, standards are changing the ways teachers teach, how and what students learn, and the ways schools operate. Let's review some of the ways standards are shaping teaching and learning.

Teacher Roles

Standards have transformed (some would say reformed) teaching from an input model to an output model. As a result, teachers are no longer able to say, "I taught Mario the use of structural cues to decode words." Now the questions are, "Is Mario able to use and apply decoding skills?" and "Will Mario do well on decoding skills on the state test?" Good teachers have good ideas about what and how to teach, and they always will. However, increasing requirements to teach to the standards and teach so that students will master the standards reduces the time and opportunity to act on those good ideas.

Curriculum Alignment

Increasing student achievement is at the center of the standards movement. Policy makers and educators view standards, tests, and teaching alignment as a viable and practical way to help ensure student achievement. **Alignment** is the arrangement of standards, curriculum, and tests so that they complement one another. In other words, the curriculum should be based on what the standards say students should know and be able to do; tests should measure what the standards indicate. **Curriculum alignment** is the process of making sure that what is taught—the content of the curriculum—matches what the standards say students should know and be able to do.

Data-Driven Instruction and the Outcomes of Standards and Testing

Accountability initiatives, including No Child Left Behind, have brought about a shift in focus from covering subject matter to meeting the needs of each student. There is

alignment The process of making sure that the curriculum and what teachers teach are what the standards specify.

curriculum alignment The process of matching curriculum to the standards and tests that measure student achievement.

only one way to determine whether or not the needs of the students are being met: through an ongoing analysis of data collected from assessing children. In data-driven instruction, teaching decisions are based on the analysis of assessment data to make decisions about how to best meet the instructional needs of each child. To use data-driven instruction, start by analyzing existing data on each student from their cumulative record files to get a general profile of each student. Then, align objectives to assessments by planning collaboratively with your grade-level colleagues to determine when you will be teaching district and state standards and how you will assess each standard. Next, gather data by using formal assessments, informal assessments, and technology. After gathering data, use it to guide your next steps in the instructional process. Which students are ready to move on? Which students need remediation? Which students need enrichment? Just remember that making data-based decisions to guide instruction is an ongoing process. You should be constantly assessing, analyzing, and adjusting throughout the school year.[22]

> **data-driven instruction** Teaching decisions are based on the analysis of assessment data to make decisions about how to best meet the instructional needs of each child.

Intentional Teaching

Intentional teaching is the process of teaching children with knowledge and purpose to ensure that young children acquire the knowledge, behaviors and skills they need for success. Intentional teachers create environments, consider the curriculum and tailor it to children as individuals, plan learning experiences, and interact with children and families with purposefulness and thoughtfulness.[23] Intentional teachers, intentionally and with purpose, plan lessons, teach, and assess in order to assure that their students are learning the Common Core Standards and achieving at high levels.

> **intentional teaching** The process of teaching children with knowledge and purpose to ensure that young children acquire the knowledge, behaviors, and skills they need for success.

Expectations of What Teachers Should Teach

When teachers ask, "What should I teach?" CCS and local standards help answer their question. However, good teachers teach more than the standards. They also teach an essential core of knowledge and skills that provides direction for the curriculum. Additionally, teachers teach individual children, plan for individual children's needs, and make decisions about what and how they should teach them. Therefore, CCS serve as the baseline of expectations for teaching and learning. In this regard, standards give teachers a shared framework, based on developmentally appropriate practice, of what they should teach to children and how we know through their learning that they are growing socially, emotionally, physically, and academically. The Professionalism in Practice feature, Five Essential Steps for Implementing the Common Core Standards, explains standards and how to better understand them.

> In this **video**, two teachers share their thoughts about common core standards and their teaching experiences using standards.

COMMON CORE STANDARDS AND CURRICULUM MATERIALS

Think for a minute about how you will teach the CCS. What will you need to help you? I'll bet you answered: books and curriculum materials. In order to help teachers know what kind of curriculum materials and content to use, the authors of the CCS developed criteria to guide publishers and curriculum developers in reading materials for grades K–2. You can access the publishers' criteria for grades 3–12 at the website listed in the Linking to Learning section at the end of this chapter. The criteria listed below concentrate on the most significant elements of the CCS for literacy in kindergarten and second grade. They are intended to direct curriculum developers to be strategic in both what to include and what to exclude in instructional materials. These guidelines are not meant to dictate classroom practice but rather to help ensure that teachers develop and receive effective tools.[24]

technology tie-in

Teaching Standards with Technology

Those who use technology in ways that expand their global connections are more likely to advance, while those who do not will find themselves on the sidelines. It's time for a paradigm shift from traditional teaching into the twenty-first century. This is not the time to wait it out.

Twenty-first century learners must be able to collaborate, problem solve, create, and be critical thinkers. Northwest Independent School District in Texas employs these best practices beginning in pre-kindergarten:

Creativity. Students develop innovative products to demonstrate creative thinking using cross-platform technology applications such as Showme, Glogster, Animoto, and Educreations. For the Spring 2012 Science Fair, students were given the option to use the tool of their choice for their presentations. The majority of students chose to create a digital application instead of the traditional science board. Many students used a virtual poster (Glogster), which allowed them to embed text, video, images, and research information all acquired from use of the iPad.

Collaboration. Collaboration combined with technology allows for limitless creative opportunities. Examples: Skype, FaceTime, video conferencing, Dropbox filesharing, and social media such as Edmodo.

Edmodo is a social network that hosts protected classrooms in a virtual environment. Teachers set up virtual classrooms that provide opportunities for online learning. As a member of the virtual classroom, students view resources, take quizzes, engage in a forum or blog, upload assignments, and share opinions with an online poll.

The use of Skype also allows a class to communicate directly with a military pen pal in Iraq. This activity enabled students to gain an authentic perspective of a real-life soldier and have a working relationship with him. Students were able to work together to create a Veteran's Day presentation using information, pictures, and videos directly from Iraq. For his birthday, they used Skype to hold a surprise party for him.

The students without financial access to technology tools at home often feel restricted. However, by using technology in the classroom, students obtain skills necessary to be successful in the outside world.

Problem Solving/Critical Thinking. Students use critical thinking skills to plan and conduct research, manage projects, solve problems, and make informed decisions using appropriate tools and resources. Research shows that there is a high demand for job applicants who are strong critical thinkers and problem solvers. Technology helps foster these skills by use of applications such as Creatagraph, CHARTGIZMO, Showme, and Blabberize.

Showme is a productivity app where students can annotate along with audio to explain a concept. An example is when students use the app to demonstrate steps taken to solve a math problem. The video can also be shared and used as a reference in Edmodo.

Differentiation. Planning for student differences, learning styles, and pacing in the classroom is a must for educators. The iPad addresses the different modalities of learning such as tactile, kinesthetic, auditory, and visual, as well as apps including Showme, Educreations, Toontastic, and StoryKit. Cara Carter, IT Support Teacher at Northwest ISD, says, "Meeting so many needs simultaneously is a challenge. Various apps engage the learners on all levels of Bloom's Digital Taxonomy."

Assessment. Data gathered from assessment drives instruction and is a vital component in today's classroom. Technology affords timely, specific, and authentic data. Assessment design can be both qualitative (Wallwisher, blogs, forums, Lino) or quantitative (PollEverywhere, Socrative, response systems).

Engagement/Own Their Learning. When children are given freedom in a nonthreatening environment to explore the digital world, they take charge of their own learning. We give choices and direction while students create products. "Children learn by being engaged, being challenged, and by discovering answers on their own. For example, Brigette Hinte, a teacher in Northwest ISD, says, "The iPads have opened up a new door in my classroom that provides these opportunities in endless ways!"

As educators, it is imperative that we meet the expectations of our digital natives. Students are on-demand learners and expect to be connected globally, immediately, and continuously with immediate access to information and resources. Teacher Allison Connell says, "Students are begging me for more time to work on class work with technology instead of asking, 'When is recess?' That really excites me! Thank you, iPad!"

Now would be a good time for you to research each of the programs mentioned above and determine how you could use particular apps, software, and programs in your teaching.

Source: Contributed by Cathy Faris, Instructional Technology Support Teacher, Northwest Independent School District, Fort Worth, Texas.

In kindergarten through grade two, the most notable shifts in the standards when compared to state standards include a focus on reading informational text and building coherent knowledge within and across grades; a more in in-depth approach to vocabulary development; and a requirement that students encounter sufficiently complex text through reading, writing, listening, and speaking.[25]

Criteria for Reading

The CCS offer specific guidance on reading foundations that should be observed in curriculum materials to prepare students to decode automatically and read with fluency by the time they finish second grade. Materials must meet the needs of a wide range of students, reinforcing key lessons in concepts of print, the alphabetic principle, and other basic conventions of the English language. Students come to school unevenly prepared, so materials must have the capacity to meet a range of needs. Materials that are aligned to the standards should provide explicit and systematic instruction and diagnostic support in concepts of print, phonological awareness, phonics, vocabulary development, and fluency.[26]

Fluency should be a particular focus of materials prepared for second graders. Materials should also provide ample opportunities for repeated oral reading (in and out of the classroom) with a variety of grade-level texts that can be easily implemented. Materials develop academic vocabulary prevalent in complex texts throughout reading, writing, listening, and speaking instruction. When they enter school, students differ markedly in their vocabulary knowledge. Materials must address this vocabulary gap early, systematically, and aggressively. These materials must offer assessment opportunities that genuinely measure progress in the foundations of reading. Activities used for assessment should clearly denote what standards are being emphasized, and materials should offer frequent and easily implemented assessments, including systems for record keeping and follow-up.[27]

Criteria for Text Selections

Texts for each grade should align with the complexity requirements outlined in the standards. The CCS hinge on students encountering appropriately complex texts at each grade level to develop the mature language skills and the conceptual knowledge they need for success in school and life. All students, including those who are behind, should have extensive opportunities to encounter and comprehend grade-level complex text as required by the standards. Far too often, students who have fallen behind are given only less complex texts rather than the support they need to read texts at the appropriate level of complexity. Complex text, whether accessed through individual reading, through read-alouds, or as a group reading activity, is a rich repository to which all readers need access.[28]

The standards maintain that high-quality text selections should be consistently offered to students because they will encourage students and teachers to spend more time on them than they would on low-quality material. This means that materials should include a greater volume of informal text, which the CCS calls for. Specifically, they call for elementary curriculum materials to be recalibrated to reflect a mix of 50 percent informational and 50 percent narrative text.[29]

Additional materials markedly increase the opportunity for regular independent reading of texts that appeal to students' interests to develop both their knowledge and joy in reading. These materials should ensure that all students have daily opportunities to read and write about texts of their choice on their own during and outside of the school day.[30]

applying research to practice

Teacher Characteristics and the Common Core Standards

Regardless of what standards you use or implement in your class-room, simply adopting the Common Core Standards will not necessarily result in higher student achievement. However, high standards, such as the Common Core Standards, positive teaching characteristics, and a supportive classroom environment can lead to higher student achievement. Here are some things that you can do:

- Get to know the children and things about them and their families.[31]
- Interact positively with all students, especially those who are difficult or shy.[32]

- Have high expectations for each student and communicate the positive message that you want each child to do well.[33]
- Create a classroom community and a community of learners by promoting positive interactions with all students and by having students help each other. For example, a morning classroom meeting is an excellent way to help students share their joys and concerns and to help students reach out to others to help them with social interactions and learning.[34]

WHAT ISSUES ARE ASSOCIATED WITH CCS?

By now, through our discussion of standards, you are aware that a number of controversies and issues swirl around CCS and their use. Let's examine some of these issues.

Standards and Achievement

Critics of standards-based education argue that standards focus too much on academic achievement and that other areas of the curriculum such as social and emotional development get left behind. High-quality teachers always teach to the whole child—the physical, social, emotional, linguistic, and cognitive. This is the foundation of early childhood education. For example, kindergarten teacher Karen Reid, Teacher of the Year at Morris Grove Elementary in North Carolina, says:

> Assessment data is necessary to guide instruction, as well as to document progress, but educating the "whole child" often begins the process of helping the children realize their worth and their potential to make contributions as a well-rounded and productive citizen. Children need to know that we care about and value them.[35]

Standards and Play

Critics of standards assert that standards promote a traditional back-to-basics approach to early childhood education at the expense of play-based and child-centered teaching and learning. Whole-child education, child-centered education, and play-based education are three building blocks of early childhood education. Play and standards are not incompatible. You can help children meet standards in many ways through play activities designed to ensure they meet standards, through intentional teaching and planning, and through direct teaching of essential skills.

Standards and the Curriculum

Many believe standards narrow the curriculum and force "teaching to the test." In some programs and classrooms, the standards may *become* the curriculum so that students pass state proficiency exams. While in a sense this issue may be true, it need not be so.

There is no reason why standards should narrow the curriculum or what is taught. Effective teachers always have and always will teach a wide and rich range of knowledge and skills based on local community needs and the needs of young children.

Standards and Testing

Critics of standards believe they lead to an overemphasis on assessment and testing. This may well be true, but proponents argue that testing is necessary to verify that children are learning. In reality, standards, instruction, and assessment, when well integrated, provide a process that helps ensure all children learn.

Standards and Teacher Autonomy

Some argue that standards impose too much structure on early childhood teachers who have a tradition of having the freedom to develop their own curriculum and classroom activities. Effective teachers always teach what they think is important in the best ways possible. I meet and interact with many local, state, and national Teachers of the Year. All of them emphasize that they teach children, not standards. LaWanda Rainey-Hall, Teacher of the Year at Glenwood Elementary, Chapel Hill-Carrboro City Schools in North Carolina, says:

> I feel that my ability to differentiate instruction and challenge each student individually to produce his/her best work makes me an outstanding teacher. I'm constantly aware of the range of abilities that my learners have and as a result, I consistently assess and teach using a variety of teaching methods that embrace and incorporate different learning styles and varied learning experiences. Knowing my students' personalities and working with families helps me design a content-rich program that includes their diverse learning needs, but also can be fun for all of us.[36]

Standards for All Students

Are Common Core Standards for all children? Yes! However, not everyone agrees that they should be. Many teachers of children with diverse needs believe that CCS and tests designed for normally developing or native English-speaking children are inappropriate for children with disabilities or different linguistic backgrounds. However, the CCS do apply to children with disabilities and special learning conditions. The U.S. Department of Education has been quite clear on this point. Under the No Child Left Behind Act (NCLB), states and local schools are held accountable for ensuring that all children—including children with disabilities—learn. Children with disabilities must be included in the assessment system required under NCLB, and schools must report their results through NCLB's adequate yearly progress (AYP) structure. The Individuals with Disabilities Education Act (IDEA) requires that when teachers and school teams develop plans for children with disabilities, they specify an individualized education program (IEP) for the child and outline *how* the child with a disability is assessed, not *whether* the child is assessed. IDEA recognizes that children learn in different ways, with different methods of instruction and assessment. The IEP team is required to determine which accommodations are necessary, how to instruct the child, and how to assess the child.[37] The Teaching and Learning in the Inclusive Classroom section describes how standards also apply to children with culturally diverse backgrounds.

TEACHING AND LEARNING IN THE INCLUSIVE CLASSROOM: ACCOMMODATING DIVERSE LEARNERS

As an early childhood teacher, you will have English language learners (ELLs) in your classroom and you will need to help them meet the Common Core Standards. One way to make standards applicable to ELLs is to provide an environment that both stimulates and accommodates them. For all children, but especially English language learners (ELLs), the classroom should be a place your students feel welcome, comfortable, and safe. Here are some things you can do to make your first grade classroom as inclusive as possible and conducive to both native speakers and English language learners so that all children meet the standards:

- Label classroom objects in multiple languages. Use English and other languages to label desks, art supplies, folders, and cubbies.
- Post class rules in English and in other languages. In addition, accompany the words with pictures to strengthen comprehension.
- Keep schedules and routines consistent until you are sure that all the ELL children understand the daily practices.
- Have ELL children (and children with learning or language differences) sit in areas that provide adequate visual and tactile access to information, such as near you during circle time, close to the blackboard or overhead, and facing your direction while you are talking. Children who are learning a new language should not have to depend on purely auditory input to gain information.
- Color-code materials to reinforce word meaning, purpose, and categorization. For example, print all homework on blue paper, vocabulary on yellow paper, math on pink paper, handouts on white paper, and notes that go home on green paper. Pencils belong in a red container, while markers belong in an orange container, and so forth.
- Keep an open dialogue about different cultures, languages, and countries so that ELL students feel welcomed and included rather than unusual or excluded by engaging in active discussion, storytelling, and sharing.
- Encourage diversity and acceptance of individual differences.
- Allow ELL students time to use and develop their native languages. Bilingualism is an important and valuable skill!

You will want to set high standards for all your children and then help them meet those standards. For example, Megan Allen, a Teacher of the Year from Florida, notes that standards are an important part of what makes education effective:

> We need to work together as states, creating focused, unified common standards and smarter assessments so teachers will have more pointed focuses for instruction. We need to work smarter, as partners in accountability and not as competitors. Within common standards we need to remember the requests of our children in keeping standards high enough to prepare them for global success. If we work as a community of advocates, helping our students succeed and putting our students' needs first, then our students, the souls of our communities, will fulfill their dreams and achieve success.[38]

The Contributions of Standards

We can conclude our discussion of standards by asking ourselves: Why is this important to us?

The standards movement has done a number of things for the early childhood profession as well as teachers and young children. Standards have helped the profession sharpen its focus about what young children should know and be able to do. As a result, many early childhood professionals have come to the conclusion that young children are much more capable than they realized or gave them credit for.

As early childhood professionals have rediscovered the children they teach, they are in the process of rediscovering themselves. Teachers are engaged in more

professionalism in practice

Five Essential Steps for Implementing the Common Core Standards

With the introduction and adoption of the Common Core State Standards by forty-six states, new challenges arise about how to implement them in a manner that acknowledges the hard work of teachers and school administrators across schools on all grade levels. It can be daunting when considering the many initiatives that have come and gone across school districts. The journey will take considerable effort and time on the part of all members of the school community: students, teachers, administrators, and families. It is one of the biggest shifts in the education of K–12 students in the last thirty years.

The CCSS are designed to prepare all students for college and careers. In the primary grades, the content and skills in English language arts and mathematics necessary to ensure student success are in great focus. The CCSS level the playing field for all students and school districts. We are looking at the same document that delineates outcomes for students at each grade level. However, the road to achieving those standards is left to the discretion of school districts and, in some cases, individual schools.

Based on our own experiences implementing the CCS, here are five recommendations that will support you in your teaching with standards.

First, familiarize yourself with the Common Core Standards. The school administrator must provide the time and space for teachers to read, interpret, and discuss the CCSS document in its entirety. Teachers must have an opportunity to speak with their colleagues, to raise questions, and to find applications to the current work in their classrooms. Teachers should not only become familiar with the standards of their grade, but that of grades above and below them in order to be a more effective teacher. In order for them to implement the content effectively, they must be aware of what the students are expected to know and do at the end of the grade.

Second, set realistic goals for the school. The school's leadership must decide, in consultation with teachers and school district officials, the one or two areas for deep focus during the school year. All areas of the CCSS cannot be addressed at once, and it will only serve to overwhelm school leaders, teachers, and students. It is best to choose a focus based on areas in need of improvement in your school and/or district.

Third, communicate expectations and goals with students and parents. Schools must conduct information sessions for parents and guardians. They, too, need to have some level of understanding. Their children are greatly impacted by the implementation of the CCSS. In order for students and parents to be active participants in their education, we need to communicate what is expected and required of students.

Fourth, collaborate with other teachers and administrators. By its design, the CCS encourage teachers to plan and implement units, which are not included in all curriculums. Collaboration between teachers to create the necessary units will result in the most effective instruction for our students. It will also encourage consistency across grade levels to ensure all students are receiving the same content and skills.

Fifth, create and administer meaningful assessments. The CCSS create a continuum of learning throughout the grades; not all skills are taught to mastery. Our assessments should reflect the goals set by the standards. Teachers should analyze assessments and discuss adjustments to reach these goals. This is where formative assessment is our friend. When teachers collaborate on the assessment tools and assess the work produced by students, they see the effect of their teaching. When all teachers are looking at the same assessment results, deeper conversations will happen and collaborative decisions made.

As educators, we often feel the pressure of implementing new and different ideas and strategies that state and federal education departments set. The frequent changes in expectations can be frustrating, discouraging, and time consuming. However, the CCSS create a national level of academic achievement for all students. When all teachers and administrators have meaningful conversations about the implementation of the CCSS, change will happen where it matters most, in the classroom.

....

Source: Contributed by Annabell Martinez, Principal, PS 124, Brooklyn, New York, and Elizabeth Bradstreet, Kindergarten Teacher, PS 124, Brooklyn, New York.

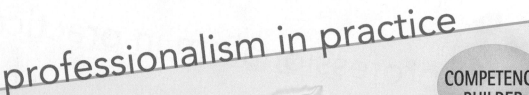

professionalism in practice

How to Plan Lessons That Meet Standards

When sitting down to create lesson plans, I always keep the following quotation in mind: "You cannot control the wind [i.e., state or district standards] but you can adjust your sails [i.e., personal lesson plans]." As you review the following steps, remember that lesson plans are to *guide* instruction; they are not a blueprint that must control your every word. You should always follow a wonderful teachable moment, even if it is not written into your lesson plan. You will never regret where it leads you and your students.

STEP 1 Become Familiar with Both State and District Standards

The objectives in my district's teacher's guide are clearly stated and are usually cross-referenced with the broader Florida Sunshine State Standards. Realize that standards encompass broad categories and often do not change significantly from one grade level to another. For example, "Reads for meaning" and "Uses context clues" apply to many grade levels; what changes is the level of presentation.

STEP 2 Incorporate in Your Plans What Will Be Assessed on High-Stakes Tests

I work into my lesson plans for all subjects the Florida Comprehensive Assessment Test task cards (e.g., compare/contrast, vocabulary, author's purpose, main idea, details, multiple representations of information, cause and effect) and the big five literacy components—phonological awareness, phonics, vocabulary, comprehension, and fluency.

STEP 3 Plan a Week Ahead

Planning ahead has several advantages:

- As you plan ahead, you think ahead. Just thinking about what you're going to teach enables you to see how standards and your instructional practices fit together.
- Planning ahead allows you to share ideas with your colleagues, get their advice, and make changes as appropriate.
- Planning ahead gives you time to gather all necessary materials and resources.

STEP 4 Meet with Other Teachers to Coordinate Plans

As the chairperson for grade three, I hold a weekly planning meeting with the other third grade teachers. We explore the information required to be presented the following week and plan together. Because my district uses the same authored curriculum across the county, we all teach from a particular reading

---

professional development than ever before, and much of this professional development involves learning how to teach with standards. In this sense, standards have reenergized the teaching profession.

Common Core Standards and Professional Development Go Hand-in-Hand

Common Core Standards don't implement themselves. Teachers spend a great deal of time in work sessions, planning sessions, and learning about the standards and how to implement them. You will be involved in **horizontal planning**, in which you collaboratively plan with your grade-level colleagues. You will also engage in **vertical planning** with teachers in grades below and above you. For example, as a second grade teacher, you will plan with kindergarten, first and third, and fourth grade teachers in order to make sure that learning is seamless across grades.

One thing that you can count on as you teach with the new Common Core Standards is that you will be very involved in meetings with your same-grade colleagues and colleagues from across your school and district about how to best implement the standards.

horizontal planning Planning in which you collaboratively plan with your grade level colleagues.

vertical planning Planning with teachers in the grade below and above what you teach.

series. This is extremely helpful with our somewhat transient population in Miami and allows for continuity as students move.

STEP 5 Create and Save a Framework for Your Lesson Plans

Because parts of lessons are repeated week after week, using a consistent framework saves valuable time. On a computer, I can cut and paste from week to week, adding or removing entries quickly.

STEP 6 Differentiate Instruction

Once the framework for lesson planning is understood, you are ready to "adjust your sails"—that is, differentiate your instruction. As an inclusion teacher, one-third of my students have exceptional needs, so I differentiate my instruction. I must adjust my presentation rather than expecting my learners to modify themselves to my presentation. Because there are varied abilities and disabilities within any given classroom, instructional practices and approaches should always be adapted to the students served within the classroom. In other words, instruction should meet the learners wherever they are and appeal to them on a multisensory level.

For instance, I plan vocabulary practice daily within every lesson plan (e.g., math vocabulary, science vocabulary, story vocabulary). Because not all students are at the same level in vocabulary development, I do the following:

- Present vocabulary on an overhead.
- Use colored markers on the overhead to separate and isolate vocabulary words.

- Use hearing and seeing sticks (i.e., rulers with an ear or an eye and a vocabulary word stapled on them). Students raise the stick when they hear or see the vocabulary word.
- Use a highlighter stick (i.e., a yardstick with an index card stapled to the end of it). When the vocabulary words are projected on the wall, I can hold the index card over a word and actually lift the word off the wall by lifting the card.

OTHER PLANNING AND INSTRUCTIONAL GUIDELINES

I recommend overplanning. Activities that you think will take a certain amount of time will often take much less or much more. This is fine you are working with children! Simply cut and paste a missed lesson into the next week's framework, or discontinue a lesson that is not working for you and move on to your next planned activity.

I also recommend moving your students often. Begin with a whole-group activity, and then transition to a partner activity. I place my students in groups of six rather than having them sit in rows. Within each grouping, I place at least two children with special needs and I have the group come up with a name and work as a small community. I also set up centers that allow for higher-order processing. Centers give me an opportunity to work with some students who may require more intensive instruction.

Lesson planning is a learned skill, and learned skills take time to master. Ask to see other teachers' lesson plans, ask them what works, and use any ideas that interest you.

....

Source: Contributed by Lynn Carrier, third grade teacher, Gulfstream Elementary, Miami, Florida, and 2007 Miami–Dade County Teacher of the Year.

ACTIVITIES FOR PROFESSIONAL DEVELOPMENT

ethical dilemma

"This educational fashion statement is wrong!"

Metropolitan Independent School District is in the process of implementing the Common Core Standards. However, not all of the early childhood teachers see eye to eye on the Common Core Standards (CCS). Some of the more vocal faculty in the school district argues that the standards would actually lower the bar for students since the Metropolitan ISD has a history of being one of the more elite school districts in the state. Third grade teacher Kathy Fair has jumped on the "dumbing down" bandwagon. Kathy also believes that the Common Core Standards are the "educational fashion of the moment" and that they won't last long. "I don't see why we have to teach to the lowest common denominator. I read a recent research report saying that there is no correlation with high-quality standards and higher student achievement," she says. "Things are going well for us, and our students are always at the top of the list when it comes to the state tests. This Common Core thing is too common!"

What should Kathy do? Contact her state senator? See if she can organize a grass-roots opposition to the CCS, perhaps using Facebook and Twitter? Do nothing? What would you do if you were Kathy?

Application Activities

1. How can you answer the question: "Are standards meeting their intended purpose of helping ensure that each and every child will achieve and learn?" One way to answer this question is to create or join a blog. I find that many outstanding teachers have blogs that you can join where you can ask this and other questions. Post the highlights of your blog on your class discussion board and ask your classmates to join your blog.

2. Review the CCS for the grade you plan to teach. Did anything surprise you about what the standards specify children should know and learn? Create an online discussion with your classmates, share your surprises with them, and ask for their opinions about the CCS.

3. Go online and find three examples of how federal and state regulation of education affects teaching in the classroom. Do you think this is a good thing? Post your opinion on your class discussion board and discuss with your classmates.

4. Review the material relating to Criteria for Text Selections earlier in this chapter. Look on the Internet for three children's books that fit the criteria for reading and text selections. Go onto your blog, Facebook, class discussion board, and so on, and ask for opinions on other children's books that you could use in the classroom that fit these criteria. Post your discoveries online.

5. Review the issues associated with the CCS. What are three ways you as an early childhood professional can help fix these issues in and out of the classroom? Ask for opinions from your classmates and post your ideas on your class discussion board. In particular, engage your classmates in this chapter's Ethical Dilemma, "This educational fashion statement is wrong!"

Linking to Learning

Common Core Standards

www.corestandards.org
This web page of the Common Core State Standards provides the mission statement and a list of Frequently Asked Questions and answers. This website really provides you everything you want and need to know about the Common Core State Standards.

MyEducationLab

Go to Topics 6 (Curriculum Planning) and 12 (Professionalism/Ethics) in the MyEducationLab (www.myeducationlab.com) for your course, where you can:

- Find learning outcomes for Curriculum Planning and Professionalism/Ethics along with the national standards that connect to these outcomes.

- Complete Assignments and Activities that can help you more deeply understand the chapter content.

- Apply and practice your understanding of the core teaching skills identified in the chapter with the Building Teaching Skills and Dispositions learning units.

- Access video clips of CCSSO National Teachers of the Year award winners responding to the question, "Why Do I Teach?" in the Teacher Talk section.

- Hear viewpoints of experts in the field in Professional Perspectives.

- Check your comprehension on the content covered in the chapter by going to the Study Plan in the Book Resources for your text. Here you will be able to take a chapter quiz, receive feedback on your answers, and then access Review, Practice, and Enrichment activities to enhance your understanding of chapter content.

chapter 6

OBSERVING AND ASSESSING YOUNG CHILDREN

Guiding, Teaching, and Learning

NAEYC Standards for Early Childhood Professional Preparation

Standard 3: Observing, Documenting, and Assessing to Support Young Children and Families

I know about and understand the goals, benefits, and uses of assessment. I know about and use systematic observations, documentation, and other effective assessment strategies in a responsible way, in partnership with families and other professionals, to positively influence the development of every child.[1]

 KINDERGARTEN TEACHER Tyron Jones wants to make sure Amanda knows the initial beginning sounds he taught the class during the last two weeks. First grade teacher Mindy McArthur wants to see how many words on the class word wall César knows. Third grade team leader Shannon Keller wants to know if all the third graders are ready for the upcoming state exam. All of these decisions relate to how to assess learning and teaching.

Teachers' minutes, hours, and days are filled with assessment decisions. Questions abound: "What is Jeremy ready for now?" "What can I tell Maria's parents about her language development?" "The activity I used in the large-group time yesterday didn't seem to work well. What could I have done differently?" Appropriate assessment can help you find the answers to these and many other questions relating to what to teach, how to teach, and what is best for children in their particular stages of development.

WHAT IS ASSESSMENT?

"Teaching without assessment is like driving a car without headlights."[2] Teaching "in the dark" does not benefit anyone in today's educational climate. Assessment is an invaluable tool to guide your teaching and your students' learning.

Your children's lives, both in and out of school, are influenced by your assessment and the assessment of others. As an early childhood professional, assessment will influence your professional life and will be a vital part of your professional practice. Effective assessment is one of your most important responsibilities, and it can enhance your teaching and children's learning.

Assessment is the ongoing, continuous process of collecting, gathering, and documenting what children do and how they do it as a basis for a variety of educational decisions that affect the child:

> Assessment involves the multiple steps of collecting data on a child's development and learning, determining its significance in light of the program goals and objectives, incorporating the information into planning for individuals and programs, and communicating the findings to families and other involved people. Assessment of child progress is integral to curriculum and instruction. In early childhood programs, the various assessments of child progress procedures that are used serve several purposes:
>
> - To plan instruction for individuals and groups
> - To communicate with families
> - To identify children who may be in need of specialized services or intervention
> - To inform program development[3]

WHY IS IT IMPORTANT FOR YOU TO KNOW HOW TO ASSESS CHILDREN AND FAMILIES?

Assessment is important because it involves the majority of the decisions you will make about children when teaching and caring for them. The decisions facing our three teachers at the beginning of this chapter all involve how best to educate children. Like them, you will be called upon every day to make decisions before, during, and after your teaching. Whereas some of these decisions will seem small and inconsequential, others will involve high stakes that influence the life course of children. All of your assessment decisions taken as a whole will direct and alter children's learning outcomes.

Figure 6.1 outlines for you the purposes of assessment and how assessment enhances your teaching and student learning. All of these purposes are important; if you use assessment procedures appropriately, you will help all your children learn well.

Principles of Assessment

As you think about the role assessment will play in your teaching, reflect on how the following general principles should guide both policies and practices for the assessment of young children. Assessments should be:

- ***About the benefits for children.*** Gathering accurate information from young children is difficult and potentially stressful. Assessments must have a clear benefit—either in direct services to the child or in improved quality of educational programs.

MyEducationLab

Visit the MyEducationLab for *Fundamentals of Early Childhood Education* to enhance your understanding of chapter concepts with a personalized Study Plan. You'll also have the opportunity to hone your teaching skills through video-based Assignments and Activities as well as Building Teaching Skills and Dispositions lessons.

FOCUS QUESTIONS

1. What is assessment?
2. Why is it important for you to know how to assess children and families?
3. What are the purposes and uses of observation and assessment and what are some ways you can assess children's development, learning, and behavior?
4. What are the types of assessment teachers use?
5. What are the contexts that influence the use of assessments?
6. What are issues of assessment?

assessment The process of observing, recording, and otherwise documenting what children do and how they do it.

FIGURE 6.1

Purposes of Assessment

Children

- Identify what children know
- Identify children's special needs
- Determine appropriate placement
- Select appropriate curricula to meet children's individual needs
- Refer children and, as appropriate, their families for additional services to programs and agencies
- Communicate with parents to provide information about their children's progress and learning

Families

- Communicate with parents to provide information about their children's progress and learning
- Relate school activities to home activities and experiences

Early Childhood Programs

- Make policy decisions regarding what is and is not appropriate for children
- Determine how well and to what extent programs and services children receive are beneficial and appropriate

Early Childhood Teachers

- Identify children's skills, abilities, and needs
- Make lesson and activity plans and set goals
- Create new classroom arrangements
- Select materials
- Make decisions about how to implement learning activities
- Report to parents and families about children's developmental status and achievement

The Public

- Inform the public regarding children's achievement
- Provide information relating to students' school-wide achievements
- Provide a basis for public policy (e.g., legislation)

Assessment plays an important and powerful role in your teaching and in children's learning. These five purposes clarify for you why it is important that you make assessment an integral part of your teaching.

- *Tailored to a specific purpose and should be reliable, valid, and fair for that purpose.* Assessments designed for one purpose are not necessarily valid if used for other purposes. In the past, many of the abuses of testing with young children have occurred because of misuse.

- *Designed to recognize that reliability and validity of assessments increase with children's age.* The younger the child, the more difficult it is to obtain reliable and valid assessment data. It is particularly difficult to assess children's cognitive abilities accurately before age six. Because of problems with reliability and validity, some types of assessment should be postponed until children are older, while other types of assessment can be pursued, but only with necessary safeguards.

- *Age appropriate in both content and the method of data collection.* Assessments of young children should address the full range of early learning and development, including physical well-being and motor development, social and emotional development, approaches toward learning, language development, and cognition and general knowledge. Methods of assessment should recognize that children need familiar contexts to be able to demonstrate their abilities. Abstract paper-and-pencil tasks may make it especially difficult for young children to show what they know.

- *Linguistically appropriate, recognizing that to some extent all assessments are measures of language.* Regardless of whether an assessment is intended to measure early reading skills, knowledge of color names, or learning potential, assessment results are easily confounded by language proficiency, especially for children who come from home backgrounds with limited exposure to English, for whom the assessment would essentially be an assessment of their English proficiency. Each child's first- and second-language development should be taken into account when determining appropriate assessment methods and in interpreting the meaning of assessment results.

- *Able to value parents as a source of information.* Because of the fallibility of direct measures of young children, assessments should include multiple sources of evidence, especially reports from parents and teachers. Assessment results should be shared with parents as part of an ongoing process that involves parents in their child's education.[4]

What Is Developmentally Appropriate Assessment?

Early childhood professionals do their best to use assessment in appropriate ways to support children's learning. We apply the framework of developmentally appropriate practice to assessment. You can develop a broad background of information about developmentally appropriate assessment by reviewing now the Early Childhood Curriculum, Assessment, and Program Evaluation Position Statement of the National Association for the Education of Young Children (NAEYC) and the National Association of Early Childhood Specialists in State Departments of Education (NAECS/SDE). This important document provides you with many important guidelines to follow as you assess young children.

Ensuring that your assessment practices are developmentally appropriate is challenging because children develop and learn in ways that are embedded within their specific cultural and linguistic contexts.[5] You need to consider such factors as children's age and development in addition to how well children can or cannot use English and their stages of linguistic development in the language they speak at home.[6] Developmentally appropriate assessment is:

- Authentic, ongoing observation and purposeful assessment and documentation in everyday classroom settings.

- Used to guide planning and teaching.
- Curriculum based—it is based on how children are achieving in the context of daily activities.
- Appropriate to the developmental status and experiences of young children.
- Responsive to individual differences in learners and allows children to demonstrate their competence in different ways.

Selecting Developmentally Appropriate Assessment Practices

Selecting appropriate assessment methods and instruments is an important part of the assessment process. Your assessment practices should meet these criteria:

- Addresses all developmental domains—physical, social, and academic. Remember, social interactions and behavior play an important role in academic achievement.
- Measures developmentally appropriate skills, learning strategies, and learning styles.
- Is conducted in natural, authentic situations.
- Is ongoing and closely related to curriculum development and program planning.
- Provides you with guidance on how to design child-centered curriculum.
- Results in information that is useful in planning children's experiences and making decisions.
- Involves parents and families and yields understandable information that is easy to relate to families and other teaching team members.
- Helps you modify environments and practices in order to maximize child learning.
- Helps you identify children who need a more focused intervention.[7]

Reporting to and Communicating with Parents and Families

Part of your responsibility as a professional is to report to parents and, when appropriate, to other primary caregivers about the growth, development, and achievements of their children. Reporting to and communicating with families is one of your most important jobs. The following guidelines will help you meet this important responsibility of reporting assessment information to parents:

Report your assessment findings accurately and honestly to the parents of your students. How might such communication build trust?

- ***Be honest and realistic with parents.*** Too often, teachers do not want to hurt parents' feelings. They want to sugarcoat what they are reporting. However, parents and guardians need your honest assessments about what their children know, are able to do, and will be able to do. With this honest assessment you can solicit their help in helping their children.
- ***Communicate with parents so they can understand.*** What you communicate to parents must make sense to them. They must understand what you are saying. Reporting to parents often has to be a combination of written and oral communication (in their language).
- ***Provide parents with ideas and information that will help them help their children learn.*** Remember that you and parents are partners in helping children be successful in school and life.

Systematic assessment of children represents a powerful way for you to learn about, guide, and direct children's learning and behavior. If you learn to use it well, you and your children will benefit.

USING OBSERVATION TO ASSESS

Professionals recognize that children are more than what is measured by any particular standardized test. Observation is an "authentic" means of learning about children—what they know and are able to do, especially as it occurs in more naturalistic settings such as classrooms, child care centers, playgrounds, and homes—and it is one of the most widely used methods of assessment. Observation is the intentional, systematic act of looking at the behavior of a child or children in a particular setting, program, or situation. Observation is sometimes referred to as "kid-watching" and is an excellent way to find out about children's behaviors and learning.

observation The intentional, systematic act of looking at the behavior of a child or children in a particular setting, program, or situation; sometimes referred to as *kid-watching*.

Purposes of Observation

Observation is designed to gather information on which to base decisions, make recommendations, develop curriculum, plan activities and learning strategies, and assess children's growth, development, and learning. For example, when professionals and parents sometimes look at children, they do not really "see" or concern themselves with what the children are doing or why. However, through carefully planned and systematic observation, you will be better able to "see" what your children are like and what they know and are able to do.

However, the significance and importance of critical behaviors go undetected if observation is done casually and is limited to "unsystematic looking." In order for you to make your observation meaningful, keep in mind that the purposes of observation are to:

- ***Determine the cognitive, linguistic, social, emotional, and physical development of children.*** Using a developmental checklist is one way professionals can systematically observe and chart the development of children. (Figure 6.4 later in this chapter shows a checklist for inclusive classrooms.)

- ***Identify children's interests and learning styles.*** Today, teachers are very interested in developing learning activities, materials, and classroom centers based on children's interests, preferences, and learning styles.

- ***Plan.*** The professional practice of teaching requires planning on a daily, ongoing basis. Observation provides useful, authentic, and solid information that enables teachers to intentionally plan for activities rather than make decisions with little or no information.

- ***Meet the needs of individual children.*** Meeting the needs of individual children is an important part of teaching and learning. For example, a child may be advanced cognitively but overly aggressive and lacking the social skills necessary to play cooperatively and interact with others. Through observation, a teacher can gather information to develop a plan for helping the child learn how to play with others.

- ***Determine progress.*** Systematic observation over time provides a rich, valuable, and informative source of information about how individuals and groups of children are progressing in their learning and behavior.

- ***Provide information to parents.*** Professionals report to and conference with parents on an ongoing basis. Observational information adds to other information they have, such as test results and child work samples, and provides a fuller and more complete picture of individual children.

- ***Provide self-insight.*** Observational information can help professionals learn more about themselves and what to do to help children.

Systematic observation each day will enable you to meet children's learning needs and be a more effective teacher. In the Professionalism in Practice feature, "Making a Difference," second grade teacher Lu Ann Harger shares her perspective on assessment and evaluation.

Advantages of Gathering Data Through Observations

Intentional observation is a useful, informative, and powerful means for informing and guiding teaching that helps ensure that all children learn. Knowing the advantages of gathering data through observation will enable the researcher to understand a child's development and learning style and assess them. Here are six advantages of gathering data through observation:

Observing is an excellent way to find out about a child's behavior and how well he or she is learning. What do you think you can learn about children from watching them interact socially with one another to complete puzzles and practice other fine-motor activities?

- *Enables professionals to collect information about children that they might not otherwise gather through other sources.* A great deal of the consequences, causes, and reactions to children's behavior can be assessed only through observation. Observation enables you to gather data that cannot be assessed by formal, standardized tests, questioning, and parent and child interviews.

- *Ideally suited to learning more about children in play settings.* Observation affords you the opportunity to note a child's social behavior in a play group and discern how cooperatively he or she interacts with peers. Observing a child at play gives professionals a wealth of information about developmental levels, social skills, and what the child is or is not learning in play settings.

The teacher in this **video** is using observation to assess the knowledge and skill level of the child playing. Note, as you watch, what you observe about the child's knowledge and skills.

- *Allows you to learn a lot about children's pro-social behavior and peer interactions.* It can help you plan for appropriate and inclusive activities to promote the social growth of young children. Additionally, your observations can serve as the basis for developing multicultural activities to benefit all children.

- *Provides a basis for the assessment of what children are developmentally able to do.* Many learning skills are developed sequentially, such as the refinement of large-motor skills before fine-motor skills. Through observation, professionals can determine whether children's abilities are within a normal range of growth and development.

- *Useful to assess children's performance over time.* Documentation of daily, weekly, and monthly observations of children's behaviors and learning provides a database for the cumulative evaluation of each child's achievement and development.

- *Helps you provide concrete information for use in reporting to and conferencing with parents.* Increasingly, reports to parents about children involve professionals' observations and children's work samples so parents and educators can collaborate to determine how to help children develop cognitively, socially, emotionally, and physically.

Steps for Conducting Observations

The four steps involved in the process of systematic, purposeful observation are listed in Figure 6.2. Review them now in preparation for our discussion of each of them.

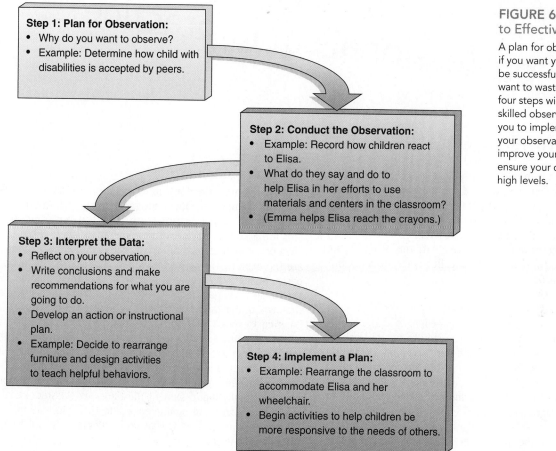

Step 1: Plan for Observation:
- Why do you want to observe?
- Example: Determine how child with disabilities is accepted by peers.

Step 2: Conduct the Observation:
- Example: Record how children react to Elisa.
- What do they say and do to help Elisa in her efforts to use materials and centers in the classroom?
- (Emma helps Elisa reach the crayons.)

Step 3: Interpret the Data:
- Reflect on your observation.
- Write conclusions and make recommendations for what you are going to do.
- Develop an action or instructional plan.
- Example: Decide to rearrange furniture and design activities to teach helpful behaviors.

Step 4: Implement a Plan:
- Example: Rearrange the classroom to accommodate Elisa and her wheelchair.
- Begin activities to help children be more responsive to the needs of others.

FIGURE 6.2 Four Steps to Effective Observation

A plan for observing is essential if you want your observation to be successful and if you don't want to waste your time. These four steps will help you be a skilled observer and will enable you to implement the results of your observation so that they improve your teaching and help ensure your children achieve at high levels.

Step 1: Plan for Observation. Planning is an important part of the observation process. Everything you do regarding observation should be planned in advance of the observation. A good guide to follow in planning for observation is to ask the questions *who, what, where, when,* and *how.*

Setting goals for observation is a crucial part of the planning process. Goals allow you to reflect on why you want to observe and thus direct your efforts to what you will observe. Stating a goal focuses your attention on the purpose of your observation. For example, suppose you want to determine the effectiveness of your efforts in providing an inclusive classroom or program and in fully including an exceptional child into the classroom. In Figure 6.4, you will see how we incorporate assessment and goal planning for Elisa, a child with cerebral palsy (CP), and develop a plan for her successful assimilation in the inclusive classroom. As the teacher, your goals might read like this:

Goal 1: To determine what modifications might be necessary in the classroom to facilitate access to all parts of the classroom for Elisa in her wheelchair.

Goal 2: To assess the development of pro-social behavioral characteristics that other children display to Elisa while interacting in the classroom.

Goal setting sharpens your observation and makes it more effective.

Step 2: Conduct the Observation. While conducting your observation, it is imperative that you be objective, specific, and as thorough as possible. For example, during your observation of Elisa and her peers, you notice that there is not enough room

professionalism in practice

Making a Difference

There are many ways to make a difference in a child's life. As a teacher, each year you are given the enormous honor of spending eight hours a day creating within a child a burning desire for learning. You have the opportunity to introduce your children to the wonders of numbers, letters, words, and the history of their nation. You have the ability to create the "what if" and the "tell me more" in minds each day. But where to start this daunting task is difficult to say.

BEGINNING OF THE SCHOOL YEAR

All things have a beginning, and nothing equals a sound beginning. Each year as the school year is ready to begin, I call all my students to introduce myself and our classroom, Camp Can Do, and put their minds at ease. Fear of the unknown is a great deterrent to success, and this phone call goes a long way in calming that fear. I ask them to bring a thinking cap along to help on tough assignments and, of course, I keep mine handy all year, too!

As they begin the first week of school, activities are planned to get to know each other and to evaluate levels of learning. Students play the M&M game by choosing a handful and speaking about themselves according to the colors. Each child gets a chance to say the alphabet, show me crayons to match color words, read a set of selected grade-level word lists, and read a passage aloud to me. As a class, we sit in community circle and use cards to stimulate discussions. That way, I can check for verbal expression, use of vocabulary words, life experiences, and comfort levels. Students also fill out a reading inventory on their likes and dislikes, play math games to show computation skills, and copy some basic words to evaluate their fine-motor skills.

FAMILY PARTICIPATION

Now that I am on the right track evaluating my students, I work on my other team members: my family members. At the beginning of each school year at Parent Night, parents and guardians are asked to provide information about their child. Sure, I have permanent records to look over, but the primary caregivers are the experts. They share fears and acts of bravery, favorites, past school experiences, and special traits of their children. With their help I will gain a better understanding of their child, and they will understand how much I value their input. During the meeting I explain how our classroom, or Camp Can Do, is run and what we do each day. I also explain the importance of their role as communicator, coach, and study partner. In the end, I read *Leo the Late Bloomer* and reiterate that my plan this year is for everyone to make it, just like Leo. Now I have the complete package: family input, student files, and my classroom evaluations. This is a sound beginning. Using this information, I can set up learning profiles for all my students that will be used throughout the year.

ASSESSMENT AND CURRICULUM

As the year's curriculum begins to unfold, I gather new information. In math, I pretest before each chapter to see what students know and do not know. Then throughout the lessons I group students according to their needs. Students work in many different groups by the year's end as their mastery of math skills is checked. Students are able to work on weak areas, like time and money, but expand areas in which they are strong, like addition computation. In spelling, lists are modified according to learning levels. Everyone gets an opportunity to try the bonus words and earn a chance for spelling prizes. In

for Elisa to manipulate her wheelchair past the easel and shelf where the crayons are kept. None of her peers noticed that Elisa could not reach the crayons and so did not help her get them. Elisa had to ask one of the children to get the crayons for her. Now you have information that will enable you to take action.

Be sure to record your data as you observe. Here are four ways you can quickly and easily gather and manage observational data:

- Wear an apron (a carpenter's apron works very well) with pockets to carry pens, note cards, and Post-it notes.
- Use Post-it notes to record observations. These can be easily added to students' notebooks, folders, and so forth.

reading and language arts, students work in small and large groups. They begin to take home simple readers or chapter books to become members of the Campfire Readers. Students work on partner reading books, enjoy the Scholastic Reader computer program books, and add up pages read, and use trade books for readers during the year as well. Weekly reading conferences are held between students and myself to check on comprehension.

The use of various assessment tools provides me with a wide range of knowledge about each student. Some assessments can be as easy to use as a book discussion to determine my students' comprehension or a game to show knowledge gained. Assessments can also take the form of a Venn diagram for comparison or a poster giving facts about the animal students researched. Ongoing assessments, such as writing portfolios, can provide a big picture of skill growth by storing information in a time line fashion. Other assessments may be standardized, such as a math or reading test. No matter what type of assessment I might use, I think it is critical that my students be aware beforehand how they will be assessed and afterward take part in a discussion of the assessment tool. When I give a test of any kind, my students have a chance to talk over the items they missed. When using a less formal assessment such as a rubric, I give these out in advance. This gives students an idea of my expectations and a way to determine what they would like to accomplish.

No matter how you choose to assess your students, the most important thing to remember is that the assessment is only as good as the teacher using it. To keep the information meaningful, I look at the assessments I use with each unit I teach. Is there an area that I forgot to include? Are my students missing a question on a test in large numbers? Did this assessment give me the information I needed to know about my students' learning? What do the students think of the assessment? Is the information easy for me to understand? Is it easy to share with my students and my parents? Good assessments gather meaningful information that enhances children's learning. If my assessments are doing that, great! If not, I need to make a change so they are.

MAKING LEARNING MEANINGFUL

All of this information would mean nothing to the students or me if they were not engaged in their learning. Seven years ago, two colleagues and I investigated the idea of integrated instruction. Taking all our textbooks, we rebuilt our second grade curriculum from the ground up using our social studies standards as the base. The result was a full year of learning that was connected and meaningful. Students could learn about community workers and be reading a story for language arts on the same topic that week. The math lesson would also use community helpers as a base for the skill taught that week. The effort to make this possible was enormous and continues today as the plan is refined each year, but the results are worth it. Learning has become an "I get it" experience for my students. They see that our story for the week is about money and so are the math lessons. They understand that we are working on the skill of compound words because they are in our story for the week. Suddenly learning has an order and pattern that make their gathering of knowledge so much more genuine and long term. This connection of learning also brings strengths and weaknesses together that help improve both. This is real, lifelong learning!

Creating an environment where learning occurs is a huge key to successful students. We use these lifelong guidelines: Be truthful. Be trustworthy. Do your personal best. Appreciate others. Be an active listener. By expecting everyone in our classroom, including myself, to follow these guidelines, we create a place that is consistent, caring, and safe. Students know what to expect from day to day. By taking the time to listen to a story from home, provide a worry box to stuff concerns in, use mistakes as learning opportunities, or help ease a fear, I am modeling these expectations. I am creating a place where my students feel comfortable, can take risks, and will grow as learners. From my most able student to my least, I hear them saying: I can do this, I will try.

Can this make a difference? We sure think so in Room 12, or Camp Can Do as we like to call it. Never underestimate the potential of a child. If they shoot for the moon and miss, they will still wind up in the stars.

....
Source: Contributed by Lu Ann Harger, second grade teacher, Hinkle Creek Elementary, Noblesville, Indiana, and a part of the USA Today ALL STAR Teacher Team.

- Use the observation checklist for inclusive classrooms shown later in Figure 6.4, checklists you make yourself, and checklists found in other books.
- Use tape recorders, video cameras, and digital cameras to gather information. A problem with using a tape recorder is that you have to transcribe your notes. Video cameras are probably best reserved for group observations. However, digital cameras are an excellent means of gathering and storing data.

Step 3: Interpret the Data. All observations can and should result in some kind of interpretation. **Interpretation** is a process that includes examining the gathered information, organizing and drawing conclusions from that information, and making decisions based on the conclusions. Interpretation serves several important functions.

interpretation A three-step process that includes examining the information that has been gathered, organizing and drawing conclusions from that information, and making decisions about teaching based on the conclusions.

- First, it puts your observations into perspective—that is, in relation to what you already know and do not know about events and the behaviors of your children.
- Second, interpretation helps you make sense of what you have observed and enables you to use your professional knowledge to interpret what you have seen.
- Third, interpretation has the potential to make you learn to anticipate representative behavior indicative of normal growth and development under given conditions, and to recognize what might not be representative of appropriate growth, development, and learning for each child.
- Fourth, interpretation forms the foundation for the implementation, necessary adaptations, or modifications in a program or curriculum.

In your observation, you can note that Elisa's only exceptionality is that she has a physical disability. Her growth in other areas is normal, and she displays excellent social skills in that she is accepted by others, knows when to ask for help, and is able to ask for help. When Elisa asks for help, she receives it.

Step 4: Implement a Plan. The implementation phase means that you commit to do something with the results, or "findings," of your observation. For example, although Elisa's behavior in your observation was appropriate, many of the children can benefit from activities designed to help them recognize and respond to the needs of others. In addition, the physical environment of the classroom requires some modification in the rearrangement of movable furniture to make it more accessible for Elisa. Implementation means you report to and conference with parents or others as necessary and appropriately apply the results of your observations to real-life situations that can improve the child's circumstances and maintain consistent progress.

TYPES OF ASSESSMENT

Early childhood teachers use many kinds of assessments to help them learn about their children and plan for teaching. The following are examples of assessment that will be an important part of your professional toolbox as you enter the profession.

Authentic Assessment

authentic assessment
Assessment conducted through activities that require children to demonstrate what they know and are able to do.

Authentic assessment is the evaluation of children's actual learning and the instructional activities in which they are involved. Figure 6.3 outlines characteristics of authentic assessment. As you examine these characteristics, think about how you will apply them to your professional practice. Following the authentic assessment strategies shown in Figure 6.3 will help ensure that the information you gather will be useful and appropriate for all children.

Authentic assessment is also referred to as *performance-based assessment*. Authentic assessment requires children to demonstrate what they know and are able to do. Meaningless facts and isolated information are considered inauthentic.

Here are some characteristics of authentic assessment:

- *Assess children based on their actual work:* Use work samples, exhibitions, performances, learning logs, journals, projects, presentations, experiments, and teacher observations.
- *Assess children based on what they are actually doing and through the curriculum.* Have you ever taken a test and walked out of the classroom and said, "We never learned that!" This is exactly the point. You need to be sure that you are assessing children on the curriculum you and they are using and the activities they are involved in.

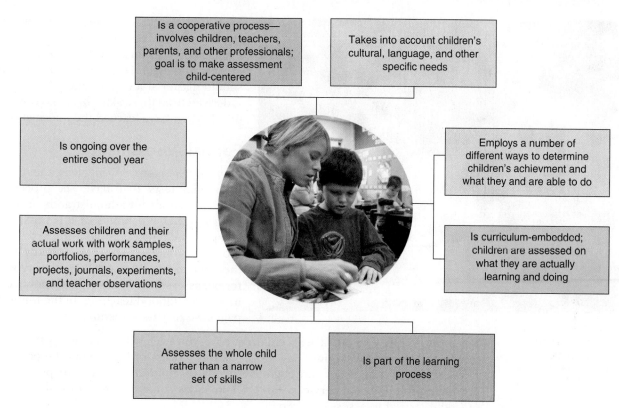

FIGURE 6.3 Characteristics of Authentic Assessment

Authentic assessment is embedded in classroom curriculum, activities, and instructional practices. These eight characteristics of authentic assessment will act as guideposts for you so that you can assure that your assessment activities are directed toward enhancing and increasing student achievement.

- *Assess what each individual child can do.* Evaluate what each child is learning, rather than comparing one child with another or one group of children with another.
- *Make assessment part of the learning process.* Encourage children to show what they know through presentations and participation.
- *Learn about the whole child.* Make the assessment process an opportunity to learn more than just a child's acquisition of a narrow set of skills.
- *Involve children and parents in a cooperative, collaborative assessment process.* The goal of authentic assessment is to be child-centered and to provide children with the resources they need to succeed.
- *Provide ongoing assessment over the entire year.* Assess children continually throughout the year, not just at the end of a grading period or at the end of the year.
- *Use many different assessment tools to evaluate your children.* Know several ways to determine children's achievement and what they know and are able to do.

Traditional Assessment

Traditional assessment refers to the method of forced choice found in multiple-choice tests, fill-in-the-blanks, true-false, matching, and the like, where students typically select an answer or recall information to complete the assessment. These tests are usually standardized or teacher-created and administered locally or statewide.[8]

traditional assessment
Assessment done with standardized tests or teacher-created tests, where students typically select an answer or recall facts, measuring how well children have learned specific information.

As part of the teaching–learning process you will conduct authentic assessment as a way to know what children know and are able to do. Authentic assessment occurs within and as part of your instructional practices.

In the traditional assessment model, the curriculum determines what is on the assessment. For an example, each state has a list of basic and essential skills that each student should master at a certain grade level. A test is derived from these skills to assess how well the children have learned the information.

Formal Assessment

Formal assessment involves the use of traditional tests that have set procedures and instructions for administration and have been *normed,* meaning that it is possible to compare a child's score with the scores of a group of children who have already taken the same exam. Table 6.1 lists other types of formal assessment measures commonly used in early childhood teaching. In the following pages we discuss screening procedures.

Screening.   In your work with children, have you ever wondered about the extent to which they are developing? **Screening** is the process of identifying the particular physical, social, linguistic, and cognitive needs of children in order to provide appropriate programs and services. Table 6.1 includes some common formal screening procedures used to assess children.

Screening procedures give you and others a broad picture of what children know and are able to do, as well as their physical and emotional status. As gross

formal assessment Assessment utilizing standardized tests that have set procedures and instructions for administration and have been normed, thus making it possible to compare a child's score with the scores of children who have already taken the same exam.

screening The process of identifying the particular physical, social, linguistic, and cognitive needs of children in order to provide appropriate programs and services.

screening procedures Procedures that give a broad picture of what children know and are able to do, as well as their physical and emotional status.

TABLE 6.1 Formal Measures of Assessment Used in Early Childhood

Assessment Instrument	Age/Grade Level	Purpose
Ages and Stages Questionnaires®, Third Edition (ASQ-3)	Birth to five years	Provides developmental and social-emotional screening for children; looks at the child's developmental delays and educates parents about developmental milestones
BRIGANCE® screens and inventories	Pre-kindergarten to grade nine	Obtains a broad sampling of children's skills and behaviors to determine initial placement, plan appropriate instruction, and comply with mandated testing requirements
Developmental Indicators for the Assessment of Learning, Third Edition (DIAL-3)	Ages three to six	Identifies children who may have special educational needs
Dynamic Indicators of Basic Early Literacy Skills (DIBELS)	Preschool and primary grades	Assesses three of the five Big Ideas of early literacy: phonological awareness, alphabetic principle, and fluency with connected text
Peabody Picture Vocabulary Test–Revised (PPVT-R)	Ages 2.5 to adult	Tests hearing vocabulary; is available in two forms

indicators of children's abilities, screening procedures provide much useful information for decisions about placement for initial instruction, referral to other agencies, and additional testing that may be necessary to pinpoint a learning or health problem. One out of every six children in the United States faces a developmental disability or disabling behavioral problem before age eighteen. Yet fewer than 50 percent of these children are identified before they start school.[9] Many school districts conduct a comprehensive screening assessment program in the spring for children who will enter kindergarten in the fall. Screening can include the following:

- Gathering information from parents about their children's health, learning patterns, learning achievements, personal habits, and special problems
- Conducting a health screening, including a physical examination, health history, and a blood sample for analysis
- Conducting vision, hearing, and speech screening
- Collecting and analyzing data from former programs and teachers, such as preschools and child care programs
- Using commercial screening instruments to help make decisions regarding children's placement in programs and need for special services

Schools and early childhood programs frequently conduct comprehensive screening programs for all children for one or two days. The data for each child are evaluated by a team of professionals who make instructional placement recommendations and, when appropriate, advise additional testing and make referrals to other agencies for assistance.

Screening measures are what you and other professionals use when you gather information and make decisions about procedures such as small-group placements, instructional levels, and so forth.

Informal Assessment

Informal assessment is a procedure for obtaining information that can be used to make judgments about children's learning, behavior, and development using means other than standardized instruments.[10] Informal assessments allow teachers to evaluate their children's progress and follow it throughout the children's learning experiences. Authentic assessment relies heavily on informal procedures including observations, checklists, and portfolios. Review and reflect on the informal methods of assessment shown in Table 6.2. Consider how you would use each one in your teaching.

informal assessment Assessment of students' learning, behavior, and development using means other than standardized tests.

Observations.   Early childhood professionals recognize that children are more than what is measured by any particular standardized test. As mentioned earlier in this chapter, *observation* is the intentional, systematic act of looking at the behavior of a child or children in a particular setting, program, or situation. It is an "authentic" means of learning about children—what they know and are able to do, especially as it occurs in more naturalistic settings such as classrooms, child care centers, playgrounds, and homes. It is one of the most widely used methods of assessment. As we have said, observation is sometimes referred to as "kid-watching" and is an excellent way to find out about children's behaviors and learning.

A sample observation form you can use is shown in Figure 6.4. This form can be a useful tool for gathering observational data and it will prove helpful when planning for teaching and finding your children's areas of improvement. In Figure 6.4, you will see how the teacher uses observations and a checklist to record the social pretend play skills of Elisa, a student in her third grade theater class.

Anecdotal Records.   Another informal assessment tool is the **anecdotal record**, a brief written description of student behavior at one specific time (see Figure 6.5).

anecdotal record An informal assessment tool that gives a brief written description of a student's behavior during a single incident.

TABLE 6.2 Informal Methods of Authentic Assessment

Method	Purpose	Guidelines
Observation Kid-watching—looking at children in a systematic way	Enables teachers to identify children's behaviors, document performance, and make decisions	Plan for observation and be clear about the purposes of the observation.
Checklist A list of behaviors identifying children's skills and knowledge	Enables teachers to observe and easily check off what children know and are able to do	Make sure that the checklist includes behaviors that are important for the program and for learning (e.g., counts from 1 to 10, hops on one foot).
Portfolio Collection of children's work samples and other products	Provides documentation of a child's achievement in specific areas over time; can include test scores, writing work samples, videotapes, etc.	Make sure the portfolio is not a dumpster but a thoughtful collection of materials that documents learning over time.
Anecdotal record Gives a brief written description of student behavior at one time	Provides insight into a particular behavior and a basis for planning a specific teaching strategy	Record only what is observed or heard; should deal with the facts and should include the setting (e.g., where the behavior occurs) and what was said and done.
Running record Focuses on a sequence of events that occurs over time	Helps obtain a more detailed insight into behavior over a period of time	Maintain objectivity and try to include as much detail as possible.
Time sampling Record particular events or behaviors at specific time intervals (e.g., 5 minutes, 10 minutes)	Helps identify when a particular child demonstrates a particular behavior; helps answer the question, "Does the child do something all the time or just at certain times and events?"	Observe only during the time period specified.
Event sampling Focuses on a particular behavior during a particular event (e.g., behavior at lunchtime, behavior on the playground, behavior in a reading group)	Helps identify behaviors during a particular event over time	Identify a target behavior to be observed during particular times (e.g., fighting during transition activities).
Work Sample Piece of children's work that demonstrates what they know and are able to do	Provides a concrete example of learning; can show growth and achievement over time	Make sure that the work sample demonstrates what children know and are able to do. Let children help select the items they want to use as examples of their learning.
Rating scale Contains a list of descriptors for a set of behaviors	Enables teachers to record data when they are observed	Make sure that key descriptors and the rating scale are appropriate for what is being observed.
Interview Engaging children in discussion through questions	Allows children to explain behavior, work samples, or particular answers	Ask questions at all levels of Bloom's Taxonomy in order to gain insight into children's learning.

FIGURE 6.4

Authentic Assessments: Example of an Inclusion Classroom Checklist

Teacher: *Graciela Gomez*

School: *Mission Hill Elementary*

Student: *Elisa B.*

Class: *First grade*

Number of children in class: *16*

Number of children with disabilities in class: *1*

Date: *09-08-14*

Types of disability: *Elisa has moderate cerebral palsy (CB) and must use a wheelchair.*

Physical Features of the Classroom

1. Are all areas of the classroom accessible to children with disabilities?

    No, Elisa cannot access the library/literacy center.

2. Are learning materials and equipment accessible for all children?

    There is not enough room for Elisa to manipulate her wheelchair past the easel and the shelf with art materials.

3. Are work and play areas separated to minimize distractions?

    Yes, but pathways are too narrow for Elisa's wheelchair.

4. Are special tables or chairs necessary to accommodate children's disabilities?

    Elisa has a large work board/table that attaches to her wheelchair.

Academic Features of the Classroom

1. What special accommodations are necessary to help children with disabilities achieve state and local standards?

    I need to check on this.

2. Are principles of developmentally appropriate practice applied to all children, including those with disabilities?

    Yes.

3. Is there a wide range of classroom literature on all kinds of disabilities?

    I have a few books but not enough. I would like more.

Classroom Interaction

1. Are children with disabilities included in cooperative work projects?

    I will work on this next week.

2. Do children without disabilities interact positively with children with disabilities?

    Elisa is a very sociable person. Students interact well with her. Elisa could not reach the crayons by herself, so she asked Billy for help. She and Billy seem to get along well.

Play Routines

1. Are children with disabilities able to participate in all classroom and grade-level activities?

    I need to talk with the P.E. teacher. I also need to observe Elisa during lunch and recess to see if she is involved in play and social activities during these times.

(continued)

FIGURE 6.4 Continued

Conclusions

1. *I need to rearrange my classroom to make sure that Elisa has access to all learning centers and materials.*

2. *The children are not as helpful to Elisa as I want them to be.*

3. *The classroom library/lit center needs more books relating to children with disabilities.*

4. *There are a lot of questions I don't have the answer to at this time (i.e., meeting state standards).*

5. *I need to include more group work and cooperative activities in my planning.*

Recommendations

1. *I will ask a custodian to help me move a heavy bookshelf. I can move and rearrange the other things. I'll give the new arrangement a trial run and see how it works for all the children.*

2. *In our daily class meetings, I will talk about helpful behaviors and helping others.*

    a. *We can read books about helping.*

    b. *I plan to start a class buddy system. I can pair Elisa and Billy!*

3. *In my lesson plans, I need to include activities for learning helpful behaviors.*

4. *I will search for books about children with disabilities.*

    a. *I'll consult with the school librarian.*

    b. *I'll talk to my grade-level leader and ask for money for books.*

5. *I will talk with the director of special education about meeting state standards. Elisa is very smart so I don't anticipate any problems.*

6. *I will develop a lesson involving group work and projects. I will include Elisa and observe the children's interactions.*

7. *I will observe Elisa at lunch and during recess.*

As previously noted, if we don't teach standards, we don't teach children. It is important for you to teach the whole child. You will be teaching in inclusive classrooms, and you will need to adjust your curriculum to teach children with disabilities. Observational checklists, such as this one, help you keep track of how the children are learning and their individual needs.

FIGURE 6.5

Authentic Assessments: Excerpt of an Anecdotal Record

. . . Today, we had a lesson on letter recognition. I had the children write their ABC's with their fingers in shaving cream on their desks. Amy started immediately and wanted to start spelling whole words. She spelled Cat, Dog, and Cow on her own. Once she had written the ABC's several times and the words she already knew, she began to ask for other words to spell. We talked about how to spell Mom, Dad, and Rob, her brother's name. She asked three or four times, "Ms. R, Ms. R, how do you spell Farm?" from across the room. When I was helping another student, she fidgeted and raised her voice to get my attention. At one point, she grabbed me by the hand to lead me to her table and wanted to know how to spell House. . . .

An anecdotal record, as the name implies, is a short account of a behavior. An anecdotal record enables you to evaluate progress and then plan for appropriate instruction that meets the needs of a particular student. An anecdote enables you to have concrete information with which you can develop your strategy for instructional and behavioral improvement.

FIGURE 6.6

Authentic Assessments: Example of a Running Record

Teacher: *Anna Beatty*
Student: *Ali R.*
Age: *5*
School: *Reed Elementary*
Date: *04/08/2014*
Time: *10:00 a.m.-10:20 a.m.*

Observations	Comments
Ali is playing at the block center with Jake and Travis. Ali has surrounded himself with the blocks and begins stacking them. The blocks are about waist high. Jake is playing with cars with Travis.	*Ali has spent a lot of time building with the blocks and is very careful about stacking them just right. But he seems to be looking at Jake and Travis a lot.*
A: "I'm building a fort!"	
J: "That doesn't look like a fort."	*Travis and Jake play together a lot. It*
A: "It's a fort; I made it to be a fort."	*doesn't look like Ali knows how to join*
T: "I think it's a garage for our cars!"	*them. Maybe that's why Ali told them it was*
Travis and Jake start to push their cars	*a fort?*
along Ali's fort. Ali keeps stacking blocks.	
A: "I said it's a fort. I built it so I get to pick. It's a fort, not a garage."	*Ali definitely doesn't look like he likes them putting cars on his fort. What will he do?*
T: "Why can't it be a garage?"	
A: "I don't have a car." Ali pauses. Then says, "If you let me be the red car, the fort can be a garage. It can be a garage first, then a fort!"	*Shows good compromising skills! The red car is a favourite of most of the boys. Good way to get what he wants and still get to play with J & T.*
Jake gives Ali the red convertible car and they start to zoom the cars all over the "garage."	
J: "Let's add a ramp."	*Pretty flexible of Ali to let J & T change his*
A: "That's a good idea. Put it here."	*fort. Another good play skill.*

A running record allows you to gather information about children's abilities and behavior over a period of time. By having information that extends over a day or a week, you are able to identify behavioral trends that you might not be aware of if you were only observing a small episode of a child's behavior over a short period of time.

These records are short and concise and tell the evaluator what needs to be known about the unique skills of a child or small group of children. They provide insight into a particular behavior and a basis for planning a specific teaching strategy. Some guidelines to remember about anecdotal records are to record only what is observed or heard, deal with the facts and include the setting, and record what was said and done by the subjects being observed.

Running Records. **Running records** are a more detailed narrative of a child's behavior that focuses on a sequence of events that occur over a period of time. These records help to obtain a more detailed insight into behavior in general, rather than specific events like the anecdotal record. When using running records, try to maintain objectivity and include as much detail as possible. Figure 6.6 gives an example of how a teacher observes a student during play time and the conflict that arises with him and two of his peers. Because the observer uses a running record to observe the student, the events are shown in chronological order and you can see how the two boys collaboratively solve their own problem.

running record An informal assessment tool that provides a more detailed narrative of a child's behavior, focusing on a sequence of events that occur over a period of time.

FIGURE 6.7

Authentic Assessments: Example of Event Sampling Using the ABC Method

Teacher: *D. Kramer*
Student: *Keith C.*
Grade: *1st*
School: *DuPont Elementary*
Date: *10-17-14*

A	B	C
Tuesday		
1:15 p.m.: *Keith just finished P.E. He looks a little upset. Ask if he's OK. I ask class to get out pencils and look at the board.*	1:20 p.m.: *Keith fidgets a little but is mostly calm, says he's fine.*	1:22 p.m.: *lessons continued*
1:24 p.m.: *Told class we would do a group project with cubes first, then they will work individually.*	1:27 p.m.: *Keith fidgets and scoots around in his chair. Some classmate giggle and turn to watch, others ignore.*	1:28 p.m.: *I ignore it, hand out Rubik's cubes to groups.* 1:33 p.m. *He stops fidgeting.*
1:33 p.m.: *Keith stopped fidgeting; I show class how to count by 5s with Rubik's cubes.*	1:40 p.m.: *Keith participates with group, seems to enjoy.*	1:42 p.m.: *Tell class only a few more minutes with the group before move onto individual work.*
1:43 p.m.: *Told class to clean up cubes and start own work.*	1:44 p.m.: *Keith plays with blocks, tossing them in the air, throwing at friends.*	1:46 p.m.: *Ask Keith to clean up; classmates laugh with Keith.*
1:50 p.m.: *Asked Keith to clean up; he is still playing with cubes.*	1:55 p.m.: *Keith making silly faces at me and classmates, playing with blocks.*	1:57 p.m.: *Take the cubes away and give Keith a warning.*
1:59 p.m.: *Gave Keith a warning, gave him worksheet, but realize we're out of time, class will be late for art.*	2:01 p.m.: *Assign Keith the worksheet for homework.*	2:02 p.m.: *Keith lines up for art without a problem, walks quietly in the hallway on way to art.*

The intended use of event sampling is to identify a pattern in a child's behavior over time. Through event sampling, you are able to identify problems and start to focus on solutions that will create desired behavior and keep the child on a positive pathway of success.

event sampling An informal assessment tool that focuses on a particular behavior during a particular event.

Event Sampling. Event sampling, unlike time sampling, uses discontinuous intervals and focuses on a particular behavior during particular events. For example, Ms. Curry would look at Sebastian's behavior during lunchtime, on the playground, and during reading time. The behavior may occur infrequently or at random times, so event sampling is only used as a cause-and-effect type of observation. Once the behavior occurs, the observer looks at what happened to cause the behavior and what happened as a result of the behavior occurring. In Figure 6.7, you can see how an observer uses the event sampling method to assess Keith's frequent behaviors.

time sampling An informal assessment tool that records particular events or behaviors during specific, continuous time intervals, such as three or four five-minute periods during the course of a morning.

Time Sampling. Time sampling records particular events or behaviors during specific, continuous time intervals (e.g., five minutes, one hour). When using the time sampling method, you take an interval such as five minutes and observe what behavior is occurring during that particular five minutes. Then you would repeat your observations over the course of a day or longer during a series of five-minute periods chosen either systematically or at random. The purpose of this method is to help identify when a child demonstrates a specific behavior. It also helps answer the question, "Does this child do something all the time or just at certain times and events?" An important key to remember when using time sampling is to observe *only* during the

FIGURE 6.8

Authentic Assessments: Example of Time Sample

Charlotte Lu—Teacher

Event	time	On task	Off Task
Center time	10.01 am	✓	
	10.02 am	✓	
	10.03 am		✓
	10.04 am		✓
	10.05 am		✓
	10.06 am	✓	
	10.07 am		✓
	10.08 am		✓
	10.09 am		✓
	10.10 am		✓
		Total: 3	Total: 7

Benjamin Woods—Para-Educator

Event	time	On task	Off Task
Center time	10.01 am	✓	
	10.02 am	✓	
	10.03 am	✓	
	10.04 am		✓
	10.05 am		✓
	10.06 am	✓	
	10.07 am		✓
	10.08 am		✓
	10.09 am		✓
	10.10 am		✓
		Total: 4	Total: 6

Time sampling is a very useful way for you to collect observation data when you need information about children's achievement and behavior over a period of time. Time sampling provides you with a useful "snapshot" of children and also serves as a useful source of information for you to share with parents.

specified time period. Figure 6.8 gives an example of how an observer uses the time sampling technique.

Rating Scales. Rating scales are usually numeric scales that contain a list of descriptors for a set of behaviors. If you have seen a rating scale before, you have noticed that they usually begin with the phrase, "On a scale of (a number) to (a number), you rate (the behavior) as . . . ." Rating scales enable a teacher to record data when they are observed. When using rating scales, make sure that the key descriptors and the rating

rating scale An informal assessment tool, usually a numeric scale, that contains a list of descriptors for a set of behaviors.

FIGURE 6.9

Authentic Assessments: Example of a Rating Scale

Teacher: *William Ivanov*

Student: *Rebecca M., Pre-K*

School: *Stephen F. Austin Elementary School*

Date: *11-10-2014*

Skill Set	No Mastery		Developing Mastery		Full Mastery
Demonstrates knowledge that print carries a message in a book	1	2	3	4	⑤
Orally retells a story	1	2	③	4	5
Listens with interest and comprehension when a story is read aloud	1	2	3	④	5
Sequences the events of a story in proper order	1	2	3	④	5
Answers questions concerning the meaning of a story	1	2	3	4	⑤

Rating scales are one of my favorite means of authentic assessment. They enable the user to gather data quickly. You should develop rating scales for all instructional activities and have them with you while you are teaching. In this way, you are embedding your rating scale in the instructional process.

scales are appropriate for what is being observed. Figure 6.9 is an example of a rating scale used for assessments.

Checklists.   Checklists are excellent and powerful tools for observing and gathering information about a wide range of student abilities in all settings. Checklists are lists of behaviors identifying children's skills and knowledge and can be used as a regular part of your teaching on a wide variety of topics and subjects. Some checklists can be developmental; others can help you assess behaviors, traits, skills, and abilities. In addition, the same checklists used over a period of time enable you to evaluate progress and achievement. Figure 6.10 is a checklist for assessing children's cognitive development in the classroom, and Table 6.3 is a social-emotional development checklist that can be used as a template or a model to make other checklists. Review Figure 6.10 and Table 6.3 now and think about how you could modify them to assess children's technology use and skills.

Here are some things for you to keep in mind when making and using checklists:

- Each checklist should contain the qualities, skills, behaviors, and other information you want to observe. In other words, tailor each checklist to a specific situation.
- Make sure you are observing and recording accurately to prevent errors in assessment.
- File all checklists in students' folders to track their progress and for future reference and use.
- Use checklists as a basis for conferencing with children and parents.
- Use the information from checklists to plan for small-group and individual instruction.

checklist A list of behaviors or other traits used in informal assessment to identify children's skills and knowledge.

FIGURE 6.10

Authentic Assessments: Example of a Cognitive Developmental Checklist, Ages 4–5

✓ Can correctly name several colors (4+)

✓ Tries to solve problems from a single point of view

✗ Follows three-part commands   *Will follow two-part commands, is working on three.*

✓ Recalls parts of a story

✓ Understands the concepts of "same" and "different"

✓ Engages in fantasy play

✓ Can count 10 or more objects   *Is up to 13!*

✓ Better understands the concept of time

✓ Knows about things used every day in the home (money, food, appliances)

Today, with the emphasis on the Common Core Standards and children's achievements, it is essential for you to gather data about children's achievement and their ability to perform certain tasks. Before, during, and after their teaching, many teachers have with them at all times short, concise checklists, such as this one, to make decisions about grouping, differentiation, and other strategies for helping children achieve.

Work Samples. A **work sample**, or a **student artifact**, is an example of children's work—art sample, writing sample, science journal—that demonstrates what they authentically know and are able to do. Figure 6.11 demonstrates how more and more children's work samples can be generated electronically. This figure illustrates how third grader, Megan, responds to the questions, "How do you like being in third grade?" and "What do you like about your teacher and classroom?" Examples of artifacts like Megan's are artwork; paper documents such as written work; electronic documents and electronic images; DVD recordings or excerpts of daily behavior; photographs of projects; voice recordings of oral skills (i.e., reading, speaking, singing); video recordings of performances (i.e., sports, musical, theatrical); scanned images of 3-D or large-scale art; and multimedia projects or Web pages exploring curriculum topics, current events, or social problems.

work sample An example of a child's work that demonstrates what the child authentically knows and is able to do.

student artifact An example of children's work—art sample, writing sample, science journal, etc.

Portfolios. Today many teachers use **portfolios**—a purposeful compilation of children's artifacts, as well as teacher observations collected over time—as a basis for assessing children's efforts, progress, and achievement. Before compiling students' portfolios, you will need to make decisions about the criteria you will use to decide what to put in the portfolios. Remember to only include samples of the child's work that you feel will be representative of the child's ability. Here are some questions to ask yourself when deciding what to include in student portfolios:

portfolio A compilation of children's work samples, other artifacts, and teacher observations collected over time.

- How will students participate in decisions about what to include?
- Do the materials show student progress over time?
- Do the materials demonstrate student learning of program and district standards and goals?
- Can you use the materials and products to adequately and easily communicate with parents about children's learning?

As you watch the **video**, notice how the teachers make use of portfolios for student self-reflection of learning and to communicate with parents.

TABLE 6.3 Authentic Assessments: Example of a Social-Emotional Developmental Checklist

Social and emotional learning are important factors to incorporate into your teaching. Checklists such as this one help you keep track of how each child is participating and growing in their social and emotional development.

Social-Emotional Developmental Checklist First Grade		
Social Behavioral Skills	Yes (Y)/No (N)	Date
Student is able to ask for what he/she needs and wants from caregivers.	Y	12-6-14
Student is able to follow directions and general expectations of caregivers.	Y	12-6-14
Student has good eye contact with peers.	Y	12-6-14
Student is able to express feelings appropriately to peers.	N	12-6-14
Student is able to share and interact cooperatively with peers.	N	12-6-14
Student is able to start conversations with peers.	Y	12-6-14
Student is able to ask questions of peers.	Y	12-6-14
Student is able to listen to peers.	N	12-6-14
Student is able to ignore peers when he/she should.	Y	12-6-14
Student is passive with peers.	N	12-6-14
Student is aggressive with peers.	N	12-6-14
Social and General Problem-Solving Skills	Yes (Y)/No (N)	Date
Student thinks about what he/she is doing.	Y	12-6-14
Student understands the consequences of behavior.	Y	12-6-14
Student behavior is goal oriented.	N	12-6-14
Student is aware when he/she is having a problem.	Y	12-6-14
Student learns from past mistakes and does not repeat them.	Y	12-6-14
Student uses good strategies to solve problems.	Y	12-6-14
Student knows when he/she is having a social problem.	Y	12-6-14
Student is knowledgeable of how he/she affects others.	Y	12-6-14
Student uses appropriate strategies to solve interpersonal difficulties.	N	12-6-14
Student uses nonaggressive solutions to solve disagreements with others.	Y	12-6-14
Emotional Well-Being and Level of Self-Esteem	Yes (Y)/No (N)	Date
Student acknowledges his/her own feelings.	Y	12-6-14
Student expresses feelings in appropriate ways. Student is able to tell others about his/her concerns/troubles.	N	12-6-14
Student thinks and verbalizes positive thoughts about self and others.	Y	12-6-14
Student seems to like him/herself (can identify positive self qualities).	Y	12-6-14
Student focuses on positive things and manages negative things.	Y	12-6-14
Student is able to take responsibility for achievements and mistakes.	Y	12-6-14

- Do the materials include examples to positively support students' efforts and progress?

Some teachers let children put their best work in their portfolios; others decide with children what will be included; still others decide for themselves what to include. Portfolios are very useful, especially during family–teacher conferences. Such a portfolio includes your notes about achievement, teacher- and child-made checklists, artwork samples, photographs, journals, and other documentation. The accompanying

FIGURE 6.11 Authentic Assessment: Example of a Work Sample

You have heard the old saying, of course, that a picture is worth a thousand words. Work samples are pictures of what a child has learned and a great way for you to observe what children have learned. These samples express children's ideas and creativity. Work samples can answer two questions: Do you think the child knows what she or he is supposed to know? How well is the child learning?

Technology Tie-In feature will give you an idea for using one type of technology, hand-held computers, in the classroom.

Interviews. **Interviewing** is a common way for observers and researchers to engage children in discussion through questions to obtain information. It allows children to explain behavior, work samples, or particular answers. Interviewing gives an eyewitness account and lets the student describe more visible information than through written records such as portfolios or checklists. When using interviewing, employ the hierarchy of questions in Bloom's Taxonomy of questioning to gain further insight into children's learning. (Refer to Figure 6.12.)

interviewing An informal assessment tool by which observers and researchers obtain information about children by asking questions and engaging them in conversation.

Rubrics. **Rubrics** are performance and scoring guides that differentiate among levels of student performance. Conventional rubrics use a range of three or more levels—for example, beginning, developing, and proficient. Each of the levels contains specific, measurable performance characteristics, such as "makes few/occasional/frequent spelling errors." Checklists, which provide specific steps for completing tasks to the highest level, are similar to rubrics.[11]

rubrics Performance and scoring guides that differentiate among levels of student performance.

Rubrics have a number of purposes:

- To enable teachers to assess performance based on preestablished criteria
- To make teachers' expectations clear
- To enable children to participate in the evaluation of their own work
- To enable children to distinguish between levels of performance and strive to do their best

To use rubrics effectively in your classroom, provide children with models or examples of each level of work and encourage them to revise their work according to the rubric assessment. You should also give children opportunities to contribute to the rubric criteria.

First grade teacher Emily Cherry for example, created a writing rubric for her students. She believes that her students should have an understanding of what is expected of them in a clear and concise manner. A rubric helps a child guide her efforts

FIGURE 6.12

Authentic Assessments: Excerpt from an Interview Assessment

Teacher: *Carla Silliman*

School: *Dewberry Elementary*

Student: *Jorge V.*

Grade: *2nd*

Date: *02-27-13*

CS: Jorge, do you remember the "Yellow School Bus" story we read on Wednesday?

JV: Yeah, they took the bus to Antarctica.

CS: Who went to Antarctica in the story?

JV: Well, the Friz, and Arnold, and Ralphie ... Dorothy Ann, Carlos, and Phoebe. And the uncle. Phoebe's uncle went on this trip, too.

CS: That's right, Jorge. Can you tell me what happened in the story?

JV: Well, like, the school bus turns into a ship and they go to Antarctica. And it's really cold, right? They have to wear parkas. That's like a really big coat. And, um, the class gets off the boat to look at penguins and they all complained about how bad it smelled.

CS: Mmhmm, then what happened next?

JV: Oh! Phoebe's uncle accidentally turns some of the kids into penguins. Some of the kids thought it was cool and some of them were afraid. Ralphie was afraid. He's always the one that's afraid. That'd be so cool to turn into a penguin. I'd be one of those giant penguins. Well, then they all go swim in the ocean. Penguins fly in the ocean but not in the air.

CS: Why do you think that's important?

JV: Most birds fly in the air. But in class we talked about how penguins can't fly because their feathers are made differently. Regular birds' feathers are, like, empty, hollow. But penguins are too heavy and they have all this extra fat on them. But penguins are special. I mean, unique, because they swim like they're flying. They're special that way. And remember, you said that made penguins unique, and I said I didn't know what unique meant so I used the dictionary to look it up. So yeah, but anyway, penguins swim so fast they can get away from sea lions and stuff.

CS: So penguins are unique. Tell me, why do you think Ralphie was afraid when they got turned into penguins?

JV: I don't know. Well, maybe because it was an accident. Or maybe he was nervous. Um, I think maybe he was afraid he couldn't turn back into a kid again ...

Of course, you've heard and watched interviews of celebrities and others. An interview is an excellent way to gather information that you might not be able to gather with paper and pencil or work samples. Interviewing children about their achievements, behaviors, and attitudes enables you to learn more about them. The interview data provide you with much useful information to guide your teaching.

technology tie-in

Using Technology to Assess Children

In the early 1970s, Intel developed the first microprocessor and Personal Computers (PCs) were born. By the twenty-first century, the Internet and the World Wide Web had exploded onto the scene and the Internet became the world's largest database. In 2008, the National Center for Education Statistics reported 100 percent of all schools had computers and the student/computer ratio was at an all-time low of 3:1.

This technological revolution provides early childhood teachers with tools to more effectively and efficiently assess young children in a formative way. Teachers can quickly and efficiently assess a child's literacy, phonological awareness, vocabulary, and math development using a netbook, notebook, Apple iPad, Apple iPod Touch, or laptop. Consider the following scenario:

It's September, and Tracy Richard is ready to begin assessing her four-year-old pre-Kindergarten children. They have been in school for one month, and the children are comfortable in their new surroundings. Tracy is anxious to see what the children in her class know about letters, vocabulary, math, and phonological awareness. This beginning-of-the-year assessment will provide her with a benchmark and enable her to modify her instruction to better meet her children's needs. Tracy grabs her netbook, reminds her assistant that she will be in the conference room next door, and calls Cassie, the first child that she will assess.

Together, Tracy and Cassie walk to the conference room chattering about the "games" they will play on the "little computer." The room is set up so that there is a small table and two child-size chairs. Tracy sits next to Cassie and places the netbook where they both can see the screen and begins the letter assessment. One by one, letters appear on the netbook screen, and Cassie quickly names them. Tracy easily scores each answer by discreetly tapping the arrows on the keyboard. Sixty seconds later, and the letter knowledge assessment is complete! Tracy walks Cassie back to the classroom and repeats the process. After she has assessed each child's letter knowledge, she will systematically work through the remaining parts of the assessment. The entire assessment will take Tracy less than 20 minutes to complete with each child.

Tracy gets the netbook back out and connects her netbook to the Internet in her classroom. She clicks on the "sync" icon on the desktop and quickly her assessments synchronize with a secure server. In just a few seconds, she has a report on how well each of her children know the letters of the alphabet. She will have a class report as well as a report on each individual child. Tracy assesses which children have an emerging understanding of letters and she will know exactly which children she will need to provide additional assistance. Tracy now has the information she needs to plan her instruction in the weeks to come.

Mobile-to-web technology allows teachers now to quickly and accurately assess children at multiple checkpoints throughout the year. With HTML-5 technology, the assessment process is simplified by allowing the teacher to assess offline. Teachers can administer assessments outside the classroom in environments that are more conducive for assessment.

There are many benefits for early childhood teachers who assess children using one of the many readily available mobile-to-web assessment tools currently on the market. The benefits of technology-based assessment over traditional assessment methods include:

- More accurate assessment results
- Less time spent preparing materials for assessment
- Less time spent in administering the actual assessment, which results in more time devoted to teaching in the classroom
- More cost-effective
- More flexibility to choose the appropriate setting for the assessment
- Immediate feedback
- Results are easy-to-interpret and share with administrators and parents
- Results enable teachers to differentiate instruction with greater ease

Tracy Richard is part of a generation that has never been without technology. She understands and values its early childhood applications. The result is that she is able to deliver instruction to her children that will have a positive impact on student achievement.

. . . .

Source: Contributed by Cheri Sherley, the University of Texas at Houston's Children's Learning Institute.

applying research to practice

Using Data to Guide Teaching and Learning

Throughout this chapter you have read a lot about the importance of using different assessment methods to guide your teaching and learning. While assessment is extremely important, sometimes we forget that the data from assessment is just as important as the assessment itself. It is the data that we get from assessment that forms the basis for our planning about what instructional strategies are best for young children. Research is very clear that the use of data in instructional decisions and processes can lead to improved student performance.[12] This kind of research is extremely important for you with the increased emphasis on the use of Common Core Standards as a means of increasing student achievement.

So, what does this mean for you?

- Use multiple sources of data to guide your planning and instructional decision making. No single assessment gives you the picture of the whole child, and the data from a single assessment are not sufficient to guide your teaching.
- Triangulate multiple sources of data. By this I mean that data about a child's social behavior, physical well-being, and classroom performance can be combined to help you fully understand why a child is having trouble learning to

read. For example, while you work on teaching a child basic decoding skills, you may also want to discuss with his family your opinion that the child needs more sleep, and your data about the child's behavior may indicate that he works best with a small group of children who are slightly advanced in achievement level.

- Share student assessment data with your colleagues and use it to help you and them as you plan horizontally (with your same-grade colleagues) and vertically with your other grade-level teachers.
- Use student data to group children in order to target students who need a particular kind of help, for example, vocabulary development.
- Use your assessment data to prioritize your instructional time. Knowing that particular children have similar instructional needs enables you to make sure that you provide them the instructional attention and time that they need to learn specific skills.
- Don't forget to involve students in the teaching-learning process. You can use your data on students to help students set learning goals for themselves. When students are involved in goal setting, they are more motivated to achieve.

and lets her know what is expected. Figure 6.13 shows how Emily completed her working rubric.

WHAT ARE THE CONTEXTS OF ASSESSMENT?

We have taken a look at individual processes of assessment—observation, screening, and individual tests—to gather data about children to help ensure achievement and learning. Now let's put all of this in context. Notice the four steps in Figure 6.14 and how they are linked to each other. The four steps, taken as a whole, make assessment a meaningful and child-appropriate process. Notice also that assessment is an ongoing process throughout the program year. Finally, notice how the purpose—the end product—of assessment is to promote, support, extend, and enrich children's learning so that children are successful in school.

Developmentally Appropriate Assessment

All assessment practices and procedures you conduct with young children should be developmentally appropriate. Here are some things to consider in your DAP assessment practices.

FIGURE 6.13

Authentic Assessments: Example of a Rubric

Conventions	Punctuation	Capitalization	Word Use	Ideas
My letters are written clearly. ✓	I use a period at the end of each ✓ sentence.	I use both capital and lowercase ✓ letters.	I use synonyms for words I write a lot. ✓	I describe where my story takes place. ✓
I leave white spaces between my ✓ words.	I use a question mark at the end of ✗ each question.	I use a capital letter to start the ✓ names of people, pets, and places.	I use new spelling words. ✓	I describe what characters feel. ✓
My sentences go from left to right. ✓	I use an exclamation point at the end of an ✓ exclamation.	I use a capital letter to start the ✓ first word of a sentence.	I use the right action word form ✗ with my nouns.	My story has a beginning, middle, and end. ✓

Have you ever gotten a grade on an assignment and didn't understand why you got it? Rubrics take the guesswork out of scoring children's work and at the same time enable children to know ahead of time the different levels of expectation for a particular topic/assignment. Rubrics take the mystery out of what students have to do and the level that they have to perform, and they make it clear what is considered high-quality work.

- *Assessment instruments are used for their intended purposes.* Assessments are used in ways consistent with the purposes for which they were designed. If the assessments will be used for additional purposes, they need to be validated for those purposes.

- *Assessments are appropriate for ages and other characteristics of children being assessed.* Assessments are designed for and validated for use with children whose ages, cultures, home languages, socioeconomic status, abilities and disabilities, and other characteristics are similar to those of the children with whom the assessments will be used.

- *What you assess is developmentally and educationally significant.* The objects of assessment include a comprehensive, developmentally and educationally important set of goals, rather than a narrow set of skills. Assessments are aligned with early learning standards, with program goals, and with specific emphases in the curriculum.

- *Use assessment data to understand and improve learning.* Assessments lead to improved knowledge about children. This knowledge is translated into improved curriculum implementation and teaching practices. Assessment helps early childhood professionals understand the ways a specific child or group of children learn; enhance overall knowledge of child development; improve educational programs for young children while supporting continuity across grades and settings; and access resources and supports for children with specific needs.

- *Your assessment should be conducted in realistic settings and situations that reflect children's actual performance.* To influence teaching strategies or to identify children in need of further evaluation, the evidence used to assess young children's characteristics and progress is derived from real-world classroom or family contexts that are consistent with children's culture, language, and experiences.

- *Use multiple sources of evidence gathered over time.* Your assessment system should emphasize repeated, systematic observation, documentation, and other forms of performance-oriented assessment.

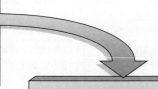

FIGURE 6.14 Integration of Observation, Assessment, Evaluation, and Achievement

Gathering data is only one step in the process to help children be successful. You have to use data to plan for and guide your instructional activities. Done well, the integration of assessment data with instructional practices leads to achievement and success for children.

Step 1:

Initial Screening and Assessment to Determine:
• Overall health status
• Developmental level(s)
• Social competence and behavior abilities and needs
• Academic skills/readiness level(s)

Step 2:

Observation and Ongoing Assessment—Daily, Monthly, and Quarterly:
• Monitoring of child's progress
• Ongoing assessment of achievement, strengths and needs, interests, and learning styles

Step 3:

Using Data to Inform Teaching and Learning Support:
• Ensure positive child outcomes
• Individualize the curriculum
• Build on prior knowledge and experiences
• Provide meaningful experiences and activities

Step 4:

Successful Completion of School Year or Program:
• Child has met standards for program or grade
• Child has achieved at high levels
• Child is confident and eager to enter the next grade or program

TEACHING AND LEARNING IN THE INCLUSIVE CLASSROOM: ASSESSMENT OF CHILDREN WITH DISABILITIES

As an early childhood professional, you will have many opportunities to assess or participate in the assessment of young children with disabilities. Assessment is a pivotal event for families and their children because assessment results are used to include or exclude children from specialized intervention that can change their developmental and academic destinies.[13]

Let's look at assessment considerations for students with special needs and English language learners (ELLs). The Individuals with Disabilities Education Act (IDEA) mandates that children with disabilities be included in state- and district-wide assessments, unless alternate assessments are more appropriate. For many students with disabilities, participation in classroom, district, or state assessments will not necessitate any changes in the manner in which teachers administer assessments. Assessment and evaluation for children with special needs must be fair and equitable for all children, and teachers must adhere to the mandates required by IDEA. Tests should:

- Be administered in the child's native language or other mode of communication.
- Be validated for the purpose they are being used for.
- Be administered by trained personnel in conformance with instructions from the test publisher.
- Be only one source of information used to decide eligibility for special education.
- Provide information about the students' educational needs, not simply intelligence.

In addition, in this chapter you have learned about the various ways teachers assess children that go beyond state, district, or standardized tests. Children both with and without disabilities will require accommodations to those assessments and the more informal assessments given by classroom teachers. These accommodations do not change the content of the test but usually fall into one of five categories. Using these accommodations will help you and other teachers equitably assess all children:

1. *Format accommodations*—The assessment directions or content is altered to include visual (such as large print), tactile (such as Braille or raised print), or auditory (such as an audio recording) presentations depending on the needs of the child.
2. *Response accommodations*—Children can respond in different ways such as using an assistive communication device, typing, sign language, or pointing.
3. *Setting accommodations*—The location of an assessment is changed so it is free from distractions and other interruptions. For example, a child might be moved to a room that is quiet or has fewer children moving about.
4. *Timing accommodations*—These accommodations change the allowable length of the testing time and provide students with the time and breaks they need.
5. *Scheduling accommodations*—These accommodations may change the particular time of day, day of the week, or number of days an assessment is given.

WHAT ARE THE ISSUES IN THE ASSESSMENT OF YOUNG CHILDREN?

As with almost everything that has been and will be discussed in this book, some issues surround essential questions about what is good practice, what is inappropriate practice, and what is best for children and families. Assessment is no different. Let's examine two important issues of assessment in early childhood.

Assessment and Accountability

There is a tremendous emphasis on the use of standardized tests to measure achievement for comparing children, programs, school districts, and countries. This emphasis will continue for a number of reasons. First, the public, including politicians and legislatures, sees assessment as a means of making schools and teachers accountable for teaching the nation's children. Second, assessment is seen as playing a critical role in the reform of education. As long as there is a public desire to improve teaching and achievement, we will continue to see an emphasis on assessment for accountability purposes.

diversity tie-in

High-Stakes Tests Leave Minority Students Behind

Today, students from preschool to high school are subjected to an almost endless array of tests. These tests are designed to measure everything from achievement, abilities, interests, and reading level to friendship preferences. When these tests are used to make critical decisions about students that have serious school and life consequences, they are called *high-stakes tests*. For example, standardized achievement tests are used to make decisions about whether Maria or Mario should be promoted to the next grade or whether Jennifer or Johnny has to attend summer school. But grade promotion and summer school attendance are not the only high-stakes decisions about young children that are based on tests.

Take the case of Amir Diego Howard, a bright third grader at Sierra Vista Elementary School. Amir's teacher thought he was a perfect candidate for the school district's gifted and talented (GT) program, so she referred him. Amir did well in the first two steps of the district's three-step process for admission into GT. First, Amir had his teacher's recommendation. Second, he scored at the 96th percentile on a national standardized achievement test. The third step was the problem. Amir failed to score an IQ of 133 on the Kaufman Brief Intelligence Test. "Sometimes they gave me these huge words that you don't even know," said Amir about the IQ test. "Like 'autobiography.' I don't know what that means. I'm only in the third grade." Unfortunately, across the country many language minority children like Amir fail to get into GT programs. Tests used to establish admission criteria discriminate against English language learners (ELLs) and minority students. As Joe Garret, Washo County GT curriculum coordinator, points out, "The kids that are English language learners, if they don't have the language and they don't have the background experiences, they are not going to do well on standardized tests we use to identify kids."

The good news is that increasing numbers of school districts are doing something about the inequities of high-stakes testing and how criteria for GT and other programs discriminate against English language learners. For example, districts are broadening and/or changing their criteria by:

- Placing more emphasis on nonverbal criteria such as learning styles and creative behavior
- Eliminating passing scores on high-stakes tests as a condition of program admission
- Placing more emphasis on teacher recommendation
- Changing admission criteria to ensure that more minority and ELL students are in GT programs
- Using language-free tests that don't discriminate against English language learners and minority children

High-Stakes Testing

High-stakes testing occurs when standardized or other kinds of tests are used to make important, and often life-influencing, decisions about children. Standardized tests have specific and standardized content, administration, and scoring procedures and norms for interpreting scores. High-stakes outcomes include decisions about whether to admit children into gifted or other special programs, whether to begin preschool or kindergarten, and whether to retain or promote children. Generally, the early childhood profession is opposed to high-stakes testing for young children because they are developing so rapidly in the early years. Also, well-trained personnel should do high-stakes testing. However, as part of the accountability movement, many politicians and school administrators view high-stakes testing as a means of ensuring that children learn and that those promotions are based on achievement. Many school critics maintain that in the pre-K and primary grades there is too much social promotion—that is, passing children from grade to grade merely to enable students to keep pace with their age peers. The Diversity Tie-In feature, "High-Stakes Tests Leave Minority Students Behind," tackles the issue of bias against minorities in high-stakes testing.

high-stakes testing Using assessment tests to make important and often life-influencing decisions about children, such as whether to admit children into programs or promote them from one grade to the next.

ACTIVITIES FOR PROFESSIONAL DEVELOPMENT
ethical dilemma

"I don't want that bonus!"

Meridith Wilson's school district has an incentive pay plan based on the results of children's achievement scores at the end of each year. Meridith, a dedicated second grade teacher, works hard to make sure her children do well. Meridith's principal recently notified her that she and four of her second grade colleagues would each receive a $7,500 bonus. The second grade team was the only group in the school notified that they would receive bonus money. At first Meridith was elated, but the more she thought about it, the more she felt as though she was not doing the right thing by accepting the bonus money. Meridith decided to ask her colleagues to join her in rejecting the bonus. On her Facebook page, she addressed her colleagues, saying, "I teach for the children. I don't teach for the money. Besides, I don't want our bonus money to have a negative impact on the collegial spirit in which we all work."

Do you agree with Meridith that she should reject the bonus money? Is Meridith being foolish? Should Meridith swallow her ethical pride and take the money and run? What would you do?

Application Activities

1. How has what you learned in this chapter influenced your ideas about how to assess children? List two ways that you will utilize these ideas in your teaching. Share them with your classmates on your class discussion board and ask them to add to your list.

2. Observe a particular child during play or another activity. Before your observation, make sure you follow the steps presented in this chapter. Use the information you gathered to plan a learning activity for the child. Post it on your class discussion board and ask for feedback on whether it is appropriate for the child.

3. Based on your knowledge and the information provided in this chapter, provide three examples of how you will use observation to assess in your classroom. Share these ideas online with your classmates. See if they have the same ideas that you did or if they have different ideas for how to assess children.

4. Review the different types of assessment presented in this chapter. Go online and look for examples of how these types of assessments have been utilized by Teachers of the Year. Then, go on Facebook, Twitter, and so on and ask for opinions on whether these examples are good ways to assess children in the classroom.

5. Frequently, articles in newspapers and magazines address assessment and testing issues. Go online, review these sources, and determine what assessment and evaluation issues are "in the news." Tweet these articles to your classmates and share what you discovered in your searches.

6. Go online and look for arguments for and against high-stakes testing. Create a survey and post it on your class action board. Have your classmates vote pro or con for high-stakes testing. What do the data reveal to you?

Linking to Learning

A Guide to the Developmentally Appropriate Assessment of Young Children

www.kidsource.com
This guide to the developmentally appropriate assessment of young children provides useful information about the appropriate uses of assessment and assessment results.

Linking Assessment and Teaching in the Critical Early Years

www.nea.org
www.keysonline.org
Excellent sources for additional information about assessment through documentation and about linking assessment and teaching.

MyEducationLab

Go to Topic 4 (Observation/Assessment) in the MyEducationLab (www.myeducationlab.com) for your course, where you can:

- Find learning outcomes for Observation/Assessment along with the national standards that connect to these outcomes.

- Complete Assignments and Activities that can help you more deeply understand the chapter content.

- Apply and practice your understanding of the core teaching skills identified in the chapter with the Building Teaching Skills and Dispositions learning units.

- Hear viewpoints of experts in the field in Professional Perspectives.

- Check your comprehension on the content covered in the chapter by going to the Study Plan in the Book Resources for your text. Here you will be able to take a chapter quiz, receive feedback on your answers, and then access Review, Practice, and Enrichment activities to enhance your understanding of chapter content.

INFANTS AND TODDLERS

Critical Years for Learning

chapter 7

NAEYC Standards for Early Child Professional Preparation Programs

Standard 1. Promoting Child Development and Learning

I use my understanding of young children's characteristics and needs, and of multiple interacting influences on children's development and learning, to create environments that are healthy, respectful, supportive, and challenging for each child.[1]

Standard 4. Using Developmentally Effective Approaches to Connect with Children and Families

I understand and use positive relationships and supportive interactions as the foundation for my work with young children and families. I know, understand, and use a wide array of developmentally appropriate approaches, instructional strategies, and tools to connect with children and families and positively influence each child's development and learning.[2]

Standard 5. Using Content Knowledge to Build Meaningful Curriculum

I understand the importance of developmental domains and academic (or content) disciplines in early childhood curriculum. I know the essential concepts, inquiry tools, and structure of content areas, including academic subjects, and can identify resources to deepen my understanding. I use my own knowledge and other resources to design, implement, and evaluate meaningful, challenging curricula that promote comprehensive developmental and learning outcomes for every young child.[3]

THE GROWING DEMAND for quality infant/toddler programs stems from the growing numbers of women with infants and toddlers in the workforce. The popularity of early care and education is also attributable to a changing view of the very young and the discovery that infants are remarkably competent individuals. We also know that the infant/toddler years are critical for growth and development. The experiences infants have—or don't have—influence everything from development to school readiness.

Given the popularity and interest in infants and toddlers and their programs, it is no wonder that more early childhood professionals are selecting the infant/toddler years as their career choice. For example, Anita Jefferson at the Redmond Toddler Group in Redmond, Washington, bursts with energy and enthusiasm for her two- and three-year-olds classes. It's clear to her toddlers that she is a kid at heart. They are very responsive to her animated songs, joyful dances, and creative art projects.[4]

Many infant teachers use textured toys to enhance the learning of children in their classroom. Because infants learn best through feeling and touch, giving them materials such as bumpy balls and touch-and-feel books enables them to explore their world through their own sense of touch.

WHAT ARE INFANTS AND TODDLERS LIKE?

Infants and toddlers are amazing! Think for a minute about your experiences with infants. What characteristics stand out most in your mind? I know that infants never cease to amaze me! Infants are capable of so many accomplishments. They are great imitators. Make a face at an infant and she will make a face back. Stick your tongue out at an infant and she will stick out her tongue at you. Talk to infants and they will "talk" back to you![5] New research suggests that infants are able to lip read by focusing on the mouth of the person speaking to them. After several months, babies shift their attention to the speaker's eyes.[6] (See the feature Applying Research to Practice in this chapter.) One of the great delights and challenges of working with infants is that you will constantly discover the wonderful things they can do.[7] Remember the story of Goldilocks? She had to find porridge, a chair, and a bed that exactly suited her. Well, babies are the same way. They want learning experiences that are just right for them. Researchers have found that babies seek learning materials and experiences that are most efficient for them to learn from. They call this the Goldilocks effect.[8] You will read more about this in the Applying Brain Research section.

Have you ever tried to keep up with a toddler? Everyone who tries ends up exhausted at the end of the day! A typical response is, "They are into everything!" And indeed they are. Toddlers are busy from morning until night getting on and into things that parents and caregivers never expected. But "getting into everything" is good for toddlers. Exploration helps toddlers learn about their world by using all of their senses. For parents and caregivers the challenge is to make sure toddlers can explore safely. Toddlers can even read your mind! Toddlers engage in "emotional eavesdropping" by listening and watching emotional reactions directed from one adult to another. They then use this emotional information to shape their own behavior.[9] Understanding other people's emotions is a critical school readiness skill. This is one reason infants and toddlers need emotionally stable teachers.

I want you to understand what children are like. To help you achieve this goal, I have included two special features, Portraits of Infants and Portraits of Toddlers. These portraits provide you with an "up-close" and personal look at real infants and toddlers as described for you by their caregivers. As you review each of these portraits, use them to consider how to apply what you have learned in this chapter. For example, for each child featured, what could you do to modify the environment to meet that child's particular needs?

Infant/Toddler Milestones

The infant and toddler years between birth and age three are full of developmental milestones and significant events. Infancy, life's first year, includes the first breath, first smile, first thoughts, first words, and first steps. Significant developments continue during toddlerhood, the period between one and three years. Two of the most outstanding developmental milestones of these years are walking and language acquisition. Mobility and language are the cornerstones of autonomy that enable toddlers to become independent. These unique developmental events are significant for children as well as those who care for and teach them. How you, other early childhood professionals, and primary caregivers respond to infants' first accomplishments and toddlers' quests for autonomy helps determine how they will develop and master life events.

MyEducationLab
Visit the MyEducationLab for *Fundamentals of Early Childhood Education* to enhance your understanding of chapter concepts with a personalized Study Plan. You'll also have the opportunity to hone your teaching skills through video-based Assignments and Activities as well as Building Teaching Skills and Dispositions lessons.

FOCUS QUESTIONS

1. What are infants and toddlers like?

2. How does brain research influence your care and education of young children?

3. How can you support the psychosocial, emotional, motor, cognitive, and language development of infants and toddlers?

4. How can you provide developmentally appropriate and enriched environments to support infants' and toddlers' development?

5. How can you provide high-quality curricula for infants and toddlers?

6. What is infant/toddler mental health, and why is it important?

Portraits of Infants and Toddlers

	Sara	Dakota	Avanti	Savo
General Description	9 months, Caucasian, female • Lives with her mother and grandmother • Expresses her feelings easily and openly • Loves to eat	15 months, Native American male • Lives with his father • Attends child care 8 hours a day • Cautious around strangers • Loves to be close to family members	22 months, African American male • Lives with his mother and father • Attends a family child care program • Has a friend at his child care center	30 months, Asian female • Lives with her parents and extended family • Very affectionate with everyone • Likes to pretend in the dramatic play area
Social-Emotional	• Begins to demonstrate separation and stranger anxiety—Sara cries when her mother leaves the room or when a stranger peeks into her stroller • Develops trust in primary caregivers if they are responsive—Sara's mother is responsive to her cues and cries • Uses social referencing and strong attachments to primary caregivers to feel secure—Sara scans her teacher's face to see if a noisy toy is safe	• Securely attached children explore away from primary caregivers, but often return for comfort and attention—Dakota plays with books, and then he brings one to his teacher • Continues to experience separation and stranger anxiety—Dakota appears cautious when a stranger enters the room or when mom leaves • Begins to demonstrate autonomy—Dakota protests when his teacher tries to put a bib on him • Uses strategies to calm himself (self-regulation)—Dakota reaches for his dad or his bunny when he is tired	• Continues to demonstrate strong attachments to primary caregivers; seeks these adults for enjoyment and security—Avanti likes to sit on his teacher's lap as she reads him a story • Self-regulation may be challenging at times—Avanti cries and falls to the floor when frustrated; he rubs his blanket on his face to calm down or go to sleep • Uses prosocial behaviors—Avanti shows concern for peers when they are hurt or distressed	• Affectionate relationships with primary caregivers help children feel secure—Savo often runs to her teacher for a hug • Children self-regulate in many ways, e.g. waiting for food to be served—Savo holds her hands behind her back when they aren't suppose to touch an object • Cooperation between children occurs—Savo and Alyssa carry a bucket of water together • Children are capable of many prosocial behaviors—Savo helps a friend who falls
Cognitive/Language	• Object permanence skills increase by 8 months of age, child begins to look for observed objects that are placed or moved out of sight—when mom put the toy behind her back, Sara crawled around her to retrieve the toy • Repeats actions that have an effect—Sara pulls the tail of the toy dinosaur to hear a song	• Often imitates adults and peers to accomplish goals—Dakota tries to get up on the couch after his dad sits down • Pretend with objects aimed at them—Dakota pretends to drink from a toy cup • Says approximately 10 words and/or use sign language but still communicates primarily with body cues and gestures	• Experiments with sequential strategies to accomplish goals—Avanti tries many strategies to get the toy out of the box • Directs pretend action to toys—Avanti moves the toy car across the floor and makes car noises • Imitates actions, even after a delay in time—Avanti watches a peer kiss a doll and then does the action when he gets home	• Uses a sequence of pretend actions such as waking a doll, feeding it, and putting it to bed again—Savo pats her doll, wraps it in a blanket, and sings a few words to it • There is often a "language explosion" from 18–36 months when children use many new words or sign language—Savo seems to learn several new words each day

Motor	• Sits, at first wobbly then well, freeing hands to manipulate objects—by 8 months of age, Sara sits and hardly ever topples over • Learns to move in a variety of ways—Sara crept on her tummy at 7 months, crawled on hands and knees by 8 months, and pulls to stand on sturdy objects (such as a coffee table) by 10 months • First uses raking grasp (using all of her fingers), then scissors grasp (using thumb and fingers), and then pincer grasp (using thumb and first finger) to pick up objects • Brings hands together in midline around 8 months of age—Sara bangs two objects together	• Many children walk—Dakota toddles across the room and adjusts his walking to different surfaces, slowing down as he walks in the mud • Enjoys crawling and walking up steps, placing one foot up and then placing the other foot on the same step—Dakota goes up and down his grandparent's steps, walking up and then crawling backwards down the steps • Turns cardboard pages of books alone or when read to by an adult—Dakota enjoys sitting in the book area at his school and turning the pages of a book by himself	• Runs with increased coordination—Avanti seems to run energetically everywhere he goes, but still falls at times • Walks up steps, putting both feet on each step—Avanti's parents stay close as he practices going up stairs • Increased fine motor skills allow children to manipulate more objects in increasingly complex ways—Avanti presses the spot on the bear's foot to hear it sing a song and then turns it upside down to hear it sing another song	• Balance improves and children climb, jump off short objects (such as rocks), master sliding down short slides, kick balls, and throw balls with increased ease—Savo climbs up on the two-foot rock and slides down on her bottom • Likes to build a tower with blocks, as fine-motor and perceptual-motor skills increase • Coordination increases with crayons, paints, using utensils, and playing with zippers become more interesting—Savo pulled down the zipper of her sleeper in the middle of the night
Adaptive (Daily Living)	• Begins to eat solid food when fed by adult—Sara opens her mouth as her mother approaches with a spoon full of soft cereal; she "tells" her mom that she doesn't want any more by turning her head, putting her lips together, or arching away	• **Uses a spoon, sometimes awkwardly, as wrist strength grows**—Dakota scoops up his yogurt with his spoon and licks off the yogurt • Uses pincer grasp (thumb and first finger together) well to pick up small objects and hold a cup with a lid on it—Dakota picks up his sippy cup with both hands and brings it up to his mouth	• Becomes increasingly independent, wanting to do things all by themselves—Avanti likes to unzip the zipper on Mom's sweater while she is wearing it • Uses a spoon to feed self, but still spills at times—Avanti uses a spoon for five minutes and then eats with his hands	• Increasingly independent with feeding—likes to eat with a spoon and a fork • Chooses which shirt, pants, or socks to wear when adult offers a choice between two—Savo chose the red shirt over the blue shirt as her mother held them out and said, "Which shirt do you want to wear today?"

Sources: Petersen, S. H., & Wittmer, D. S. (2009). Endless opportunities for infant and toddler curriculum. Upper Saddle River, NJ: Merrill/Pearson; Wittmer, D. S., & Petersen, S. H. (2009). Infant and toddler development and responsive program planning-A relationship-based approach. Upper Saddle River, NJ: Pearson; and Wittmer, D. S. (2008). Focusing on peers. The importance of relationships in the early years. Washington, DC: ZERO TO THREE.

Questions:

• Self-regulation and self-soothing play important roles in children's development. What are two important roles that self-soothing plays? What are two behaviors that children use to self-soothe and comfort themselves?
• What reasons can you give for why Dakota continues to experience separation and stranger anxiety?
• Is Avanti's language development "normal" for a child of 22 months of age? Avanti uses two-word phrases to express himself. What are these two-word phrases called?
• How is Savo's caregiver supporting her need for autonomy and independence? What are some things that you can do to support toddlers' in their quest for autonomy and independence?

TABLE 7.1 Average Height and Weight of Infants and Toddlers

Age (months)	Males		Females	
	Height (inches)	Weight (pounds)	Height (inches)	Weight (pounds)
Birth	19.75	7.75	19.50	7.50
3	24.00	13.25	23.25	12.00
6	26.50	17.50	25.75	15.75
9	28.25	20.50	27.50	18.75
12	29.75	22.75	29.00	21.00
18	32.25	25.75	31.75	24.25
24	34.25	28.00	33.75	26.50
30	36.00	29.75	35.75	28.50
36	37.75	31.50	37.25	30.50

Source: Centers for Disease Control and Prevention, National Center for Health Statistics, "Clinical Growth Charts," 2001, www.cdc.gov/growthcharts.

What Is Normal Development?

infancy A child's first year of life.

toddlerhood The period of a child's life between one and three years of age.

As you work with infants, toddlers, and other children, constantly keep in mind that "normal" growth and development milestones are based on averages. Table 7.1, for instance, gives average heights and weights of infants and toddlers. Remember, though, that "average" is only the middle ground of development. Also consider the whole child and take into account cultural and family background, including nutritional and health history, to determine what is normal for individual children. Furthermore, when we provide children with good nutrition, health care, and a warm, loving emotional environment, development tends toward what is "normal" for each child.

Nature Versus Nurture

nature The genetic background and innate qualities with which every child comes into the world. These innate qualities are influenced by culture, socioeconomic status, and parenting styles.

nurture The environment, culture, socioeconomic, family, and societal environments in which children are reared.

Does **nature** (genetics) or **nurture** (environment) play a larger role in development? This question is at the center of a never-ending debate. At this time there is no one right and true answer because the answer depends on many things. On the one hand, many traits are fully determined by heredity. For example, your eye color is a product of your heredity. Physical height is also largely influenced by heredity, as are temperament and shyness. Certainly height can be influenced by nutrition, growth hormones, and other environmental interventions, but by and large an individual's height is genetically determined.

On the other hand, nurturing and the environment in which children grow and develop also play an important role in development. For example, environmental factors that play a major role in early development include nutrition, quality of the environment, stimulation of the brain, affectionate and positive relationships, and opportunities to learn. Think for a moment about other kinds of environmental influences that affect development, such as family, neighborhood, school, and friends.

A decade or two ago, we believed that nature and nurture were competing entities and that one of these was dominant over the other. Today we understand that they are not competing entities; both are necessary for normal development, and it is the interaction between the two that makes children the individuals they are.

BRAIN DEVELOPMENT

Let's continue our look at young children with a discussion of the importance of the brain in ongoing growth and development. Brain and child development research has created a great deal of interest in the first three years of life. Research on the brain has enormous implications for early childhood education and for public policy. Brain research provides a strong basis for making decisions about what programs to provide for young children, as well as what environmental conditions promote optimal child development. Brain research also underscores the importance of early experiences and the benefits of early intervention services, thus pointing toward a positive economic return on investments in young children.

Public interest in the application of brain research to early childhood education has intensified. In many cases that research affirms what early childhood educators have always intuitively known: Good parental care, warm and loving attachments, and positive age-appropriate stimulation from birth onward make a tremendous difference in children's cognitive development for a lifetime. Let's review some interesting facts about infant and toddler brain development and consider the implications they have for your practice as a professional. Also review Figure 7.1, which shows the regions of the brain and their functional processes.

The brain is a fascinating and complex organ. Anatomically, the young brain is like the adult brain, except it is smaller. The average adult brain weighs approximately 3 pounds. At birth, the infant's brain weighs 14 ounces; at six months, 1.31 pounds; and at three years, 2.4 pounds. So you can see that during the first two years of life the brain undergoes tremendous physical growth. The brain finishes developing at about age ten, when it reaches its full adult size.

At birth, the brain has one hundred billion *neurons,* or nerve cells, which is the total amount it will ever have. It is important for parents and other caregivers to play with, respond to, interact with, and talk to young children because this is the way brain connections develop and learning takes place. Brain connections become permanent as children use them repeatedly. However, brain connections that are not used or

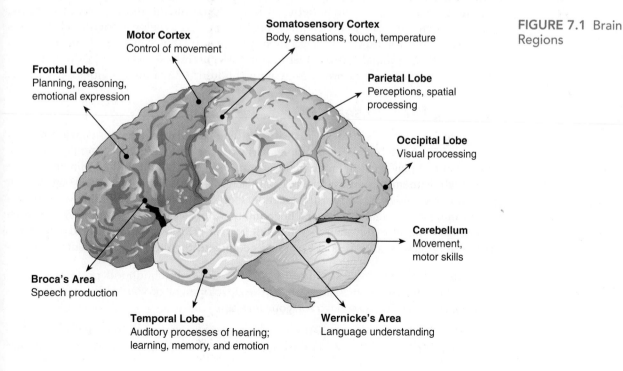

FIGURE 7.1 Brain Regions

Motor Cortex
Control of movement

Somatosensory Cortex
Body, sensations, touch, temperature

Frontal Lobe
Planning, reasoning, emotional expression

Parietal Lobe
Perceptions, spatial processing

Occipital Lobe
Visual processing

Cerebellum
Movement, motor skills

Broca's Area
Speech production

Temporal Lobe
Auditory processes of hearing; learning, memory, and emotion

Wernicke's Area
Language understanding

neural shearing *or* pruning
The process of brain connections withering away when they are not used or used very little.

synaptogenesis The formation of connections, or synapses, among neurons; this process of brain development begins before birth and continues until age ten.

synapses Brain connections; the junction across which nerve impulses pass.

critical periods Periods that represent a narrow window of time during which a specific part of the body is most vulnerable to the absence of stimulation or to environmental influences.

sensitive periods Periods of development during which it is easier to learn something than it is at other times.

used very little may wither away. This withering away is known as neural shearing or pruning. This helps explain why children who are reared in language-rich environments do well in school, while children who are not reared in such environments may be at risk for academic failure.

Also, by the time of birth, through a process called synaptogenesis, these billions of neurons have formed over fifty trillion synapses or connections across which nerve impulses pass. This process will continue to occur until the age of ten. The experiences that children have help form these neural connections. Experiences count. If children don't have the experiences they need to form neural connections, they may be at risk for poor developmental and behavioral outcomes. In this regard, remember that while experiences count, not all experiences are equal! Children need high-quality experiences that contribute to their education and development.

In addition, children need the right experiences at the right times. These "right times" are known as critical periods. Critical periods represent a narrow window of time during which a specific part of the body is most vulnerable to the absence of stimulation or to environmental influences.[10] For example, the critical period for language development is the first year of life. It is during this time that the auditory pathways for language learning are formed. Beginning at birth, an infant can distinguish the sounds of all the languages of the world. But at about six months, through the process of neural shearing or pruning, infants lose the ability to distinguish the sounds of languages they have not heard. By twelve months, their auditory maps are pretty well in place.[11] It is literally a case of "use it or lose it." An infant whose mother or other caregiver talks to her is more likely to have a larger vocabulary than an infant whose mother doesn't talk to her.

Having the right experiences at the right time also relates to broad, developmental "windows of opportunity" or sensitive periods during which it is easier to learn something than it is at another time. Sensitive periods represent a less precise and often longer period of time when skills, such as acquiring a second language, are influenced. However, if the opportunity for learning does not arise, these potential new skills may not be lost forever. They may be harder to learn or they may not be learned fully.[12] During the last decade, scientists and educators have spent considerable time and energy exploring the links between brain development and classroom learning. Brain research provides many implications for how to develop enriched classrooms for children and for how to engage them in activities that will help them learn and develop to their optimal levels. Most importantly, brain research has made educators aware of the importance of providing young children stimulating activities early in life.

Applying Brain Research

Brain research also tells us a great deal regarding stimulation and the development of specific areas of the brain. For example, brain research suggests that listening to music and learning to play musical instruments at very early ages stimulate the brain areas associated with mathematics and spatial reasoning.[13] In addition, brain research suggests that gross-motor activities and physical education should be included in a child's daily schedule throughout the elementary years. Regrettably, school systems often cut programs such as physical education and music in times of budget crisis, even though research shows that these programs are essential to a child's complete cognitive development.[14]

Brain-Based Guidelines for Teaching.   As an early childhood professional, reflect on the following conclusions about the development of young children and consider the implications they have for your teaching:

1. Child development is shaped by a dynamic and continuous interaction between biology and experience. For example, the years from birth to age eight are

extremely important environmentally, especially for nutrition, stimulation of the brain, affectionate relationships with parents and others, and opportunities to learn. Think a moment about how other kinds of environmental influences—such as family, school, and friends—affect development.

2. Culture influences every aspect of human development and is reflected in child-rearing beliefs and practices designed to promote healthy adaptations. For example, the kinds of foods parents feed their children, the ways they discipline, and their beliefs about the importance of education are based on cultural beliefs and customs.

3. The growth of self-regulation is a cornerstone of early childhood development that cuts across all domains of behavior. For example, children learn to regulate their behaviors with the help of parents and teachers who provide help in controlling their behavior and who guide them in making good choices.

4. Children are active participants in their own development, reflecting the intrinsic human drive to explore and master one's environment. This drive to explore is especially evident in toddlers' constant exploring and "getting into things."

5. Child–adult relationships and the effects of these relationships on children are the building blocks of healthy development. For example, children whose parents read to them form positive relationships with and happy memories of reading.

6. The timing of early childhood experiences is important. However, children remain vulnerable to risks throughout the early years of life and into adulthood. For example, much of what represents a threat to healthy brain development involves what we call *toxic stress,* resulting from chronic negative experiences. Stressors include child abuse and neglect. We know that the presence of these stressors can change brain chemistry and affect behavior. This is why professionals must help protect children from stress and harm. The accompanying Professionalism in Practice feature outlines for you five best practices that you can implement in your work with infants and toddlers.

PSYCHOSOCIAL AND EMOTIONAL DEVELOPMENT

Now, review Erik Erikson's theory of psychosocial development. The first of Erikson's psychosocial stages, basic trust versus basic mistrust, begins at birth and lasts about one and a half to two years. For Erikson, basic trust means that "one has learned to rely on the sameness and continuity of the outer providers, but also that one may trust oneself and the capacity of one's organs to cope with urges."[15] Whether children develop a pattern of trust or mistrust, says Erikson, depends on the "sensitive care of the baby's individual needs and a firm sense of personal trustworthiness within the trusted framework of their culture's lifestyle."[16]

Basic trust develops when children are reared, cared for, and educated in an environment of love, warmth, and support. An environment of trust reduces the opportunity for conflict among child, parent, and caregiver. The accompanying Professionalism in Practice feature, "Five Best Practices That Support Infant and Toddler Care and Education," describes how to provide high-quality care and education for children.

Social Behaviors

Social relationships begin at birth and are evident in the daily interactions of infants, parents, and teachers. Infants are social beings who possess many behaviors that they use to initiate and facilitate social interactions. Everyone uses *social behaviors* to begin and maintain a relationship with others. Consequently, healthy social development is essential for young children. Regardless of their temperament, all infants are capable of and benefit from social interactions.

In this **video,** observe infants and toddlers in a center setting. Observe how the caregivers interact with the children and reflect on how child-teacher relationships matter. Later, return to this video to observe motor and language development.

professionalism in practice

Five Best Practices That Support Infant and Toddler Care and Education

BEST PRACTICE 1 Health and safety are the foundation of program planning

Supporting Principles:

- The physical environment meets all state and local legal standards.
- The caregiver ratio meets state and local standards and enables children to have free movement and exploration while monitoring for safety.
- Caregivers collaborate with families regarding nutrition and milestones of physical development.

BEST PRACTICE 2 Curriculum is in the context of relationships and routines

Supporting Principles:

- Primary caregivers maintain relationships with children over an extended period of time.
- Attachment and the development of trust are supported through individual responses to each child's unique needs. Specifically, there is no group schedule relating to routine.
- An individual curriculum plan addresses each child's development through specific interactions based on relationships and routines.

BEST PRACTICE 3 Interactions and materials are developmentally, individually, and culturally appropriate

Supporting Principles:

- All caregivers have completed at least one class in child development and use that knowledge of typical development in day-to-day interactions; for example, solid foods are not introduced until the tongue thrust reflex is fully inhibited.
- Caregivers observe individual children on a daily basis, documenting their individual development and adjusting interactions and materials accordingly.
- If individual development appears to be atypical, caregivers seek and receive resources, which scaffold appropriate early intervention.

- Caregivers are thoroughly familiar with the families in their program and have prepared and implemented a family plan, which is incorporated in each child's curriculum.

BEST PRACTICE 4 Families are the child's primary source of attachment

Supporting Principles:

- Caregivers maintain "optimum distance" in their attachment with the young children who are under their care; for example, caregivers avoid phrases such as "my baby," "come to mama," and so on and scaffold the child's primary attachment to the family in all interactions.
- Caregivers are aware of their personal biases and expectations in regard to infancy and toddlerhood and avoid applying them to their professional work with very young children.

BEST PRACTICE 5 Infant and toddler care and education is distinctly different from preschool, infant stimulation plans, or babysitting

Supporting Principles:

- Interactions and materials in programs for very young children are presented in the context of routines and relationships, not typical preschool curriculum, such as "group time," "table time," and "free play." "Happenings" and individual interactions in the context of routines and attachment to a primary caregiver are the basis of the infant-toddler curriculum.
- Infant stimulation, such as DVDs, flash cards, and adult-centered activities are not developmentally appropriate or necessary in working with very young children who are typically developing.

Source: Contributed by Patrice Thatcher-Stephens, Chair, Staff Development, College of Siskiyou, Weed, California.

Crying is a primary social behavior in infancy. It attracts parents or caregivers and promotes a social interaction of some type and duration, depending on the skill and awareness of the caregiver. Crying also has a survival value; it alerts caregivers to the presence and needs of the infant. However, merely meeting the basic needs of infants in a matter-of-fact manner is not sufficient to form a firm base for social development. You must react to infants with enthusiasm, attentiveness, and concern for them as unique persons.

Imitation is another social behavior of infants. They have the ability to mimic the facial expressions and gestures of adults. When a mother sticks out her tongue at a baby, after a few repetitions, the baby will also stick out his tongue![17] This imitative behavior is satisfying to the infant, and the mother is pleased by this interactive game. Since the imitative behavior is pleasant for both persons, they continue to interact for the sake of interaction, which in turn promotes more social interaction. Social relations develop from social interactions, but we must always remember that both occur in a social context, or culture.

Attachment and Relationships

Bonding and attachment play major roles in the development of social and emotional relationships. **Bonding** is a relationship between a parent and child that usually begins at the time of birth and establishes the basis for an ongoing mutual attachment.[18] It is a one-way process, which some maintain occurs in the first hours or days after birth. **Attachment**, on the other hand, is the enduring emotional tie between the infant and the parents and other primary caregivers; it is a two-way relationship and a strong affectional tie between a parent/caregiver and the child that endures over time. There are four states of attachment as shown in Figure 7.2.

Attachment behaviors serve the purpose of getting and maintaining proximity; they form the basis for the enduring relationship of attachment. Parent and teacher attachment behaviors include kissing, caressing, holding, touching, embracing, making

bonding A relationship between a parent and offspring that usually begins at the time of birth and that establishes the basis for an ongoing mutual attachment.

attachment An enduring emotional tie between a parent/caregiver and an infant that endures over time.

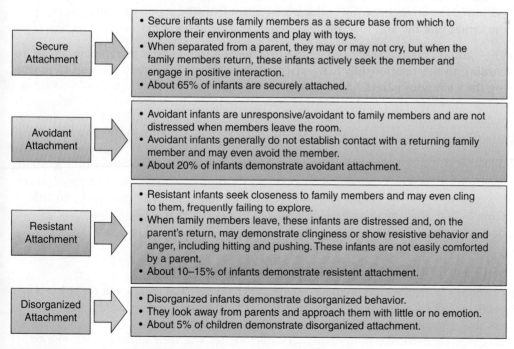

FIGURE 7.2 Individual Differences in Attachment

Source: Based on Mary Ainsworth, *Patterns of Attachment: A Psychological Study of the Strange Situation* (Hillsdale, NJ: Lawrence Erlbaum, 1978).

eye contact, and looking at the face. Infant attachment behaviors include crying, sucking, eye contact, babbling, and general body movements. Later, when infants are developmentally able, attachment behaviors include following, clinging, and calling.

Adult speech has a special fascination for infants. Interestingly enough, given the choice of listening to music or listening to the human voice, infants prefer the human voice.[19] This preference plays a role in attachment by making the baby more responsive. Infants attend to language patterns they will later imitate in their process of language development; they move their bodies in rhythmic ways in response to the human voice. Babies' body movements and caregiver speech synchronize to each other: Adult speech triggers behavioral responses in the infant, which in turn stimulate responses in the adult, resulting in a "waltz" of attention and attachment.[20]

Multiple Attachments. Increased use of child care programs inevitably raises questions about infant attachment. Parents are concerned that their children will not attach to them. Worse yet, they fear that their baby will develop an attachment with the caregiver rather than with them. However, children can and do attach to more than one person, and there can be more than one attachment at a time. Infants attach to parents as the primary teacher as well as to a caregiver, resulting in a hierarchy of attachments. Infants show a preference for the primary caregiver, usually the mother.

Parents should not only engage in attachment behaviors with their infants, but they should also select child care programs that employ caregivers who understand the importance of the caregiver's role and function in attachment. High-quality child care programs help parents maintain their primary attachments to their infants in many ways. The staff keeps parents well informed about infants' accomplishments, but parents are allowed to "discover" and participate in infants' developmental milestones. A teacher, for example, might tell a mother that today her son showed signs of wanting to take his first step by himself. The teacher thereby allows the mother to be the first person to experience the joy of this accomplishment. The mother might then report to the center that her son took his first step at home the night before.

The Quality of Attachment. The quality of infant–parent attachment varies according to the relationship that exists between them. A primary method of assessing the quality of parent–child attachment is the Strange Situation, an observational measure developed by Mary Ainsworth (1913–1999) to assess whether infants are securely attached to their caregivers. The testing episodes consist of observing and recording children's reactions to several events: a novel situation, separation from their mothers, reunion with their mothers, and reactions to a stranger. Based on their reactions and behaviors in these situations, children are described as being securely or insecurely attached, as detailed in Figure 7.2. The importance of knowing and recognizing different classifications of attachment is that you can inform parents and help them engage in specific behaviors that will promote the growth of secure attachments.

Temperament and Personality Development

temperament A child's general style of behavior.

Children are born with individual behavioral characteristics that, when considered as a collective whole, constitute **temperament**. This temperament—that is, what children are like—helps determine their personalities, which develop as a result of the interplay of their particular temperament characteristics and their environment. Figure 7.3 outlines for you the three classifications of children's temperament.

The classic study to determine the relationship between temperament and personality development was conducted by Alexander Thomas, Stella Chess, and

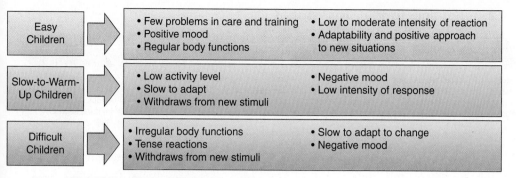

FIGURE 7.3 Children's Temperaments

Source: Based on A. Thomas, S. Chess, and H. Birch, "The Origin of Personality," *Scientific American*, 23(1970): 102–109.

Herbert Birch.[21] Thomas and his colleagues developed three classes or general types of children: the *easy child*, the *slow-to-warm-up child*, and the *difficult child* (see Figure 7.3).

It is important to develop a match between children's temperament and the caregiver's child-rearing style. The parenting process extends beyond natural parents to include all those who care for and provide services to infants; therefore, it is reasonable to expect that all who are part of this parenting cluster will take infants' basic temperaments into account.

MOTOR DEVELOPMENT

Think for a minute of all the life events and activities that depend on motor skills. Motor skills play an important part in all of life. Even more so, motor development is essential for infants and toddlers because it contributes to their intellectual and skill development. Table 7.2 lists infant and toddler motor milestones.

Here are some general principles that govern motor development:

- Motor development is sequential.
- Maturation of the motor system proceeds from gross (large) to fine (small) behaviors. For example, as part of learning to reach, Maria sweeps toward an object with her whole arm. Over the course of a month, however, as a result of development and experiences, Maria's gross reaching gives way to a specific reaching, and she grasps particular objects.
- Motor development is from cephalo to caudal—from head to foot (tail). This process is known as *cephalocaudal development*. At birth, Maria's head is the most developed part of her body; she holds her head erect before she sits, and her being able to sit precedes her walking.
- Motor development also proceeds from the proximal (midline, or central part of the body) to the distal (extremities), known as *proximodistal development*. Maria is able to control her arm movements before she can control her finger movements.

Motor development also plays a major role in social and behavioral expectations. For example, toilet training is a milestone of the toddler period. Many parents want to accomplish toilet training as quickly and efficiently as possible, but frustrations arise when they start too early and expect too much of children. Toilet training is largely a matter of physical readiness, and most child-rearing experts recommend waiting until children are two years old before beginning the training process.

TABLE 7.2 Infant and Toddler Milestones

Month 1	Month 2	Month 3	Month 4	Month 5	Month 6
• Looks at faces • Lifts head when lying on stomach • Responds to sounds	• Vocalizes, gurgles, and coos • Follows objects across field of vision • Holds head up for short periods	• Watches faces intently • Raises head and chest when lying on stomach • Visually tracks moving objects • Begins to babble	• Smiles and laughs • Can bear some weight on legs • Coos when spoken to	• Can distinguish between bold colors • Plays with hands and feet • Can roll once	• Turns towards sounds and voices • Imitates sounds • Rolls over in both directions • Reaches for objects

Month 7	Month 8	Month 9	Month 10	Month 11	Month 12
• Sits without support • Enjoys playing games like pat-a-cake and peek-a-boo • Responds to name • Finds partially hidden objects	• Says "mama" and "dada" to both parents • Grasps objects from hand to hand • Begins to crawl	• Stands while holding onto something • Is beginning to understand object permanence	• Waves good-bye • Crawls well, with belly off the ground	• Says "mama" and "dada" to correct parent • Stands alone for a few seconds	• Imitates others' activities • Indicates wants with gestures • Speaks first word • Takes first steps

Month 13	Month 14	Month 15	Month 16	Month 17	Month 18	Month 24
• Uses two words skillfully • Walks with assistance	• Eats with fingers • Empties containers of contents • Walks without assistance	• Plays with ball • Uses three words regularly	• Turns pages of a book • Becomes attached to soft toy or object	• Can build a block tower using 3–4 blocks • Enjoys pretend games • Likes riding toys	• Reads board books • Climbs; uses chairs and tables to reach toys	• Names at least six body parts • Sorts by shape and color • Uses two- to four-word sentences • Kicks ball • Begins to run

COGNITIVE DEVELOPMENT

Reflect on our discussion of cognitive development and think about how a child's first schemes are sensorimotor. Piaget said that infants construct (as opposed to absorb) schemes using reflexive sensorimotor actions.

Infants begin life with only reflexive motor actions that they use to satisfy biological needs. Consider sucking, for example, an innate sensorimotor scheme. Christina turns her head to the source of nourishment, closes her lips around the nipple, sucks, and swallows. As a result of experiences and maturation, Christina adapts or changes this basic sensorimotor scheme of sucking to include both anticipatory sucking movements and nonnutritive sucking, such as sucking a pacifier or blanket.

Children construct new schemes through the processes of assimilation and accommodation. Piaget believed that children are active constructors of intelligence through *assimilation* (taking in new experiences) and *accommodation* (changing existing schemes to fit new information), which results in *equilibrium*.

Stages of Sensorimotor Intelligence

Sensorimotor cognitive development consists of six stages (shown in Figure 7.4, Stages of Sensorimotor Cognitive Development) described in the following text.

Stage 1: Birth to One Month.
During this stage, Christina sucks and grasps everything. She is literally ruled by reflexive actions. Reflexive responses to objects are

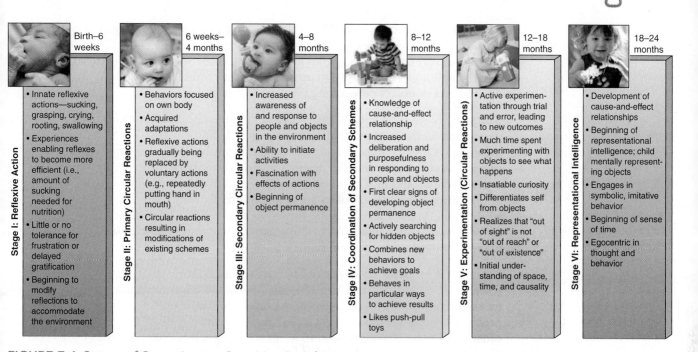

FIGURE 7.4 Stages of Sensorimotor Cognitive Development

undifferentiated, and Christina responds the same way to everything. Sensorimotor schemes help Christina learn new ways of interacting with the world, which promotes her cognitive development.

Grasping is a primary infant sensorimotor scheme. At birth, Christina's grasping reflex consists of closing her fingers around an object placed in her hand. As Christina matures in response to experiences, her grasping scheme is combined with the delightful activity of grasping and releasing everything she can get her hands on!

Stage 2: One to Four Months.
Sensorimotor behaviors not previously present in Christina's repertoire of behavior begin to appear: habitual thumb sucking (indicates hand–mouth coordination), tracking moving objects with the eyes, and moving the head toward sounds (indicates the beginning of the recognition of causality). Christina starts to direct her own behavior rather than being totally dependent on reflexive actions.

Primary circular reactions begin. A circular response occurs when Christina's actions cause her to react or when another person prompts her to try to repeat the original action. The circular reaction is similar to a stimulus–response, cause-and-effect relationship.

Stage 3: Four to Eight Months.
Christina manipulates objects, demonstrating coordination between vision and tactile senses. She also reproduces events with the purpose of sustaining and repeating acts. The intellectual milestone of this stage is the beginning of object permanence, the concept that things that are out of sight continue to exist.

Secondary circular reactions begin during this stage. Christina repeating an action with the purpose of getting the same response from an object or person characterizes this process. Christina will repeatedly shake a rattle to repeat the sound. Repetitiveness is characteristic of all circular reactions. "Secondary" here means that the reaction comes from a source other than the infant. Christina interacts with people and objects to make interesting sights, sounds, and events happen and last. Given an object, Christina will use all available schemes, such as mouthing, hitting, and banging; if one of these schemes produces an interesting result, she continues to use the scheme to elicit the same response. Imitation becomes increasingly intentional as a means of prolonging interest.

circular response Behavior that typically begins to develop in early infancy, in which an infant's own actions cause the infant to react or when another person prompts the infant to try to repeat the original action; similar to a stimulus–response relationship.

object permanence The concept that things out of sight continue to exist; this intellectual milestone typically begins to develop at four to eight months of age.

Stage 4: Eight to Twelve Months.

During this stage, characterized by coordination of secondary schemes, Christina uses means to attain ends. She moves objects out of the way (means) to get another object (end). She begins to search for hidden objects, although not always in the places they were hidden, indicating a growing understanding of object permanence.

Stage 5: Twelve to Eighteen Months.

This stage, the climax of the sensorimotor period, marks the beginning of truly intelligent behavior. Stage 5 is the stage of experimentation. Christina experiments with objects to solve problems, and her experimentation is characteristic of intelligence that involves tertiary circular reactions, in which she repeats actions and modifies behaviors over and over to see what will happen.

Christina and other toddlers are avid explorers, determined to touch, taste, and feel all they can. Novelty is interesting for its own sake, and Christina experiments in many different ways with a given object. For example, she will use any available item—a wood hammer, a block, a rhythm band instrument—to pound the pegs in a pound-a-peg toy.

Stage 6: Eighteen to Twenty-four Months.

This is the stage of symbolic representation, which occurs when Christina can visualize events internally and maintain mental images of objects not present. Representational thought enables Christina to solve problems in a sensorimotor way through experimentation and trial and error and predict cause-and-effect relationships more accurately. She also develops the ability to remember, which allows her to try out actions she sees others do. During this stage, Christina can "think" using mental images and memories, which enable her to engage in pretend activities. Christina's representational thought does not necessarily match the real world and its representations, which accounts for her ability to have other objects stand for almost anything: a wooden block is a car; a rag doll is a baby. This type of play, known as **symbolic play**, becomes more elaborate and complex in the preoperational period.

symbolic play When a child uses an object, such as a block, to represent something else, such as a car.

LANGUAGE DEVELOPMENT

Language development begins at birth. The first cry, the first coo, the first "da-da" and "ma-ma," the first words are auditory proof that children are participating in the process of language development (as shown in Figure 7.5). How does the infant go from the first

End of 3 months

- Smiles when you appear
- Makes "cooing" sounds
- Quiets or smiles when spoken to
- Recognizes your voice
- Cries differently for different needs (parents learn to "read" their babies and know what each cry means)

End of 6 months

- Makes gurgling sounds when playing
- Babbles repetitive syllables, such as "ba, ba, ba"
- Use of voice to express pleasure and displeasure
- Moves eyes in the direction of sounds
- Responds to changes in the tone of caregiver
- Notices that some toys make sounds
- Pays attention to music

End of 12 months

- First words
- Tries to imitate words
- Says a few words, such as "dada," "mama," and "uhoh"
- Understands simple instructions, such as "Please drink your milk"
- Understands "no"
- Turns and looks in the direction of sounds

End of 18 months

- Points to objects or pictures when named
- Recognizes names of familiar people, objects, and body parts
- Follows simple directions accompanied by gestures
- Says up to eight to ten words

FIGURE 7.5 Language Development in Infants and Toddlers

cry to the first word a year later? How does the toddler develop from saying one word to several hundred words a year later? How does language development begin? What forces and processes prompt children to participate in this uniquely human endeavor? Let us examine some of the explanations.

Heredity and Language Development

Heredity plays a role in language development in a number of ways. First, humans have the respiratory system and vocal cords that make rapid and efficient vocal communication possible. Second, the human brain makes language possible. The left hemisphere is the center for speech and phonetic analysis and is the brain's main language center. However, it does not have the exclusive responsibility for language. The right hemisphere plays a role in our understanding of speech intonations, which enables us to distinguish between declarative, imperative, and interrogative sentences.[22] Without these processing systems, language as we know it would be impossible.

Industrial Differences.   Children's industrial differences play a role in their learning and sequence of language development. For example, one of my students, Autumn, has an eleven-month-old daughter and a seven-year-old daughter. Autumn says, "My seven-year-old said her first word at nine months. Darley, my eleven-month-old, will probably be twelve months when she says her first word."

Language development begins at birth. Infants and toddlers need to be surrounded by a rich linguistic environment that enables them to develop the literacy skills necessary for successful learning.

The Sequence of Language Development

Children develop language in predictable sequences and in an age–stage process, which is described next.

First Words.   The first words of children are just that, first words. Children talk about people: dada, papa, mama, mommy, and baby (referring to themselves); animals: dog, cat, kitty; vehicles: car, truck, boat, train; toys: ball, block, book, doll; food: juice, milk, cookie, bread, drink; body parts: eye, nose, mouth, ear; clothing and household articles: hat, shoe, spoon, clock; greeting terms: hi, bye, night-night; and a few words for actions: up, no more, off.

Holophrasic Speech.   Children are remarkable communicators without words. When children have attentive parents and teachers, they develop into skilled communicators, using gestures, facial expressions, sound intonations, pointing, and reaching to make their desires known and get what they want. Pointing at an object and saying, "uh-uh-uh" is the same as saying, "I want the rattle" or "Help me get the rattle." As a responsive caregiver you can respond by saying, "Do you want the rattle? I'll get it for you. Here it is!" One of the attributes of an attentive caregiver is the ability to read children's signs and signals, anticipating their desires even though no words are spoken.

The ability to communicate begins with "sign language" and sounds and progresses to the use of single words. Toddlers are skilled at using single words to name objects, to let others know what they want, and to express emotions. One word, in essence, does the work of a whole sentence. These single-word sentences are called holophrases.

The one-word sentences children use are primarily referential (used primarily to label objects, such as "doll"), or expressive (communicating personal desires or levels of social

holophrases One-word sentences that toddlers use to communicate.

interaction, such as "bye-bye" and "kiss"). The extent to which children use these two functions of language depends in large measure on the teacher and parent. For example, children's early language use reflects their mother's verbal style. This makes sense and the lesson is this: How parents speak to their children influences how their children speak.

Symbolic Representation. Two significant developmental events occur at about the age of two. First is the development of **symbolic representation**. Representation occurs when something else stands for a mental image. For example, a word is used to represent something else not present. A toy may stand for a tricycle; a baby doll may represent a real person. Words become signifiers of things, such as ball, block, and blanket.

The use of mental symbols also enables the child to participate in two processes that are characteristic of the early years: symbolic play and the beginning of the use of words and sentences to express meanings and make references.

Vocabulary Development. The second significant achievement that occurs at about age two is the development of a fifty-word vocabulary and the use of two-word sentences. This vocabulary development and the ability to combine words mark the beginning of rapid language development. Vocabulary development plays a very powerful and significant role in school achievement and success. Research repeatedly demonstrates that children who come to school with a broad use and knowledge of words achieve better than their peers who do not have an expanded vocabulary. Adults are the major source of children's vocabularies.

Telegraphic Speech. You have undoubtedly heard a toddler say something like "Go out" in response to a suggestion such as "Let's go outside." Perhaps you've said, "Is your juice all gone?" and the toddler responded, "All gone." These two-word sentences are called **telegraphic speech**. They are the same kind of sentences you would use if you wrote a text message. The sentences are primarily made up of nouns and verbs. Generally, they do not have prepositions, articles, conjunctions, and auxiliary verbs.

Motherese or Parentese. Many recent research studies have demonstrated that mothers and other caregivers talk to infants and toddlers differently than adults talk to each other. This distinctive way of adapting everyday speech to young children is called **motherese**[23] or **parentese**. Characteristics of motherese are the following:

- The sentences are short, averaging just over four words per sentence with babies. As children become older, the length of sentences mothers use also becomes longer. Mothers' conversations with their children are short and sweet.
- The sentences are highly intelligible. When talking to their children, mothers tend not to slur or mumble their words. This may be because mothers speak slower to their children than they do to adults in normal conversation.
- The sentences are "unswervingly well formed"; that is, they are grammatical sentences.
- The sentences are mainly imperatives and questions, such as "Give Mommy the ball" or "Do you want more juice?" Since mothers can't exchange a great deal of information with their children, their utterances are such that they direct their children's actions.
- Mothers use sentences in which referents ("here," "that," "there") are used to stand for objects or people: "Here's your bottle." "That's your baby doll." "There's your doggie."
- Mothers expand or provide an adult version of their children's communication. When a child points at a baby doll on a chair, the mother may respond by saying, "Yes, the baby doll is on the chair."
- Mothers' sentences involve repetitions. "The ball, bring Mommy the ball. Yes, go get the ball. The ball, go get the ball."

symbolic representation The understanding, which develops at about age two, that something else can stand for a mental image; for example, a word can represent a real object or a concept.

telegraphic speech Two-word sentences, such as "Go out" or "All gone," used by toddlers.

motherese or **parentese** The distinctive way of adapting everyday speech to young children.

In working with parents of infants, what would you do to encourage them to use motherese with their children?

Negatives. If you took a vote on toddlers' favorite word, "no" would win hands down. When children begin to use negatives, they simply add "no" to the beginning of a word or sentence ("no milk"). As their "no" sentences become longer, they still put "no" first ("no put coat on"). Later, they place negatives appropriately between subject and verb ("I no want juice").

By the end of the preschool years, children have developed and mastered most language patterns. The basis for language development is the early years, and no amount of later remedial training can make up for development that should have occurred during this sensitive period for language learning.

Baby Signing. Think of all the ways you use signs—gestures to communicate a need or emotion. You blow a kiss to convey affection and hold your thumb and little finger to the side of your head to signal talking on the telephone. I'm sure you can think of many other examples. Now apply this same principle to young children. Children have needs, wants, and emotional feelings long before they learn to talk. There is a growing movement of teaching children to use signs and gestures to communicate desires or signify objects and conditions. Beginning at about five months, babies can baby sign. That is, they can use signals that stand for something else (e.g., a tap on the mouth for food, squeezing the hand for milk).

There is not universal agreement about whether to teach babies a common set of signs or to use ones that parents and children themselves make up. Linda Acredelo and Susan Goodwyn, popularizers of **baby signing**, identify these benefits: It reduces child and parent frustration, strengthens the parent–child bond, makes learning to talk easier, stimulates intellectual development, enhances self-esteem, and provides a window into the child's world.[24]

A major part of your role as an early childhood professional is to provide a developmentally appropriate environment and activities for young children. This means that you must know infant/child development and individual children. You must also know how to apply that knowledge to a curriculum that will enable children to learn what they need to know for successful learning and living.

baby signing The use of symbolic gestures by infants to nonverbally communicate to parents and others their needs and wants.

How to Promote Language Development in Infants and Toddlers

Providing a language-rich context supporting children's language and literacy is one of the most important things you can do as an early childhood professional. Following are some ways you can achieve this goal.

Treat Children as Partners in the Communication Process. Engage in conversations, smile, sing nursery rhymes, and make eye contact. Infant behaviors such as smiling, cooing, and vocalizing serve to initiate conversation.

Conduct Conversations. Talk to children clearly and distinctly. Conversations are the building blocks of language development.

Talk to Infants in a Soothing and Pleasant Voice. Mothers' language interactions with their toddlers are much the same as with infants. When conversing with toddlers who are just learning language, simplify your verbalization—but not by using "baby talk," such as "di-di" for diaper or "ba-ba" for bottle. Rather, speak in an easily understandable way. Instead of saying, "We are going to take a walk around the block, so you must put your coat on," you would instead say, "Let's get coats on."

Use Children's Names.   Use children's names while conversing with them. This personalizes the conversation and builds self-identity. The most important word to a child is his or her name. "My, Sarah! You look beautiful!" Infants who do not respond when their name is called may be more likely to be diagnosed with an autism spectrum disorder or another developmental problem at age two.[25]

Use a Variety of Means to Stimulate and Promote Language Development.   Read stories, sing songs, and give children many opportunities to verbally interact with you and other children.

Converse and Share Information.   Encourage children to talk and share information with you, other children, and adults.

Converse in Various Settings.   Encourage children to learn to talk in various settings. Take them to different places—the library, the park, the supermarket, the post office—so they can use their language with a variety of people. This approach also gives children ideas and events for using language.

Have Children Use Language in Different Ways.   Teach children how to use language to ask questions and to explain feelings and emotions. Tell children what they have done and describe things. "Mario! Great job! You got the book all by yourself!"

Teach the Language of Directions and Commands.   Give children experiences in how language is used for giving and following directions. Help children understand that language can be used as a means to an end—a way of attaining a desired goal. "Bruce, let's ask Christina to help us put the blocks back in the basket."

Converse with Children About What They Are Doing and How They Are Doing It.   Help children learn language through feedback—asking and answering questions and commenting about activities—which shows children that you are paying attention to them and what they are doing. "Okay, let's read a story. Hillary, what book is your favorite?"

Use the Full Range of Adult Language.   Talk to children in the full range of adult language, including past and future tenses. Talk about what happened yesterday, before a diaper change, and what will happen next. "Okay, Cindy! We changed your diaper, now we are going to put on this pretty pink top."

Use New Words and Phrases.   Read stories and talk about new words. Children's vocabularies are a prediction of their learning to read.[26] Children with good vocabularies can engage others in conversations. So, you will want to develop children's vocabularies by reading to them and engaging them in conversations in which you use a rich vocabulary to identify people, places, and things.

The caregiver in this video encourages language development while performing one of her many daily routines. Notice how she uses a higher pitch, the child's name, and singing as she converses with the child.

PREPARING ENRICHED ENVIRONMENTS TO SUPPORT INFANT AND TODDLER DEVELOPMENT

Research studies repeatedly show that children who are reared, cared for, and taught in environments that are enriched are healthier, happier, and more achievement oriented than children who are not raised in such environments. Environments for infants and toddlers should be *inviting, comfortable, healthy, safe, supportive, challenging,* and *respectful.* You must plan in order to create environments with these features. Figure 7.6 shows infant and toddler floor plans that you can refer to as you reflect on how you can create enriched environments for infants and toddlers.

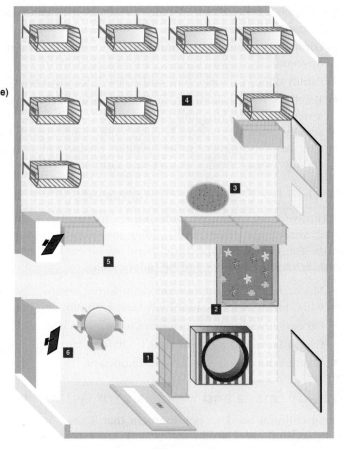

FIGURE 7.6 Infant/Toddler Floor Plan (0–18 months/12–30 months) for an Enriched Environment

1 Individual Cubbies
2 Infant Play Area (mobile)
3 Infant Play Area (non-mobile)
4 Sleep Area
5 Diaper-Changing Area
6 Eating Area

Also, as you plan, think about how you can make the environment as home-like as possible. Infants and toddlers like and need environments that are cozy, warm, and safe places to be. You can customize your children's home-like environment with curtains, family pictures on the walls, a couch, and so forth. Make sure that your home away from home includes objects from children's various cultures.

As you reflect and plan about creating enriched environments for children, review Figure 7.6, a floor plan for infants, ages birth to eighteen months, and a floor plan for toddlers, ages twelve to thirty months. Use them as a resource and planning guide for your enriched environment.

Following are some things you can do to provide an enriched environment for infants and toddlers.

Provide for Health and Safety

Safe environments are essential for infants, toddlers, teachers, and families. Here are some guidelines for providing safe environments for infants and toddlers:

- Areas used for diapering and toileting are separate from areas used for cooking, eating, and children's activities.
- Mattresses used for infants are firm; avoid soft bedding, such as comforters, pillows, fluffy blankets, and stuffed toys.
- All infant and toddler toys are made of nontoxic, lead-free materials and are sanitized regularly.

- All required policies and plans of action for health emergencies requiring rapid response (such as choking or asthma attacks) are posted.
- Locations and telephone numbers of emergency response systems are posted and up-to-date.
- Family contact information and consent for emergency care are readily available.
- Teachers, staff, volunteers, and children wash their hands with soap and running water after diapering and toilet use, before and after food-related preparation or activity, after hands have become contaminated with blood or other body fluids, after handling pets or other animals, before and after giving medications, before and after bandaging a wound, and after assisting a child with toileting.[27]

Provide for Basic Emotional Needs

basic trust An Erikson concept that involves trust, security, and basic optimism that an infant develops when nurtured and loved.

Supportive environments enable infants to develop **basic trust** and toddlers to develop **autonomy**. Infant and toddler care should be loving and responsive to their needs. The trusting infant can depend on others to meet her needs. Toddlers want to do things for themselves and be independent.

autonomy An Erikson concept that says as toddlers mature physically and mentally, they want to do things by themselves with no outside help.

- Meet infants' and toddlers' needs in warm, sensitive ways. Provide for their choices while taking into account their temperament, emotions, and individuality.
- Express love and be affectionate to your children. Tell them, "I love you!"
- Give infants and toddlers your undivided attention—respond to their actions.
- Treat each child as special and important.

Provide Space and Materials for Active Involvement

Tour a classroom designed for mobile infants in this **video**. Do the space, equipment, and materials provide a healthy, safe environment for infants to actively explore?

Young children need an environment that allows plenty of activity for them to grow both physically and intellectually. Here are some things you can do:

- Provide safe floor space indoors and grassy areas outdoors so children can explore and move freely.
- Provide low, open shelves that allow children to see and select their own materials.
- Have a cubby for each child's personal belongings. Personalize these with a picture of each child.
- Provide toys and objects that children can manipulate, feel, suck, and grasp.
- Provide objects and containers that children can use to put things in and dump out.
- Provide responsive toys that make sounds, pop up, and change color as children manipulate or act on them.
- Allow infants and toddlers to crawl, pull up, walk, move freely, and explore environments safely.
- Provide activities based on children's interests and abilities. This is a key to responsive and relational caregiving.
- Provide all kinds of books—stories, poems, and so on.
- Provide music as background and music to sing and dance to.

DEVELOPMENTALLY APPROPRIATE CURRICULUM FOR INFANTS AND TODDLERS

All early childhood professionals who provide care for infants and toddlers—indeed, for all children—must understand and recognize this important concept, which provides a solid foundation for any program. The NAEYC defines *developmentally appropriate* as having three dimensions:

applying research to practice

Sleeping, Speaking, and Being Choosy: What Research Tells Us

HOW SHOULD BABIES SLEEP?

Sudden infant death syndrome (SIDS) is the unexpected, sudden death of a child under age one. It usually occurs at night or at naptime. The American Academy of Pediatrics recommends that when parents and other caregivers put babies to sleep, they place them on their backs. In ongoing efforts to reduce and prevent SIDS, the American Academy of Pediatrics, in 2011, expanded their recommendations for a safe infant-sleeping environment to include the following:[28]

- Supine sleeping position (on the back)
- Use of a firm sleep surface
- Avoidance of soft bedding
- Room-sharing without bed-sharing
- Routine immunization
- Consideration of a pacifier
- Avoidance of overheating
- Avoidance of exposure to tobacco smoke, alcohol, and illicit drugs

So what does this mean for you?

- You have a tremendous responsibility to work with parents to inform and advise them about infant sleeping positions and their infant's safety and well-being.
- Make sure that you and your colleagues are thoroughly trained and are able to follow the rules and guidelines of the American Academy of Pediatrics and other health agencies in providing for infant/toddler safety.

BABIES LEARN TO SPEAK BY READING YOUR LIPS

Researchers recently reported that reading lips and watching mouths play an important role in learning to speak. Researchers gathered data on infants' language development by using a special eye-tracking device, which indicates where babies are focusing their eyes when adults are speaking. Infants' tendency to look at adults' lips when they are talking is most prominent in the first year of life.[29]

So, what does this mean for you?

- As I have repeatedly said throughout this book, talk, talk, talk and read, read, read to babies.
- Speak face-to-face with babies. Hold babies so that their face is anywhere from 12 to 18 inches from your face and where they can directly scan your lips while you are speaking to them.
- Interestingly, the authors of this study note that since children with autism look more at lips and less at faces, this tendency to lip read for a longer time than normal may be an early indicator of autism.
- Urge parents, grandparents, and other caregivers to be actively involved with their children. Some parents think that little happens developmentally in the first year of life. This study emphasizes even more that the first year plays a powerful role in children's language development.

APPLYING THE GOLDILOCKS EFFECT

Researchers at the University of Rochester discerned that infants must be highly selective in choosing what information in the environment to pay attention to in order to learn efficiently. They found that infants look away from (ignore) stimuli that are too complex and stimuli that are not stimulating enough. These results suggest that infants "implicitly seek to maintain intermediate rates of information absorption and avoid wasting cognitive resources on overly simple or overly complex events."[30]

So, what does this mean for you?

- The research suggests that infants are very actively engaged in seeking information, and they are very selective. So, it makes sense for you to apply Piaget's cognitive theory—make sure that infants' experiences are linked to what they know and provide them with novel experiences but ones that are not overly complex or too stimulating.

- What is known about child development and learning—referring to knowledge of age-related human characteristics that permits general predictions within an age range about what activities, materials, interactions, or experiences will be safe, healthy, interesting, achievable, and also challenging for children.

- What is known about the strengths, interests, and needs of each individual child in the group to be able to adapt for and be responsive to inevitable individual variation.

- Knowledge of the social and cultural contexts in which children live to ensure that learning experiences are meaningful, relevant, and respectful for the participating children and their families.[31]

Based on these dimensions, you must provide different programs of activities for infants and toddlers. To do so, you must get parents and your professional colleagues to recognize that infants, as a group, are different from toddlers and need programs, curricula, and environments specifically designed for them. For example, we know that sudden infant death syndrome (SIDS) occurs in very young babies—a developmental, researched fact. We also use the practice recommended by the American Academy of Pediatrics: that infants under the age of one year be put down for a nap or for the night on their *backs*.[32] As another example, we know that mobile infants and toddlers developmentally need lots of physical activity and opportunities to explore, so quality programs accommodate this need. Designing programs and practices specifically for different age groups is at the heart of developmentally appropriate practice. The early childhood education profession is leading the way in raising consciousness about the need to match what professionals do with children's development as individuals. We have a long way to go in this regard, but part of the resolution will come with ongoing training of professionals in child development and curriculum planning.

Finally, it is important to match teachers and child care providers with children of different ages. Not everyone is emotionally or professionally suited to provide care for infants and toddlers. Both groups need adults who can respond to their particular needs and developmental characteristics. Infants need especially nurturing professionals; toddlers, however, need adults who are also nurturing and who can tolerate and allow for their emerging autonomy and independence.

Multiculturally Appropriate Practice

Children and families are not all the same. They do not all come from the same socioeconomic and cultural backgrounds, and they do not all rear their children the same way. Consequently, it is important for teachers and caregivers to get to know children and families and to be culturally sensitive in their care and education practices. Even so, it may be that because of background and culture, families and professionals may not always agree on a particular policy or practice. For example, many infant/toddler programs teach self-help skills early and encourage children to become independent as soon as possible. These practices may conflict with some families' cultural beliefs and practices.

Curriculum for Infants and Toddlers

Curriculum for infants and toddlers consist of all the activities and experiences they are involved with while in your care. The curriculum provides for the whole child—the physical, emotional, social, linguistic, and cognitive aspects. Consequently, infant/toddler teachers plan for all activities and involvement: feeding, washing, diapering/toileting, playing, learning, having stimulating interactions, outings, being involved with others, and having conversations. You must plan the curriculum so it is developmentally appropriate.

All dimensions of the infant/toddler curricula are based on *responsive relationships*. This means that you are responsive to the *needs* and *interests* of each infant and toddler.

Provide Daily Routines

The infant/toddler curriculum is also built around routines of the daily organization and purposes of the programs. Routines include (1) arrivals and departures; (2) diapering and toileting; (3) feeding, mealtimes, and snacks; and (4) naps and sleep time.

Organizing the curriculum around routines and including routines in the curriculum provides children with consistency, security, a sense of safety, an increase of trust, and a general sense of well-being. Language development also provides you with an excellent opportunity to incorporate literacy into the curriculum.

Encourage Language Development

- Read, read, and read to infants and toddlers. Read aloud with enthusiasm, because this shows children how much you love to read.
- Read in all places and times—before naptime, when invited by children for special occasions, before and after outings, and so forth.
- Read from all kinds of books—stories, poems, and the alphabet.
- Provide books (washable, cloth, small board books, etc.) for children to "read," handle, manipulate, and mouth.
- Sing for and with children. Play a wide variety of music. Sing while changing diapers and doing other teacher–child activities.
- Read and sing nursery rhymes that provide children experiences with manipulating language.
- Talk, talk, talk.

As you promote and support children's language development you can also model and teach appropriate social interactions.

Promote Respectful Social Development and Interactions

- Use respectful language such "Please," "Thank you," and "Excuse me."
- Play games and engage in activities that include small groups of children.
- Play with toys that involve more than one child. For example, use a wagon and let one child pull another.

Encouraging children to help each other in activities such as block play allows them to learn and play cooperatively, which makes it easier for them to engage in challenging activities.

Provide Engaging and Challenging Activities

A challenging environment is one in which infants and toddlers can explore and interact with a wide variety of materials. It is important for you to provide all children with developmentally appropriate challenges. A challenging curriculum enables children to go from their present levels of development and learning to higher levels.

- Include a wide variety of multisensory, visual, auditory, and tactile materials and activities to support all areas of development—physical, social, emotional, and linguistic.
- Include materials for large and small muscles for reaching, grasping, kicking, pulling up, holding on, walking, and so forth.
- Provide materials for tactile and sensory stimulation.
- Hold, play with, and be responsive to infants and toddlers—you are the best toy a child has.
- Provide mirrors for infants and toddlers to look at themselves and others.
- Provide visually interesting things for children to look at, such as mobiles, family pictures, and murals.
- Take infants and toddlers on walks so they can observe nature and people.

professionalism in practice

How to Plan a Curriculum for Infants and Toddlers: Day to Day the Relationship Way

Talitha (nine months old) leans against her teacher while laughing and giving her a quick hug while Marcus (thirteen months old) figures out how to make music with a small drum. Kareem (eighteen months old) climbs into a teacher's lap with a book in his hand while Tanya (twenty-four months old) splashes water with her peers at a small water table.

All of these fortunate infants and toddlers have something in common. They attend programs in which teachers know how to plan a curriculum that is responsive and promotes relationships.

WHAT IS AN INFANT/TODDLER CURRICULUM?

A curriculum for infants and toddlers includes everything that they experience (from their perspective) from the moment they enter the program until they leave to go home. Every experience makes an impression on how children view themselves, others, and the world. Caring teachers plan a curriculum that is (1) relationship based and (2) responsive to infants' and toddlers' needs, interests, and developmental levels as well as their families' goals for their children.

WHY ARE RELATIONSHIPS IMPORTANT IN CURRICULUM?

A relationship is a bond of caring between two people that develops over time. In a relationship-based program, teachers support all the relationships that are key to children's development—parent–child, teacher–child, teacher–family, and child–child relationships. Children need these sustaining, caring relationships to give them a sense of self-worth, trust in the positive intentions of others, and motivation to explore and learn. They need protection, affection, and opportunities to learn to thrive.

HOW CAN YOU PLAN AND IMPLEMENT A RESPONSIVE CURRICULUM?

In a responsive curriculum, teachers interact with children and plan day to day the relationship way. Teachers make daily and weekly changes in the environment and in their interactions in response to each child's needs, interests, goals, and exploration of concepts. How do you do this? First, you *respect,* then you *reflect,* and then you *relate.*

STEP 1 Respect

Respect that infants and toddlers are competent, motivated learners; recognize that play is the way young children learn; and honor individual differences. Recognize that infants and toddlers are active learners and thinkers who are using many different strategies to figure out how things work. In an emotionally supportive and interesting environment,

Thinking about and planning for how you will relate and respond to infants and toddlers is based on the guidelines and the steps outlined in the Professionalism in Practice feature, "How to Plan a Curriculum for Infants and Toddlers: Day to Day the Relationship Way," in this chapter.

Technology and Infants and Toddlers

A responsive environment can also include children's use of technology, especially applications that encourage and support responses and interactions. The accompanying Technology Tie-In illustrates three apps for iPads and iPhones that provide for interaction and responsiveness with infants and toddlers.

INFANT MENTAL HEALTH

infant mental health The overall health and well-being of infants and young children in the context of family, school, and community relationships.

Infant mental health is the "state of emotional and social competence of young children."[33] It occurs in the context of the interplay between nature and nurture. The nurture context consists of many "nested" and interrelated processes and factors,

they are motivated problem solvers, make good choices, and care about others. When infants and toddlers aren't sleeping or eating, they are usually playing with toys, people, and objects. As they make choices, infants and toddlers focus on *their* important goals for learning and nurturing—for example, opening and closing a door on a toy, filling a hole on the playground, or playing with a friend. As they play, they explore concepts such as how objects fit into various spaces, cause and effect, object permanence, how to comfort another child, or what they can do with different sizes of paper (e.g., crumple, stack, make into a ball, etc.). Nurturing and responsive adults stay close by, support children's play, and meet their emotional needs by using all of the strategies described in the next sections. Respect that children are unique human beings with different styles (e.g., some eat fast and others slow), different interests, and one-of-a-kind personalities.

STEP 2 Reflect

Reflection is a process of wondering with families and other teachers about the child's unique interests, explorations, and culture. It is a process of observing children to know them well. You can use an observation and planning guide such as the one shown here to capture your observations.

As you reflect ask yourself the following questions: What is the child trying to do, and how is the child trying to do it? What is the child learning? (*Not:* What am I teaching?) What concepts (e.g., space, time, social interactions, expressing emotions, ways to open containers) is the child exploring? What is the child telling you he or she needs? (More positive attention, more affection, new strategies to use when another child takes a toy, more room to learn to walk?) What is new in the child's development? For example, is he or she learning to climb or jump, comfort peers, use two words together, or ask questions?

STEP 3 Relate

Relate to children by providing the basics—moment-to-moment responsive adult interactions.

- Comfort distressed children.
- Respond to children's cues and signals.
- Talk responsively with children, abundantly describe your own and the children's actions, and provide reasons and explanations.
- Sing, read, play with children, and respond to children's need for sleep, food, and comfort.
- Guide children to learn how to be pro-social by noticing when they are kind, modeling helpfulness, and demonstrating how to care for others.
- Be open and receptive to what each child is learning in the moment, and follow each child's lead.
- Encourage the children to experiment and problem-solve.
- When a child becomes frustrated, scaffold the child's learning and motivation by helping just enough to support the child's learning how to do the task.
- Remember that sometimes you facilitate children's concentration and peer play by sitting near and observing with engaged interest.

Source: Contributed by Donna S. Wittmer and Sandra H. Petersen, authors of Infant and Toddler Development and Responsive Program Planning: A Relationship-Based Approach (Upper Saddle River, NJ: Merrill/Prentice Hall, 2006). Donna was a professor of early childhood education at the University of Colorado–Denver for seventeen years. Sandy works for ZERO TO THREE.

including parents' mental health, educational background, and socioeconomic status; parents' parenting knowledge and competence; home conditions; child care; school and community quality and resources; and the values and practices of family cultures. Figure 7.7 identifies for you some of the environmental conditions that constitute "threats" to children's mental health. Review it now and reflect on what you can do to reduce or eliminate mental health threats in children's lives.

Infant health can be viewed as an interrelated set of relationships between children, parents, early childhood programs, and community agencies. The essential question for you and other early childhood professionals is how to best provide for infants' health. The Diversity Tie-In feature, "Accommodating Diverse Infants and Toddlers," provides you with ways to ensure that our work with infant and toddlers is culturally appropriate. Infant health is all about *relations*—relations among children, parents, child care programs, and other community agencies. Here are some relational guidelines you can follow:

- ***Individualize attention.*** Attention is given to the individual needs of infants and parents. Responsive caregiving of infants acknowledges and addresses their needs

technology tie-in

Rearing Infants and Toddlers in the World of Apps

Many of today's infants and toddlers around the world are learning basic language and cognitive skills with apps for iPads and iPhones. Infants and toddlers are truly children of the technological generation. Many toddlers are more skillful in manipulating apps than their parents and caregivers! The following are some applications that help infants and toddlers and their parents learn in the technological age. A number of caveats are in order, however:

- Not all children are fortunate enough to live in families with the means to provide their infants and toddlers access to iPhones and iPads. You can make iPads and iPhones accessible to your children in your programs.

- As in all things, with all children, you must balance their involvement with apps (especially children age two and under) and their need for interaction with other environmental stimuli, such as YOU and an enriched environment. Also review the American Academy of Pediatrics position statement on media use by children younger than two years and a joint position statement issued by the National Association for the Education of Young Children and the Fred Rogers Center for Early Learning and Children's Media, "Technology and Interactive Media as Tools in Early Childhood Programs Serving Children from Birth through Age 8." Both websites are at the end of this chapter in the Linking to Learning section.

"I Hear Ewe"

Whenever your children tap on an animal or vehicle icon, the game announces what animal or vehicle it is and plays a recording of how it really sounds!

A great way to introduce infants and toddlers to animals and vehicles!

"Letters A to Z"

Animated flashcards designed to help children learn the letters of the alphabet in a fun and engaging way!

Each flashcard contains characters and creatures that come to life in illustrated scenes accompanied by sound effects to describe the letters!

"Drawing Pad"

Drawing Pad is a mobile art studio designed exclusively for the iPad! The beautiful user interface puts the fun into creating art.

An entertaining and kid-friendly app that enables children to choose different colors, tools, and includes stamps.

Source: Used with permission from Darren Murtha Apps.

and behavioral temperament, and conveys the respect and security essential for early emotional development.

- ***Emphasize strengths.*** Early relationships emphasize the strengths and resources of infants and toddlers. Everyone has strengths, even the newborn. Helping parents

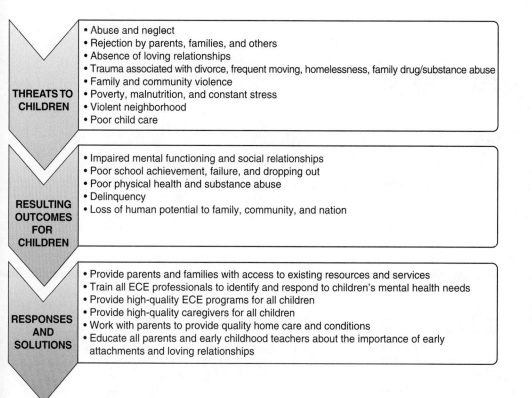

THREATS TO CHILDREN
- Abuse and neglect
- Rejection by parents, families, and others
- Absence of loving relationships
- Trauma associated with divorce, frequent moving, homelessness, family drug/substance abuse
- Family and community violence
- Poverty, malnutrition, and constant stress
- Violent neighborhood
- Poor child care

RESULTING OUTCOMES FOR CHILDREN
- Impaired mental functioning and social relationships
- Poor school achievement, failure, and dropping out
- Poor physical health and substance abuse
- Delinquency
- Loss of human potential to family, community, and nation

RESPONSES AND SOLUTIONS
- Provide parents and families with access to existing resources and services
- Train all ECE professionals to identify and respond to children's mental health needs
- Provide high-quality ECE programs for all children
- Provide high-quality caregivers for all children
- Work with parents to provide quality home care and conditions
- Educate all parents and early childhood teachers about the importance of early attachments and loving relationships

FIGURE 7.7 Threats to Children's Mental Health, Resulting Outcomes, and Solutions

understand their infants' strengths, and the strengths that they bring to their caregiving, builds confidence within parents and supports their interactions with their infants.

- **Provide continuous and stable caregiving.** For the infant, continuous and stable caregiving builds confidence that their needs will be met. Especially in the earliest years, it is important for infants who are cared for out of the home to have a long-term relationship with a primary caregiver. For the parents, knowing that there are consistent people available to turn to—the child's caregiver, a home visitor, extended family, network of formal and informal support—is equally important.

- **Be accessible.** Relationships need to be accessible and responsive to when and how the infant and parent need attention and support. To achieve this for infants, adults need to understand the rhythm of the infants, being mindful of the cues infants send when seeking attention as well as those cues infants send when they are overstimulated. The parents and caregivers also need to be participants in supportive relationships. The extent to which the program staff and administration are available for parents helps to meet the individual needs of the adults, facilitating parents' responsive relationships with the infant.

- **Be culturally responsive.** You need to recognize the importance of understanding the values, beliefs, and practices of diverse cultures. Integrate diversity into your caregiving. In all interactions with children and their families, honor their home culture.[34]

Responsive caregiving and teaching also means that you will provide for the needs of all children regardless of disability and that you will help them to develop behaviorally by promoting self-regulation. The following section of Curriculum and Instruction in the Inclusive Classroom helps you learn how to promote self-regulation in young children.

diversity tie-in

Accommodating Diverse Infants and Toddlers

Infants' and toddlers' mental health and well-being is influenced by their parents. So, collaborating with parents and accommodating to their cultures and needs is an important professional role. As an early childhood professional, your students will come from home environments that are very diverse. For example, Hayden is a fifteen-month-old of West European ancestry and comes from a single-mother household. Eighteen-month-old Guadalupe is Mexican American and comes from the traditional two-parent household. Sixteen-month-old Lee is biracial with a Latino mother and a Chinese American father who works overseas six months of the year. James is a fifteen-month-old seventh-generation American, while at the other end of the spectrum eighteen-month-old Yahya's parents are refugees from Darfur. Families today represent a diverse group of parental pairings, races, religions, socioeconomic statuses, and cultures. It is important to remember that culture influences parenting styles, beliefs about child rearing, education, and family responsibilities. As the teacher of all these children, you will want to make each and every parent and child feel welcome, safe, and valued. While at first you may find it overwhelming to effectively collaborate with so many diverse families, here are some tips:

- Care for and about all of your children, regardless of race, creed, or socioeconomic status. When you genuinely care for their children, parents are more likely to respond favorably to you.
- Talk with parents in order to learn about and incorporate aspects of children's lives at home into your classroom.

Maintain continuity by using the same or similar books, providing opportunities to celebrate diverse holidays, and being respectful of religious and cultural traditions.

- Some parents may be dealing with feelings of separation anxiety or even guilt. You can help calm their fears by demonstrating that you know how to provide a high-quality education for their children. Provide classroom environments that are stimulating, safe, and inclusive.
- Keep a log in which you document children's developmental milestones. For example, on Tuesday, Lee was able to redress himself after toileting for the first time. Share this milestone with his parents. Take a digital photo of Lee dressed and proud of his success, write up his accomplishment on a piece of decorated paper, or provide a "certificate" of accomplishment. Parents will appreciate what their children have achieved—and will love that you appreciate it too!
- Maintain open communication with parents. Have a folder you send back and forth between home and school that contains behavior charts, art work, lists of daily schedules, and so forth.
- Help parents develop networks with other parents. A monthly coffee chat, a parents' night out, book clubs, joint resource libraries, or an Internet blog are excellent ways to encourage open discourse between parents. Such activities help break down cultural, economic, and language barriers and encourage development of family friendships.

TEACHING AND LEARNING IN THE INCLUSIVE CLASSROOM

self-regulation A child's ability to gain control of bodily functions, manage emotions, maintain focus and attention, and integrate cognitive, physical, and social-emotional abilities.

Meet Isabella, a two-month old Caucasian infant. She is new to your care and you are beginning to build a relationship with her. Like all babies, Isabella must begin to learn how to self-regulate. **Self-regulation** is a child's ability to gain control of bodily functions, manage emotions, maintain focus and attention; and integrate cognitive, physical, and social-emotional abilities. The growth of self-regulation is a developmental milestone across early childhood that begins in infancy and influences all aspects of behavior.[35] Babies must learn to increasingly self-regulate and control their emotions over time. Responsive caregivers act as helpers, external regulators, who help babies learn to gain self-control. Therefore, when you care for Isabella, you act as an extension of or as a support for her internal ability to regulate.

Several factors influence a baby's ability to move from external to internal self-regulation. Temperament is one factor. Temperament traits like mood, irritability, and adaptability affect a baby's capacity for emotional regulation. **Goodness of fit**—how well a teacher recognizes and responds or adapts to a child's temperament—also affects the learning of self-regulation. You develop a goodness of fit by working with babies' temperaments, not against them. You can work to lesson or soften some of the difficult features of temperament, and you can emphasize the strengths of temperament, but you can't change an infant's temperament! This means that you make changes in your own style of relating and change the environment to work with the baby's temperament.[36]

> **goodness of fit** How well a teacher recognizes and responds or adapts to a child's temperament—also affects the learning of self-regulation.

Granted, it is taxing to care for a baby who fusses nonstop or who sleeps for only an hour here and there; or a toddler who bites or who constantly throws tantrums. Negative behaviors give you cues and clues that the infant or toddler is having difficulty with self-regulation. You help Isabella learn self-regulation when you provide her with manageable challenges that are part of everyday life, like waiting to be fed or self-soothing into sleep. When you offer manageable challenges while providing external support, you help Isabella and all babies build self-regulation and personal responsibility.[37]

Here are some strategies you can use to help Isabella and other infants and toddlers develop self-regulation.

- Build a close relationship with Isabella. This helps her regulate her emotions and actions because she learns to trust you to fulfill her needs. She can rely on you for consistent care and constant attention. As a result, Isabella gradually learns to quiet and control herself. To build close relationships: [38]

  - ***Observe closely and respond.*** Babies always give you cues to let you know when they are ready to play or when they are tired, hungry or full. Be aware of and accepting of individual differences reflected in each baby's needs. For example, when Isabella is two months old, she cries loudly when she is hungry; if you respond promptly so that she does not become distressed, she will learn to trust you. Then, by the time she is four months old, she will only have to whimper to cue you to her needs.[39]

  - ***Provide structure and predictability.*** Babies need consistent caregivers who provide continuity of care. You strengthen your relationship with Isabella as she trusts the continuity of your relationship with her. For example, if you follow a regular sleep schedule each day, Isabella will feel safe because she learns what to expect.[40]

  - ***Show empathy and caring.*** When caregivers identify children's needs and respond to them as significant, infants and toddlers feel good about themselves and are better able to handle their emotions. When Isabella reaches eight months of age and cries when her mother leaves in the morning, you can use a soft, soothing voice to empathize and reassure her, "It's so hard for you. I know you feel so sad." You can hold her and rub her back to offer empathy and strengthen your relationship with her.[41]

  - ***Define age-appropriate limits.*** Help Isabella know what is expected. When she is a ten-month-old, you can tell her, "No biting. That hurts me." As Isabella grows, be consistent in expressing expectations and setting rules or consequences. The goal is to guide children and set limits so that they feel supported and valued, not judged and rejected. When Isabella grows into a curious toddler and wants to explore, you can verbalize and model limits. Tell her, "Wait for me, Isabella. We go out together," as you take her hand and help her open the door.[42]

- Play! When you play with babies and toddlers, you help them learn to find answers to problems and also help them develop the attention they need to attend to tasks.[43] To help Isabella develop self-regulation through play:

  - ***Model language.*** Early on, Isabella won't have many words, so you should describe what she is doing and what you and she are doing together. This responsive approach helps Isabella build understanding between her actions and words. Soon Isabella will be talking! She will also begin to use "self-talk" to help her control her own behavior. As her language and emotional development progresses, you can encourage Isabella to use her words to express her feelings and thoughts rather than immediately acting on her impulses.[44]

- **Be a consultant.** As children begin to pretend, their play scripts are very straightforward and uncomplicated. When Isabella is younger, her pretend script may consist of using a brush to brush her own hair. When you take part in her play, you can help her grow her script by showing her how to brush the hair of a doll and your own hair. When you insert new roles or ideas into pretend situations and toys, Isabella learns to apply her behavior to the new scenario, which increases her self-regulation.[45]

Helping Isabella and other babies develop self-regulation helps them grow into children ready for school and for life. As a result, Isabella will be able to understand what teachers and others ask of her in given situations, monitor her own behavior to see if it matches, and maintain or change what she is doing based on her evaluation of the behavior.

ACTIVITIES FOR PROFESSIONAL DEVELOPMENT

ethical dilemma

"To vaccinate or not to vaccinate?"

Alyssa Eaton wants to send her two-year-old toddler, Kyle, to Hopkins Day School, one of the city's best child care programs for infants and toddlers. However, Alyssa is not happy to learn that Hopkins requires parents to provide proof of immunization before children are accepted into the program. Alyssa objects to and does not support childhood immunizations on religious grounds and because she thinks vaccines cause autism.

What should Alyssa do? Use Facebook to rally parents in an effort to ask the Hopkins board to repeal their policy? Exercise her rights as a parent to decline immunization for Kyle on philosophical and/or religious grounds? Abandon her beliefs about immunizations and have Kyle vaccinated? What should Alyssa do? What would you do?

Application Activities

1. Observe children between the ages of birth and eighteen months. Identify the six stages of sensorimotor intelligence by describing the behaviors you observed. Cite specific examples of secondary and tertiary reactions. For each of the six stages, develop two activities that would be cognitively and developmentally appropriate for use with infants and toddlers. Present this information in a Prezi presentation to your classmates.

2. Research on brain development indicates that children whose mothers nurture them have a larger hippocampus area of the brain than children who are not richly nurtured. The hippocampus is important for learning and mental health. Read more in this chapter about brain development and read online articles about applying brain research. Identify six best practices for ways mothers can nurture their children. Post this information to your class blog.

3. You are invited to speak to a group of infant/toddler caregivers about relationship-based caregiving. Develop your presentation and list five specific suggestions you will make about key relationship-based practices for infants and toddlers. Share

your ideas in a Prezi presentation with others or online in an early childhood discussion group.

4. Consult either the hardback or online version of the Developmentally Appropriate Practice Guide of the National Association for the Education of Young Children (*Developmentally Appropriate Practice in Early Childhood Programs*, 3rd edition). Read and reflect on the section on developmentally appropriate practice in the infant and toddler years, ages birth to three. Identify what you believe are the six most essential practices of providing developmentally appropriate curriculum for infants and toddlers. Post your six selections to your class discussion board and have your classmates vote on their top three. Share the top three results with your entire class.

5. Enriched environments play an important role in providing high-quality curricula for infants and toddlers. Choose either the infant or toddler environment diagram in this chapter and for each of the areas identified provide three suggestions for how you would enrich it. Post your enriched environment diagram to your class discussion board and ask for comments.

6. Research is clear about how positive mental health contributes to children's growth and development. Factors that support infant mental health include nurturing parents and caregivers. Identify three activities that caregivers can do which nurture and support infant/toddler mental health. Share your ideas in an online discussion with your classmates.

Linking to Learning

American Academy of Pediatrics

www.pediatrics.aappublications.org
American Academy of Pediatrics position statement, "Media Use by Children Younger Than 2 Years."

National Association for the Education of Young Children

www.naeyc.org
Joint position statement issued by the National Association for the Education of Young Children and the Fred Rogers Center for Early Learning and Children's Media, "Technology and Interactive Media as Tools in Early Childhood Programs Serving Children from Birth through Age 8."

MyEducationLab

Go to Topics 2 (Child Development/Theories) and 8 (DAP/Teaching Strategies) in the MyEducationLab (www.myeducationlab.com) for your course, where you can:

Find learning outcomes for Child Development/Theories and DAP/Teaching Strategies along with the national standards that connect to these outcomes.

Complete Assignments and Activities that can help you more deeply understand the chapter content.

Apply and practice your understanding of the core teaching skills identified in the chapter with the Building Teaching Skills and Dispositions learning units.

Hear viewpoints of experts in the field in Professional Perspectives.

- Explore interactive CONNECT Modules to practice classroom skills and enhance professional development.

- Check your comprehension on the content covered in the chapter by going to the Study Plan in the Book Resources for your text. Here you will be able to take a chapter quiz, receive feedback on your answers, and then access Review, Practice, and Enrichment activities to enhance your understanding of chapter content.

chapter 8

THE PRESCHOOL YEARS

Getting Ready for School and Life

NAEYC Standards for Early Childhood Professional Preparation Programs

Standard 4: Using Developmentally Effective Approaches to Connect with Children and Families

I understand and use positive relationships and supportive interactions as the foundation for my work with young children and families. I know, understand, and use a wide array of developmentally appropriate approaches, instructional strategies, and tools to connect with children and families and positively influence each child's development and learning.[1]

Standard 5: Using Content Knowledge to Build Meaningful Curriculum

I understand the importance of developmental domains and academic (or content) disciplines in early childhood curriculum. I know the essential concepts, inquiry tools, and structure of content areas including academic subjects and can identify resources to deepen my understanding. I use my knowledge and other resources to design, implement, and evaluate meaningful, challenging curricula that promote comprehensive developmental and learning outcomes for every young child.[2]

WHAT IS PRESCHOOL?

Preschools are programs for children ages three to five to help ensure that they have the readiness behaviors and skills necessary for learning before they enter kindergarten. Today, it is common for many children to be in a school of some kind as early as age two or three. In fact, 80 percent of all four-year-old children are in some kind of preschool.[3] Thirty-nine states currently invest in preschool education in the form of public preschools or support for Head Start.[4] This widespread access to preschool is known as **universal preschool**, and more states are moving in this direction. In 2011, the fifty states spent over $5 billion on preschool education.[5] There are approximately 456,800 preschool teachers in the United States who teach in many kinds of preschool programs.[6] What are these teachers like? Here are mini portraits of some preschool Teachers of the Year:

universal preschool The idea that all children and families should have access to preschool, in the same way that kindergarten is available now.

- ***Marcy Wells.*** Marcy Wells knows that her preschoolers love creatures great and small. By combining that love for animals with lessons in kindness and respect, Wells tries to foster respect and awareness in her classroom and outside of it.[7]

- ***Wendy Butler-Boyesen.*** Science means success for Wendy Butler-Boyesen's students at EWEB Child Development center in Eugene, Oregon. She excites her young students by exploring different scientific themes each month, from hiking through local wetlands to studying the solar system.[8]

- **Geralyn Dunckelman.** This Houma, Louisiana, teacher teaches Title I preschoolers often identified as at-risk, but refuses to use such labels, saying, "The only thing these children are at risk of is making a difference in this world." Dunckelman embraces parents as the primary teachers of their children. When she became aware that one parent was illiterate while another spoke and read only Spanish, she recorded books in English for the family while recruiting a Spanish-speaking volunteer to create Spanish-language versions. These same parents eventually volunteered to read and teach Spanish to the class.[9]
- **Lisa Frank.** Lisa Frank of McCloskey Elementary School in Philadelphia has students in her Bright Futures pre-K classroom try anything from yoga to sign language. She always makes it an enjoyable experience. For instance, once she transformed her classroom into a magical ocean environment, complete with blue cling wrap and sea-creature stickers on the window, an ocean-sound CD during naptime, and an edible ocean made of blueberry Jell-O and Swedish fish.[10]
- **Karla Lyles.** Karla Lyles listens, observes, and engages her students in conversations. For example, when her students expressed interest in building houses, she took them on a construction-site field trip to explore the renovation of homes in their Chicago community. The class created a book filled with photos and captions from their excursion, and even enjoyed an on-site school visit by the backhoe driver they befriended on their trip.[11]
- **Camryn Winters.** Camryn Winters believes in the potential of every child and that all children deserve a quality education. Her preferred method of teaching is inquiry-based learning where her students learn through various interactions with people and objects. She says, "I believe in their capability, curiosity and interest. I take much pride in meeting each child where they are and helping them grow emotionally, socially, and developmentally. I hope to foster independence, competence and confidence within each child allowing them to dream big and believe they can be anything they want to be."[12]

Why Are Preschools Growing in Popularity?

A number of reasons help explain the current popularity of preschool programs. With the falling economy and parents losing their jobs, finding affordable child care while trying to find a job has become a major burden on families. This in turn places a great demand on the early childhood profession to provide more programs and services, including programs for three- to five-year-olds. Many parents, however, are frustrated and dissatisfied with efforts to find quality programs for their children. They believe the federal and state governments, local communities, policy makers, and politicians should all work together to improve the quality of preschool education in the United States.[13]

Working Parents. Working parents believe the public schools hold the solution to their child care needs so they advocate (rather strongly) for public schools to provide preschool programs. Some parents cannot afford quality child care; they believe preschools, furnished at the public's expense, are a reasonable, cost-efficient way to meet their child care needs. The alignment of

FOCUS QUESTIONS

1. What are preschools and why are they so popular?

2. What are preschoolers like and how can you support their physical, motor, social, emotional, cognitive, and language development?

3. What is school readiness?

4. What are preschool standards and how do they affect teaching and learning?

5. What does the preschool curriculum consist of?

the public schools with early childhood programs is becoming increasingly popular. Some think it makes sense to put the responsibility for educating and caring for all of the nation's children under the sponsorship of one agency—the public schools.

Highly Educated Workforce.   Second, a more highly educated workforce will increase economic growth.[14] Business leaders see early education as one way of developing highly skilled and more productive workers.[15] Many business leaders see preschool as economic development because the nation needs a highly educated workforce to compete in a global economy, and this education begins in preschool.[16] Many preschool programs include work-related skills and behavior in their curriculum. For example, approaches to learning or dispositions for learning are important preschool goals. Approaches to learning such as self-regulation and complying with rules and routines are essential workplace behaviors. Likewise, being literate begins in the early years, and literacy is an essential workforce skill. Learning to read is a high priority for our nation's schools. It makes sense to lay the foundation for reading as early as possible in the preschool years.

Equal Opportunity.   Third, many believe that early public schooling, especially for children from low-income families, is necessary if the United States is to promote equal opportunity for all. They argue that low-income children begin school already far behind their more fortunate middle-class counterparts and that the best way to keep them from falling hopelessly behind is for them to begin school earlier. Extensive research makes it apparent that investing in our children is important for all children— and not as expensive as some people believe.[17]

Cost Effective.   High-quality early education benefits children of all social and economic groups. It helps prepare young children to succeed in school and become better citizens; they earn more money, pay more taxes, and commit fewer crimes.[18] Consider what the research outlined below reveals about the cost benefits of spending taxpayer money in the early years.

Perry Preschool Project[19]

- For every dollar spent, more than $16 was saved in tax dollars.
- Sixty-five percent of the program group graduated from high school on time, compared to 45 percent of the control group.
- The control group suffered twice as many arrests as the program group.

Chicago Child–Parent Center Program[20]

- For every dollar invested in the program, $7.10 was returned.
- Participants had a 51 percent reduction in child maltreatment.
- Participants had a 41 percent reduction in special education placement.

New Jersey Abbott Preschool Program[21]

- Increased receptive vocabulary scores by an additional four months, a particularly significant finding since this measure is strongly predictive of general cognitive abilities.
- Increased scores on measures of early math skills by 24 percent over the course of the year.
- Increased print awareness scores by 61 percent over the course of the year— children who attended the program know more letters, know more letter-sound associations, and are more familiar with words and book concepts at entry to kindergarten.

Los Angeles Universal Preschool[22]

- The percentage of children scoring near proficient on social and emotional skills needed to do well in kindergarten increased from 22 percent in the fall to 72 percent in the spring.

- English language learners (ELLs) who scored significantly lower than their non–English learner peers in fall 2008 closed the gap in skills such as demonstrating proficiency in using crayons, washing hands, controlling impulses, expressing needs, counting to 10, and recognizing letters of the alphabet, as well as shapes and colors by spring 2009.

- In general skills, such as writing their first names, recognizing rhyming words, and using books, ELLs' gains exceeded those made by non–English learners.

These preschool programs show us that in the long run and across multiple academic, social, and economic domains, it actually costs taxpayers more *not* to provide high-quality education than it does to provide money for preschools.[23]

What Are Preschools Like?

As preschool programs have grown in number and popularity, they have also undergone significant changes in purpose. In previous decades, the predominant purposes of preschools were to help socialize children, enhance their social-emotional development, and get them ready for kindergarten or first grade.[24] Today, there is a decided move away from socialization as the primary function for enrolling children in preschool. Preschools are now promoted as places to accomplish the following goals:

- Support and develop children's innate capacity for learning. The responsibility for "getting ready for school" has shifted from being primarily children's and families' responsibilities to being a cooperative venture among child, family, home, schools, and communities.[25]

- Provide children the academic, social, and behavioral skills necessary for entry into kindergarten. Today a major focus is on developing preschool children's literacy and math skills.[26]

- Use preschools to deliver a full range of health, social, economic, and academic services to young children and their families. Family welfare is also a justification for operating preschools.

- Solve or find solutions for pressing social problems. The early years are viewed as a time when interventions are most likely to have long-term positive influences. Preschool programs are seen as ways of lowering the number of dropouts, improving children's health, and preventing serious social problems such as substance abuse and violence.[27]

These goals of the "new" preschool illustrate some of the dramatic changes that are transforming how preschool programs operate and how preschool teachers teach. Given the changing nature of the preschool, it is little wonder that the preschool years are playing a larger role in early childhood education. They will continue to do so. In Charlottesville, Virginia, the preschool program is designed to provide a "stimulating environment and to provide and guide the educational experiences of each child."[28] To provide these educational experiences, a qualified lead teacher and teaching assistant work with up to sixteen children in one classroom. Charlottesville preschool programs focus on teaching students to make good decisions about their behaviors, to cooperate with other children and adults, to communicate with others about their experiences and feelings, to take initiative and solve problems, and to gain reading and math readiness skills and concepts.[29] Check out the Linking to Learning section at the end of this chapter to review their website.

WHAT ARE PRESCHOOLERS LIKE?

Today's preschoolers are not like the children of previous decades. Many have already experienced one, two, or three years of child care. They have watched hundreds of hours of television. Many are technologically sophisticated and many use game-based computer entertainment. They have experienced the trauma of family divorce or the psychological effects of abuse. Many have experienced the glitz and glamour of boutique birthday parties or the poverty of being homeless. Both collectively and individually, the experiential backgrounds of preschoolers are quite different from those of previous generations. These factors raise a number of imperatives for you and preschool teachers:

- Observe and assess children so that you really understand what they know and are able to do.
- Conference and collaborate with families in order to discover children's unique experiences, abilities, and needs.
- Develop programs to meet the needs of today's children, not yesterday's children. As children change, we must change our preschool programs to meet their needs and within the context of their experiences.

Take a minute and review and reflect on the accompanying Portraits of Preschoolers feature to familiarize yourself with what they are like. Answer the developmentally appropriate questions that accompany the portraits.

Physical and Motor Development

One noticeable difference between preschoolers and infants and toddlers is that preschoolers have lost most of their baby fat and taken on a leaner, elongated look. This process of "slimming down" and increasing motor coordination enables preschoolers to participate with more confidence in the locomotor activities so vitally necessary during this stage of growth and development. Both girls and boys continue to grow several inches per year throughout the preschool years. Table 8.1 shows the average height and weight for preschoolers. Compare these averages with the height and weight of preschoolers you know or work with.

Preschool children are learning to use and test their bodies. The preschool years are a time for learning what they can do individually and how they can do it. Locomotion plays a large role in motor and skill development and includes such activities as moving the body through space—walking, running, hopping, jumping, rolling, dancing, climbing, and leaping. Preschoolers use these activities to investigate and explore the relationships among themselves, space, and objects in space.

TABLE 8.1 Average Height and Weight of Preschoolers

	Males		Females	
Age	Height (inches)	Weight (pounds)	Height (inches)	Weight (pounds)
3 years	38.00	33.00	38.00	32.00
4 years	41.00	37.00	41.00	36.00
5 years	44.00	42.00	43.00	41.00

Source: Family Practice Notebook, "Height Measurement in Children," 2012; accessed March 8, 2012, at www.fpnotebook.com/endo/exam.

Preschoolers also like to participate in fine-motor activities such as drawing, coloring, painting, cutting, and pasting. Consequently, they need programs that provide action and play, supported by proper nutrition and healthy habits of plentiful rest and good hygiene. Good preschool programs provide for these unique physical needs of preschoolers and support their learning through active involvement.

Social and Emotional Development

A major responsibility of preschool teachers is to promote and support children's social and emotional development. Positive social and emotional development enables children to learn better and to succeed in all of school and life activities.

During the preschool years (ages three to five), children are in Erikson's psychosocial development stage of initiative versus guilt (see Chapter 3). During this stage, children are fully involved in locomotive activities and the enjoyment of doing things. They want to plan and be involved in activities. They want to move and be active.

You can help support children's initiative in these ways:

Physical activites contribute to children's physical, social, emotional, linguistic, and cognitive development. It is essential that programs provide opportunities for children to engage in active play in both indoor and outdoor settings. What are some things that children can learn through participation in playgroup activities?

- Give children freedom to explore in safe and secure indoor and outdoor environments.

- Provide projects and activities that enable children to discover and experiment. Preschool children like to work and play with their hands.

- Encourage and support children's attempts to plan, make things, and be involved. Preschool children like to build things and see the accomplishments of their efforts.

Self-Regulation. During the preschool years, children are learning **self-regulation**, the ability to control their emotions and behaviors, to delay gratification, and to build positive social relations with one another.

Teaching self-regulation (i.e., self-control or impulse control) is a major teacher task during the preschool years. The following guidelines will help you promote children's self-regulation:

self-regulation The ability of preschool children to control their emotions and behaviors, to delay gratification, and to build positive social relations with one another.

- ***Provide a variety of learning experiences.*** Young children are very good at creating diversion when none is available. Often teachers think they cannot provide interesting learning experiences until the children are under control, when, in fact, the real problem is that the children are out of control because there is nothing interesting for them to do. You must intentionally plan for children's learning experiences.

- ***Arrange the environment to help children do their best.*** Make sure block-building activities are accorded enough space and are protected from traffic. Avoid arrangements that invite children to run or get out of control, such as large open spaces.

- ***Get to know each child.*** Establish relationships with parents and support children's strengths as well as their needs.

- ***Set clear limits for appropriate and inappropriate behavior.*** Enforce them with rational explanations in a climate of mutual respect and caring.

Portraits of Preschoolers

	Ericka	Aidross	Jamilah	Lukas
General Description	3 years, Caucasian, female • Nurturing, friendly, diligent • Loves to help and eager to learn • Lives with father, mother, older sister, and older brother	3 years, Middle Eastern, male • Friendly, talkative, cheerful • Fascinated with trucks • Has traveled to many countries • Lives with father, mother, and younger brother • Both parents are attending graduate school	4 years, African American, female • Very bright and talkative, with a great personality • Makes friends easily • Always happy • Lives with mother, father, and two older siblings	4 years, Hispanic, male • Well-liked by all students, talkative, very expressive, and friendly • Family moved from Colombia to United States • Is the youngest and has an older brother
Social-Emotional	• Follows rules and procedures • Developing meaningful friendships • Aware of responsibilities as a classroom community • Uses problem-solving skills	• Beginning to encourage classmates to follow classroom rules • Becomes upset when asked to stop a preferred activity during transition times • Shows concern when classmates are sad/upset • Developing a preference for playing with two to three classmates	• Engages in cooperative play on her own • Takes turns voluntarily • Enjoys helping others • Learns from her mistakes • Helps others make the right choices	• Interacts amiably with all students • Very helpful when peers need help • Works more diligently and completely • Vocabulary is developed in both Spanish and English (bilingual) • Beginning to feel comfortable speaking in English • Likes to imitate Power Rangers and Karate Kid
Cognitive/Language	• Sings songs at circle time • Understands concepts about print • Able to carry out two-step directions • Enjoys read-aloud books • Has one-to-one correspondence • Knows shapes • Counts from 1 to 20	• Can count objects up to 10 with one-to-one correspondence • Tells a story using pictures • Can identify names of classmates in print • Enjoys answering questions during whole group time	• Rote counts to 35 and can use one-to-one correspondence up to 35 • Can answer "why" questions • Can pick out non-rhyming words out of a set of three • Can sort objects by attributes	• Can count from 0 to 15 in Spanish and English • Has difficulty with letter identification and sounds in the Spanish and English alphabet • Recognizes all shapes, colors (English), and body parts (Spanish)

Motor	• Jumps, climbs, and runs • Eats using utensils and stacks her own tray • Cuts with scissors and writes name with various instruments • Builds towers	• Writes name independently • Uses tweezers to pick up small objects • Uses scissors to cut out simple shapes • Kicks a ball to a friend • Can hop on one foot	• Creates movements to the beat of music • Can gallop, jump, skip, and hop on one foot • Use writing tools correctly • Able to cut out shapes and objects such as butterflies and frogs	• Large muscle and small muscle are both highly developed • Coordination between feet and whole body during physical activity is very coordinated • Is very creative with building complicated shapes utilizing Legos® • Enjoys music and loves and attempts to break dance and jump around.
Adaptive (Daily Living)	• Washes hands after using the bathroom • Able to identify community helpers in and out of the school • Follows daily classroom routines (puts up folder and signs in for class) with ease	• Uses toilet independently • Usually washes hands without prompting • Dresses self independently; can use Velcro® fasteners but needs help with laces • Uses eating utensils appropriately • Follows classroom routines easily (takes out folder and puts his backpack away)	• Able to make appropriate decisions when it comes to safety • Able to dress herself • Can tie her shoes • Understands the order of daily routines	• Prefers to dress himself • Recognizes community environment (Civic Center) • Washes hands after using the bathroom without being asked, reminds others to do so • Does not have any difficulty expressing his needs and wants • Gets upset if he doesn't sit next to his friends

Source: Contributed by Principal Felicia Sprayberry and teachers at the Popo and Lupe Gonzalez School for Young Children, Denton Independent School District, Denton, Texas.

Questions:

• Aidross encourages his classmates to follow classroom rules. How would you develop a learning situation in which Aidross can be a team leader and help other children who don't follow the classroom rules?
• Transition times are often difficult times for children and teachers during which children can and do engage in inappropriate activities. What would you do to help Aidross, who doesn't like to stop an activity and transition, and others develop transition routines?
• Jamilah seems to have the ability to make "right" choices. How would you let Jamilah help her peers learn to make "right" choices?
• Lukas likes to engage in rough-and-tumble play. What are your views on rough-and-tumble play? How would you encourage children to not be "too rough" during rough-and-tumble play?
• Ericka seems to be a "model" student. How would you differentiate activities so that Ericka can continually keep learning at higher levels?

- ***Develop a few simple group rules.*** With preschool children, the simpler the rules, the better. I think it is best to begin the program year with a basic set of five (or fewer) rules such as:
  - Be nice to others.
  - Listen to the teacher.
  - Follow directions.
  - Hands are for helping.
  - Feet are for walking.

As you and the children discuss these rules and as the children get used to following them, you and they can modify, change, and add to the rules. Here are some other suggestions for helping preschoolers develop self-regulation:

- ***Use children's home languages as often as possible.*** Make every effort to show children you support their culture and respect their language.
- ***Coach children on how to express their feelings verbally.*** Help children use either their home language or English, and to solve social problems with others using words. For many children, this will mean not only providing the words and offering some possible solutions, but being there to assist when situations arise.
- ***Model self-control by using self-talk.*** "Oh, I can't get this lid off the paint. I am feeling frustrated [take a deep breath]. Now I'll try again."[30]

Cognitive Development

Children's preoperational characteristics have particular implications for you and other early childhood professionals. You can promote children's learning during the preoperational stage of cognitive development by following the steps presented in the accompanying Professionalism in Practice feature, "How to Promote Preschoolers' Cognitive Development." As you review these steps, start to plan for how you can apply them to your classroom.

Preschoolers are in the preoperational stage of intellectual development. Characteristics of the preoperational stage are that (1) children grow in their ability to use symbols, including language; (2) children are not capable of operational thinking (an *operation* is a reversible mental action), which explains why Piaget named this stage *preoperational;* (3) children center on one thought or idea, often to the exclusion of other thoughts; (4) children are unable to *conserve,* or understand that the quantity of something does not change simply because its appearance changes; and (5) children are egocentric.

Language Development

Children's language skills grow and develop rapidly during the preschool years. *Vocabulary,* the number of words children know, continues to grow. Sentence length also increases and children continue to master syntax and grammar.

During the preschool years, children's language development is diverse and comprehensive and constitutes a truly impressive range of learning. An even more impressive feature of this language acquisition is that children learn intuitively, without a great deal of instruction, the rules of language that apply to words and phrases they use. You can use many of the language practices recommended for infants and toddlers to support preschoolers' language development. The accompanying Diversity Tie-In feature provides you with specific examples of how you can support children's English language learning.

In this video, listen to how this three-year-old child's teacher extends and enriches his language and scaffolds him toward more complex and involved sentences and responses. This is an excellent example of how effective teachers help children learn language and social interaction.

professionalism in practice

How to Promote Preschoolers' Cognitive Development

STEP 1 Furnish Concrete Materials to Help Children See and Experience Concepts and Processes

Children learn more from touching and experimenting with an actual object than they do from a picture, story, video, or teacher's lecture. If children are learning about apples, bring in a collection of apples for children to touch, feel, smell, taste, discuss, classify, manipulate, and explore. Collections of things such as leaves, rocks, and bugs also offer children an ideal way to learn the names for things, classify, count, and describe.

STEP 2 Use Hands-On Activities That Give Children Opportunities for Active Involvement in Their Learning

Encourage children to manipulate and interact with the world around them. In this way, construct concepts about relationships, attributes, and processes. Through exploration, preoperational children begin to collect and organize data about the objects they manipulate. For example, when children engage in water play with funnels and cups, they learn about concepts such as measurement, volume, sink/float, bubbles, prisms, evaporation, and saturation.

STEP 3 Give Children Many and Varied Experiences

Provide diverse activities and play environments that lend themselves to teaching different skills, concepts, and processes. Children should spend time daily in both indoor and outdoor activities. Give consideration to the types of activities that facilitate large- and fine-motor, social, emotional, and cognitive development. For example, outdoor play activities and games such as tag, hopscotch, and jump rope enhance large-motor development; fine-motor activities include using scissors, stringing beads, coloring, and using writing materials such as crayons, pencils, and markers.

STEP 4 Scaffold Appropriate Tasks and Behaviors

Preoperational children learn to a great extent through modeling. Children should see adults reading and writing daily. It is also helpful for children to view brief demonstrations by peers or teachers on possible ways to use materials. For example, after children have spent a lot of time in free exploration with math manipulatives, show children patterning techniques and strategies they may want to experiment with during their own play. Some of these attributes are outlined in the Professionalism in Practice feature, "Using Blocks to Help Preschoolers Build Mathematical Skills."

STEP 5 Provide a Print-Rich Environment to Stimulate Interest and Development of Language and Literacy in a Meaningful Context

The physical environment should display room labeling, class stories and dictations, children's writing, and charts of familiar songs and finger-plays. Provide a variety of literature for students to read, including books, magazines, and newspapers. Paper and writing utensils should be abundant to motivate children in all kinds of writing. Daily literacy activities should include opportunities for shared, guided, and independent reading and writing; singing songs and finger-plays; and creative dramatics. Make *word walls* with familiar words and words that children encounter in their reading and writing. Display these words on classroom walls and other surfaces. Word walls are an essential part of your classroom environment. Read to children every day.

STEP 6 Allow Children Periods of Uninterrupted Time to Engage in Self-Chosen Tasks

Children benefit more from large blocks of time provided for in-depth exploration in meaningful play than they do from frequent, brief ones. It takes time for children to become deeply involved in play, especially imaginative and fantasy play. Morning and afternoon schedules should each contain at least two such blocks of time.

STEP 7 Guide Children in Problem-Solving Skills in Math and Science

Apply and provide a variety of appropriate math and science strategies to solve problems. Use graphic organizers in math. A graphic organizer such as a Venn diagram is a visual representation of material. The use of graphs is important. Children can graph many things—even their lunch requests! Many stories also offer a way to develop problem-solving skills. As you teach number concepts, use stories and visual representations. For example, there are five apples on the tree. Two apples fell on the ground. How many apples are on the tree? In science, ask questions such as "What do you think will happen if . . . ?"

Teaching English Language Learners. A reality of teaching in the preschool today is that some students will come to your classroom not speaking any English. Others will be in stages of English acquisition ranging from speaking very little English to speaking it very well. In 2010, 22 percent of children spoke a language other than English at home[31] and 5.3 percent had difficulty speaking English.[32] In all, over ten million children speak a language other than English in the home.[33] Other than English, in the United States, Spanish is the most often spoken home language. Other common home languages are Chinese and Vietnamese.[34] Furthermore, your chances of having to teach children English increases dramatically in high-minority population states such as Arizona, California, Florida, Illinois, New Jersey, New York, and Texas.[35]

As discussed in earlier chapters of this book, children whose home language is not English are called *English language learners* (ELLs). They are learning English as their second language. Preschool ELLs are like other preschoolers. Everything we have said about children's cognitive, physical, linguistic, and social-emotional development applies to them. They are bright, active, and they want to learn!

The following guidelines will provide you with teaching strategies you can apply to your teaching of ELLs:

- *Keep ELLs active and involved.* Provide motor and kinesthetic activities such as playing games involving basic English words, acting out stories, and helping with classroom chores.
- *Create a buddy system.* Pair ELLs with other children who are native English speakers or who know English well.
- *Teach daily living and vocabulary words and phrases.* Teach vocabulary and phrases that enable ELLs to greet others and identify objects in the classroom and home. Teach words they need to get along in everyday life such as days of the week. Have children make their own dictionaries of pictures labeled with words. They can have a picture dictionary for school and one for home. Help children learn oral language skills first. Then emphasize writing skills, followed by learning-to-read skills.
- *Incorporate children's culture into classroom activities.* Classroom activities and themes that focus on the children—such as "all about me"—enable you to support and celebrate children's unique cultural identities.
- *Integrate technology into children's English learning.* Use language-learning software to help your students learn English, such as the Zip Zoom English software by Scholastic that aids in developing critical language and reading skills for ELLs in grades K–3. The Technology Tie-In feature explores ways in which technology can assist in any child's literacy development.

READY TO LEARN: READY FOR SCHOOL

readiness Being ready to learn; possessing the knowledge, skills, and abilities necessary for learning and for success in school.

School readiness—whether a child is "ready to learn" with the necessary knowledge, skills, and abilities—is a major topic of debate in discussions of preschool and kindergarten programs. The early childhood profession is reexamining readiness, its many interpretations, and the various ways the concept is applied to educational practices.

When asked "Does readiness matter?" the answer should be a big "Yes!" Research shows that students who enter kindergarten proficient across all readiness skills perform "significantly better" on standardized tests of English and math in third, fourth, and fifth grades than do children who have inadequate readiness skills or behaviors.[36]

Figure 8.1 shows important factors for kindergarten readiness. These are some of the things children should know and be able to do *before* coming to kindergarten. Thus they shape, influence, and inform the preschool curriculum and the activities o

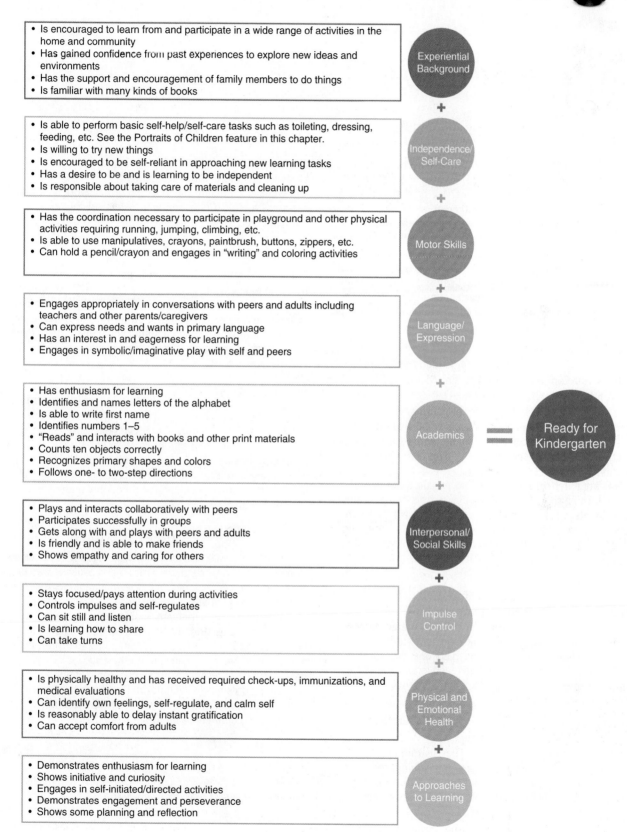

- Is encouraged to learn from and participate in a wide range of activities in the home and community
- Has gained confidence from past experiences to explore new ideas and environments
- Has the support and encouragement of family members to do things
- Is familiar with many kinds of books

Experiential Background

+

- Is able to perform basic self-help/self-care tasks such as toileting, dressing, feeding, etc. See the Portraits of Children feature in this chapter.
- Is willing to try new things
- Is encouraged to be self-reliant in approaching new learning tasks
- Has a desire to be and is learning to be independent
- Is responsible about taking care of materials and cleaning up

Independence/ Self-Care

+

- Has the coordination necessary to participate in playground and other physical activities requiring running, jumping, climbing, etc.
- Is able to use manipulatives, crayons, paintbrush, buttons, zippers, etc.
- Can hold a pencil/crayon and engages in "writing" and coloring activities

Motor Skills

+

- Engages appropriately in conversations with peers and adults including teachers and other parents/caregivers
- Can express needs and wants in primary language
- Has an interest in and eagerness for learning
- Engages in symbolic/imaginative play with self and peers

Language/ Expression

+

- Has enthusiasm for learning
- Identifies and names letters of the alphabet
- Is able to write first name
- Identifies numbers 1–5
- "Reads" and interacts with books and other print materials
- Counts ten objects correctly
- Recognizes primary shapes and colors
- Follows one- to two-step directions

Academics = Ready for Kindergarten

+

- Plays and interacts collaboratively with peers
- Participates successfully in groups
- Gets along with and plays with peers and adults
- Is friendly and is able to make friends
- Shows empathy and caring for others

Interpersonal/ Social Skills

+

- Stays focused/pays attention during activities
- Controls impulses and self-regulates
- Can sit still and listen
- Is learning how to share
- Can take turns

Impulse Control

+

- Is physically healthy and has received required check-ups, immunizations, and medical evaluations
- Can identify own feelings, self-regulate, and calm self
- Is reasonably able to delay instant gratification
- Can accept comfort from adults

Physical and Emotional Health

+

- Demonstrates enthusiasm for learning
- Shows initiative and curiosity
- Engages in self-initiated/directed activities
- Demonstrates engagement and perseverance
- Shows some planning and reflection

Approaches to Learning

FIGURE 8.1 Building Blocks of Kindergarten Readiness

diversity tie-in

Best Practices for English Language Learners (ELLs)

As a bilingual preschool teacher I have the opportunity to teach students who face the challenge of learning more than what is expected from an average student. My students' tasks go beyond learning grammar and mathematics. They also courageously try to grasp an entirely new language and culture. English language learners (ELLs) come into the classroom with different gifts, challenges, and expectations for learning.

Every day I am inspired by my students' strength and fortitude as I observe them overcome what can seem like impossible obstacles. It is truly an honor to teach young ELLs.

Here are six best practices you can use to promote learning success for ELLs:

BEST PRACTICE 1 Involve Parents in Their Children's Education as Early and Thoroughly as You Can. At Your First Parent Meeting, Discuss Opportunities or Parental Involvement!

Parents are the biggest influence for promoting learning and success in education. My colleagues and I find that students with the most aptitude come from homes where parents are actively engaged in their children's lives and who value education.

Educate parents to recognize that playtime can be utilized as learning time. Send weekly newsletters home outlining what students will study in class and suggest ways they can expand on them at home. Simple activities, such as counting the blocks she plays with or observing growing plants, will greatly enhance their child's capacity to learn.

BEST PRACTICE 2 Set High Expectations

Most preschool students are naturally ready to learn and experience new ideas. Always consider children's undeveloped differences and attitudes. Truly believe in your students! You must absolutely know that each and every one can learn! Make modifications and differentiate each lesson you teach. When you expect the very best from your students, they can and will rise to the challenge.

BEST PRACTICE 3 Incorporate Collaborative Learning

Form small learning groups or pairs. First, learning groups enable you to create advanced critical thinking opportunities for the students in your classroom. After all, two (or more) thinking minds are better than one! Second, most students

are eager and excited to talk and work with their classmates. Students achieve greater success with a challenging curriculum while also gaining the essential groundwork for working as part of a team. Collaborative problem solving becomes a gratifying and invigorating part of the day.

BEST PRACTICE 4 Assess Students Often

One of your duties is to determine each child's knowledge base from the moment they enter your classroom. To maximize learning potential, comprehensively assess students throughout the day, week, and year. Use data from these assessments to direct both whole group and individual instruction. Use your assessment information to intentionally plan and differentiate your instruction.

BEST PRACTICE 5 Use Visuals and Movement

Teaching young children requires a great amount of energy. Reading becomes a highly expressive skill. Make books of all genres (fiction and nonfiction) come to life. Visuals and movement also provide a basis for comprehension. Students can easily grasp and internalize the concepts using visual aids because they provide a clear and functional understanding in a meaningful way.

BEST PRACTICE 6 Build Word Walls

Use word walls. ELLs are learning two languages at once so it is important to provide them with a rich academic vocabulary. Having a high vocabulary in a native language helps students learn another language more easily.

Providing a print-rich environment through word walls and labeling helps students across a range of reading levels. Emergent readers benefit by understanding that print conveys a message. Advanced readers build their vocabulary by having the word resources in the classroom. Regularly replacing words on the wall naturally introduces and familiarizes students to hundreds of words. Reading, writing, and comprehension develop rapidly!

. . . .

Source: Contributed by Monica Gil, Gonzalez 2011–2012 SYC Teacher of the Year, Popo and Lupe Gonzalez School for Young Children.

preschool teachers. Review these now and think about their implications for what you will teach preschoolers to know and do.

Discussions about readiness have changed the public's attitude about what it means. Responsibility for children's early learning and development is no longer placed solely on children and their parents but rather is seen as a shared responsibility among children, parents, families, early childhood professionals, communities, states, and the nation.

School Readiness Skills and Dispositions

Readiness is not something that exists in the abstract. It consists of specific and well-identified skills and dispositions. Some of these specific and well-identified dispositions in "getting ready for school" are discussed next.

Approaches to Learning.

> Four-year-old Luis is hard at work completing a puzzle. The puzzle, given to him by his teacher, is a little harder than the ones he has worked on before. He picks up a puzzle piece and looks at the puzzle, trying to decide where it might go. He tries it one way. It doesn't fit. He turns it around and tries again. Success! He has been working at the puzzle for a long time. His teacher comments, "Luis, you are working so hard to finish that puzzle."[37]

Luis has demonstrated that he has certain dispositions that will serve him well when he enters kindergarten. He is able to persist with a task, he will try something different when what he first tried did not work, and he has the self-control necessary to pay attention. These dispositions are part of what we call **approaches to learning**. Approaches to learning are the inclinations, dispositions, and learning styles necessary to interact effectively with the learning environment. Approaches to learning include the following:[38]

1. *Curiosity/initiative.* The child is eager to learn and willing to try a variety of new and challenging activities.
2. *Persistence.* The child is able to persevere and complete a variety of tasks and activities, even if the first attempts are unsuccessful.
3. *Attention.* The child has the ability to concentrate when necessary and to pay attention during teacher-directed activities.
4. *Self-direction.* The child is able to set goals, make choices, and manage his or her time with increased independence.
5. *Problem solving.* The child is able to solve problems in a variety of ways, including finding more than one solution, investigation, and collaboration with peers.
6. *Creativity.* The child is able to address tasks with increased flexibility and originality.

Language.
Language is the most important readiness skill. Children need language skills for success in school and life. Important language skills include the following:

- **Receptive language**, such as listening to the teacher and following directions.
- **Expressive language**, which includes the ability to talk fluently, to articulately communicate needs and ideas with teacher and peers, and to express oneself in the language of the school.
- **Symbolic language**, which is communication in which children use a word, sign, picture, and so on to represent a concept or meaning. For example, young children tend to show fingers to tell how old they are.
- *Vocabulary development,* which should be three to four thousand words by the time preschoolers enter kindergarten.[39]

approaches to learning
Inclinations, dispositions, and learning styles necessary to interact effectively with the learning environment.

receptive language
Language, such as listening to the teacher and following directions.

expressive language
Language that includes the ability to talk fluently, to articulately communicate needs and ideas with teacher and peers, and to express oneself in the language of the school.

symbolic language
Communication in which children use a word, sign, picture, etc. to represent a concept or meaning.

How to Use Technology as a Scaffolding Tool in the Preschool Classroom

Technology can be an exciting tool to help children acquire early literacy skills. Using cameras, printers, scanners, and software provides endless possibilities for personalizing literacy activities.

SELECT THE EQUIPMENT

You need several pieces of equipment to create literacy materials and activities.

Digital Camera

An inexpensive camera may work just as well as a special model designed for children. There are a number of features to consider:

- Resolution—the sharpness of the pictures expressed in pixels (the higher the resolution, the better the picture).
- Optical zoom—magnifies the images using a multifocal-length lens.
- Image capacity—memory capability for images shot at high resolution.
- Expansion slot for memory card.
- LCD display for children to review pictures.

Digital Video Camera

- Use to document events in the classroom.
- Use a tripod to ease use and avoid accidents.

Printer and Scanner

- A color printer is essential for book making and literacy material creation.

- Scanners can transfer children's writing samples and artwork into a digital format.

Digital Touchscreen Devices

- Digital devices, including the iPod touch, iPad, and similar models, can be used by an adult in the classroom as a record-keeping tool. Some of these devices have built-in features, such as a calendar, address book, memo pad, clock, and calculator. Some models have Internet access, cameras, color screens, and audio capabilities, enabling them to record and show multimedia content.
- This important documentation tool can record a child's progress.
- Children's work can be captured in photo or even video form.
- Software applications or appropriate apps are key to use with children's portfolio items.
- These devices can be used as tools for exploration and learning by young children. Children's apps need to be carefully evaluated for developmental appropriateness.

LEARN TO USE THE EQUIPMENT

Most equipment is fairly user-friendly, requiring very little, if any, instruction to operate.

- Become familiar with all options and test them.
- Make sure equipment is easy for children to use.

The manufacturer may have tutorials that are downloadable from its website. Online training sites may also offer tips and training on using technology.

Early Literacy Skills.   Reading and writing skills that are developed in the years from birth to age five have a clear and consistently strong relationship with later literacy skills. Six variables representing early literacy skills predict later measures of literacy development. These six variables are correlated with later literacy development:[40]

alphabetic knowledge (AK)
Knowledge of the names and sounds associated with printed letters.

phonological awareness (PA)
The ability to detect, manipulate, or analyze the auditory aspects of spoken language (including the ability to distinguish or segment words, syllables, or phonemes), independent of meaning.

- **Alphabetic knowledge (AK)**: Knowledge of the names and sounds associated with printed letters.
- **Phonological awareness (PA)**: The ability to detect, manipulate, or analyze the auditory aspects of spoken language (including the ability to distinguish or segment words, syllables, or phonemes), independent of meaning.
- **Rapid automatic naming (RAN)** *of letters or digits*: The ability to rapidly name a sequence of random letters or digits.

CHOOSE THE SOFTWARE

Before you choose software or apps, decide on the literacy activity:

- For creating simple books or class slide shows, use a photo-management type of program—such as iPhoto, Kodak EasyShare, or Photo Kit Junior. Also presentation software, such as Keynote or Microsoft PowerPoint, can be used for viewing the final product.
- For interactive books, authoring software is best—such as Classroom Suite, HyperStudio, or even Microsoft Word. Recently developed apps may also be appropriate and easy to use with digital devices.

CREATE LITERACY ACTIVITIES FOR THE CHILDREN

When they create their own electronic books, children learn many print concepts, including reading text left to right and top to bottom, separating words with a space, and learning that words have meaning.

Electronic Book Templates

- Each child can create a book about him- or herself or can base it on a field trip, class project, or favorite book.
- Children can add their own pictures, voices, and text.
- Page-turning buttons in the bottom corners of each page allow children to navigate forward and backward through the book.

Child-Created Books

Children in preschool classes can learn to use digital cameras, download pictures to the computer, and use software to create books.

- Explain how to plug the camera into the computer and download the pictures.
- Show children how to use the photo management application.

- Teach children how to enter text and sounds into the program.
- Encourage children to work in small groups to benefit from cooperative play.

DOCUMENT THE LEARNING

- *Daily documentation.* Take digital photos in the classroom on an ongoing basis. Pictures of children's construction, artwork, or play activities can be shared immediately with them. The teacher may also want to share the images with the class as a review of the week's activities and projects.
- *Wall displays.* Displaying digital pictures in a hallway or on a classroom wall gives children documentation of events and an opportunity to review and revisit. Children's language skills are sparked as they review the pictures. They may also dictate a narrative about the pictures and events.
- *Portfolios.* Have digital photos, scanned photos, writing samples, and artwork in children's individual electronic portfolio files. At the end of the year, copy the images to a CD or DVD for families, or create an electronic book or movie about each child. Families might also create their own books during a workshop at the end of the year. With simple instructions and a template, they can choose the images to place in children's books.

Technology is a scaffolding tool for literacy when educators and families know how to use equipment and apply it to young children's needs. Children gain print concepts and other early literacy skills, and the technology serves as a valuable documentation tool.

. . . .

Source: Contributed by Linda Robinson, Assistant Director, Center for Best Practices in Early Childhood, Western Illinois University, Macomb, Illinois.

- *RAN of objects or colors*: The ability to rapidly name a sequence of repeating random sets of pictures of objects (e.g., "car," "tree," "house," "man") or colors.
- *Writing or writing name*: The ability to write letters in isolation on request or to write one's own name.
- **Phonological memory (PM)**: The ability to remember spoken information for a short period of time.

Readiness and Culture

Every child is always ready for some kind of learning. Children always need experiences that will promote learning and get them ready for the next step. As early childhood educators, we should constantly ask such questions as: What does this child know? What can I do to help this child move to the next level of understanding?

rapid automatic naming (RAN) The ability to rapidly name a random sequence, such as a random sequence of letters, digits, colors, or pictures of objects.

phonological memory (PM) The ability to remember spoken information for a short period of time.

In the first five years of life, children learn to talk their people's language and play their people's daily life scripts—homemaking and going places, talking to friends and buying and selling, making and fixing, singing and dancing, and storytelling and celebrating rituals. Children's imitative and playful grounding in their culture is the foundation for identity development and for trust in the world as a predictable and a meaningful place.[41]

Many factors influence children's readiness for school. Reflect on the influence of parents, siblings, home, and schools on how children learn. Readiness is also a function of culture. Culture is a group's way of life, including basic values, beliefs, religion, language, clothing, food, and various practices. Teachers have to be sensitive to the fact that different cultures have different values regarding the purpose of school, the process of schooling, children's roles in the schooling process, and the family's and culture's roles in promoting readiness. You must learn about other cultures, talk with families, and try to find a match between the process and activities of schooling and families' cultures. Providing culturally sensitive, supportive, and responsive education is the responsibility of all early childhood professionals.

From teachers' standpoints, it is critical to identify those aspects of children's cultural backgrounds that have the greatest relevance for children's adjustment, motivation, and learning at school. Cultural dimensions that influence children's school readiness include (1) parents' attitudes and beliefs about early learning, (2) the nature and extent of parent–child interactions and other experiences that support the kinds of learning that schools tend to expect from children, and (3) social conventions that affect the ways in which knowledge and skills pertinent to early learning are communicated among and used by family members. The primary language used at home is also a profoundly important factor that affects children's adjustment to school.[42]

culture A group's way of life, including basic values, beliefs, religion, language, clothing, food, and various practices.

TEACHING AND LEARNING IN THE INCLUSIVE CLASSROOM: THE TEACHER'S ROLE IN ENCOURAGING PEER INTERACTIONS IN PRESCHOOL CLASSROOMS

There are specific steps teachers can take to enhance children's peer interactions in the classroom. They include:

1. ***Provide children with opportunities to play with peers.*** There is no substitute for the experience children gain from interacting with peers. Teachers can strategically set up play opportunities with peers by establishing a "peer buddy" program. With a "peer buddy" program, the teacher pairs children with a play partner and requires the dyad to play together for a set period of time. For example, the first fifteen minutes of center time or playground time could be devoted to playing with an assigned peer buddy. The children would be expected to go to a center or an area of the playground together for fifteen minutes. When the time is over, they are free to play as they please.

2. ***Use teacher talk to encourage peer interactions.*** Teacher talk refers to specific help that teachers provide to children to assist them to become better play partners. Teacher talk can take several different formats: (a) recasting: when the teacher changes the child's word into a word that is more familiar to a peer (e.g., child says *pweeze* and the teacher says *please*); (b) repeating: when a teacher restates what a child has said for the peer's benefit (e.g., child says, "He hurt his leg," and the teacher says, "His dog hurt his leg"); (c) questioning: when the teacher begins a back and forth interaction with a child to try to get a peer involved in the

interaction (e.g., teacher says, "What did you make the baby for dinner?", child answers, "Pizza," teacher replies to the peer, "He made the baby pizza"); and (d) prompting: when a teacher provides a specific cue to a child (e.g., teacher says, "I think your friend wants to play with you").

3. *Use teaching opportunities that occur during ongoing classroom routines.* For example, a teacher notices that a child is interested in joining other children in the block area and thus prompts the child to approach the other children and say, "Play please."

4. *Provide children with instructional interactions that are brief.* With this approach, the teacher waits for one of the children to focus on an object or begin a social interaction with a peer. Once this occurs, the teacher gets the child's attention so that the teaching can begin. For example, a child may say, "I need a block." The teacher turns to the peer, hands the peer a block, and says, "Say here you go." The peer is expected to take the block, hand it to his or her peer, and repeat what the teacher said.

5. *Intervene when necessary, but let children attempt to interact with peers on their own first as they begin to use their newly learned skills.* Gradual disengagement of teachers from involvement in children's play with peers is beneficial especially when children are attempting to use newly learned social skills. This allows the children to benefit from trying to use social skills on their own rather than relying on the teacher.

Source: Contributed by Tina Stanton-Chapman, Professor of Education, University of Virginia.

Transitions to Kindergarten

A **transition** is a passage from one learning setting, grade, program, or experience to another. You can help ensure that the transitions preschool children make from home to preschool to kindergarten are happy and rewarding experiences.

> **transition** A passage from one learning setting, grade, program, or experience to another.

You can help your children and families make transitions easily and confidently in these ways:

- Educate and prepare children ahead of time for any new situation. Children can practice routines they will encounter when they enter kindergarten. For example, children can practice some likely kindergarten routines such as putting away their things each day.

- Alert parents to new and different standards, dress, behavior, and parent–teacher interactions they will encounter in kindergarten. Inform parents that school attendance is important for children's achievement. Also, make them aware of your state's attendance requirements.

- Give children an opportunity to meet their new teachers. Invite a kindergarten teacher to your classroom to read to the children.

- Let parents know ahead of time what their children will need in the new program (e.g., lunch box, change of clothing, etc.).

- Provide parents of children with special needs and bilingual parents with additional help and support during the transition. Introduce them to new teachers and contact personnel.

- Offer parents and children an opportunity to visit programs. Children will better understand the physical, curricular, and affective climates of their new programs if they visit in advance.

"Puzzle, Puzzle, Where Does This Piece Go?"

There is a lot of discussion about getting preschoolers ready for kindergarten and what readiness skills are important for their school success. Recent research ties early math skills with later school success. Researchers examined data on over 17,000 preschool children and concluded that early math skills consistently predict later school success.[43]

So what does this mean for you?

• Make sure you include math activities in your curriculum to help ensure that your children are ready for kindergarten. Other predictors of later school achievement include

early reading and behavioral and attention skills, so don't neglect these!

• Include puzzle play and the opportunity to select puzzle play in free choice activity time in your preschool curriculum. Research reveals that children who play with puzzles develop better spatial skills, which are essential for math and math-related learning.[44]

• Include block play as outlined in the Professionalism in Practice feature, "Using Blocks to Help Preschoolers Build Mathematical Skills" in this chapter.

• Cooperate with the staff of any program the children will attend to work out a transition plan.

• Exchange class visits between preschool and kindergarten programs. Class visits are excellent ways to have preschool children learn about the classrooms they will attend as kindergartners. Having kindergarten children visit the preschool and telling preschoolers about kindergarten provides for a sense of security and anticipation.

• Work with kindergarten teachers to make booklets about their program. These booklets can include photographs of children, letters from kindergarten children and preschoolers, and pictures of kindergarten activities. These books can be placed in the reading centers where preschool children can "read" about the programs they will attend.

• Hold a "kindergarten day" for preschoolers in which they attend kindergarten for a day. This program can include such things as riding the bus, having lunch, touring the school, and meeting teachers.

Remember that transitions can be traumatic experiences for children. When transitions are hurried, unplanned, and abrupt, they can cause social, emotional, and learning problems. Successful transitions can be good learning experiences for children.

"Letting Kids Help Each Other Is the Way to Go!"

It is somewhat common sense to know that children learn how to speak and understand language by talking and speaking with their parents and teachers. However, researchers found that children's receptive and expressive language develops faster when they are interacting with their classmates who have better language skills than they do.[45]

So, what does this mean for you?

- Children's classmates are an important resource for language development for all children, especially ELLs and children with low-level language abilities. Remember Vygotsky said that scaffolding occurs best when children are interacting with "more competent others." In this case, the more competent others are their peers with better language skills.
- Group children according to their language ability levels, giving children with low-level language skills an opportunity to interact with children who have high language skills.
- Manage your classroom and learning groups to make sure that you create an environment in which all children have an opportunity to engage in conversation and are comfortable with conversing with all of their classmates regardless of language ability.

Peer Interactions in the Classrooms

Successful peer interactions are critical to the social development of preschoolers. Peers afford preschoolers exciting and fun play experiences. When preschoolers do not have the needed skills to play with others or do not have playmates in the class, they often become excluded from play opportunities and do not develop more complex social skills needed for future peer interactions. Teachers may need to support these children by providing assistance to help them benefit from social interactions.

COMMON CORE AND PRESCHOOL STATE STANDARDS

The purposes of preschool are changing dramatically. More and more, preschools are seen as places that get children ready for kindergarten. What was traditionally taught in kindergarten is now taught in the preschool. The preschool curriculum is now stressing academic skills related to reading, writing, and math as well as social skills. Increasingly, the responsibility for setting the preschool curriculum is being taken over by state departments of education through early learning guidelines or *standards,* statements of what preschoolers should know and be able to do.

As a result of the Common Core Standards for K–12 for what students should be able to know and do, it should come as no surprise that the standards movement is also influencing pre-K (birth to age 4) education as well. As a result, states have developed early learning guidelines (ELGs) to describe what children should know and be able to do as a means of getting them ready for school and kindergarten. The development and implementation of early learning guidelines has raised many issues regarding developmentally appropriate practice.

Currently, the majority of states have guidelines or standards for what preschool children should know and do before they enter kindergarten. These early learning standards include literacy, mathematics, science, social studies, fine arts, health and safety, personal and social development, physical development, and technology applications. Two important points are associated with state preschool standards. One is that preschool goals and learning standards are being set by the Common Core Standards and what children in K–3 need to know and do. State departments of education, and as a result, states are determining the preschool curriculum. Second, the preschool curriculum is becoming focused much more on academics, and this will continue. Figure 8.2 shows you an example from the Florida preschool standards in math, reading, and science.

The accompanying Professionalism in Practice feature about early learning standards gives you sound professional advice for teaching preschool standards.

Florida Early Learning and Developmental Standards for Four-Year-Olds

Math	Reading	Science
• Shows understanding of and uses appropriate terms to describe ordinal positions • Shows understanding by participating in the comparison of quantities • Shows understanding of addition and subtraction using a concrete set of objects • Understands various two-dimensional shapes, including circle, triangle, square, rectangle, oval, and other less common shapes	• Shows an understanding of words and their meanings • Demonstrates age-appropriate ability to write letters • Demonstrates comprehension of text read aloud • Shows motivation for reading • Initiates, ask questions, and responds to adults and peers in a variety of settings	• Demonstrates the use of simple tools and equipment for observing and investigating • Explores growth and change of living things • Explores the outdoor environment and begins to recognize changes (e.g., weather conditions) in the environment, with teacher support and multiple experiences over time • Demonstrates ongoing environmental awareness and responsibility (e.g., reduce, reuse, recycle), with teacher support

FIGURE 8.2 Preschool Standards: Florida

As you review and reflect on Florida's Early Learning and Developmental Standards, now would be a good time for you to review the learning standards in your state. You can also go online and get the full version of the Florida standards (see the Linking to Learning section at the end of this chapter) and compare and contrast them with your state standards. What implication does teaching the standards have for you and your career as a teacher?

DEVELOPMENTALLY APPROPRIATE PRACTICE AND THE PRESCHOOL CURRICULUM

Although the curricula of individual preschools are varied and are influenced by state standards or guidelines, all programs should have certain essential curricular content areas. These include (1) social and emotional; (2) language and communication; (3) emergent literacy reading and writing; (4) mathematics; (5) science; (6) social studies; (7) fine arts; (8) physical development; and (9) technology. In other words, the content areas for preschool are much like those for kindergarten and first grade.

It is more than likely that your state has preschool guidelines for what preschool children should know and do for each of these curriculum areas. Now would be a good time for you to review the preschool guidelines/standards for your state or another state. Pay particular attention to the math standards. Learning mathematics is a high priority in all of education from pre-K through grade twelve. More and more, the preschool years are viewed as the foundation for mathematics learning.

Daily Schedule

What should the preschool day schedule be like? Although a daily schedule depends on many things—your philosophy, the needs of children, families, beliefs, and state and local standards—the following descriptions illustrate what you can do on a typical preschool day. The preschool schedule described here is for a whole-day program;

many other program arrangements are possible. Some preschools operate half-day, morning-only programs five days a week; others operate both a morning and an afternoon session; others operate only two or three days a week. However, an important preschool trend is toward public school full-day, full-year programs.

How you structure the day for your children will determine in part how and what they learn. You will want to develop your daily schedule with attention and care. Figure 8.3 is an example of a schedule for a full-day program.

Opening Activities.   As children enter, the teacher greets each individually. Daily personal greetings make the children feel important, build a positive attitude toward school, and provide an opportunity to practice language skills. Daily greetings also give you a chance to check each child's health and emotional status.

Children usually do not arrive all at one time, so the first arrivals need something to do while others are arriving. Offering a free selection of activities or letting children self-select from a limited range of quiet activities (such as puzzles, pegboards, or

Schedule

Time	Activity	Notes
8:00	Opening Activities	Peg boards, puzzles, coloring, reading, journal writing, etc.
8:45	Group Meeting	Circle time, group singing, planning, sharing, announcements, etc.
9:30	Learning Centers	Reading center, math center, science center, civics center, history center, etc.
10:30	Bathroom/ Wash Hands	Self-help skills, toileting, hand washing, etc.
10:45	Snack	Nutritious, encourages independence (i.e., self-serving, self-prepared, etc.)
11:15	Outside Time	Climbing, jumping, swinging, throwing, kicking, pretending, etc.
12:00	Bathroom	Teach health, self-help, and intrapersonal skills, but children can use restroom at any time
12:15	Lunch Time	Meal served family style: teachers and children eat together. Use time to relax, build relationships, engage in conversation, etc.
1:00	Relaxation and/or Nap Time	Rest, quiet time, coloring, listening to music on headphones, self-soothing and relaxation techniques, breathing exercises, teacher-read story time, read to self, etc.
2:45	Centers/ Projects	Art activities, drama activities, music activities, cooking, project approach (see Ch. 5), holiday activities, work projects, collecting activities, field trips, etc.
3:15	Group Time	Listening and attention skills, discuss the day, discuss learning, evaluate performance and behavior, etc.
3:30	Good-Bye Time	
4:00	Close	Classroom clean up, self-directed activities as parents arrive (i.e., coloring, reading, etc.)

FIGURE 8.3 Sample of a Daily Schedule

professionalism in practice

The What and Why of Early Learning Standards

The majority of states have developed early learning standards for preschool-age children. Many states are in the process of developing standards for infants and toddlers. Early childhood educators in each state worked hard to define reasonable expectations for children from ages birth through five years that reflect the values and uniqueness of their state, as well as comply with accepted developmental understandings of how young children learn and develop. There are many similarities and unique features across all the state standards. Most states provide easy Internet access to the early learning standards they developed. Early educators should become familiar with the standards in their state and incorporate them in their curriculum planning and assessment practices.

MAKE THE BEST USE OF STANDARDS

There are benefits to implementing early learning standards. There are also potential problems if they are used inappropriately. The benefits include:

- Reinforcement of the incredible potential for learning and growth in young children
- Help in establishing expectations for children at different ages and creating a commonality for communication among early educators
- Creation of a framework for accountability—a way for early educators to show parents, the community at large, and themselves just what children are learning
- The potential to be incorporated into curriculum that is developmentally appropriate for preschoolers—play and investigation, emergent curriculum and projects, small- and large-group times, and daily routines such as snack

time, toileting and hand washing, outdoor times, and transitions
- The capability to be assessed in ways that are authentic, based on teacher observation and documentation of children's progress through photographs and work samples that can be used to show children's progress on the early learning standards

Use caution when using early learning standards. Early educators committed to implementing them within a developmentally appropriate framework of curriculum and assessment must be careful to avoid the following:

- Teaching and curricular practices that overemphasize direct instruction and which do not value child-initiated play and investigation with adult guidance and support
- Assessment practices that focus on testing or on-demand tasks that do not naturalistically reflect how children demonstrate the early learning standards in everyday activities, play, investigation, and daily routines

Learning the standards for your state takes time. Figuring out ways to incorporate them into activities and daily routines, as well as assessing children's progress in authentic and naturalistic ways, may require training, dialogue among colleagues, and even some trial and error as you get started and see what works and doesn't work in your setting. Early learning standards have changed the climate of early childhood education. The accountability associated with them may be frightening or seem oppositional to traditional early childhood practices. This is not the case! They can be implemented within the context of best practices for young children. Time and effort on your part and on the part of administrators will

---

markers to color with, journal "writing," etc.) are appropriate ways to involve children as they arrive.

Note how the teacher in this **video** involves her students in the discussion of apples while preparing them for the next activity.

Group Meeting/Planning.   After all children arrive, you and they plan together and talk about the day ahead. This is also the time for announcements, sharing, and group songs, and for children to think about what they plan to learn during the day.

Learning Centers.   After the group time, children are free to go to one of various learning centers, organized and designed to teach concepts. Table 8.2 lists types of learning centers and the concepts each is intended to teach. You should plan based on the state standards and for the concepts and skills you want children to learn in each

be required to implement standards in ways that are just right for preschoolers.

STANDARDS IN A PRESCHOOL CURRICULUM

There are two ways to think about standards in a preschool curriculum: naturalistically and intentionally.

Naturalistic Approaches

Naturalistically, standards are embedded in all that goes on in a preschool classroom. You can look back over the day with children and think about what you saw children do and heard them say. Then, you can identify which standards they were demonstrating as they played in the dramatic play area, or created at the art table, or built with the blocks.

This requires conscientious attention to what children are doing and familiarity with your state's early learning standards. The more you reflect and think about this and the more you dialogue with colleagues, the more you will see the children's progress!

Intentional Approaches

Thinking intentionally about standards is a proactive approach. You can plan for activities and materials that will directly address specific early learning standards. Again, you do not need to think in terms of direct instruction only. Your plans for children's play, projects, group times, and field trips can incorporate early learning standards. You can:

- Put together specific materials or activities that address a particular standard.
- Use the standards as a basis for writing the goals on lessons and activity plans.
- Plan for how you will record what the children do in relation to that standard.

ASSESSING STANDARDS AUTHENTICALLY

As you work with children throughout each day, be in a continual process of observing and listening, as well as evaluating what you are seeing and hearing. Authentic assessment involves gathering information about a child as you work and play with him, observe him, listen to him, ask him open-ended questions to learn more about his thinking, and challenge him to try the next step. Then, evaluate all of the information you have learned about the child. This is where the standards come into play. They are the reference by which the child's accomplishments are measured. You ask yourself the following questions:

- Has the child accomplished a particular standard or not?
- If not, where is he on a spectrum of progress toward accomplishing the standard?
- If he has accomplished the standard, what is the next step in acquisition of skills and knowledge that he is ready for?
- What curricular plans will best meet this child where he is and help him move on in his progress and accomplishments?

Authentic assessment through observation and reflection about each child's progress is time consuming. It is also the best and most appropriate way to get a true picture of how each child is developing in relation to the expectations in the standards. The time and effort put into documenting through observational notes, photographs, and work samples is worth it if the end result is a truer, more reliable evaluation of the child's capabilities.

CONCLUSION

Early learning standards have many benefits. They can be a wonderful guide to reasonable expectations and common goals for children in each state. They can be incorporated into developmentally appropriate preschool curriculum and authentic assessment practices. This takes commitment and hard work on the part of all involved to do what is right for young children!

....

Source: Contributed by Gaye Gronlund, early education consultant and author (www.gayegronlund.com). Adapted with permission from Gaye Gronlund, Make Early Learning Standards Come Alive: Connecting Your Practice and Curriculum to State Guidelines *(St. Paul, MN: Redleaf Press, 2006); special edition published unchanged in 2007 by Merrill/Prentice Hall as part of the Merrill Education/ Redleaf Press College Textbook Series. © 2012 Gaye Gronlund.*

center. Also, every center should be a literacy center; that is, there should be materials for the development of writing and reading in every center.

Learning centers provide a number of useful functions. They enable you to meet the diverse learning needs and interests of your children and your community. In addition, learning centers:

- Encourage and promote collaboration, social interaction, and independent work
- Provide you with a classroom organization that enables you to work with individual children and small groups while other children are meaningfully and actively involved
- Provide for active and child-initiated learning

TABLE 8.2 Types of Classroom Learning Centers

Theme-Based Centers	Concepts
Use theme centers as an extension of classroom themes: • Space • Dinosaurs • The Ocean • All About Me • My Family Generally a classroom theme lasts for one to two weeks and occasionally longer. Children can use theme centers for varying amounts of time from fifteen to thirty minutes and during their free time.	• Use language skills, participate in sociodramatic play, and verbalize. • Identify role(s) as a family member. • Cooperate with others in joint activities. • Learn how to cooperate and practice good habits of daily living such as sharing, taking turns, and following rules.

Subject Centers	Concepts
• *Literacy/Language:* Be sure to change books frequently. Add ten new books every two to three weeks. The goal is to have preschoolers familiar with 100 books. Also include books from all genres: picture books, fiction, science, and so on. • *Writing:* Provide various and plentiful materials for writing: paper, blank books, folded paper, envelopes, markers, pencils, and so forth. Every center should have materials for writing. • *Math:* Provide plastic number tiles, math cards, pegboards. There should be many concrete materials to promote hands-on experiences. The math center should also have picture books about math; read stories involving math.	• Verbalize; listen; understand directions; how to use books; colors, size, shapes, and names; print and book knowledge; vocabulary development; print awareness. • Learn alphabet, word knowledge, that words have meaning, that words make sentences, and so forth. • Learn that writing has many useful purposes, and that written words convey meaning. • Understand meanings of whole numbers. • Recognize the number of objects in small groups without counting and by counting. • Understand that number words refer to quantity. • Use one-to-one correspondence to solve problems by matching sets and comparing number amounts and in counting objects to ten and beyond. • Understand that the last word stated in counting tells "how many." Count to determine number amounts and compare quantities (using language such as "more than" and "less than"). • Order sets by the number of objects in them. • Find shapes in the environment and describe them. • Build pictures and designs by combining two- and three-dimensional shapes. • Solve problems such as deciding which piece will fit into a space in a puzzle. • Discuss the relative positions of objects with vocabulary such as "above," "below," and "next to." • Identify objects as "the same" or "different," and "more" or "less," on the basis of attributes that can be measured. • Measure attributes such as length and weight. Make comparisons of objects based on length, weight, etc.

TABLE 8.2 Types of Classroom Learning Centers *(Continued)*

Subject Centers	Concepts
• *Science:* Provide books on science; provide materials for observing, for discovering relationships, and for learning about nature, plants, animals, and the environment.	• Develop skills in observation, size, shape, color, whole/part, figure/ground, spatial relations, and classifying, graphing, problem-solving skills. • Learn how to observe, make comparisons, classify, and problem-solve. • Investigate and explore.
• *Life Science:* Provide various plants and animals, terrariums, and habitats.	• Understand plant and animal care and habitats.
• *Art/Music/Creative Expression:* Provide materials for painting, coloring, drawing, cutting, and pasting. Engage children in activities involving singing and movement. Provide puppets and puppet theater to encourage dramatic and creative expression.	• Listen to a wide range of musical styles. • Learn color relationships and combinations. • Engage in creative expression, aesthetic appreciation, satisfaction. • Create representations of homes and places in the community. • Participate in group singing, finger-plays, and rhythm.

Activity Centers	Concepts
• *Construction/Blocks:* Provide a variety of different kinds of blocks.	• Describe size, shape, length, seriation, spatial relationships. • Develop problem-solving skills.
• *Woodworking:* Make real tools and building materials available. Be sure to provide goggles and other precautions for children's safety.	• Learn to follow directions; learn how to use real tools; learn about planning and the construction process. • Discover whole/part relationships.
• *Dramatic Play:* Provide various materials and props for home activities, including a child-size stove, table, chairs, refrigerator, sink, etc. Provide clothing, hats, and shoes, as well as outfits and props from many occupations such as nurse/doctor, firefighter, and construction worker.	• Learn language skills, socio-dramatic play, functions, processes, social skills. • Engage in pretend and imaginary play. • Learn roles and responsibilities of community workers.
• *Water/Sand Play*	• Learn what floats; investigate capacity; compare volume. • Develop social skills and responsibility (i.e., cleanup).

Technology Centers	Concepts
• *Computer/Technology:* Provide computers, printer, scanner, fax machine, digital camera, and video camera. A computer center can have one or more workstations or can have one or more laptops or handheld devices.	• Learn socialization, keyboarding, how technology can solve problems. • Learn basic technology skills. • Write (using e-mail, word processing). • Use technology to learn basic math and language skills. • Use technology to play games.

Although we want children to be involved in child-initiated and active learning, sometimes it is necessary to directly teach children certain concepts or skills.

When developing learning centers, keep these guidelines in mind:

- Teach children how to use each center. Provide appropriate rules for use, care of materials, and so on. Such guidelines can be covered with the whole group as well as in small groups or with individuals.
- Develop centers around your state's/district's pre-K guidelines or standards, children's interests, and your learning goals for the children. For example, a state standard or learning expectation for preschool might specify that "children demonstrate emergent reading skills." To help meet this goal, you could develop a center that has a variety of age-appropriate printed materials such as books, magazines, catalogs, and so forth. You would also provide opportunities in the center for children to "read" and participate in literacy-related activities.
- Use children's interests to develop learning centers. For example, on a nature walk around the center, the children were very interested in dragonflies, grasshoppers, and crickets. You can develop a learning center in which children draw pictures of insects, record observations about insects, and sort pictures of insects by type.
- Develop ways for evaluating children's work processes and products while they are at the centers. Chapter 6 provides many ideas for how to observe and assess children's products and achievement.

Bathroom/Hand Washing.   Before any activity in which food is handled, prepared, or eaten, children should wash and dry their hands. Instructing children in proper hand-washing procedures can prevent the spread of illness and form lifelong habits. Hand washing has assumed a major role in the prevention of diseases such as the flu.

Snacks.   After learning center activities, a snack is usually served. It should be nutritionally sound and something the children can serve (and often prepare) themselves.

Outdoor Activity/Play/Walking.   Outside play should be a time for learning new concepts and skills, not just a time to run around aimlessly. Children can practice climbing, jumping, swinging, throwing, and using body control. Teachers may incorporate walking trips and other events into outdoor play.

Bathroom/Toileting.   Bathroom/toileting times offer opportunities to teach health, self-help, and intrapersonal skills. Children should also be allowed to use the bathroom whenever necessary.

Lunch.   Lunch should be a relaxing time, and the meal should be served family style, with professionals and children eating together. Children should set their own tables and decorate them with place mats and flowers they can make in the art center or as a special project. Children should be involved in cleaning up after meals and snacks. On the other hand, in many programs, preschool children go to the school cafeteria for their lunch. Try to make this a relaxing experience also.

Relaxation.   After lunch, children should have a chance to relax, perhaps to the accompaniment of teacher-read stories, CDs, or music. This is an ideal time to teach children breathing exercises and relaxation techniques, select their own quiet activity, or read to themselves.

Nap Time. Children who want or need to should have a chance to rest or sleep. Quiet activities should be available for those who do not need to or cannot sleep on a particular day. In any event, nap time should not be forced on any child.

Centers or Special Projects. Following nap time is a good time for center activities or special projects. Special projects can also be conducted in the morning, and some may be more appropriate then, such as cooking something for snack or lunch. Special projects might involve cooking, holiday activities, collecting things, work projects, art activities, and field trips.

Group Time. The day can end with a group meeting to review the day's activities. This meeting develops listening and attention skills, promotes oral communication, stresses that learning is important, and helps children evaluate their performance and behavior.

Good-Bye Time. This is a time for your children to participate in cleaning responsibilities. After the classroom is clean, your students can engage in self-directed activities until their parents arrive to pick them up. Such activities might include coloring or reading, playing in various centers, "reading" books and other materials, and other "free choice" activities.

Play in Preschool Programs

Play has traditionally been at the heart of preschool programs. Children's play is and will continue to be important in preschool programs because it results in learning. Therefore, preschool programs should support learning through play.

This video shows many types of play. What skills are fostered through these play activities?

The notion that children learn and develop through play began with Froebel. Since his time, most early childhood programs have incorporated play into their curricula. Montessori viewed children's active involvement with materials and the prepared environment as the primary means by which they absorb knowledge and learn. John Dewey believed that children learn through play and that children should have opportunities to engage in play associated with everyday activities (e.g., the house center, post office, grocery store, and doctor's office). Piaget believed play promotes cognitive knowledge and is a means by which children construct knowledge of their world. He thought that through active involvement, children learn. Vygotsky viewed the social interactions that occur through play as essential to children's development. He believed that children, through social interactions with others, learn social skills such as cooperation and collaboration that promote and enhance their cognitive development. The accompanying Professionalism in Practice feature shows you how to use block play to help children learn essential math skills.

Providing opportunities for children to choose among well-planned, varied learning activities enhances the probability that they will learn through play.

Accommodating Play. Preschool is the first opportunity Han Ling has had to go to school. Han Ling is **typically developing** (meaning that she reaches the majority of developmental milestones at the appropriate time and does not have deficits in social areas), and she enjoys coloring, story time, and playing on the swing set outside. In preschool, Han Ling must learn the rules of a more structured environment, such as sitting for longer periods of time, and she must learn pre-math and language skills. With so much to teach her, it is easy to forget that Han Ling's first job as a preschool-aged child is play. Play is the true language of children. It is how they learn social

typically developing Reaching the majority of developmental milestones at the appropriate time and not presenting deficits in social areas.

professionalism in practice

Using Blocks to Help Preschoolers Build Mathematical Skills

Froebel, the father of kindergarten, introduced blocks to the early childhood curriculum with his creation of gifts. Froebel created these gifts to facilitate children's creativity and provide opportunities for them to construct geometric forms. Preschool classrooms today have a variety of different types of blocks. Enabling children to explore and experiment with these materials provides them opportunities to develop the foundation for mathematical concepts related to algebra, geometry, and measurement.

When planning learning experiences for young children to use blocks, consider the following ideas prior to using these materials:

USE A VARIETY OF INSTRUCTIONAL APPROACHES

- Give children time to explore freely with blocks during center time or other times in the day. Providing opportunities for free play allows children to develop various intuitive geometric concepts and problem-solving skills.
- Informally guide children's individual block play to help them connect prior learning experiences or deepen their understanding of a concept. Pose questions about the children's play to provoke mathematical conversations. For example, when a child sorts blocks into different groups, ask the child about these groupings with questions such as:
  - Why did you put these blocks together?
  - What other blocks could you put into this group?
- Use the blocks in small group or whole group instruction to introduce or review mathematical concepts such as counting or identifying various shapes.

PROVIDE CHILDREN WITH DIFFERENT TYPES OF BLOCKS TO EXPLORE

Incorporate a variety of manipulatives—including different types of blocks—for young children to use in your preschool classroom. Providing these materials will allow children to explore mathematical concepts such as sorting, patterns, measurement, and geometry. The accompanying table lists some of the common types of blocks used in preschool classrooms and some of the mathematical concepts children develop when using these materials.

ASK CHILDREN A VARIETY OF QUESTIONS

It is important for you to ask students thought-provoking questions that will allow them to explore a variety of mathematical concepts. Asking children questions about their block structures not only provides them with the opportunity to engage in mathematical conversations about their work, but also gives you the occasion to explore children's mathematical knowledge. For example, if a preschooler made a pattern with pattern blocks, you might ask the following questions:

- Tell me about your creation. What did you make? (Give the child an opportunity to use her words to describe the blocks.)
- What type of pattern did you make?
- If I wanted to add to your pattern, what blocks would I have to use?
- Is there a block that looks the same as the three green triangles?

norms, hone peer interactions, express their emotions, engage in their environment, and learn problem solving. However, play does not always erupt spontaneously, so here are some tips to encourage Han Ling in play:

- Provide different play opportunities by arranging your room in centers. Block centers with blocks of varying weights and sizes, dramatic play centers with dress-up clothes, home centers with pretend food and cooking appliances, and manipulative centers with toys like dolls, action figures, or cars are just a few examples of centers that elicit play.

Type of Block	Mathematical Concepts	Examples
Building/architect blocks	Patterns, sorting, geometry, measurement, spatial relationships, counting	Children will build various structures with these materials. Consider playing an "I Spy" type of game where children find different shapes in their creations.
Pattern blocks	Patterns, sorting, geometry, measurement, spatial relationships, counting	Children can practice creating patterns with these blocks or creating "new" shapes.
Snap cubes	Patterns, sorting, measurement, counting	Children can use blocks to determine the length/width of various objects in the room.
Color tiles	Patterns, sorting, measurement, counting	Children might use these blocks to measure objects in the classroom or to start thinking about how many color tiles might cover a certain object in the classroom (area).
Tangrams	Patterns, sorting, geometry, measurement, spatial relationships, counting	Provide children with opportunities to create "new" shapes with tangrams. Children can trace the perimeter of these designs and have friends try to create their new shapes.
Three-dimensional geometric models	Patterns, sorting, geometry, measurement, counting	These solids not only provide examples of various three-dimensional shapes, but also allow children different types of materials to sort.
Color cubes	Patterns, sorting, measurement, counting	Children can use these cubes to start understanding the concept of capacity. For instance, have children explore how many cubes different objects in the classroom can hold.
Attribute blocks	Patterns, sorting, geometry, measurement, counting	Children can practice sorting these blocks into various groups. Allow children to develop groups and labels instead of telling them to sort by color or by shape. Children will develop groupings that are more interesting with this flexibility.

As you ask these questions, encourage children to use their own words to describe their work. Also, verify your understanding of the child's descriptions. For example:

Ms. Jones: What type of pattern did you make?
Alicia: We used one yellow block and then three green blocks.
Ms. Jones: So you used one yellow hexagon and three green triangles, and then another yellow hexagon and three green triangles?
Mason and Alicia: Yes.

Providing children with opportunities to explore and construct with blocks helps lay the foundation for future mathematical success. These experiences not only allow children to deepen their understanding of algebra, geometry, and measurement, but they also offer children opportunities to practice their problem-solving skills. In addition, children will engage in meaningful mathematical conversations with their peers and their teacher.

....

Source: Contributed by Elisabeth Johnston, assistant professor in the Department of Elementary and Early Childhood Education at Slippery Rock University. Her current research relates to how preschool teachers can support young children's mathematical development. Elisabeth taught second grade for six years at a gifted and talented magnet school in Texas, where she was responsible for teaching math to a diverse range of second graders.

- Change your centers as you rotate your units. For example, if you are in a transportation unit, put toy boats, bicycles, cars, trucks, and trains in the manipulative center. Your students will begin to act out and internalize the information you've given them in their play.

- Start a rotation of three or four children grouped by their personalities, strengths, and weaknesses for each center. Don't put students in a center by themselves. Play is a wonderful opportunity to help Han Ling learn social skills and problem solving, which is much more difficult to do solo. It is natural and acceptable for centers and the children in them to occasionally blend into one another.

- When children repeatedly combine activities, like the block center with the manipulative center or the home center and the dress-up center, go ahead and combine them. This may make your groups larger but also more vibrant and conducive of greater social skill building.
- Move children into different groups. You may not find the perfect group for every child right away.
- Play! Children don't always naturally know how to play, especially if they are unfamiliar with the toys or the other children, or if they are developmentally delayed. You notice that Han Ling seems unsure and doesn't participate very much. To start:
  - Choose similar or complementary toys. If Han Ling has a mommy doll, you pick up the daddy doll and the baby doll. Once you show interest, Han Ling will likely take the initiative and tell you what part to play or what to say. Let her lead you and don't ask too many direct questions.
  - If Han Ling does not take the initiative in play, you can ask for directions in a roundabout way, saying, "Hmm, I'm not sure which one to be, the dad or the baby . . . ." She will likely take the lead and tell you what role to take.
  - To begin a play sequence, start with a scenario that Han Ling will be familiar with, like fixing breakfast or going to the grocery store. Once she is on familiar ground, Han Ling may become more directive and steer the pretending in other directions.
- Use play as an opportunity to observe your students. Through their play, they are communicating to you their strengths and weaknesses, their home lives, relationships, fears and insecurities, as well as greatest joys and interests. Use this information to become a better teacher for them.
- Remember that play is a way children "work things out," explore, and communicate. If Han Ling uses language or acts out behavior that is overly aggressive or abusive, make a note of the situation, time, and date. Report it to the school counselor and your principal. Ask them whether you should notify the parents or Child Protective Services.

Play can be an adventure for both Han Ling and for you. If you accommodate play in your classroom, both you and your students will learn a lot and enjoy the school day.

Planning for Play.   You are the key to promoting meaningful play, which promotes a basis for learning. How you prepare the environment for play and the attitudes you have toward it help determine the quality of the children's learning.

Intentionally plan to implement the curriculum through play. Integrate specific learning activities with play to achieve learning outcomes. Play activities should match children's developmental needs and be free of gender and cultural stereotypes. Teachers have to be clear about curriculum concepts and ideas they want children to learn through play.

- Provide time for learning through play. Include play in the schedule as a legitimate activity in its own right.
- Supervise play activities and participate in children's play, as we discussed above. In these roles, help, show, and guide. Model when appropriate and intervene only when necessary.
- Observe children's play. Teachers can learn how children play and the learning outcomes of play to use in planning classroom activities.

- Create environments that ensure children will learn through play. Create both indoor and outdoor environments that encourage play and support its role in learning.
- Organize the classroom or center environment so that cooperative learning is possible and active learning occurs.
- Provide materials and equipment that are appropriate to children's developmental levels and that support a nonsexist and multicultural curriculum.
- Question children about their play. Discuss what children did during play, and "debrief" children about what they have learned through play.
- Provide for safety in indoor and outdoor play.

Today, with all of the discussions about standards and academics, sometimes play gets pushed out of the curriculum. Through play, you can help children meet state standards and achieve high academic levels. When children play, they are involved in activities they are interested in. Through play, children learn by doing. Learning through interests and learning by doing are two hallmarks of developmentally appropriate practice.

As children play, teachers follow their lead and help them learn new concepts, knowledge, and skills. For example, a state standard asks students to be able to count and engage in one-to-one correspondence. During play in the housekeeping center, the children are setting the table for lunch. The teacher asks children to count out the number of forks they will need for the place settings (counting) and then asks them to put a fork at each place setting (one-to-one correspondence). The accompanying Professionalism in Practice feature, "Using Blocks to Help Build Mathematical Skills," demonstrates how block play helps children learn math standards.

Kinds of Play.

Play occurs in many types and forms. Your understanding of each of these will enable you to implement a meaningful program of learning through play. We will now discuss the different types of play.

Social Play.

Children engage in many kinds of play. Mildred Parten, a children's play researcher, identified six stages and descriptions of children's social play:

- *Unoccupied play* is play in which the child does not play with anything or anyone; the child merely stands or sits, without doing anything observable.
- *Solitary play* is play in which the child plays alone, seemingly unaware of other children.
- *Onlooker play* is play in which the child watches and observes the play of other children. The center of interest is others' play.
- *Parallel play* is play in which the child plays alongside but in ways similar to other children nearby, and with toys or other materials similar to those other children.
- In *associative play,* children interact with each other—perhaps by asking questions or sharing materials—but do not play together.
- In *cooperative play,* children actively play together, often as a result of organization by the teacher.[46]

Observing children's social play is a good way to sharpen your observation skills and to learn more about children's play and the learning that occurs through play.

Social play supports many important functions. First, it provides the means for children to interact with others and learn many social skills. Children learn how to compromise ("OK, I'll be the baby first and you can be the mommy"), be flexible ("We'll do

These children are learning how to strengthen their gross-motor skills through functional play by stacking blocks on top of each other. Children enjoy experiencing the functions and movements of their bodies through repetitions and manipulations.

it your way first and then my way"), resolve conflicts, and continue the process of learning who they are. Second, social play provides a vehicle for practicing and developing literacy skills. Children have others with whom to practice language and from whom to learn. Third, play helps children learn impulse control; they realize they cannot always do whatever they want. And fourth, in giving a child other children with whom to interact, social play negates isolation and helps children learn how to have the social interactions so vital to successful living.

On the other hand, children cannot learn all they need to know through play. There is a place in the curriculum for teacher-initiated instruction. For example, after her assessment of children's number knowledge, a preschool teacher might decide that her children need more counting practice. She could then lead them in a lesson with counting bears in which the children count out five bears from the basket of bears on their table. Both child-initiated play and teacher-initiated instruction are used in programs we discussed in Chapter 4. In addition to social play, other types of play and their benefits and purposes are shown below. Carefully study these kinds of play and plan for how you will include them in your program.

Functional Play. Functional play occurs during the sensorimotor period and in response to muscular activities and the need to be active. Functional play is characterized by repetitions, manipulations, and self-imitation. Functional play allows children to practice and learn physical capabilities while exploring their immediate environments. Very young children are especially fond of repeating movements for the pleasure of it. They engage in sensory impressions for the joy of experiencing the functioning of their bodies. Repetition of language is also a part of functional play.

Symbolic Play. Piaget referred to symbolic play as "let's pretend" play. During this stage, children freely display their creative and physical abilities and social awareness in a number of ways—for example, by pretending to be something else, such as an animal. Symbolic play also occurs when children pretend that one object is another—that a building block is a car, for example—and may also entail pretending to be another person—a mommy, daddy, or firefighter.

Informal or Free Play. Informal play occurs when children play in an environment that contains materials and people with whom they can interact. Learning materials may be grouped in centers with similar equipment: a kitchen center, a dress-up center, a block center, a music and art center, a water or sand area, and a free-play center, usually with items such as tricycles, wagons, and wooden slides for promoting large-muscle development. The atmosphere of a free-play environment is informal, unstructured, and unpressured. Play and learning episodes are generally determined by the interests of the children. Outcomes of free play are socialization, emotional development, self-control, and concept development.

Sociodramatic (Pretend) Play. Dramatic play allows children to participate vicariously in a wide range of activities associated with family living, society, and their own and others' cultural heritage. Dramatic play is generally of two kinds: *sociodramatic* and *fantasy.* Sociodramatic play usually involves everyday realistic activities and events, whereas fantasy play typically involves fairy tale and superhero play. In sociodramatic play, children have an opportunity to express themselves, assume different roles, and interact with their peers. Sociodramatic play acts as a nonsexist and multicultural arena in which all children are equal.

Outdoor Play. Children's play outside is just as important as inside play. Outdoor environments and activities promote large- and small-muscle development and body coordination as well as language development, social interaction, and creativity. The outdoor area is a learning environment and, as such, the playground should be designed according to learning objectives. Indoor learning can also occur outdoors. Easels, play dough, and dramatic play props can further enhance learning opportunities.

ACTIVITIES FOR PROFESSIONAL DEVELOPMENT

ethical dilemma

"There's only one way."

Tracy Hodgkin teaches a class of twenty-two three- and four-year-old children from diverse cultures in a school district with a history of low achievement test scores. The new superintendent has promised the board of education that he will turn the district around in three years. The superintendent has hired a new preschool coordinator because he believes that one of the best ways to close the district's achievement gap is to begin as early as possible. The new preschool coordinator has recommended the adoption of a skills-based curriculum that includes the use of direct instruction, other teacher-centered approaches, and a scripted curriculum. According to her, "There is only one way to teach children what they need to know, and that is to directly teach them. We can't fool around with all this play and child-centered stuff."

Direct instruction of basic skills and teacher-centered instructional practices are contrary to what Tracy learned in her teacher education classes at the university. In addition, these approaches do not fit with her view of child-centered and developmentally appropriate practice.

What should Tracy do? Should Tracy inform the preschool coordinator that she will not use the materials when and if they are adopted? Should Tracy use Facebook to convene a meeting of other teachers and ask their opinions about the materials? Should Tracy keep her thoughts to herself and vow to use the new curriculum only when she has to? Or should Tracy adopt another plan? What would you do?

Application Activities

1. When my students and I discuss preschool programs and when they hear preschool teachers talk about their programs, they are always amazed by how different the preschool of today is from what many of them remember it was like.

Through Internet research and online observations of preschool programs, develop a Prezi presentation that includes what you believe are five outstanding features of preschool programs today. Share your presentation with your classmates and ask them to add to your outstanding features.

2. Just as preschools of today are not like preschools of yesterday, so preschool children today are not like the preschool children of yesterday. Identify five characteristics of preschoolers today that are different from preschoolers a decade ago. One of the characteristics you might want to begin with is "more technologically savvy." Use Word Clouds for Kids (www.abcya.com/word_clouds.htm)—a graphical representation of word frequency—and post your results to your online class bulletin board.

3. School readiness, that is, readiness for kindergarten, is a huge topic in early childhood education today. Identify five characteristics that you think all preschoolers should possess in order to be ready for kindergarten. Post your results online and ask your classmates to rank order your characteristics according to their preferences. Based on the results, share your final list with your classmates.

4. Standards are statements of what children should know and be able to do. Read and reflect on pre-K guidelines in your state (if your state doesn't have pre-K guidelines, use the ones from Florida) and identify five of what you consider to be the most important pre-K guidelines.

5. Play is and should be an important part of children's lives. Unfortunately, many children don't get an opportunity to play and too many children play too little. You have been invited by a local community agency to present your views about the advantages of play for children and how parents and teachers can incorporate more play activities into home and school. Make a list of four recommendations that you will make during your presentation. Share them online with your classmates and ask for their comments.

Linking to Learning

Charlottesville City Schools

www.ccs.k12.va.us
The City of Charlottesville values education highly and the Charlottesville City School Division offers the very best in curriculum and community. Charlottesville City Schools are very much a part of the community, as well as the world!

Florida Early Learning and Developmental Standards

www.fldoe.org
These standards create a common framework and language for providers of VPK Education Programs as well as School Readiness Programs serving four-year-olds.

MyEducationLab

Go to Topics 2 (Child Development/Theories) and 6 (Curriculum Planning) in the MyEducationLab (www.myeducationlab.com) for your course, where you can:

- Find learning outcomes for Child Development/ Theories and Curriculum Planning along with the national standards that connect to these outcomes.

- Complete Assignments and Activities that can help you more deeply understand the chapter content.

- Apply and practice your understanding of the core teaching skills identified in the chapter with the Building Teaching Skills and Dispositions learning units.

- Hear viewpoints of experts in the field in Professional Perspectives.

- Explore interactive CONNECT Modules to practice classroom skills and enhance professional development.

- Check your comprehension on the content covered in the chapter by going to the Study Plan in the Book Resources for your text. Here you will be able to take a chapter quiz, receive feedback on your answers, and then access Review, Practice, and Enrichment activities to enhance your understanding of chapter content.

KINDERGARTEN TODAY

Meeting Academic and Developmental Needs

NAEYC Standards for Early Childhood Professional Preparation

Standard 1. Promoting Child Development and Learning

I use my understanding of young children's characteristics and needs, and of multiple interacting influences on children's development and learning, to create environments that are healthy, respectful, supportive, and challenging for each child.[1]

Standard 4. Using Developmentally Effective Approaches to Connect with Children and Families

I understand and use positive relationships and supportive interactions as the foundation for my work with young children and families. I know, understand, and use a wide array of developmentally appropriate approaches, instructional strategies, and tools to connect with children and families and positively influence each child's development and learning.[2]

Standard 5. Using Content Knowledge to Build Meaningful Curriculum

I understand the importance of developmental domains and academic (or content) disciplines in early childhood curriculum. I know the essential concepts, inquiry tools, and structure of content areas, including academic subjects, and can identify resources to deepen their understanding. I use my own knowledge and other resources to design, implement, and evaluate meaningful, challenging curricula that promote comprehensive developmental and learning outcomes for every young child.[3]

AS WE BEGIN our discussion of kindergarten children and programs, perhaps you are thinking back to your kindergarten or pre-first-grade school experiences. I am sure that you have many pleasant memories and they include your teachers and classmates, what you learned, and how you learned it. It is good that you have fond memories of your kindergarten and/or other preschool experiences. However, we can't use just memories to build our understanding of what today's high-quality kindergartens are or should be like. If you have not visited a kindergarten program lately, now would be a good time to do so. You will discover that kindergarten education is undergoing a dramatic change. Compare the following changes that are transforming the kindergarten you went to versus kindergarten today:

- ***Emphasis on academics including math, literacy, and science.*** Reasons for the emphasis on academics include:
  - Common Core Standards that specify what children should know and be able to do
  - Political and public support for early education and skill learning because they reduce grade failure and school dropout[4]

- *Enriched curriculum with emphasis on literacy designed to have children read by entry into first grade and on grade level by grade three.* Reasons for emphasis on literacy in the kindergarten include:
  - Recognition that literacy and reading are pathways to success in school and life
  - Kindergarten for all children, or **universal kindergarten**, is now becoming a permanent part of the American education system. Seventy-three percent of five-year-old children attend a kindergarten program.[5] Fifty-five percent attend a full-day kindergarten program.[6]
- *More funding provided by more states for districts to provide more kindergarten programs.*[7]
- *Longer school days and transition from half-day to full-day programs.* Reasons for longer school days and full-day programs include:
  - An increase in the number of working parents
  - Recognition that earlier is the best option
  - Research that shows a longer school day helps children academically[8]
- *Exploding kindergarten enrollment.*
- *More challenging kindergarten programs, with children being asked to do and learn at higher levels.*[9]
- *More testing.* Reasons for the increased testing include:
  - The accountability movement
  - Recognition that district testing that begins in third grade and earlier puts more emphasis on what kindergarten children should learn[10]

As a result of these and other changes we discuss in this chapter, the contemporary kindergarten is a place of high expectations and achievement for all children. Kindergarten education is literally changing before our eyes!

THE HISTORY OF KINDERGARTEN EDUCATION

Kindergarten has a long and interesting history that helps us better understand the kindergartens of today.

Friedrich Froebel

Friedrich Froebel's educational concepts and kindergarten program were imported from Germany into the United States in the nineteenth century, virtually intact, by individuals who believed in his ideas and methods. His influence remained dominant for almost half a century. While Froebel's ideas still seem perfectly acceptable today, they were not acceptable to those in the mid-nineteenth century who subscribed to the notion of early education. Especially innovative and hard to accept was the idea that learning could be based on play and children's interests—in other words, that learning could be child centered. Most European and American schools were subject oriented and emphasized teaching basic skills. In addition, Froebel was the first to advocate a communal education for young children outside the home. Froebel's ideas for educating children as a group in a special place outside the home were revolutionary.

Margarethe Schurz

Margarethe Schurz established the first kindergarten in the United States. After attending lectures on Froebelian principles in Germany, she returned to the United States and, in 1856, opened her kindergarten at Watertown, Wisconsin. Schurz's program was conducted in German, as were many of the new kindergarten

MyEducationLab

Visit the MyEducationLab for *Fundamentals of Early Childhood Education* to enhance your understanding of chapter concepts with a personalized Study Plan. You'll also have the opportunity to hone your teaching skills through video-based Assignments and Activities as well as Building Teaching Skills and Dispositions lessons.

FOCUS QUESTIONS

1. What major changes has kindergarten education undergone from Froebel to the present?
2. What are kindergarten children like?
3. What children attend kindergarten?
4. What are environments for kindergarten children like?
5. What is included in the kindergarten curriculum?

universal kindergarten The availability of kindergarten to all children.

programs of the time, since Froebel's ideas of education especially appealed to bilingual parents. Schurz influenced Elizabeth Peabody, who was not only fascinated by but converted to Froebel's ideas.

Elizabeth Peabody

Elizabeth Peabody opened her kindergarten in Boston in 1860. She and her sister, Mary Mann, also published a *Kindergarten Guide.* Peabody almost immediately realized that she lacked the necessary theoretical grounding to adequately implement Froebel's ideas. She visited kindergartens in Germany, then returned to the United States to popularize Froebel's methods. Peabody is generally credited as kindergarten's main promoter in the United States.

Susan Blow

The first public kindergarten was founded in St. Louis, Missouri, in 1873 by Susan E. Blow, with the cooperation of the St. Louis superintendent of schools, William T. Harris. Elizabeth Peabody had corresponded for several years with Harris, and the combination of her prodding and Blow's enthusiasm and knowledge convinced Harris to open a public kindergarten on an experimental basis. Endorsement of the kindergarten program by a public school system did much to increase its popularity and spread the Froebelian influence within early childhood education. In addition, Harris, who later became the U.S. Commissioner of Education, encouraged support for Froebel's ideas and methods.

Patty Smith Hill

The kindergarten movement, at first ahead of its time, became rigid and teacher centered rather than child centered. By the turn of the twentieth century, many kindergarten leaders thought that programs and training should be open to experimentation and innovation rather than rigidly following Froebel's ideas. Patty Smith Hill thought that, while the kindergarten should remain faithful to Froebel's ideas, it should nevertheless be open to innovation. She believed that the kindergarten movement, to survive, had to move into the twentieth century, and she was able to convince many of her colleagues. More than anyone else, Hill is responsible for kindergarten as it was known prior to its twenty-first-century transformation.

Kindergarten Today

Kindergarten as it was known five years ago is not the same as kindergarten today. Kindergarten twenty years from now will be vastly different from today. Kindergarten is in a transitional stage from a program that formerly focused primarily on social and emotional development to one that emphasizes academics, especially early literacy, math and science, and activities that prepare children to think and problem-solve. These changes represent a transformation of great magnitude and will have a lasting impact on kindergarten curriculum and teaching.

WHAT ARE KINDERGARTEN CHILDREN LIKE?

Kindergarten children are like other children in many ways. They have similar developmental, physical, and behavioral characteristics that characterize them as kindergartners—children ages five to six. Yet, at the same time, they have characteristics that make them unique individuals. Now would be a good time for you to review the Portraits of Kindergartners feature, which provides you information about some children who are in kindergarten today. These authentic portraits give you insight into children's social-emotional, cognitive, and physical development and adaptive (daily living) skills.

Physical Development

Kindergarten children are energetic. They have a lot of energy, and they want to use it in physical activities such as running, climbing, and jumping. Their desire to be involved in physical activity makes kindergarten an ideal time to involve children in projects of building—for example, making **learning centers** to resemble a store, post office, veterinary office, and so forth.

From ages five to seven, children's average weight and height approximate each other. For example, at six years, boys, on average, weigh 46 pounds and are 45 inches tall, while girls, on average, weigh about 44 pounds and are 45 inches tall. At age seven, boys weigh on average 50 pounds and are about 48 inches tall; girls weigh on average 50 pounds and are about 48 inches tall. Review Table 9.1, which shows the average height and weight of kindergarten children.

learning centers Areas of the classroom specifically set up to promote student-centered, hands-on, active learning.

Social and Emotional Development

Kindergarten children, ages five to six, are in Erikson's industry versus inferiority stage of social and emotional development. During this stage kindergarten children are continuing to learn to regulate their emotions and social interactions.

Some things you can do to promote kindergartners' positive social and emotional development are the following:

- Provide opportunities for children to be physically and mentally involved in activities involving problem solving and social activities with others.
- Teach and role-model how to make and keep friends.
- Model positive social and emotional responses. Read stories and discuss feelings such as anger, happiness, guilt, and pride.
- Give children opportunities to be leaders in projects and activities.
- State your expectations for appropriate behavior and discuss them with your children.

Most kindergarten children, especially those who have been to preschool, are very confident, are eager to be involved, and want to and can accept a great deal of responsibility. They like going places and doing things, such as working on projects, experimenting, and working with others. Socially, kindergarten children are at the same time solitary and independent workers and growing in their ability and desire to work cooperatively with others. They want to be industrious and successful. Their combination of

TABLE 9.1 Average Height and Weight of Kindergartners

Age	Males		Females	
	Height (inches)	Weight (pounds)	Height (inches)	Weight (pounds)
5 years	44.00	42.00	43.00	41.00
6 years	46.00	46.00	46.00	47.00
7 years	48.00	51.00	48.00	52.00
8 years	51.00	58.00	50.00	58.00

Note: Remember that averages are just that—averages. Children are different because of their individual differences. Ongoing growth and development tend to accentuate these differences.
Source: Family Practice Notebook, "Height Measurement in Children," 2012; accessed March 8, 2012, at www.fpnotebook.com/endo/exam.

Portraits of Kindergartners

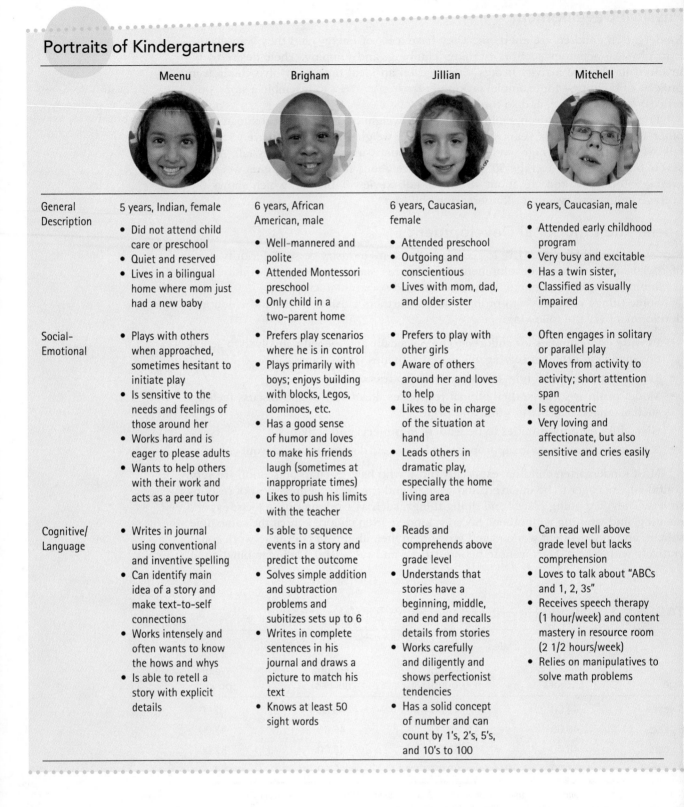

	Meenu	Brigham	Jillian	Mitchell
General Description	5 years, Indian, female • Did not attend child care or preschool • Quiet and reserved • Lives in a bilingual home where mom just had a new baby	6 years, African American, male • Well-mannered and polite • Attended Montessori preschool • Only child in a two-parent home	6 years, Caucasian, female • Attended preschool • Outgoing and conscientious • Lives with mom, dad, and older sister	6 years, Caucasian, male • Attended early childhood program • Very busy and excitable • Has a twin sister, • Classified as visually impaired
Social-Emotional	• Plays with others when approached, sometimes hesitant to initiate play • Is sensitive to the needs and feelings of those around her • Works hard and is eager to please adults • Wants to help others with their work and acts as a peer tutor	• Prefers play scenarios where he is in control • Plays primarily with boys; enjoys building with blocks, Legos, dominoes, etc. • Has a good sense of humor and loves to make his friends laugh (sometimes at inappropriate times) • Likes to push his limits with the teacher	• Prefers to play with other girls • Aware of others around her and loves to help • Likes to be in charge of the situation at hand • Leads others in dramatic play, especially the home living area	• Often engages in solitary or parallel play • Moves from activity to activity; short attention span • Is egocentric • Very loving and affectionate, but also sensitive and cries easily
Cognitive/ Language	• Writes in journal using conventional and inventive spelling • Can identify main idea of a story and make text-to-self connections • Works intensely and often wants to know the hows and whys • Is able to retell a story with explicit details	• Is able to sequence events in a story and predict the outcome • Solves simple addition and subtraction problems and subitizes sets up to 6 • Writes in complete sentences in his journal and draws a picture to match his text • Knows at least 50 sight words	• Reads and comprehends above grade level • Understands that stories have a beginning, middle, and end and recalls details from stories • Works carefully and diligently and shows perfectionist tendencies • Has a solid concept of number and can count by 1's, 2's, 5's, and 10's to 100	• Can read well above grade level but lacks comprehension • Loves to talk about "ABCs and 1, 2, 3s" • Receives speech therapy (1 hour/week) and content mastery in resource room (2 1/2 hours/week) • Relies on manipulatives to solve math problems

Motor	• Excellent fine motor skills; holds pencil with tripod grip • Prefers conventional spelling to inventive spelling and uses classroom resources to find words she needs • Runs, jumps, skips, and hops with ease	• Plays baseball and basketball on an organized team; able to catch and throw a ball • Runs, jumps, and gallops easily • Writes legibly in his journal with spaces between words and correct sizing of letters • Difficulty sitting still during circle time activities, sometimes needs to go sit at his table	• Can tie her own shoes and assists others in tying theirs • Writes in complete sentences with correct sizing, spacing, punctuation, and capitalization • Participates in dance and gymnastics activities after school • Enjoys running, swinging, and dancing on the playground	• Writing has shown improvement with the use of a weighted pencil • Often walks on tiptoes and falls easily • Receives occupational therapy several times per month at school and private therapy weekly • Runs and jumps and participates in all physical education activities
Adaptive (Daily Living)	• Consistently cleans up her personal space and assists others with their materials • Dresses and grooms herself each morning • Raises hand to speak and asks for help when problems arise • Knows class rules and expectations and encourages others to follow them	• Comes to school well groomed and well cared for • Takes care of his own bathroom needs with no accidents • Is able to open his own containers at lunch • Can snap, zip, and tie shoelaces	• Comes to school on time and well prepared with homework, folder, backpack, and other materials • Independent with bathroom and self-help skills • Helps with chores at home, such as emptying dishwasher and putting away clothes	• Is able to take care of bathroom needs but has occasional accidents • Difficulty buttoning, zipping, tying, and fastening • Often misplaces his materials within the classroom • Very capable but needs constant supervision in order to produce quality work

Source: Portraits contributed by Lynne Rhodes, kindergarten teacher, Curtsinger Elementary, Frisco Independent School District, Frisco, Texas.

Carefully read the backgrounds of the four children—Meenu, Brigham, Jillian, and Mitchell.

Questions:
• How do the backgrounds of these four children influence how you would teach them?
• Are there any "red flags" in the backgrounds of any of these children?
• You have two children, Meenu and Mitchell, who are solitary in their approaches to life and learning. How will you accommodate them and help them become more outgoing and involved?
• Brigham likes to "push the limits" with his teacher. How will you plan to deal with children who "push your limits"?
• Of the four students, which one do you think will require more individual attention from you? Why? How?

Today, kindergarten is the the first grade in the K–12 continuium of school. Reflect about what you can do to support children's academic achievements.

a "can do" attitude and their cooperation and responsibility make them a delight to teach and work with.

Cognitive and Language Development

Kindergarten children are in a period of rapid intellectual and language growth. They have a tremendous capacity to learn words and like the challenge of learning new words. This helps explain kindergarten children's love of big words and their ability to say and use them. This is nowhere more apparent than in their fondness for dinosaurs and words such as *brontosaurus* or *triceratops*. Kindergarten children like and need to be involved in many language activities.

Additionally, kindergartners like to talk. Their desire to be verbal should be encouraged and supported by allowing many opportunities to engage in various language activities such as singing, telling stories, being involved in drama, and reciting poetry.

What children know when they enter kindergarten helps determine their success in school and what and how they are taught. Keep in mind that many kindergartners know more than people think, but many others know a great deal less. For example, many immigrant children in border states, such as Texas and California, are illiterate in their native language.

WHO ATTENDS KINDERGARTEN?

Froebel's kindergarten was for children three to seven years of age. In the United States, kindergarten is for five- and six-year-old children before they enter first grade. Since the age at which children enter first grade varies, the ages at which they enter kindergarten also differ. Many parents and professionals support an older rather than a younger kindergarten entrance age because they think older children are more "ready" for kindergarten and will learn better.[11] Whereas in the past children had to be five

Today, you will teach in an inclusive classroom. As such, you will work with children of various abilities and disabilities. Now is an ideal time for you to plan for how you will gain the skills necessary to teach children in an inclusive setting.

years of age prior to December 31 for kindergarten admission in many districts, today the trend is toward an older admission age.[12]

Kindergarten Entrance Age

Undoubtedly, there will be ongoing debates and discussions about the appropriate age for kindergarten entrance. Current legislative policies and initiatives support delaying kindergarten entrance ages.

applying research to practice

Research plays an important role in your professional development as a kindergarten teacher. Research can inform and guide your instructional practices and increase children's learning. Here are two examples of how research can help you. The first stresses how positive emotions enhance learning and the second article stresses the need for your preventing failure for every one of your kindergarten students.

"FOR KIDS, LAUGHTER IS THE BEST MEDICINE"

The latest neuroscience research provides us information about how humor and positive emotions in general affect children's well-being. The research reported that "humor is a very important component of emotional health, maintaining relationships and health."[13] The research goes on to note that humor is an important part of positive emotions and helps children be resilient to emotional and physical stress.

So what does this mean for you?

- Provide opportunities for children to laugh, relax, and feel good about themselves, their accomplishments, and other children.
- Involve children in humorous activities involving storytelling, reading humorous literature, and appropriately watching funny videos.

Some books that can add humor to your life and the lives of your children are these:

- *Big Chickens* by Leslie Helakoski. When four big chickens see a wolf sneaking near their coop, they run into the woods to hide. But for a bunch of big chickens, running away from danger isn't as easy as it looks! What if they get stuck in a ditch? What if they step into a cow patty? Brimming with the silliness children love.
- *The Dog Who Loved the Good Life* by Bryan Langdo. Mr. Hibble has a new dog. His name is Jake. Jake is not like other dogs: He likes to eat dinner at the table. He always remembers to brush his teeth. And he just loves to watch cartoons! Mr. Hibble hopes he can train Jake to act the way a real dog should.
- *Very Boring Alligator* by Jean Gralley. Nothing will make this boring gator leave: saying "pretty please" doesn't do it; even making heebie-jeebie eyes doesn't help. Alligator just doesn't seem to get it. Luckily, a very resourceful little girl is ready to put her foot down.

"THE FOURTH R—RETENTION"

Increasingly, we read about politicians and the public demanding more retention or grade failure in an effort to bring more accountability to the public schools. However, new data collected by the U.S. Department of Education's Civil Rights Office points out the ratio of ethnic disparities in student retentions. Your children who are Hispanic or black are much more likely to be failed than their white counterparts. Black students are nearly three times as likely as white students to be retained.[14]

So what does this mean for you?

- Focus all of your efforts on providing each child with the support and help they need to be successful in achieving the Common Core Standards for kindergarten.
- Use all of the instructional strategies available to you such as accommodation, differentiation of instruction, scaffolding, and so on, to ensure that each child gets the appropriate instruction to prevent failure.
- Work with and involve parents to help them understand the demands of kindergarten education and to help them support their children's school success.
- Stress to children and their parents the importance of school attendance. Children can't learn when they're not in school. Regular school attendance is one of the best things children can do to help ensure that they achieve and learn.

Redshirting. You may have heard of the practice of *redshirting* college football players. This is the practice of holding a player out a year so he can grow and mature. The theory is that the extra year will result in a better football player. The same practice applies to kindergarten children. The U.S. Department of Education estimates that about 9 percent of entering kindergarten children are *redshirted*—held out of school for a year.[15] Parents and administrators who practice redshirting think that the extra year will give children an opportunity to mature intellectually, socially, and physically. On the one hand, redshirting might have some benefit for children who are immature and whose birth dates fall close to the school entrance date cutoff. On the other hand, some affluent parents redshirt their children, their sons in particular, because they want them to be the oldest members of the kindergarten class. They reason that their children will be class leaders, will get more attention from the teachers, and will have another year under their belt, which will help them handle the increasing demands of the kindergarten curriculum.

Rather than the constant juggling of entrance ages, what is needed are early childhood programs designed to meet and serve the needs of all children, regardless of the ages at which they enter school. At the heart of this issue of age and time is whether maturation or school is the more potent factor in children's achievement. Research studies comparing age and school effects suggest educational intervention contributes more to children's cognitive competence than does maturation.[16]

These and other issues will continue to fuel the educational debates and will make learning about and teaching in kindergarten even more fascinating as the years go by.

diversity tie-in

The Kindergarten Achievement Gap Begins Before Kindergarten

In the opening pages of the third edition of NAEYC's *Developmentally Appropriate Practice in Early Childhood Programs Serving Children from Birth Through Age 8,* the authors discuss the early childhood achievement gap as one of the critical issues faced by children and early childhood professionals. Here is what they say:

All families, educators, and the larger society hope that all children will achieve in school and go on to lead satisfying and productive lives. But that optimistic future is not equally likely for all of the nation's schoolchildren. Most disturbing, low-income and African American and Hispanic students lag specifically behind their peers on standardized comparisons of academic achievement throughout the school years, and they experience more difficulties while in the school setting.[17]

The achievement gap between students of various races, cultures, and socioeconomic backgrounds is a serious issue, which all of us as early childhood educators must address. Many low-income children come to school already behind their more advantaged counterparts because they are not prepared to meet the demands of contemporary schooling.

The extent and seriousness of the achievement gap is further illustrated in the results of a survey of Michigan kindergarten teachers:

- Thirty-two percent of kindergarten teachers were not satisfied with the abilities of their kindergarten students

when they started school, with an additional 50 percent being only somewhat satisfied.
- According to the teachers, only 65 percent of children entered kindergarten classrooms ready to learn the curriculum.
- Eighty-six percent of teachers report that students who are behind academically at kindergarten entrance impact a teacher's ability to effectively provide instruction to the rest of the class.[18]

Awareness of the extent of the problem is only one part of our efforts to reduce and eliminate achievement gaps. Taking effective action is the other part of the solution. Here are two things that we can do as early childhood professionals:

- Advocate that *all* children, particularly English language learners and children from low-income backgrounds, have the opportunity to participate in high-quality preschool programs. As we discussed in Chapters 2 and 8, there There is growing consensus that providing universal preschool for all children will help them socially and academically as they continue through the elementary grades.
- Advocate for "ready schools and ready communities" so that the schools children attend and the communities they live in are united in their efforts to provide the health, nutrition, and educational experiences all children need in order to be successful in school and life.

In addition, there are many specific things that preschool and kindergarten teachers can do to help children catch up with their more advantaged peers. Intentional teaching of these skills will go a long way toward helping to eliminate the achievement gap.

Universal Kindergarten

Just as support is growing for universal preschools, it should come as no surprise that there is wide public support for compulsory and tax-supported universal public kindergarten. Forty-three states require school districts to offer at least a half-day kindergarten.[19] The national trend is for districts to offer full-day programs. Nine states require school districts to offer full-day kindergarten.[20] However, only fourteen states require mandatory kindergarten attendance of age-eligible children.[21] Nonetheless, because of the widespread availability of kindergarten, 94 percent of American children attend at least a half-day kindergarten before entering first grade.[22] As a result, public school kindergarten is now considered the first grade of school. It is important for you to know that kindergarten is considered a time for serious learning and accomplishment.

Today, full-day kindergarten offers several potential benefits. It provides continuity for children accustomed to full-day experiences outside of the home, provides continuity with schedules in first grade and beyond, reduces the number of disruptions and transitions children experience in a typical day, and allows teachers more time for both formal and informal instruction that provide meaningful learning opportunities. It also provides an important opportunity to align the policies and practices of the grades that follow kindergarten with those of the early learning programs that typically come before. Furthermore, results of empirical research on the effects of full- versus half-day kindergarten are encouraging. Studies not only show full-day programs have no detrimental effects on children who attend, but students show significantly stronger academic gains over the course of the kindergarten year than their counterparts in half-day programs.[23]

Alternative Kindergarten Programs

Giving the changing kindergarten curriculum, the almost universal nature of kindergarten, and the prevalence of a variety of abilities and disabilities, it is not surprising that some children are not ready for many of the kindergarten demands placed on them. As a result, teachers and schools have developed alternative kindergarten programs.

Developmental Kindergarten.   The *developmental kindergarten (DK)* is a pre-kindergarten for kindergarten-age children who are developmentally or behaviorally delayed; it is viewed as one means of helping them succeed in school. School districts have specific criteria for placing children in developmental kindergartens; some of their placement criteria include the following:

- Kindergarten-eligible children are given a kindergarten screening test to identify those who have special learning or behavioral needs. Some states, such as Massachusetts, require that all children take a screening test prior to kindergarten enrollment.[24]

- Pre-kindergarten children are given a readiness test, such as the Kindergarten Readiness Test (KRT),[25] to help determine their readiness for regular kindergarten. (The placement of children in any program should not be made solely on the basis and results of one test.)

- Parents and preschool teachers who believe that children are not ready for kindergarten consult about the placement of individual children.

For example, the Troy Michigan District has a DK program that provides meaningful and challenging experiences that build upon children's prior knowledge. Their integrated program of teacher-directed and child-initiated learning allows children many opportunities to manipulate materials, explore and discover ideas, interact with others, and develop at their own unique rate. This program fosters the development of a positive self-image and enhances children's growth toward their individual potential.[26]

Transition Kindergarten.   A *transition kindergarten* is designed to give children the time they need to achieve what is required for entry into first grade. These children are really getting two years to achieve what others would normally achieve in one. A transition class is different from a nongraded program in that the transition class consists of children of the same age, whereas the nongraded classroom has children of different ages.

The concept of transition classes implies, and practice should involve, linear progression that promotes ongoing achievement and success. Children are placed in a transition kindergarten so they can continue to progress at their own pace. The curriculum, materials, and teaching practices should be appropriate for each child's developmental age or level.

Proponents of transitional programs identify these benefits:

- Promotes success, whereas retention is a regressive practice that promotes failure.
- Provides for children's developmental abilities.
- Enables children to be with other children of the same developmental age.
- Provides an appropriate learning environment.
- Puts children's needs ahead of the desire to place them in a particular grade.
- Provides additional time for children to integrate learning—often referred to as the *gift of time.*

Students at Honor Roll Elementary School who attend Transitional Kindergarten (TK) classes engage in a well-integrated, nurturing environment that focuses on socialization and active learning. Teachers work with children so they are able to complete their work independently, read and write, and discover their five senses. Academic skills are further developed through phonics-based reading, hands-on math activities, spelling, and simple grammar. Music, art, and physical play are also important parts of the TK curriculum.[27]

Mixed-Age/Multiage Grouping.   *Mixed-age grouping* provides another approach to meeting the individual and collective needs of children. In a multiage group, there is a diversity of abilities, at least a two-year span in children's ages, and the same teacher. Multiage groups:

- Provide materials and activities for a wider range of children's abilities.
- Create a feeling of community and belonging; most mixed-age groups have a feeling of family because children spend at least two years in the group.
- Support children's social development by providing a broader range of children to associate with; older children act as teachers, tutors, and mentors; younger children are able to model the academic and social skills of their older class members.
- Provide for a continuous progression of learning.

Today, more teachers and schools are using multiage grouping to support kindergarten learning. "By grouping students by ability rather than age, we're better able to respond to the student's needs," Principal Dawn Gonzales says. "Research shows that multiage classrooms can be beneficial to academic achievement. Collaboration and friendships across all age groups are gained that create a unique community. Older students have an opportunity to become role models and to reinforce their own understanding through teaching. Younger students get to preview concepts they'll study later."[28]

Looping.   *Looping* occurs when a teacher spends two or more years with the same group of same-age children. In other words, a teacher involved in looping begins teaching a group of kindergartners and then teaches the same group as first graders and perhaps as second graders. Another teacher might do the same with second, third, and fourth graders. These are some advantages of looping:

- Teachers, students, and parents develop a deep relationship because of the longer amount of time together.
- Teachers understand the children's family dynamics and the expectations of the parents.
- Teachers develop a deeper understanding of children's learning styles.
- The second year around the students are already familiar with classroom procedures and expectations. Furthermore, the teacher already knows the needs of the students and can jump right in.

Retention.   Along with the benefits of early education and universal kindergarten come other issues as well. One of these is retention. Children who are retained, instead of participating in kindergarten graduation ceremonies with their classmates, are destined to spend another year in kindergarten. Many of these children are retained, or failed, because teachers judge them to be immature, or they fail to measure up to the districts' or teachers' standards for promotion to first grade.

Across our country, 10 to 30 percent of children are retained in kindergarten.[29] These children are failing kindergarten because they are presumably not ready for the demands of first grade. Yet the early years of schooling are crucial in determining the child's long-term attitudes toward self, teachers, and learning. Children who emerge from the early years feeling good about themselves, respecting teachers, and enjoying learning will regard education as exciting and as a positive challenge. On the other hand, children who leave the early years of schooling feeling badly about themselves, with a low regard for teachers, and turned off to learning may find recess the best part of the school day.[30]

Do children do better the second time around? Despite our intuitive feelings that children who are retained will do better, research evidence is unequivocally contrary to that notion: Children *do not* do better the second time around. In fact, studies show that children do worse and that retention causes children to drop out.[31]

Supporting Children's Approaches to Learning

Children's approaches to learning are an important dimension of learning. These approaches to learning are curiosity/initiative, persistence, attention, self-direction, problem-solving ability, and creativity. The experiences children have before they come to kindergarten often influence the success of their kindergarten years. Three areas are particularly important in influencing children's success in kindergarten: children's skills and prior school-related experiences, children's home lives, and preschool and kindergarten classroom characteristics. Research demonstrates the following in relation to these three areas:[32]

- Children who are socially adjusted do better in school. For example, kindergarten children whose parents initiate social opportunities for them are better adjusted socially and therefore can do better.
- Rejected children have difficulty with school tasks.
- Children with more preschool experiences have fewer adjustments to make in kindergarten.
- Children whose parents expect them to do well in kindergarten do better than children whose parents have low expectations for them. Children who have teachers with high expectations also do better in school.

FIGURE 9.1

Sample Reading Log

My Weekly Home Reading Journal

Name: *Daniel Sheffield*

Week of: *December 12*

Day:	Book Read:	Who I Read To:
Monday	*The Biggest, Best Snowman*	*Mom*
Tuesday	*A Bed for the Winter*	

Reading logs encourage children and their families to read together.

- Books, videos, computer-based learning materials, and other materials designed for children in the home improve the chances that children will be successful in school.
- Developmentally appropriate classrooms and practices promote easier and smoother transitions for children from home to school, from grade to grade, and from program to program.

The nature, extent, creativity, and effectiveness of transitional experiences for children, parents, and staff will be limited only by the commitment of all involved. If we are interested in providing good preschools, kindergartens, and primary schools, then we will include transitional experiences in the curricula of all these programs.

How successful children are in kindergarten depends on how well all who have a stake in children's education cooperate. More and more we realize that when early childhood teachers work with parents, children's achievement increases. For example, you can involve your students' parents in a family literacy project that supports children's learning to read. One way to do this is to encourage children and their parents to "read together." The use of a reading log such as the one shown in Figure 9.1 motivates children to read at home and involves the whole family.

ENVIRONMENTS FOR KINDERGARTNERS

Both the physical environment and the social environment of the kindergarten classroom influence children's physical, cognitive, linguistic, and social-emotional development. In classrooms where the environment supports children's learning, research shows that the occurrence of problem behaviors is reduced and the rate of children's social cooperation with their peers increases.[33]

The Healthy Environment

A healthy setting is important for all children. A safe, clean, well-maintained classroom with a positive atmosphere and social climate increases student and staff self-esteem and student achievement.[34] A healthy environment includes having children practice healthy habits. In Arlington, Virginia, schools have installed hand sanitizer dispensers in all classrooms and have large supplies of gel available. "Now when children come in from recess or go to lunch without time for a restroom break, they get a squirt of the gel," says Principal Lolli Laws. Principal Karen Hodges has her children sing the ABC song while they wash their hands, because washing hands for the time it takes to sing the song is long enough to kill the germs.[35]

A healthy environment also includes a relaxed and happy eating environment. Areas should be disinfected properly before eating. Substantial research clearly indicates that a healthy diet and environment contribute to children's overall health and well-being.[36]

Healthy Foods.   The federal government requires that every school district participating in the national school lunch and breakfast program develop a wellness plan to help children eat healthier foods.[37] Schools now include more fruits, vegetables, and whole grains on lunch trays. Connecticut schools prohibit the sale of soda and other sugary drinks, and deep fryers are disappearing from school cafeterias nationwide. Many schools have already banned junk food in vending machines.[38] Alternative healthy foods that parents can bring are sealed yogurts, bagels, and fruits.

Organic Foods.   Growing and eating organic foods is part of the greening of America and its schools. Creating lesson plans about organic foods, the benefits of organic food, and organic agriculture enables children to be familiar with organic products. If there's an organic farm near the school, a field trip is a good way to really teach children about organic farming. You can also talk about the environmental impact of choosing organic products and ways children can talk to their parents (or even to the school cafeteria staff) about using more organic products. If there is space, starting a classroom organic garden is a wonderful way for children to take home lessons about organic foods. Students can research organic gardening methods on the Internet or in books, start a classroom compost pile, and take care of their plants using organic methods.[39] For example, Casa Dei Bambina Montessori School in Santa Maria, California, has an organic snack menu that includes:

Monday: Blueberry Muffins and Oranges
Tuesday: Cheese and Crackers with Carrots
Wednesday: Polenta Pizzas and Fruit[40]

The Respectful Environment

A *respectful environment* is one in which teachers show respect for children, colleagues, and families. In addition, children are respectful of adults and peers. This psychologically friendly environment contributes to a respectful environment and includes the attitudes, feelings and values of the school and community.

In a respectful classroom, teachers treat children courteously, talk with them about in- and out-of-school activities and events, and show a genuine concern for them as individuals with specific needs. Unfortunately, not all children get the respect they need and want at home or at school. Some children, especially children with behavior and attention problems, can be subjected to verbal abuse by teachers and children.[41] This is one reason why your respectful classroom means so much to each child.

The Supportive Environment

A *supportive environment* creates a climate where children can do their best work. Teachers have high expectations and students are expected to succeed.[42] The supportive environment consists of the immediate physical surroundings, social relationships, and cultural settings in which children function and interact. To help create a supportive social environment, *all* children of all cultures, genders, socioeconomic levels, and backgrounds are valued and included in all activities. In addition, a supportive kindergarten environment:

- *Meets children's safety needs.* Children feel safe and secure socially and emotionally. They have teachers who care about and help them.
- *Has a balance between teacher-initiated and child-initiated activities.* Children should be able to choose to do things that they consider challenging and also things they do very well.
- *Provides a classroom arrangement and materials for active learning.* In a supportive environment, children are listening to stories, telling stories, dictating stories, looking at and reading books independently, singing, relating events that happened outside school, and talking, talking, talking. Children are also using computers interactively with appropriate games and tasks, solving puzzles, counting napkins to put on the table to match the number of children, measuring heights and weights. In other words, the teachers, the classroom arrangement, and the materials support children's active learning.
- *Is a place that emphasizes social and emotional development as well as academic achievement.* Generally, age is the only criterion that determines whether a child may enroll in kindergarten. This means that some children come to kindergarten emotionally immature and more than a little self-centered. However, in any group of five-year-olds, there are children who function more like four-year-olds and others who are like six-year-olds. And overall development isn't the only type of difference that exists. Some children are sociable, while others do not get along well with their peers.
- *Has a well-trained teacher in charge.* Training for kindergarten teachers has steadily become more rigorous over the past few decades. In addition, children who have highly trained and qualified teachers do better academically.[43]

A curriculum that helps children feel good about themselves also helps them become aware that other children have needs and rights, too. In a good kindergarten environment children learn to wait, to share, to take turns, to help others as they also gain confidence in their own abilities and self-worth.[44]

The Challenging Environment

A challenging learning environment provides curricula that are not too easy or too hard. Teachers adjust learning levels to children's abilities while also making it possible for children to meet state and local expectations. Challenging environments match children's abilities and achievement levels so they are successful. A challenging kindergarten classroom is responsive to children's cultures and socioeconomic backgrounds. In these types of environments, teachers are attentive to individual students and provide them with one-on-one attention and instruction.

In challenging environments, teachers assess children's learning on a daily basis to inform instructional decisions and provide the necessary assistance. Challenging learning environments that encourage the active involvement of students can sometimes be difficult for teachers to create. The following are some suggestions for how you can create a challenging environment:

- Be knowledgeable about children's academic, social, and cultural backgrounds.
- Meet each child at his or her developmental level, foster that stage, and scaffold the child to the next level.

- Use diverse and appropriate teaching approaches to provide meaningful learning opportunities for each child.
- Differentiate instruction and activities.
- Engage children in projects and small group activities, while also enabling children to do their best work.
- Use technology to focus on academics and cognitive learning and engage children.
- Interact with children in ways that help them to think and problem-solve at their own levels.

The Physical Environment

Environments that support kindergarten children's learning are essential if we want all kindergarten children to be successful.

Classroom Arrangement and Organization. The classroom is organized to promote interaction and learning. Desks, tables, and workstations are clustered together; work areas have a variety of learning materials to encourage group projects, experiments, and creative activities.

Also, a high-quality kindergarten classroom is one in which children feel at home. Children's work is prominently displayed, and they feel a sense of ownership. Here are some things you can do to provide high-quality kindergarten environments:

- Provide many materials that support children learning to read and write. Learning to read and write is a high priority of kindergarten, so be sure to offer a wide variety of all kinds of books and writing materials.
- Organize the children into groups of different sizes and ability levels. This provides for social interaction and cooperative learning and encourages children to help others (scaffolding).
- Use a variety of different instructional approaches, such as small group, large group, seat work, center time, free activity choice time, individual teacher one-on-one work with children, and free play time.
- Develop your classroom arrangement so that it supports district and state learning standards. For example, to meet reading content standards, make books easily accessible to students. Also, make sure the classroom has a comfortable area for group and individual reading times.
- Adapt your classroom arrangement so it meets the learning and social needs of your children. For example, set aside time for students to work in groups, assign group projects, and assign projects dealing with different cultures.
- Collaborate with your children to "personalize" your classroom. Make your classroom home-like and cozy. Use plants, rugs, beanbag chairs, pillows, and so on.
- Make supplies and learning materials accessible to children by storing them on open shelves with labels (using pictures and words).

The Social Environment

The social environment consists of the immediate physical surroundings, social relationships, and cultural settings in which children function and interact. To help create a supportive social environment, all children of all cultures, genders, socioeconomic levels, and backgrounds should be valued and respected. Teachers treat children courteously, talk with them about in- and out-of-school activities and events, and show a genuine concern for them as individuals with specific needs. Unfortunately, not all children get the respect they need and want at home or at school. Some children,

In this **video**, three teachers discuss their students' social skills. Pay attention to how the teachers use modeling and praise to encourage cooperation and respect in the classroom.

especially children with behavior and attention problems, can be subjected to verbal abuse by teachers and children.[45] Also, for shy children, the social environment can provide them with the social interaction they need, but they may have a difficult time initiating the interaction, and teachers need to help them find playmates. On the other hand, under the direction of an unaware or uncaring teacher, classroom activities and social interactions may encourage isolation and separation.

A key element of the social environment is developing positive teacher–child relationships, Here are some things you can do:

- Spend time in one-to-one interactions with children.
- Get on children's level for face-to-face interactions.
- Use a pleasant, calm voice and simple language.
- Follow children's lead and interest during play.
- Help all children understand and meet classroom expectations.
- Redirect children when they engage in challenging behavior.
- Listen to children and encourage them to listen to others.
- Acknowledge children for their accomplishments and effort.

CURRICULUM IN THE KINDERGARTEN

All kindergarten classrooms should be child-centered and support developmentally appropriate practice in planning and implementing curriculum. Developmentally appropriate practice involves teaching and learning that is in accordance with children's physical, cognitive, social, linguistic, individual, and cultural development. Professionals help children learn and develop in ways that are compatible with how old they are and who they are as individuals (e.g., their background of experiences and culture). Early childhood professionals who embody the qualities of good kindergarten teachers are those who teach in developmentally appropriate ways.

Common Core Standards in Kindergarten

Today, the Common Core Standards (CCS) are the basis for the majority of instruction that occurs in kindergarten and grades one through three. The CCS are designed to ensure that all students receive high-quality education from school to school and state to state. Although the standards are common across school districts and states, they in no way discourage or interfere with kindergarten teachers bringing their creativity and passion to the learning environment. Currently, the CCS are for English language arts and mathematics. Teachers are implementing them; this is why the CCS are playing such a powerful role in kindergarten education today. Figure 9.2 shows an example from the kindergarten mathematics standards.

Developmentally Appropriate Practice in the Kindergarten Classroom

As we discussed, the growing academic demands on kindergarten children and the experiences that many kindergarten children had as preschoolers combine to transform the role of the kindergarten and the kindergarten teacher. Also, beginning in the kindergarten, children developmentally undergo what is popularly known as the "five to seven shift" during which children are more physically and cognitively developed and they demonstrate a remarkable interest in and enthusiasm for learning and being involved in the learning process. All of these factors in kindergarten children's lives converge to create developmentally and behaviorally unique individuals. Teachers use

Common Core State Standards for Math in Kindergarten

- Represent addition and subtraction with objects, fingers, mental images, drawings, sounds (e.g., claps), acting out situations, verbal explanations, expressions, or equations.

- Solve addition and subtraction word problems, and add and subtract within 10 (e.g., by using objects or drawings to represent the problem).

- Decompose numbers less than or equal to 10 into pairs in more than one way (e.g., by using objects or drawings), and record each decomposition by a drawing or equation (e.g., $5 = 2 + 3$ and $5 = 4 + 1$).

- For any number from 1 to 9, find the number that makes 10 when added to the given number (e.g., by using objects or drawings), and record the answer with a drawing or equation.

FIGURE 9.2 Kindergarten Math Standards

Source: Common Core State Standards, © Copyright 2010. National Governors Association Center for Best Practices and Council of Chief State School Officers. All rights reserved.

their knowledge of children's growth and development and the unique characteristics of each child to create developmentally appropriate programs for their children. Your implementation of developmentally appropriate practice in your kindergarten includes the following practices:

- ***Make learning meaningful to children and related to what they know.*** Children find things meaningful when they are interesting and the children can relate to them.
- ***Individualize your curriculum as much as possible.*** All children do not learn the same way, nor are they interested in learning the same things as everyone else all the time.
- ***Make learning physically and mentally active.*** Actively involve children in learning that includes building, making, experimenting, investigating, and working collaboratively with their peers.
- ***Provide for hands-on activities with concrete objects and manipulatives.*** Emphasize real-life activities as opposed to workbook and worksheet activities.

Kindergarten curriculum includes not only activities that support children emotionally and socially in learning to be more competent people, but also more academic experiences, such as those in literacy and reading, math, science, social studies, and the arts. All experiences, however, should first be approached by considering five- and six-year-olds' developmental capabilities.

Literacy and Reading in Kindergarten

Today, improving literacy is a major goal across all grade levels. All states and school districts have adopted an educational agenda with a strong literacy focus and have set the goal of having all children read on grade level by grade three.

This means that the reading goals for kindergarten learning are higher than they have ever been, and they will continue to increase. Now would be a good time for you to review your kindergarten state standards for literacy and reading. Teaching and learning today function in a standards-based environment.

Literacy and Reading. Early childhood professionals place a high priority on children's literacy and reading success. Literacy means the ability to read, write, speak, and listen. Professionals view literacy as a process that begins at birth (perhaps before) and continues to develop across the life span, through the school years.

literacy The ability to read, write, speak, and listen.

Reading and written language acquisition is a continuum of development. Think of children as being on a continuous journey toward full literacy development! Regardless of what method you use to teach children how to read, the goal is that they should learn to read—and read on or above grade level—so they can do well in school and life.

The process of becoming literate is also viewed as a natural process; reading and writing are processes that children participate in naturally, long before they come to school. No doubt you have participated with or know of toddlers and preschoolers who are literate in many ways. They "read" all kinds of environmental print such as signs (McDonald's), labels (Cheerios), and menus and other symbols in their environments.

Language arts refers to the subjects, including reading, spelling, and composition, aimed at developing reading and writing skills in early childhood education. Figure 9.3 defines common terms used when discussing literacy. These are terms you will want to know and use. They are an important part of being able to "talk the talk" of your profession. You will use these terms in your work with parents, colleagues, and the community.

Supporting Children's Learning to Read.   A primary goal of kindergarten education is for children to learn how to read. Teachers must instruct, support, and guide children in helping them learn what is necessary for them to be successful in school and in life. Here are some of the things you can do to motivate children's learning to read:

- Include a variety of different types of books, such as picture books without words, fairy tales, nursery rhymes, picture storybooks, realistic literature, decodable and predictable books, information books, chapter books, biographies, big books, poetry, and joke and riddle books.
- Provide other types of print such as newspapers, magazines, and brochures.
- Introduce and discuss several books each week (may be theme related, same authors, illustrators, types of books, etc.).
- Have multiple copies of popular books.
- Provide a record-keeping system for keeping track of books read (may include a picture-coding system to rate or evaluate the book).
- Showcase many books by placing them so covers are visible, especially those that are new, shared in read-aloud sessions, or theme-related.
- Organize books on shelves by category or type (may color-code).
- Provide comfortable, inviting places to read (pillows, rugs, a sofa, large cardboard boxes, etc.).
- Encourage children to read to "friends" (include stuffed animals and dolls for "pretend" reading).
- Have an Author's Table with a variety of writing supplies to encourage children to write about books.
- Have a Listening Table for recorded stories and tapes.[46]

Developing Literacy and Reading in Young Children.   Literacy and reading are certainly worthy national and educational goals, not only for young children but also for everyone. However, how best to promote literacy has always been a controversial

Alphabet Knowledge

- The knowledge that letters have names and shapes and that letters can represent sounds in language.
- *Example: Children recognize and name the letters of the alphabet.*

Alphabetic Principle

- Awareness that each speech sound or phoneme in a language has its own distinctive graphic representation and an understanding that letters go together in patterns to represent sounds.
- *Example: Letters and letter patterns represent sounds of the language. Introduce just letters that are used a lot such as M, A, T, S, P, and H. Teach consonants first for sound–letter relationships.*

Comprehension

- In reading, the basic understanding of the words and the content or meaning contained within printed material.
- *Example: Keisha is able to retell the story. Johnny is able to tell who the main character is.*

Decoding

- Identifying words through context and phonics.
- *Example: James can figure out how to read a word he does not know by using his knowledge of letters and sounds. Also, he uses context clues (information from pictures and the sentence before and the sentence after a word) to "decode" it. He looked at the picture with a "pile" of wood to figure out "pile," a word he did not know.*

Phoneme

- The smallest unit of speech that makes a difference to meaning.
- *Example: The word "pig" has three phonemes: /p/ /i/ /g/.*

Phonemic Awareness

- The ability to notice, think about, and work with the individual sounds in spoken words.
- *Example: Alex can identify the words in a set that begin with the same sound: boy, big, bike.*

Phonics

- The learning of alphabetic principles of language and knowledge of letter–sound relationships.
- *Example: Children learn to associate letters with phonemes (basic speech sounds) to help break the alphabetic code.*

Phonological Awareness

- The ability to manipulate language at the levels of syllables, rhymes, and individual speech sounds.
- *Example: Maria can distinguish words that rhyme from those that don't rhyme. Whitney can match words that sound alike. Caroline can segment words into sounds. Angie can blend sounds into words.*

Print Awareness

- The recognition of conventions and characteristics of a written language.
- *Example: Mario pretends to read a bedtime story to his teddy bear. Also, he recognizes the Pizza Hut sign on his way to school.*

FIGURE 9.3 Reading/Literacy Instructional Terminology

topic. What do children need to know to become good and skillful readers? Research identifies the following:[47]

- *Phonemic awareness.* The ability to focus on and use phonemes (the smallest units of spoken language) in spoken words. The English language has at least forty-one phonemes. Some words (e.g., *a* or *oh*) have only one phoneme. Most words, however, consist of a blend of phonemes (e.g., three phonemes in *chip: ch, i,* and *p*).
- *Phonics.* Learning letter–sound relationships and spelling patterns.
- *Fluency.* Reading with speed, accuracy, and proper expression.
- *Comprehension.* The ultimate goal of reading: integrating the skills involved with reading and understanding what is being read.
- *Vocabulary.* Knowing and understanding the words in written and spoken language.

Components of Literacy and Reading Instruction.
There are a variety of approaches to literacy and reading instruction. Basal approaches and materials used for literacy and reading development often emphasize one particular method. Your kindergarten program will contain varying amounts of each of the following.

Phonics. A popular approach to reading instruction is based on phonics, which stresses teaching letter–sound correspondences. By learning these connections, children are able to combine sounds into words (C-A-T). The proponents of phonics instruction argue that letter–sound correspondences enable children to make automatic connections between words and sounds and, as a result, to sound out words and read them on their own. From the 1950s until the present time there has been much debate about whether phonics or the sight word approach (described below) to literacy development is best. Today, there is a decided reemphasis on the use of phonics instruction. One reason is that the research evidence suggests that phonics instruction enables children to become more proficient readers.[48] Many states (such as my state of Texas) outline specific phonics skills required for each grade level. You will want to enhance your teaching of phonics skills by taking classes, attending workshops, reading, and so forth.

Sight Words. A common component of a balanced literacy program is the teaching of sight words. Many teachers use the Dolch Word List as a source for 220 of the most commonly used English words. This list is organized by grade level, frequency, and difficulty. When children are able to recognize these words instantly, they are able to read increasingly higher-level texts with more fluency. You can supplement the Dolch list with vocabulary words from books students read.

Many early childhood teachers label objects in their classrooms (door, bookcase, etc.) as a means of teaching a sight vocabulary. Word walls are popular in kindergarten and primary classrooms. A word wall is a bulletin board or classroom display area on the classroom wall on which high-frequency and new words are displayed. The words are arranged alphabetically.

Language Experience. Another method of literacy and reading development, the language experience approach (LEA), follows the philosophy and suggestions inherent in progressive education philosophy. This approach to reading instruction is child centered, links oral and written language, and maintains that literacy education should be meaningful to children and should grow out of experiences that are interesting to them. LEA is based on the premise that what is thought can be said, what is said can be written, and what is written can be read. Children's experiences are a key element in such child-centered approaches. Many teachers transcribe children's dictated

In this video, watch a kindergarten class blend sounds to make words. What does the teacher do to engage the children in the lesson?

phonics instruction A teaching method that emphasizes letter–sound correspondence so children can learn to combine sounds into words.

sight word approach Also called *whole-word* or *look-say,* an approach to reading that involves presenting children with whole words so they develop a "sight vocabulary" as opposed to "sounding out" words using phonics.

word wall A bulletin board or classroom display area on the classroom wall on which high-frequency and new words are displayed. The words are arranged alphabetically.

language experience approach (LEA) A reading instruction method that links oral and written language.

"experience" stories and use them as a basis for writing and for reading instruction. When children write stories, write in their journals, and write and illustrate cards and notes they are using their language experiences to learn to write and read. Many programs for English language learners use the LEA approach.

The Balanced Approach.   As with most things, a balanced approach is the best, and many early childhood advocates are encouraging literacy approaches that provide a balance between whole-language methods, phonics instruction, and the whole-word (sight) approach to meet the specific needs of individual children. No one approach to reading is the best for all children. It really takes a combination of the three approaches to reading—a balanced approach—to successfully teach all children to read. Consequently, you should have knowledge of multiple methods for teaching reading, which enables you to create and implement a balanced approach for all children.

Reading and Writing Workshops

Currently, there is a great deal of emphasis on implementing the Common Core Standards in reading and language arts. The CCS call for a balance between fictional and informational (nonfiction) literature. Reading and writing workshops in which children are reading about current events, science, social studies, and other content areas enables children to read and write across the curriculum.

Reading and writing workshops follow this format.

- Begin with a whole-class meeting in which the teacher provides a short lesson of the day's topic.
- Continue with a structured work period in which children read/write independently, engage in guided reading/writing groups, work with peers in small groups, and individually conference with the teacher.
- End with a whole-class meeting in which children reflect on and talk about their accomplishments.

Reader's Workshop.   Reader's Workshop allows the teacher to structure the literacy block in a way that meets each child's needs. It begins with a mini-lesson, which introduces the concepts, strategies, and techniques used by skilled readers in order to decode and comprehend text. The teacher reads aloud quality literature to the class while modeling the behaviors he or she wishes to teach. Then, students are given time to practice these skills independently in their own reading while the teacher works with individual students and small groups to give each student targeted instruction based on their needs. During their independent reading, students respond in different ways to the books they read both by drawing and writing. At the end of Reader's Workshop, students are encouraged to share their reading experiences of the day and what they learned as a whole group, in partners, or in small groups.

Shared Reading.   Shared reading is an important component of Reader's Workshop in kindergarten. Because children love books and reading, shared reading is a good way for you to capitalize on their interests and help them learn to read. Shared reading is a means of introducing young beginners to reading by using favorite books, rhymes, and poems. Teachers model reading for the students by reading aloud a book or other text and ultimately inviting students to join in.

Shared reading builds on children's natural desire to read and reread favorite books. The repeated reading of texts over several days, weeks, or months deepens children's understanding of them because each time the reading should be for a different purpose: to extend, refine, or deepen children's abilities to read and construct meaning.

---

balanced approach An approach to literacy in which there is a balance between whole-language methods and phonics instruction.

whole-language approach Philosophy of literacy development that advocates using all aspects of language—reading, writing, listening, and speaking—to help children become motivated to read and write.

shared reading A teaching method in which the teacher and children read together from a book that is visible to all.

The shared reading routine requires that you have on hand a big-book form of the book to be read, as well as multiple little-book copies for individual rereading later. You then follow these five steps:

1. Introduce the book. Show and discuss the book cover: the title, author, illustrator, and other appropriate book features. Have the children make predictions on what the story is about.

2. Read the book aloud to the children, holding it so they can see each page. Pause briefly to discuss the story or to respond to reactions and gestures.

3. Finish reading and ask questions. Ask children to retell the story.

4. Reread the story and invite your children to read along.

5. Extend the book. Involve your children in activities related to the book such as drawing, painting, and writing their own stories.

Writing Workshop. Writing workshops help children gain the skills and confidence they need to be good writers. Reading and Writing Workshop are similarly structured and start with a mini-lesson based on Common Core Standards, the curriculum written by the district, and the needs of the students. Then, children transition into independent writing time while the teacher works with small groups or conferences with individual children. Through the workshop model, teachers intentionally teach and explicitly model all parts of the writing process and use their own writing, students' writing, and quality published children's literature as examples.

Over the course of the school year, children write in a variety of both narrative and expository genres and learn to revise, edit, and publish their work for audiences to read. With guidance, young children are capable of and enjoy writing personal narratives, fictional stories, poetry, and informational texts. Beginning in kindergarten, students also use a variety of digital tools to publish their work.

In addition to writing in a variety of genres, many school districts use the Six-Trait Writing Method[49] to teach writing.

The six traits are the following:

1. *Ideas.* Teach children to develop ideas in their writing and to focus and elaborate on their ideas. Collaborate and brainstorm with children and make lists of items they can write about, such as: people I know, things I do, things I have, and places I go, for children to refer to when they need ideas for writing.

2. *Organization.* Have children look at the structure of their writing and examine and experiment with organizational structures in multiple fiction and nonfiction genres. For example, teach children to check for a beginning, middle, and end when they write stories or organize information learned from a science or social studies unit into an alphabet book.

3. *Voice.* Encourage children to find their personal voice and write for their audience. Let children's voices of culture, gender, and home background come through in their writing.

4. *Word Choice.* Encourage children to use "big," unique, and precise words in their writing. Many of these words can come from the books they read and that you read to them. Remember that 50 percent of children's reading should be from informational sources. Have children use personal and classroom word walls to develop an extensive vocabulary to use in their writing.

5. *Sentence Fluency.* Teach children to begin sentences in different ways and use sentences of varying lengths and structures.

6. *Conventions.* Teach children proper rules of grammar, spelling, and punctuation. Have children proofread their work and the work of other children. You and the children can discuss proper conventions of writing in group meetings.[50]

Lesson Planning

In addition to knowing the curriculum, the "what" to teach, another dimension of being a high-quality kindergarten teacher is knowing *how* to teach. This involves planning for teaching. Reflective practice involves thinking before teaching, thinking during teaching, and thinking after teaching. Part of your role as a kindergarten teacher will be to write lesson plans, either individually or as a team member. Some school districts have prepared lesson plans that you will be required to use. Other districts may ask you to prepare lesson plans a week or two in advance. Whatever the case, a good lesson plan helps you be an effective teacher.

Many school districts use the 5E Model of Instruction for lesson plans. The five E's are:

1. Engagement
2. Exploration
3. Explanation
4. Expansion
5. Evaluation

Read the accompanying special feature, "5E Lesson Plan: Literacy," and learn how teacher Lynne Rhodes integrates the 5E model into her lesson planning.

> "5E's: Engagement, Exploration, Explanation, Expansion, Evaluation"

5E LESSON PLAN: Literacy

Rationale: The use of 5E model lessons is effective for several reasons. First, these lessons are research-based, and have been proven to enhance both teacher and student performance. Second, the lessons are designed to develop knowledge while at the same time forming collaborative relationships. Third, these lessons lend themselves easily to differentiation among various types of learners, including those included from all special education arenas, allowing students to progress through varying levels of Bloom's Taxonomy. Finally, they are layered (structured to build onto prior knowledge) to ensure that all learners are successful.

Lesson Title: Just Ducky

Time Frame for Lesson: 2 days

Day 1: Engage, Explore
Day 2: Explain, Extend, and Evaluate

> Base your lessons on state/ Common Core Standards

Standards: Texas Essential Knowledge and Skills (TEKS)

English Language Arts—Reading/Comprehension of Literary Text/Theme and Genre

- K.4B—ask questions and respond to text read aloud
- K.9A—identify the topic of an informational text heard
- K.10A—identify the topic and details in an expository text heard or read, referring to the words and/or illustrations
- K.10B—retell important facts in a text, heard or read

Writing/Writing Process

- K.20A—gather evidence from provided text sources
- K.20B—use pictures in conjunction with writing when documenting research

Science

- K.10 The student knows that organisms resemble their parents and have structures and processes that help them survive within their environments.

Materials: the book *Ducks Quack* by Pam Scheunemann, Web access, butcher paper, markers and crayons, yellow construction paper ducks, blue construction paper ovals, pencils

Vocabulary: oviparous, preening, omnivorous, webbed feet

Engage

Begin by reading the book *Ducks Quack* by Pam Scheunemann. Encourage students to listen closely for new things they learn about ducks. Next, do an online search for facts about ducks.

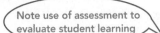

Provide opportunities for students to be actively involved with each other

Explore

Next, invite students to do a Think/Pair/Share activity.[*] Students will turn to their neighbor, chat about something they have just learned, and continue until the teacher calls time by ringing a bell, clapping her hands, etc. Once everyone has had an opportunity to share with a neighbor, have several students come up to the front of the class to share something that they learned from the book or the website.

Explain

For this portion of the lesson, students, along with the teacher, will create a "tree map."[†] To do this, put a picture of a duck at the top of the paper and divide the chart into three sections. "Ducks . . . have/can/are." Direct students to volunteer answers to complete each section of the chart. Once the chart is complete, have students take turns reading the facts that they have volunteered. (See photo for completed tree map.)

Extend

The following day, take out the tree map and re-read and review it. Next, give students a yellow construction paper duck and have them cut it out. Then, give them a blue construction paper oval. This will be the pond. Have them fold the oval in half and glue the duck behind the fold of the paper so that it can open from the bottom. They may add waves, fish, etc. to their pond and details to their ducks if they wish. Once they have made the "duck in the pond," direct them to open up the pond and write some duck facts inside. (See photo for example.) Early finishers may choose a partner and take turns reading their duck facts to each other. Differentiate where necessary.[‡]

Evaluate

Note use of assessment to evaluate student learning

The final portion of the 5E lesson involves an informal assessment. When all students have completed their ducks in a pond, have them sit in a circle on the carpet. Begin giving them statements about ducks, and have them determine whether the statements are true or false. If the statement is true, then students give a "thumbs up" signal. If the statement is false, then they signal with "thumbs down." The teacher will observe

· · · · · · · · · · · · · · ·

[*]Think/Pair/Share activities allow students to chat with each other about what they learned, then share their thoughts with the rest of the class. This is a cooperative strategy that was developed by Frank Lyman and his colleagues in Maryland.

[†]A tree map may also be referred to as a "thinking map." It is a technique whereby students can classify ideas and include specific details about each idea. See www.mapthemind.com for more examples of tree maps.

[‡]Higher level students may independently use additional books containing information about ducks in order to learn more facts. Lower level students may need to dictate their information to the teacher if they have difficulty writing sentences on their own.

which students miss one or more of the questions, and, if necessary, will review or reteach those concepts with the students still having difficulty.

Examples of true/false questions:

- Ducks are oviparous. (True)
- Ducks have babies called chicks. (False)
- Ducks have webbed feet. (True)
- Ducks are herbivorous. (False)
- Ducks cannot fly. (False)

> Use Bloom's Taxonomy to ask higher order questions

Continue questioning the students, being sure to stretch their thinking with questions reaching higher than just the knowledge level of Bloom's Taxonomy. Following are some sample questions:

- Why is it important for ducks to preen their feathers? (Application)
- What would happen if ducks could not swim? (Evaluation)
- Describe how ducks are omnivorous. (Comprehension)
- Name some of the similarities and differences between ducks and chickens. (Analysis)

Source: Contributed by Lynne B. Rhodes, kindergarten teacher at Curtsinger Elementary, Frisco ISD, Texas.

Mathematics in Kindergarten

Like all other kindergarten subjects, the teaching of math in kindergarten today is not what it was in the past. A good place to begin to understand what mathematics is like in the kindergarten today is with the Common Core Standards (CCS). Now would be a good time for you to go back and review Figure 9.2.

Science in Kindergarten

Scaffolding with Science. We do not want to forget that in all of our teaching of young children, we should be alert as to how to integrate theory into practice. For example, science offers many wonderful opportunities to apply Vygotsky's ideas, especially scaffolding. In addition, science activities provide many opportunities for children to be involved in science processes and act like scientists. The accompanying Professionalism in Practice feature shows you how to do this.

Social Studies in Kindergarten

In kindergarten, the social sciences most often included are history, geography, economics, and civics.[51] For each of these disciplines you will want to include knowledge, concepts, and themes. Your teaching of social studies should be content based and child centered, and you will want to make sure that you consult your state's content standards for social studies.

Historically, social studies in kindergarten have focused on the **expanding horizons approach**, also called the **expanding environments approach**, for

This **video** shows a kindergarten class engaged in a science lesson. Notice the classroom strategies the teacher uses to transition between activities and to focus the students' attention.

expanding horizons approach *or* **expanding environments approach** An approach to teaching social studies in which the student's world is the center of the initial units, with children at each grade level being exposed to a slowly widening environment.

professionalism in practice

How to Integrate Science and Literacy in Kindergarten

Lightning is flashing and thunder is rolling in my bilingual kindergarten classroom. The children are trying to say how the storm is scaring them. But they don't know how to describe what's going on. They can only say that there's a lot of rain and wind. They've never heard the words for thunder or lightning—in either Spanish or English! Since many of these children are performing at high levels in other areas, this underdevelopment of oral language in science is amazing. No wonder we see such high failure rates on state science test scores.

If our children are to develop a love of science and the ability to think and express themselves scientifically, they need to learn about scientific concepts, methods, and attitudes while they are young. This gives them a foundation for future work in the sciences, math, language, and the arts.

WHY IS TEACHING SCIENCE IN KINDERGARTEN IMPORTANT?

- Science is an ideal vehicle for developing children's questioning minds about the natural world.
- Implementing the National Science Education Standards can help our students take their place in a scientifically literate society.
- When children explore science they acquire oral and written language for scientific expression—and learn to read in new contexts.
- Science teaches children to appreciate the diversity of life and its interconnectedness.
- When children learn about nature they respect and care for our planet and its natural resources.
- Learning scientific methods teaches children to view themselves as scientists.
- Exciting lessons in science can foster a lifelong love for the subject.

KINDERGARTNERS CAN ACT LIKE SCIENTISTS

Teaching children what a scientist is and what scientists do is fundamental to science education. Scientists observe with their five senses (sight, touch, taste, smell, and hearing). They draw what they see, write about their observations, classify, ask questions, make predictions, create models, design experiments, count accurately, test their hypotheses, repeat their experiments, and keep on trying. Children learn this *scientific method* and practice it from pre-kindergarten to grade twelve.

ELEMENT 1 Plan an Activity and Address Standards

Always plan activities that provide opportunities to engage, explore, explain, elaborate, and evaluate—the 5E model. See the 5E lesson plan suggestions in the chapter. Central to teaching science is developing scientific concepts and methodology rather than merely studying some favorite topic or, worse yet, displaying some dramatic effect, such as a foaming "volcano." Use the Common Core state and district standards to plan your science learning objectives. Plan activities as you consider the standards.

Example: *Use "Planting Pumpkin Seeds" (a small part of an ongoing unit) to teach the following objectives as stated in the Texas Essential Knowledge and Skills publication:*

- *Students will ask questions about organisms, objects, and events.*
- *Students will plan and conduct simple descriptive investigations and communicate their findings.*

ELEMENT 2 Include Hands-On Experiences

Because children come from diverse backgrounds, they may not all have experience with a particular topic. To "level the playing field," begin every science unit with a shared, hands-on experience.

Example: *Bring a real pumpkin to the classroom and let the children touch it. Ask them to describe it and encourage them to ask questions.*

sequencing and selecting content. In this approach the children are at the center of expanding horizons; at each grade level they are immersed in a widening environment. In recent years, the expanding horizons approach has come under criticism. Critics of this approach maintain that it is simplistic, lacks rigorous social science content, and does not engage children in a serious exploration of social studies.

Although the expanding horizon approach is much maligned, nonetheless the teaching of social studies generally begins with who the children are and where they

Teacher: "What do you notice about the pumpkin?"
Jonathan: "It's orange."
Sara: "It's like a ball."
Carolina: "It has brown spots on it."
Anthony: "It has lines on it."
Edward: "It's big."
Teacher: "What do you wonder about the pumpkin?"
Kevin: "Is it real?"
Carolina: "Are there seeds inside?"
Daniela: "Will it get bigger?"
Pedro: "Is it heavy?"

ELEMENT 3 Incorporate Writing and Drawing

- Model writing for the class by recording on a chart what children say about the pumpkin.
- Encourage interactive writing. Have the children take turns with a marker on a large piece of paper writing their observations as a group and using invented spelling.
- Teach children to make direct observations by individually drawing in their science journals or on recording sheets only what they see.
- Depending on the children's developmental levels, they will either write about their observations, or you will record their observations.

ELEMENT 4 Incorporate Literature

- Incorporate both international and fiction materials for read-alouds, free reading, and research. Some examples you can use are: *Apples and Pumpkins* (Anne Rockwell), *Calabazas/Pumpkins* (Melvin and Gilda Berger), *From Seed to Plant* (Allan Fowler), *From Seed to Pumpkin* (Wendy Pfeffer), *Pumpkin Circle* (George Levenson) (Spanish version: *El círculo de las calabazas*), *Pumpkin Jack* (Will Hubbell), *Perfect Pumpkins* (Jeff Bauer), *Pumpkin, Pumpkin* (Jeanne Titherington), *Too Many Pumpkins* (Linda White).
- Choose nonfiction books with photos (including children if possible): *Perfect Pumpkins* (Jeff Bauer), *Pumpkin Circle* (George Levenson) (Spanish version: *El círculo de las calabazas*).

- Use charts of songs and poems for shared reading to teach scientific vocabulary and concepts.
- Explain science textbook features such as table of contents, diagram labels, glossary, and index.

ELEMENT 5 Ask Questions to Promote Student-Designed Experiments

- Start children wondering. Model asking testable questions for the children:
  "What would happen if we watered these seeds?"
  "What would happen if we didn't water some others?"
  "What would happen if these seeds got a lot of light?"
  "What would happen if these seeds got only a little light?"
- Ask: "Which of these would grow faster and how could we find out?"
- Now say:
  "Let's put three seeds in each cup with some soil."
  "We'll put one cup where it will get a *lot* of light and *water* the seeds."
  "We'll put one cup where it will get a *lot* of light and *not water* the seeds."
  "We'll put one cup where it will get a *little* bit of light and *water* the seeds."
  "We'll put one cup where it will get a *little* bit of light and *not water* the seeds."
- Prompt the class to make predictions and record their answers.

Brandon: "I think the seeds will grow in three days."
Samantha: "I think the seeds will grow in five days."

- The children will check the seeds every few days and record the results in their science journals.
- Discuss the results.

Source: Contributed by Lori Cadwallader, bilingual teacher, Newton Rayzor Elementary, Denton ISD, Texas.

are geographically. In addition, approaches to social studies in kindergarten also try to be child centered and developmentally appropriate.

Today's teaching of social studies is designed to provide children with content knowledge and skills from the four social sciences: history, geography, economics, and civics. So, in your teaching of social studies you will want to make sure that children are provided with authentic content and are engaged in activities that help them learn knowledge, apply knowledge, and engage in critical thinking.

Ideas for Teaching Social Studies.   The following are some ideas that you can use to help you teach the social studies content standards of your state and school district:

- *Geography.* Gayle teaches her kindergarten class about different cultures by placing one end of a ribbon on a map of the United States and the other end on the country they are learning about. Gayle discusses with the students about the different modes of transportation that could be used to travel to the country. Pictures are placed on the map above that country pertaining to the culture there. Students are then instructed to draw a picture, write a story, or create a poem to put on the map as well.

- *Economics.* Ashley teaches her children about assembly lines through the use of creative arts. She draws pictures of stick figures with each line drawn using a different color crayon. After displaying the drawing on the wall she then separates her class into small groups and gives each group member a different color crayon and one piece of paper per group. The piece of paper is passed down the line of students, and each student draws one line with his or her crayon matching Ashley's drawing. The class then discusses the importance of assembly lines, why each member must do his or her part, and the different products that are made by assembly lines.

- *Civics.* Eric has his kindergarten children make a U.S. flag collage using large paper, magazines, crayons, scissors, and glue. He then discusses with the class that the flag is a national symbol, explains what the stars and stripes stand for, and discusses the role national symbols play in society. Students then tell Eric where they've seen the American flag flown before, and he makes a list of these places on the chalkboard. After the discussion, students individually draw pictures of other flags they have seen.

- *History.* Sarah teaches her kindergarten children about ancient cultures through photographs and online reproductions of wall paintings from ancient civilizations that illustrate aspects of life as it was lived in ancient times. She then asks the students to give her ideas about which animals lived at that time, which animals the people hunted, and what games the people played. Sarah then has her students illustrate a picture of a day in their own lives using markers, crayons, or paint. The pictures include scenes such as coming to school, reading in class, recess, lunch, and playing with pets or siblings at home. After their drawings are complete, Sarah hangs the students' pictures next to the pictures of the ancient civilization. The class then holds a discussion about the similarities and differences in the ancient civilizations and their own.

Arts in Kindergarten

Teaching of the arts in kindergarten consists of knowledge, skills, and concepts from these four areas: music, art, dance, and theater. The standards were developed by the American Alliance for Theater and Education, Music Educators National Conference, the National Art Education Association, and the National Dance Association.

In your role as a kindergarten teacher, you will want to integrate the arts into everything that you do. Children love to participate in activities relating to the arts, so you should capitalize on their natural creative inclinations and provide them with these experiences. As with anything else, the integration of the arts depends on these factors: time, opportunity, and materials.

Time.   By integrating the arts into your curriculum, you are solving the time issue by enabling children to participate in all of these activities while they are learning reading/literacy, math, science, and social studies. For example, here are some ideas for integrating the arts into each of these areas:

- **Reading/literacy.** Students can act out the stories of their favorite book; students can illustrate a story that they and/or the class have written.
- **Math.** Students can use art materials to make charts and graphs and design and make different kinds of shapes. Students can also develop rules to describe the relationships of one shape to another—for example, "You can put two identical triangles together to make a rectangle."
- **Science.** Children can use their artistic skills to draw and paint various examples of life cycles of organisms or write and produce a public service announcement on the importance of personal health in the kindergarten classroom.
- **Social studies.** Students can learn about and sing many of the songs popular in their state's history; students can learn the folk dances of various cultural groups in their state.

Opportunity. There are many opportunities during the school year for children to engage in projects that involve the arts. For example, puppetry can be integrated into all of the content areas, and stories provide many opportunities for children to engage in theater and dramatic play. For instance, in preparation for and while reading the story "The Three Billy Goats Gruff," children can make paper masks to depict the goats and could build a bridge out of blocks and/or other materials. Also, students could have a starring role playing the troll. Every thematic unit provides opportunities for all of the arts, and children should be encouraged to explore ways to express ideas from the thematic units in an artistic way.

Materials. Materials are just as important as time and opportunity. They include all of the materials related to the visual arts—paints, crayons, markers, brushes, and so on—as well as materials necessary for music and dance. For example, you could provide materials such as DVDs of folk dances, popular songs, and sing-along tunes. To encourage theater expression, children need props—clothes, hats, puppets, and plenty of materials such as cardboard boxes, glue, and tape for making their own stage settings and backgrounds. Keep in mind that the *process* of exploring the creative arts is more important than the finished *product*. Children are learning to enjoy learning when the process is respected by teachers.

Technology in the Kindergarten. Technology pervades everything that children do in and out of the classroom. Using technology in your classroom will help you teach and help children learn. Technological tools commonly found in many kindergarten classrooms include computers, computer programs, printers, DVDs, televisions, and digital cameras. Use technology to help you achieve learning standards and objectives and focus on the curriculum. State standards also include standards for the application of technology to everyday life activities and classroom learning activities. Your use of technology should also build on children's out-of-school experiences. In addition, provide technology experiences for all children while ensuring that those who lack technology competence receive appropriate assistance. Children who are more technologically experienced can partner with students who are less technologically savvy. Parents can also help children become more familiar with technology by extending in-school technology learning at home.

Incorporating technology into the early elementary classroom allows students to engage in all kinds of learning in multisensory ways. You will benefit from software that includes:

- Active learning with students making decisions
- Multisensory and multidimensional learning

- Age-appropriate expectations
- Flexibility, ease of use, and open-ended operation
- Provision for children to explore without fear of making mistakes, and that responds to their exploration in ways that encourage further investigation

technology tie-in

Whiteboards in the Kindergarten Classroom

Today's young children are "digital natives." They are immersed in a world of technology that brings them information and media on demand. As a result, when they begin their school-based experience they require that same high level of engaging information from their learning environment. Integration of a variety of technology tools is necessary for a high-quality education. One of those tools, the interactive whiteboard, is an essential resource in today's early childhood classrooms.

SIX BEST PRACTICES FOR USING INTERACTIVE WHITEBOARDS IN KINDERGARTEN

BEST PRACTICE 1 Where?

Mount whiteboards at a level where children can easily reach and interact with them. This can be at floor level or a low wall so students can best view the board while in whole-group instruction.

BEST PRACTICE 2 Who?

The real power of whiteboards, and other technology, lies in engaging students' interactive learning. For example, instructional activities that require students to move objects to retell a story, match patterns, and roll interactive dice in a math lesson are all ways to engage students in meaningful learning.

BEST PRACTICE 3 What?

The interactive whiteboard is a powerful tool to support learning in both literacy and math content for young children. Devote time to good basic training using the intuitive software that comes with the interactive whiteboard. The whiteboard program comes with many interactive tools and premade templates that can make designing an activity a breeze for you. Invest time upfront to learn the features of the software to save valuable time and increase the quality of the instructional activities.

BEST PRACTICE 4 With?

Collaborate with colleagues! Sharing digital files via e-mail or intranet enables you and other teachers to work together. Teams of teachers can divide tasks by subject areas or Common Core Standards and share work with others. Online networks like Smart Exchange provide lessons you can customize for your individual classroom.

BEST PRACTICE 5 When?

Using whiteboard technology to extend and differentiate learning is great but whiteboards do not take the place of good teaching. Young children benefit most from their time engaged in hands-on learning with real objects and through instruction time with you and their classmates.

BEST PRACTICE 6 How?

Use the interactive whiteboard to assist in accommodations for students with all types of special needs. Use an iPad and remote desktop apps like SplashTop to accommodate students who may not be able to access the whiteboard in a typical way. For example, a student with limited movement can move shapes on the whiteboard from the back of the room using supplemental devices. Children can write using a keyboard.

Utilizing the most current technology like interactive whiteboards in early childhood classrooms provides students with the twenty-first century tools they need to be twenty-first century learners.

. . . .

Source: Contributed by Pamela Beard, M.Ed., elementary teacher at Forest Ridge Elementary, College Station, Texas.

TEACHING AND LEARNING IN THE INCLUSIVE CLASSROOM: KINDERGARTEN FOR CHILDREN WITH DISABILITIES

Now that you have read about changes and issues in kindergartens today, let's focus our attention on the transition to kindergarten for children with disabilities. Most parents of typically developing children feel positive about their child's transition to kindergarten, but they nonetheless remain anxious about this major entry point into the world of school. Parents of children with disabilities share these worries with other parents and also have practical questions related to how, where, when, and who will provide their children's services. For the many parents who have worked hard to establish support systems in their preschools, the thought of starting all over again from scratch can seem daunting. The Individuals with Disabilities Education Act (IDEA) clearly articulates the importance of transitions for children with disabilities from early intervention programs to early childhood special education and inclusive kindergarten classrooms.

You can help facilitate all children's transitions to kindergarten by making a conscious effort to think about the acronym SCHOOL:

S: *Start early.* Schools must carefully bridge the distance between a play-based curriculum and the increasing academic demands of kindergarten. It is not unreasonable to start the transition process a full year to year and a half before kindergarten begins. For example, in the fall of a child's last year of preschool, teachers at the child's current school should contact the kindergarten to schedule times to meet and visit each program.

C: *Collaborative team approach.* Planning and making decisions with a collaborative team should involve families, preschool teachers, kindergarten teachers, school administrators, and any related service providers that the child sees (e.g., occupational therapists, physical therapists). For example, the team may observe several schools and choose the one that best meets the needs of the child.

H: *Honor active involvement of families.* This may include teaching children about the school and kindergarten and addressing their questions and concerns about how specialized services will be provided for their children. For example, parents may want to meet with the therapists or visit the school with their child prior to the beginning of school.

O: *Observe current and future schools.* Observe at the preschool and have the teachers and families observe at the kindergarten prior to the start of the kindergarten year. This will allow you to identify the needs and strengths of the child and prepare for any modifications or accommodations. For example, you may observe that the classroom arrangement of the preschool is easily replicated and meets the needs of *all* children.

O: *Outline goals and anticipated outcomes.* Work as a team to develop the goals and outcomes in the child's individualized education program. This may not be necessary for every child, but *all* children need goals and outcomes to ensure an optimal kindergarten experience. For example, a common kindergarten goal is following rules, routines, and directions. This can then include modifications or adaptations for children who need them.

L: *Listen and learn.* The child's previous teachers, therapists, and parents have a wealth of child-specific, relevant information that includes strategies or adaptations that have previously been successful. Having collaborative dialogues also allows you to share the services and supports available at your school. For example, a parent might tell you that a child uses modified scissors when cutting or enjoys social praise.

ACTIVITIES FOR PROFESSIONAL DEVELOPMENT
ethical dilemma

"To redshirt or not to redshirt?"

Delani and Bill Stevens watched a national television program about redshirting kindergarten children. Delani and Bill hadn't thought much about redshirting Jason, their five-year-old son, and holding him back from kindergarten, until they watched the program. Jason has a summer birthday and will have just turned five in August, which would make him one of the youngest in his class. "We don't know what to do," says Delani. "We don't know whether to play the numbers game and give him that extra year to grow in size and maturity or to let him go to school and take our chances. We would prefer for Jason to be one of the older kids in the class and be a leader rather than a follower. We don't think it's really cheating the system," says Delani. "We'll do whatever we think we have to do to make sure that Jason is prepared and successful in life."

What do you think? Are Delani and Bill "gaming the system"? Do you agree with Delani and Bill that they should give their child every advantage to be successful? Do you see anything wrong with parents giving their children every advantage that they can? What would you recommend Delani and Bill do? What would you do if Jason were your son?

Application Activities

1. Review the important figures in kindergarten education mentioned in this chapter. Which person do you think contributed the most? How? Go online and find additional information regarding your most important person. Share your findings with your classmates via your online class discussion board and see if they support your selection.

2. Do you support an earlier or a later entrance age to kindergarten? Find three reasons for your opinion. Go online to find arguments for and against your opinion. Did any of these change your view? Get on Facebook, Twitter, and so on and ask for others' opinions on early or later kindergarten entrance.

3. Do you think that redshirting is an appropriate practice? Why? Why not? If a parent asked you about redshirting her son who has an August birthday, how would you answer her?

4. Reflect on your role of creating classrooms that are healthy, respectful, supportive, and challenging. What one thing in each of these areas do you think is essential? Put your suggestions on your class discussion board and ask for comments from your classmates.

5. One of the requirements of the new CCS is that kindergartners have to be reading before they enter first grade. Teacher Trisha Martinez teaches in a half-day kindergarten program. She is exasperated. "How am I going to teach all my children to read in a half-day program?," she wonders. Where do you stand on the half-day vs. full-day kindergarten debate? Conduct a poll of your classmates concerning how many of them support a whole or half-day program. Based on the results of your findings, post your comments to a blog devoted to the issue of half- or whole-day kindergarten.

Linking to Learning

Dolch Sight Words

www.dolchsightwords.org

Dedicated to providing various educational activities to teach reading that include teachers teaching their students and parents teaching their children.

Kindergarten Connection

www.kconnect.com

Dedicated to providing valuable resources to primary teachers; offers new hints, tips, and information each week.

National Kindergarten Alliance

www.nkateach.org

The result of a summit of leaders from various kindergarten associations, organizations, and interest groups that met in January 2000, this national organization serves kindergarten teachers throughout the United States.

MyEducationLab

Go to Topics 2 (Child Development/Theories) and 7 (Curriculum/Content Areas) in the MyEducationLab (www.myeducationlab.com) for your course, where you can:

- Find learning outcomes for Child Development/Theories and Curriculum/Content Areas along with the national standards that connect to these outcomes.

- Complete Assignments and Activities that can help you more deeply understand the chapter content.

- Apply and practice your understanding of the core teaching skills identified in the chapter with the Building Teaching Skills and Dispositions learning units.

- Examine challenging situations and cases presented in the IRIS Center Resources.

- Explore interactive CONNECT Modules to practice classroom skills and enhance professional development.

- Check your comprehension on the content covered in the chapter by going to the Study Plan in the Book Resources for your text. Here you will be able to take a chapter quiz, receive feedback on your answers, and then access Review, Practice, and Enrichment activities to enhance your understanding of chapter content.

chapter 10

THE EARLY ELEMENTARY GRADES: ONE THROUGH THREE

Preparation for Life

NAEYC Standards for Early Childhood Professional Preparation Programs

Standard 1. Promoting Child Development and Learning

I use my understanding of young children's characteristics and needs, and of multiple interacting influences on children's development and learning, to create environments that are healthy, respectful, supportive, and challenging for all children.[1]

Standard 4. Using Developmentally Effective Approaches to Connect with Children and Families

I understand and use positive relationships and supportive interactions as the foundation for my work with young children and families. I know, understand, and use a wide array of developmentally appropriate approaches, instructional strategies, and tools to connect with children and families and positively influence each child's development and learning.[2]

Standard 5. Using Content Knowledge to Build Meaningful Curriculum

I understand the importance of developmental domains and academic (or content) disciplines in early childhood curriculum. I know the essential concepts, inquiry tools, and structure of content areas, including academic subjects, and can identify resources to deepen my understanding. I use my own knowledge and other resources to design, implement, and evaluate meaningful, challenging curricula that promote comprehensive developmental and learning outcomes for every young child.[3]

TEACHING IN GRADES ONE THROUGH THREE

As we have discussed, reform is sweeping across the educational landscape, and nowhere is this more evident than in grades one to three, also known as the **primary grades**. Changes include how schools operate and are organized, how teachers teach, how children are evaluated, and how schools involve and relate to parents and the community. The federal and state governments are specifying standards, curriculum, and testing agendas. In an era of accountability, state and public schools are held to higher standards for learning and achievement. Reform, accountability, and achievement are in; schooling as usual is out.

primary grades Grades one to three.

Contemporary Schooling Today

Let's look at the nature of grades one through three today. Here are some examples of what teaching and learning is like in real classrooms as you prepare to teach children ages six to nine. Here are some mini-portraits of Teachers of the Year in grades one, two, and three.

First grade teacher Nancy Berry at Liza Jackson Preparatory School, Fort Walton Beach, Florida, welcomes children from diverse backgrounds and learning styles to "Berryland USA: A Place Where Children Love to Learn." Berry accepts students unconditionally and treats them as if they are smart to make learning a self-fulfilling prophecy. She reassures kids that she made mistakes as a child, coaxing them to read, write, organize thoughts, and make decisions at a higher level. She uses singing, moving, reading, experiencing, applying, and writing to reach all types of learners. "I don't teach to a test," she says. "I teach to life."[4]

Elizabeth Parker, a second grade teacher at Fort Smith, Arkansas, is recognized as an outstanding literacy educator. According to her principal, "Beth is a teacher leader who constantly researches best teaching practices to better help her students achieve academic success in her classroom and to assist fellow teachers with curriculum and instructional questions." Parker's creative, well-planned, motivating lessons and excellent classroom management skills help her students read above grade level. Parker's students have also experienced significant gains in math, with many scoring above the district average.[5]

Valorie Lewis of Stigler, Oklahoma, a third grade teacher, shares her story of overcoming poverty, teasing, and low expectations with her rural Oklahoma students to inspire them to believe in themselves because "there is no such thing as a child without the potential for success." Lewis holds a weekly "Community Circle" for her students to share thoughts and feelings and learn empathy. She fosters an environment where students respect and value others by having the children draw names each week and fill out "Positive Comment Cards" about that person each day to share with the class. She developed a daily review program to practice basic skills and Third Grade Brain Olympics, used in other classes and schools.[6]

Native Hawaiian Yuuko Arikawa is adept at showing her students why reading is fundamental to their long-term success. At Kaala Elementary School in Wahiawa, Hawaii, she instills in them a love of books and a strong grasp of the written word. From researching up-and-coming best practices and field-testing new strategies, to sharing her findings with fellow teachers and helping to integrate effective tactics into their lessons, Arikawa is an integral part of her school's achievement growth.[7]

Learning Contexts

How and what you teach is dependent in many ways on the school and social contexts of teaching in grades one, two, and three. Here are some of the major contexts of teaching in grades one, two, and three.

Diversity.   The percentage of racial/ethnic minority students enrolled in the nation's public schools increased to 43 percent in 2009.[8] This increase in minority enrollment largely reflects the growth in the percentage of students who were Hispanic. Hispanic students represent 22 percent of public school enrollment. The distribution of minority students in public schools differs across regions of the country, with minority public school enrollment (55 percent) exceeding white enrollment (45 percent) in the West.[9] The number of school-age children who speak a language other than English at home is 5 million, or 76 percent of the population at this age range.[10] This means you will be teaching children

MyEducationLab

Visit the MyEducationLab for *Fundamentals of Early Childhood Education* to enhance your understanding of chapter concepts with a personalized Study Plan. You'll also have the opportunity to hone your teaching skills through video-based Assignments and Activities as well as Building Teaching Skills and Dispositions lessons.

FOCUS QUESTIONS

1. What is teaching in grades one through three like?

2. What are children in grades one through three like?

3. What is included in high-quality environments that support learning in the primary grades?

4. What is included in the curriculum of the primary grades?

5. What can children learn about school and life from nature?

from different cultures and backgrounds, and you will have to take those differences into account in your planning and teaching. In addition to cultural and linguistic differences, diversity is also reflected in children's socioeconomic status and in their physical, cognitive, social, emotional, adaptive, and communication abilities.

Take a look at the Diversity Tie-In feature, "The Rich Get Richer." It addresses issues and consequences of children from low socioeconomic homes, neighborhoods, and schools having fewer educational materials to learn from than children from higher socioeconomic backgrounds.

Achievement. High-level achievement of all students is a national priority today as illustrated by the teacher vignettes at the beginning of this chapter. Schools and teachers place a premium on closing the achievement gap that exists between races and socioeconomic levels. High-quality teachers are dedicated to ensuring that each child learns.

diversity tie-in

The Rich Get Richer

INEQUALITIES OF EDUCATIONAL RESOURCES

The title of this Diversity Tie-In may seem perplexing to you. After all, when we think about the rich getting richer, we think of money and other things associated with the rich and famous. However, the same applies to schools and schooling. It is an established fact in the research literature that socioeconomically disadvantaged students and schools do less well on measures of academic achievement compared with their more advantaged peers.[11] Think for a moment about some of the things that contribute to rich learning experiences and environments, such as the children and the teacher. Students score higher in schools with more resources such as educational materials, higher SES classmates, and highly educated and highly effective teachers. There are other dimensions to rich learning environments that contribute to student achievement. For example, children also need high-quality classroom environments with materials that support learning. To learn to read and write well, children need books, technology and other materials that support achievement. Unfortunately, these materials are not evenly distributed across all classrooms in the country. In fact, resources are generally distributed by the socioeconomic status (SES) of the children who attend these classrooms.

INEQUALITIES OF LEARNING MATERIALS

Let's look at the inequality of distribution of classroom learning materials by SES status. Children from high-SES environments get more of the materials that support literacy than do their less-advantaged low-SES peers. In addition, children in low-income families have access to fewer reading materials than those children in upper-income families. In the very real world of learning to read, children who have adequate learning materials do indeed get richer in that they are able to learn to their fullest capacity. In order to help close the socioeconomic gaps in academic achievement, we want to make sure that children of low-income families have access to high-quality learning materials that are age and culturally appropriate.

MAKING CLASSROOMS MORE EQUAL

So, what does this mean for you as a classroom teacher? Here are five things you can do:

1. Make sure that you use all of your classroom materials to their fullest. Using materials and allowing children to have access to them is an essential first step in making sure that children are getting a foundation for reading and literacy.
2. Read, read, and read to your children. Reading to children is one of the best ways to improve vocabulary, word knowledge, and meaning, and to promote interest in and enthusiasm for reading.
3. Select reading materials to include both fiction and information books and literature. Children need a balance, 50/50, of the two types of reading and resource material.
4. Work with families and the community to get the materials you and your children need. Be an advocate for getting your children the materials they need to learn how to read and write. Your advocacy includes conducting fund-raisers, seeking support from local businesses, and spreading the word that children need materials if they are to learn effectively and well.
5. Conduct family literacy programs for your parents. In these programs, help parents learn the importance of reading and literacy, and the vital role books and other reading materials play in children's lives.[12]

The Common Core Standards also create a context in which preparing primary children for career and college places an emphasis on assuring all students achieve to high levels. You will be involved in the implementation of the Common Core Standards and will be part of grade-level teams collaborating to apply them to instructional practice. This emphasis on achievement results in many educational pressures, which affect children and you. These include the end of social promotion and making sure all children can read on level by the end of third grade.

Standards. In 45 states, the curriculum of grades one through three is aligned with the Common Core Standards (CCS). As a result, you will be teaching content designed to help students learn what the CCS specify. In fact, many school districts provide their teachers with lesson plans that suggest activities and instructional strategies based on the CCS. You won't always get to teach exactly what you want to teach, when you want to teach it, and how you want to teach it. However, good teachers always find ways to include in the curriculum what they believe is important and developmentally appropriate. As many teachers have learned and are learning, teaching with the CCS does not have to be dull and boring; you can make learning interesting and relevant to all your students' lives.

Today's primary grade teachers must balance the children's interests with a curriculum aligned to state standards. This video discusses the challenges and rewards of teaching primary grade students.

The CCS have transformed (some say reformed) teaching from an input model to an output model. As a result, teachers are no longer able to say, "I taught Mario the use of structural cues to decode words." Now the questions are, "Is Mario able to use and apply decoding skills?" and "Will Mario do well on decoding skills on the state test?" High-quality teachers have good ideas about what and how to teach, and they always will. However, the time and opportunity to act on those good ideas are reduced by increasing requirements to teach to the standards and teach so students master the standards. This is where intentional teaching comes into play.

Testing. Testing is, and will continue to be, a part of contemporary school culture and instructional practices. For example, in the months of April and May, from P.S. 124 in Brooklyn, New York, to Lead Mine Elementary in North Carolina, to Frisco ISD in Texas, teachers focus on year-end teaching. You, too, will be involved in helping students learn appropriate grade-level content so they can pass local, state, and national tests. In addition, you will use test data as a basis for your planning and instruction.

Data-Driven Instruction. In **data-driven instruction**, teaching decisions are based on the analysis of assessment data to make decisions about how to best meet the instructional needs of each child. The accompanying Technology Tie-in feature, "How to Use Data-Driven Instruction," will help you learn how to incorporate data-driven instruction into your planning and teaching.

data-driven instruction An approach to teaching in which analysis of assessment data drives the decisions about how to meet the instructional needs of each child.

Changing Teacher Roles. As previously discussed, the role of the early childhood teacher is changing rapidly and dramatically. This is particularly true for teachers in grades one to three. For example, it is likely that you will be a member of a grade-level team that meets regularly to plan, learn, debate, discuss, decide, and develop lessons and learning activities. You will collaborate with your colleagues on all types of projects and learning activities. Today, school is a place where a premium is placed on collaboration and being a team player.

In this video, notice how the staff is collaborating to examine assessment data to see if students are learning state standards and if teaching strategies are effective.

Curriculum Alignment. Teaching issues are as old as teaching itself and involve frequently asked questions, such as "What should I teach?" and "How should I teach it?" As usual, the answer is, "It depends." It depends on what you and other teachers think is important and what the CCS say is important. Therein lies the heart of the issue: how to develop meaningful curriculum that is aligned with the CCS. Learning how to develop strong lesson plans that also meet state standards is important for all

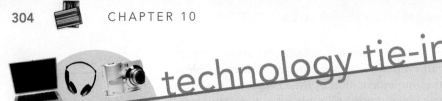

COMPETENCY BUILDER

How to Use Data-Driven Instruction

You don't have to go back to *Little House on the Prairie* to find a teaching style based on "getting through" the curriculum. Covering the curriculum is not the same as student learning. Accountability initiatives have brought about a shift in focus from covering subject matter to meeting the educational needs of each student. There is only one way to determine whether or not the learning needs of each student are being met, and that is through an ongoing analysis of data collected by assessing children.

BACKGROUND

Lead Mine Elementary School has a diverse population with over 40 percent of our students eligible for free or reduced lunches, and for many students English is not their primary language. Yet despite these challenges, we have achieved consistently high test score results over the years. Our teachers had to learn to teach smarter and to use technological resources as their ally.

WHAT IS DATA-DRIVEN INSTRUCTION?

Data-driven instruction is a system of teaching in which instructional decisions are based on an analysis of student assessment data collected to determine how best to meet the needs of each individual student.

THE PROCESS OF IMPLEMENTING DATA-DRIVEN INSTRUCTION

STEP 1 Start the School Year by Analyzing Existing Data

Before your students arrive, examine their cumulative record files to get a general profile of each student. The first week of school we conduct universal screenings on all of our students, including our kindergartners. Aimsweb (see the Linking to Learning section at the end of the chapter) is a useful tool to screen students because it is research based and includes math. It is a benchmark and progress-monitoring system based on direct, frequent, and continuous student assessment. The results are reported to students, parents, teachers, and administrators via a Web-based data management and reporting system to determine response to intervention. DIBELS is another popular universal screener, but it does not include math. Universal screening is a quick way to check student progress throughout the year, but is just one aspect of the assessment picture.

STEP 2 Align Assessments to Objectives

Plan collaboratively with your grade-level colleagues to determine when and how you will teach Common Core, district, and

teachers. The accompanying 5E Lesson Plan walks you through how to plan a third grade geometry lesson with the 5E model of planning.

Increasing student achievement is at the center of the CCS movement. Policy makers and educators view standards, tests, and teaching alignment as viable and practical ways to help ensure student achievement. *Alignment* is the arrangement of CCS, curriculum, and tests so that they complement one another. In other words, the curriculum is based on what the CCS say students should know and be able to do; tests measure what the standards indicate. *Curriculum alignment* is the process of making sure that what you teach—the context of the curriculum—matches what the CCS and state standards say students should know and be able to do.

5E LESSON PLAN: Geometry

Lesson Title: Geometry: Getting Started

Time Frame for Lesson: 3 days

state standards as well as how you will assess each standard. It is common and customary for grade-level teachers to meet regularly to make plans for how to teach standards and how to gather data based on student achievement. Many districts use Professional Learning Teams (PLTs) in which teachers work collaboratively to formalize lesson plans and ideas for their students.

STEP 3 The Data Collection Process

Data collection serves two purposes. Teachers give formative assessments to determine what students know and make adjustments in instruction to help all succeed. Technology makes this academic temperature taking much easier. You can do quick checks of knowledge with the help of student response devices (clickers) or with such programs as Study Island and Success Maker. Teachers give summative assessments at the end of a unit or the end of the year to tell them how well the students learned those objectives. Reflective teachers look at summative data to assess their own effectiveness. See the Linking to Learning section at the end of the chapter for more information on these programs.

STEP 4 Analyze Data

At the completion of the data collection process for a unit of study, meet with your grade-level colleagues and look at the data for trends. Did the majority of the students reach the standard? Does the data reveal student achievement needs you have to address? What standards did the students have trouble achieving? Did one teacher do a better job teaching the objective? What tips can she give the others to improve instruction as a team?

STEP 5 Use Data Analysis to Decide the Next Course of Study

After examining the data, use it to guide your next steps in the instructional process. Which students are ready to move on? Which students need remediation? Which students need enrichment? Gail Ausley, a kindergarten teacher at Lead Mine, says, "How are you going to plan instruction if you don't have any data? You can't plan unless you know what you're planning for." Jessica Yutzy, Gail's teammate, says, "It helps me to pinpoint the areas of greatest need for targeting instruction." In creating your plan to meet the needs of each student you may also involve resource teachers such as the academically gifted teacher, the ELL teacher, a special education teacher, the computer lab manager, or any other specialists in your school who can help you meet the specific needs of each child. Differentiation of instruction is critical.

STEP 6 Repeat the Process

Making data-based decisions to guide instruction is an ongoing process. Throughout the school year, you are constantly assessing your students, analyzing their data, and readjusting the plan to best meet their individual needs.

. . . .

Source: Contributed by Gary W. Baird, principal, Lead Mine Elementary School, Raleigh, North Carolina.

Day 1: Engage and Explore

Day 2: Explain and Elaborate

Day 3: Evaluate

Materials: chart paper, markers, toothpicks (in baggies labeled: sides), mini-marshmallows (in baggies labeled: vertices), student journals or writing paper, camera

Standards: Texas Essential Knowledge and Skills (TEKS)

3.8 Geometry and Spatial Reasoning. The student uses formal geometric vocabulary. The student is expected to identify, classify, and describe two dimensional geometric figures by their attributes.

3.20 Writing/Expository and Procedural Texts. Students write expository texts to communicate ideas and information to specific audiences for specific purposes. Students are expected to: (A) create brief compositions that: (ii) include supporting sentences with simple facts, details, and explanations.

Targeted Vocabulary: polygon, vertex, vertices, side

Engage

Play "I Spy." On a large piece of chart paper, draw a picture of a simple house that is made out of basic 2D shapes. Ask your students, "Which shapes do you see?" As the students give you answers, highlight the shapes they are referencing and write the name of the shape out to the side.

Consider using a different color for each shape. This will help your lower-level and English language learners differentiate by color. Keep the chart paper posted throughout the entire geometry unit so that you can add vocabulary as needed and students can refer to it throughout.

Explore

Mistakes are bound to happen in the Explore portion of the lesson; this is part of learning. Let it happen! Take note of these misconceptions and address them during the Explain portion.

Arrange your students into groups of three to four. Make sure your lower-level learners are grouped with you. Challenge your groups to build the shapes mentioned in the Engage part of your lesson with the following materials:

- Show and distribute mini-marshmallow baggies and introduce them as "vertices."
- Show and distribute toothpick baggies and introduce them as "sides."

Say, "I will be listening for my mathematicians to use these vocabulary terms. Please refer to your materials as vertices and sides." By doing this, students will get used to the vocabulary terms associated with classifying 2D shapes. Give the students time to build. *You will want to actively monitor your students, encouraging the use of vocabulary. While you are working with your group, use quality questioning to guide your students to discover the attributes of basic geometry.*

Explain

This is a very important part of the lesson. It is a time for students to reflect and for you to straighten out any misconceptions. More than likely, students will have built

their circle using many sides and vertices, when in fact, a circle is unlike any other shape: it is made from one continuous curved line and is not considered a polygon. Also, if students built their rectangle using 6 vertices instead of 4, you'll need to address this and guide discussion on ways to change the length of the sides without compromising the number of needed vertices.

Have your students write the word POLYGON in their math journals. Ask, "What if I told you that all but one shape that you built today was a polygon? Which shape is unlike any other? (A circle.) "A circle is made up of one continuous curved line. It does not belong in the same category as the rest. What do the others have in common?" (They are made up of straight lines and vertices.) "Shapes that are made up of straight sides and vertices are called polygons." Define this word together in journals.

This is a great opportunity to introduce any and all vocabulary you need. To reach all levels of learning: show, build, hand-draw, and define each term. Examples: parallelogram, trapezoid, hexagon, pentagon, decagon, etc.

Elaborate

Take students outside with a mission to find as many 2D shapes as they can on the playground. Ask students to create a tally chart of each shape found and a hand-drawn picture. Come back together and allow the students to share their findings with a partner or group.

Your lower level-students may need a list of specific shapes that you want them to locate. Have checklists ready to go for these students, with the shapes you want them to find already listed. English language learners would benefit from a picture posted next to the shape. Your higher-level students will be inclined to find the harder, more intricate shapes. Give them freedom to find as many as possible.

Evaluate

Evaluations do not always need to be paper and pencil; sometimes you need to think outside of the box! In this case, you need to asses if the students can use formal geometric vocabulary to identify, classify, and describe 2D shapes by their attributes. What better way to test this than by having the students become the shapes?

Choose a location with a lot of floor space. Call on groups of students to participate in making shapes lying on the floor with their bodies. Explain that their body is the "straight side" and in order to create a "vertex," two sides must touch. If you pull a group of three names, have them build a triangle. If you pull a group of five, ask if they can build a pentagon. Ask, "How many sides does your shape have? How many vertices?" Once your students gain speed with the activity, consider having two groups compete: "Who can build the most accurate hexagon with the fastest speed, while also working the quietest?" The possibilities of how to use this activity are endless. If you're in need of a graded assignment, ask your students to write a paragraph comparing polygons with a circle. Students will need to show their learning by stating facts about polygons.

Something to consider: Snap a picture of the students building each shape in your vocabulary list. Print the pictures and have the students label the vertices and list important information about that shape on the back. These can be used as review flashcards.
....

Source: Celeste E. Hanvey, M.Ed, third grade teacher, Curtsinger Elementary School, Frisco, Texas. Photos by Celeste E. Hanvey and Kathy Stroud.

Academics. The contemporary curriculum in grades one to three is heavy on reading and the STEM subjects (science, technology, engineering, and math). There is also an emphasis on the arts, social studies, character education, and health and wellness through physical education. Many of these areas, however, are integrated with the basic curriculum. For example, to integrate academics with children's projects and activities, fifth grade teacher Patricia Doyle at Pine Grove Elementary in St. Petersburg, Florida, taught a Family Recipe classroom project. The project included third, fourth, and fifth grade students in an activity that also involved their extended family members. Doyle wanted the students to learn about their ancestors and their ethnicity by producing cookbooks made up of family favorite recipes. The project covered many skills in many subjects: social studies, writing, technology, reading, research, speaking and presentation, math, and science.[13]

Technology Use and Integration.   Children are different today from a decade ago because of new and different kinds of technology.[14] Today's generation is the "dot-com" or Net Generation. They have grown up surrounded by technology and are familiar and comfortable with it. Children's involvement with computer games enables them to think abstractly and to make rapid-fire decisions. About three fourths (77 percent) of homes in the United States have Internet access.[15] This connectivity enables children to have almost immediate access to vast amounts of information that enrich their lives and learning. Also, consider how the use of cell phones and text messaging change the way children communicate. Here is how two third graders texted with each other about a school project:

Student 1: do u wanna b partners for the project?

Student 2: yeah. txt me later. doin chores.

Because today's children are immersed in technology, you need to find many opportunities to integrate technology into their learning activities. Provide opportunities for children to access the Internet, use digital cameras to gather information and document learning, create and transport reports on the Internet, and engage in electronic creativity discussions and the sharing of ideas.

Just as not all of your children have access to the Internet, so, too, will not all of your children have the same access to technology. Making sure children have access to technology is an important factor when designing a classroom environment and planning curricula that promotes learning and motivation. You have to provide opportunities for children who don't have or use technology at home to have technology opportunities in your classroom.

Health and Wellness.   Physical education at all levels is undergoing a renaissance. One reason for its rejuvenation, especially in the primary and elementary grades, is the concern about the national epidemic of childhood obesity and increases in childhood diabetes.[16] Physical education classes and programs are viewed as a way of providing children with the knowledge and activities they need to get in shape and stay that way for the rest of their lifetimes.

Ongoing Political and Educational Changes.   What politicians and lawmakers believe is best for children and how to teach them changes with every state and national election. Changes in politics in turn change how we teach children and what we teach them. For the past decade, politicians have placed a major emphasis on standards and academic achievement. The No Child Left Behind Act of 2001 (NCLB) focused teaching and learning on meeting state, and now the CCS standards, especially in reading and math. Today there is a great emphasis on getting all students **college and career ready** (CCR), and this process begins in grades one, two, and three.

As a result of what we have discussed, you must look at teaching in grades one to three differently from how you would approach preschool and kindergarten education. You will want to consider new and appropriate approaches for teaching in these three important grades.

college and career ready
The content knowledge and skills students need to be successful in all future endeavors.

WHAT ARE CHILDREN LIKE IN GRADES ONE THROUGH THREE?

All children share common developmental characteristics, yet each child is a unique individual. Although the common characteristics of children guide our general practice of teaching, we still must always account for the individual needs of children.

Portraits of Children

We have discussed a lot of information about the curriculum and environments of the primary grades, but what about the children? Classrooms and programs are for the children, and we must always remember that children are the reason we teach. On the following pages are portraits of first, second, and third grade children ages seven, eight, and nine for you to review. As you read these, reflect about how you would teach each one in your classroom.

Physical Development

Two words describe the physical growth of primary age children: *slow* and *steady*. Children at this age experience continual growth, develop increasing control over their bodies, and explore the things they are able to do.

From ages six to nine, children's average weight and height approximate each other, as shown in Table 10.1. The weight of boys and girls tends to be the same until about age nine, when girls pull ahead of boys in both height and weight. Wide variations appear in both individual rates of growth and development and among the sizes of individual children. These differences in physical appearance result from genetic and cultural factors, nutritional intake and habits, health care, and experiential background. In the "Portraits of Children" compare and contrast the development of primary grade children in all the domains.

The primary years are also a time to use and test developing motor skills. Children's growing confidence and physical skills are reflected in games involving running, chasing, and kicking. A nearly universal characteristic of children in this period is their almost constant physical activity.

Differences between boys' and girls' motor skills during the primary years are minimal; their abilities are about equal. Therefore, you should not use gender as a basis for limiting boys' or girls' involvement in activities. Children in the primary grades are also more proficient at school tasks that require fine-motor skills, such as writing, making artwork, and using computers. In addition, primary-age children want to and are able to engage in real-life activities. They want the "real thing." In many ways this makes teaching them easier and more fun, since many activities have real-life applications.

TABLE 10.1 Average Heights and Weights for Primary-Age Children

Conduct your own survey of the height and weight of primary-age children. Compare your findings with this table. What conclusions can you draw?

| Age | Males | | Females | |
	Height (inches)	Weight (pounds)	Height (inches)	Weight (pounds)
6 years	46.00	46.00	46.00	47.00
7 years	48.00	51.00	48.00	52.00
8 years	51.00	55.00	50.00	58.00
9 years	53.00	62.00	52.00	64.00

Note: Remember that averages are just that—averages. Children are different because of their individual differences. Ongoing growth and development tend to accentuate these differences.
Source: Based on information from Family Practice Notebook, "Height Measurement in Children," 2012; accessed March 8, 2012, at www.fpnotebook.com/endo/exam.

Portraits of First, Second, and Third Graders

	Samantha	Blake	Jamee	Jacob
General Description	• 9-year-old Caucasian female • Loves music, her heritage, and drawing • Youngest of two children	• 9-year-old Caucasian male • Loves Legos®, *Star Wars*, and telling imaginative stories • Youngest of two children	• 8-year-old African American female • Well-spoken and great sense of humor • Interested in music and art • Lives with both parents and younger sister (2 years) • One of the tallest students in her class	• 7-year-old Hispanic male • Great sense of humor; laughs at himself • An only child • Loves music, trains, drawing, and writing
Social/ Emotional	• Is aware of others' feelings and is empathetic toward them; often helps others solve problems • Expresses ideas clearly and likes to be part of the group • Asks questions in order to understand social situations and be a better problem solver • Likes to process her thinking before making a decision when it comes to a social situation	• Has difficulty expressing his feelings and often acts out when anxious or upset • Wants to play with all of his classmates but is unsure how to approach them • Would rather work independently in a secluded part of the classroom • Once he talks about what is bothering him with an adult, he is able to return to regular activities	• Friendly and outgoing • Has many friends • Often mediates disputes during recess • Empathetic	• Makes friends; keeping friendships is very important to him • Emotionally sensitive, seeks approval, easily hurt • Does not respond well to criticism • Interacts equally well with boys and girls, but appears to prefer engaging with girls
Cognitive	• Can concentrate on a single task for 30 minutes or more • Though she needs to be pushed to read more "just right" books, enjoys reading • Can solve complex math problems by breaking down the problem solving process	• Can concentrate on a single task for 5 minutes and benefits from one-on-one support to make sure he is on task and understand directions • Benefits from concepts being modeled and then guided practice before being able to work on an assignment independently	• Reads on grade level with good comprehension • Initially had trouble writing for sustained periods of time • Some challenges with basic math concepts, but perseveres	• Reads on grade level with good comprehension • Writing is at grade level • Admits that he is challenged by mathematics, but grades are of average performance

	• Enjoys learning new things and facing challenges in her academic work	• Can complete 1- by 2-digit multiplication problems but might need a visual of the process before beginning • Can tell vivid stories but needs a scribe to write them down		
Motor	• Can balance on one foot with ease • Has fantastic hand-eye coordination • Can grasp a pencil and write in cursive or print neatly • Skillfully uses a computer mouse and keyboard controls	• Has difficulty sitting straight in a chair, as he often leans over • Has difficulty sitting in one place for lengthy periods of time; taps or swings feet frequently • Uses simple combinations of movements such as running or jumping • Skillfully uses a mouse and keyboard	• Strong fine motor skills • Participates in all physical education activities	• Performs average on gross- and fine-motor skills, but still is unable to tie shoelaces • Participates in group games • Participates in all school activities
Adaptive (Daily Living)	• Independent about getting materials and is always willing to help put materials away that were left behind • Polite and gracious when talking to people and is a good listener • Is flexible with routines and schedules	• Needs organizational support in order to keep track of his learning materials • Has a great sense of humor and wants to make others happy • Is unaware that his behaviors might distract others and often needs a reminder of this • Benefits from a consistent schedule	• Responds well to praise • Is a responsible student; comes to school with necessary materials • Is well groomed • Attentive in class and an active participant	• Responds well to praise • Comes to school with necessary materials • Obeys class and school rules • Has a specific sense of style (hats and vests)
	• Has a positive attitude about learning and life, enjoying creative experiences	• Participating more in class discussions and taking more risks, especially when explaining his thoughts and feelings to others		

Source: Contributed by PS 124, Brooklyn, New York, Annabell Martinez, principal.

One of the foundational tenants of early childhood education is that each child is a unique individual. As early childhood professionals, we celebrate and value children's individuality. We dedicate ourselves to teaching to the individuality of each child. The authentic and real life portraits of Samantha, Blake, Jamee, and Jacob are designed to illustrate how unique children are. Read about and reflect on each child individually. Consider how you would respond to and teach each child.

(continued)

Portraits of First, Second, and Third Graders (Continued)

Questions:

- Today, a national goal is to have all children read on grade level by grade three. Samantha has to be "pushed" to read more of the right kind of books. What kind of "right" books would you recommend for Samantha? How would you differentiate and accommodate her reading instruction?
- Based on his brief portrait, what kind of learning "problems" does Blake have? What can you do to help Blake from "acting out"? Extend the length of time he can concentrate on a topic? Sitting in one place for a length of time?
- Consider that Jamee has some "challenges" with basic math concepts. What can you do to help ensure that young girls like Jamee do not develop math anxiety and instead enjoy and do well in math?
- Three of the children—Samantha, Jamee and Jacob—enjoy music. Give two examples for how you can incorporate music and the arts in your teaching to promote children's learning.

Maturity in the Primary Grades.   Although we refer to early childhood education as the years from birth to age eight, the primary grades, one through three, represent, in many ways, a divide in early childhood development. The primary grades are a period in which children are undergoing dramatic developmental change. Primary-age children, while still children in many ways, are entering faster into the "tween" years or preadolescence than in previous decades. In third grade you will notice more evidence of the early onset of puberty, especially in girls. Growing up fast can be attributed in part to **puberty**, the period of profound physical and emotional developmental changes in the transition from childhood to adolescence. Health professionals attribute the early onset of puberty to lack of sound nutritional habits, childhood obesity (diet, especially consumption of meat and dairy products that contain hormones and industrial chemicals), and family genetics.[17]

puberty The period of profound physical and emotional developmental changes in the transition from childhood to adolescence.

The physical changes that accompany puberty can be confusing and traumatic for young girls, especially when they do not understand what is happening. This is where you will have to work closely with parents to help them educate their children about their children's developmental changes, and at the same time, you will have to collaborate with parents to help them understand their children's health and development and the emotional repercussions associated with it. Of course the amount and kind of developmental information you provide depends on your school's policy regarding developmental topics. So, make sure you are well informed about what you can and cannot say and teach.

Today, there is a greater emphasis on children's cognitive development and activities that promote reading, math, and science. What are some things you can do to help children be successful in these areas?

Social Development

Children in grades one to three (ages six through nine) are in Erikson's industry versus inferiority stage of social-emotional development. This period is a time when children gain confidence and ego satisfaction from completing challenging tasks. Children want to act responsibly and are quite capable of achieving demanding tasks and accomplishments, and they take a lot of pride in doing well. All of this reflects the "industry" aspect of social-emotional development.

Children during this stage are at varying levels of academic achievement. Those who are high in academic self-esteem credit their success to **mastery-oriented attributions** such as trying hard (industriousness), paying attention, determination, and stick-to-itiveness. If children have difficulty completing a task, they believe that by trying harder they will succeed.

At the same time, children in this stage compare their abilities and accomplishments to their those of their peers. When they perceive that they are not doing as well as they can or as well as their peers, they may lose confidence in their abilities and achievement. This is the "inferiority" side of this stage of social-emotional development. Some children attribute their failures to a lack of ability and develop **learned helplessness**, in which they learn through repeated failure to behave helplessly. This is where you can be helpful and supportive of children, providing them with tasks they can accomplish and encouraging them to do their best.

Here are some things you can do to accomplish this goal:

- Provide activities children can reasonably accomplish so they can experience the satisfaction that comes from a job well done.
- Apply Gardner's theory of multiple intelligences to your teaching. Let children excel at things they are good at. All children develop skills and abilities in particular areas. Build a classroom environment that enables children to be competent in their particular intelligence.
- Be supportive and encouraging of children's efforts. For example: "Good job, Carol! See what great work you can do when you really try!"

Emotional Development

Think for a moment about how important emotions are in your life and how emotions influence what and how you learn. When you are happy, life goes well! When you are sad, it is harder to get enthused about doing what you have to do. The children you teach are no different. Emotions are an important part of children's everyday lives. One of your responsibilities is to help them develop positive emotions and to express their emotions in healthy ways.

The following activities give you specific ideas for how to support the positive social-emotional development of children in the industry versus inferiority stage of development:

1. *Use literature to discuss emotions.* Children in grades one to three like to talk about their emotions and the emotions of characters in literature. They are able to make emotional inferences about characters' emotional states and discuss how they are or are not appropriate to the story. They can then relate these emotional states to their own lives and to events at home and in the classroom. Some good books to use to discuss emotional states include these:

   - *How Are You Peeling? Foods with Moods* by Saxton Freymann and Joost Elffers offers brief text and photographs of carvings made from vegetables that introduce the world of emotions by presenting leading questions such as "Are you feeling angry?"
   - *Today I Feel Silly, & Other Moods That Make My Day* by Jamie Lee Curtis follows a little girl with curly red hair through thirteen different moods, including silly, grumpy, mean, excited, and confused.
   - *When Sophie Gets Angry . . . Really, Really Angry* by Molly Bang conveys young Sophie's anger when her mother allows her younger sister to play with her stuffed gorilla, the eventual calm she feels after running outside and crying, and the calm and relaxed return home.

mastery-oriented attributions Personal characteristics that include trying hard, paying attention, determination, and stick-to-itiveness.

learned helplessness A condition that can develop when children lose confidence in their abilities and, in effect, learn to feel that they are helpless.

2. ***Encourage children to express their emotions.*** Beginning and ending the day with a classroom meeting discussion is a good way to help children express their thoughts and feelings. This provides children a safe and secure outlet to say how they felt during their day. Also, begin every day with a morning meeting. You can ask children for their joys and concerns, which provide the context for them to freely discuss their feelings.

3. ***Write about feelings.*** Give children opportunities to keep journals in which they write about home, family life, classroom events, and how they feel about them. One teacher has her children create word clouds, which they share with her and with their classmates if they choose. Cassie, Mario, and Emily collaborated and used Wordle to develop a word cloud in response to their reading of Jamie Lee Curtis's book, *Today I Feel Silly, & Other Moods That Make My Day* (Figure 10.1).

4. ***Provide for cultural differences.*** Be aware of how various cultures express emotions. Some cultures are very emotive, whereas others are not. Work with parents to learn how their cultures express certain emotions, such as joy and sadness, and what are culturally acceptable and unacceptable ways to express emotions.

Mental Health in Early Childhood.   Just as we are concerned about the mental health of children from birth to age six, so, too, are we concerned about the mental health of children in the middle years. We are particularly concerned about **childhood depression**. Two and a half percent of children are diagnosed with depression.[18] Childhood depression manifests itself in the following ways:

> Persistent sadness; withdrawal from family, friends, and activities that they once enjoyed; increased irritability or agitation; changes in eating and sleeping habits (e.g., significant weight loss, insomnia, excessive sleep); may complain of feeling sick; refuse to go to school; cling to a parent or caregiver; or worry excessively that a parent may die.[19]

Children's good mental health begins at home and continues in your classroom. Part of your role is to work with parents to promote their children's mental health and

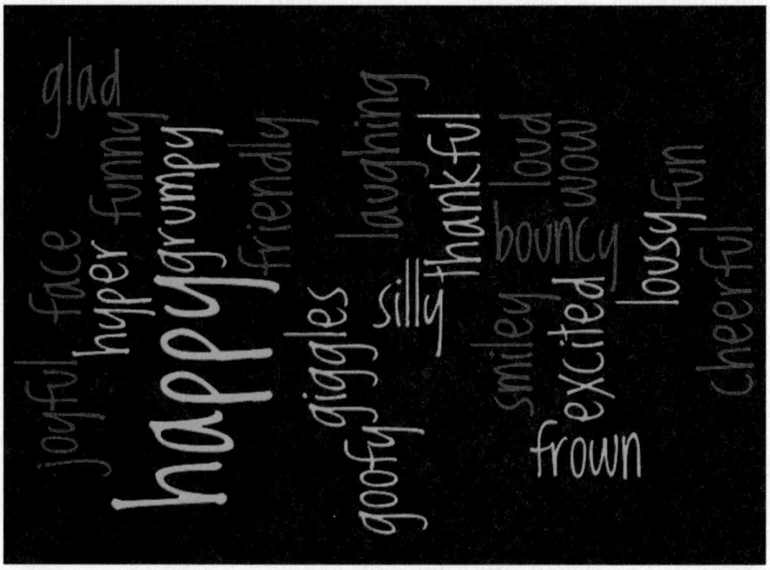

childhood depression A disorder affecting as many as one in thirty-three children that can negatively impact feelings, thoughts, and behavior and can manifest itself with physical symptoms of illness.

FIGURE 10.1 Journal Entry

Today's students want to use technology and unique programs to write, express themselves, and be creative. Programs such as Wordle, which lets students develop word clouds, provide them with an alternative way of expressing their thoughts and feelings.

to support children's good mental health in your classroom. In your work and collaboration with parents, here are some things you can advise parents to do:

- **Encourage children to play.** Play time is as important to a child's development as food. Play helps a child be creative, develop problem-solving skills and self-control, and learn how to get along with others.
- **Enroll children in an after-school activity, especially if they are otherwise home alone after school.** This is a great way for children to stay productive, learn something new, gain self-esteem, and have something to look forward to during the week.
- **Provide a safe and secure home environment.** Fear can be very real for a child. Try to find out what is frightening him or her. Be loving, patient, and reassuring, not critical.
- **Give appropriate guidance and discipline when necessary.** Be firm, but kind and realistic with your expectations. The goal is not to control the child, but to help him or her learn self-control.
- **Communicate.** Parents need to make time each day after work and school to listen to their children, talk with them about what is happening in their lives, and share emotions and feelings.[20]

In your teaching of young children, here are some things you can do:

- **Create a sense of classroom belonging.** Feeling connected and welcomed is essential to children's positive adjustment, self-identification, and sense of trust in others and themselves.
- **Promote resilience.** Adversity is a natural part of life and being resilient is important to overcoming challenges and good mental health. Connectedness, competency, helping others, and successfully facing difficult situations all foster resilience.
- **Develop competencies.** Children need to know that they can overcome challenges and accomplish goals through their actions. Achieving academic success and developing individual talents and interests helps children feel competent and more able to deal positively with stress.
- **Ensure a positive, safe classroom and school environment.** Feeling safe is critical to students' learning and mental health. Promote positive behaviors such as respect, responsibility, and kindness. Prevent negative behaviors such as bullying and harassment.
- **Teach and reinforce positive behaviors and decision making.** Provide consistent expectations and support. Teach social skills, problem solving, and conflict resolution, which are supporters of good mental health.
- **Encourage helping others.** Children need to know that they can make a difference. Pro-social behaviors build self-esteem, foster connectedness, reinforce personal responsibility, and present opportunities for positive recognition.
- **Encourage good physical health.** Good physical health supports good mental health.[21]

Cognitive Development

Concrete operational thought is the cognitive milestone that enables children in the primary elementary grades to think and act as they do. Children in the *concrete operations stage*, from about age seven to about age twelve, begin to use mental images and symbols during the thinking process and can reverse operations. For example, operations include many mathematical activities involving addition and subtraction, greater than and less than, multiplication, division, and equalities. A child is able to reverse operations when she can understand that when, for example, she adds two to three to get five, she can reverse this operation by subtracting two from five to get three. This is why it is a good idea for you to use concrete materials (e.g., rods, beads, buttons, blocks) to help children physically see operations as an aid for mental representation.

Concrete operational children begin to develop the ability to understand that change involving physical appearances does not necessarily change quality or quantity. They also begin to reverse thought processes by going back over and "undoing" a mental action just accomplished. Other mental operations children are capable of during this stage include:

- *One-to-one correspondence.* One-to-one correspondence is the basis for counting and matching objects. The concrete operations child has mastered the ability, for example, to give an iPod from the technology cart to each member of her work group.
- *Classification of events and time according to their occurrence.* For example, a child in the concrete operations stage can classify events as occurring before or after lunch.
- *Classification involving multiple properties.* Multiple classifications occurs when a child can classify objects on the basis of more than one property such as color and size, shape and size, shape and color, and so forth.
- *Seriation.* This is the ordering of people, objects, or events. For example, Mandy developed a chart showing the heights of children in her class from shortest to tallest.
- *Class inclusion operations.* Class inclusion also involves classification. For example, if you showed five apples, five oranges, and five lemons to a child in the concrete operations stage and asked him if there were more apples or fruit, he would be able to respond "fruit."

The process of development from the preoperational stage to the concrete stage is gradual and continual and occurs over a period of time as a result of maturation and experiences. No simple sets of exercises will cause children to move up the developmental ladder. Rather, ongoing developmentally appropriate activities lead to conceptual understanding.

Moral Development

moral development The process of developing culturally acceptable attitudes and behaviors, based on what society endorses and supports as right and wrong.

Moral development is the process of developing culturally acceptable attitudes and behaviors toward others and the environment based on what society endorses and supports through rules, laws, and cultural norms as right and wrong.

Jean Piaget and Lawrence Kohlberg are the leading proponents of a developmental stage theory of children's moral development. Table 10.2 outlines their stages of moral development during ages six to ten. Implicit to children's moral development is the process of moving or developing from what is known as "other regulation" (by parents, teachers, etc.) to self-regulation. Review Table 10.2 now and consider how you can apply the implications of this information to your teaching.

Character Education.   Character education is closely aligned with pro-social and conflict resolution education and is now a high priority for all early childhood educators. Character education is rapidly becoming a part of many early childhood programs. Character education activities designed to teach specific character traits are now commonplace in the curriculum of the primary grades. The three R's have been expanded to the six R's: reading, writing, arithmetic, respect, responsibility, and reasoning. Respect, responsibility, and reasoning are now part of the primary curriculum because the public believes children not only have to learn *how* to count, they also believe schools must teach children *what* counts.

TABLE 10.2 Moral Development in the Primary Years

Theorist	Moral Stage and Characteristics	Implications for Teachers
Jean Piaget	1. *Relations of Constraint: Grades 1–2* Concepts of right and wrong are determined by judgments of adults. Therefore morality is based on what adults say is right and wrong.	• Provide children with many opportunities to engage in decision making and make decisions about what is right and wrong.
	2. *Relations of Cooperation: Grades 3–6* Children's exchange of viewpoints with others helps determine what is good/bad and right/wrong.	• Provide opportunities every day for children to make decisions and assume responsibilities. Responsibility comes from opportunities to be responsible.
Lawrence Kohlberg	1. *Preconventional Level: Ages 4–10* Morality is a matter of good or bad based on a system of punishment and reward as administered by adults in authority positions.	• Provide many examples of moral behavior and decisions. Use children's literature to help you achieve this goal.
	• *Stage 1. Punishment and obedience* Children operate within and respond to consequences of behavior.	• Use children's out-of-classroom experiences as a basis for discussion involving values and decision making.
	• *Stage 2. Instrumental–relativist orientation* Children's actions are motivated by satisfaction of needs ("You scratch my back, I'll scratch yours").	• Provide children many opportunities to interact with children of different ages and cultures.

Some common character traits taught in the primary grades are responsibility, cooperation, respect for others, compassion, self-discipline, tolerance, courage, friendship, optimism, honesty, perseverance, future-mindedness, and purposefulness.

ENVIRONMENTS THAT SUPPORT LEARNING IN THE PRIMARY GRADES

Environments play a major role in children's learning and success and are also a major determinant of what and how well children learn. Classrooms not only support children's learning, but they also help ensure that all children learn to their full capacities. Use these features to help you provide the best learning environment possible for all children.

The Physical Environment

The following conditions support learning in the primary classroom:

- Materials are in abundant supply for reading, writing, language development, and content area development (e.g., books about math, science, social studies, and the arts).
- Learning centers reflect content areas.
- Children are seated in chairs at tables or in clusters of desks for roughly three to six children.
- Literature of all genres supports content area learning centers, and materials provide for and emulate real work experiences (i.e., the waiting room, the restaurant).
- Materials and instruction provide for interdisciplinary integrated approaches.
- Program, learning, and environment are coordinated so that materials support and align with outcomes and standards.

- Teacher instruction (teacher-directed instruction and intentional teaching) and active student involvement are balanced.
- Centers support literacy. All centers have materials that support reading and writing.
- Children's products are displayed and valued.
- Schedules are posted where children can read them.
- Technology supports and enriches basic skill and concept learning. Children use technology to make presentations, projects, and reports.

The Social Environment

The following conditions support an enriching emotional and social environment:

- Families, other adults, and the community are connected to classroom learning.
- Children are valued and respected. The classroom is a community of learners.
- Children live and learn in peace and harmony.
- High expectations for all are an essential part of the classroom culture.
- Assessment is continuous and appropriate and is designed to support teaching and learning.
- Thinking is considered a basic skill and is integrated through all areas of the curriculum.

Environments That Support Pro-Social and Conflict Resolution Education

All early childhood professionals, parents, and politicians believe that efforts to reduce incidents of violence and uncivil behavior begin in the early years. Consequently, they place emphasis on teaching children the fundamentals of peaceful living, kindness, helpfulness, and cooperation. Follow these suggestions to foster the development of pro-social skills in your classroom:

- ***Be a good role model for children.*** Demonstrate in your life and relationships with children and other adults the behaviors of cooperation and kindness that you want to encourage in children. Civil behavior begins with courtesy and manners. You can model these and help children do the same.
- ***Provide positive feedback and reinforcement when children perform pro-social behaviors.*** When you reward children for appropriate behavior, they tend to repeat the behavior. ("I like how you helped Jake. I'll bet that made him feel better.")
- ***Provide opportunities for children to help and show kindness to others.*** For example, cooperative programs between your children and eldercare homes and other community agencies are excellent opportunities to practice kind and helping behaviors.
- ***Conduct conflict-free classroom routines and activities.*** Provide opportunities for children to work together and practice skills for cooperative living. Design learning centers and activities for children to share and work cooperatively.
- ***Provide practice in conflict resolution skills.*** Classroom exercises here include taking turns, talking through problems, compromising, and working out problems.
- ***Use examples from literature to make your point.*** Read stories to children that exemplify pro-social behaviors and provide such literature for them to read.
- ***Counsel and work with parents.*** Encourage them to limit or eliminate altogether their children's watching violence on television, attending R-rated movies, playing video games with violent content, and buying CDs with objectionable lyrics.

- **Catch children "doing good."** Help children feel good about themselves, build strong self-images, and be competent individuals. Notice when children behave pro-socially and tell them that you are pleased with their actions. Children who are happy, confident, and competent feel good about themselves and are more likely to behave positively toward others.

TEACHING AND LEARNING IN THE INCLUSIVE CLASSROOM: DIFFERENTIATED INSTRUCTION

Differentiated instruction is an approach to teaching and learning for students of differing abilities in the same class. All classes have differing abilities. The intent of differentiating instruction is to maximize each student's growth and individual success, meet each student where he or she is, and assist the child in the learning process.

There is no single set of strategies that constitutes differentiated instruction. Instead, the practice rests on principles that require you to continuously assess students and adjust instruction accordingly. In a class where the teacher differentiates instruction, she or he frequently rotates students into small groups based on demonstrated knowledge, interest, and/or learning style preferences. The teacher then targets instruction to the needs of each group with the aim of moving all students toward high levels of achievement. A differentiated classroom is a dynamic environment where students move in and out of learning groups based on achievement data, interests, and learning styles.

When you give directions in a differentiated classroom, start the class with a small task, such as a review question or skill practice, and then meet with one small group at a time to provide specific directions for each group. Write out directions for each group. Have the directions on the group's table or cluster at the beginning of the class or include the directions at a learning center or with a packet of learning materials that the students select. Then, use group lessons, activities, or graphic organizers to introduce concepts to the entire class before expecting small groups to work independently with a new concept or skill.

Teaching Practices

A lot of change has occurred in the primary grades, with more on the way. One of the more dramatic changes is the integration of early childhood education and special education. As a result, instructional practices are blending and those used by special educators are now routinely used in all primary grade programs.

Another dramatic change is the widespread use of technology to facilitate teaching and learning. Students routinely have access to and use a wide variety of technological devices. Increasingly content comes from the Internet. Classrooms and whole school districts do use textbooks, but increasing numbers are electronic textbooks.[22]

Intentional Teaching.   Intentional teaching is the process of teaching children the skills they need for success. Letter grades and report cards are still very popular, although narrative reports (in which professionals describe and report on student achievement), checklists (which describe the competencies students have demonstrated), parent conferences, portfolios containing samples of children's work, and other tools for reporting achievement are being used to supplement letter grades.

Developmentally Appropriate Practice in the Primary Grades

As early childhood professionals, we devote a lot of attention to, and place a great deal of emphasis on developmentally appropriate practice, especially with infants, toddlers,

applying research to practice

Does Class Size Make a Difference?

Class size is one of the variables in American education that the public, politicians, and teachers believe influences student learning outcomes. At least twenty-four states, including my state of Texas, have mandated class size limits in the public schools. In Texas, the maximum class size in grades K–4 is twenty-two students (22:1). However, as a result of the Great Recession, many states, including Texas, have honored school district requests for exceptions to the maximum class size. As a result, many teachers find themselves with two to three more students in their classes. In one study of class size, conducted in Tennessee, class size was reduced by seven students to an overall class size of twenty-two. As a result, there was an increase of student achievement equivalent to three additional months of schooling over a four-year period.[23] Similar studies have also found achievement benefits to reducing class size. However, other studies have found mixed achievement effects or no achievement effects at all as a result of class size reduction. Class size reduction seems to have its greatest benefits for disadvantaged students in the early grades. It is likely that given the current economic climate in the United States class size will creep up by one to three students per class over the next few years and, as teachers and school administrators know, once class size is increased, it is difficult to reduce because of funding and other resource issues.

So, what does this mean for you?

1. Research is clear that teachers matter and that children who have highly effective teachers achieve at higher levels than those who don't. You should do everything you can to be a highly effective teacher and to do the best you can to teach each child.
2. Research is also clear that regardless of class size, if teachers don't make productive use of classroom time and student involvement, then class size reduction has no benefits.

3. Make the best use of students' time to maximize learning. Engage students productively in learning activities throughout the entire school day.
4. Have high expectations for your children. When children believe that their teachers respect and value them, they achieve at higher levels than those children who believe their teachers don't care about them.[24] Always remember that student–teacher relations matter.

CURRICULUM IN THE PRIMARY GRADES

The curriculum content of grades one, two, and three is pretty much determined by the Common Core Standards and state and local standards. Take a few minutes now to review the CCS and the standards for grades one, two, or three in your state by using the link in the Linking to Learning section. The Common Core Standards for first grade reading, second grade math, and third grade reading and writing are shown in Figure 10.2.

The ways teachers help children achieve standards are many and varied. Teachers and children develop projects, write and put on plays, go on field trips, attend community events such as festivals and symphony orchestras, prepare for and hold arts and crafts exhibits, develop and update Web pages, and prepare for and take state exams. In other words, teaching in grades one, two, and three is fun, challenging, hard work, but worth the effort! A parent describes third grade teacher Robert Stephenson, Michigan Teacher of the Year, this way:

Mr. Stephenson creates an environment where the students thrive and enjoy education. He has the ability to make students feel great about themselves and their work. Mr. Stephenson makes learning fun by incorporating an extraordinary array of hands-on experiences. The kids love it, and more importantly— they learn![25]

preschoolers, and kindergarteners. However, my observing and participating in grade one to grade three classrooms leads me to wonder if there may be a tendency to believe that once children enter first grade, and as they progress through the primary grades, there is less of a need to consider the role of developmentally appropriate practices in teaching. Unfortunately, academics can get in the way.

Part of your knowledge base as a teacher of primary grade children is to know child development and how the development of first, second, and third graders affects their learning and your teaching. Developmental knowledge is essential for you to understand children and to conduct appropriate instructional practices. However, developmentally appropriate practice goes far beyond mere knowledge of how children develop.

First Grade Reading	Second Grade Math	Third Grade Reading	Third Grade Writing
• Ask and answer questions about key details in a text • Identify words and phrases in stories or poems that suggest feelings or appeal to the senses • Use illustrations and details to describe characters, setting, or events • With prompting and support, read prose and poetry of appropriate complexity for grade one	• Represent and solve problems involving addition and subtraction • Understand place value • Measure and estimate lengths in standard units • Reason with shapes and their attributes	• Ask and answer questions to demonstrate understanding of a text, referring to the text as basis for answers • Determine the meaning of general academic and domain-specific words and phrases in a relevant text • Use information gained from illustrations and the words in a text to demonstrate understanding of the text	• Write opinion pieces on topics or texts, supporting a point of view with reasons • Write informative/explanatory texts to examine a topic and convey ideas and information clearly • Write narratives to develop real or imagined experiences or events using effective technique, descriptive details, and clear event sequences • Write routinely over extended time frames and shorter time frames for a range of discipline-specific tasks, purposes, and audiences

FIGURE 10.2 Common Core Standards: Grades 1–3

For example, one of the cornerstones of developmentally practice is *intentionality*, being intentional in everything you do, from creating enriched environments, to planning and collaborating with your colleagues, to assessing children, and differentiating and accommodating programs and projects to meet their learning needs. Intentional teaching is purposeful and thoughtful and is directed toward helping students achieve Common Core Standards, state standards, and local standards.

Literacy and Reading in the Primary Grades

Just like preschool and kindergarten programs, today's primary grades emphasize literacy development, reading, and math. In fact, this emphasis is apparent in all the elementary grades, from pre-K to grade six. Parents and society want children who can speak, write, read well, and compute. More teachers use a balanced approach to reading. They integrate many different activities into a complete system of literacy development. For example, here are some things you can do as a teacher:

• Use the fundamentals of letter–sound correspondence, word study, and decoding, as well as many literacy activities, to involve children in reading, writing, speaking, and listening.

• Incorporate many reading approaches, such as shared reading, guided reading (discussed next), independent reading, and modeled reading (reading aloud).

- Use many forms of writing, such as shared writing, guided writing, and independent writing.
- Integrate literacy across the curriculum; for example, students write in journals or composition books about their experiences and investigations in math and science. Children write daily for different purposes. They write creative stories, answers to math word problems, personal narratives, journal entries, scientific observations, research reports, and responses to literature. They write fiction in different genres such as fables, poetry, and science fiction.
- Integrate literacy across cultures. That is, use technology to communicate with and about people in other cultures.
- Use children's written documents as reading material, as well as literature books, vocabulary-controlled and sentence-controlled stories, and those containing predictable language patterns. Choose the best children's literature available to read to and with children.
- Organize literacy instruction around themes or units of study relevant to students.
- Have children create stories, write letters, keep personal journals, and share their written documents with others.

Guided Reading.   Guided reading is designed to help children develop and use strategies of independent reading and become good readers. Teachers provide support for small groups of readers as they learn to use various reading strategies (context clues, letter–sound relationships, word structure, and so forth).

The accompanying Professionalism in Practice feature, "How to Implement a Successful Guided Reading Program," helps you learn how to implement guided reading with your children.

Math in the Primary Grades

Today's math curriculum focuses on hands-on activities, problem solving, group work and relevancy to real life. Notice how the teacher in this **video** incorporates these ideas into her math lesson.

Teachers are reemphasizing mathematics as an essential part of primary education. Just as reading is receiving a great deal of national attention, so too is mathematics. Some call this reemphasizing of mathematics the "new-new math," which emphasizes hands-on activities, problem solving, group work and teamwork, application and use of mathematical ideas and principles to real-life events, daily use of mathematics, and an understanding of and use of math understandings and competencies. The new math seeks to have students be creative users of math in life and workplace settings but also includes the ability to recall addition sums and multiplication products quickly. The accompanying Professionalism in Practice feature "Bright Ideas for Teaching Math," will help you.

Science in the Primary Grades

With a national emphasis on testing children in math and science, some critics of public schools contend that teachers spend too little time teaching science. They argue that children should receive high quality science teaching and learning opportunities. One way schools are responding is by increasing opportunities for children to participate in science fairs and other organized activities designed to promote science teaching and learning.

At the Science Fair.   It is very common for children in the primary grades to participate in school-based and local science fairs. Science fairs promote and support the STEM subjects in the primary grades and provide children with opportunities to be involved in STEM activities involving scientific thinking, exploring STEM activities in depth, and engaging in hands-on/minds-on learning. Science fair activities are a good way for children to explore areas that are of interest to them and to put the scientific method into practice. Science fair entries are usually in the form of a display or

How to Implement a Successful Guided Reading Program

WHY SHOULD I TEACH GUIDED READING?

Guided reading is essential for all students, not just for beginning readers. Unfortunately, students come into third grade with gaps in their learning, and it is your responsibility to fill those gaps. It is critical for you to realize that a student's grade level is not the same as his instructional level; therefore, it is impossible to teach all students on the same level.

Guided reading is a very effective way to differentiate classroom instruction and meet the needs of all students. It allows you time to accelerate and provide strategic interventions for students who are reading below grade level, and at the same time, allows students who are reading above grade level the opportunity to reach their full potential and not be held back by struggling readers. Guided reading is a great way to motivate and help all students be good readers.

HOW OFTEN SHOULD I TEACH GUIDED READING?

You should teach guided reading every day. Schedule forty-five minutes daily, which allows you to meet with three groups each day for fifteen minutes. It is imperative that you meet with struggling readers daily in order to reinforce skills. Students who are reading above grade level can work much more independently with less need for direct instruction, so meet with this group once a week in order to monitor progress and provide feedback. The rest of your time is divided between a couple of groups who are reading on grade level. Table 10.3 shows a guided reading schedule that will help you be organized and stay on track.

HOW DO I GROUP STUDENTS FOR GUIDED READING?

When setting up guided reading groups, know and understand where your students are in their learning journey. Grouping the below-grade-level and the above-grade-level students is the easiest because these are usually the most obvious. When grouping the on-level students, consider reading level, classroom performance, and ongoing formal and informal assessment in creating equal-ability groups. It is important for you to understand that groups can and should change throughout the year. As students become more proficient readers, put them in groups with peers of the same ability levels. The goal is that by the end of the year, there will be several groups reading on or above grade level and at a high ability level, and no groups are working below grade level.

HOW CAN I SIMULTANEOUSLY MANAGE GUIDED READING GROUPS AND INDEPENDENT READING GROUPS?

Strong classroom management skills are an essential component of a successful guided reading program in any grade level. Your expectations should be fair and consistent so that students know exactly what your expectations of them are for learning and behavior. Students must know that you will hold them accountable for their time during guided reading. Your guided reading procedures must be taught through direct, intentional instruction and practice. For the first few weeks, you should continuously monitor, compliment on-task behavior, and remind students of expectations.

I believe guided reading is the most effective way to differentiate classroom instruction, motivate and excite children about reading, and help each student master skills enabling them to achieve full potential and become more successful readers.

....

Source: Contributed by Candice M. Bookman, third grade teacher, Lawrence Elementary School, Mesquite Independent School District, Mesquite, Texas.

TABLE 10.3 Example Schedule

	Monday	Tuesday	Wednesday	Thursday	Friday
9:00–9:15	Below-Level Group	Below-Level Group	Below-Level Group	Below-Level Group	Below-Level Group
9:15–9:30	Low Group (on level)	Low Group (on level)	High Group (on level)	Low Group (on level)	Mid Group 2 (on level)
9:30–9:45	Mid Group 1 (on level)	Mid Group 2 (on level)	Mid Group 1 (on level)	Mid Group 1 (on level)	Above-Level Group

professionalism in practice

Bright Ideas for Teaching Math

Albert Einstein once said, "Do not worry about your problems with mathematics, I assure you mine are far greater." If it is true that one of the most intellectually gifted men in recent history had trouble with math, is it any wonder that our children sometimes suffer the same fate? Can it be that learning how to "do" math is such a difficult process that the vast majority of us will struggle and only a select few will go easily into the daunting world of equations, variables, and theorems? My answer to this question is a resounding NO! It is my belief and experience that young children take to math like they do to water. As long as they have guidance and aren't made afraid of the process before they begin it, they will do fine.

I've taught hundreds of students over the past nine years. During that time, the study of math has been an exploration of sorts. I've learned that numbers are like friends. Once you get to know them, they're lots of fun to be around. I do not claim to be an expert in the area of teaching math. I am simply one of many dedicated teachers who understand that in order to learn, children must be free to explore, ask questions, and make mistakes. From personal experience I know there is no greater resource than my fellow teachers. Some of what I'm about to share I've learned from them. Hopefully, these ideas for teaching math will help you and your students in some way.

IDEA 1 Students Must Be Comfortable with Numbers in Order to Use Them

In order to be comfortable with numbers, children must recognize them, understand how they can be used, and have no fear of using them incorrectly. Most adults would agree that making mistakes and messing up occasionally is sometimes the best way to learn. Students will come to you with the idea they simply can't understand math. Your first job is to convince them they *can* and *will* be successful in math.

IDEA 2 Give Students Real-World Problems That Have Meaning for Them

Numbers are better understood when they represent physical things. Whether you're talking about fourteen ducks, thirty-two marbles, or even seven of your friends, numbers have meaning. Give students problems that show this representation. Ask them for a specific "unit" or item they're counting. Their world is full of easy-to use-examples. Take advantage of this and help them relate to what they're learning.

IDEA 3 Practice Is Important!

Young students must be strong in the operations of addition, subtraction, multiplication, and division. To gain strength they must practice whenever the opportunity presents itself. Use the classroom for organized practice. Quizzes, verbal answers to problems, and morning math are all ways to help students get in the necessary repetition. Small group or partner pairs are great for multiplication fact practice. I like to use the down time of waiting in line for student restroom breaks to go over division facts! However you get the practice in, make it efficient and effective.

IDEA 4 Not All Students Learn the Same Way

Today's teachers must employ different techniques to reach all of their students. My students use paper and pencil, flash cards, manipulatives, SmartBoard technology/Internet resources, rap songs, and even YouTube to help them navigate through their study of math. You will know what's best for your students. The important thing to remember is it won't be the same for all of them, and it's up to you to find what works.

IDEA 5 Know What You Want to Accomplish with Your Students and Let It Guide Your Instruction

Like many other teachers, I've been asked to realign my teaching to specifically address Common Core Standards for math. In my opinion, these standards are an excellent way to bring cohesiveness to the different math concepts students are expected to master. Before you begin teaching, know exactly what your students need to accomplish Fully understand the standard you're attempting to meet and plan ahead, giving lots of thought to the activities that will help your students reach the goal. Assess formatively as often as necessary to make sure you're on the right road. Let what you learn *during* teaching guide what you do *while* you're teaching. Remember, learning is rarely a straight and narrow path. You and your students may have to go in several different directions to reach your goal. With input from your students, it's up to you to navigate the course.

I hope these ideas are helpful to you in your career. Always remember, you are a teacher. You change lives. You have the most important job in the world!

Source: Contributed by Nickie A. Blackburn, elementary teacher at Pike Elementary in Kentucky.

accompanying artifacts such as students' experimental journals and materials/apparatus used in their projects. Guidelines for science fair entries include the following:

- Well-identified, stated, and understandable problem
- Hypothesis stating and testing
- Data collection
- Data analysis
- Evidence of scientific thinking
- Conclusions about the research

Part of your role is to encourage all students to engage in science projects. Business and industry are demanding that public schools educate more scientists, especially women. Beginning in kindergarten we have to develop a positive climate for girls to engage in STEM activities and to begin to consider STEM fields as appropriate career paths. In fact, helping children think about and consider careers is part of developmentally appropriate practice.

The accompanying photo shows a science fair winner with the student's winning entry.

Science fair activities enable children to do independent scientific work while collaborating with teachers, family members, and peers. The science fair project also encourages children to think scientifically, act like a scientist, and explore solutions to complex problems.

Girls Need Science, Too.   Girls are underrepresented in science-based careers, especially in engineering, physics, technology, and math. This trajectory of underrepresentation begins in early childhood. Most children, boys and girls alike, are equally interested in science. The problem is how girls are taught and involved in science. The following are some things you can do to encourage and involve girls in science.

- Make sure all children have equal access to science materials and are involved in science experiments and activities.
- Since girls often excel in writing, encourage them to record their research and data collection in a science journal and in electronic format.
- Encourage all students to collaborate online by using blogs, Facebook, Twitter, YouTube, and so on to record and share their learning and the results of their experiments.

Engineering for All.   With the Common Core Standards there is an increasing emphasis on getting children career and college ready. This emphasis on career and college readiness includes and involves children early in STEM activities. In STEM activities there is also an emphasis on involving all children in engineering processes and activities. The process of being involved in engineering is being able to understand and use the engineering design process to solve problems. Figure 10.3 is an illustration of the engineering design process for Engineering is Elementary that you can use with your children.

Arts in the Primary Grades

In the primary grades, the creative arts most often include music, theater, dance, and art. For each of these disciplines you will want to include knowledge, concepts, and themes. Your teaching of the arts should be content based and child centered, and you will want to make sure that you consult your state's content standards for the arts.

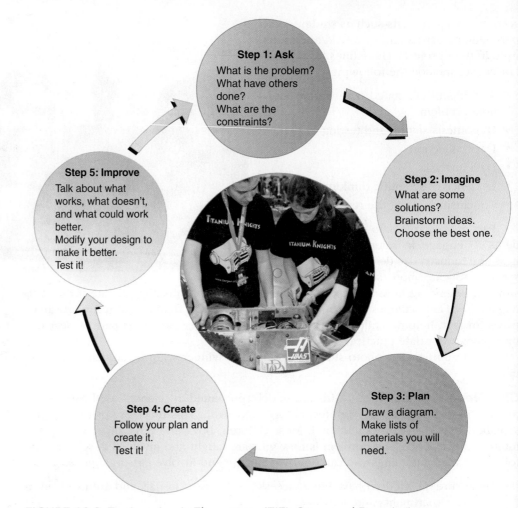

FIGURE 10.3 Engineering is Elementary (EiE): Steps and Descriptions

The engineering design process is a series of steps that engineers use to guide them as they solve problems.

STEAM. The arts are known to promote creativity, and many advocates of the arts today are encouraging the sciences to include arts with STEM to create STEAM. Proponents of such a combination of STEM and the arts argue that this can enhance student learning and promote creative thinking and innovation.

This integration of the arts with STEM is not new to early childhood teachers. They routinely integrate all subjects including the arts, music, and dance across all content areas. Today's teaching of the arts is designed to provide children with content knowledge and skills from the four disciplines of music, theater, dance, and art. So, in your teaching of the arts you will want to make sure that children are provided with authentic content and are engaged in activities that help them learn and apply knowledge of the arts. LaTonya Daniels encourages her students to appreciate and examine different styles of music as well as to create dance presentations that are specifically related to the music. She plays music and asks her students to listen to it carefully, thinking about what it is about and how it makes them feel. She plays the music again and asks her students to move to the music. If the music is fast, she encourages them to move fast. At the same time, she asks her students to show her how the music makes them feel—happy, sad, and so forth.

Social Studies in the Primary Grades

Social studies are the integrated study of the social sciences and humanities to promote civic competence. The primary purpose of social studies is to help children develop the ability to make informed and reasoned decisions for the public good as citizens of a culturally diverse, democratic society in an interdependent world.[26]

Teaching social studies is an important part of your responsibility as an early childhood teacher. While teachers devote a lot of instructional time to literacy/reading and math, you need not neglect social studies. Keep in mind that you can integrate social studies content with reading and math, so that children are reading and engaged in math processes "across the social studies curriculum." Be sure you are familiar with your state standards for the grade level you are teaching in order to incorporate them into your planning and teaching. Following are some ideas for incorporating social studies into your curriculum.

Culture.   The best place to begin teaching about culture is with you and your students. At the beginning of the school year, third grade teacher Alessia Rossi shares information about her Italian background with her students by showing where her ancestors came from. She uses social studies tools such as maps and globes to help her students put Italy in the world geographic context. She invites members of the local Italian Sons and Daughters of America (ISDA) to share Italian culture and heritage. She introduces Italian words and ties these to the reading lessons. She has books about the Italian culture in the reading center and DVDs with Italian songs and dances. In the process of Rossi's sharing, her students feel comfortable and start to share their cultures and backgrounds. At the end of the school year, the class hosts a Cultural Heritage Festival.

Time, Continuity, and Change.   Just as culture is all around us, so we are surrounded by time, continuity, and change. Second grade teacher Kelie Shipley involves her students in a community history project in which her students research not only the history of their town, but also how the town is changing and why. In the course of their research the children discovered that on one of the dedication plaques, the name of the person for whom their school is named was misspelled. They wrote letters to school and city officials, resulting in a new plaque. At the new dedication, relatives of the school's namesake came and talked about what school was like when they were in the second grade.

People, Places, and Environment.   Your local museums, art institutes, and historical centers are wonderful resources for involving your students in learning about people, places, and the environment. For example, the Allen Memorial Art Museum in Oberlin, Ohio, collaborates with the Asian Art/Educational Outreach Funding Initiative of the Freeman Foundation and has developed Asian art educational programming for children and teachers. One of the lessons involves children ages five through eight in *gyotaku*, a Japanese art of fish painting, and *haiku*, a form of Japanese poetry. You can learn more about this program and reflect on how you could involve your students in similar activities and learning experiences with the website in the Linking to Learning section at the end of the chapter.

Individual Development and Identity.   First grade teacher Ashley Gotkins incorporates the North Carolina Grade 1 Social Studies Standards into her teaching. They focus on neighborhoods and communities around the world. Gotkins, whose grandmother was one-sixteenth Cherokee, uses her cultural heritage to teach about Native Americans and the Cherokee tribes. She builds her Native American lessons around these North Carolina Standards:[27]

- Describe the roles of individuals in the family.
- Identify various groups to which individuals and families belong.

- Compare and contrast similarities and differences among individuals and families.
- Explore the benefits of diversity in the United States.

Individuals, Groups, and Institutions.   On the first day of school, first grade teacher Tanika Ramsey holds a "morning meeting" in which all of the children introduce themselves. Then she talks about families and what a family is. The children brainstorm about what things they can do to live peacefully in their classroom family. In the following days, Ramsey expands the discussion to include what children can do to live harmoniously in the school. The children discuss school rules; interview administrators, staff, and other teachers; and develop a "blueprint for school living." They share their "blueprint" with other first grade classes.

Power, Authority, and Governance.   Classroom living requires a lot of compromises and getting along with others. First grade teacher Jacki Aochi believes she should share her "power" with children and can accomplish this goal by teaching her children how to resolve conflicts. She uses the Betsy Evans "Conflict Resolution with Young Children" program. In addition, Aochi conducts a morning meeting that consists of three parts. Each part takes about five minutes:

- *Announcements.* Both she and the students make announcements related to classroom and school events and activities as well as life events such as birthdays, sporting events, and family activities.
- *Concerns.* The children discuss events inside and outside of the classroom and suggest resolutions for how they and others can turn the concern into a positive situation.
- *Being a good citizen.* Children have an opportunity to state what they are going to do during the day or week to be good citizens in the classroom, school, home, and community.

Production, Distribution, and Consumption.   Matt Blair teaches his third graders about the production, distribution, and consumption of consumer products by creating, selling, and distributing handmade cards. The children design and illustrate get-well, birthday, and thank-you cards and provide original verses and sentiments. They also package, sell, and distribute their cards. As part of the project, children visit design studios and printers and consult with marketing executives of local businesses. All proceeds from the sales of the cards go to a community charity selected by the children.

Science, Technology, and Society.   Second grade teacher Beverly Haung integrates her teaching of science, technology, and society with the teaching of the scientific method. She involves the children in a project in which they survey their homes and community to determine the ways in which computers influence how people live and work. The children post their own research questions, develop their surveys—both online and hard-copy versions—analyze their data, draw conclusions, write their results in their science journals, and publish the results in their school newspaper.

Global Connections.   Melissa Gloria's students are third graders whose first language is primarily English, but they are learning Spanish as a second language. They are studying world cultures and use ePals Global Community to exchange letters, postcards, photographs, and journal entries via e-mail with their electronic pals in Colombia. They collaborate by exchanging information about culture and history.

Civic Ideals and Practices.   First grade teacher Gretchen Reich uses the local community to teach civic pride. Her students engage in a project of learning about community agencies and how they help others. The students select agencies they would like to know more about, such as the Salvation Army, and invite agency members to their classroom to talk about what they do. As a result of their community civic involvement, the children decided to collect pennies to support the Salvation Army Red Kettle drive. In six weeks, the children raised $50. Also, once a month, the children bake cookies and take them to homes for senior citizens.

Teaching Thinking

As we previously discussed, reasoning has been added as one of the six R's of early childhood programs. Educators believe that if students can think, they can meaningfully engage in subject matter curriculum and the rigors and demands of the workplace and life. As a result, many teachers are including the teaching of thinking in their daily lesson plans.

Figure 10.4 shows examples of questions you can use to promote thinking. They are based on Benjamin Bloom's hierarchy of questioning levels. A major teaching objective is to ask students questions that move them up the hierarchy into higher level thinking from knowledge to evaluation. Your questions not only challenge children to think, but they also promote linguistic, social, and behavioral skills. For example, recall of knowledge is the lowest level of thinking and evaluation is the highest; therefore, instead of asking children merely to recall information, teachers should encourage them to think critically about information, solve problems, and reflect. To promote thinking in your classroom follow these guidelines:

- Give children the freedom and security to be creative thinkers.
- Encourage children to search for other answers and alternative solutions rather than settling for one "right" answer. Ask open-ended questions ("Why do you think that?") rather than questions that require a yes or no response.
- Create classroom cultures in which children have the time, opportunity, and materials with which to be creative.
- Integrate thinking into the total curriculum so that children learn to think during the entire school day.

THE CHILD IN NATURE

Today, with the urbanization of America and with more children living in tighter urban spaces, many are isolated from nature. This isolation from nature is also true for suburban children as well who may spend their time in front of the television or glued to iPhones and iPads. Involving children in environmental education and involving them in activities relating to the outdoors and nature provides them opportunities to get in touch with the outdoors and be involved in meaningful ecological activities.

Why Is Environmental Education Important?

Environmental education is important for the following reasons:

- Enables children to act responsibly and be stewards of the environment.
- Increases student engagement in STEM—science, technology, engineering, and mathematics all lend themselves to the outdoors and to environmental/ecological issues.
- Connects classroom learning to the real world.
- Enables children to make decisions that influence the health and well-being of the environment today and tomorrow.

environmental education Curriculum and programs that aim to teach children about the natural world and particularly how ecosystems work.

EVALUATION

Question Cues: assess, decide, rank, grade, test, measure, recommend, convince, select, judge, explain, discriminate, support, conclude, compare, summarize

- Compare and discriminate between ideas
- Assess value of theories, presentations
- Make choices based on reasoned argument
- Verify value of evidence
- Recognize subjectivity

Sample Question: Olivia, which of these pictures is your favorite? Why? Mario, how would you deal with the situation? Sophia, is there a better way to arrange your display?

SYNTHESIS

Question Cues: Combine, integrate, modify, rearrange, substitute, plan, create, design, invent, compose, formulate, prepare, generalize, rewrite, what if?

- Use old ideas to create new ones
- Generalize from given facts
- Relate knowledge from several areas
- Predict, draw conclusions

Sample Question: Edward, what do you think will happen if we mix red and yellow together? Jenna, how would you solve the girl's problem we just read about in our story?

ANALYSIS

Question Cues: Analyze, separate, order, explain, connect, classify, arrange, divide, compare, select, explain, infer

- Seeing patterns
- Organization of parts
- Recognition of hidden meanings
- Identification of components

Sample Question: Caleb, why did the girl change her mind about what she was going to do? Jessica, can you explain how the two boys we read about are similar and different?

APPLICATION

Question Cues: Apply, demonstrate, calculate, complete, illustrate, show, solve, examine, modify, relate, change, classify, experiment, discover

- Use information
- Use methods, concepts, theories in new situations
- Solve problems using required skills or knowledge

Sample Question: Isabella, how would you organize these pictures to show your parents which one you like best and which one you like least? Matthew, if you could change one thing in our classroom, what would it be?

COMPREHENSION

Question Cues: Summarize, describe, interpret, contrast, predict, associate, distinguish, estimate, differentiate, discuss, extend

- Understand information and grasp meaning
- Translate knowledge into new context
- Interpret facts; compare, contrast
- Order, group, infer causes
- Predict consequences

Sample Question: Jennifer, what do you think happens next in our story? Josh, can you tell me what this word means? Liam, how is the main character in our story similar to the character in yesterday's story?

KNOWLEDGE

Question Cues: List, define, tell, describe, identify, show, label, collect, examine, tabulate, quote, name, who, when, where, extend

- Observation and recall of information
- Knowledge of dates, events, and places
- Knowledge of major ideas
- Knowledge of subject matter

Sample Question: Jackie, how would you describe the color of the monkey in the story we read? Dylan, can you name the three characters in our story? Heather, how many days have you been in school?

FIGURE 10.4 Applying Bloom's Taxonomy to Early Childhood Classrooms

Source: Based on "Learning Skills: Bloom's Taxonomy," University of Victoria, Counselling Services, www.coun.uvic.ca. From B. S. Bloom, ed., *Taxonomy of Educational Objectives: The Classification of Education Goals, Handbook I. Cognitive Domain* (New York and Toronto: Longmans, Green, 1956).

Green Schools and Green Curricula

All across the United States, schools are going green. Green schools are those whose the buildings create a healthy environment conducive to learning while saving energy, resources, and money. Green schools and curricula are a response to eco-issues around the world and represent ways to save energy, conserve resources, infuse curricula with environmental education, build school gardens, and offer more healthy school lunches.

Horticultural Therapy   Horticultural therapy involves children in horticultural activities such as gardening and landscaping with the intent of improving their cognitive, social, educational, and emotional development. Horticultural therapy is designed to improve the whole child, body, mind, and spirit. For example, at Cherry Ridge Elementary in Louisiana, children with autism planted a garden and raised lettuce, cabbage, radishes, pumpkins, and carrots. As a result of their gardening experiences, teachers report that the children have improved their grades and communication skills. Teachers also report that by taking care of and working in the garden, children are improving their concentration, self-esteem, and social skills.

Here are some things you could do to promote environmental education and involvement with your children:

- Involve your children in recycling activities.
- Read books that involve environment issues and which provide examples of children involved in environmental activities.
- Involve your children in outdoor activities relating to the Common Core and state standards. Many STEM activities lend themselves to children's involvement in environmental issues such as alternative energy. For example, children can make pinwheels and use them as a basis for discussing the pros and cons of wind turbines and the generation of electricity.
- Create an outdoor educational environment on any land available to you on or adjacent to your school. Such mini-environments are a good way to involve the community and community agencies and to enable children to be more ecologically aware.

ACTIVITIES FOR PROFESSIONAL DEVELOPMENT

ethical dilemma

"Poorest excuse award."

Eight-year-old Isabella Garcia got off the school bus distraught and sobbing. When her mother, Mary Garcia, asked what was wrong, Isabella handed her the "Poorest Excuse Award" she had received from her teacher. Mary was flabbergasted. "I couldn't believe it," she said. "I thought it was a joke of some kind. But Isabella told me that her teacher called her up in front of the whole class to give her the poorest excuse award for not having her homework done. When I contacted the principal, he literally 'blew me off.' He tried to make a joke about it, saying the teacher was just having fun with the children. This isn't my idea of fun!" Mary exclaimed. "Isabella was humiliated. This is very disturbing. I can't believe a professional teacher would treat a child the way she did! If the school thinks I am going to forget about all of this, they have another thought coming!"

What should Mary do? Should she immediately contact the school superintendent and school board president to schedule an interview? Should she contact the local news station and ask them to have a reporter meet her in front of the school to air her grievances? Should Mary occupy the principal's office? Should she use social media to publicly humiliate the teacher? What should Mary do? What would you do?

Application Activities

1. One of the curriculum goals of many states is that all children should be able to read on grade level by grade three.
   a. Why do you think this is such an important goal?
   b. Why do you think this goal is set for grade three rather than another grade level, such as grades one or two?
   c. What are three things you and other teachers can do to help all children achieve the goal of reading on or above grade level by grade three?
   d. Create a Prezi presentation of your conclusions, post it on your class discussion board, and invite comments from other teachers.

2. Early childhood teachers are able to articulate their reasons for wanting to teach a particular grade. Many of my early childhood education students say they want to teach only in kindergarten. Others are not sure. One of my students, Chris, wants to teach fourth or fifth grade. He says he prefers working with children who are more mature.
   a. Observe a first, second, or third grade classroom and give five or six reasons why you would or would not want to teach in these classrooms.
   b. Create a blog to share your thoughts and see what other professionals have to say.

3. What do you think are the most important subjects of the primary grades? Why? How would you agree or disagree with those who think any subjects other than reading, writing, and arithmetic are a waste of time? Use Prezi to make your points and organize your thoughts. Share your Prezi presentation with your classmates.

4. We have discussed the importance of using technology to support teaching and learning. Search teacher blogs and identify five features that you would use in your blogging with children and families.

5. Give five reasons why is it important for children to be involved in nature and environmental learning. Use Wordle to create a visual of your review. Put your word cloud on your class discussion board.

Linking to Learning

Aimsweb

www.aimsweb.com
A benchmark and progress-monitoring system based on direct, frequent, and continuous student assessment.

Oberlin College

www.oberlin.edu
This site provides a description of art education provided by the Arts of Asia in Reach program.

Betsy Evans

www.kidsandconflict.com
This site provides means of conflict resolution in young children.

Study Island

www.studyisland.com
This website provides Web-based instruction and assessment opportunities for students K–12.

Wordle

www.wordle.net

Generate "word clouds" to spark classroom discussions and engage students.

Common Core Standards

www.corestandards.org

These national standards are focused on setting the same educational expectations for all students in the United States.

ePals Global Community

www.epals.com

Connect with students, teachers, and classrooms from all over the world. Interact and learn together on a global scale.

MyEducationLab

Go to Topics 2 (Child Development/Theories) and 7 (Curriculum/Content Areas) in the MyEducationLab (www.myeducationlab.com) for your course, where you can:

- Find learning outcomes for Child Development/Theories and Curriculum/Content Areas along with the national standards that connect to these outcomes.

- Complete Assignments and Activities that can help you more deeply understand the chapter content.

- Apply and practice your understanding of the core teaching skills identified in the chapter with the Building Teaching Skills and Dispositions learning units.

- Examine challenging situations and cases presented in the IRIS Center Resources.

- Check your comprehension on the content covered in the chapter by going to the Study Plan in the Book Resources for your text. Here you will be able to take a chapter quiz, receive feedback on your answers, and then access Review, Practice, and Enrichment activities to enhance your understanding of chapter content.

chapter 11

EDUCATING CHILDREN WITH DIVERSE BACKGROUNDS AND SPECIAL NEEDS

Ensuring Each Child Learns

NAEYC Standards for Early Childhood Professional Preparation Programs

Standard 1: Promoting Child Development and Learning

I use my understanding of young children's characteristics and needs, and of multiple interacting influences on children's development and learning, to create environments that are healthy, respectful, supportive, and challenging for all children.[1]

Standard 2: Building Family and Community Relationships

I know about, understand, and value the importance and complex characteristics of children's families and communities. I use this understanding to create respectful, reciprocal relationships that support and empower families, and to involve all families in their children's development and learning.[2]

Standard 4: Using Developmentally Effective Approaches to Connect with Children and Families

I understand and use positive relationships and supportive interactions as the foundation for my work with young children and families. I know, understand, and use a wide array of developmentally appropriate approaches, instructional strategies, and tools to connect with children and families and positively influence each child's developmental learning.[3]

SECOND GRADE New York Teacher of the Year Katie Ferguson teaches in a high-needs school. Katie is also certified in special education, which she calls an important component in providing individualized instruction for the students in her inclusive classroom. Using a vast array of educational tools and strategies, she holds her students up to the highest standards, helping each to achieve his or her fullest potential.[4]

Children with diverse backgrounds and special needs are in every classroom in the United States. You will teach students with a variety of special needs. They might come from low-income families and various racial and ethnic groups; they might speak little or no English; they may have exceptional abilities or disabilities. You will be challenged to provide an education for all students that is appropriate to their physical, intellectual, linguistic, social, and emotional abilities and to help them achieve their best.

INCLUSIVE EDUCATION

You will teach in an inclusive classroom. Today's teacher is a teacher of all children regardless of ability or disability. The inclusive classroom is one outcome of the ongoing integration of the fields of early childhood education and early childhood special education. In addition to guiding your teaching and professional development with the NAEYC Standards for Professional Preparation, you should also be guided by the Council for Exceptional Children's (CEC) Content Standards for all Beginning Special Education Teachers. They are outlined for you in Figure 11.1. Reflect on these standards and how you can achieve them.

Children with special needs and their families should receive the education and services necessary for them to succeed in school and life. Unfortunately, sometimes children with disabilities are not provided appropriate services and fail to reach their full potential. Figure 11.2 shows various statistics about disabilities that you may find troubling. This is one reason for laws to help ensure that children have an appropriate education and related services and that schools and teachers have high expectations for them. As you reflect on the figures, answer the accompanying questions.

The federal government has passed many laws protecting and promoting the rights and needs of children with disabilities. One of the most important federal laws is the Individuals with Disabilities Education Act (IDEA), originally enacted in 1975 and reauthorized by Congress in 2004.

As with many special areas, the field of children with special needs has a unique vocabulary and terminology. The terms defined in Figure 11.3 help you gain a deeper meaning of and appreciation for your teaching of children as you collaborate with their families.

THE INDIVIDUALS WITH DISABILITIES EDUCATION ACT (IDEA)

The Individuals with Disabilities Education Act (IDEA) governs how states and public agencies provide early intervention, special education, and related services to children with disabilities.[5] The purpose of IDEA is to ensure that all children with disabilities have available to them a free appropriate public education that emphasizes special education—now often called *exceptional student education*—and related services designed to meet their unique needs; to ensure that the rights of children with disabilities and their parents or guardians are protected; to assist states and localities to provide for the education of all children with disabilities; and to assess and ensure the effectiveness of efforts to educate children with disabilities.[6]

MyEducationLab

Visit the MyEducationLab for *Fundamentals of Early Childhood Education* to enhance your understanding of chapter concepts with a personalized Study Plan. You'll also have the opportunity to hone your teaching skills through video-based Assignments and Activities as well as Building Teaching Skills and Dispositions lessons.

FOCUS QUESTIONS

1. What is the Individuals with Disabilities Education Act (IDEA), and why is it important?

2. Who are children with disabilities, and how do you teach them?

3. Who are English language learners, and how do you teach them?

4. What is multiculturalism, and how do you teach multicultural children?

Standard 1	*Foundations:* I understand the field as an evolving and changing dicipline based on philosophies, evidence-based principles and theories, relevant laws and policies, diverse and historical points of view, and human issues that have historically influenced and continue to influence the field of special education and the education and treatment of individuals with exceptional needs in both school and society.
Standard 2	*Development and Characteristics of Learners*: I know and demonstrate respect for students as unique human beings. I understand the similarities and differences in human development and the characteristics between and among individuals with and without exceptional learning needs.
Standard 3	*Individual Learning Differences:* I understand the effects that an exceptional condition can have on an individual's learning in school and throughout life. I understand that the beliefs, traditions, and values across and within cultures can affect relationships among and between students, their families, and the school community.
Standard 4	*Instructional Strategies:* I possess a repertoire of evidence-based instructional strategies to individualize instruction for individuals with exceptional learning needs.
Standard 5	*Learning Environments and Social Interactions*: I actively create learning environments for individuals with exceptional learning needs that foster cultural understanding, safety and emotional well-being, positive social interactions, and active engagement of individuals with exceptional learning needs.
Standard 6	*Language*: I understand typical and atypical language development and the ways in which exceptional conditions can interact with an individual's experiece with and use of language.
Standard 7	*Instructional Planning*: I develop long-range individualized instructional plans anchored in both general and special education curricula.
Standard 8	*Assessment*: I use multiple types of assessment information for a variety of educational decisions.
Standard 9	*Professional and Ethical Practice*: I am guided by the profession's ethical and professional practice standards.
Standard 10	*Collaboration:* I routinely and effectively collaborate with families, other educators, related service providers, and personnel from community agencies in culturally responsive ways.

FIGURE 11.1 Content Standards for Educators of Individuals with Exceptional Gifts and Talents

Source: What Every Special Educator Must Know (2009, 6th ed. Revised). Council for Exceptional Children (CEC).

56% of children receiving early intervention transitioned to kindergarten "very easily" versus 4% whose transition was "very difficult"	59% of children in early intervention have trouble communicating their needs	8% of children receiving special education services have emotional disturbances	African American students are 2.83 times more likely to receive special education and related services for mental retardation than all other racial/ethnic groups combined and 2.24 times more likely for emotional disturbance	Asian children (ages 6–21) account for 8.1% of students receiving special education services for autism and developmental delays, more than any other race/ethnicity	Hispanic preschoolers represent 20% of the general population but are less likely to be served under Part B of IDEA than children of all other racial/ethnic groups combined	46% of American Indian/Alaska Native children with disabilities drop out of high school, nearly double the dropout rate of Caucasians with disabilities	African American students (ages 6–21) represent only 14.8% of the general population but comprise 44.8% of students with specific learning disabilitie

*Might Hispanics with disabilities be overrepresented or underrepresented in these data? Why might this occur?
*Why do you think African American students are overrepresented in the population of students with disabilities? What other statistic helps explain this?
* What is the primary developmental delay with children in early intervention?
* Why is early intervention important for success in school?

FIGURE 11.2 Children with Disabilities: Facts, Figures, and Questions

Source: Department of Education, Office of Special Education and Rehabilitative Services, Office of Special Education Programs, 30th Annual Report to Congress on the Implementation of the Individuals with Disabilities Education Act, 2008, Washington, D.C., 2012.

FIGURE 11.3

Terminology Related to Children with Special Needs

Adaptive education	Modifying programs, environments, curricula, and activities to provide learning experiences that help all students achieve desired education goals.
Children with disabilities	Replaces former terms such as *handicapped*. To avoid labeling children, do not use the reversal of these words (e.g., *disabled children*).
Co-teaching	The process by which a regular classroom professional and a special educator or a person trained in exceptional student education team teach, in the same classroom, a group of regular and mainstreamed children.
Disability	A physical or mental impairment that substantially limits one or more major life activities.
Early intervention	Providing services to children and families as early in the child's life as possible to prevent or help with a special need or needs.
Exceptional student education	Replaces the term *special education*; refers to the education of children with special needs.
Full inclusion	The mainstreaming or inclusion of all children with disabilities into natural environments such as playgrounds, child care centers, preschool, kindergarten, and primary grade classrooms.
Individualized education program (IEP)	A written plan for a child stating what will be done, how it will be done, and when it will be done.
Individualized family service plan (IFSP)	A written plan for providing early intervention services for a child and his or her family based on the child's strengths and needs. It lists outcomes and describes the services and coordination that will get to those outcomes. Family members decide what is written on the plan, they can veto any input from professionals, and the plan can be amended at any time by the family.
Least restrictive environment (LRE)	Children with disabilities are educated with children who have no disabilities. Special classes, separate schooling, or other removal of children with disabilities from the regular educational environment occurs only when the nature or severity of the disability is such that education in regular classes with the use of supplementary aids and services cannot be achieved satisfactorily.
Mainstreaming	The social and educational integration of children with special needs into the general instructional process; usually a regular classroom program.
Natural environment	Any environment in which it is natural for any child to be, such as home, child care center, preschool, kindergarten, and primary grades.
Response to intervention (RTI)	Seeks to prevent academic failure through early intervention, frequent progress measurement, and increasingly intensive research-based instructional interventions for children who continue to have difficulty.
Universal design (UD)	The use of teaching strategies and instructional support (technology, etc.) designed to make the curriculum and instructional strategies accessible to each student.

The accompanying Professionalism in Practice feature describes how CEC National Teacher of the Year Gayle Solis Zavala brings her classroom of children with disabilities and general education children together and enriches the education and development of both.

professionalism in practice

Kids with Special Needs Need Extra Special Touch

STEP 1 Provide a Warm Welcome

I want to emphasize the importance of the warm welcome each day. A handshake or friendly pat on the back is a personal gesture that lets the students know they are important and you are glad to see them.

STEP 2 Support Independence

Call this first day of school Independence Day. Students with disabilities, just as students without disabilities, find themselves facing this day with many of the same feelings and anxieties. Students with disabilities, however, especially students with English as a second language, may have little or no way to communicate their needs or feelings. They may walk or dash away or squat down refusing to move in fear of what is waiting ahead. In the cafeteria it's like entering another world altogether, where once again they will be asked to wait in a line, but this time there are choices to make, a cashier to greet, a table that stretches for miles to sit at, and food wrapped in plastic bags and cartons to figure out how to open.

The choices for breakfast, and later for lunch, are eventually communicated by the students in a way that begins to give them independence and a communicative voice (i.e., pointing, verbalizing part or all of a word, sign language, or a picture communication board). Cafeteria staff members give students PIN numbers to use whenever they get breakfast or lunch. Students carry their numbers with them to key in on what looks like a debit card machine. Consult with the cafeteria staff members ahead of time to gain their support and patience. This is a functional and practical opportunity to learn numbers and add another important independent skill. For students with cognitive and/or physical limitation, a communication board or simple one-message voice output device can be used to convey any needed communicative message.

STEP 3 Scaffold

Use scaffolding as a teaching strategy when orienting and teaching students with disabilities. As students learn to sign, verbalize, and select what they want to say on their picture boards, the teacher or staff can model or provide assistance to help a student learn a more independent response. Continuing on with the cafeteria scenario, a teacher's first reaction may be to open up a student's juice carton or wipe a soiled mouth or clothing. But, if the students are to learn to take care of

themselves, they need to repeatedly practice these self-help skills. The reward is evident as the students finally open their own cartons and wave their hands in the air with delight and look to their teacher for praise.

STEP 4 Praise

Praise is one of your biggest teaching tools in managing behavior:

> "I like the way Jesus is staying in line. Great job, Jesus!"
> "I like the way Ashley is keeping her hands to herself [gesturing with folded arms or hands in pocket]."
> "Look how nicely Antwan said 'Thank you' to Ms. Vargas. Nice words, Antwan."

The students are always watching to see what gets teachers' and staff's attention. It is always more beneficial to voice positive praise, especially with the most challenging students.

STEP 5 Develop a Social Contract

Establish a written social contract (pictures can be added to cue understanding) between the students and the teaching staff. Even if students are nonverbal or have limited communication skills, you can model appropriate choices about positive social interaction, use picture prompts, or capture the targeted behavior when it happens to add to the social contract. Allowing students to participate in creating the social contract is another example of giving them independence and self-advocacy. Some social contract behaviors are:

- Listen quietly to one another.
- Use nice words with each other.
- Establish eye contact.
- Enjoy humor (have fun), but not hurtful (don't make fun of one another).

A social contract is also an important opportunity to emphasize to paraprofessionals, volunteers, and other classroom personnel how the climate of the classroom should be. Everyone signs the contract and we review it at least once a day to maintain its importance.

Establishing independence, providing opportunities to communicate, and a safe, nurturing climate is a recipe for success with all children.

....

Source: Contributed by Gayle Solis Zavala, CEC Teacher of the Year.

FIGURE 11.4

Number of Children Served by IDEA

- All disabilities: 6,552,766
- Specific learning disabilities: 2,431,317
- Speech and language impairments: 1,416,060
- Intellectual disability: 463,321
- Emotional disturbance: 407,617
- Multiple disabilities: 131,458
- Hearing impairments: 79,215
- Orthopedic impairments: 65,345
- Other health impairments: 689,183
- Visual impairment: 29,217
- Autism: 378,876
- Deaf-blindness: 2,283
- Traumatic brain injury: 25,391
- Development delay: 368,873

Note: Data include children and youth ages 3–21.

Source: National Center for Education Statistics; Table A-9-1. Number and percentage distribution of children and youth ages 3–21 served under the Individuals with Disabilities Education Act (IDEA), Part B, and number served as a percentage of total school enrollment, by disability type: selected school years, 1980–1981 through 2009–2010; 2012.

IDEA defines children with disabilities as those children with mental retardation, hearing impairments (including deafness), speech or language impairments, visual impairments (including blindness), serious emotional disturbance, orthopedic impairments, autism, developmental delays, traumatic brain injury, other health impairments, or specific learning disabilities; and who, by reason thereof, need special education and related services.[7] Figure 11.4 shows how many children between the ages of three and twenty-one are served by IDEA.

About 13 percent of the nation's children receive services for disabilities.[8] What this means for you is that in your classroom of 20 to 25 students, you will have at least two to three children with some kind of disability.

IDEA's Six Principles

IDEA establishes six basic principles to follow as you provide educational and other services to children with special needs:

1. *Zero reject.* IDEA calls for educating *all* children and rejecting none. No child can be excluded from receiving an appropriate, public education. The zero reject principle prohibits schools from excluding any student with a disability.

2. *Nondiscriminatory evaluation.* Schools must use evaluations that are not culturally or racially biased in order to determine whether a child has a disability. Further, if it is determined that a child has a disability, nondiscriminatory evaluation must be used to determine the kind of special education and services the student should receive.

3. *Free and appropriate public education.* Instruction and related services need to be individually designed to provide educational benefits in making progress toward meeting the unique needs of each student. IDEA provides for a free appropriate public education (FAPE) for all students between the ages of three and twenty-one. *Free* means without cost to the child's parents. *Appropriate* means that children must receive an education suited to their age, maturity level, condition of disability, past achievements, and parental expectations.

As a teacher, your knowledge of child development will be essential in helping you determine if a child's development is outside of the norm. This **video** helps explain the referral process which may or may not result in the child needing special services.

children with disabilities As defined by IDEA, children who need special education and related services because of mental retardation, hearing impairments, speech or language impairments, serious emotional disturbances, orthopedic impairments, autism, traumatic brain injury, other health impairments, or specific learning disabilities.

zero reject principle A rule under IDEA that prohibits schools from excluding any student with a disability.

free appropriate public education (FAPE) The requirement under IDEA that children must receive a free education suited to their age, maturity level, condition of disability, achievements, and parental expectations.

4. ***Least restrictive placement/environment.*** All students with disabilities have the right to learn in the least restrictive environment (LRE)—an environment consistent with their academic, social, and physical needs. Such a setting may or may not be the general classroom, but 96 percent of children with disabilities spend at least part of their school day in general classrooms.[9]

5. ***Procedural due process.*** Schools must follow set procedures to protect and safeguard the rights of children and parents. IDEA also provides schools and parents with ways of resolving their differences by mediation and/or hearings before impartial hearing officers or judges.

6. ***Parent and student participation and shared decision-making.*** IDEA specifies a process of shared decision-making whereby educators, parents, and students collaborate in deciding on a student's individualized educational plan (IEP).

Additional Provisions of IDEA

Individualized Education Programs (IEPs). Because IDEA requires individualization of instruction, schools must provide for all students' disabilities and specific needs. Individualized instruction occurs when teachers develop and implement plans to meet the individual academic and behavioral plans of a particular child. Individualization of instruction also means developing and implementing an individualized education program (IEP) for each student. The IEP must specify what will be done for the child; how and when it will be done; by whom it will be done; and this information must be in writing.

IEPs have several purposes. They:

- Protect children and parents by ensuring planning and delivery of services occur.
- Guarantee that children will have plans tailored to their individual strengths, weaknesses, and learning styles.
- Help teachers and other instructional and administrative personnel focus their teaching and resources on children's specific needs, promoting the best use of everyone's time, efforts, and talents.
- Help ensure that children with disabilities receive a range of services from other agencies if needed, and the plan must specify how each child's total needs will be met.
- Clarify and refine decisions about what is best for children, where they should be placed, and how they should be taught and helped.
- Ensure that children will not be categorized or labeled without discussion of their unique needs.
- Require review of the contents on at least an annual basis, encouraging professionals to consider how and what children have learned, to determine whether what was prescribed was effective, and to prescribe new or modified strategies.

In developing the IEP, a person trained in diagnosing disabling conditions, such as a school psychologist, must be involved, as well as a classroom professional, the parent, and, when appropriate, the child. Because so many classrooms of today are inclusive, more than likely you will have children with disabilities in your classroom. This means you will participate in the development of an IEP.

IDEA Part C: Early Intervention for Infants and Toddlers. Special provisions of IDEA provide the states with incentives to provide early intervention services to infants and toddlers, birth through age two with developmental delays or who have diagnosed physical or mental conditions with high probabilities of resulting in developmental delays. These intervention services are provided through an individualized family service plan (IFSP).

Individualized Family Service Plan. The process of helping children, infants, and toddlers with disabilities begins with referral and assessment and results in the development of an **individualized family service plan (IFSP)** designed to help families reach the goals they have for themselves and their children. Infants and toddlers receive early intervention services through the IFSP, which includes the following:

- Multidisciplinary assessment developed by a multidisciplinary team and the parents.
- Planned services to meet developmental needs, including, as necessary, special education, speech and language pathology and audiology, occupational therapy, physical therapy, psychological services, parent and family training and counseling services, transition services, medical diagnostic services, and health services.
- Supporting information—a statement of the child's present levels of development; a statement of the family's strengths and needs in regard to enhancing the child's development; a statement of major expected outcomes for the child and family; the criteria, procedures, and timelines for determining progress; the specific early intervention services necessary to meet the unique needs of the child and family; the projected dates for initiation of services; the name of the case manager; and transition procedures from the early intervention program into a preschool program.

An IFSP requires an integrated, team approach to intervention. A **transdisciplinary team model** is one method of integrating information and skills across professional disciplines. In this model, all team members (including the family) teach, learn, and work together to accomplish a mutually agreed-on set of intervention outcomes. With a transdisciplinary model, one or a few people are primary implementers of the program; other team members provide ongoing direct or indirect services. For example, an occupational therapist might observe a toddler during meals and then recommend to the parents how to physically assist the child.

Benefits of Family-Centered Services.   Family-centered services are an important component of early childhood programming. Programs that embrace and utilize family-centered services achieve important improvements in children's developmental and social adjustment outcomes; decrease parental stress as a result of accessing needed services for their children and themselves; and recognize the family's role as decision maker and partner in the early intervention process.

Assistive Technology.   IDEA encourages IEP developers to determine whether assistive technology is necessary and appropriate in order to meet children's needs. Public Law 100–407, the Technology-Related Assistance for Individuals with Disabilities Act of 1988 (Tech Act), defines **assistive technology** as "any item, device or piece of equipment, or product system, whether acquired commercially off the shelf, modified, or customized, that is used to increase, maintain, or improve functional abilities of individuals with disabilities."[10]

Assistive technology covers a wide range of products and applications, from simple devices such as adaptive spoons and switch-adapted battery-operated toys to complex

Sidebar:

All early childhood programs should address the individual needs of children with disabilities. How can you use IEPs to ensure that those needs are being met?

individualized family service plan (IFSP) As required by IDEA, a plan created for infants and toddlers with disabilities and their families, specifying what services they will receive to help them reach their specific goals.

transdisciplinary team model In this model, all team members (including the family) teach, learn, and work together to accomplish a mutually agreed-on set of intervention outcomes.

assistive technology any item, device or piece of equipment, or product system, whether acquired commercially off the shelf, modified, or customized, that is used to increase, maintain, or improve functional abilities of individuals with disabilities

devices such as computerized environmental control systems. Figure 11.5 shows several examples of these systems and devices.

Assistive technology helps children with vision impairments see and children with physical disabilities read and write. Assistive technology helps children who are

	BigKeys Keyboard BigKeys Keyboard is an assistive technology that has keys four times bigger than standard keyboard keys. It arranges letters in alphabetical order to assist young children and generates only one letter, regardless of how long a key is pressed. The BigKeys Keyboard also accommodates children who cannot press down two or more keys simultaneously.
	Big Red Switch Big Red Switch is a large, colorful switch to turn devices on and off. It is five inches in diameter with a surface that is easy to see and activate. It also has an audible click to help children make the cause-and-effect link.
	QuickTalker 12 QuickTalker 12 is an augmentative communication device that gives children a voice! It allows them to communicate by pressing on pictures.
	Touch Windows 17 Touch Windows 17 is a touch screen that attaches to the computer monitor and allows children to touch the screen directly rather than using a mouse. It can be used on a flat surface, such as a wheelchair tray, and is scratch-resistant and resistant to breaking.
	All-Turn-It Spinner An inclusion learning tool, All-Turn-It Spinner allows all children to participate in lessons on numbers, colors, shapes, matching, and sequencing. It is a spinner that is controlled by a switch for easy manipulating and has optional educational overlays, stickers, and books that can be purchased separately.
	Talk Pad Talk Pad is a portable communication device that is designed to be used by children who need assistance with speech. It uses an electronic chip that records the voice and allows children with language limitations to be active participants in everyday activities.

FIGURE 11.5 Examples of Assistive Technologies

applying research to practice

Daily Report Cards (DRC) Improve Students' Behavior

Most children are accustomed to receiving a six-week report card. However, we know that constant feedback about behavior and achievement provides students information they need to improve their behavior and learn new skills and information. The What Works Clearinghouse (WWC), a U.S. Department of Education agency, reviews educational research on a wide range of topics. The WWC reports that the use of daily report cards (DRCs) can improve the behavior of students with ADHD.[11] A DRC is aligned with behavioral and academic goals and with a student's individualized education program (IEP). The teacher sends home the DRC with information about the student's daily behavior and academic progress. Parents review and respond to the DRC and return it to the teacher.

So, what does research about the effectiveness of a daily report card have to do with you?

1. Many teachers provide parents ongoing information about their children's progress and behavior in the days and weeks between a six-week report card. While this is a lot of work, it certainly pays dividends in terms of building home–school relationships and student achievement.
2. Frequent reports to parents help ensure that teachers and parents/families are in agreement about children's behavioral and academic progress.
3. Sending home a DRC for children with disabilities in your classroom is a good idea and one you should consider. A weekly report card would work well for other students.
4. For some families, an electronic DRC or a weekly report would probably work better than a hard copy. Sending an electronic DRC ensures that it gets home!

Consistent, ongoing, helpful feedback, including suggestions for improving behavioral and academic achievement, is beneficial for every child and their families, too.

---

developmentally delayed learn the skills they need to achieve at appropriate levels and enables other children with disabilities to substitute one ability for another and receive the special training they need. In addition, computer-assisted instruction provides software tools for teaching students at all ability levels, including programmed instruction for students with specific learning disabilities.

Inclusive classrooms offer many benefits for children. They demonstrate increased acceptance and appreciation of diversity, develop better communication and social skills, show greater development in moral and ethical principles, create warm and caring friendships, and demonstrate increased self-esteem.

CHILDREN WITH DISABILITIES

These are exciting times for children with disabilities, their families, and their teachers because today's educational practices make a real difference in the lives of children with disabilities. As a result, life for children with disabilities is remarkably different from what it was only a few years ago. Furthermore, we know tomorrow holds the promise of even more opportunities for accomplishment and fewer barriers. So, in this context of optimism, let's take a closer look at children with disabilities and discuss how you can teach them.

Children with Autism Spectrum Disorders (ASD)

Autism is a complex developmental disability that appears during the first three years of life. It is the result of a neurological disorder that affects the normal functioning of the brain, impacting development in the areas of social interaction and communication

autism A complex developmental disability that appears during the first three years of life. It is the result of a neurological disorder that affects the normal functioning of the brain, impacting development in the areas of social interaction and communication skills.

Inclusive classrooms educate students with disabilities in the least restrictive educational environment. What would you say to a parent of a child without a disability who questions the idea of an inclusive classroom?

skills. Autism affects each child differently and to varying degrees. Autism is currently diagnosed four times more often in boys than girls, though we do not know why.[12] Its prevalence is not affected by race, region, or socioeconomic status. Since autism was first diagnosed in the United States, the occurrence has climbed to 1 in 88 children across the country,[13] and autism diagnoses are increasing at the rate of 10 to 17 percent per year.[14] Autism is the fastest growing serious developmental disability in the United States.[15] More children will be diagnosed with autism in the coming years than children with AIDS, diabetes, and cancer combined. *Spectrum delays* (another term used to refer to autism and developmental delays) cost the nation more than $60 billion per year, a figure expected to reach $200–$400 billion in the next decade,[16] but receive less than 5 percent of the research funding of many less prevalent childhood diseases.[17]

Children with autism typically demonstrate the following characteristics:

- Deficits in receptive and expressive communication skills
- Difficulties in verbal and nonverbal communication
- Repetitive or "stereotyped" behaviors[18]
- Difficulty initiating and sustaining symbolic play and social interactions[19]
- Difficulties in social interactions
- Limited interests
- Difficulties with joint attention (showing expressions by following eye gaze, gesturing, or leading)
- Trouble keeping up with conversations[20]

The cause of autism remains unknown. Each child with autism may have his or her own individual cause. However, twin and family studies suggest an underlying genetic vulnerability to autism.[21] Researchers have identified several genes associated with autism and have found anomalies in multiple areas of the brain of people who have autism. Other studies found that people with autism have atypical levels of serotonin or other neurotransmitters in their brains. This suggests that autism results from the interference of typical brain development caused by glitches in the genes that organize brain growth and guide how neurons communicate with one another as the fetus develops in utero.[22] Still other research suggests that in infancy and toddlerhood brain synapses are pruned in such a way as to "turn on or off" the autism gene, indicating that autism is a synaptic disorder.[23] Still other researchers have found that there may be environmental triggers for autism spectrum disorders (ASDs),[24] but contrary to popular belief, there is no scientific evidence of a relationship between immunizations/vaccines and autism.[25] It is likely that the cause of spectrum disorders is due to a combination of all of these factors. Regardless of the cause, autism is a prevalent presence in American society and will continue to be.

Autism and Immunizations/Vaccines. Despite popular opinion, research does not support the belief that ADHD is caused by immunizations or vaccines.[26] Some parents believe that preservatives used in immunizations and vaccines cause or trigger autism and ADHD. Although public health officials advise parents that immunizations and vaccines do not cause health problems, including autism and ADHD, a growing number of parents are opting out of required immunizations and vaccinations. Public health officials are concerned for the children who are not vaccinated or immunized and the health threat they create for themselves, their peers, and the public at large.

Diagnosis.   Autism can be diagnosed as early as six to eighteen months of age, and the earlier children with autism receive intense and consistent intervention, the more likely they are to have positive experiences in the school, the home, and later in occupational areas.[27] Signs of autism in infants and toddlers can include fixation on objects, a lack of response to people, failing to respond to their names, avoiding eye contact, and engaging in repetitive movements such as rocking or arm flapping.[28]

Interventions.   There are a number of effective interventions for autism. One is applied behavior analysis (ABA), based on the theory that behavior rewarded is more likely to be repeated than behavior ignored. To reinforce behavior, ABA therapists initiate a sequence of stimuli, responses, and rewards. For example, an ABA therapist who is working on joint attention with David, a child with ASD, will ask David to "show me" the red block (stimulus). If David points to the red block (response), the ABA therapist gives him a reward, such as a sticker, or an appropriate reward that is rewarding to David. If David does not respond or points to a different colored block, the therapist ignores the behavior and repeats the stimulus.

applied behavior analysis (ABA) The theory that behavior rewarded is more likely to be repeated than behavior ignored.

Play therapy is another effective intervention for children on the spectrum. Play therapy uses developmentally appropriate practices and models to incorporate social experiences and enjoyable interactions to enhance a child's pretend skills, joint attention, communication skills, and appropriate behavior. Play therapy can take place individually between a therapist and one child, in a group with other children, or along with the parents. Unlike ABA, play therapy is generally child-led.[29] For example, a play therapist working with Kate, a child with autism, would use different toys to engage her. Over time, the play therapist would challenge Kate's behaviors and content of play by initiating different play scenarios. The play therapist reflects and comments on Kate's emotions and activities in order to elicit and reward language development, play skills, and relationship development so that Kate can feel understood and valued for who she is.

play therapy A method that incorporates social experiences and enjoyable interactions into a therapeutic approach to working with children with developmental delays in order to enhance communication skills and other appropriate behavior.

Other Interventions.   Music, art, and occupational therapies are also highly effective interventions for children with autism.[30] Music therapists or art therapists use their respective expressive mediums (musical instruments, singing, painting, clay, etc.) to provide children who have spectrum delays with different means of experiencing relationships, self-expression, and expanding other skills. These therapies are unique in that they give children with spectrum delays an opportunity to develop skills that have social utility. As a result, children gain in peer interaction, self-esteem, and improved everyday functioning. Physical and occupational therapists use a more body-centered approach to reach children with developmental delays. By swinging, receiving deep compressions to their body, climbing, and jumping, children's bodies are challenged and made more comfortable, thereby eliciting more language, social reciprocity, and joint attention. These types of therapies can also be done individually, in groups, or with parents to maximize the effects of therapy. For example, an occupational therapist might put Benjamin in a hammock swing and push him in it to stimulate his vestibular needs while engaging him in developmentally appropriate conversation.

Other methods of effective intervention include a highly supportive teaching environment; predictability and routine; family involvement; and working with young children in small teacher-to-child ratios, often one-to-one in the early stages.

Children with Attention Deficit Hyperactivity Disorder (ADHD)

Attention deficit hyperactivity disorder (ADHD) is a neurobehavioral disorder involving how the brain affects emotions, behaviors, and learning. Children with ADHD generally suffer with difficulties in three specific areas: attention, impulse control, and hyperactivity.[31] Research suggests that there may be a genetic cause; studies of twins show that almost 80 percent of the influence of ADHD is due to genetic factors.[32] Other ADHD causes can be brain injury; environmental exposure, such as lead; alcohol and tobacco use during pregnancy; and premature birth and low birth weight. However, many things such as environment and poverty may make ADHD symptoms more prominent and contribute to the failure to resolve it. Still, the evidence is not strong enough to conclude that they are the main causes of ADHD.[33]

To be classified as having ADHD, a student must display, for a minimum of six months, at least six of the following characteristics to a degree that is maladaptive and inconsistent with developmental level. There are three types of ADHD: predominantly inattentive type, predominantly hyperactive-impulsive type, and combined type.

ADHD, Predominantly Inattentive Type.

Frequently, the term *attention deficit disorder (ADD)* is used to refer to the predominantly inattentive type of ADHD and not the hyperactive component. A child diagnosed with the predominantly inattentive type of ADHD:

- Often does not give close attention to details or makes careless mistakes in schoolwork, work, or other activities.
- Often has trouble keeping attention on tasks or play activities.
- Often does not seem to listen when spoken to directly.
- Often does not follow through on instructions and fails to finish schoolwork, chores, or duties in the workplace (not due to oppositional behavior or failure to understand instructions).
- Often has trouble organizing activities.
- Often avoids, dislikes, or doesn't want to do things that take a lot of mental effort for a long period of time (such as schoolwork or homework).
- Often loses things needed for tasks and activities (e.g., toys, school assignments, pencils, books, or tools).
- Is often easily distracted.
- Is often forgetful in daily activities.[34]

ADHD, Predominantly Hyperactive-Impulsive Type.

Children with the hyperactive-impulsive type tend to exhibit a combination of impulsivity and overactivity. This type is the stereotype of ADHD. A child with predominantly hyperactive-impulsive type:

- Often fidgets with hands or feet or squirms in seat when sitting still is expected.
- Often gets up from seat when remaining in seat is expected.
- Often excessively runs about or climbs when and where it is not appropriate (adolescents or adults may feel very restless).
- Often has trouble playing or doing leisure activities quietly.
- Is often "on the go" or often acts as if "driven by a motor."
- Often talks excessively.
- Often blurts out answers before questions have been finished.
- Often has trouble waiting one's turn.
- Often interrupts or intrudes on others (e.g., butts into conversations or games).[35]

ADHD, Combined Type.   Children who have the combined type of ADHD exhibit both inattentive behaviors and hyperactive and impulsive behaviors. They may not show sufficient symptoms in either category to make a diagnosis of one type or another but do exhibit enough symtoms in both types to interfere with daily life and learning.[36]

ADHD and Gender.   ADHD is diagnosed about three times more often in boys than in girls, though they are no more likely to have it, and conservatively affects 4 to 12 percent of all students.[37] Boys are more likely to have the hyperactive component, and thus are identified with ADHD more often and more quickly, whereas girls tend to show the symptoms of ADHD in different ways. However, both boys and girls can have any combination of symptoms. Some speculate that the typical hyperactive symptoms of boys disrupt the classroom more, and as a result, teachers are more likely to recommend testing and diagnosis.[38] Hallmark symptoms for boys tend to be impulsivity and inability to sit still or concentrate. Researchers speculate that because girls are socialized to please parents and teachers, they are more likely to compensate for their ADHD in behavior-appropriate ways. Symptoms for ADHD in girls are nonstop, uncontrollable talking; friendship difficulties; inordinate messiness; and difficulty paying attention, which may sometimes present as simply "not getting it."[39] Some researchers have found that when these symptoms are identified, teachers tend to see them as evidence of a lack of the girl's academic abilities or intelligence rather than a symptom of a learning and behavior disorder. Some estimate that as many as 50 to 75 percent of girls who have ADHD are not diagnosed.[40] As a result, girls may not get the help they need. In addition, girls are often diagnosed five years later than boys, at around age twelve in comparison to boys at age seven.[41]

The Effects of ADHD.   When ADHD is left untreated, children are more likely than their counterparts who have gotten help for their ADHD or those who don't have ADHD to experience lower educational achievement and are less likely to graduate from high school or college. They are also more inclined to have low self-esteem, antisocial thoughts, a pessimistic outlook on their future, and problems with their romantic relationships and jobs.[42] With the right combination of medication and intervention, children with ADHD have a better chance for a successful academic, personal, and career life. Interventions for ADHD include differentiated academic instruction, behavioral interventions, classroom accommodation, and various medications.[43]

Cooperative Learning Strategies for Children with ADHD.   In your work with children, be sure to use cooperative learning strategies. Have students work together in small groups to maximize their own and each other's learning. Use strategies such as **T**hink-**P**air-**S**hare, in which you ask students to think about a topic, pair with a partner to discuss it, and share ideas with the group. Also, individualize instructional practices. For example, use partnered reading activities—pair the child with ADHD with another student who is a strong reader. Have the partners take turns reading orally and listening to each other. Use storytelling sessions in which children retell a story that they have recently read. Keep a word bank or dictionary of new or hard-to-read sight-vocabulary words. Encourage computer games for reading comprehension. Schedule computer time for children to have drill-and-practice with sight-vocabulary words. Finally, make available to students a second set of books and other materials that they can use at home.

Develop Organizational Skills.   Keep in mind that organization and study-skill strategies are particularly important for children with ADHD. They need to learn and use organization and study skills both throughout lessons and throughout their daily lives. The following are suggestions for ways to help students with ADHD develop and use organizational and study-skill strategies:

- *Assignment notebooks.* Provide the child with ADHD with an assignment notebook to help organize homework and seat work.
- *Color-coded folders.* Provide the child with color-coded folders to help organize assignments for different academic subjects (e.g., reading, mathematics, social science, and science).
- *Homework partner.* Assign the child a partner to help record homework and seatwork in the assignment notebook and to help file work sheets and other papers in the proper folders.

Time management is an essential skill for children with ADHD because they tend to need extra help managing their time. Here are some tips to help students with ADHD learn to manage their time effectively:

- *Use a clock or wristwatch.* Teach the child with ADHD how to read and use a clock or wristwatch to manage time when completing assigned work.
- *Use a calendar.* Teach the child how to read and use a calendar to schedule assignments.
- *Practice sequencing activities.* Provide the child with supervised opportunities to break down an assignment into a sequence of short, interrelated activities.
- *Create a daily activity schedule.* Tape a schedule of planned daily activities on the child's desk.
- *Provide parents with time management strategies to use at home.*

Behavioral Intervention.   The purpose of behavioral intervention in the school setting is to assist students with ADHD in developing the behaviors that are most conducive to their own learning and that of classmates. Well-managed classrooms prevent many disciplinary problems and provide an environment that is favorable for learning. Consequently, behavioral intervention should be viewed as an opportunity for teaching in the most effective and efficient manner, rather than as an opportunity for punishment.[44]

- *Define the appropriate behavior while giving encouragement.* Make encouragement specific for the positive behavior the student displays; that is, your comments should focus on what the student did right and should include exactly what part(s) of the student's behavior were desirable. Rather than praising a student for not disturbing the class, praise the student for quietly completing a math lesson on time.
- *Give praise immediately.* The sooner approval is given regarding appropriate behavior, the more likely the student is to repeat it.
- *Vary statements of praise.* The comments you use to praise appropriate behavior should vary. When students hear the same praise statement repeated over and over, it may lose its value.
- *Be consistent and sincere with praise.* Appropriate behavior should receive consistent praise. Consistency among teachers is important to avoid confusion on the part of students with ADHD. Similarly, students will notice insincere praise, which will make praise less effective.

Classroom Accommodation.   Children with ADHD often have difficulty adjusting to the structured environment of a classroom, determining what is important, and focusing on assigned work. Because they are easily distracted by other children or by nearby activities, many children with ADHD benefit from accommodations that reduce distractions in the classroom environment and help them stay on task.[45]

- *Seat the child near you.* Assign the child with ADHD a seat near your desk or the front of the room. This seating assignment allows you to monitor and reinforce the child's on-task behavior.
- *Seat the child near a student role model.* This arrangement enables children to work cooperatively and to learn from their peers.
- *Provide low-distraction work areas.* As space permits, make available a quiet, distraction-free room or area for quiet study time and test taking. Students should be directed to this area privately and discreetly in order to avoid the appearance of punishment.

Medication.   The use of drugs to help children control their behavior is appropriate and common. Some teachers and other education professionals object to medication for fear that children are overmedicated. Ritalin, Metadate, Concerta, and Daytrana are four of the most prescribed drugs for treating ADHD in children.[46] These drugs are a vital and effective component in helping children with ADHD. Medications affect each children differently, so children may need to try different types and at different dosages before a right fit is found. With the right combination of medication, behavioral interventions, and creative teaching, children with ADHD can be successful learners and students, which will set them up for success later in life.

TEACHING AND LEARNING IN THE INCLUSIVE CLASSROOM: INSTRUCTIONAL STRATEGIES FOR TEACHING CHILDREN WITH DISABILITIES

Sound teaching strategies work well for *all* students, including those with disabilities, but you must plan to create inclusive teaching environments. Here are some strategies that can help make your classroom a true *learning* environment.

Universal Design.   We have talked about universal design before. The concept of universal design (UD) is important to remember in regard to teaching children with disabilities because it describes the adaptation of teaching strategies and technology to make the learning environment, the curriculum, and the instruction processes accessible to each young child—much in the same way that universal design in architecture incorporates curb cuts, automatic doors, ramps, and other accommodations for people with disabilities. Universal design is about ensuring that learning is accessible to all students, and that success and achievement are feasible for all students regardless of their differences. Universal design was established in order to integrate a greater number of students with disabilities into general education classroom settings. Universal design is based on two best practices: (1) instruction is developmentally appropriate, and (2) teaching is based on a constructivist approach to learning. Developmentally appropriate practices and constructivist learning are based on the belief that children need multiple means of engagement and expression, as well as practical experiences that support what they have learned.

For example, when teachers teach oral language and conversation skills, they use different modes of presenting the material and provide positive reinforcement.

universal design (UD) The process of adapting teaching strategies and technology to make the learning environment, the curriculum, and the instruction methods accessible to each young child, regardless of physical limitations or learning disabilities.

Teachers might record children's thoughts and ideas via written language, audio, or video in order to provide alternate ways for children to interact with the material. If the teacher is focusing writing, she would embed writing into a variety of activities, accept all students' attempts, and remain sensitive to the physical demands of writing that may be difficult for some students. She would also provide computers and other electronic devices to promote alternate routes to written expressive language.

When it comes to universal design, flexibility is the key. For example, in a math lesson from the Common Core Standards on solving word problems, the teacher would present steps and procedures for solving word problems using multiple media, such as oral directions, charts or diagrams, storybooks, blocks, or even cooking activities. The idea is to reach each child at the level he or she understands best. The teacher may introduce the concept of value comparison through graphs and group discussion one day, and then use a cooking experiment to demonstrate the concept practically ("Which is more: two cups of flour, or three cups of water?").

Response to Intervention/Response to Instruction (RTI).

Response to Intervention/Response to Instruction is a multitier instructional approach to the early identification and support of students with learning and behavior needs. RTI works by efficiently differentiating instruction for all students at their developmental level. Students who are responsive to initial high-quality instruction continue to be taught in the manner that is effective for them. Students who have difficulty, for whatever reason, are engaged in increasingly smaller groups with increasingly need-oriented instruction until they succeed. RTI is successful because it incorporates increasing intensities of instruction based on research-based interventions that match the individual needs of the students, as shown in Figures 11.6 and 11.7.

Other Teaching Strategies.

The following ideas will also help you teach children with disabilities and create inclusive settings that enhance the education of *all* students:

- *Accentuate the positive.* One of the most effective strategies is to emphasize what children can do rather than what they cannot do. Children with disabilities have talents and abilities similar to those of other children.
- *Use appropriate assessment.* Include work samples, cumulative records, and appropriate assessment instruments. Parents and other professionals who have worked with individual children are sources of valuable information and can contribute to accurate and appropriate plans for them. Appropriate assessment includes using culturally sensitive tools and measures.
- *Use concrete examples and materials.*
- *Develop and use multisensory approaches to learning.* Use multisensory learning centers. Multisensory learning centers can assist in meeting diverse needs in an inclusive classroom; they can address various instructional levels with emphasis on visual, auditory, and kinesthetic pathways to learning.
- *Model what children are to do.* Rather than just telling them what to do, have a child who has mastered a certain task or behavior model it for others. Also, ask each child to perform a designated skill or task with supervision. Give corrective feedback. Then let children practice or perform the certain behavior. In addition, children who have mastered the task can demonstrate and model to other children how to complete it.
- *Make the learning environment a pleasant, rewarding place to be.*
- *Create a dependable classroom schedule.* All children develop a sense of security when daily plans follow a consistent pattern. Children with disabilities in

Response to Intervention/ Response to Instruction (RTI) A multitier approach to the early identification and support of students with learning and behavior needs; it evaluates assessment data and employs differentiated instruction, so that students who are struggling can receive more intense intervention.

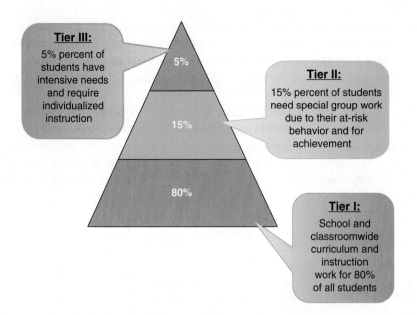

FIGURE 11.6 The Three Tiers of Continuous Intervention/Instruction

Through RTI, teachers and schools provide ongoing assessments and instructional processes to ensure that each child is successful.

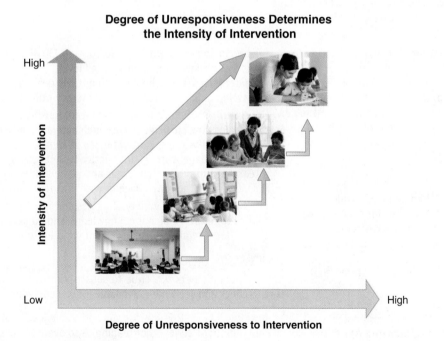

FIGURE 11.7 In RTI, the Degree of Unresponsiveness Determines the Intensity of Intervention

particular benefit from dependable schedules because they provide routine, stability, and a sense of control. However, allowing for flexibility is also important.

• ***Encourage parents to volunteer at school and to read to their children at home.***

• ***Identify appropriate tasks children can accomplish on their own.*** Create opportunities for them to become more independent of you and others.

- *Use cooperative learning.* Cooperative learning enables all students to work together to achieve common goals. Cooperative learning has five components:
  1. *Positive interdependence.* Group members establish mutual goals, divide the prerequisite tasks, share materials and resources, assume shared roles, and provide feedback to one another.
  2. *Face-to-face interaction.* Group members encourage and facilitate one another's efforts to complete tasks through direct communication.
  3. *Individual accountability/personal responsibility.* Individual performance is assessed, and results are reported back to both the individual and the group, which holds members accountable for completing their fair share of responsibility.

technology tie-in

Internet Resources for Helping Children with Disabilities Learn to Read

The following resources are beneficial for all children in helping them learn to read. They are also especially beneficial for children with disabilities. Each of these websites can be found in the Linking to Learning feature at the end of the chapter. With the help of technology, teachers can give children tasks appropriate to their reading level with the goal of increasing their achievement. Choose resources for your children carefully and preview them before allowing children to use them.

FREE RESOURCES

Starfall—This is a favorite with children and has a wide range of activities, starting with interactives for each letter of the alphabet. Decodable stories, or stories written to illustrate specific phonics rules, can be read aloud while the child follows along with the text. Older children can enjoy a large selection of poems, folk tales, and other stories that can be read aloud to them.

Storytime Online—A project created by the Screen Actors Guild. Well-known actors read popular children's books. A favorite of many children is Elijah Wood reading *Me and My Cat.* A Storytime Online favorite of teachers is the reading of *The Rainbow Fish* by Ernest Borgnine.

Read Write Think—A joint effort by the International Reading Association and the National Council of Teachers of English. Interactive activities are available for children to develop their knowledge of the alphabet and for making words. Many examples of interactive graphic organizers are available for children to organize their thoughts after reading or to brainstorm ideas for writing. Quality lesson plans are available for teachers at all levels, K–3. Resources for parents and afterschool programs give ideas for fun ways to develop children's creativity and literacy skills at home.

Scholastic: Contains interactives that improve reading skills across the curriculum. One such activity is a Listen and Read Activity, a favorite of many students, especially English language learners. Interactive whiteboard activities integrate multiple content areas and allow students to work individually at their own pace or with partners and teams.

PBS Kids—Contains a variety of games and interactive activities to reinforce alphabet knowledge and comprehension skills. There are also many stories for children to listen to.

PAID SUBSCRIPTION WEBSITES

Many school districts subscribe to subscription websites, so be sure to check and see what is available for you and your children.

Reading A to Z—This site contains printable leveled books for children at all levels of reading. Also available are forms for teachers to take running records and keep track of the errors children make while reading aloud and the strategies they observe children using to decode text. Lesson plans and worksheets accompany each text.

Tumble Books—Hundreds of popular children's books are animated and read aloud on this popular website. Games, puzzles, and lessons, as well as lesson plans for teachers accompany each book.

4. *Interpersonal and small-group skills.* Students are responsible for getting to know and trust one another, communicating accurately and clearly, accepting and supporting one another, and resolving conflicts in a constructive manner.

5. *Group processing.* Group reflection includes describing which contributions of members are helpful or unhelpful in making decisions and which group actions should be continued or changed.

- *Develop a peer buddy system.* In a peer buddy system, classmates serve as friends, guides, or counselors to students who are experiencing problems. Variations are to pair an older student with a younger one who is experiencing a problem or to pair two students who are experiencing similar problems.[47]

Testing Strategies for Children with Disabilities. We've talked about the difficulty of using tests and assessments with children with disabilities. We have known for a long time that too many children with disabilities are taking inappropriate state tests that produce results that don't reflect what the children really know and are able to do. More states are responding by providing modified tests. A growing number of states provide students effective and equitable access to grade-level or course curriculum and assessments. The push for modified tests comes in part from some schools that miss making Adequate Yearly Progress (AYP) as required by NCLB because too many exceptional students do not score at the proficient level. Teachers involved in the modified testing report that the process is much smoother than in previous years and that they believe the results support the use of the modified tests.[48]

TEACHING ENGLISH LANGUAGE LEARNERS (ELLS)

The United States is experiencing a rapid increase in immigration. By 2015, the Census Bureau estimates, immigrant children will account for 30 percent of the school-age population.[49] If you are working in Arizona, California, Nevada, Texas, New York, or New Jersey—the states that currently have the greatest immigrant representation—you will certainly teach students from immigrant families.[50] Here are some of the difficulties immigrant families face:

- One in every five children in immigrant families have difficulty speaking English.[51]
- Twenty-seven percent of immigrant children live in linguistically isolated homes. This means that in their homes, they are the only ones under the age of fourteen who know English.[52]
- Twenty-six percent of immigrant children's parents do not have a high school diploma or equivalent. Thirteen percent of immigrant children's parents do not have the equivalent of a ninth grade education.[53] This means that immigrant children will not get as much help with language development and school or homework activities as native-born children; and children of immigrants may be less prepared than their counterparts to start kindergarten. Three- and four-year-old children in immigrant families are less likely to participate in nursery school or preschool programs than their peers.[54]
- Spanish is second only to English as the most spoken language in the United States.[55] Spanish speakers often face discrimination in public and private sectors for not knowing English.

Supporting English Language Learners

José is a bright and energetic second grader. He excels in math, enjoys playing soccer, and collects baseball cards. He struggles with English as his second language.

He and his family immigrated only six months ago. José is one of 17 million children of immigrant families in the United States.[56]

As José's teacher, you will provide him with the knowledge and experiences necessary so he can be successful in school and life in the United States. Here are some steps you can take to help José:

- Play to José's strengths and interests.
  - José is good at math, so appeal to his analytical nature by providing reading material that is factual and observable. Magazines for children—like *Kids Discover, Muse, Ladybug,* and *Highlights*—are rich in graphs, tables, and photos and provide information José will find interesting.
  - José is interested in soccer, so provide stories and books about soccer to enrich his English-speaking and -reading skills.
  - Help José organize soccer games during recess. Encourage him to take a leadership role, like team captain, and to teach others how to play. A leadership role and helping others will increase his acceptance into the classroom and will allow him to make friendships more easily.
- Make sure José understands you. After giving directions to the entire class, ask José quietly if he understands the directions and if he needs you to repeat anything more slowly or in more detail.
- Make sure your body language conveys to José that you accept him as a person and learner. When José feels accepted and welcomed by you, he is more likely to come to you for help rather than not seeking help at all.
- Initiate a buddy system. Assign a classmate to José to run interference in language and cultural differences. This buddy will be a mentor to José when he needs it. A buddy system increases familiarity and encourages José's acceptance into your classroom.
- Accommodate cultural differences. Be knowledgeable of José's culture. Do a little research. Familiarize yourself with cultural norms so that you can appropriately respond to José. For example, certain symbols in certain cultures may mean different things. While you may use a particular symbol to signal acceptance or a job well done, José may take it as an insult.
- Incorporate Spanish (or another language) into your classroom. Doing so helps lay the foundation for language learning. For example, when introducing new vocabulary words, ask José for a translation in Spanish. The role of translator will give José a position of worth and knowledge in the classroom and will enhance his self-esteem.
- Encourage José to speak English when appropriate, but allow him to communicate with others freely in either Spanish or English.
- Have a "Spanish Hour" once a week in which José reads a book in Spanish to the class. The class can translate the story into English. This process encourages cultural discussions, acceptance, sharing, and language skills.

Dual Language Programs

The following programs use English and another language to teach ELLs. Review and reflect on these programs. Your school will use one of these programs or a variant to teach ELLs.

Two-Way Immersion or Two-Way Bilingual

- The goal is to develop strong skills and proficiency in both L1 (native language) and L2 (English).

- Includes students with an English-language background and students from one other language background.
- Instruction is in both languages, typically starting with smaller proportions of instruction in English, and gradually moving to half in each language.
- Students typically stay in the program throughout elementary school.

Dual Language

- When called "dual language immersion," usually the same as two-way immersion or two-way bilingual.
- When called "dual language," may refer to students from one language group developing full literacy skills in two languages—L1 and English.

One-Way Immersion

- Either native English speakers or native speakers of the second language make up all or most of the students enrolled and instruction takes place in two languages.
- At least half the instructional time is in the second language—in early grades it may take up as much as 90 percent.
- Must be a distinct separation of the two languages.

Two-Way Immersion

- Native speakers of English and native speakers of the second language learn both languages in the same classroom.
- At least one-third of the students must be native speakers of the second language.
- The goal is to produce fully bilingual, biliterate students by the end of elementary school.

Late Exit Transitional, Developmental Bilingual, or Maintenance Education

- The goal is to develop some skills and proficiency in L1 and strong skills and proficiency in L2 (English).
- Instruction at lower grades is in L1, gradually transitioning to English; students typically transition into mainstream classrooms with their English-speaking peers.
- Differences among the three programs focus on the degree of literacy students develop in the native language.

Early Exit Transitional

- The goal is to develop English skills as quickly as possible, without delaying learning of academic core content.
- Instruction begins in L1, but rapidly moves to English; students typically are transitioned into mainstream classrooms with their English-speaking peers as soon as possible.

Heritage Language or Indigenous Language Program

- The goal is literacy in two languages.
- Content is taught in both languages, with teachers fluent in both languages.
- Differences between the two programs: Heritage language programs typically target students who are non-English speakers or who have weak literacy skills in

Early childhood educators must consider the diverse characteristics of students—including gender, ethnicity, race, and socioeconomic factors—when planning learning opportunities for their classes. What are some ways diversity can enrich the curriculum?

bilingual education
Education in two languages (for example, the student's native language and English).

multicultural awareness The appreciation for and understanding of people's cultures, socioeconomic status, and gender. This includes understanding one's own culture.

 This **video** reinforces the importance of a teacher knowing the background and prior knowledge of each student. It is important to link the student's culture to the classroom and to broaden students' understanding of different cultures.

L1; indigenous language programs support endangered minority languages in which students may have weak receptive and no productive skills. Both programs often serve Native American students.[57]

MULTICULTURAL EDUCATION

The population of the United States is changing and will continue to change. For example, projections are that by 2050, over one-quarter of the population will be Hispanic.[58]

The population of young children in the United States reflects the population at large and represents a number of different cultures and ethnicities. Thus, many cities and school districts have populations that express great ethnic diversity, including Asian Americans, Native Americans, African Americans, and Hispanic Americans. For example, the Miami–Dade County, Florida, school district has children from 172 countries, each with its own culture.[59] As a result of changing demographics, more students will require special education, **bilingual education** (being taught in both their native language and in English), and other special services. Issues of culture and diversity shape instruction and curriculum. These demographics also have tremendous implications for how you teach and how your children learn.

Multicultural Awareness

Multicultural awareness is the appreciation for and understanding of people's cultures, socioeconomic status, and gender and includes understanding one's own culture. Multicultural awareness programs and activities focus on other cultures while making children aware of the content, nature, and richness of their own. Learning about other cultures concurrently with their own culture enables children to integrate commonalities and appreciate differences without inferring the inferiority or superiority of one or the other.

Promoting multiculturalism in an early childhood program has implications far beyond your school, classroom, and program. Multiculturalism influences and affects work habits, interpersonal relations, and a child's general outlook on life. Take these multicultural influences into consideration when designing curriculum and instructional processes for the children you teach.

Being a multiculturally aware teacher means you are sensitive to the socioeconomic backgrounds of children and families. For example, we know that children who come from families with low socioeconomic status learn less.[60] The same is true with children's school achievement and maternal education, as the Diversity Tie-In feature illustrates. By learning about family background you can provide children from diverse backgrounds the extra help they may need to be successful in school.

Use Appropriate Instructional Materials. Carefully consider and select appropriate instructional materials to support the infusion of multicultural education. The following are some suggestions for achieving this goal.

diversity tie-in

Race, Socioeconomic Status, and Student Achievement

Children's *socioeconomic status (SES)*, their social and economic backgrounds, is a reflection of family income, maternal education level, and family occupation. You may be surprised by the inclusion of maternal education level in this list, but in fact it is a powerful predictor of how well students do in school. As a mother's education increases, so does student achievement. This helps explain why, from a social and educational policy perspective, a U.S. priority is to prevent teenage mothers, indeed all girls, from dropping out of school.

Minority students tend to have lower reading and mathematics achievement scores than do their nonminority peers.[61] Whether this is due to testing bias, cultural bias, or other sociocultural factors, we do not know, but the fact remains that we must do serious educational work to increase minority children's achievement scores.

Only 7 percent of children who are dual-language learners are reading proficiently by the time they finish third grade. This is compared to 37 percent of students who speak English as their first language.[62] Mathematics aptitudes are just as staggering, with dual language learners achieving at 14 percent compared to their native English classmates who achieve at 44 percent.[63] The correlation between third grade reading and mathematics ability levels and dropping out of high school or not finishing on time is validated through research time and time again.

Family income also correlates with how well students do in school, whether or not they drop out, the kind and type of schools they attend, and the quality of their teachers. There is also a correlation between children's family income and their achievement scores. Students' socioeconomic status is used to determine eligibility for many state and federal programs such as Head Start and Title I programs. One Head Start eligibility criterion, for example, is that the child's family meets federal poverty income criteria for enrollment, and many schools provide free or reduced-charge school lunches based on family income.

Socioeconomic status has many implications for children's academic, social, and behavioral development. Socioeconomic status affects nutrition, cognitive development, discipline practices, and the amount of quality time spent with parents and family. All of these factors play a large part in each child's ability to come to your classroom every day ready to learn and grow and develop. Take a moment to reflect on other effects that race, socioeconomic status, and parental, in particular maternal, education play in your classroom. How can you make a difference in the lives of your students regardless of their socioeconomic status?

Multicultural Literature. Choose literature that stresses similarities and differences regarding how children and families live their *whole lives*. Here are some examples of good books you can use with your children:

- *Princesas: Olvidadas o desconocidas* (*Princesses: Forgotten or Unknown*) by Philippe Lechermeier and Rebecca Dautremer: Describes unique princesses that all have their own positive and negative attributes.

- *El mejor mariachi del mundo* (*The Best Mariachi in the World*) by J. D. Smith: A tale about finding one's own talent.

- *Teo en la nieve* (*Teo in the Snow*) by Violeta Denou: Teo and his friends go on a winter excursion in the mountains and do not always make safe choices in the pursuit of having fun.

- *León y Beto* (*Leon and Bob*) by Simon James: A story about a boy whose father is away in the army and his imaginary friend who is his confidant and playmate.

- *¡Ay, No!* (*Oh, No!*) by Rotraut Susanne Berner: A lesson about a hen who complains about everything, her friend who has a solution to every complaint, and their discovery that things are not always black and white.

Themes. Early childhood teachers often select and teach with thematic units that help strengthen children's understanding of themselves, their culture, and the cultures of others. Here are some appropriate theme topics:

- Getting to Know Myself, Getting to Know Others
- What Is Special About You and Me?
- Growing Up in the City
- Growing Up in the Country
- Tell Me About Africa (South America, China, etc.)

Personal Accomplishments. Add to classroom activities, as appropriate, the accomplishments of people from different cultural groups, women of all cultures, and individuals with disabilities.

When selecting materials for use in a multicultural curriculum for early childhood programs, make sure:

- People of all cultures are represented fairly and accurately.
- People of color, many cultural groups, and people with exceptionalities are represented.
- Historical information is accurate and nondiscriminatory.
- Materials do not include stereotypical roles and language.
- There is gender equity—that is, boys and girls are represented equally and in nonstereotypical roles.

Teach to Children's Learning Styles and Intelligences.

Every child has a unique learning style. Although every person's learning style is different, we can cluster learning styles for instructional purposes.

Different Children, Different Learning Styles. It makes sense to consider students' various learning styles and account for these differences when organizing the environment and developing activities: "Learning style is the way that students of every age are affected by their (1) immediate environment, (2) own emotionality, (3) sociological needs, (4) physical characteristics, and (5) psychological inclinations when concentrating and trying to master and remember new or difficult information or skills."[64]

Learning styles consist of the following elements:

- Environmental—sound, light, temperature, and design
- Emotional—motivation, persistence, responsibility, and the need for either structure or choice
- Sociological—learning alone, with others, or in a variety of ways (perhaps including media)
- Physical—perceptual strengths, intake, day or night energy levels, and mobility
- Psychological—global/analytic, hemispheric preference, and impulsive/reflective

Teaching to children's learning styles is a good way to infuse multiculturalism into your program.[65] Also, review and reflect on Gardner's multiple intelligences theory and how you can apply it to your teaching.

Educating students with diverse backgrounds and special needs makes for a challenging and rewarding career. As society, families, and children change; as diversity increases; and as more students with special needs come to school, you will have to change how and what you teach. How to constantly improve your responses to students' special needs and improve learning environments and curricula will be one of

learning style The way a child learns—specifically, how the child's environment, emotions, sociological needs, physical characteristics, and psychological inclinations come into play as he or she works to master new or difficult information or skills.

your ongoing professional responsibilities. Your students with special needs are waiting for you to make a difference in their lives!

ACTIVITIES FOR PROFESSIONAL DEVELOPMENT

ethical dilemma

"Speak English first!"

Beth Janison is a new first grade teacher in River Bend School District. River Bend has had a large influx of minority students during the past few years. In fact, the minority students are almost the majority. Not everyone thinks that the rapid increase in the minority student population is beneficial to the school district or town. Some of Beth's colleagues think that the school district is bending over (too far) backward to meet minority students' needs. At Beth's first meeting with Harry Holister, her new mentor teacher, he remarked, "Respecting minorities and catering to them are two different things. I'm going to stress with my parents that this is America and speaking English comes first. If their kids can't speak English, they fail!"

What should Beth do? Should she agree with Harry and adopt a policy of English first? Should Beth seek out the director of multiculturalism for her district and discuss Harry's comments with him or her? Should Beth contact the local LULAC (League of United Latin American Citizens) and ask for their support? Or should Beth pursue another course of action? What should Beth do? What would you do?

Application Activities

1. Visit an inclusive classroom and observe a child with a special need during play time. Develop an observational checklist to guide your observation. Note the materials available, the physical arrangement of the environment, and the number of other children involved. Try to determine whether the child is really engaged in the play activity. Hypothesize about why the child is or is not engaged. Make three recommendations for how you would ensure the full inclusion and engagement of this child in your classroom. Discuss your observations with your colleagues.

2. As we discussed in this chapter, the number of children diagnosed with autism is increasing. There is a lot of public interest in autism, its causes, treatments, and especially how to educate children with autism. Search the Internet for the latest developments regarding autism diagnosis. What are they? Share your findings on your class online discussion board, and ask your classmates if they have anything to add to your list. What implications does your information have for children, families, and you?

3. We discussed applied behavior analysis (ABA) as one educational intervention for educating children with autism. Go to YouTube.com or Teachertube.com and observe teachers implementing ABA approaches in their classrooms. What questions and conclusions do you have after watching these videos? What do you think are two benefits of ABA? Give two reasons why you would or would not want to receive ABA training. Post your reasons on your class website.

4. Multiculturalism is an important part of every classroom. Go online and search for three activities you can use to promote multiculturalism in your classroom. Share these activities on your class discussion board and with your friends on Facebook or other social networking sites and ask for opinions about your findings. See what other activities your friends and classmates suggest. Compile a multiculturalism resource list to use and share.

Linking to Learning

Starfall

www.starfall.com
A free website to teach children to read with phonics. For preschool, kindergarten, and first grade. Exciting phonics games and online interactive books.

Storytime Online

www.storylineonline.net
Streaming video program featuring famous people reading children's books aloud.

Read Write Think

www.readwritethink.org
Providing educators and students access to the highest quality practices and resources in reading and language arts instruction.

Scholastic

www.scholastic.com
The corporate mission of Scholastic is to encourage the intellectual and personal growth of all children, beginning with literacy, the cornerstone of all learning.

PBS Kids

www.pbskids.org
Play educational games, watch PBS KIDS shows, and find activities like coloring and music.

Reading A to Z

www.readinga-z.com
Reading A-Z is among the family of Learning A-Z websites providing affordable, online curriculum resources.

Tumble Books

www.tumblebooks.com
TumbleBookLibrary is an online collection of animated, talking picture books that teach young children the joys of reading in a format they'll love.

MyEducationLab

Go to Topics 10 (Cultural & Linguistic Diversity) and 11 (Special Needs/Inclusion) in the MyEducationLab (www.myeducationlab.com) for your course, where you can:

- Find learning outcomes for Cultural & Linguistic Diversity and Special Needs/Inclusion along with the national standards that connect to these outcomes.

- Complete Assignments and Activities that can help you more deeply understand the chapter content.

- Apply and practice your understanding of the core teaching skills identified in the chapter with the Building Teaching Skills and Dispositions learning units.

- Examine challenging situations and cases presented in the IRIS Center Resources.

- Access video clips of CCSSO National Teachers of the Year award winners responding to the question, "Why Do I Teach?" in the Teacher Talk section.

- Hear viewpoints of experts in the field in Professional Perspectives.

- Check your comprehension on the content covered in the chapter by going to the Study Plan in the Book Resources for your text. Here you will be able to take a chapter quiz, receive feedback on your answers, and then access Review, Practice, and Enrichment activities to enhance your understanding of chapter content.

chapter 12

GUIDING CHILDREN'S BEHAVIOR

Helping Children Be Their Best

NAEYC Standards for Early Childhood Professional Preparation Programs

Standard 1: Promoting Child Development and Learning

I use my understanding of young children's characteristics and needs, and of multiple interacting influences on children's development and learning, to create environments that are healthy, respectful, supportive, and challenging for each child.[1]

Standard 4. Using Developmentally Effective Approaches to Connect with Children and Families

I understand and use positive relationships and supportive interactions as the foundation for my work with young children and families. I know, understand, and use a wide array of developmentally appropriate approaches, instructional strategies, and tools to connect with children and families and positively influence each child's development and learning.[2]

WHY GUIDE CHILDREN'S BEHAVIOR?

Think for a moment of the early childhood classes you have observed. In some of the classes children were actively involved in meaningful activities based on Common Core, state, and district standards. In other classrooms, the children and teachers seemed disorganized with little real learning occurring. What makes the difference? Three things: a community of learners, a well-organized classroom, and a well-thought-out and well-implemented plan for guiding children's behavior and learning.

As an early childhood professional, you will assume the major responsibility for guiding children's behavior in up-close and personal ways. You will spend many hours with young children as a parent/family surrogate. You need to know how to best guide children's behavior and help them become responsible. There are a number of reasons for knowing how to best guide children's behavior:

- Helping children learn to guide and be responsible for their own behavior is as important as helping them learn to read and write. Think for a moment about how many times you have said or have heard others say, "If only the children would behave, I could teach them something!" Appropriate behavior and learning go together. One of your primary roles as an early childhood teacher is to help children learn the behaviors and skills necessary for them to act responsibly.

- Helping children learn to act responsibly and guiding their behavior lays the foundation for lifelong responsible and productive living. As early childhood educators, we believe that the early years are the formative years. Consequently, what we teach children about responsible living, how we guide them, and the skills we help them learn will last a lifetime.

- The roots of delinquent and deviant behavior are in the early years. From research we know which behaviors lead to future problems. For example, research shows that children who rebound between home and school with an aggressive attitude toward their peers and teachers and a tendency to cause disruption are more likely to suffer a range of negative outcomes as adults. They are at greater risk of failing school, becoming addicted to drugs, engaging in antisocial behavior, and succumbing to depression or anxiety.[3]

- The public is increasingly concerned about the erosion of civility, and what it perceives as a general breakdown of personal responsibility for bad behavior. One reason the public funds public educational system at all levels is to help keep society strong and healthy. Parents and the public look to you and your early childhood colleagues for assistance in helping children learn to live cooperatively and civilly in a democratic society. Getting along with others and guiding one's behavior is a culturally and socially meaningful accomplishment.

What Is Guiding Behavior?

Guiding children's behavior is a process of helping them build positive behaviors. It involves **behavior guidance**, a process by which all children learn to control and direct their behavior and become independent and self-reliant.

As you work with young children, one of your goals is to help them become independent and have the ability to regulate or govern their own behavior. **Self-regulation** is the child's ability to plan, guide, and monitor his or her own behavior according to changing classroom and life circumstances.

GUIDING BEHAVIOR IN A COMMUNITY OF LEARNERS

I emphasize in this chapter that cognitive and social development, and behavioral characteristics are interconnected. High-quality early childhood teachers recognize that it does not make sense to teach children reading, writing, and arithmetic and not also teach them skills necessary for responsibly guiding their own behavior.

The Community of Learners

Classrooms are and should be a **community of learners** in which children of all ages take shared responsibly for the physical, social, and learning environments. In this environment, you must help children develop the behaviors necessary for living and learning in the community.

MyEducationLab

Visit the MyEducationLab for *Fundamentals of Early Childhood Education* to enhance your understanding of chapter concepts with a personalized Study Plan. You'll also have the opportunity to hone your teaching skills through video-based Assignments and Activities as well as Building Teaching Skills and Dispositions lessons.

FOCUS QUESTIONS

1. What is guiding behavior and why is it important?

2. What does it mean to guide behavior in a community of learners?

3. What is the social constructivist approach to guiding behavior?

4. What are twelve steps you can use to guide children's behavior?

behavior guidance A process by which teachers help all children learn to control and direct their behavior and become independent and self-reliant.

self-regulation The ability of preschool children to control their emotions and behaviors, to delay gratification, and to build positive social relations with each other.

community of learners A classroom or learning setting in which all children take shared responsibility for their own and each other's physical, social, and learning environments.

In this **video**, a first grade teacher works with her class to refine their classroom rules and a middle school teacher uses a class meeting to solve a problem. Notice how both teachers model good listening skills and respect.

A learning community is child centered. All that we do in classrooms should focus on children's growth and development as persons and as learners. The practice we use and teach for guiding children's behavior is for their benefit. As a result of our guiding children's behavior—and helping them guide their own behavior—children can be successful, confident, responsible, and contributors to the learning community.

Democratic Living.   In our efforts to help prepare all children to live effectively and productively in a democracy, we place increasing emphasis on providing experiences that will enable them to productively live and learn in democratic school and classroom communities. The idea of teaching democratic living through classrooms that are miniature democracies is not new. John Dewey was an advocate of this approach and championed democratic classrooms as a way of promoting democratic living. However, running a democratic classroom is easier said than done. It requires a confident teacher who believes it is worth the effort.

- Let children, as a class, make appropriate decisions about class rules and how the classroom operates. Students can suggest procedures for how to decide who does what classroom chores, such as conducting a lunch count, and so on.
- Actively and intentionally teach respect, such as how children can get along with their peers.
- In your classroom meetings, let children talk about their joys and concerns. Listen to what children say. Use this information to guide you in how you respond to and interact with your children.
- Always complement children for what they do and provide proactive, encouraging feedback and suggestions for how they can achieve at the next level.

Key Foundational Practices.   Learning communities are grounded in key foundational practices. These include:

- *Cooperative living and learning.* You can promote cooperative living in which children help each other direct their behavior. Think about Vygotsky's theory of social relations. Children are born seeking social interactions, and social relations are necessary for children's learning and development. Peers help each other learn.

    Children's natural social groups and play groups are ideal and natural settings in which to help children assist each other in learning new behaviors and being responsible for their own behavior. The classroom as a whole is an important social group.

    In addition, you can initiate, support, and foster a cooperative, collaborative learning community in the classroom. In a learning community, children are involved in developing and setting guidelines and devising classroom norms and, by extension, individual norms of behavior. Teachers "assist" children but do not do things for them, and they ask questions that make children think about their behavior—how it influences the class, themselves, and others. This process of cooperative living occurs daily. Discussions grow out of existing problems, and guidance is provided based on the needs of children and the classroom.

- *Respect for children.* Constantly honor and respect children as human beings. When you respect and honor children, then they are much more likely to engage in behavior that is respectful and honorable. Here are some guidelines you can follow for showing respect to children:
    - Be positive in all that you do and say to and with children.
    - Be polite and mannerly in all you do and say.
    - Listen to each child and acknowledge his or her feelings and opinions.
    - Set appropriately high expectations for each child.

- *Time and opportunity to talk about behavior and develop strategies for guiding their behavior.* A good way to provide children time and opportunity to talk about behavior and classroom problems is through a class meeting. (An excellent resource for learning about and how to conduct class meetings is the NAEYC resource book *Class Meetings: Young Children Solving Problems Together* by Emily Vance and Patricia Jimenez Weaver.) Classroom meetings can serve many useful functions. The teacher and children can talk about expected behaviors from day to day ("When we are done playing with toys, what do we do with them?"), review what children did in a particular center or situation, and help them anticipate what they will do in future situations ("Tomorrow morning when we visit the Senior Citizen Center …"). In all these situations, children are cooperatively engaged in thinking about, talking about, and learning how to engage in appropriate behavior.

  Democratic learning environments require that students develop responsibility for their own and others' behaviors and learning, that classrooms operate as communities, and that all children are respected and respectful of others.

- *Character education as a means of promoting responsible behavior.* Character education continues to be an important means of promoting fundamental behaviors that early childhood professionals and society believe are essential for living in a democratic society.

- *Civility.* Civil behavior and ways to promote it are of growing interest at all levels of society. The specific teaching of civil behavior—how to treat others well and in turn be treated well—is seen as essential for living well in contemporary society. At a minimum, civil behavior includes manners, respect, and the ability to get along with people of all races, cultures, and socioeconomic backgrounds.

civil behavior In interactions with others, treating them well and, in turn, being treated well.

WHAT IS THE SOCIAL CONSTRUCTIVIST APPROACH TO GUIDING BEHAVIOR?

You can use theories of learning and development to guide your teaching. Reacquaint yourself now with the theories of Piaget, Vygotsky, Maslow, and Erikson so their ideas will be fresh in your mind as we apply them to guiding children's behavior.

The Social Constructivist Approach: Piaget and Vygotsky

Piaget's and Vygotsky's theories support a social constructivist approach to learning and behavior. Teachers who embrace a social constructivist approach believe that children construct or build a set of behaviors as a result of learning from experience and from making decisions that lead to responsible actions. Your primary role in the constructivist approach is to guide and help children as they construct or build their behaviors and use them in socially appropriate and productive ways. This process begins in homes and classrooms.

Vygotsky's theories of *scaffolding* and the *zone of proximal development (ZPD)* especially lend themselves as a positive means of helping you to guide children's behavior. Also, two additional essentials to Vygotskyian constructivist theories: adult–child discourse and child self-discourse (or private speech) are useful. Foundational to Vygotskyian and constructivist theory are the central beliefs that the development of a child's knowledge and behaviors occurs in the context of social relations and with adults and peers. This means that learning and development are socially mediated as children interact with more competent peers and adults. As children gain the ability to master language and appropriate social relations, they intentionally regulate their behavior.

social constructivist approach A theory that states children construct or build their behavior as a result of learning from experience and from making decisions that lead to responsible behavior.

adult–child discourse A conversation between an adult/parent and a child.

self-discourse or private speech An internal conversation between a person and himself or herself.

Guiding Behavior in the Zone of Proximal Development

The zone of proximal development (ZPD) is the cognitive and developmental space that is created when the child is in social interaction with a more competent person (MCP) or a more knowledgeable other (MKO). As Vygotsky explains, the ZPD is the "actual development level as determined by independent problem solving and the level of potential development as determined through problem solving under adult guidance or in collaboration with more capable peers."[4] Problem solving is what guiding behavior is all about. Teachers take children from the behavioral and social skills they have in their ZPD and guide them to increasingly higher levels of responsible behavior and social interactions. Also, although we often think of guiding behavior as a one-on-one activity, this is not the case. Your role in guiding behavior includes large and small groups, as well as individual children. Figure 12.1 illustrates the ZPD and provides ideas for how to guide children's behavior within it. The ZPD is constantly moving and changing, depending on children's behavioral accomplishments and the assistance and scaffolding provided by others.

Guiding Behavior with Scaffolding

Scaffolding is one of the ways teachers can guide children in the ZPD. Recall that scaffolding is the use of informal methods such as conversations, questions, modeling,

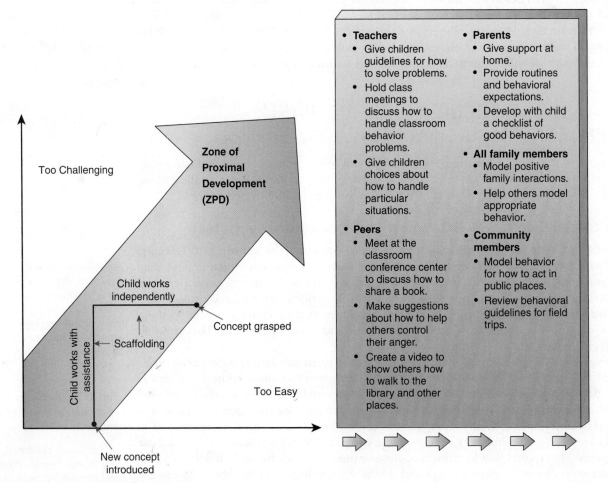

FIGURE 12.1 Zone of Proximal Development

guiding, and supporting to help children learn concepts, knowledge, and skills that they might not learn by themselves. When more competent others provide "help," children are able to accomplish what they would not have been able to do on their own. In the ZPD, children are capable of far more competent behavior and achievements as they receive guidance and support from teachers and parents. The Professionalism in Practice feature, "How to Guide Hard-to-Manage Children to Help Ensure Their Success," shows you how to scaffold learning as you intentionally teach children the skills and behaviors essential to guiding their own behavior.

Adult–Child Discourse

The scaffolding script that follows is illustrative of adult–child discourse. Discourse also involves talking about how children might solve problems, guide their own behavior, interact and cooperate with others, understand norms of social conduct, and learn values related to school and family living. Teachers must initiate and guide these discourses and help children learn new skills that will assist them in developing self-regulation. Here is an example of a "learning conversation" that invites student participation. This discourse centers on how student authors should act while they are sharing their stories:

Ms. Anthony: Maybe we should now think about how to behave as the author during author's chair. What do authors do? Who can remember? Stephanie, would you like to start?

Stephanie: The author sits in the author's chair and speaks loud and clear.

Joyce: The author should not be shy and should be brave and confident.

Ms. Anthony continues to invite students to participate by providing ideas and suggestions, using this type of scaffolding. The children create a list of responsibilities to guide their behaviors while sharing stories.[5]

Private Speech and Self-Guided Behavior

Jennifer, a four-year-old preschooler, is busily engrossed in putting a puzzle together. As she searches for a puzzle piece, she asks herself out loud, "Which piece comes next?" I'm sure you have heard children talk to themselves. More than likely, you have talked to yourself while working on a task! Such conversations are commonplace in the lives of young children and adults.

Private speech plays an important role in problem solving and self-regulation of behavior. Children learn to transfer problem-solving knowledge and responsibility from adults to themselves:

> Self-regulation is focused on the ability of a child to regulate him or herself through private speech by comprehending what is asked in a given task or situation. The student must also be able to monitor his or her behaviors to see if there is coordination with the given task at hand and be able to maintain or avert what he is doing based on his own judgments.
>
> Self-regulation is important in school and teachers are the first to acknowledge this. A self-regulated student can stay in his designated area and focus on the task given to him by the teachers, capable of paying attention when the teacher is discussing or reading aloud without losing the attention focused on the teacher, especially to the learning process the student experiences. The child will soon learn to talk and may use "self-talk" to help regulate his or her behavior.[6]

TWELVE STEPS FOR GUIDING BEHAVIOR

As with many things in life, you accomplish goals by having a well-thought-out, conceptual plan for what you want to achieve. Guiding children's behavior is no

professionalism in practice

How to Guide Hard-to-Manage Children to Help Ensure Their Success

Tyrone entered the kindergarten classroom on the first day of the school year, trailing several feet behind his mom, who appeared to be unaware of his presence. She called out a greeting to another mom, and the two of them had an extended discussion about events in the neighborhood. Tyrone glanced around the room and headed purposefully toward the housekeeping center, where he grabbed a baby doll, threw it out of the doll bed, and then ran to the block box and grabbed a large block in each hand. At this point I deflected his trail of destruction and redirected his progress: "Good morning, welcome to my class. My name is Ms. Cheryl. What's your name?" The whirlwind stopped briefly to mumble a response that I could not understand and glared at me in open hostility. "Let's go talk to Mom," I suggested, touching his shoulder and directing him toward his mom.

BACKGROUND

My school is in an area that includes mostly low-socioeconomic households; ours is a Title I school, with 95 percent of our students on free or reduced-fee lunches. In any given year, one-half to two-thirds of our students entering kindergarten have had no preschool experience. Nevertheless, as an early childhood educator, it is my job to help these students develop behaviors that will ensure their success in education. That does not mean that I need only to teach them to write their names, recognize all their letters and numbers, sit quietly in their chairs, and raise their hands before they speak. These tasks are not ends in themselves but are important steps in encouraging children to love learning and to gain the self-regulation that supports it.

UNDERSTANDING BEHAVIOR

In our opening scenario, what important facts do you recognize as signals that Tyrone has some behaviors that require adjustment to ensure his success in school? He seems unaware of the expected protocol for entering a classroom—that is, looking for an adult in charge to give him directions. His mother's apparent lack of interest in her child's behavior could be an indicator that Tyrone does not expect the adults around him to be involved with his activities. He may have been in an atmosphere that requires very little from him when it comes to following rules and, as indicated by his hostility, may see adult intervention as only restrictive rather than supportive and nurturing. Tyrone may even have an undiagnosed speech problem that prohibits adults and other children from understanding his needs. If adults in his world have failed to observe and interact with him, he is also probably lacking basic language skills and vocabulary, which would limit his understanding. He appears to deal with his world in a very physical manner.

BEHAVIORS NECESSARY FOR SUCCESS IN SCHOOL

The following behaviors are necessary for children to succeed in school:

Behavior 1: *Recognition of authority*—Tyrone was not even aware that an adult was in charge of the classroom.
Behavior 2: *Trust in adults*—The process of building trust is lengthy, but Tyrone needs to learn to see adults as nurturing and supportive.
Behavior 3: *Use of verbal skills rather than physical reactions*—If Tyrone is lacking in language, I can help provide language experiences, defining words, explaining everything in detail, showing and describing pictures, reading books aloud, helping with activities, and talk, talk, talking.

Behaviors 1 and 2 are especially complex; they stem from children's environments and experiences. However, I am committed to being one of the reasons a child succeeds and will dedicate great amounts of time and energy to changing different. It involves many dimensions and there is a lot to think about. The following twelve steps for guiding behavior are designed to give you practical, achievable, and successful ideas you can relate to and use in your daily practice. As you read and reflect on each of the twelve steps, consider how you can apply them to your teaching and how you can begin to personalize them to your professional practice so they become your own and are strategies that you use automatically in helping children be their best.

behaviors that interfere with student learning. I follow certain steps to guide destructive behaviors into more successful ones.

STEP 1 Plan

Before that first day of school, I plan—what activities I will offer my students, what part of the day I will use for centers, how I can show my students the best ways to use materials, where I want them to keep their belongings, how I can explain my expectations about dealing with conflict, how I will deal with behavior that is inappropriate, and what I am going to say about procedures for our classroom.

STEP 2 Be Explicit

Many of my students are not accustomed to having an adult schedule their time for six hours, and many behavior problems stem from this new pressure to conform to an unfamiliar structure. Therefore, I want to be sure that all of my students fully understand what I expect. For example, I state exactly how I want them to move about the classroom, the cafeteria, the playground, and the school hallways. If they do not follow my instructions, I require them to practice. Many behaviors that inhibit success in school occur because students are not made aware of appropriate and inappropriate school procedures.

Some teachers seem to lack a presence of authority with their students. These teachers appear to be unaware that in every group situation, someone needs to be in charge. Authority is demonstrated in a demeanor that gives the immediate impression, "Yes, I do know what I am doing and I have reasons for all of my actions." Authority is demonstrated with the calm assurance that comes from knowing that you will get the results you desire if you are persistent. Hard-to-manage students take great patience. Often hours of thinking, talking to colleagues, reading, and planning are required. You may only lay the foundation for helping a troubled student. Other teachers who follow you will, hopefully, add to the building of success in that student.

STEP 3 Model Behaviors

I model or have my students role-play expected behavior in interpersonal actions. Students who take other students' belongings, hit other students, or push and shove other students are taught to handle these issues through conflict-resolution methods. However, it takes numerous rounds of modeling and role-playing to make an impact on behavior that has been ingrained for five years at home and is still the norm when students return home.

STEP 4 Role-Play

I spend some time each day having students role-play scenarios with incorrect behavior. We brainstorm about what is the correct behavior. Hitting, pushing, name calling, and destroying property are all common problems among my students. I ask my students how they feel if someone calls them a name (or exhibits any of the other negative behaviors).

STEP 5 Develop Classroom Rules

I have five classroom rules:

1. We listen to each other.
2. We use our hands for helping, not hurting.
3. We use caring language.
4. We care about each other's feelings.
5. We are responsible for what we say and do.

STEP 6 Reinforce

Helping hard-to-manage children learn to guide their own behavior takes consistent reteaching and reinforcement. I correct every misbehavior that I see, by either using the "I don't like it when you . . ." statement or by stating which rule has been broken. I use a very calm voice when I talk to my students and do not allow them to "tell" on each other. When a student comes to me with a tale of misbehavior, I ask, "Did you tell [*specific name*] how you feel?" Usually, by the end of the first nine-week grading period, my students are using the behaviors and statements we have learned, and the tone of my classroom changes from a volatile one to a caring one. Spending some time at the beginning of the year changing behaviors and stating expectations gives my students the guidance they need to begin and to continue successful student careers.

....

Source: Contributed by Cheryl Doyle, National Board Certified preschool teacher, Teacher of the Gifted, grades K–5, Caribbean Elementary, Miami, Florida.

Step 1: Use Constructivist Guidance Guidelines

Based on the constructivist theory, here are some strategies you can use to guide children's behavior:

- Guide problem solving:
  - "Tanya, what are some things you can do to help you remember to put the books away?"

- "Travis, you and Maria want to use the easel at the same time. What are some ideas for how you can both use it?"
- Ask questions that help children arrive at their own solutions:
  - "Jacob, you can't use both toys at the same time. Which one do you want to use first?"
  - "Rene, here is an idea that might help you get to the block corner. Ask Amelia, 'Would you please move over a little so I can get to the blocks?'"
- Model appropriate skills:
  - Practice social skills and manners. For example, say "Please" and "Thank you."
- Listen attentively to children and encourage listening.
  - For example, say "Harry has something he wants to tell us. Let's listen to what he has to say."

Use other constructivist strategies such as scaffolding, class discussions and adult–child discourse. Using these strategies effectively requires much determination and practice. They are worth the effort, and you will be rewarded with their beneficial results as you learn to guide children's behavior.

Step 2: Guide the Whole Child

Children are not one- or two-dimensional persons. Children are a unified whole. There is much discussion today about teaching the whole child—physically, socially, emotionally, mentally, linguistically, and spiritually. The same applies to guiding behavior of the whole child. This renewed interest in the whole child reflects the profession's ongoing dedication to developmentally appropriate practice. The Association for Supervision and Curriculum Development (ASCD) leads a national effort to include the whole child in all instructional programs and practices. The association's website is listed at the end of the chapter in the Linking to Learning section. As you work with your children, reflect on how you can promote their positive development in all dimensions.

Differentiate Guidance. Just as we differentiate instruction for each child, we also want to differentiate guidance for each child. This means that the one-size-fits-all approach to guidance doesn't work. Assess each child's behavioral strengths and weaknesses and select appropriate guidance for each child. For example, Amanda is a very responsible child who works and learns best with little guidance and through appropriate suggestions for how she can complete certain assignments and activities. Raul, on the other hand, is a boisterous, active boy who needs constant reminders of rules and how to interact with others. While you will have rules that apply to the entire class, and while you will have behavioral guidelines that apply to everybody, individual children need more or less explicit guidelines and some may need more of your attention than others. Figure 12.2 illustrates the different components of teaching the whole child.

Step 3: Know and Use Developmentally Appropriate Practice

Knowing child development is the cornerstone of developmentally appropriate practice. Children cannot behave well when adults expect too much or too little of them based on their development or when parents expect them to behave in ways inappropriate for them as individuals. Thus, a key for guiding children's behavior is to *really know what they are like*. This is the real meaning of developmentally appropriate practice. You will want to study children's development and observe children's behavior to learn what is appropriate for all children and individual children based on their age, needs, gender, and culture.

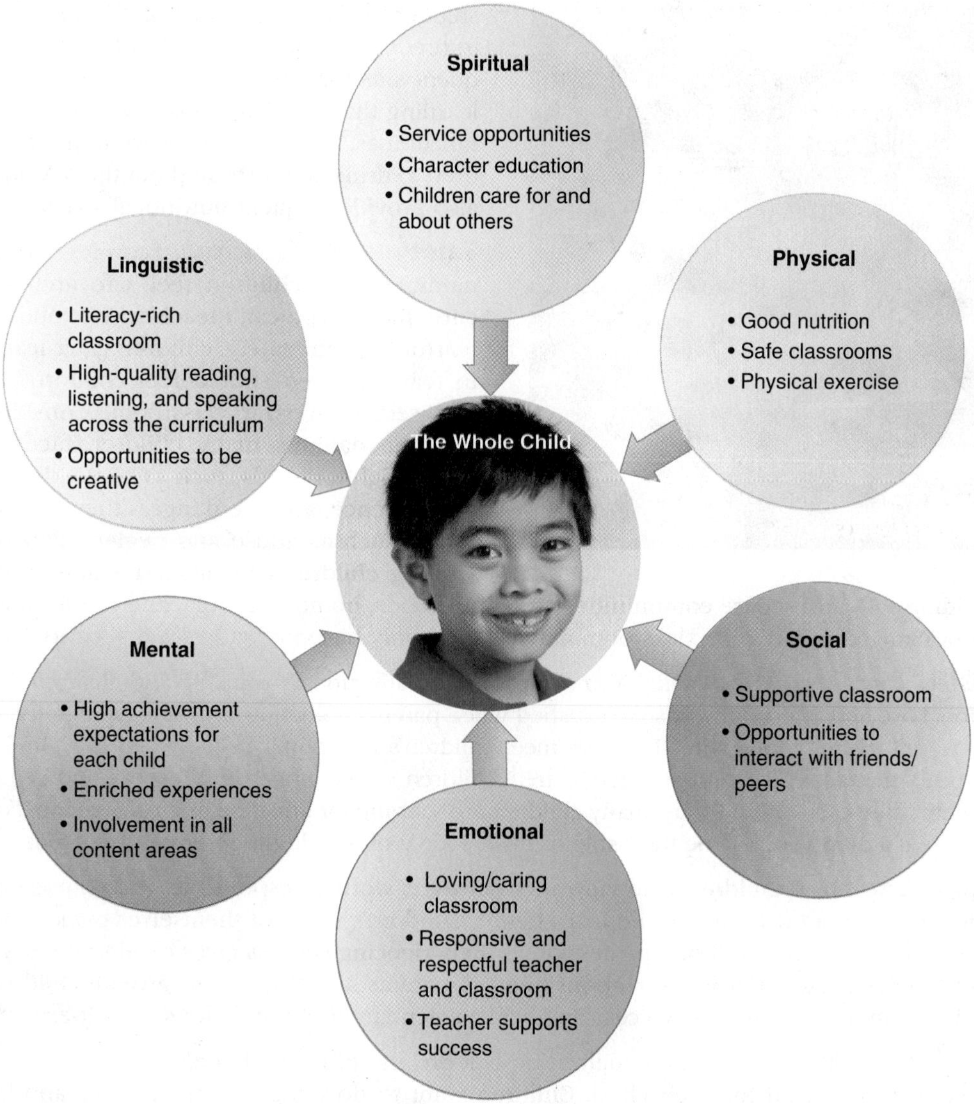

FIGURE 12.2 Guiding the Whole Child

Step 4: Meet Children's Needs

A major reason for knowing children and child development is so that you will be able to meet their needs. Abraham Maslow felt that human growth and development were oriented toward *self-actualization*, the striving to realize one's potential. Review and reflect on Maslow's hierarchy of needs now. Consider how children's physical needs, safety and security needs, belonging and affection needs, and self-esteem needs culminate in self-actualization. An example of each of these needs illustrates how to apply them to guiding children's behavior.

Physical Needs.   Children's abilities to guide their own behaviors depend in part on how well their physical needs are met. Children do their best in school when they are well nourished. Families and schools should provide for children's nutritional needs by giving them breakfast. Recent brain research also informs us that the brain needs protein and water to function well. Mental performance can fall by 10 percent when your

Helping children become more independent by warmly supporting their efforts is one of the most effective forms of guidance. Identify some ways you can support your students' efforts to do things for themselves.

students are thirsty, and thirst will also add to tiredness, headaches, and irritability. Frequent small intakes of water are better for learning than limiting drinks to breaks and lunchtimes.[7] You should encourage children to drink water throughout the day and also provide frequent nutritional snacks.

Safety and Security. Learning communities help children feel safe and secure. Just as you can't teach when you are fearful for your safety, children can't learn in fear. Children should feel comfortable and secure in your classroom. Consider also the dangers many children face in their neighborhoods, such as crime, drugs, and violence, and the dangers they face at home, such as abuse and neglect. Part of guiding children's behavior includes providing safe and secure communities, neighborhoods, homes, schools, and classrooms. For many children your classroom may be their only haven of safety and security.

Belonging and Affection. You need love and affection in your life and children do, too. Love and affection needs are satisfied when parents hold, hug, and kiss their children and tell them, "I love you." Teachers meet children's affectional needs when they smile, speak pleasantly, are kind and gentle, treat children with courtesy and respect, and genuinely value each child. Today, many children are starving for affection and recognition. For these children you may be their sole or main source of meeting their emotional needs.

Self-Esteem. Children who view themselves as worthy, responsible, and competent feel good about themselves and learn better. Children's views of themselves come from parents and early childhood professionals. Experiencing success gives children feelings of high self-esteem. It is the responsibility of parents and teachers to give all children opportunities for success. Success and achievement are the foundations for self-esteem.

Self-Actualization. Self-actualization is a process of becoming all you can be, and we want this goal for each child. Children want to do things for themselves and be independent. You and parents can help children become independent by helping them learn to dress themselves, go to the restroom by themselves, and take care of their classrooms. Teachers also help children set achievement and behavior goals ("Tell me what you are going to build with your blocks") and encourage them to evaluate their behavior ("Let's talk about what you did in the literacy center").

Step 5: Help Children Build New Behaviors

Helping children build new behaviors means that you help them learn that they are primarily responsible for their own behavior and that the pleasures and rewards for appropriate behavior are internal, coming from within themselves as opposed to always coming from outside (i.e., from the approval and praise of others). This concept is known as **locus of control**, the source or place of control, which should be the child, not the teacher.

The process of developing an internal locus of control begins at birth, continues through the early childhood years, and is a never-ending process throughout life. When their locus of control is external, children are controlled by others; they are always told what to do and how to behave. We want children to control their own behavior and to take responsibility for their behavior. What we want to avoid is having children blame their behavior on others ("Chandra took my pencil") or on circumstances ("I didn't have

locus of control The source of control over an individual's behavior; the locus may be external (controlled by others) or internal (within oneself).

time"). Legitimate excuses are appropriate, but always blaming others or external events is not. Learning to do it right and trying again after a failure are important positive behaviors.

Affirming and acknowledging children's appropriate behavior is a good way to build new behaviors—everyone likes to be praised and affirmed for a job well done, good efforts, and their best work. Helping children learn new behaviors and change or modify old behaviors is also an important part of guidance. Following are some ways of affirming and acknowledging behavior verbally, socially, and nonverbally:

Verbal

- "I like the way you . . ." "Great," "Cool," "Wow," "Way to go," "Super," "Terrific," "Excellent," "Fantastic," "Awesome," "You're working hard," "Good job," "Tremendous," "Beautiful"

Social (as a result of good behavior in classrooms, small groups, etc.)

- Parties, group approval, class privileges, or individual privileges; time to do a favorite activity (e.g., read books, play games)

Nonverbal

Facial: Smiling, winking, or raising of eyebrows

Gestures: Clapping of hands, waving, forming an okay sign (thumb + index finger), victory sign, nodding head, or shrugging shoulders

Proximity: Standing near someone, shaking hands, getting down on child's level, hugging, rubbing on child's back, or holding child's arm up

Responsible choices and support are key ways to help children develop responsible behavior that internalizes their locus of control.

Guiding children's behavior consists of essential guidelines, including helping children build new, appropriate behaviors and helping them to be responsible for their behaviors. Why is it important for children to learn to guide their own behavior rather than having teachers and parents always telling them what to do?

Step 6: Empower Children

Helping children build new behaviors creates a sense of responsibility and self-confidence. As children are given responsibility, they assume responsibility and develop greater self-direction, as you guide them to the next level in their personal zones of proximal development. Some teachers and parents hesitate to let children assume responsibilities, but without responsibilities children are bored and frustrated and become discipline problems—the very opposite of what is intended. Learning communities are child-centered, not teacher-centered. It is important to instill in children a sense of independence and responsibility for their own behavior. For example, you might say, "You have really worked a long time cutting out the flower you drew. You kept working on it until you were finished. Would you like some tape to hang it up with?"

You can do a number of things to help children develop new behaviors that result in empowerment.

- *Give children responsibilities.* All children, from an early age, should have responsibilities—that is, tasks that are their job to do and for which they are responsible. Being responsible for completing tasks and doing such things as putting away toys and learning materials promotes a positive sense of self-worth and conveys to children that in a community people have responsibilities for making the community work well.

applying research to practice

Children and Self-Control: It's All About the Brain!

How is your self-control? Have you ever said to yourself, "Why did I do that?" Have you ever said to yourself, "I'm not going to eat a Snickers bar until after I study," but you ate it before you were done studying? Children encounter many of the same problems with self-control you do. We talk a lot about helping children develop self-control, but how can we do this? Well, as it turns out, research can help us. Researchers inform us that preschoolers who learn to delay gratification are more likely to do well in school, avoid substance abuse, and generally do better in life than children who can't delay their gratification.[8] Similar research reveals that delaying gratification and self-control are better predictors of a student's academic performance than an IQ test![9]

So, what does this mean for you? How can you actively employ strategies to help children learn to delay gratification? Here are some examples.

- Develop a reasonable set of classroom rules and make sure that every child follows them.
- Develop classroom routines for what children are to do and how they are to behave, especially when they enter the school or classroom; during transitions from one learning center to another; and from classroom to lunch or recess. Helping children self-manage their behavior leads to self-control and delayed gratification.

- Provide children with classroom "cues and clues" for how to make decisions and be responsible. For example, provide children with social stories. A social story is a personalized, detailed, and simple script that breaks down behavior and provides rules and directions. Social stories can range from drawings featuring stick figures, to computer images, or even better, to digital photos featuring a specific child. Also, a good way to give specific directions is with step-by-step photos for how to engage in and complete certain tasks such as hand washing, how to put away learning materials, and so on.
- Provide appropriate "rewards" for children who focus on learning tasks for specific periods of time; who lead by example during routines such as standing in line or waiting their turn; and who complete a task from beginning to end.
- Embed management skills into classroom routines such as taking turns; being respectful and listening while others speak; and helping children learn that they can't always have what they want when they want it.

Helping children delay gratification and learn self-control may be one of the most valuable things you can do to help them be successful throughout their lifetimes.

---

social story A personalized, detailed, and simple script that breaks down behavior and provides rules and directions.

- ***Give children choices.*** Life is full of choices—some require thought and decisions; others are automatic, based on previous behavior. But every time you make a decision, you are being responsible and exercising your right to decide. Children like to have choices, and choices help them become independent, confident, and self-disciplined. Making choices is key for children to help them develop responsible behavior and inner control. Learning to make choices early in life lays the foundation for decision-making later. Here are some guidelines for giving children choices.
  - Give children choices when there are valid choices to make. When it comes time to clean up the classroom, do not let children choose whether they want to participate, but let them pick between collecting the scissors or the crayons.
  - Help children make choices. Rather than say, "What would you like to do today?" say, "Sarah, you have a choice between working in the woodworking center or the computer center. Which would you like to do?"
- ***Support children.*** As an early childhood professional, you must support children in their efforts to be successful. Arrange the environment and make opportunities available for children to be able to do things. Successful accomplishments are a major ingredient of positive behavior.

The accompanying Technology Tie-In feature will give you another perspective on how you can use technology to help support children in their efforts to guide their own behavior.

technology tie-in

High-Tech? Low-Tech? Both!

One of the challenges many teachers face is how to manage and guide children with disabilities. For example, some of the characteristics of children with autism and ADHD is that they have difficulty paying attention, staying focused, and developing social relationships. All these behavioral skills are necessary for learning in the home and at school and getting along with others.

The use of robots and service animals are two alternatives that increasing numbers of teachers and families are turning to in order to help children stay on track, stay focused, and develop the skills they need to be successful in school and life.

ROBOTS

Researchers find that many children describe their interactions with robots as reassuring and supportive—the kind of response necessary for living and learning. For children with autism, especially, interaction with robots enables them to attend, respond, read emotions, and communicate. For example, when children play with KASPAR the robot (see the Linking to Learning section, as well as Figure 12.3), they tend to relax and enjoy their interaction.

Another robot, Keepon, encourages children to interact with him and as a result, they develop the ability to interact socially with their classmates, teachers, and others. The relaxing, nonjudgmental environment that robots provide gives children freedom to interact with them and practice social cues and responses. An informal, open, and conversational environment helps these children develop and master basic communication skills necessary for survival and for flourishing in the real world.[10]

ANIMAL-ASSISTED THERAPY

Service animals, such as dogs and cats, provide an opportunity for children to develop social skills and character skills relating to kindness and compassion; nurturance; loyalty and responsibility, especially responsible pet ownership; and to develop motor and physical skills through human-animal interactions. Service animals provide children the opportunity to be in a less restrictive environment, where they may interact and engage in learning opportunities with their peers. Children who need animal-assisted therapy often improve in their ability to trust others; learn appropriate touch; cooperate; problem-solve; concentrate; and express their emotions.[11] Learning these basic skills assists children in developing their ability to communicate effectively with their peers and adults, giving them the opportunity to learn and have a more productive and fulfilling role in their classrooms and homes.

For children with autism, service animals also provide comfort and security and another avenue for expressing emotions

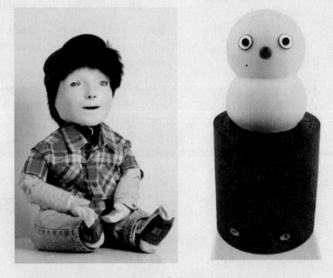

FIGURE 12.3 KASPAR and Keepon

and interacting socially. For example, at Carson Elementary School, third grader Jeremy attends school with his service dog, Sam. Jeremy has muscular dystrophy, which makes it difficult for him to play with other children. As a result, he was becoming withdrawn and antisocial. However, teachers report that with Sam around, Jeremy is more outgoing, talkative, and sociable.

Service dogs need to be certified by agencies such as the National Service Animal Registry (see the Linking to Learning section). Furthermore, not all schools and school districts allow animals in classrooms. So, you will want to check your school district's policy before you make any decisions about service animals in your classroom.

What does all of this mean for you? There is more than one way to address and solve children's behavioral problems. Certainly, you, the teacher are the creator of the environment and manager of the classroom. However, for children with particular behavioral problems such as those with autism and poor behavioral skills, robots and animal-assisted therapy may be the solution you have been looking for and that one or two of your children need.

. . . .

Source: Kaspar photo contributed by University of Hertfordshire; KEEPON photo contributed by Beatbots, LLC.

Step 7: Establish Appropriate Expectations

Expectations set the boundaries for desired behavior. They are the guideposts children use in learning to direct their own behavior. Like everyone, children need guideposts along life's way as shown in Figure 12.4.

Set high and appropriate expectations for children. When children know what to expect, they can better achieve those expectations. Up to a point, the more we expect of children, the more and better they achieve.

The following are some things you can do to promote appropriate expectations.

Set Limits. Setting limits is closely associated with establishing expectations and relates to defining unacceptable behavior. Setting clear limits is important for three reasons:

1. Setting limits helps you clarify in your own mind what you believe is acceptable, based on your knowledge of child development, children, their families, and their culture.

FIGURE 12.4

Examples of Classroom Rules, Pre-K–3

Pre-Kindergarten	• Helping Hands • Listening Ears • Looking Eyes • Quiet Voices • Walking Feet
Kindergarten	• Be kind to everybody • Raise your hand when you want to speak • Use inside voices • Walk inside the room • Listen to the teachers • Follow the school rules
First Grade	• Respect other people • Keep your hands and feet to yourself • Raise your hand for permission to speak in class • Walk quietly in the hallways • Move about quietly in the classroom
Second Grade	• Be a good listener • Be a good friend • Be polite • Be a hard worker • Be the best you can be
Third Grade	• Listen to and follow directions • Raise your hand • Work quietly • Keep hands and feet to yourself • Walk silently in the halls • Be kind to others

Source: Based on Carrollton Elementary School, Carrollton, Texas (pre-kindergarten); Chaplain Elementary School, Chapin, South Carolina (kindergarten); Garrison-Pilcher Elementary School, Thomasville, Georgia (first grade); Elwood Public School, Elwood, Nebraska (second grade); and H.L. Horn Elementary, Vinton, Virginia (third grade).

2. Limits help children act with confidence because they know which behaviors are acceptable.

3. Limits provide children with security. Children want and need limits.

As children grow and mature, the limits change and are adjusted to developmental levels, programmatic considerations, and life situations. Knowing what they can and cannot do enables children to guide their own behavior.

Develop Classroom Rules. Plan classroom rules from the first day of class. As the year goes on, you can involve children in establishing classroom rules, but in the beginning, children want and need to know what they can and cannot do. For example, rules might relate to changing groups and bathroom routines. Whatever rules you establish, they should be fair, reasonable, and appropriate to the children's age and maturity. Keep rules to a minimum; the fewer the better.

supportive classroom A classroom in which the teacher provides the conditions for enabling all children to learn. In addition, children help each other and are responsible for demonstrating appropriate behavior.

Step 8: Arrange and Modify the Classroom Environment

The classroom environment plays a key role in children's ability to guide their behavior. Arrange the environment so that it supports the purposes of the program and makes appropriate behavior possible. Appropriate room arrangements signal to children that they are expected to guide and be responsible for their own behavior and enable teachers to observe and provide for children's interests. Also, it is easier to live and work in an attractive and aesthetically pleasing classroom or center. We all want a nice environment—children should have one, too. The guidelines shown in Figure 12.5 can help you think about and arrange your classroom to support children as they guide their own behavior.

The Supportive Classroom. Arrange the physical setting into a **supportive classroom**, conducive to the behaviors you want to teach. A supportive classroom is one in which the teacher provides the conditions for enabling all children to learn. In addition, children help each other and are responsible for demonstrating appropriate behavior. If you want to encourage independent work, provide places and time for children to work alone. Disruptive behavior is often encouraged by classroom arrangements that force children to walk over or through other children to get to equipment or materials.

Step 9: Model Appropriate Behavior

Telling is not teaching. Actions speak louder than words. Children see and remember how other people act. Modeling plays a major role in helping children guide their behavior.

Teachers and parents lay the first—and most important—foundation for children's appropriate habits and behaviors. You must be the best role model you can for children and help parents be good role models, too. Whether you want to or not, or like it or not, you have to accept responsibility for helping raise responsible children who will become responsible adults.

Literature is a good way for you and parents to encourage prosocial behaviors and discuss role models for children. The picture books listed in Figure 12.6 provide you many opportunities to model appropriate behavior through good books.

The classroom environment is one of the most important factors that enable children to develop and use appropriate behavior. The classroom should belong to children, and their ownership and pride in it makes it more likely they will act responsibly.

Make the classroom a rewarding place to be. It should be comfortable, safe, and attractive.

Locate materials so that children can easily retrieve them. When children have to ask for materials, this promotes dependency and can lead to behavior problems.

Create center areas that are well defined and accessible to children and have appropriate and abundant materials. Provide children with guidelines for how to use centers and materials, and make center boundaries low enough so that you and others can see over them.

Have an open area in which you and your children can meet as a whole group. This area is essential for story time, general class meetings, and so on. Starting and ending the day with a class meeting provides an opportunity for children to discuss their behaviors and suggest ways they and others can do a better job.

Establish a system so that materials are easily stored, and so that children can easily put them away. A rule of thumb is that there should be a place for everything and everything should be in its place.

Provide for all kinds of activities, both quiet and loud. Try to locate quiet areas together (reading area and puzzle area) and loud centers together (woodworking and blocks).

Create opportunities for children to display their work.

FIGURE 12.5 How to Arrange the Classroom to Support Positive Behavior

Use the following strategies to help children learn through modeling:

- **Show.** For example, show children where the block corner is and how and where the blocks are stored.
- **Demonstrate.** Perform a task while students watch. For example, demonstrate the proper way to put the blocks away and how to store them. Extensions of the demonstration method are to have children practice the demonstration while you supervise, or to ask a child to demonstrate to other children.
- **Supervise.** Supervision is a process of reviewing, reminding, maintaining standards, and following up. If children are not performing the desired behavior, review the behavior. Be consistent in your expectations of desired behavior. Children will soon learn they do not have to put away their blocks if you allow them not to do it even once.

Happy to Be Me!: A Kid Book About Self-Esteem by Christine Adams and Robert J. Butsh. Saint Meinrad, IN: Abbey Press, 2001 (Ages 4–8).	• This colorful book leads the young reader through a process of self-discovery: exploring uniqueness, building a healthy self-image, and preparing for challenging situations. Every child in the world is special, gifted, and wonderful. And each one deserves to feel "happy to be me" !
It's Hard to Be Five: Learning How to Work My Control Panel by Jamie Lee Curtis. Illustrated by Laura Cornell. New York: HarperCollins, 2004 (Ages 4–8).	• This book is about a five year old's challenges in learning self-control. He faces challenges of contolling his temper when dealing with younger siblings, avoiding dirt, and starting school. However, he sees many advantages of being five, such as walking by himself and many fun activities at school that his younger brother cannot yet experience.
Hands Are Not for Hitting by Martine Agassi. Illustrated by Marieka Heinien. Minneapolis, MN: Free Spirit Publishing, 2009 (Ages 4–8).	• This book shows children that their hands can do many things—including hurt someone. By learning what violence does to others, they learn how to stop it before it happens.
Why Can't I? (Our Emotions and Behaviour) by Sue Graves. Illustrated by Desideria Gucciardini. Minneapolis, MN: Free Spirit Publishing, 2011 (Ages 4–8).	• This brightly illustrated book helps kids understand how their emotions and actions are related and how they can be managed. It invites kids to explore their own experiences and how they can handle them.
Let's Talk About Being Helpful by Joy Berry. New York: Joy Berry Enterprises, 2009 (Ages 4–8).	• This book explains what it is to help others and how kids can have a big impact on the world around them. It includes interactive activities and a companion CD to help emphasize the lesson.

FIGURE 12.6 Children's Books That Encourage Prosocial Behaviors in Young Children

Step 10: Avoid Problems

It's easy to encourage children's misbehavior. Often teachers expect perfection and adult behavior from children. If you focus on building responsible behavior, there will be less need to solve behavior problems.

Ignoring inappropriate behavior is probably one of the most overlooked strategies for guiding children's behavior. Some teachers feel guilty when they use this strategy. They believe that ignoring undesirable behaviors is not good teaching. Ignoring some inappropriate behavior can be an effective strategy, but it must be combined with positive reinforcement of desirable behavior. Thus, you ignore inappropriate behavior and at the same time reinforce appropriate behavior. A combination of positive reinforcement and ignoring can lead to desired behavior.

When children do something good or are on task, tell them. Catch children being good; look for good behavior. This strategy helps improve individual behavior and group behavior as well.

Step 11: Develop a Partnership with Parents, Families, and Others

Involving parents and families is a wonderful way to gain valuable insights about children's behaviors. Some things you can do to collaborate with parents on guiding children's behaviors are these:

• Share your philosophy of guiding behavior with parents. Your classroom website is a good place to do this.

Social relationships play a powerful role in children's and teachers' everyday behavior. Teachers must promote positive child–child and teacher–child relationships. What are some things you can do to promote positive social relationships in your classroom or program?

- Share classroom rules and expectations with parents.
- Hold meetings for and with parents and share with them the information in this chapter and how to apply it to their learning about how to guide children's behavior in the home.
- Always be available in person, on the phone, or via e-mail to discuss with parents questions or concerns they might have about their children's behavior.

Step 12: Use and Teach Conflict Management

Quite often, conflicts result from children's interactions with others. Increasingly, teachers advocate teaching children ways to manage and resolve their own conflicts.

Teaching conflict resolution strategies is important in the learning community for several reasons. First, it makes sense to give children the skills they need to handle and resolve their own conflicts. Second, teaching conflict resolution skills to children enables them to use these same skills as adults. Third, the peaceful resolution of interpersonal conflicts contributes, in the long run, to peaceful homes and communities. Children who are involved in efforts to resolve interpersonal behavior problems peacefully and intuitively learn that peace begins with them. Strategies used to teach and model conflict resolution include the following:

- ***Model resolutions.*** You can model resolutions for children: "Sasha, please don't knock over Brittany's building because she worked hard to build it"; "Lauren, what is another way (instead of hitting) you can tell Amber that she is sitting in your chair?"
- ***Do something else.*** Teach children to get involved in another activity. Children can learn that they do not always have to play with a toy someone else has. They can get involved in another activity with a different toy. They can do something else now and play with the toy later. Chances are, however, that by getting involved in another activity they will forget about the toy for which they were ready to fight.
- ***Talk it over.*** Children can learn that talking about a problem often leads to a resolution and reveals that there are always two sides to an argument. Talking also helps children think about other ways to solve problems. Children should be involved in the solution of their interpersonal problems and classroom and activity problems.
- ***Taking turns.*** Taking turns is a good way for children to learn that they cannot always be first, have their own way, or do a prized activity. Taking turns brings equality and fairness to interpersonal relations.
- ***Share.*** Sharing is a good behavior to promote in any setting. Children have to be taught how to share and how to behave when others do not share. Children can be helped to select another toy rather than hitting or grabbing.
- ***Teach children to say "I'm sorry."*** Saying "I'm sorry" is one way to heal and resolve conflicts. It can be a step toward good behavior. Children need to be reared in an environment in which they see and experience others apologizing for their inappropriate actions toward others.

"Be a Buddy, Not a Bully!" was the theme for Thomas Elementary School's anti-bullying awareness week. Students participated in daily activities that promote anti-bullying, beginning with dressing in camouflage to "Be a HERO" (Help Encourage and Respect Others), then wearing jogging suits and tennis shoes to "Walk Away from a Bully." On "Mix It Up Day," students were encouraged to sit by someone other than their friends at lunch to meet new friends. On "Black Out Bullying Day," students wore black clothing and wrote on strips of paper one way they could make a stand against bullying to make a grade-level chain link. On the last day, students wore school spirit shirts and stood together to illustrate the theme "Together We Stand, Divided We Fall."[12]

Applying the Twelve Steps

The twelve steps for guiding children's behavior we have discussed here will help you build learning communities in which you and your children can live happily and productively. These twelve steps lay the foundation for building learning communities and provide you with guidelines that will ensure you and the children are successful.

The first eight years of children's lives provide us many opportunities for helping children develop the skills and behaviors that will enable them to live healthy and productive lives. Enabling children to guide their own behavior and to live cooperatively and peacefully with other children will help them be better persons and good citizens. Guiding children's behavior is fundamental to making sure that all children have the opportunity to succeed in school and life.

I wish you much success as you joyfully and confidently empower children to guide their behavior.

TEACHING AND LEARNING IN THE INCLUSIVE CLASSROOM: ACCOMMODATING DIVERSE LEARNERS

Many young children exhibit problem behaviors in early childhood, and for most children these behaviors are transient or respond well to developmentally appropriate management techniques. In this chapter you have learned about some of these techniques. Unfortunately, some students do not respond to guidance strategies and require additional assistance. Positive reinforcement can be used for *all* children and *increases* the occurrence of appropriate behavior. Positive reinforcement is different from rewards. You can give rewards to children when they engage in desirable behavior, but if the reward does not lead to an increase in positive behavior, it is not actually a positive reinforcer. Here are some different types of positive reinforcement that you can use in your classroom.

Tangible Reinforcement

Tangible reinforcers are edible or material objects a child wants, such as candy, stickers, stamps, or certificates. A child's positive behavior is reinforced by access to these items that may not be related to the specific behavior. For example, you can give all children stickers who sit appropriately during circle time.

Activity-Based Reinforcement

Activity-based reinforcement is access to fun or preferred activities that reinforce a child's behavior. For example, allowing a child to have free time in the puzzle center if he finishes seat work is an example of an activity-based reinforcement.

Token Reinforcement

Token reinforcement gives children points or tokens for appropriate behavior. These rewards have little value in themselves but can be exchanged for something the child

diversity tie-in

Children's Behavior and Socioeconomic Status

Socioeconomic status correlates positively and negatively with good parenting. Research confirms that good parenting enhances academic achievement, whereas poor parenting often leads to poor academic achievement.[13] Unfortunately, the Great Recession of 2008–2012 had a tremendous impact on the nation's economy and the socioeconomic status (SES) of many families and children. Census Bureau data indicate that 46.2 million Americans—the highest number in the last 52 years—are now living in poverty.[14] What effect does the Great Recession have upon children's classroom and home behaviors? The answer is "a lot." Parents and other family members in low SES households interact and discipline their children differently than parents and family members in higher SES groups.[15]

- The stresses of living in poverty, poor housing conditions, and parent unemployment inject more stress into the lives of all family members, especially children. Stressed parents have more intense emotional reactions to their children's behavior than parents that are not always stressed and, as a result, stressed parents use harsher discipline.[16]
- Highly stressed parents assume that their children intentionally misbehave. It is as though stressed parents are looking for ways that their children misbehave and get upset when they do. This leads to more frequent bouts of discipline.[17]

- Low socioeconomic parents believe in and use more harsh methods of discipline than their higher socioeconomic counterparts.[18] This may be because of their lower levels of education or it may be because of the ways they themselves were parented.[19] In either case, harsh discipline tends to lead to more negative outcomes for children.

Given the discipline practices of low socioeconomic parents, you can do the following:

- Be especially sensitive to and observant of the low socioeconomic children's behavior in your classroom, monitoring for signs of abuse and neglect.
- Collaborate with your administrators and colleagues to develop parent-education programs for all parents to help them understand and to use appropriate methods of discipline and child guidance.
- Child discipline and guidance is often a function of culture and race. You will want to educate yourself on the discipline practices of different ethnic groups. For example, some ethnic groups believe in and practice harsher methods of discipline than do parents from other ethnic groups.

wants. For example, giving children tickets that they can exchange for free-choice time or trips to the "treasure chest" is a common token reinforcement system.

Social Reinforcement

Social reinforcement is given when teachers express praise and approval for appropriate behavior. They may be verbal; "Good job!" written with a smiley face; or expressions such as a smile, a pat on the back, or a wink.

Natural Reinforcement

Natural reinforcement results directly from the child's behavior. For example, a child is struggling to open her juice. The child says "Help," and an adult helps the child. The opening of and getting the juice is reinforcing. This successful interaction increases the likelihood that the child will *ask* for help in the future, rather than requesting assistance in a more inappropriate manner.

Notice, in this video, how the teacher listens closely to each child and facilitates conflict resolution. Pay close attention to how the teacher reflects each of the girls' feelings.

The goal is for children to behave appropriately with natural or social reinforcement. Meeting the needs of *all* children requires knowledge of different types of reinforcement to tailor your interventions to the individual needs of each child.

ACTIVITIES FOR PROFESSIONAL DEVELOPMENT

ethical dilemma

"Boy in a duffel bag!"

Shortly after six-year-old Chris left for school, his mother, Amy Baker, received a phone call from school asking her to come and pick up Chris because he was "jumping off the walls." Chris has autism and is in a special education class to help meet his needs. Amy rushed to the school and hurried down the hallway toward the classroom door. Outside the classroom, she heard Chris crying out "Mama, mama!" Amy couldn't believe her ears! Her son's voice was coming from a duffel bag outside the classroom door. Amy frantically untied the duffel bag drawstrings and pulled Chris out. When Amy demanded an explanation from teachers and school administration, they downplayed the whole issue. They said they put Chris in a "therapy bag to calm him down." Amy became indignant. "Therapy bag or duffel bag—it's all the same to me! Why would anyone put Chris in a bag? If this school thinks they are getting away with this, they've got another thought coming!"

What should Amy do? Start a website petition asking for people to sign up to attend the next school board meeting? Contact the Council for Exceptional Children and see if they can help? Pull Chris from the public school, place him in a private school, and forget the whole thing? Go to the local television stations and request airtime to explain to the public what is really going on in their schools? What should Amy do? What would you do?

Application Activities

1. Based on your professional experiences and on Internet research, identify five features of classroom settings and atmosphere that influence classroom behavior. How will you use each of these five features in your classroom? Post your information to your class discussion board or create a Prezi presentation to share online with your classmates.

2. List five behaviors you think are desirable in toddlers, five in preschoolers, and five in kindergartners. For each behavior, give two examples of how you would encourage and promote development of that behavior in your program or classroom. Compare and contrast your "desirable traits" with those identified by your classmates.

3. Research Internet sources devoted to discipline and guiding behavior, including the use of physical punishment. Determine what various meanings of "discipline" are. Identify specific examples for how others identify how to discipline in various situations. Do you agree with the methods recommended? What three implications does your research have for your role as a teacher of young children?

4. In this chapter you learned twelve steps for guiding children's behavior. Although they are all important, rank-order the twelve in importance to you. Your first choice will be 1, your second, 2, and so on. Share your rankings online with your colleagues and ask how they agree or disagree with your ranking.

Linking to Learning

Association for Supervision and Curriculum Development (ASCD)

www.ascd.org
Leads a national effort to include the whole child in all instructional programs and practices.

Kinesics and Synchronisation in Personal Assistant Robotics (KASPAR)

kaspar.herts.ac.uk
KASPAR is a minimally expressive, therapeutic robot that helps children with autism understand how to read emotions and engage with the people around them.

Keepon

beatbots.net
Keepon is a small creature-like robot designed to interact with children by directing attention and expressing emotion.

NSAR Service Dog Certification

www.nsarco.com
The most complete, professional Service Dog registry available. Certify your disability and register your dog as a service animal in minutes.

MyEducationLab

Go to Topic 9 (Guiding Children) in the MyEducationLab (www.myeducationlab.com) for your course, where you can:

- Find learning outcomes for Guiding Children along with the national standards that connect to these outcomes.

- Complete Assignments and Activities that can help you more deeply understand the chapter content.

- Apply and practice your understanding of the core teaching skills identified in the chapter with the Building Teaching Skills and Dispositions learning units.

- Explore interactive CONNECT Modules to practice classroom skills and enhance professional development.

- Check your comprehension on the content covered in the chapter by going to the Study Plan in the Book Resources for your text. Here you will be able to take a chapter quiz, receive feedback on your answers, and then access Review, Practice, and Enrichment activities to enhance your understanding of chapter content.

chapter 13

PARENTS, FAMILIES, AND THE COMMUNITY

Building Partnerships for Student Success

ONE THING we can say with certainty about today's educational landscape is that parents, families, and communities are as much a part of the educational process as are the students, teachers, and staff. Efforts to involve families and communities in the process of educating the nation's children are at an all-time high. One primary reason for these renewed efforts is the overwhelming evidence that the effect of involving parents, families, and communities in the schools increases student achievement and promotes positive educational outcomes. Research studies confirm the benefits of parent/community support.[3]

A positive and convincing relationship exists between family involvement and benefits for students, including improved academic achievement. This relationship holds across families of all economic, racial/ethnic, and educational backgrounds, as well as students of all ages. Students with involved parents, no matter their background, are more likely to earn higher grades and test scores, adapt well to school, attend regularly, have better social skills and behavior, and graduate and go on to higher education. Family involvement also has a protective effect; the more families can support their children's progress, the better their children do in school and the longer they stay in school.[4]

The public believes that nothing has a greater effect on students' level of achievement than parents. In fact, the public thinks that parents matter more than teachers![5] This makes parental involvement in children's education even more important.

NEW VIEWS OF PARENT/FAMILY PARTNERSHIPS

Current accountability and reform movements have convinced families that they should no longer be kept out of their children's schools. Families believe their children have a right to effective, high-quality teaching and care by high-quality teachers.[6] Parents have become more militant in their demands for high-quality education. Schools and other agencies have responded by seeking ways to involve families in this quest for quality. Educators and families realize that mutual cooperation is in everyone's best interest.[7]

Ownership

In addition to using traditional methods of involving parents in fund-raising and children's activities, schools now involve parents in decisions about hiring new teachers, school safety measures, and appropriate curriculum to help ensure that all children learn.

Parents, families, and the community are now viewed as the "owners" of schools. As one parent said to me, "I don't consider myself a visitor at school. I'm an owner!"

Increasing Student Achievement

Today, a major emphasis is on increasing student achievement. One of the best ways to do this is through involving parents in at-home learning activities with their children. Parent involvement is, now more than ever, a two-way street—from school to home and from home to school. The same reciprocal process applies to school–community collaboration.

For example, Karen Marler, principal of Lacoochee Elementary, Florida, helps parents take ownership of their children's education in order to increase student achievement.

Teodora Romero wanted to help her children succeed in school, but she didn't know how. A Mexican immigrant who speaks Spanish almost exclusively, Romero felt overwhelmed by the assignments her third grade son Luis and kindergarten daughter Berniece brought home.

So, Principal Marler developed Parent University, which offers classes to help parents help their children and themselves: Help Children Read, Volunteering at School, and Parent Involvement.[8]

Teacher Paula McCullough at Lakehoma Elementary, Oklahoma, also helps parents take ownership of their children's education in order to increase student achievement. Her Professionalism in Practice feature, "Home and School: An Unbeatable Team!" shows you how helping parents can help your students.

MyEducationLab

Visit the MyEducationLab for *Fundamentals of Early Childhood Education* to enhance your understanding of chapter concepts with a personalized Study Plan. You'll also have the opportunity to hone your teaching skills through video-based Assignments and Activities as well as Building Teaching Skills and Dispositions lessons.

FOCUS QUESTIONS

1. What are new views of family and community involvement?

2. How do changing parents and families change the ways you involve parents and families?

3. What are the six types of parent/family involvement and how can you use each in your program?

professionalism in practice

Home and School: An Unbeatable Team!

STEP 1 Form Partnerships with Parents

My philosophy of teaching is very simple: It is to teach the whole individual child, not a subject. Each child is unique, with different strengths and weaknesses, different likes and dislikes. To achieve my goal, I must form a partnership with the home. By working together, we can build a team whose mutual goal is the educational success of the child.

STEP 2 Communicate with Families

A strong relationship needs to exist between the school and home in order for the child to get the best education possible. This "unbeatable team" is established through communication. Communication needs to be varied, timely, and honest. Proper communication is the tool that allows me to motivate parents to find the necessary time to work with and support their children's educations. I use weekly newsletters, phone calls, notes home, weekly homework bags, parent conferences/meetings, and parent volunteers.

STEP 3 Send Newsletters

I send out a weekly newsletter to inform my parents of "current events" in our classroom. Included in the newsletters are weekly progress reports, a list of spelling words, current areas of study, and special events/dates. I also include helpful tips on learning, such as how to help their child study spelling words, how to encourage reading for enjoyment and comprehension, or what games to play at home to practice reading/math skills.

STEP 4 Encourage Feedback

To encourage a two-way communication between home and school, I include a place for comments in the newsletters. Individual notes are sent home and phone calls made when needed. Sometimes it is necessary to keep parents informed on a daily basis about their child's progress, behavior, and/or work habits. I send home a daily note that is signed by the parent and returned to school. I have found it helpful to write these notes on a carbonless-copy message book so that I always have a copy (for those times when the student conveniently does not make it home with the note). Using different forms of communication keeps parents well informed of their child's progress, classroom policies/procedures, curriculum goals, and ideas on how best to help their child succeed at school.

STEP 5 Provide Homework Bags

I send homework bags home each week. Each bag contains a worksheet to practice the skills (math/reading) taught in class,

---

This video shows a good example of bringing parents and children together to increase parent involvement and student achievement.

CHANGING PARENTS AND FAMILIES: CHANGING INVOLVEMENT

The family of today is not the family of yesterday, nor will the family of today be the family of tomorrow. Family structures are literally changing in front of our eyes! Today's parents are single, married, heterosexual, gay, lesbian, cousins, aunts, uncles, grandparents, brothers, sisters, and others. These changes in who and what parents are and what a family is have tremendous implications for parenting, child rearing, education, and for how you involve parents in your classroom.

Working Parents

An increasing percentage of mothers with children are currently employed. In 51.4 percent of married-couple families, both the husband and the wife are employed.[9] Sixty-five percent of mothers with children under the age of six and 77 percent of mothers with their youngest child between the ages of six to seventeen are in the workforce.[10] This creates a greater demand for early childhood programs. Unfortunately, much

a practice reader, a reading activity, and a parent response form. The homework bags become increasingly more difficult as the student advances in abilities. A variety of reading activities are included to keep students excited about learning. The reading activities are determined by the lesson and the practice reader enclosed in the homework bag. They include games (board games, teacher-made folder games, card games, etc.), art projects (with the materials included), writing projects (a suitcase with a variety of writing materials), and simple cooking recipes.

These homework bags encourage parent–child interaction as they work together on the same skills that are covered at school. The parents have firsthand experience in watching the academic growth of their child and discovering their child's weaknesses and strengths. The child gets to practice needed skills in a safe, warm environment with the added bonus of parental approval.

STEP 6   Teach Parents

At the first of the year, I hold a meeting for my parents. I explain classroom procedures and how first graders learn to read and solve math problems. The parents are supplied with handouts on activities they can do at home to improve math and reading skills. I do not assume the parents are knowledgeable about how to help their child at home. I conduct a minilesson on the parents' role in teaching children to read. I model for them how they should guide their children when reading together by asking predicting questions, discussing cause/effect, using context clues, and so forth. At the end of the meeting, parents are given the opportunity to ask questions concerning their children's education. This gives me the opportunity to clarify any concepts or activities I had not clearly explained.

Usually, the questions asked need to be heard by the entire group. Parents realize that everyone has some of the same concerns: getting a reluctant child to read, homework hassles, improving weak math/reading skills, and challenging high achievers. Parents see that they are not alone in their child's educational journey.

STEP 7   Recruit Parents

Every year, I recruit parent volunteers to become involved in my class. These "helping hands" are used to encourage my students to develop skills and/or interests. Parents listen to my students read, play games with them, help individual students learn math facts or spelling words, make learning centers, and aid students in creating art projects. The use of parent volunteers helps to strengthen the relationship between school and home. It also makes parents more aware of the importance their role plays in the education of children.

By using a variety of activities, I get parents involved in their children's educations. If both members of the team—parents and teacher—meet their educational responsibilities, an unbeatable team is formed with the same goal in mind—*children excited about learning.*

Source: Paula McCullough is a transitional first grade teacher at Lakehoma Elementary, Mustang, Oklahoma, and a USA Today All-USA Teacher.

---

child care in the United States is low quality.[11] One of your professional responsibilities is to partner with parents to raise the quality of child care and to make it affordable and accessible. Another responsibility is to collaborate with parents and help them educate their children.

For many working parents, getting involved in their children's school can seem like the impossible dream. So much of what schools do occurs between the hours of 8 a.m. and 4 p.m.; but all of that is changing, as more schools and teachers find that they have to find more creative and parent-friendly ways of involving working parents. Here are some ways you and your colleagues can involve working parents.

• Leave the schoolhouse door open longer. Today, many parents, especially working parents, don't necessarily need to come to the school during school hours, but they do need to have teachers and administrators available to them at other times. You will want to rethink the times at which you can be available for working parents either face to face or electronically, and you will have to be creative in working with individual parents and parent organizations for them to be involved with their children's education.

Grandparents acting as parents for their grandchildren are a growing reality in the United States today. What are some things you can do to ensure that grandparents will have the educational assistance and support they need so that their grandchildren will be successful in school?

• Conference with parents at a distance by using Skype to conduct the conference. For example, it may be possible for working parents to conference with teachers via Skype.

• E-mail information directly to parents rather than sending home notes with children.

• Send out project bags to working parents that they can complete at home, such as cutting out laminates and making or stuffing folders.

• Offer alternative times for conferencing and meetings, such as Saturday mornings or evenings. Even weeknights are better for some working parents.

Fathers

Fathers are rediscovering the joys of parenting and interacting with young children. At the same time, early childhood educators have rediscovered fathers! The number of fathers who stay at home and provide primary care for their children has doubled in the last decade. In 2001, 81,000 fathers stayed at home compared to 176,000 in 2011. Men are playing an active role in providing basic care, love, and nurturance to their children. Increasingly, men are more concerned about their roles as fathers and their participation in family events before, during, and after the birth of their children. Fathers want to be involved in the whole process of child rearing.

Because of the profession's increased understanding of the importance of fathers in children's development, there is now more research than ever before about fathers' roles in the lives of children. For example, research indicates that:

• Children with involved, caring fathers have better educational outcomes.

• Fathers who are involved, nurturing, and playful with their infants have children with higher IQs, as well as better linguistic and cognitive capacities.

• Toddlers with involved fathers go on to start school with higher levels of academic readiness. They are more patient and can handle the stresses and frustrations associated with schooling more readily than children with less involved fathers.

• The influence of a father's involvement on academic achievement extends into adolescence and young adulthood. Children with involved, loving fathers are significantly more likely to do well in school, have healthy self-esteem, and exhibit empathy and prosocial behavior compared to children who have uninvolved fathers.[12]

• Students living in father-absent homes are twice as likely to repeat a grade in school.[13]

As you can see, helping fathers be involved with their children benefits children, families, schools, and society.

Ideas for Involving Fathers.   Regardless of the roles that fathers play, make special efforts to involve them. Here are some father-friendly ideas you can use to encourage their involvement.

• ***Invite fathers to your class or program.*** Make sure they are included in all your parent/family initiatives.

• ***Make fathers feel welcome in your program.*** For example, kindergarten students at Palm Pointe Elementary (Florida) celebrated Father's Day with their dads by participating in the "Donuts with Dad" Day. Students presented their dads with arts and crafts to show appreciation for all fathers.[14]

- ***Send a simple survey home to fathers.*** Ask them how they would like to be involved in their children's education. Keep in mind the six types of parent/family involvement shown in Figure 13.1, which we discuss later in the chapter.

- ***Provide special fatherhood and parenting classes for fathers.*** For example, the Colorado Fatherhood Initiative has helped Keith Lewis become a father to his seven-year-old son. "I feel like I have a better understanding about being a better man and a father," Lewis said.

"The program helped shape me and move me. It will do the same thing for any father, 17 or 45. We can all learn a thing or two from being better fathers." The Colorado Fatherhood Initiative supports fatherhood programs statewide such as Abusive Men Exploring New Directions (AMEND), Special Needs Dadvocate, and Los Padres Fatherhood Program.[15]

- ***Have fathers invite other fathers to be involved.*** Fathers may think no other fathers are involved until they themselves get involved. For example, the Bellow Spring Elementary School offers the Watch D.O.G.S. (Dads of Great Students), a program that encourages fathers, grandfathers, uncles, and other father figures to spend time at the school monitoring lunch and recess and helping in the classroom. "It is a very big deal when your dad is a watch dog," said Chris Polimeni, a father who has a daughter in the second grade and a son in kindergarten. Principal Jacqueline Klamerus says, "The children take tremendous pride . . . having their dads spend the day with them."[16]

- Include books and other literature about dads in your classroom library. Two good books are:

  - *My Father Knows the Names of Things* by Jane Yolen. A child celebrates his father's expertise. Not only does dad know "a dozen . . . words for night," he knows about soaps, dinosaurs, bugs, and flowers.[17]

  - *My Father Is Taller Than a Tree* by Joseph Bruiac. Thirteen unique father-and-son pairs who come from diverse backgrounds and live in different places. Even though the dads are not all the same, their relationships show us an important truth: Even the simplest and most familiar activities become special when dads and kids do them together.[18]

Families continue to change, and as they do, you must adapt and adopt new ways of involving family members and providing for their needs. For example, growing numbers of fathers have responsibility for rearing their children. What can you do to ensure the involvement of single fathers in your programs?

In this **video**, notice how the school staff actively encourages parents to participate in school events. How do parents feel about the school as a consequence of their participation in school activities?

Single Parents

The number of one-parent families, both male and female, continues to increase. Certain demographic groups are disproportionately represented in single-parent families. These increases are due to several factors. First, pregnancy rates are higher among lower socioeconomic groups. Second, teenage pregnancy rates in poor Caucasian, Hispanic, and African American populations are sometimes higher because of lower education levels, economic constraints, and fewer life opportunities.[19] Eighty percent of single-parent families were headed by females and 20 percent were headed by males.[20]

A third reality is that more educated women are choosing to have children without marrying. In fact, 41 percent of all births are to unmarried women.[21] This phenomenon is likely to continue to grow. So, working with single moms will be a major part of your teacher role.

Involving Single-Parent Families.   Many of the children you teach will be from single-parent families. Depending on where you teach, as many as 50 percent of your children could be from single-parent families. Here are some things you can do to ensure that single-parent families are involved.

- Many adults in one-parent families are employed during school hours and may not be available for conferences or other activities during that time. You must be willing to accommodate family schedules by arranging conferences at other times, perhaps early morning, noon, late afternoon, or early evening. Some employers, sensitive to these needs, give release time to participate in school functions, but others do not. In addition, professionals and principals need to think seriously about going to families, rather than having families always come to them.

- Remember that single parents have a limited amount of time to spend on involvement with their children's school and with their children at home. Therefore, when you talk with single-parent families, make sure that (1) the meeting starts on time, (2) you have a list of items to discuss, (3) you have sample materials available to illustrate all points, (4) you make specific suggestions relative to one-parent environments, and (5) the meeting ends on time.

- Because one-parent families are more likely to need child care assistance to attend meetings, child care should be planned for every parent meeting or activity.

- Suggest ways that single parents can make their time with their children meaningful. If a child has trouble following directions, show families how to use home situations to help in this area. For example, children can learn to follow directions while helping with errands, meal preparation, or housework.

- Get to know families' lifestyles and living conditions. For instance, you can recommend that every child have a quiet place to study, but this may be an impossible demand for some households. You need to visit some of the homes in your community before you set meeting times, decide what family involvement activities to implement, and determine what you will ask of families during the year. Keep in mind the condition of the home environment when you request that children bring certain items to school or carry out certain tasks at home. And when asking for parents' help, be sensitive to their talents and time constraints.

- Help develop support groups for one-parent families within your school, such as discussion groups and classes on parenting for singles. And be sure to include the needs and abilities of one-parent families in your family involvement activities and programs.

- Avoid making the assumption that students live with both biological parents. Avoid the traditional "Dear Parents" greeting in letters and other messages; instead use "Dear Parent," "Dear Family," "Friends," or some other form of greeting.

The importance of involving parents in their children's education and schooling cannot be overemphasized. Parent involvement has beneficial outcomes for both children and their parents, as the Applying Research to Practice feature illustrates.

Teenage Parents

Teenage pregnancy is declining and is at its lowest in two decades. Nonetheless, teenage pregnancy rates are still cause for alarm. Consider these facts:

- 367,752 births occurred to mothers aged fifteen to nineteen years, a birthrate of 34.3 per 1,000 women in this age group.[22]

applying research to practice

Involvement Causes Parents to "Invest" in Their Children

Research concerning parent involvement generally looks at the effects parent and family involvement has on child outcomes such as achievement, school attendance, and so forth. However, new research sheds light on the effects of parent involvement on parents themselves and how those effects in turn benefit children. Researchers investigated Head Start's parent involvement program and found that parent involvement increases parents' involvement with their children. In other words, parent involvement encourages parents to "invest" themselves in their children. This investment takes the form of parents being more attentive to their children and being willing to spend more time with them in reading to them, doing math activities, and so forth.[23] So, what does this mean for you?

- Knowing that parents are more likely to "invest" in their children when they are involved means that you

should make every effort to involve *all* parents in your program.

- Begin early in your program of involving parents, before the school year begins or at the very beginning of the school year. For example, first grade teacher Carrie Jostmeyer in Frisco (Texas) ISD calls every one of her students' parents and talks about the child's first day; tells the parents how proud she is to be their child's teacher; and invites the parents to come and visit and be involved in the child's classroom.

- Be a strong advocate for encouraging parents to enroll their children in preschool and other programs. This helps ensure that parents are involved and engaged early in the schooling process. As a result, they will invest earlier in their children.[24]

- As a group, Latino teenagers have the highest birthrate, with 56 births per 1,000.[25]
- Among the states, Mississippi has the highest birthrate of teens fifteen to nineteen years of age, with 68 births per 1,000. New Mexico reaches second with 64 per 1,000, and Texas is third with 63 per 1,000. The national teen birthrate average is 42 per 1,000.[26]

From a public policy perspective:

- Pregnancy and birth are significant contributors to high school dropout rates among girls. Only about 50 percent of teen mothers receive a high school diploma.
- The children of teenage mothers are more likely to have lower school achievement, drop out of school, have more health problems, be incarcerated at some time during adolescence, give birth as a teenager, and face unemployment as a young adult.[27]

From an early childhood point of view, teenage pregnancies create greater demand for infant/toddler child care and for programs to help teenagers learn how to be good parents.

Supporting and Helping Teenage Parents. At one time, most teenage parents were married. But today, the majority are not, and they come from culturally and linguistically diverse backgrounds. Despite society's advances over the last few decades, for teen moms, not much has changed. Two-thirds of teenage mothers live in poverty; less than 50 percent graduate high school; and only 2 percent of girls who are moms by the age of eighteen will graduate college by the age of thirty.[28] Further, more teenage mothers are choosing to raise their children with assistance from their mothers and grandmothers. Regardless of their circumstances, teenage parents have the following needs:

- ***Support in their role as parents.*** Support can include information about child-rearing practices and child development and help in implementing the information in their interactions with their children. Teen Parents of Lubbock (Texas) enrolls young mothers age twelve to twenty-one in weekly education meetings and monthly social activities or play-dates with their mentor moms. The program enables teenagers to meet other young mothers like themselves and be in a support network that keeps them focused on school while raising their children.[29]

- ***Support in their continuing development as adolescents and young adults.*** Remember that younger teenage parents are really children themselves. They need assistance in meeting their own developmental needs, as well as those of their children. In spite of the reality television programs such as *Teen Mom* and *16 and Pregnant* to glamorize teen moms, they need a great deal of help and support.

- ***Help with completing their education.*** Some early childhood programs provide parenting courses as well as classes designed to help teenage parents complete requirements for a high school diploma. Remember that a critical influence on children's development and achievement is the mother's education level. For example, the Tupelo (Mississippi) School District offers the Link Center, a high school advancement academy for teenage mothers so they can continue their education while receiving additional help not received in a traditional classroom, like parenting skills.[30]

As early childhood programs enroll more children of teenage families, they must seek ways to creatively and sensitively involve these families.

Prison/Incarcerated Families

In the United States, one in 31 adults is in prison or on parole.[31] This means that at least 1.7 million minor children in the United States, about a quarter of whom are under age five, have a parent in prison.[32] Ninety-two percent of incarcerated parents are fathers. Parents held in the nation's prisons report having an estimated 1,706,600 minor children, accounting for 2.3 percent of the U.S. resident population under the age of eighteen.[33] For children of incarcerated parents, their life outcomes are, in many cases, bleak. For example, they are two to three times more likely to engage in delinquent behavior than children of unincarcerated parents.[34]

Get on the Bus.   Faced with these alarming statistics, community programs are taking an active role in preventing juvenile delinquency as well as giving children an opportunity to see their incarcerated parents. Get on the Bus, a Los Angeles–based nonprofit organization founded by Sister Suzanne Steffen, brings children and their guardians/caregivers from throughout the state of California to visit their mothers and fathers in prison every year around Mother's and Father's Day. Get on the Bus is a project of the Center for Restorative Justice Works. Maria Palmer, program director, says that every child has a right to see, to talk with, and to touch their parents. In May 2010, Get on the Bus took 70 busloads of children from every major city in California to three women's prisons and four men's prisons. Maria says that for many children, this is the only way that they get to visit their parents, many of whom are incarcerated over 300 miles away. Kids on the bus learn that they are not alone and are not the only children with a parent in prison. Maria has this advice for you as a classroom teacher:[35]

- Be aware that in your classroom you may have children whose parents are in prison. Understanding that many children have incarcerated parents is the first step to helping them.
- Not all children of incarcerated parents know that their mother or father is in prison. Many families are careful of what they say about where the mother or father is, so approach each family carefully and get to know their needs. Ask them how you can help them.
- Let children know that they are loved by you and others. Remember, all children need love and affection and the security of knowing you care.[36]

Homeless Families and Children

Homelessness is always a problem in the United States. The National Center on Family Homelessness reports that more than 1.6 million children—or one in 45 children—are homeless annually in America. It is estimated that 40 percent of homeless children, or roughly 640,000 over that time frame, are under age six. The accompanying collapse of the housing market and widespread home foreclosures spurred by the Great Recession of 2008–2012 increased the number of homeless families throughout the country. With one in forty-five children in the United States being homeless, chances are you will have a child of a homeless family in your classroom.

Public Law 107-110, the McKinney-Vento Homeless Assistance Act of 2001, provides that "each state educational agency shall assure that each child of a homeless individual and each homeless youth has access to the same free, appropriate public education, including a public preschool education, as provided to other children and youth." The act also requires school districts to establish "liaisons" between children who are homeless and their schools.

Involving Homeless Families and Children.   Here are some strategies you can use to involve homeless families and their children.

- Keep in mind that homeless families are dealing with many problems, including their homelessness, which cause them stress, such as providing basic care, protection, food, clothing and health care for their children. You may have to challenge your own attitudes toward homeless families and children.

- Work with your school district liaison to become involved with homeless families and to secure specific help for homeless children in your classroom and school.

- Provide basic learning materials for homeless children and their families. A backpack with books and school supplies enables children to feel as though they are a "normal" part of the schooling process, and it enables parents to read to and work with their children. You can work with community groups to furnish free school supplies.

- Work with your school liaison to link homeless families to community services that can help them find shelter, food, clothing, and health care, as well as legal services regarding immigration, housing, and other problems.

- Collaborate with your school administration and colleagues to create a parent lounge or parent center that homeless families can use as a means of having Internet access, making connections with community services, and feeling as though they are a part of their child's learning community and schooling process.

Being absent from school is a huge problem for homeless children, and school absenteeism is a swelling epidemic, as the accompanying Diversity Tie-In feature illustrates.

Grandparents as Parents

More adult children than ever are living with their parents and grandparents. Reasons for this increase include parental drug use, divorce, mental and physical illness, abandonment, teenage pregnancy, child abuse and neglect, incarceration, and death. One in eight twenty-two- to twenty-nine-year-olds say that because of the Great Recession of 2008–2012, they have boomeranged back to live with their parents after being on their own.[37] A record 49 million Americans, or 16.1 percent of the total U.S. population, live in a family household that contains at least two adult generations or a grandparent and at least one other generation.[38]

diversity tie-in

Parents, Children, and School Absenteeism

We talk about children in the classrooms as though they were just a natural part of the process of education. We take it for granted that children will be in our classroom every day for us to teach. But what if there were no children? For many schools, this is exactly the problem! Children are not in school. And as you are probably thinking right now, if children are not in the classroom, they are not learning. This is exactly right!

While chronic school absence (missing class 10 percent of the total days of the school year) is not a problem everywhere, it can reach surprisingly high levels even in the early grades. Nationwide, nearly 10 percent of kindergartners and first graders are chronically absent. In some communities, chronic early absence can affect 25 percent of all children in kindergarten through third grade across the entire district. Within particular schools in the same district, chronic early absence can range from less than 1 percent to more than 50 percent.[39] Research concludes that chronic absence adversely impacts student performance. This is especially true for children living in poverty. All children, regardless of socioeconomic background, do worse academically in first grade if they are chronically absent in kindergarten. Chronic absence in kindergarten especially affects reading performance for Hispanic first graders. Among poor children, chronic absence in kindergarten predicts the lowest levels of educational achievement at the end of the fifth grade.[40]

Again, you are probably thinking that one solution to chronic absenteeism is to get children in school. This is exactly right also! Achieving the goal of reducing chronic absenteeism and having children in school requires collaboration among teachers, schools, families, and communities. Here are some things you can do.

- Make every effort to involve or engage with all parents. Don't let any of your parents "fall through the cracks." When parents feel as though you value them and their children and want them to get involved, they are more likely to be involved and send their children to school.
- Stress to children and families the importance of school attendance. Talk about the importance of school attendance at your morning meetings. Send notes and newsletters to parents providing them with reasons why it is important for their children to attend school.
- When children are absent, contact parents, inquire why their children are not in school, and ask what you can do to help.
- Offer classroom incentives for good attendance. Incentives can include certificates, awards, class field trips, and so forth.

---

chronic school absence Missing class 10 percent of the total days of the school year.

grandfamilies Another term for children living with their grandparents.

Many children today are *skipped-generation children*, meaning that neither of their parents is living with them and they are living with grandparents or in some other living arrangement. There are about 640,000 skipped-generation grandfamilies in the United States, all with one or more children under eighteen. The number of children in these grandfamilies (another term for children living with their grandparents) remains constant at about 1 million.[41] Grandparents in these skipped-generation households have all of the parenting responsibilities of parents—providing for their grandchildren's basic needs and care, as well as making sure that they do well in school. As a result, these grandparents need your support and educational assistance.

Ideas for Involving Grandparents. You can literally help grandparents learn to parent all over again, keeping in mind that they are rearing their grandchildren in a whole different generation from the one in which they reared their children. Here are some things to do:

- Provide refresher parenting courses to help grandparents understand how children and schooling have changed since they reared their children.
- Link grandparents to support groups, such as Raising Our Children's Children (ROCC) and the AARP Grandparent Information Center. Web addresses for these

organizations are located in the Linking to Learning section at the end of this chapter.

- Offer grandparents opportunities to engage with children academically and socially. Many universities offer Grandparent University where grandparents can relive memories of being at a university and their grandchildren can experience what college has to offer—dorm life, food, and classes. For example, children or grandchildren of Oklahoma State University (OSU) alumni are invited to OSU's Grandparent University summer program. Students choose from the fourteen majors available, including architecture, broadcasting, and horticulture, and also stay in dorms, attend classes in their major, and participate in campus activities.[42]

Many grandparents who are raising grandchildren live in poverty. For them, many teachers turn to the community for help. For example, children in Bejae Keil's kindergarten class at King Academy are all fortunate enough to have "Grandma" Velma Turner, a volunteer through the Visiting Nurse Services of Iowa's Foster Grandparent Program. She has spent the past three years volunteering as a foster grandparent around Des Moines, working with students in several public schools. Turner has young grandchildren and great-grandchildren of her own, but she said she finds the time to spend at the school because she loves kids. "I have a real love of children. What people don't realize is that they're good for me, just as I can help them." Turner helped organize a midday class picnic for the children, many of whom had never eaten a picnic lunch.[43]

Linguistically Diverse Parents and Families

Linguistically diverse parents are individuals whose English proficiency is minimal and who may lack a deep knowledge of the norms and social systems in the United States. *Linguistically diverse families* often face language and cultural barriers that greatly hamper their ability to become actively involved in their children's education, although many have a great desire and willingness to participate.

Because the culture of linguistically diverse families often differs from that of the majority in a community, those who seek a truly collaborative involvement must take into account the cultural features that inhibit collaboration. Styles of child rearing and family organization, attitudes toward schooling, organizations around which families center their lives, life goals and values, political influences, and methods of communication within the cultural group all have implications for parent participation.

Linguistically diverse families often lack information about the U.S. educational system—including basic school philosophy, practices, and structure—which can result in misconceptions, fear, and a general reluctance to become involved. Furthermore, the U.S. educational system may be quite different from the ones these families are used to. In fact, they may have been taught to avoid active involvement in the educational process, preferring to leave all decisions concerning their children's education to professionals.

The U.S. ideal of a community-controlled and community-supported educational system must be explained to families from cultures in which this concept is not so highly valued. The traditional roles of children, teachers, and administrators in the United States also have to be explained. Many families need to learn to assume their roles and obligations associated with their children's schooling.

Here are some culturally sensitive suggestions for involving linguistically diverse families.

- ***Know what each parent in your program wants for his or her child.*** Find out families' goals. What are their caregiving practices? What concerns do they have about their child? Encourage parents to talk about all of this, to ask questions, and to be honest with you about their goals for their children.

linguistically diverse parents Parents whose English proficiency is minimal and who may lack a comprehensive knowledge of the norms and social systems in the United States.

Students today come from very diverse backgrounds. This **video** gives practical suggestions for making all parents/caregivers feel welcome in the school.

- **Build relationships.** Relationships enhance your chances for conflict management or resolution. Be patient. Building relationships takes time, but it enhances communications and understandings. You'll communicate better if you have a relationship, and you'll have a relationship if you learn to communicate!

- **Educate yourself and your parents.** Learn about the cultures and customs of your families. Help families and children learn the customs and practices of the United States and their local community.

The accompanying Diversity Tie-In, "Getting Hispanic Parents Involved in Schools," provides you some helpful ideas for involving Hispanic parents.

Your role as an early childhood professional includes learning how to effectively involve linguistically diverse parents and families of many different cultures. How will you prepare yourself for this important role?

Lesbian, Gay, Bisexual, and Transgender (LGBT) Families

More than likely, you will have in your classroom children from lesbian, gay, bisexual, and transgendered (LGBT) families. Here are some important facts and figures you need to consider as you seek to involve and embrace all parents and families.

- Being raised in LGBT families does not impact normal childhood development. Studies show that the sexual orientation of a parent is irrelevant to the development of a child's mental health, social development, sexual orientation, and to the quality of the parent–child relationship.[44] Children raised in lesbian households are psychologically well adjusted and have fewer behavioral problems than their peers raised in heterosexual households. Children from lesbian families rate higher in social, academic, and total competence. They also show lower rates in social, rule-breaking, aggressive problem behavior.[45]

- LGBT parents are more likely to be involved in their children's education, are more involved in school activities, and are more likely to report more consistent communication with school personnel than their heterosexual counterparts.[46]

- LGBT parents suffer from various types of exclusion from their school communities, such as being excluded or prevented from fully participating in school activities and events, being excluded by school policies and procedures, and being ignored and feeling invisible. LGBT parents report mistreatment from other parents in the school community and from their children's peers at school.[47]

- Children may be stigmatized because of their parents' sexuality and be victims of teasing and bullying. Studies provide mixed results on whether children from LGBT families suffer from more teasing and bullying than peers from heterosexual families. However, data show that about 45 percent of LGBT parents are either African American or Latino. This is important because it is possible that there is a greater degree of stigmatization of homosexuality in minority groups.[48]

- LGBT families are raising 4 percent of all adopted children in the United States.[4] Adopted children with same-sex parents are more likely to be foreign-born.[5] These children may face not only prejudices about their country of origin but also the prejudices against the sexual orientation of their families.

So, what does this mean for you? Children in your classroom are your students regardless of their parents' sexual orientation and your own personal beliefs. They

diversity tie-in

Getting Hispanic Parents Involved in Schools

Because parents play such a powerful role in their children's educational development, early childhood programs must make every effort to involve the parents and families of *all* children. Unfortunately, many minority parents are not included at all, or not to the extent they should be. The urgency of involving minority parents becomes more evident when we look at the population growth of minorities. Strong growth in Hispanic enrollment is expected to continue for decades, according to a recently released U.S. Census Bureau population projection. The Census Bureau projects that the Hispanic school-age population, ages five to seventeen, will increase by 166 percent by 2050 to 28 million, while the non-Hispanic school-age population will grow by just 4 percent to 45 million over this same period. In 2050, there will be more school-age Hispanic children than school-age non-Hispanic white children.[51]

Given the U.S. economy and clashing news about immigration policy, immigrant families are resentful and believe that educational, community, and human service programs harbor some degree of prejudice, which creates a deep sense of mistrust. As a result, programs need to be deeply concerned with developing trust with families by focusing on building interpersonal relationships. These interpersonal relationships need to be based on respect, dignity, and kindness.

The St. Joseph School District in St. Joseph, Missouri, in attempts to generate and sustain respectful, dignified, and kind relationships between schools and linguistically diverse families, established the English for Speakers of Other Languages (ESOL) Program. The district's ESOL philosophy—integration, not assimilation—is visible in its ESOL office, appropriately called the Welcome Center. The Welcome Center serves as an enrollment center for language minority families. The Welcome Center also serves as a resource center and gathering place for students' families.[52]

Furthermore, family outreach is the focus of bimonthly meetings that are held at the ESOL office. Family Fun Nights are regular events at the center schools, and all materials are offered in several languages. English classes are offered to students' parents and other members of the family through the district's adult English as a Second Language (ESL) program. St. Joseph's Parents-as-Teachers program employs one bilingual parent educator and aggressively recruits non-English-speaking families. The ESOL staff is on hand to help parents negotiate parent–teacher conferences and can provide a translated report card upon request. The motto of the program is that when students feel good and when their families feel good, both are more likely to be involved in education. Many families helped by the Welcome Center have reported that the ESOL program was a great help in navigating their first months in St. Joseph and that the staff guided the family through the enrollment process and continues to help them understand the public school system.

Across the country, educators will place more emphasis on how to make Hispanic and other minority parents feel welcome and involved in their children's schools. Programs that have successfully involved Hispanic parents recommend the following strategies:

- *Personal touch.* Use face-to-face communication in the Hispanic parents' primary language when first making contact. It may take several personal meetings before parents gain sufficient trust to actively participate.
  - Make home visits if possible, taking Spanish-speaking parents with you to interpret for you. Remember, parents trust parents!
  - Have parents invite other parents to school, where you can talk personally to a small group.
  - Always greet parents whenever they come to school for any reason.
- *Nonjudgmental communication.* Avoid making Hispanic parents feel that they are to blame or are doing something wrong. Support parents for their strengths rather than judging them for perceived failings.
  - Be an active listener—pay close attention to what parents are saying and how they are saying it.
  - Be willing to compromise.
- *Bilingual support.* Communicate with Hispanic parents in both Spanish and English.
  - Send all notes and flyers home in Spanish.
  - Spanish-speaking parents can help you compose notes and announcements.
  - Designate a Hispanic parent as the contact for your classroom to keep other parents informed about upcoming meetings.
  - Establish a Spanish book corner where students and parents can check out bilingual or Spanish books to read together.
- *Staff development focused on Hispanic culture.* All staff must understand the key features of Hispanic culture—Latino history, traditions, values, and customs—and their impact on students' behavior and learning styles. For example, Hispanic children like peer-oriented learning, so mixed-age grouping and cooperative learning strategies work well. You should learn as much as possible about the children and their culture.
- *Community outreach.* Many Hispanic families can benefit from family literacy programs, vocational training, ESL programs, improved medical and dental services, and other community-based social services.

deserve the best you can give them. All parents deserve to be and should be involved. One mother said, "I want my sons' school environment to give them the opportunity to learn without harassment. And I want to be a welcomed and integral part of my children's educational experience as they grow."[53]

Involving LGBT Parents/Families.   Here are some strategies for you to follow for involving LGBT parents.

- Treat each family member and child equally with dignity, respect, and honor. Under no circumstances should you participate in making disparaging, derogatory, or negative remarks to or about LGBT parents to other teachers, parents, students, or community members.

- Collaborate with other staff members to arrange for a uniform response to teasing and bullying. Teachers and administrators should be a united front against discrimination and bullying to better support each child's education and sense of belonging.

- Studies show that LGBT parents whose children's schools have a comprehensive safe-school policy that protects students from bullying and harassment report the lowest level of mistreatment.

- Providing a comprehensive curriculum based on diversity acceptance is also helpful.[54] Work with your colleagues and school district administrators to support and use a comprehensive approach to exploring and welcoming diverse families.

- Invite and encourage LGBT families to attend school functions, volunteer, and participate in classroom activities as you do other families. Let them know you value and desire their input, presence, and participation. Make it clear that your classroom is a friendly, accepting, equalizing place by having classroom decorations reflect the diversity of all families, from biracial to LGBT to single parents.

- Be sure to include both parents in the parent/family relationship, not just the biological parent (if the child is not adopted). Encourage both parents' participation and input.

Military Families

You may have heard the phrase, "When one member joins, the whole family serves," when it comes to service members and their families.[55] This could not be more true today with the United States at war in several countries. Children are profoundly impacted by their families' involvement in military service. At the present time, there are over 1.4 million servicemen and servicewomen in the armed forces, so it is likely that you will have a child of a military family in your classroom.[56] Today's service families are unique in that they face a lifestyle that is often in upheaval and results in increased family separations due to frequent deployment, recalls to active duty, and relocations. These are highly stressful and challenging times for service families.[57]

Supporting Military Children and Families.   Here are some suggestions for how you can support children of military families.

- ***Help children keep in contact with families.*** Offer opportunities for children to write letters, e-mail, or talk to their parent on the phone. As a project for your students, you can honor your military parents by sending them a class package with a special gift, video, or letter. Many faith-based veterans groups and other community agencies will pay the postage for packages and letters for service personnel. For example, Cindy Bost of Youngsville, Pennsylvania, started Pennies for Postage to help families and organizations pay for postage to send care packages to service members overseas. Cindy started with bake sales and donation buckets in stores around town, and local organizations are collaborating as well.[58] You can also help kids keep a journal, scrapbook, or photo album of daily events to share with their mom or dad when they return.

- *Get in touch with other military families in your school and community.* The Department of Defense has the Sure Start program, which operates Child Development Programs (CDP) and the Department of Defense Educational Activities (DoDEA). CDP provides child care and before- and after-school care for children six weeks to fourteen years old. DoDEA provides free public education to all children in grades K–12, plus selected preschool-aged children who have disabilities.[59] Through these programs, you can help children in your class make contact with other children whose parents are on active military duty and give them a forum to talk about their thoughts and feelings.

- *Collaborate with your community to gain access to programs that support military families.* The Armed Services YMCA's Operation Hero holds biweekly meetings where children come together to work on various projects designed to increase their ability to adapt to making changes in schools and new friends. Such support groups offer many outlets for children and families to form new relationships, establish ties in a new place, and feel comfortable in a school. Relocating is difficult for children. Mikayla Bonner says, "The challenges are different with trying to fit in with your new environment and trying to be yourself and make friends at the same time."[60] Imagine having to do that several times a year! So, if a military support group for families and children does not exist in your school or community, you can help organize one.

- *Understand and spot academic and behavior cues early.* Children may experience a decline in classroom performance while a parent is on active military duty; it may be hard for them to focus with so much to be worried about.[61] Be understanding and supportive; provide a listening ear to your children with deployed family members. Provide extra tutoring and other opportunities for children to learn and practice academics to help keep them on track.

- *Encourage parents to limit the amount of television children watch.* Young children should not watch war-related coverage without adult supervision. Children's fears and worries for their family members can lead to negative emotions, such as depression, anxiety, or aggression.[62] Provide a nurturing relationship and classroom. Sadly, children do know about and are harmed by war and violence. You can produce an antidote for fear and violence by providing a positive and nurturing class and school environment.

In our connected media society, involving parents electronically provides you many possibilities and opportunities as the Technology Tie-In feature illustrates.

TYPES OF PARENT/FAMILY INVOLVEMENT

Parent/family involvement is a process of helping parents and family members use their abilities to benefit themselves, their children, and the early childhood program. Families, children, and the program are all part of the process; consequently, all three parties should benefit from a well-planned program of involvement. Nonetheless, the focus in interactions between parent/family and the child is the family—and you must work with and through families if you want to be successful.

As you think about your role in parent and family involvement, reflect on the six types of parent involvement in Figure 13.1. These six types of parent/family involvement constitute a comprehensive approach to your work with parents. A worthy professional goal would be for you to *try* to have some of your parents involved in all six

parent/family involvement
A process of helping parents and family members use their abilities to benefit themselves, their children, and the early childhood program.

technology tie-in

Involving Families Electronically

The Internet provides an excellent way for you to reach out to parents and keep them informed and involved. For example, teachers use the Internet to post calendars, newsletters, discussion topics, assignments, assessment tools, spelling lists, and tips. Here are some ways you can electronically connect with families:

- **E-mail.** E-mail is fast and convenient, and for many families it is the preferred mode of communication. E-mail increases communication between families and teachers and between faculty and outside personnel involved in working with individual students.
- **Teacher website.** Most school districts have a website that provides general information about the district and individual schools. Many teachers have their own classroom website as well. Web pages are excellent ways to give parents and community members general information and let them virtually experience school and classroom events and accomplishments. For example, through the Internet, you can access many teachers' websites. Now would be a good time for you to do this.

    First grade teacher Marci McGowan uses her classroom website as an interactive tool to connect with families outside of the classroom. She displays photos of student work and projects, access to other colleagues' teacher websites for resources and information, and educational books and activities students can work on during the summer break. Most importantly, Marci's teaching philosophy is located on her website to guide and direct her teaching of young children. She also writes a letter to the children at the beginning of the year introducing

herself, explaining what supplies to bring, and when and where to meet her on the first day of school.[63]
- **Twitter.** Twitter, a social-networking website delivering short (140 characters or less), text-based posts, is useful on many levels. Teachers can use Twitter to send out homework so that parents are automatically updated. Parents can follow teachers and see what their children are up to from any computer (from work, home, coffee shops) at any time of the day. Twitter can also bring students into contact with their community on a local and global level. Students in two Maine elementary schools have been exchanging messages through Twitter. Teachers say the exercise was initiated to help students develop their writing skills by composing messages that must be 140 characters or less.[64]
- **Video chat.** Teachers can use free video chat providers such as Skype or Gmail to hold convenient conferences with parents. If a parent is away on a business trip or can't get away from the office, with the click of a button the parent can take part in a conference with teachers and other parents on their lunch break. In Olathe, Kansas, teachers use Skype to allow both students and their families to attend parent–teacher conferences.[65]
- **Teacher–parent blog.** Teachers can use a blog to connect with students and their families. Blogs can feature lesson summaries, concept introduction and exploration, and classroom notes, reminders, and news. Parents can leave comments, be more informed, and communicate with other parents in the class.

of these types of parental involvement throughout the program year. Your success as an involver of parents at all levels will depend in part on how well you collaborate with your colleagues, your parents, and your community.

Type 1: Personal/Individual Involvement and Empowerment

- *Adult education classes.* Provide families with opportunities to learn about a range of topics, such as child development, helping children learn to read, and basic math skills.
- *Training programs.* Give parents and other family members skills as classroom aides, club and activity sponsors, curriculum planners, and policy decision makers. When parents and other family members are viewed as experts, empowerment results.
- *Classroom and center activities.* Although not all families can be directly involved in classroom activities, encourage those who can. But remember that those who are involved must have guidance, direction, and training. Involving parents and others as paid aides can be an excellent way to provide both employment and

Parents really appreciate the inclusion that the blogs provide. The fascination and engagement with technology for children is something that helps motivate parents to be involved. As one parent explains, "Our child is genuinely excited to come home and show us what's going on at school. He reads his own words and listens to his own voice on the Internet. He finds this fascinating. This knowledge helps him to better utilize Internet resources, and increases his understanding and awareness of the technologies. It also keeps us parents in the loop."[66]

You can involve your students in building a great classroom-parent relationship. The more "student-led" the online activities are, the more engaged and interested parents will be. First grade teacher Carrie Jostmeyer recommends these ideas:

- **Animoto videos**—Students create online presentations instead of slideshows, using photos, graphics, music, and videos about what they are learning.
- **Student and classroom blogs**—Parents have access to what the students are learning about and discussing.
- **Flip camera videos**—Students can record themselves reading a book out loud and send it to their parents wherever they are. What an awesome e-mail to open up in the middle of the workday!
- **Weekly news report**—Students take the lead as anchors, news reporters, and camera crew, writing what they learned in different content areas throughout the week and recording a news broadcast. You can burn copies of the broadcast for students to take home to watch with their parents.[67]

Here are some guidelines to follow when you communicate with families electronically:

- Check with your school or program technology coordinator for guidelines and policies for Web page development and communicating electronically with parents.

- Remember that not all parents are connected to the Internet. There is still a "digital divide" in the United States; low-income parents and minorities are less likely to have Internet access. Consider how to provide families without Internet access the same information you provide to families who have Internet service. Here are some things you can do:
  - Use the cell phone to stay in touch with parents.
  - Work with local libraries and make arrangements for parents to have Internet access.
  - Research to see if any of your community partners can help you arrange for adopting a family to provide them Internet services.
- Observe all the rules of politeness and courtesy that you would in a face-to-face conversation.
- Observe all the rules of courteous Internet conversations. For example, don't use all capital letters (this is similar to SHOUTING).
- Remember that just like handwritten notes, electronic mail can be saved. In addition, electronic notes are much more easily transferred.
- Be straightforward and concise in your electronic conversations.
- Establish ground rules ahead of time about what you will and will not discuss electronically.

There are unlimited possibilities for you to conduct a meaningful program of involvement for all parents and families. Families can make a significant difference in their children's education, and with your assistance they can join teachers and schools in a productive partnership.

As you think about how you will involve parents and families, reflect on the powerful influences families have in children's lives. It is in the context of the family unit that children learn about morality and character—essential developmental dimensions of their lives.

---

training. Many programs, such as Head Start, actively support such a policy. Get as many parents involved in your classroom as you can.

- *Libraries and materials centers.* Families benefit from books and other articles relating to parenting. Some programs furnish resource areas with comfortable chairs to encourage families to use these materials.

Type 2: Home/Family Involvement and Empowerment

- *Performances and plays.* These, especially ones in which children have a part, tend to bring families to school; however, the purpose of children's performances should not be solely to get families involved.
- *Telephone hotlines.* When staffed by families, hotlines can help allay fears and provide information relating to child abuse, communicable diseases, and special events. Hotlines answered by a knowledgeable parent or family member, even if only during certain hours of the week, provide other parents and family members with a

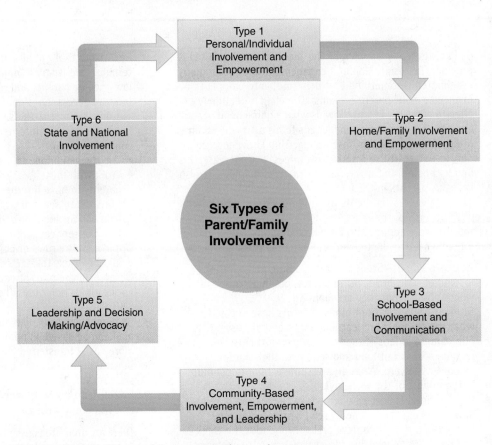

FIGURE 13.1 Six Types of Parent/Family Involvement

There are basically six types of parent/family involvement. Consider how you can involve some of your parents in all of the six types.

Source: G. S. Morrison, *Early Childhood Education Today,* 12th ed. (Upper Saddle River, NJ: Pearson, 2011); and G. S. Morrison, *Parent Involvement in the Home, School, and Community* (Columbus, OH: Merrill, 1978).

means of getting advice and help. Telephone networks or phone trees are also used to help children and parents with homework and to monitor latchkey children.

- ***Newsletters/e-newsletters.*** When planned with parents' help, newsletters are an excellent way to keep families informed about program events, activities, and curriculum information. Newsletters in parents' native languages help keep language-minority families informed.

- ***Books and other materials for parents and children to use at home.*** Provide material for parents to read to their children. For example, in the Professionalism in Practice feature "Home and School: An Unbeatable Team!" at the beginning of this chapter, you learned how teacher Paula McCullough uses book bags to encourage parental awareness of student learning. Also, sending out a monthly calendar of activities to be done at home is another good way to keep families involved in their children's learning.

- ***IEPs for children with special needs.*** Involvement in writing an IEP is not only a legal requirement but also an excellent learning experience and an effective communication tool.

- ***A website for parents.*** A website informs them about the activities of your classroom. Give suggestions for how parents can extend and enrich classroom projects and activities at home.

Type 3: School-Based Involvement and Communication

- *Welcoming committees.* A good way to involve families in any program is to have other families contact them when their children first join a program. Parents are good organizers of these types of activities.
- *Tutor time.* Provide tutor time in which parents and their children can work with teachers on special topics such as math homework, teaching literacy skills, and so on.
- *Participation in workshops.* These workshops introduce families to the school's policies, procedures, and programs. Most families want to know what is going on in the school and would do a better job of helping their children at home if they knew school policies and classroom procedures.

Type 4: Community-Based Involvement, Empowerment, and Leadership

- *Family nights, cultural dinners, chili cook-offs, and potluck dinners.* Such events bring families and the community to the school in nonthreatening, social ways. For example:
  - At Country Heights Elementary School (Davies County, Kentucky), preschool teacher Connie Johnson invites a community librarian to come in and read books to her children. Connie also regularly sends home with her children information about public library activities and events. The public library staff visits over seventy-two preschool sites throughout the county.[68]
  - Hills Elementary (Iowa) has a large population of students who live in an impoverished part of town. The school started a community center, which offers a monthly family night dinner program and provides opportunities for parents, teachers, and students to develop study and life skills.[69] And, speaking of community librarians and libraries, Justin Minkel, Arkansas Teacher of the Year, suggests in his feature Professionalism in Practice: "The Home Library" that you work with parents and families to develop home libraries for children.
- *Parent support groups.* Parents need support in their roles. Support groups can provide parenting information, community agency information, and speakers.
- *Home visitations.* Home visitations are an excellent way to promote community/school/family involvement. For example, the Henderson County Schools (Kentucky) conduct an annual home visitation blitz. The home visitation blitz sends out 500 teachers and other school staff into the homes of 3,000 students. Community members from attorneys to politicians to store owners and business executives provide and serve a barbecue lunch for the home visitors. (See tips for conducting home visits in this chapter.)

Type 5: Leadership and Decision Making/Advocacy

- *Fairs and bazaars.* Involve families in many aspects of the decision-making process. Allow and encourage input in regard to fund-raising, planning, and so forth.
- *School parent councils.* Review the school's budget, recommend programs, sponsor events, solve problems, and raise funds for special school activities.[70]
- *School site councils.* Many decisions affecting the education of students are made in the schools. School-based decision-making is the responsibility of the School Site Council. For example School Site Councils hire teachers (in some cases), approve school rules, and decide if students will wear uniforms.[71]
- *Hiring and policy making.* Parents and community members can and should serve on committees that hire staff and set policy.

- **Curriculum development and review.** Parents' involvement in curriculum planning helps them learn about and understand what constitutes a quality program and what is involved in a developmentally appropriate curriculum. When families know about the curriculum, they are more supportive of it.

Type 6: State and National Involvement

Stand for Children is an independent organization that works with parents to engage them in advocacy and building better public schools in Chicago and Illinois. Stand for Children held a series of telephone town halls in which they called 70,000 people and asked them to listen in to a town hall meeting held by a panel of speakers. Parents were given the opportunity to join the real-time discussions and to ask questions. Town hall meetings included discussions about longer school days, how to build better public schools, and how to promote safety and reduce violence in schools and communities.[72]

The National Civic League partners with local communities nationwide to increase by 50 percent the number of low-income children reading on grade level in third grade in at least a dozen states during the next ten years. In 2011, the city of Baltimore won the All-American City Award, presented by the National Civic League, for creating a Grade-Level Reading Campaign to achieve three goals by 2020:

1. Average daily attendance of 97 percent for students in grades K–3.
2. More than 80 percent of students reading at grade level by the end of third grade.
3. More than 80 percent of all children fully prepared for kindergarten.[73]

The Kentucky Department of Education sends out an issue of *ParentInfo*, an e-mail newsletter, with timely tips on how parents can help children succeed in school. Topics include college and career readiness, testing, school-based decision-making councils, anti-bullying technology, and more.[74]

Parents and students at Lura A. White Elementary School in Shirley, Massachusetts, participated in the annual Books and Beyond, a national program that promotes student reading outside of school and the involvement of parents in their children's reading. Awards are given to teachers and parents who make the program a success and also students who read the most books. All participants and their families enjoy a school-wide barbecue. Kindergarten students read 6,720 books; first graders read 7,895 books; second graders read 5,635 books; and third graders read 8,116 books.[75]

Home Visitation

All across the United States, growing numbers of school districts are encouraging and supporting teachers to visit children's homes and ask parents for help in educating their children. Two home visits per year are required in the Head Start program, and home visits are becoming more commonplace in many school districts.[76] Teachers who do home visiting are trained prior to going on the visits. Although not every state or district pays extra for home visits, more schools are building home visits into the school calendar, with a certain number of days being set aside for home visiting. Some districts and programs provide released time for visitation by hiring substitute teachers to enable classroom teachers to make home visits.

A home visiting program demonstrates that teachers, principal, and school staff are willing to "go more than halfway" to involve all parents in their children's education. Home visits help teachers demonstrate their interest in students' families and understand their students better by seeing them in their home environment.

These visits should not replace parent–teacher conferences or be used to discuss children's progress. When done early before any school problems can arise, they avoid putting parents on the defensive and signal that teachers are eager to work with all parents.

Teachers who have made home visits say they build stronger relationships with parents and their children, and improve attendance and achievement. Although many "home" visits do occur in the home, they do not always have to. Sometimes parents are more comfortable meeting teachers away from the home in places such as community centers, churches, or the local YMCA or YWCA. These visits are still considered "home" visits.

Here are some guidelines for how you can be successful in your program of home visitation.

Prepare for the Visit.   Planning for home visitations is as important as conducting the visit. It makes sense to have goals, objectives, and guidelines for these visitations as a means for successfully planning for them.

Buder Elementary School in St. Louis, Missouri, has these goals for its home visitations:

- Improve academic achievement and test scores
- Increase student attendance
- Increase parental involvement
- Increase homework completion
- Improve behavior, decrease discipline referrals, and improve attitudes about school[77]

Schedule the visits:

- Some schools have scheduled home visits in the afternoon right after school. Others have found that early evening is more convenient for parents. Some schools schedule visits right before a new school year begins. A mix of times may be needed to reach all families.
- Work with community groups (e.g., Boys and Girls Clubs, housing complexes, 4-H, YMCAs, and community centers) to schedule visits in neutral but convenient spaces.

Make parents feel comfortable:

- Send a letter home to parents explaining the desire to have teachers make informal visits to all students' homes. Include a form that parents can mail back to accept or decline the visit.
- State clearly that the intent of your thirty-minute visit is to introduce yourself to family members and not to discuss the child's progress.
- Suggest that families think about special things their children would want to share with you, the teacher.
- Reduce parents' worries. One school included a note to parents that said, "No preparation is required. In fact, our homes need to be vacuumed and all of us are on diets!" This touch of humor and casualness helps set a friendly and informal tone.
- Make a phone call to parents who have not responded to explain the plan for home visits and reassure parents that it is to get acquainted and not to evaluate students.
- Enlist community groups, religious organizations, and businesses to help publicize the home visits.[78]

Parent–Teacher Conferences

Significant parent involvement occurs through well-planned and well-conducted conferences between parents and early childhood teachers, informally referred to as parent–teacher conferences. Such conferences are often the first contact many families have with school. Conferences are critical both from a public relations point of view and as a vehicle for helping families and professionals accomplish their goals. The

professionalism in practice

The Home Library: Transforming At-Risk Readers

Melinda started second grade with everything against her. She lives in poverty, her mom is illiterate in English and Spanish, and she was severely abused at the age of six. At the beginning of the year, she owned only one book.

Despite these barriers, Melinda made extraordinary academic progress. She moved from a kindergarten level to a fourth grade level in the two years she was in my class. Her demeanor changed, too; she began smiling and laughing more often, and she became a confident scholar.

One reason for her success is simple—instead of one book at home, Melinda now has a home library of 40 books.

THE 1,000 BOOKS PROJECT

Each of the 25 children in my class received 40 books over the course of second and third grade, for a total of 1,000 new books in their homes. I purchased the books through a combination of my own funds, donations from individuals and local organizations, and bonus points from Scholastic book orders. The kids received three types of books each month: copies of several class read-alouds, books their guided reading group had just read, and individual choices selected from Scholastic's website. The total cost for each student's home library was less than $50 each year.

I watched child after child become a different kind of writer, thinker, and human being because of her or his growth as a reader.

TIPS FOR BUILDING A HOME LIBRARY AND FAMILY LITERACY

TIP 1 Create a home library project

Start small—before launching The 1,000 Books Project, I did a pilot version where my eight lowest readers each received ten books. Funding for the project can come from school or district funds, local businesses, or mini-grants from organizations that support literacy. Whatever the size of the project, these three elements are essential:

Many early childhood teachers conduct home visits to help parents learn how to support their children's learning at home. What useful information can parents provide you about children's learning, experience, and growth and development?

following guidelines will help you as an early childhood professional prepare for and conduct successful conferences:

- **Plan ahead.** Be sure of the reason for the conference. What are your objectives? What do you want to accomplish? List the points you want to cover and think about what you are going to say.

- Have each child create a physical space at home for the books.
- Let the students choose most of the titles.
- Make sure the books aren't too hard or too easy for the student.

TIP 2 Find a time when parents can come into your classroom to read with their children

My students' parents are invited to visit the classroom every Tuesday at 2:30 to read with their children. Sometimes the parent reads a book to the child; other times the child reads to the parent. I make sure I have books in the class library that are written in Spanish or other families' home languages for those parents who aren't as comfortable reading in English. Parents usually read to their own child first, then they read with other students whose parents weren't able to come that day, building a class community where families begin to know one another.

TIP 3 Make sure your books reflect your students' lives and interests

Because most of my students speak Spanish as a first language, three book baskets in my classroom library are filled with books in Spanish (nonfiction, fantasy, and realistic fiction). I make sure the books reflect the kids' interests as well as their family's cultural heritage. Be sure to include nonfiction, too—most students love nonfiction texts related to their interests. As an added bonus, photographs are better than drawings when it comes to helping children build vocabulary.

TIP 4 Create "talk time" for both children and their families

Kids need time to share their connections, questions, and opinions about each book they read. We do about fifty "think-pair-shares" a day where students turn to their conversation partner for that week and talk one-on-one about a question I pose. Inviting parents as "guest speakers" is a great way to enrich the context of a book. I invited a student's mom to speak about her experience moving to the United States from Mexico. She spoke in Spanish, with her daughter translating, and the students immediately noticed that this parent's reasons for leaving Mexico were the same as the motivations of European immigrants in the books we had been reading.

TIP 5 Teach parents, too

Students who make the most reading growth in my class are those who read almost every night at home. Many parents have already made reading a nightly activity, but some parents need guidance on how to help their children become readers. Each year I ask parents to set aside about twenty minutes a night for their child to read, and I provide them with a list of questions in both Spanish and English that they can ask their child after reading, such as, "What was your favorite part?" or "What questions did you have while you were reading?"

....

Source: Contributed by Justin Minkel, second and third grade teacher at Jones Elementary in northwest Arkansas. He is the 2007 Arkansas Teacher of the Year, a 2006 Milken Educator, and a 2011 National Board Certified Teacher.

- ***Get to know the families.*** This is not wasted time; the more effectively you establish rapport with families, the more you will accomplish in the long run.
- ***Avoid an authoritative atmosphere.*** Do not sit behind your desk while families sit in children's chairs. Treat families and others like the adults they are.
- ***Communicate at parents' levels.*** Do not condescend or patronize. Instead, use familiar words, phrases, and explanations families understand. Do not use jargon or complicated explanations, and speak in your natural style.
- ***Accentuate the positive.*** Make every effort to show and tell families that children are doing well. When you deal with problems, put them in the proper perspective: what a child is able to do, what the goals and purposes of the learning program are, what specific skill or concept you are trying to get the child to learn, and what problems the child is having in achieving the goal or purpose. Most importantly, explain what you plan to do to help the child achieve and what specific role families can have in meeting the achievement goals.
- ***Give families a chance to talk.*** You will not learn much about families and children if you do all the talking, nor are you likely to achieve your goals. Some teachers are accustomed to dominating a conversation, and many families will not be as verbal as you, so you will have to encourage some families to talk.

- *Learn to listen.* An active listener holds eye contact, uses body language such as head nodding and hand gestures, does not interrupt, avoids arguing, paraphrases as a way of clarifying ideas, and keeps the conversation on track.
- *Follow up.* Ask families to schedule a definite time for the next conference as you are concluding the current one. Having another conference is the best method of solidifying gains and extending support, but other acceptable means of follow-up are telephone calls, written reports, notes sent with children, and brief visits to the home. Although these types of contacts may appear casual, they should be planned for and conducted as seriously as any regular family–teacher conference.
- *Develop an action plan.* Never leave families with a sense of frustration, not knowing what you are doing or what they are to do. Every communication with families should end on a positive note, so that everyone knows what can be done and how to do it.

Making Contact by Telephone

Making a telephone call is an efficient way to contact families when it is impossible to arrange a face-to-face conference. Here are some tips you can use for your telephone contacts with parents:

- Since you cannot see someone on a telephone, it takes a little longer to build rapport and trust. The time you spend overcoming families' initial fears and apprehensions will pay dividends later.
- Constantly clarify what you are talking about and what you and the families have agreed to do, using such phrases as "What I heard you say then . . ." and "So far, we have agreed that . . ."
- Do not act hurried. There is a limit to the amount of time you can spend on the phone, but you may be one of the few people who care about the parent and the child. Your telephone contact may be the major part of the family's support system.

Given the fact that about 13 percent of the children in the United States has a disability, more than likely, you will be working with and involving parents with disabilities. The following section on Teaching and Learning in the Inclusive Classroom provides you with a list of guidelines when collaborating with parents of children with disabilities.

TEACHING AND LEARNING IN THE INCLUSIVE CLASSROOM: INVOLVING FAMILIES OF CHILDREN WITH DISABILITIES

Now that you have read about the different ways to involve parents and bolster home–school collaboration, let's discuss some requirements for working with parents when the children have a disability. The Individuals with Disabilities Education Act (2004) supports the belief that the education of children with disabilities is made more effective by strengthening the role of parents in the special education process. IDEA requires that parents participate in each step of the special education process and ensures this by giving parents the following protections.

- *The right to give informed written consent and the right to confidentiality.* Parents must give written permission before their child is evaluated, before services begin or are changed, and before information about their child is shared with anyone else.
- *The right to receive written prior notice.* Parents must receive written notice before any evaluations or assessments can take place and before each meeting to review the individualized family service plan (IFSP) or individualized education program (IEP).

- **The right to a coordinated IFSP or IEP.** A written plan is developed by a team of professionals and the parents to develop goals for the child and services that will best help reach those goals. This plan also describes when, where, and how services will be delivered.
- **The right to receive services in natural environments and in the least restrictive environment.** Services are focused on the family's and child's daily routines and designed to be carried out within regular activities. The IFSP/IEP team must provide written justification if services are provided anywhere other than the natural environment or least restrictive environment.
- **The right to review records.** Parents may inspect, review, and receive a copy of their child's records.
- **A process to resolve disputes.** Parents who feel their child's rights have been violated may file a written complaint or request mediation or a due process hearing.

Ensuring that children's needs are met and that their rights are upheld requires a system of communication that is consistent and mutually agreed on. Children's success at home and school is strengthened when this communication is reciprocal and positive. Parents and teachers have knowledge that when shared can benefit *all* children. Sharing back and forth between teachers and families is optimal because each has information the other may not have. The more information families and teachers have, the more they can collaborate to help children.

Community/Business Involvement

A comprehensive program of parent and family involvement is not complete without community involvement. More early childhood teachers realize that neither they alone nor the limited resources of their programs are sufficient to meet the needs of many children and families in the twenty-first century. Consequently, early education professionals are seeking ways to link families to community services and resources.

The task facing early childhood professionals is this: Seeking merely to involve parents in school activities is no longer a sufficient program of parent involvement. Today, we can make the lives of families and their children better by making families the focus of our involvement activities. In our effort to do this, community resources provide valuable tools, and businesses can partner with schools to enhance both educational opportunities and the lives of families.

Community Resources.   The community offers a vital and rich array of resources for helping you teach better and for helping you meet the needs of parents and their children. Schools and teachers cannot address the many issues facing children and youth without the partnership and collaboration of powerful sectors of society, including community agencies, businesses, and industry.

Following are suggested actions you can take to learn to use your community in your teaching:

- **Know your students and their needs.** Through observations, conferences with parents, and discussions with students, you can identify barriers to children's learning and discover what kind of help to seek.
- **Know your community.** Walk or drive around the community. Ask a parent to give you a tour to help familiarize you with agencies and individuals. Read the local newspaper and attend community events and activities.
- **Ask for help and support from parents and the community.** Keep in mind that many business and community leaders will not be involved unless you personally ask them. The only encouragement many individuals and local businesses need is your invitation.

- *Develop a directory of community agencies.* Consult the business pages of local phone books, contact local chambers of commerce, and ask parents what agencies are helpful to them.
- *Compile a list of people who are willing to come to your classroom to speak to or work with your students.* You can start by asking parents to volunteer and to give suggestions and recommendations of others.
- *Write grants.* Many businesses have foundations that provide grants to help children and families. Ask your parents to help you write grants and involve your school colleagues, as well.

Only by helping families meet their needs and those of their children will you create opportunities for these children to reach their full potential. For this reason alone, family involvement programs and activities must be an essential part of every early childhood program.

School–Business Partnerships.   School–business partnerships are excellent means of strengthening programs and helping children and families. For their part, businesses are eager to develop the business–school connection in an effort to help schools better educate children.

Schools and businesses all over the country have partnered to help both the schools and local businesses build involvement and community. For example in Durham, North Carolina, the school district sponsors an annual information session with the Durham Regional Association of Realtors. At this annual event, area real estate professionals learn all about Durham public schools so they can better respond to requests from home buyers (parents) who are moving to Durham.[79]

In Norwalk, Connecticut, Pepperidge Farms has teamed up with Norwalk Hospital and Jefferson Elementary School to combat childhood obesity. This partnership created a program called L.E.A.N. (Learning with Energy from Activity and Nutrition). Pepperidge Farms employees worked with over 200 second and third graders, helping them learn and develop lifelong habits of healthy eating and exercise. The students work together and with their mentors to learn about medical conditions that poor nutrition causes, such as obesity, diabetes, heart disease, and cancer. Many students choose to alter their eating habits, opting for milk and water over sodas and other sweetened drinks. Additionally, they have increased their consumption of fruits and vegetables as well as their level of physical activity. Pepperidge Farms chose Jefferson Elementary because it was the largest elementary school in the area, serving the largest percentage of both minorities and low-income families who qualified for free or reduced rate lunches. This partnership doesn't stop when school lets out. Students are invited to attend three separate Project L.E.A.N. summer camps.[80]

Since the Great Recession of 2008–2012, financial literacy has been a hot topic in grades K–3. Teachers are teaching such "money smarts" skills as budgeting, saving, earning, and spending. In northeast Maryland, the Aberdeen Proving Ground Federal Credit Union (APGFCU), and Bayview Elementary have a business–school partnership. Activities and services include financial education presentations in classrooms, free money management seminars for parents and school staff, and recognition and reward incentives for student achievement.[81]

Partnerships between schools and local businesses range from the simple and informal to highly structured and professional. Teachers often manage partnerships. A partnership can be between a local business or community organization and the entire school, a single class, or even just a few students. Community partners range from large corporations to smaller local businesses such as an independently owned pharmacy, the local branch of the YMCA, or a neighborhood grocery store.

The challenge for you and all early childhood professionals is quite clear: how to make families the focus of your involvement activities so that their lives and their children's lives are made better. Anything less will not help families and children access and benefit from the opportunities of the twenty-first century.

ACTIVITIES FOR PROFESSIONAL DEVELOPMENT

ethical dilemma

"I don't want to get involved with them."

Tyler Cove Elementary School has recently received a number of new families displaced by a hurricane. Six-year-old Tamika, her mother, and three siblings arrived in town with only the clothes on their backs. Although Cassie has no hurricane-displaced children in her third grade class, she is very much concerned about their well-being. She mentions to Tamika's teacher that several community agencies are involved in hurricane relief and could provide Tamika and her family with clothing and other resources. Tamika's teacher is unresponsive: "I know, Cassie, but I don't have the time to mess around with this stuff. I've got all I can do to keep up with the things I have to do in the classroom. I don't want to make a lot of extra work for myself. Besides, I really don't want to get involved with these kinds of families; they just don't fit into our community. They'll be gone before too long."

What should Cassie do to help Tamika and her family? Report Tamika's teacher to the principal? Offer to buy Tamika and her family clothing? Call her friend at the Salvation Army for help? Or develop another strategy? What should Cassie do? What would you do?

Application Activities

1. Search the Internet for how current accountability and reform movements are changing and shaping parents' attitudes about their involvement in and their relationship with the schools. Why are parents demanding more involvement in their children's schools? Conduct an online poll with your classmates regarding their opinions about how involved they think parents and families should or should not be in their local schools.

2. Choose one family demographic from the Changing Parents and Families section of the chapter that interests you or that you feel you need to learn more about in order to meet the needs of the children in your classroom. Create a PowerPoint presentation documenting research and general information about this particular demographic and its implications in your classroom. Then, create a list of ideas or events that you will use to encourage involvement of this family type in your classroom. Post your ideas to a teacher blog such as TeacherLingo and ask for comments.

3. Choose one type of involvement (e.g., volunteering, learning at home, etc.) from the six types of parent/family involvement discussed in this chapter and develop a plan for parent/family involvement in a grade you plan to teach using the following outline:

   a. Identify overall and specific objectives for your plan.

   b. Using the type of involvement you chose, develop specific activities for involving families and providing services to them.

   c. Explain how you would involve different family types in your event (fathers, single parents, LGBT parents, military families, etc.).

   d. Explain how you will use the community resources in your plan.

Post your plan on your classroom discussion board and ask for comments from classmates. Critique and offer comments on a classmate's plan for a different type of parent/family involvement.

Linking to Learning

Colorado Fatherhood Initiative

www.coloradodads.com
Coloradodads.com is a service of the Colorado Fatherhood Council, which serves to help fathers and their children.

AARP Grandparent Information Center

www.aarp.org/relationships/friends-family
AARP is a nonprofit, nonpartisan organization that has taken an extra step to help its members who have become primary caregivers of their children and/or their grandchildren.

Armed Services YMCA

www.asymca.org
The ASYMCA works with military families to help provide deployment support, food and clothing pantries, child care, counseling, tutoring, and other basic life services.

MyEducationLab

Go to Topic 3 (Family/Community) in the MyEducationLab (www.myeducationlab.com) for your course, where you can:

- Find learning outcomes for Family/Community along with the national standards that connect to these outcomes.
- Complete Assignments and Activities that can help you more deeply understand the chapter content.
- Apply and practice your understanding of the core teaching skills identified in the chapter with the Building Teaching Skills and Dispositions learning units.

- Check your comprehension on the content covered in the chapter by going to the Study Plan in the Book Resources for your text. Here you will be able to take a chapter quiz, receive feedback on your answers, and then access Review, Practice, and Enrichment activities to enhance your understanding of chapter content.

APPENDIX

Time Line of the History of Early Childhood Education

1524	Martin Luther argued for public support of education for all children in his *Letter to the Mayors and Aldermen of All the Cities of Germany in Behalf of Christian Schools.*
1628	John Amos Comenius's *The Great Didactic* proclaimed the value of education for all children according to the laws of nature.
1762	Jean-Jacques Rousseau wrote *Émile,* explaining that education should take into account the child's natural growth and interests.
1801	Johann Pestalozzi wrote *How Gertrude Teaches Her Children,* emphasizing home education and learning by discovery.
1816	Robert Owen set up a nursery school in Great Britain at the New Lanark Cotton Mills, believing that early education could counteract bad influences of the home.
1836	William McGuffey began publishing the *Eclectic Reader* for elementary school children; his writing had a strong impact on moral and literary attitudes in the nineteenth century.
1837	Friedrich Froebel, known as the "Father of the Kindergarten," established the first kindergarten in Blankenburg, Germany.
1856	Mrs. Margaretha Schurz established the first kindergarten in the United States in Watertown, Wisconsin; the school was founded for children of German immigrants, and the program was conducted in German.
1860	Elizabeth Peabody opened a private kindergarten in Boston, Massachusetts, for English-speaking children.
1871	The first public kindergarten in North America was started in Ontario, Canada.
1873	Susan Blow opened the first public kindergarten in the United States in St. Louis, Missouri, as a cooperative effort with the superintendent of schools, William Harris.
1876	A model kindergarten was shown at the Philadelphia Centennial Exposition.
1892	The International Kindergarten Union (IKU) was founded.
1896	John Dewey started the Laboratory School at the University of Chicago, basing his program on child-centered learning with an emphasis on life experiences.
1907	Maria Montessori started her first preschool in Rome, called Children's House; her now-famous teaching method was based on the theory that children learn best by themselves in a properly prepared environment.
1911	Margaret and Rachel McMillan founded an open-air nursery school in Great Britain in which the class met outdoors; emphasis was on healthy living.
1915	Eva McLin started the first U.S. Montessori nursery school in New York City.
1918	The first public nursery schools were started in Great Britain.
1919	Harriet Johnson started the Nursery School of the Bureau of Educational Experiments, later to become the Bank Street College of Education.
1922	Abigail Eliot, influenced by the open-air school in Great Britain and basing her program on personal hygiene and proper behavior, started the Ruggles Street Nursery School in Boston.
1924	*Childhood Education,* the first professional journal in early childhood education, was published by the IKU.
1926	The National Committee on Nursery Schools was initiated by Patty Smith Hill at Columbia Teachers College; now called the National Association for the Education of Young Children (NAEYC), it provides guidance and consultant services for educators.
1926	The National Association of Nursery Education (NANE) was founded.
1930	The IKU changed its name to the Association for Childhood Education.
1943	Kaiser Child Care Centers opened in Portland, Oregon, to provide twenty-four-hour child care for children of mothers working in war-related industries.
1946	Dr. Benjamin Spock wrote the *Common Sense Book of Baby and Child Care.*

1950	Erik Erikson published his writings on the "eight ages or stages" of personality growth and development and identified "tasks" for each stage of development; the information, known as "Personality in the Making," formed the basis for the 1950 White House Conference on Children and Youth.
1952	Jean Piaget's *The Origins of Intelligence in Children* was published in English translation.
1960	Katherine Whiteside Taylor founded the American Council of Parent Cooperatives for those interested in exchanging ideas in preschool education; it later became the Parent Cooperative Preschools International.
1965	The Head Start program began with federal money allocated for preschool education; the early programs were known as child development centers.
1971	The Stride Rite Corporation in Boston was the first to start a corporate-supported child care program.
1972	The National Home Start Program was initiated for the purpose of involving parents in their children's education.
1975	Public Law 94-142, the Education for All Handicapped Children Act, was passed, mandating a free appropriate public education for all children with disabilities and extending many rights to parents of such children.
1984	The High/Scope Educational Foundation released a study that documented the value of high-quality preschool programs for poor children. This study would be cited repeatedly in coming years by those favoring expansion of Head Start and other early years programs.
1986	Public Law 99-457, the Education of the Handicapped Act Amendments, established a national policy on early intervention that recognizes its benefits, provides assistance to states for building systems of service delivery, and recognizes the unique roles of families in the development of their children with disabilities.
1988	Even Start was established by the U.S. Department of Education as a parent education/literacy program.
1995	Head Start Reauthorization established a new program, Early Head Start, for low-income pregnant women and families with infants and toddlers.
2001	The No Child Left Behind Act (NCLB) was passed, providing funding for early literacy and learning to read.
2003	Beginning of the Literacy Decade: All early childhood professionals are called to action by the United Nations to fight against illiteracy worldwide.
2007	Montessorians around the world celebrate one hundred years of Montessori education.
2009	The world marks the two hundredth anniversary of Louis Braille, inventor of the Braille system of writing used by the blind and visually impaired worldwide. Braille represents one of the world's great assistive technologies.
2009	The American Recovery and Reinvestment Act of 2009 provides $2.1 billion for Head Start and Early Head Start.
2010	Head Start celebrates forty-five years of success.
2011	Nine states (CA, MA, MD, DE, MN, NC, OH, RI, WA) receive a share of $500 million in federal grant money from the Race to the Top Federal Initiative to increase the effectiveness of preschool programs.
2012	States re-energize their efforts to fund pre-K and kindergarten programs in the wake of budget cuts of the Great Recession.

ENDNOTES

Chapter 1

1. Excerpted and adapted from NAEYC, "NAEYC Standards for Early Childhood Professional Preparation Programs." Position Statement. Washington, DC: NAEYC. Reprinted with permission from the National Association for the Education of Young Children (NAEYC). Copyright © 2009 by NAEYC. Full text of all NAEYC position statements is available at www.naeyc.org/positionstatements.

2. Excerpted and adapted from NAEYC, "NAEYC Standards for Early Childhood Professional Preparation Programs." Position Statement. Washington, DC: NAEYC. Reprinted with permission from the National Association for the Education of Young Children (NAEYC). Copyright © 2009 by NAEYC. Full text of all NAEYC position statements is available at www.naeyc.org/positionstatements.

3. Excerpted and adapted from NAEYC, "NAEYC Standards for Early Childhood Professional Preparation Programs." Position Statement. Washington, DC: NAEYC. Reprinted with permission from the National Association for the Education of Young Children (NAEYC). Copyright © 2009 by NAEYC. Full text of all NAEYC position statements is available at www.naeyc.org/positionstatements.

4. Excerpted and adapted from NAEYC, "NAEYC Standards for Early Childhood Professional Preparation Programs." Position Statement. Washington, DC: NAEYC. Reprinted with permission from the National Association for the Education of Young Children (NAEYC). Copyright © 2009 by NAEYC. Full text of all NAEYC position statements is available at www.naeyc.org/positionstatements.

5. Excerpted and adapted from NAEYC, "NAEYC Standards for Early Childhood Professional Preparation Programs." Position Statement. Washington, DC: NAEYC. Reprinted with permission from the National Association for the Education of Young Children (NAEYC). Copyright © 2009 by NAEYC. Full text of all NAEYC position statements is available at www.naeyc.org/positionstatements.

6. Excerpted and adapted from NAEYC, "NAEYC Standards for Early Childhood Professional Preparation Programs." Position Statement. Washington, DC: NAEYC. Reprinted with permission from the National Association for the Education of Young Children (NAEYC). Copyright © 2009 by NAEYC. Full text of all NAEYC position statements is available at www.naeyc.org/positionstatements.

7. Science Daily, "System Aims to Improve Teachers and Teacher Training Programs," April 4, 2011; accessed May 26, 2012, at http://www.sciencedaily.com/releases/2011/04/110404105809.htm.

8. Michelle Shearer, "Making a Difference—Shaping the Future," 2011; accessed May 26, 2012, at http://www.ccsso.org/Documents/NTOY/Applications/2011NTOYfinMDapp.pdf.

9. Excerpted and adapted from NAEYC, "NAEYC Standards for Early Childhood Professional Preparation Programs." Position Statement. Washington, DC: NAEYC. Reprinted with permission from the National Association for the Education of Young Children (NAEYC). Copyright © 2009 by NAEYC. Full text of all NAEYC position statements is available at www.naeyc.org/positionstatements.

10. Forum on Child and Family Statistics, *America's Children: Key National Indicators of Well-Being* (2011); accessed May 26, 2012, at http://www.childstats.gov/americaschildren/eco1.asp.

11. Evelyn Pringle, "Schools Failing Children with Disabilities," 2006; accessed May 26, 2012, at http://www.lawyersandsettlements.com/articles/civil-human-rights/school_disability-00121.html.

12. Daniel Leija, "I Am a Teacher," 2011; accessed May 26, 2012, at http://www.tea.state.tx.us/TOY_Leija_essay.pdf.

13. National Association for the Education of Young Children, *NAEYC Standards for Early Childhood Professional Preparation Programs, 2009*; accessed May 29, 2012, at http://www.naeyc.org/files/naeyc/file/positions/ProfPrepStandards09.pdf.

14. Ibid.

15. Ibid.

16. Michelle Shearer, "Making a Difference—Shaping the Future," 2011; accessed May 26, 2012, at http://www.ccsso.org/Documents/NTOY/Applications/2011NTOYfinMDapp.pdf.

17. McAllen ISD, 2010–2011 Technology Teachers of the Year, 2011; accessed May 28, 2012, at http://mws.mcallenisd.net/cidc/ttoy/1011.html.

18. S. Feeney and K. Kipnis, *Code of Ethical Conduct and Statement of Commitment* (Washington, DC: NAEYC, 2005). Used with permission.

19. S. Feeney and N. K. Freeman, *Ethics and the Early Childhood Educator: Using the NAEYC Code* (Washington, DC: NAEYC, 2005).

20. MyWestHartford, "Kristi Luetjen Named the Connecticut Teacher of the Year"; accessed May 28, 2012, at http://mywesthartfordlife.com/education.php?cid=&id=96.

21. National Council for Accreditation of Teacher Education, *NCATE Unit Standards: Glossary* (Washington, DC: NCATE, 2006); accessed May 28, 2012, at http://www.ncate.org/Standards/NCATEUnitStandards/UnitStandardsinEffect2008/tabid/476/Default.aspx.

22. National Association for the Education of Young Children, *NAEYC Standards for Early Childhood Professional Preparation Programs, 2009*; accessed May 28, 2012, at http://www.naeyc.org/files/naeyc/file/positions/ProfPrepStandards09.pdf.

23. Excerpted and adapted from NAEYC, "NAEYC Standards for Early Childhood Professional Preparation Programs." Position Statement. Washington, DC: NAEYC. Reprinted with permission from the National Association for the Education of Young Children (NAEYC). Copyright © 2009 by NAEYC. Full text of all NAEYC position statements is available at www.naeyc.org/positionstatements.

24. Excerpted and adapted from NAEYC, "NAEYC Standards for Early Childhood Professional Preparation Programs." Position Statement. Washington, DC: NAEYC. Reprinted with permission from the National Association for the Education of Young Children (NAEYC). Copyright © 2009 by NAEYC. Full text of all NAEYC position statements is available at www.naeyc.org/positionstatements.

25. National Association for the Education of Young Children, *NAEYC Position Statement on Developmentally Appropriate Practice, 2009 Revision* (Washington, DC: NAEYC, 2009).

26. Children's Defense Fund, "Children in the United States," 2011; accessed May 28, 2012, at http://www.childrensdefense.org/child-research-data-publications/data/state-data-repository/cits/2011/childre-in-the-states-notes-sources.pdf.

27. U.S. Census Bureau, *State and County Quickfacts*; accessed May 28, 2012, at http://quickfacts.census.gov/qfd/states/00000.html.

28. SchoolDigger.com, "Anthony (Susan B.) Elementary (Sacramento, CA)"; accessed May 28, 2012, at http://www.schooldigger.com/go/CA/schools/3384005282/school.aspx.

29. SchoolDiggcr.com, "Alta Loma Elementary (San Angelo, TX)"; accessed May 28, 2012, at http://www.schooldigger.com/go/TX/schools/3870004296/school.aspx.

30. L. Derman-Sparks and the A.B.C. Task Force, *Anti-Bias Curriculum: Tools for Empowering Young Children* (Washington, DC: NAEYC, 1989).

31. Ibid.

32. Ibid.

33. National Association for the Education of Young Children, *NAEYC Standards for Early Childhood Professional Preparation Programs, 2009*; accessed May 28, 2012, at http://www.naeyc.org/files/naeyc/file/positions/ProfPrepStandards09.pdf.

34. M. Henniger, "Cooking in the Classroom: Math … Science … FUN!"; accessed May 28, 2012, at http://www.primarily-kids.com/article_cooking.html.

35. A. M. Bush, "Boy's "Second Voice" Helps Him Communicate" *Fosters*, January 1, 2010; accessed May 28, 2012, at http://www.fosters.com/apps/pbcs.dll/article?AID=/20100101/GJLIFESTYLES/912299977/-1/CITLIFESTYLES10&template=citAParticle.

36. Times Herald, "Students: Teacher of the Year Makes Learning Fun"; accessed May 29, 2012, at http://www.times-herald.com/opinion/20120429Editorial-Sun-MOS.

37. H. Lambert, "Supportive Teachers Play Critical Role in Children's Academic Success," January 24, 2012; accessed May 14, 2012, at http://education.tamu.edu/news-archive/2012/01/supportive-teachers-play-critical-role-children%E2%80%99s-academic-success.

38. Association for Supervision and Curriculum Development, "About the Whole Child"; accessed May 28, 2012, at http://www.wholechildeducation.org/about/.

39. Association for Supervision and Curriculum Development, "Whole Child Resolution Tool Kit: Frequently Asked Questions," 2009, http://www.wholechildeducation.org/blackboard/faqs/#faq1.

40. St. Philips College, "Early Childhood Studies, A.A.S."; accessed May 28, 2012, at http://myspccatalog.alamo.edu/preview_program.php?catoid=73&poid=3803&returnto=2010.

41. Annie Martin, "Peer Program Helps Teachers Sharpen Skills," May 26, 2012; accessed May 30, 2012, at http://www.news-journalonline.com/news/local/flagler/2012/05/26/peer-program-helps-teachers-sharpen-skills.html.

42. Word Press.com, "Teacher of the Year Bios," May 1, 2009; accessed May 28, 2012, at http://ezureick.wordpress.com/2009/05/01/teacher-of-the-year-bios/.

43. U.S. Census Bureau, *American Community Survey Briefs,* "School-Aged Children with Disabilities in U.S. Metropolitan Statistical Areas: 2010," 2011; accessed May 29, 2012, at http://www.census.gov/prod/2011pubs/acsbr10-12.pdf.

44. Debra Johnson and Angela Rudolph, "Beyond Social Promotion and Retention—Five Strategies to Help Students Succeed," 2001; accessed May 28, 2012, at http://www.ldonline.org/article/Beyond_Social_Promotion_and_Retention%97Five_Strategies_to_Help_Students_Succeed?theme=print.

45. Laura Varlas, "Highly Effective Teachers: Defining, Rewarding, Supporting, and Expanding Their Roles," 2009; accessed May 28, 2012, at http://www.ascd.org/publications/newsletters/policy-priorities/vol15/issue3/full/Highly-Effective-Teachers@-Defining,-Rewarding,-Supporting,-and-Expanding-Their-Roles.aspx.

Chapter 2

1. Excerpted and adapted from NAEYC, "NAEYC Standards for Early Childhood Professional Preparation Programs." Position Statement. Washington, DC: NAEYC. Reprinted with permission from the National Association for the Education of Young Children (NAEYC). Copyright © 2009 by NAEYC. Full text of all NAEYC position statements is available at www.naeyc.org/positionstatements.

2. Excerpted and adapted from NAEYC, "NAEYC Standards for Early Childhood Professional Preparation Programs." Position Statement. Washington, DC: NAEYC. Reprinted with permission from the National Association for the Education of Young Children (NAEYC). Copyright © 2009 by NAEYC. Full text of all NAEYC position statements is available at www.naeyc.org/positionstatements.

3. Tina Repetti Renzullo, "Teacher of the Year Essay," 2011; accessed May 29, 2012, at http://teacher2teacher.lacoe.edu/teacher-of-the-year-essay--national-teacher-of-the-year.aspx.

4. A. J. Mullen, 2009 Connecticut Teacher of the Year acceptance speech; accessed May 28, 2012, at http://www.sde.ct.gov/sde/cwp/view.asp?a=2678&Q=322238&pp=12&n=1.

5. MSNBC, "Poverty Rate Hits 18-Year High as Median Income Falls"; accessed May 28, 2012, at http://bottomline.msnbc.msn.com/_news/2011/09/13/7742437-poverty-rate-hits-18-year-high-as-median-income-falls.

6. National Poverty Center, "Poverty in the United States, Frequently Asked Questions," 2010; accessed May 28, 2012, at http://www.npc.umich.edu/poverty/.

7. U.S. Department of Health and Human Services, "The 2012 HHS Poverty Guidelines"; accessed May 28, 2012, at http://aspe.hhs.gov/poverty/12poverty.shtml.

8. Ibid.

9. Ibid.

10. Brookings, "Families of the Recession: Unemployed Parents & Their Children," 2010; accessed May 28, 2012, at http://www.brookings.edu/papers/2010/0114_families_recession_isaacs.aspx.

11. Ibid.

12. The Pew Charitable Trusts, "Since the Start of the Great Recession, More Children Raised by Grandparents," 2010; accessed May 28, 2012, at http://www.pewtrusts.org/our_work_report_detail.aspx?id=60725.

13. Ibid.

14. Pew Research Center, "Childhood Poverty Among Hispanics Sets Record, Leads Nation," 2011; accessed May 28, 2012, at http://www.pewhispanic.org/2011/09/28/childhood-poverty-among-hispanics-sets-record-leads-nation/.

15. J. Kayitsinga, "Poverty and Health of Children from Racial/Ethnic Minority and Immigrant Families in the Midwest," *Julian Samora Research Institute*, November 2010; accessed May 28, 2012, at http://www.jsri.msu.edu/pdfs/rr/rr44.pdf.

16. "Poor Schools Shortchanged on Funding, Ed. Dept. Says," *Education Week*, 2011; accessed May 28, 2012, at http://blogs.edweek.org/edweek/campaign-k-12/2011/11/for_years_advocates_for_poor.html.

17. J. Dewey, "The School and Social Progress." Chapter 1 in *The School and Society*. Chicago: University of Chicago Press (1907): 19–44; 2006; accessed May 29, 2012, at http://www.brocku.ca/MeadProject/Dewey/Dewey_1907/Dewey_1907a.html.

18. M. Edelman, "Leaving the Littlest Ones Behind," 2010; accessed May 28, 2012, at http://news.change.org/stories/leaving-the-littlest-ones-behind.

19. Foundation for Child Development, "Child and Youth Well-Being"; accessed May 28, 2012, at http://www.soc.duke.edu/~cwi/.

20. K. Land, "Foundation for Child Development Child Well-Being Index," 2010; accessed May 28, 2012, at http://fcd-us.org/sites/default/files/FINAL%202010%20CWI%20Annual%20Release.pdf.

21. Education.com, "Achievement Gap"; accessed November 8, 2011, at http://www.education.com/definition/achievement-gap/.

22. McKinsey and Company, "The Economic Impact of the Achievement Gap in America's Schools," April 2009; accessed May 28, 2012, at http://mckinseyonsociety.com/the-economic-impact-of-the-achievement-gap-in-americas-schools/.

23. Ibid.

24. Ibid.

25. Fouad, Hackett, Haag, Smith, Kantamneni, and Fitzpatrick, "Barriers and Supports for Continuing in Mathematics and Science: Gender and Educational Level Differences," updated 2010; accessed May 28, 2012, at http://www.sciencedirect.com/science/article/pii/S0001879110001168.

26. Ibid.

27. S. Lewis, *A Call for Change: The Social and Educational Factors Contributing to the Outcomes of Black Males in Urban Schools*, Council of the Great City Schools, 2010; accessed May 28, 2012, at http://graphics8.nytimes.com/packages/pdf/opinion/A-Call-For-Change.pdf.

28. Center for Educator Compensation Reform, *Does Evidence Suggest That Some Teachers Are Significantly More Effective Than Others at Improving Student Achievement?* accessed May 28, 2012, at http://cecr.ed.gov/guides/researchSyntheses/Research%20Synthesis_Q%20A1.pdf.

29. D. Johnson and A. Rudolph, "Beyond Social Promotion and Retention—Five Strategies to Help Students Succeed," 2001; accessed May 28, 2012, at http://www.ncrel.org/sdrs/areas/issues/students/atrisk/at800.htm.

30. Teachers of Color, "The 7 Habits of Successful Teachers"; accessed May 28, 2012, at http://www.teachersofcolor.com/2011/03/the-7-habits-of-successful-teachers/.

31. S. Gable, "Nature, Nurture, and Early Brain Development," ClassBrain.com, May 3, 2009; accessed May 28, 2012, at http://classbrain.com/artread/publish/article_30.shtml.

32. P. Kuhl, "Brain Mechanisms in Early Language Acquisition," *Neuron Review*, September 9, 2010; accessed May 28, 2012, at http://life-slc.org/docs/Kuhl-brainmechanisms2010.pdf.

33. S. Gable, "Nature, Nurture, and Early Brain Development," ClassBrain.com, May 3, 2009; accessed May 28, 2012, at http://classbrain.com/artread/publish/article_30.shtml.

34. B. Mauk, "Music Training Changes Brain Networks," The Dana Foundation, 2009; accessed May 28, 2012, at http://www.dana.org/news/features/detail.aspx?id=21762.

35. E. Jensen, "A Physical Education Is Supported by Brain Research," Brain Based Jensen Learning, April 19, 2010; accessed May 28, 2012, at http://www.jensenlearning.com/news/physical-education-is-supported-by-brain-research/brain-based-learning.

36. J. Gentry, "R.E.A.D to Develop Baby-Toddler Reading and Writing Brains," *Psychology Today*, August 2011; accessed May 28, 2012, at http://www.psychologytoday.com/blog/raising-readers-writers-and-spellers/201108/read-develop-baby-toddler-reading-and-writing-brain.

37. "Biological Causes of Depression," December 12, 2011; accessed May 28, 2012, at http://www.allaboutdepression.com/cau_02.html.

38. T. Fujioka, B. Ross, R. Kakigi, C. Pantev, and L. J. Trainor, "One Year of Musical Training Affects Development of Auditory Cortical Evoked Fields in Young Children," 2006; accessed May 28, 2012, at http://brain.oxfordjournals.org/content/129/10/2593.abstract.

39. P. C. M. Wong, E. Skoe, N. M. Russo, T. Dees, and N. Kraus, "Musical Experience Shapes Human Brainstem Encoding of Linguistic Pitch Patterns," *Nature Neuroscience* 10, April 2007, 420–422; retrieved from Nature Neuroscience database at http://www.nature.com/neuro/journal/v10/n4/abs/nn1872.html.

40. Z. Peters, "How Music Can Help Your Child Learn," 2011; accessed May 29, 2012, at http://www.education.com/magazine/article/Can_Music_Help_Learn/.

41. NIDCR, "Dental Caries (Tooth Decay)," 2011; accessed May 28, 2012, at http://www.nidcr.nih.gov/DataStatistics/FindDataByTopic/DentalCaries/.

42. Centers for Disease Control and Prevention "Untreated Dental Caries (Cavities) in Children Ages 2–19, United States"; accessed May 28, 2012, at http://www.cdc.gov/Features/dsUntreatedCavitiesKids/.

43. American Lung Association, "Asthma and Children Fact Sheet," November 2011, http://www.lungusa.org/lung-disease/asthma/resources/facts-and-figures/asthma-children-fact-sheet.html.

44. M. E. Dallas, "Even Homes Without Pets Have Pet Allergens," Baby Center, November 6, 2011; accessed May 28, 2012, at http://www.babycenter.com/204_even-homes-without-pets-have-pet-allergens_10359550.bc.

45. Centers for Disease Control and Prevention, "Asthma: Basic Information," updated March 12, 2012; accessed May 28, 2012, at http://www.cdc.gov/asthma/faqs.htm.

46. Centers for Disease Control and Prevention, National Center for Environmental Health, "Lead," 2012; accessed May 28, 2012, at http://www.cdc.gov/nceh/lead/.

47. National Institute for Environmental Health, "Lead Poisoning," 2010; accessed May 28, 2012, at http://kids.niehs.nih.gov/explore/pollute/lead.htm.

48. Centers for Disease Control and Prevention, 2012 update; accessed May 29, 2012, at http://www.cdc.gov/diabetes/projects/cda2.htm.

49. American Diabetes Association, "Diabetes Basics," definitions; accessed May 29, 2012, at http://www.diabetes.org/diabetes-basics/type-1/.

50. Children with Diabetes, "What You Should Know," 2005; accessed May 29, 2012, at http://www.childrenwithdiabetes.com/cgi-bin/cwdprintpage.pl?url=http://www.childrenwithdiabetes.com/d_0n_d00.htm.

51. American Heart Association, "Overweight in Children," 2012 update; accessed May 28, 2012, at http://www.heart.org/HEARTORG/GettingHealthy/WeightManagement/Obesity/Overweight-in-Children_UCM_304054_Article.jsp#.

52. J. Harrington, "Identifying the 'Tipping Point' Age for Overweight Pediatric Patients," 2010, Science Daily, February 11, 2010; accessed May 28, 2012, at http://www.sciencedaily.com/releases/2010/02/100211121832.htm.

53. American Academy of Children and Adolescent Psychiatry, "Obesity in Children and Teens," 2011; accessed May 28, 2012, at http://www.aacap.org/cs/root/facts_for_families/obesity_in_children_and_teens.

54. R. Nauert, "Misperception of Weight Ups Teen Depression Risk," Psych Central, 2009; accessed May 28, 2012, at http://psychcentral.com/news/2010/06/29/misperception-of-weight-ups-teen-depression-risk/15189.html.

55. New Mexico AppleSeed, "Full Stomachs = Full Minds: A Guide to 'Breakfast After the Bell,'" 2011; accessed May 28, 2012, at http://nmappleseed.org/www.nmappleseed.org/Publications_files/Final%20breakfast%205%3A9.pdf.

56. L. Brown, W. Beardslee, and D. Prothrow-Smith, Impact of School Breakfast on Children's Health and Learning: An Analysis of the Scientific Research, November 17, 2008; accessed May 28, 2012, at http://bestpractices.nokidhungry.org/download/file/fid/263.

57. University of Michigan Health Systems, "Obesity and Overweight," 2011; accessed May 28, 2012, at http://www.med.umich.edu/yourchild/topics/obesity.htm.

58. V. Strauss, "School Junk Food Ban Works, Study Finds," The Washington Post, 2010; accessed May 28, 2012, at http://voices.washingtonpost.com/answer-sheet/health-1/school-junk-food-ban-works--.html.

59. Robert Wood Johnson Foundation, "Arkansas Schools, Parents Adjusting Well to State Efforts to Curb Obesity," June 17, 2008; accessed May 28, 2012, at http://www.rwjf.org/newsroom/product.jsp?id=31911.

60. Nutrition Services Department, RUSD Center for Food and Justice, "Riverside Unified School District Farmers' Market Salad Bar Program," 2010; accessed May 28, 2012, at https://saladbars2schools.org/pdf/Riverside-SBP.pdf.

61. T. Shanks, Y. Kim, V. Loke, and M. Destin, "Assets and Child Well-Being in Developed Countries," Children and Youth Services Review, 2010; accessed May 28, 2012, at http://csd.wustl.edu/Publications/Documents/WP09-66.pdf.

62. White House Task Force on Childhood Obesity Report to the President, "Solving the Problem of Childhood Obesity within a Generation," May 2010; accessed May 28, 2012, at http://children.webmd.com/news/20100511/michelle-obama-plan-to-end-child-obesity-epidemic.

63. United Sates Census Bureau, Reports on Demographic Changes, 2010; accessed May 29, 2012, at http://www.census.gov/people/.

64. Ibid.

65. M. Marquez, Elementary Teacher of the Year, 2011, "Philosophy of Teaching"; accessed May 29, 2012, at http://www.pisd.edu/about.us/awards.ratings/maria.marquez.shtml.

66. L. Ayala, Texas Education Agency, 2010 Texas Assessment Conference ELL Student Assessment Update; accessed December 16, 2011, at http://www.tea.state.tx.us/WorkArea/linkit.aspx?LinkIdentifier=id&ItemID=2147490746&libID=2147490743.

67. M. P. Smart, "The Word and the World: Technology Aids English-Language Learners," Edutopia, 2008; accessed May 28, 2012, at http://www.edutopia.org/technology-software-english-language-learners.

68. Centers for Disease Control and Prevention, "Violence Prevention," May, 18, 2012; accessed May, 28, 2012, at http://www.cdc.gov/ViolencePrevention/.

69. Ibid.

70. Ibid.

71. D. Christakis, "The Effects of Fast-Paced Cartoons," Pediatrics, September, 2011; accessed May 28, 2012, at http://pediatrics.aappublications.org/content/128/4/772.full.

72. Ibid.

73. Ibid.

74. Ibid.

75. American Academy of Pediatrics, "TV and Toddlers," 2006; accessed December 15, 2011, at http://www.aap.org/en-us/advocacy-and-policy/aap-health-initiatives/Pages/Media-and-Children.aspx.

76. E. Brown, "SpongeBob Impairs Little Kids' Thinking, Study Finds," Los Angeles Times, September 12, 2011; accessed May 28, 2012, at http://articles.latimes.com/2011/sep/12/news/la-heb-spongebob-squarepants-children-brain-20110912.

77. California State University, "Television Statistics," 2010; accessed May 28, 2012, from http://www.csun.edu/science/health/docs/tv&health.html.

78. Ibid.

79. National Institute on Media and the Family, "Children and Media Violence," November 2006; accessed May 28, 2012, at http://www.mediafamily.org/facts/facts_vlent.shtml.

80. Eyes on Bullying, Education Development Center Inc., "Child Care," 2010; accessed May 28, 2012, at http://www.eyesonbullying.org/childcare.html.

81. WebMD, Health and Parenting, "Bullying—What Children Should Do If They Are Bullied," 2010; accessed May 28, 2012, at http://www.webmd.com/parenting/tc/bullying-what-children-should-do-if-they-are-bullied.

82. "More Than 25% of Teenagers Have Suffered Cyber Bullying in the Past Year," Science Daily, 2010; accessed May 28, 2012, at http://www.sciencedaily.com/releases/2010/12/101214085734.htm.

83. National Center for Mental Health Promotion and Youth Violence Prevention, "Preventing Cyber Bullying in the School and the Community," 2009; accessed May 28, 2012, at http://www.promoteprevent.org/Publications/center-briefs/Cyberbullying%20Prevention%20Brief.pdf.

84. U.S. Department of Health and Human Services, Administration on Children, Youth, and Families. *Child Maltreatment 2009* (Washington, DC: U.S. Government Printing Office, 2010); accessed May 28, 2012, at http://www.acf.hhs.gov/programs/cb/pubs/cm09/cm09.pdf.

85. *U.S. Statutes at Large,* 88(1976): 5; accessed May 28, 2012, at http://constitution.org/uslaw/sal/088_statutes_at_large.pdf.

86. The White House, "Education," 2011; accessed May 28, 2012, at http://www.whitehouse.gov/issues/education.

87. J. D. Black, "The Business of Child Care," *Great Falls Tribune,* February 1, 2009; accessed November 10, 2011, at http://pqasb.pqarchiver.com/greatfallstribune/access/1688989991.html?FMT=ABS&date=Feb+01,+2009.

88. President Barack Obama, "Education," July 18, 2011; accessed May 28, 2012, at http://www.whitehouse.gov/issues/education.

89. The White House, "Promoting Innovation, Reform, and Excellence in America's Public Schools"; accessed May, 28, 2012, at http://www.whitehouse.gov/the-press-office/fact-sheet-race-top.

90. Ibid.

91. The White House, "We Can't Wait: Nine States Awarded Race to the Top–Early Learning Challenge Grants," December 16, 2011; accessed May 28, 2012, at http://www.whitehouse.gov/the-press-office/2011/12/16/we-cant-wait-nine-states-awarded-race-top-early-learning-challenge-grant.

92. Paige Johnson, "Teaching for 21st Century Skills," *Educational Leadership,* 67(1), September 2009, 11.

Chapter 3

1. Excerpted and adapted from NAEYC, "NAEYC Standards for Early Childhood Professional Preparation Programs." Position Statement. Washington, DC: NAEYC. Reprinted with permission from the National Association for the Education of Young Children (NAEYC). Copyright © 2009 by NAEYC. Full text of all NAEYC position statements is available at www.naeyc.org/positionstatements.

2. Excerpted and adapted from NAEYC, "NAEYC Standards for Early Childhood Professional Preparation Programs." Position Statement. Washington, DC: NAEYC. Reprinted with permission from the National Association for the Education of Young Children (NAEYC). Copyright © 2009 by NAEYC. Full text of all NAEYC position statements is available at www.naeyc.org/positionstatements.

3. Pre-K Now, "The History of Pre-K," updated 2010; accessed May 28, 2012, at http://www.preknow.org/resource/abc/timeline.cfm.

4. Arne Duncan, "Keeping the Promise to All America's Children," speech given at the Council for Exceptional Children, April 10, 2010; accessed May 31, 2012, at http://www2.ed.gov/news/speeches/2010/04/04212010.html.

5. Cynthia Watkins, "Mediterranean District Teacher of the Year," DoDEA Teacher of the Year; accessed May 28, 2012, at http://www.dodea.edu/teachers/toy.cfm?cId=2011.

6. J. A. Comenius, *The Great Didactic of John Amos Comenius,* ed. and trans. M. W. Keating (New York: Russell & Russell, 1967), 58.

7. J.-J. Rousseau, *Emile, or Education,* trans. B. Foxley (New York: Dutton, Everyman's Library, 1933), 5.

8. R. D. Archambault, ed., *John Dewey on Education: Selected Writings* (New York: Random House, 1964), 430.

9. L. Benson, I. Harkavy, and J. Puckett, *Dewey's Dream: Universities and Democracies in an Age of Education Reform* (Philadelphia: Temple University Press, 2007).

10. W. Harms and I. DePencier, *Experiencing Education: 100 Years of Learning at the University of Chicago Laboratory Schools* (Orlando Park, IL: Alpha Beta Press, 1996), available online at http://www.ucls.uchicago.edu/about/history/education.shtml.

11. J. Wolfe, *Learning from the Past: Historical Voices in Early Childhood Education* (Mayerthorpe, Alberta, Canada: Piney Branch Press, 2002).

12. M. Montessori, *The Discovery of the Child,* trans. M. J. Costelloe (Notre Dame, IN: Fides, 1967), 22.

13. The International Montessori Council, *The Montessori Way,* 2010; accessed May 28, 2012, at http://www.montessori.org/imc/index.php?option=com_content&view=article&id=261:the-montessori-way&catid=16:articles-introducing-montessori-education&Itemid=44.

14. The Center for Public Education, "Starting Out Right: Pre-K and Kindergarten Full Report," 2011; accessed May 31, 2012, at http://www.centerforpubliceducation.org/Main-Menu/Organizing-a-school/Starting-Out-Right-Pre-K-and-Kindergarten/Starting-Out-Right-Pre-K-and-Kindergarten-full-report.html.

15. U.S. Department of Education, *Improving Basic Programs Operated by Local Educational Agencies* (Title I, Part A); accessed May 28, 2012, at http://www2.ed.gov/programs/titleiparta/index.html.

16. U.S. Department of Education, *Improving Basic Programs Operated by Local Educational Agencies (Title I, Part A);* accessed May 28, 2012, at http://www2.ed.gov/programs/titleiparta/index.html.

17. D. M. Brodzinsky, I. E. Sigel, and R. M. Golinkoff, "New Dimensions in Piagetian Theory and Research: An Integrative Perspective," in I. E. Sigel, D. M. Brodzinsky, and R. M. Golinkoff, eds., *New Directions in Piagetian Theory and Practice* (Hillsdale, NJ: Erlbaum, 1981), 5.

18. Ibid.

19. Y. Jumani, "Does Experiential Learning Facilitate Learners to Construct Their Own Knowledge," *Bizcovering: Education and Training,* August 5, 2009; accessed May 28, 2012, at http://bizcovering.com/education-and-training/does-experiential-learning-facilitate-learners-to-construct-their-own-knowledge.

20. P. G. Richmond, *An Introduction to Piaget* (New York: Basic Books, 1970), 68.

21. G. A. Davis and J. D. Keller, *Exploring Science and Mathematics in a Child's World* (Columbus, OH: Pearson, 2009), 12.

22. L. S. Vygotsky, *Mind in Society* (Cambridge, MA: Harvard University Press, 1978), 244.

23. Ibid.

24. J. R. H. Tudge, "Processes and Consequences of Peer Collaboration: A Vygotskian Analysis," *Child Development,* 63(6), 1992, 1365.

25. Ibid.

26. E. Bodrova and D. J. Leong, "Scaffolding Emergent Writing in the Zone of Proximal Development," *Literacy Teaching and Learning,*

3(2), 1998, 1–18; available online at http://www.mcrel.org/our_work/scaffolding.pdf.

27. WAECE-AMEI (World Association of Early Childhood Educators) Newsletter, "Study on the Relationship Between Nutrition and Learning," Bulletin No. 398, February 6, 2009.

28. K. Barker, "Classroom Policies for Our Kindergarten Classroom"; accessed May 28, 2012, at http://lk094.k12.sd.us/Classroom%20Rules.htm.

29. J. Atkinson, "Effective Praise," *Inside Jennifer's 1st Grade Classroom*; accessed May 28, 2012, at http://blogs.scholastic.com/1_2/2008/08/effective-prais.html.

Chapter 4

1. Excerpted and adapted from NAEYC, "NAEYC Standards for Early Childhood Professional Preparation Programs." Position Statement. Washington, DC: NAEYC. Reprinted with permission from the National Association for the Education of Young Children (NAEYC). Copyright © 2009 by NAEYC. Full text of all NAEYC position statements is available at www.naeyc.org/positionstatements.

2. Excerpted and adapted from NAEYC, "NAEYC Standards for Early Childhood Professional Preparation Programs." Position Statement. Washington, DC: NAEYC. Reprinted with permission from the National Association for the Education of Young Children (NAEYC). Copyright © 2009 by NAEYC. Full text of all NAEYC position statements is available at www.naeyc.org/positionstatements.

3. National Association for the Education of Young Children, "About Us Overview"; accessed May 30, 2012, at http://www.naeyc.org/academy/primary/aboutoverview.

4. The Pew Center on the States. (2011, September). *Transforming Public Education: Pathway to a Pre-K–12 Future*. Washington, DC: PEW Center on the States; accessed May 30, 2012, at http://www.pewcenteronthestates.org/uploadedFiles/wwwpewcenteronthestatesorg/Initiatives/Pre-K_Education/Pew_PreK_Transforming_Public_Education.pdf.

5. National Association of Elementary School Principals Foundation. (2011, July). *Building & Supporting an Aligned System: A Vision for Transforming Education Across the Pre-K-Grade, Three Years*. Atlanta, GA: NAESP Foundation and ING Foundation. Accessed May 30, 2012, at http://fcd-us.org/sites/default/files/NAESP%20Task%20Force%20Report.pdf.

6. H. Boyd. (n.d.). *Keeping Schools Safe*. Redwood City, CA: Education.com; accessed May 30, 2012, at http://www.education.com/magazine/article/Keeping_Schools_Safe/.

7. K. Brenneman, J. Stevenson-Boyd, and E. C. Frede. "Math and Science in Preschool: Policies and Practice" (2009, March). New Brunswick, NJ: NIEER. Accessed May 30, 2012, at http://nieer.org/resources/policybriefs/20.pdf.

8. Bureau of Labor Statistics, "Employment Characteristics of Families Summary: Table 5. Employment Status of the Population by Sex, Marital Status, and Presence and Age of Own Children under 18, 2009–10 Annual Averages," March 2011; accessed May 30, 2012, at http://www.bls.gov/news.release/famee.nr0.htm.

9. Entrerprise Partners, "The Importance of Early Care and Education," 2006; accessed May 30, 2012, at http://www.practitionerresources.org/cache/documents/639/63935.doc.

10. Child Care Bureau, Forum on Child and Family Statistics, "America's Children: Key National Indicators of Well-Being,"

2010; accessed May 30, 2012, at http://www.childstats.gov/americaschildren/famsoc3.asp#18.

11. Mount Kisco Child Care Center, "The Mount Kisco Child Care Center Connection," Fall 2011; accessed May 30, 2012, at http://www.mkdcc.org/pdf/2011-Fall-MKCCC-Newsletter.pdf.

12. Family Services of Westchester, "My Second Home … Independence … Dignity … Respect"; accessed May 30, 2012, at http://familyservicesofwestchester.org/wp-content/uploads/2011/05/MSH-FACT-SHEET-2011.pdf.

13. Bright Horizons Family Solutions, "Employer-Sponsored Child Care," 2009, updated 2012; accessed May 30, 2012, at http://www.brighthorizons.com/employer/care.aspx.

14. Broward Independent School District, "Before and After School Child Care," 2011; accessed May 30, 2012, at http://www.broward.k12.fl.us/k12programs/bascc/.

15. "Kindergarten Wraparound Program"; accessed May 30, 2012, at http://www.town.raynham.ma.us/Public_Documents/RaynhamMA_recreation/Childcare%20Program%20Description.

16. Exchange Trend Report, "The Proud Story of Military Child Care," 2011; accessed May 30, 2012, at https://libproxy.library.unt.edu:9443/login?url=http://search.ebscohost.com/login.aspx?direct=true&db=ehh&AN=59177253&site=ehost-live&scope=site.

17. Military Homefront, "An Overview"; accessed May 30, 2012, at http://www.militaryhomefront.dod.mil/tf/childcare.

18. M. Story, K. Kaphingst, R. Robinson-O'Brien, and K. Glanz, "Creating Healthy Food and Eating Environments: Policy and Environmental Approaches," *Annual Review of Public Health*, 29, April 2008, 253–272 (first published November 21, 2007); accessed May 30, 2012, at http://publhealth.annualreviews.org.

19. All for Natural Health, "Organic Food Benefits Children Too," 2007–2010; accessed May 30, 2012, at http://www.all4naturalhealth.com/organic-food-benefits.html.

20. Little Dreamers, Big Believers, "Organic Food Day Care," June 2, 2008; accessed February 4, 2010, at http://www.littledreamersdaycare.org/tag/organic-food-day-care/.

21. Centers for Disease Control and Prevention, "Reducing Pesticide Exposure at Schools," 2007; accessed May 30, 2012, at http://www.cdc.gov/niosh/docs/2007-150/.

22. "Healthy Classroom Fact Sheet," May 2007; accessed May 30, 2010, at http://www.in.gov/idem/files/healthy_classroom_fact_sheet.pdf.

23. Contributed by Amy Turcotte, developmental specialist.

24. National Resource Center for Health and Safety in Child Care, University of Colorado Health Sciences Center at Fitzsimons, "A Parent's Guide to Choosing a Safe and Healthy Child Care"; accessed May 30, 2012, at http://nrckids.org/RESOURCES/ParentsGuide.pdf.

25. Ibid.

26. Kiddie Academy, "About Us," 2008; accessed May 30, 2012, at http://www.kiddieacademy.com/aboutus/choose_child-care-services-resources.aspx.

27. Debra J. Ackerman and W. Steven Barnett, *Does Preschool Education Policy Impact Infant/Toddler Care?*, March 2009; accessed May 30, 2012, at http://nieer.org/resources/policybriefs/21.pdf.

28. NICHD Early Child Care Research Network, "Child Outcomes When Child Care Center Classes Meet Recommended Standards for Quality," *American Journal of Public Health*, 88(7), 1998, 1072–1077.

29. S. Bredekamp, and C. Copple, *Developmentally Appropriate Practice in Early Childhood Programs Serving Children from Birth Through Age 8,* 3rd ed. (Washington, DC: NAEYC, 2009).

30. National Institute of Child Health and Human Development, "NICHD Study of Early Child Care and Youth Development (SECCYD)"; accessed May 30, 2012, at http://www.nichd.nih.gov/research/supported/seccyd.cfm. See also *Results from the NICHD Study of Early Child Care and Youth Development* (New York: Guilford Press, 2005), 28–35.

31. Reprinted by permission from Child Care and Child Development, *Results from the NICHD Study of Early Child Care and Youth Development* (New York: Guilford Press, 2005), 28–35.

32. HighScope Education Research Foundation, *The HighScope K–3 Curriculum: An Introduction* (Ypsilanti, MI: HighScope, 1989), 1.

33. Ibid.

34. Ibid.

35. HighScope Educational Research Foundation, "KDIs (Key Experiences)"; accessed May 30, 2012, at http://www.highscope.org/Content.asp?ContentId=614.

36. Ibid.

37. HighScope Educational Research Foundation, "Preschool: Adults and Children—Partners in Learning"; accessed May 30, 2012, at http://www.highscope.org/Content.asp?ContentId=63.

38. M. Montessori, *Dr. Montessori's Own Handbook* (New York: Schocken Books, 1965), 131.

39. H. Helm and L. Katz, *Young Investigators: The Project Approach in the Early Years* (New York: Teachers College Press, 2001).

40. U.S. Department of Health and Human Services, Administration for Children and Families, Early Childhood Learning and Knowledge Center, "Head Start Program Fact Sheet: Fiscal Year 2010"; accessed May 30, 2012, at http://www.acf.hhs.gov/programs/ohs/about/fy2010.html.

41. A. Gelber and A. Isen, *Children's Schooling and Parents' Investment in Children: Evidence from the Head Start Impact Study,* University of Pennsylvania, December 2011; accessed May 30, 2012, at http://www.nber.org/papers/w17704.pdf?new_window=1.

42. U.S. Department of Health and Human Services, *Head Start Impact Study Final Report,* January 2010, xxiii–xxvi; accessed May 30, 2012, at http://www.acf.hhs.gov/programs/opre/hs/impact_study/reports/impact_study/hs_impact_study_tech_rpt.pdf.

43. Ibid.

44. Early Childhood Learning and Knowledge Center, "Policies and Procedures for Designation Renewal of Head Start and Early Head Start Grantees," updated December 1, 2011; accessed May 30, 2012, at http://eclkc.ohs.acf.hhs.gov/hslc/standards/Head%20Start%20Requirements/1307.

45. Teachstone, "What Is the CLASS™ Tool?," 2012; accessed May 30, 2012, at http://www.teachstone.org/about-the-class/.

46. U.S. Department of Health and Human Services, Administration for Children and Families, "Head Start Programs Fact Sheet," Fiscal Year 2010; accessed May 30, 2012, at http://www.acf.hhs.gov/programs/ohs/about/fy2010.html.

47. G. Fernandez, "Therapy Dogs Reduce Stress in Autistic Children," Child Development Institute Parenting Today, October 2010; accessed May 30, 2012, at http://childdevelopmentinfo.com/child-health-news/therapy-dogs-reduce-stress-in-autistic-children.shtml.

Chapter 5

1. Excerpted and adapted from NAEYC, "NAEYC Standards for Early Childhood Professional Preparation Programs." Position Statement. Washington, DC: NAEYC. Reprinted with permission from the National Association for the Education of Young Children (NAEYC). Copyright © 2009 by NAEYC. Full text of all NAEYC position statements is available at www.naeyc.org/positionstatements.

2. Excerpted and adapted from NAEYC, "NAEYC Standards for Early Childhood Professional Preparation Programs." Position Statement. Washington, DC: NAEYC. Reprinted with permission from the National Association for the Education of Young Children (NAEYC). Copyright © 2009 by NAEYC. Full text of all NAEYC position statements is available at www.naeyc.org/positionstatements.

3. A. G. de Leon, "After 20 Years of Educational Reform, Progress, But Plenty of Unfinished Business," Carnegie Corporation of New York, *Carnegie Results,* (1)3; accessed May 29, 2012, at http://www.carnegie.org/results/03/index.html.

4. K. Paris, "Summary of Goals 2000: Educate America Act," North Central Regional Educational Laboratory, 1994; accessed May 29, 2012, at http://www.ncrel.org/sdrs/areas/issues/envrnmnt/stw/sw0goals.htm.

5. U.S. Department of Education, "Four Pillars of NCLB," 2004; accessed May 29, 2012, at http://www.ed.gov/nclb/overview/intro/4pillars.html.

6. Ibid.

7. Gale Cengage Learning, "No Child Left Behind"; accessed May 29, 2012, at http://www.galeschools.com/article_archive/no_child_left_behind.htm.

8. Federal Education Budget, "No Child Left Behind—Overview," June 7, 2011; accessed May 29, 2012, at http://febp.newamerica.net/background-analysis/no-child-left-behind-overview.

9. E. Ramirez and K. Clark, "What Arne Duncan Thinks of No Child Left Behind," *Education Week,* February 5, 2009; accessed May 29, 2012, at http://www.usnews.com/articles/education/2009/02/05/what-arne-duncan-thinks-of-no-child-left-behind.html.

10. *New York Times,* "No Child Left Behind Act," October 24, 2011; accessed May 29, 2012, at http://topics.nytimes.com/top/reference/timestopics/subjects/n/no_child_left_behind_act/index.html.

11. Paul E. Peterson, Ludger Woessmann, Eric A. Hanushek, and Carlos X. Lastra-Anadón, "Globally Challenged: Are Students Ready to Compete?" August 2011; accessed June 4, 2012, at http://www.hks.harvard.edu/pepg/PDF/Papers/PEPG11-03_GloballyChallenged.pdf.

12. D. Scott, "States Begin Implementing Common Core Standards," February 7, 2012; accessed May 29, 2012, at http://www.governing.com/templates/gov_print_article?id=138797064.

13. Education Northwest, "Common Core State Standards History"; accessed May 29, 2012, at http://edcuationnorthwest.org/resource/1280.

14. The Opportunity Equation, "Common Core Standards: Why Did States Choose to Adopt?"; accessed May 29, 2012, at http://opportunityequation.org/standards-and-assessments/common-core-standards-why-did-states.

15. A. Ross, "New Rules Make Kindergarten Count for More," *The Palm Beach Post,* August 20, 2011; accessed May 29, 2012, from http://www.palmbeachpost.com/news/schools/new-rules-make-kindergarten-count-for-more-1765416.html.

16. National Governors Association Center for Best Practices, "Common Core State Standards," *Council of Chief State School Officers*, 2010; accessed May 29, 2012, at http://www.corestandards.org/the-standards.

17. Common Core Standards, "About the Standards"; accessed May 29, 2012, at http://corestandards.org/about-the-standards.

18. National Center for Education Statistics, "Achievement Gaps: How Hispanic and White Students in Public Schools Perform in Mathematics and Reading on the National Assessment of Educational Progress," *National Assessment of Educational Progress*, June 2011; accessed May 29, 2012, from http://nces.ed.gov/nationsreportcard/pubs/studies/2011459.asp.

19. U.S. Department of Education, "Great Teachers and Great Leaders," updated May 2011; accessed May 29, 2012, at http://www2.ed.gov/policy/elsec/leg/blueprint/publication_pg5.html.

20. Head Start, "Family and Parent Services"; accessed May 29, 2012, at http://heartlandheadstart.org/page4.html.

21. W. Loeb, et al., "Doing What Works: Linking Formative Assessment to Benchmarks," May 2008; accessed May 29, 2012, at www.ed.gov/launcher.cfm?media/MathScience/MPR/MF/See/720_mf.

22. Contributed by Gary W. Baird, principal, Lead Mine Elementary School, Raleigh, North Carolina.

23. C. Copple and S. Bredekamp, *Developmentally Appropriate Practice in Early Childhood Programs; Serving Children from Birth to Age 8,* 3rd ed., 33, 2009.

24. D. Coleman and S. Pimentel, "Publishers' Criteria for the Common Core State Standards in English Language Arts and Literacy, Grades K–2"; August 25, 2011, accessed May 29, 2012.

25. Ibid.

26. Ibid.

27. Ibid.

28. Ibid.

29. Ibid.

30. Ibid.

31. R. Croninger and V. Lee, *Social Capital and Dropping Out of High School: Benefits to At-Risk Students of Teachers' Support and Guidance*, 2001, accessed May 29, 2012, at http://www.eric.ed.gov/ERICWebPortal/search/detailmini.jsp?_nfpb=true&_&ERICExtSearch_SearchValue_0=EJ636312&ERICExtSearch_SearchType_0=no&accno=EJ636312.

32. K. Rudasill and S. Rimm-Kaufman, "Teacher–Child Relationship Quality: The Roles of Child Temperament and Teacher–Child Interactions," 2009; accessed May 29, 2012, at http://www.mendeley.com/research/teacherchild-relationship-quality-roles-child-temperament-teacherchild-interactions/.

33. Ibid.

34. K. Donohue, K. Perry, and R. Weinstein, "Teachers' Classroom Practices and Children's Rejection by Their Peers," *Applied Developmental Psychology*; accessed May 29, 2012.

35. Chapel Hill–Carrboro City Schools, "2009–2010 Teachers of the Year (Karen Reid)"; accessed January 24, 2012, at http://www.chccs.k12.nc.us/education/components/scrapbook/default.php?sectiondetailid=72588&PHPSESSID=bac1144723306d8fe6c57718e656fb9f.

36. Chapel Hill–Carrboro City Schools, "2009–2010 Teachers of the Year (LaWanda Rainey-Hall)"; accessed May 29, 2012, at http://www2.chccs.k12.nc.us/education/components/ scrapbook/default.php?sectiondetailid=72588&PHPSESSID=bac1144723306d8fe6c57718e656fb9f.

37. National Dissemination Center for Children with Disabilities, "Accommodations in Assessment" (September 2010); accessed May 29, 2012, at http://nichcy.org/schoolage/iep/iepcontents/assessment.

38. M. Allen, "2010 National Teacher of the Year Finalists Chosen," The Council of Chief State School Officers, January 12, 2010; accessed May 29, 2012, at http://www.nstoy.org/newsletter/spring10/page13.html.

Chapter 6

1. National Association for the Education of Young Children. (2011, June). *NAEYC Standards for Initial & Advanced Early Childhood Professional Preparation Programs.* Washington, DC: NAEYC; accessed January 25, 2012, at http://www.naeyc.org/files/ncate/file/NAEYC%20Initial%20and%20Advanced%20Standards%206_2011-final.pdf.

2. Literacy Links, "Spotlight on Using Assessment to Guide Instruction," 2006; accessed September 16, 2009, at http://www.maine.gov/education/rf/newsletters/1106newsletter.rtf.

3. NAEYC Academy for Early Childhood Program Accreditation, "Standard 4: NAEYC Accreditatoin Criteria for Assessment of Child Progress"; accessed May 3, 2009, at http://www.grandmahouse.org/docs/assessment.pdf.

4. J. Walker, S. Shenker, and K. Hoover-Dempsey, *Why Do Parents Become Involved in Their Children's Education? Implications for School Counselors,* 2010; accessed October 10, 2011, at http://schoolcounselor.metapress.com/content/768th8v77571hm7r/.

5. National Association for the Education of Young Children. (2009). *Developmentally Appropriate Practice in Early Childhood Programs: Serving Children from Birth Through Age 8*, 3rd ed. C. Copple and S. Bredekamp, eds. Washington, DC: 22.

6. Ibid.

7. Kentucky Early Childhood Data System, *Selecting the Most Appropriate Assessment Tool*, April 2009; accessed August 4, 2009, at https://www.kedsonline.org/Documents/Selecting%20the%20Most%20Appropriate%20Assessment%20Tool_4_09.pdf.

8. J. Mueller, "What Is Authentic Assessment?" Authentic Assessment Toolbox, 2011; accessed February 2, 2012, at http://jfmueller.faculty.noctrl.edu/toolbox/whatisit.htm.

9. Centers for Disease Control and Prevention, "Developmental Disabilities Increasing in US," Department of Health and Human Services, June 14, 2011; accessed November 1, 2011, at http://www.cdc.gov/features/dsDev_Disabilities.

10. Council of Chief State School Officers, *The Words We Use: A Glossary of Terms for Early Childhood Education Standards and Assessment*, "Informal Assessment"; accessed April 1, 2009, at http://www.ccsso.org/projects/scass/projects/early_childhood_education_assessment_consortiu/publications_and_products/2873.cfm.

11. Mary Rose, "Make Room for Rubrics"; accessed July 23, 2009, at http://teacher.scholastic.com/professional/assessment/roomforubrics.htm.

12. A. Datnow, V. Park, and P. Wohlstetter. *Achieving with Data: How High-Performing School Systems Use Data to Improve Instruction for Elementary Students*. Los Angeles: USC Center on Educational Governance, 2007. Accessed August, 2012, at https://www.newschools.org/files/AchievingWithData.pdf.

13. S. J. Bagnato, J. T. Neisworth, and K. Pretti-Frontczak, *LINKing Authentic Assessment and Early Childhood Intervention: Best Measures for Best Practices*, 4th ed. (Baltimore, MD: Paul Brookes, 2009).

Chapter 7

1. Excerpted and adapted from NAEYC, "NAEYC Standards for Early Childhood Professional Preparation Programs." Position Statement. Washington, DC: NAEYC. Reprinted with permission from the National Association for the Education of Young Children (NAEYC). Copyright © 2009 by NAEYC. Full text of all NAEYC position statements is available at www.naeyc.org/positionstatements.

2. Excerpted and adapted from NAEYC, "NAEYC Standards for Early Childhood Professional Preparation Programs." Position Statement. Washington, DC: NAEYC. Reprinted with permission from the National Association for the Education of Young Children (NAEYC). Copyright © 2009 by NAEYC. Full text of all NAEYC position statements is available at www.naeyc.org/positionstatements.

3. Excerpted and adapted from NAEYC, "NAEYC Standards for Early Childhood Professional Preparation Programs." Position Statement. Washington, DC: NAEYC. Reprinted with permission from the National Association for the Education of Young Children (NAEYC). Copyright © 2009 by NAEYC. Full text of all NAEYC position statements is available at www.naeyc.org/positionstatements.

4. Redmond Toddler Group, "Our Teachers"; accessed June 6, 2012, at http://www.redmondtoddler.org/teachers.php.

5. American Federation of Teachers, "Nurturing Language Development—Infants and Toddlers," accessed June 4, 2012, at http://www.aft.org/earlychildhood/language-dev.htm.

6. Ibid.

7. E. Bergelson and D. Swingley, "At 6–9 Months, Human Infants Know the Meanings of Many Common Nouns," January 17, 2012; accessed June 4, 2012, at http://www.pnas.org/content/109/9/3253.full?sid=9309a162-3d09-4957-b93b-8c9b67b24fb9.

8. C. Kidd, S. T. Piantadosi, and R. N. Aslin, "The Goldilocks Effect: Human Infants Allocate Attention to Visual Sequences That Are Neither Too Simple Nor Too Complex," *PLOS One,* May 23, 2012; accessed on September 25, 2012, at www.plosone.org/article/info%3Adoi%2F10.1371%2Fjournal.pone.0036399.

9. I. Florez, "Child Development, Developing Young Children's Self-Regulation Through Everyday Experiences," July 2011; accessed June 4, 2012, at http://www.naeyc.org/files/yc/.../Self-Regulation_Florez_OnlineJuly2011.pdf.

10. S. Gable, "Nature, Nurture, and Early Brain Development," ClassBrain.com, January 10, 2011; accessed June 4, 2012, at http://classbrain.com/artread/publish/article_30.shtml.

11. P. Kuhl, *Early Language Acquisition: The Brain Comes Prepared* (St. Louis, MO: Parents as Teachers National Center, 1996).

12. S. Gable, "Nature, Nurture, and Early Brain Development," ClassBrain.com, January 10, 2011; accessed June 4, 2012, at http://classbrain.com/artread/publish/article_30.shtml.

13. E. Wilcox, "Straight Talk About Music and Brain Research," *Teaching Music,* 7(3), December 1999, 29, 31–35.

14. J. Donnelly and K. Lambourne, "Classroom-Based Physical Activity, Cognition, and Academic Achievement," January 31, 2011; accessed June 4, 2012, at http://www.nemours.org/filebox/service/preventive/nhps/.../classroompa.pdf.

15. E. Erikson, *Childhood and Society,* 2nd ed. (New York: Norton, 1963; first pub. 1950), 249.

16. Ibid.

17. A. N. Meltzoff, "'Like Me': A Foundation for Social Cognition," *Developmental Science,* (10)1, January 2007, 126–134.

18. Random House Dictionary, "bonding," Dictionary.com, 2009; accessed June 4, 2012, at http://dictionary.reference.com/browse/bonding.

19. J. Oats and A. Grayson, *Cognitive and Language Development in Children,* 2nd ed. (Oxford, England: Blackwell, 2004).

20. M. Goldstein, J. Schwade, and M. Bornstein, "The Value of Vocalizing: Five-Month-Old Infants Associate Their Own," June 2009; accessed June 4, 2012, at http://www.ncbi.nlm.nih.gov/pubmed/19489893.

21. A. Thomas, S. Chess, and H. Birch, "The Origin of Personality," *Scientific American,* 223(2), August 1970, 102–109.

22. G. Josse and N. Tzourio-Mazoyer, "Review: Hemispheric Specialization for Language," *Brain Research Reviews,* 44(1), January 2004, 1–12.

23. E. L. Newport, "Mother, I'd Rather Do It Myself: Some Effects and Non-Effects on Maternal Speech Style," in C. E. Snow and C. A. Ferguson, eds., *Talking to Children* (Cambridge, England: Cambridge University Press, 1979), 112–129.

24. L. Acredolo and S. Goodwyn, *Baby Signs: How to Talk with Your Baby Before Your Baby Can Talk* (Chicago: Contemporary Books, 1996).

25. JAMA and Archives Journals, "Babies Who Don't Respond to Their Names May Be at Risk for Autism or Other Disorders," *ScienceDaily,* April 4, 2007; accessed March 9, 2009, at http://www.sciencedaily.com/releases/2007/04/070402162106.htm.

26. National Institute for Literacy, Vocabulary Instruction, Eunice Kennedy Shriver National Institute of Child Health and Human Development; accessed June 4, 2012, at http://www.nifl.gov/partnershipforreading/explore/vocabulary.html.

27. U.S. Department of Health and Human Services, Administration for Children and Families, *FY 2007 PRISM Protocol: Safe Environments,* 2007.

28. American Academy of Pediatrics, "A Parent's Guide to Safe Sleep," 2012; accessed April 10, 2012, at http://www.healthychildcare.org/pdf/SIDSparentsafesleep.pdf.

29. E. Bergelson and D. Swingley, "At 6–9 Months, Human Infants Know the Meanings of Many Common Nouns," January 17, 2012; accessed June 4, 2012, at http://www.pnas.org/content/109/9/3253.full?sid=9309a162-3d09-4957-b93b-8c9b67b24fb9.

30. C. Kidd, S. Piantadosi, and R. Aslin, "The Goldilocks Effect: Human Infants Allocate Attention to Visual Sequences That Are Neither Too Simple Nor Too Complex," May 23, 2012; accessed June 4, 2012, at http://www.plosone.org/article/info%3Adoi%2F10.1371%2Fjournal.pone.0036399.

31. S. Bredekamp and C. Copple, eds., *Developmentally Appropriate Practice in Early Childhood Programs,* 3rd ed. (Washington, DC: NAEYC, 2009), 9.

32. A. Hsu, "Rethinking SIDS: Many Deaths No Longer a Mystery," *NPR,* July 15, 2011; accessed June 4, 2012, at http://www.npr.org/2011/07/15/137859024/rethinking-sids-many-deaths-no-longer-a-mystery.

33. Tulane Institute of Infant and Early Childhood Mental Health, "10 Things You Should Know About Infant Mental Health"; accessed June 4, 2012, at http://www.infantinstitute.org/tenth.htm.

34. D. Stark, R. Cohen, and J. Jerald, "Guiding Principles," updated April 26, 2012; accessed June 4, 2012, at http://eclkc.ohs.acf.hhs.gov/hslc/ttasystem/teaching/eecd/Domains%20of%20Child%20Development/Social%20and%20Emotional%20Development/edudev_art_00114_072305.html.

35. Beyond the Journal, "Young Children on the Web," July 2006; accessed June 4, 2012, at http://journal.naeyc.org/btj/200607/Gillespie709BTJ.pdf.

36. Ibid.

37. Ibid.

38. Ibid.

39. Ibid.

40. Ibid.

41. Ibid.

42. Ibid.

43. Parents as Teachers, "Helping Your Child Learn Self-Regulation Through Play," accessed June 4, 2012, at http://www.parentsasteachers.org/site/pp.asp?c=ekIRLcMZJxE&b=307151.

44. Ibid.

45. Ibid.

Chapter 8

1. Excerpted and adapted from NAEYC, "NAEYC Standards for Early Childhood Professional Preparation Programs." Position Statement. Washington, DC: NAEYC. Reprinted with permission from the National Association for the Education of Young Children (NAEYC). Copyright © 2009 by NAEYC. Full text of all NAEYC position statements is available at www.naeyc.org/positionstatements.

2. Excerpted and adapted from NAEYC, "NAEYC Standards for Early Childhood Professional Preparation Programs." Position Statement. Washington, DC: NAEYC. Reprinted with permission from the National Association for the Education of Young Children (NAEYC). Copyright © 2009 by NAEYC. Full text of all NAEYC position statements is available at www.naeyc.org/positionstatements.

3. National Institute for Early Education Research, "The State of Preschool 2011"; accessed June 6, 2012, at http://nieer.org/yearbook.

4. Ibid.

5. Ibid.

6. U.S. Department of Labor, Occupational Outlook Handbook, 2009–10 Edition, "Preschool Teachers," April 6, 2012; accessed June 6, 2012, from http://www.bls.gov/oco/ocos069.htm.

7. The Humane Society of the United States, "Oregon Preschool Teacher Named Kind Teacher of the Year," May 11, 2011; accessed on June 6, 2012, at http://www.humanesociety.org/news/news/2011/05/kind_teacher_of_the_year_051111.html.

8. Healy Communications Inc., "First-Ever National Preschool Teacher of the Year Award Winners Announced by Story Reader™," September 18, 2006; accessed June 7, 2012, at http://www.prnewswire.com/news-releases/first-ever-national-preschool-teacher-of-the-year-award-winners-announced-by-story-readertm-57017202.html.

9. Ibid.

10. Ibid.

11. Ibid.

12. Union Public Schools, "RPECEC Teacher of the Year," 2011; accessed June 7, 2012, at http://www.unionps.org/index.cfm?id=613&theparentid=399.

13. National Association of Child Care Resource and Referral Agencies, "Parent's Perception of Childcare in the United States," 2009; accessed June 6, 2012, at http://www.naccrra.org/node/1794.

14. W. T. Dickens, I. Sawhill, and J. Tebbs, The Brookings Institution, "Policy Brief #153, The Effects of Investing in Early Childhood Education on Economic Growth," April 2006; accessed June 7, 2012, at http://www.brookings.edu/views/papers/200604dickenssawhill.pdf.

15. Ibid.

16. Billings, R. (2012). "Business Leaders Back Early Education as Economic Development." Mainebiz; accessed June 6, 2012, at http://www.mainebiz.biz/apps/pbcs.dll/article?AID=/20120206/CURRENTEDITION/120209987/0/FRONTPAGE.

17. L. J. Calman and L. Tarr-Whelan, Early Childhood Education for All: A Wise Investment (New York: Legal Momentum, April 2005); accessed June 6, 2012, at http://web.mit.edu/workplacecenter/docs/Full%20Report.pdf.

18. Ibid.

19. HighScope. Lifetime Effects: The HighScope Perry Preschool Study Through Age 40, 2005; accessed June 6, 2012, at http://www.highscope.org/content.asp?contentid=219.

20. The Chicago Child–Parent Center Program; accessed June 6, 2012, at http://www.waisman.wisc.edu/cls/Program.htm.

21. National Institute for Early Education Research. The APPLES Blossom: Abbott Preschool Program Longitudinal Effects Study (APPLES) Preliminary Results Through 2nd Grade, June 2009; accessed June 6, 2012, at http://nieer.org/pdf/apples_second_grade_results.pdf.

22. C. Rivera. "L.A. Study Affirms Benefits of Preschool," Los Angeles Times, April 19, 2010; accessed June 6, 2012, at http://www.latimes.com/news/local/la-me-0420-preschool-20100419,0,2289045.story.

23. R. Lynch, "Enriching Children, Enriching the Nation: Public Investment in High-Quality Prekindergarten," Economic Policy Institute; 2007; accessed June 6, 2012, at http://www.epi.org/publication/book_enriching.

24. National Governors Association, A Governor's Guide to School Readiness: Building the Foundation for Bright Futures (Washington, DC: National Governors Association Center for Best Practices, 2005); accessed June 7, 2012, at http://www.nga.org/cms/home/nga-center-for-best-practices/center-publications/page-edu-publications/col2-content/main-content-list/building-the-foundation-for-brig.html.

25. C. Bruner, S. Floyd, and A. Copeman, "Seven Things Policy Makers Need to Know About School Readiness, Revised and Expanded Toolkit," State Early Childhood Policy Technical Assistance Network (Des Moines, IA: Child and Family Policy Center, January 2005), 7; accessed June 7, 2012, at http://www.finebynine.org/uploaded/file/7%20Things.pdf.

26. D. S. Strickland and S. Riley-Ayers, Early Literacy: Policy and Practice in the Preschool Years (New Brunswick, NJ: NIEER,

April 2006); accessed June 7, 2012, at http://nieer.org/resources/policybriefs/10.pdf.

27. J. P. Shonkoff and D. A. Phillips, eds., *From Neurons to Neighborhoods* (Washington, DC: National Academy Press, 2000), 338; accessed June 7, 2012, at http://www.nap.edu/openbook.php?record_id=9824&page=R1.

28. Charlottesville City Schools, "Preschool Program"; accessed June 6, 2012, at http://www.ccs.k12.va.us/programs/preschool.html.

29. Ibid.

30. U.S. Department of Health and Human Services, Administration for Children and Families, "Head Start Child Outcomes Framework Domain 6: Social and Emotional Development," March 4, 2005; accessed May 13, 2009, at http://www.headstartinfo.org/leaders_guideeng/domain6.htm.

31. Kids Count Data Center, "Children That Speak a Language Other Than English at Home (percent)—2010"; accessed June 6, 2012, at http://datacenter.kidscount.org/data/acrossstates/Rankings.aspx?ind=81.

32. "Indicator FAM5: Language Spoken at Home and Difficulty Speaking English," 2010; accessed June 6, 2012, at http://www.childstats.gov/americaschildren/famsoc5.asp.

33. Ibid.

34. U.S. Census Bureau, "Detailed List of Languages Spoken at Home for the Population 5 Years and Over by State: 2007"; accessed June 6, 2012, at http://www.census.gov/hhes/socdemo/language/.

35. Ibid.

36. Santa Clara County Partnership for School Readiness and Applied Research Survey, "Does Readiness Matter? How Kindergarten Readiness Translates into Success," April 2008; accessed June 7, 2012, at http://www.appliedsurveyresearch.org/storage/database/early-childhood-development/schoolreadiness/sanmateosanta-clara/DoesReadinessMatter_ALongitudinalAnalysisFINAL3.pdf.

37. M. Conn-Powers, "All Children Ready for School: Approaches to Learning,"*Early Childhood Briefing Paper Series,* Indiana University, 2006; accessed June 6, 2012, at http://www.iidc.indiana.edu/styles/iidc/defiles/ECC/SRUD-ApproachestoLearning.pdf.

38. Ibid.

39. S. Hawley, "Kindergarten Prep: New Guidelines Outline What All Pre-Kindergartners Should Know," *ACF Newsource,* December 31, 2006; accessed June 7, 2012, at http://acfnewsource.org.s60463.gridserver.com/education/k_prep.html.

40. National Early Literacy Panel, *Developing Early Literacy: Report of the National Early Literacy Panel* (Washington, DC: National Institute for Literacy, 2008); accessed June 7, 2012, at http://lincs.ed.gov/publications/pdf/NELPReport09.pdf.

41. E. Jones and S. Cronin, "Play and Culture," *ExchangeEveryDay,* April 16, 2009; accessed June 6, 2012, at http://www.childcareexchange.com/eed/news_print.php?news_id=2234.

42. D. Phillips and N. A. Crowell, eds., *Cultural Diversity and Early Education: Report of a Workshop, National Research Council* (Washington, DC: National Academies Press, 1994).

43. Japel, C. "School Readiness and Later Achievement," *Developmental Psychology,* 2007:43, 6, 1428–1446; accessed June 7, 2012, at http://www.policyforchildren.org/pdf/School_Readiness_Study.pdf.

44. *Science Daily,* "Puzzle Play Helps Boost Learning Math-Related Skills," February 16, 2012; accessed June 6, 2012, at http://www.sciencedaily.com/releases/2012/02/120216094631.htm.

45. A. J. Mashburn, et al., "Peer Effects on Children's Language Achievement During Pre-Kindergarten," *Child Development,* 2009: 70, 3; accessed June 7, 2012, at http://www.srcd.org/index.php?searchword=online+publications&option=com_search&Itemid=.

46. M. Parten, "Social Participation among Preschool Children," *Journal of Abnormal and Social Psychology,* 27, 1932, 243–269.

Chapter 9

1. Excerpted and adapted from NAEYC, "NAEYC Standards for Early Childhood Professional Preparation Programs." Position Statement. Washington, DC: NAEYC. Reprinted with permission from the National Association for the Education of Young Children (NAEYC). Copyright © 2009 by NAEYC. Full text of all NAEYC position statements is available at www.naeyc.org/positionstatements.

2. Excerpted and adapted from NAEYC, "NAEYC Standards for Early Childhood Professional Preparation Programs." Position Statement. Washington, DC: NAEYC. Reprinted with permission from the National Association for the Education of Young Children (NAEYC). Copyright © 2009 by NAEYC. Full text of all NAEYC position statements is available at www.naeyc.org/positionstatements.

3. Excerpted and adapted from NAEYC, "NAEYC Standards for Early Childhood Professional Preparation Programs." Position Statement. Washington, DC: NAEYC. Reprinted with permission from the National Association for the Education of Young Children (NAEYC). Copyright © 2009 by NAEYC. Full text of all NAEYC position statements is available at www.naeyc.org/positionstatements.

4. National Dropout Prevention Center/Network. "Early Childhood Education: An Overview," 2012; accessed June 6, 2012, at www.dropoutprevention.org/effective-strategies/early-childhood-education.

5. U.S. Census Bureau, "School Enrollment: Nursing and Primary School Enrollment of People 3 to 6 Years Old," revised May 23, 2012; accessed June 6, 2012, at http://www.census.gov/hhes/school/data/cps/2010/tables.html.

6. Ibid.

7. J. Hustedt and W. Barnett, "Financing Early Childhood Education Programs: State, Federal, and Local Issues." *Educational Policy* 25(1), July 2011; accessed February 6, 2012, at http://epx.sagepub.com/content/25/1/167.short.

8. C. Gabrieli and W. Goldstein, *Time to Learn: Benefits of a Longer School Day,* 2012; accessed June 6, 2012, at http://www.readingrockets.org/article/24556.

9. The Oregonian Editorial Board, "Get Ready for an Early Start," November 28, 2011; accessed June 6, 2012, at http://www.oregonlive.com/opinion/index.ssf/2011/11/get_ready_for_an_early_start.html.

10. This digest was adapted from a position paper of the Association for Childhood Education International by Vito Perrone, "On Standardized Testing," which appeared in *Childhood Education,* Spring 1991, 132–142.

11. B. Levine, "Is Your Child Ready for Kindergarten?" 2012; accessed June 6, 2012, at http://www.sesamestreet.org/parents/topics/development/development01.

12. A. Gordon, "OLR Backgrounder: Narrowing Kindergarten Entrance Age," February 4, 2011; accessed June 6, 2012, at http://www.cga.ct.gov/2011/rpt/2011-R-0024.htm.

13. R. Preidt, "For Kids, Laughter Really May Be the Best Medicine," January 31, 2012; accessed June 6, 2012, at http://www.nlm.nih.gov/medlineplus/news/fullstory_121398.html.

14. U.S. Department of Education, Civil Rights Office, "Civil Rights Data Collection," 2009–2010; accessed June 6, 2012, at http://ocrdata.ed.gov.

15. S. Pappas, "Kindergarten Dilemma: Hold Kids Back to Get Ahead?," *MSN NBC news*, September 9, 2010; accessed June 6, 2012, at http://www.msnbc.msn.com/id/38993761/ns/health-childrens_health/t/kindergarten-dilemma-hold-kids-back-get-ahead.

16. D. Stipek, "At What Age Should Children Enter Kindergarten? A Question for Policy Makers and Parents," *Social Policy Report,* 16(2), 2002, 11.

17. C. Copple and S. Bredekamp, eds., *Developmentally Appropriate Practice in Early Childhood Programs: Serving Children from Birth Through Age 8*, 3rd ed. (Washington, DC: NAEYC, 2009), 8.

18. R. Snyder, "Education Reform," 2011; accessed March 9, 2012, at http://www.ecic4kids.org.

19. Nevada Legislative Counsel Bureau, "Full-Day Kindergarten," February 2010; accessed June 6, 2012, at http://www.leg.state.nv.us/.../Research/.../ResearchBriefs/FullDayKindergarten.pdf.

20. Ibid.

21. Education Commission of the States, "Access to Kindergarten: Age Issues in State Statutes," *State Notes Kindergarten,* updated 2011; accessed June 6, 2012, at http://mb2.ecs.org/reports/Report.aspx?id=32.

22. National Center for Education Statistics, "Enrollment Trends by Age," 2012; accessed June 6, 2012, at http://nces.ed.gov/programs/coe/indicator_ope.asp.

23. Children's Defense Fund, "The Facts about Full-Day Kindergarten," January 2012; accessed June 6, 2012, at http://www.childrensdefense.org/child...data.../the-facts-about-full-day.pdf.

24. Health and Human Services, "Massachusetts Chapter 766," 2010; accessed June 6, 2012, at http://www.mass.gov/?pageID=eohhs2terminal&L=4&L0=Home&L1=Government&L2=Laws%2C+Regulations+and+Policies&L3=Massachusetts+Commission+for+the+Blind+-+Related+Laws+and+Regulations&sid=Eeohhs2&b=terminalcontent&f=mcb_g_chapter_766&csid=Eeohhs2.

25. Scholastic Testing Service Inc, "Readiness Assessment," 2010; accessed June 6, 2012, at http://ststesting.wordpress.com/category/school-readiness-testing/.

26. Troy School District, "Developmental Kindergarten Program," 2010–2011; accessed June 6, 2012, at http://www.troy.k12.mi.us/tsdnews/dkbrochure.pdf.

27. The Honor Roll School, "Transition Kindergarten," 2010; accessed June 6, 2012, at http://www.thehonorrollschool.com/page.cfm?p=19548.

28. Carol Peck, "Multiage Classrooms Aid Both Students, Teachers," *Arizona Republic*, January 17, 2010; accessed June 6, 2012, at http://www.azcentral.com/arizonarepublic/local/articles/2010/01/17/20100117edpeck0117.html.

29. *Psychology Today*, May 20, 2008; accessed June 13, 2012, at http://www.psychologytoday.com/blog/digital-children/200805/kindergarten-retention.

30. Ibid.

31. Nailing Xia and Sheila Kirby, RAND Education, "Retaining Students in Grade: A Literature Review of the Effects of Retention on Students' Academic and Nonacademic Outcome," 2009; accessed June 6, 2012, at http://www.rand.org/pubs/technical_reports/2009/RAND_TR678.sum.pdf.

32. K. L. Maxwell and S. K. Elder, "Children's Transition to Kindergarten," *Young Children,* 49(6), 56–63.

33. J. T. Downer, K. M. La Paro, R. C. Pianta, and S. E. Rimm-Kaufman, "The Contribution of Classroom Setting and Quality of Instruction to Children's Behavior in Kindergarten Classrooms," *Elementary School Journal,* 105(4), March 2005, 377–394.

34. Council of Chief State School Officers, "Addressing the Challenges: A Safe, Supportive, and Healthy School Environment," January 27, 2009; accessed January 27, 2009, at http://www.ccsso.org/Projects/school_health_project/addressing_the_challenges/6498.cfm.

35. Gary Hopkins, "School-Wide Handwashing Campaign Cut Germs, Absenteeism," *Education World*, April 30, 2009; accessed June 6, 2012, at http://www.educationworld.com/a_admin/admin/admin431.shtml.

36. Centers for Disease Control and Prevention, "Healthy Food Environment," 2010; accessed June 6, 2012, at http://www.cdc.gov/healthyplaces/healthtopics/healthyfood_environment.htm.

37. U.S. Department of Agriculture, "USDA School Meals: Healthy Meals, Healthy Schools, Healthy Kids," February, 16, 2012; accessed June 6, 2012, at http://www.fns.usda.gov/cga/factsheets/school_meals.htm.

38. Ibid.

39. Sarah White, "Lesson Plan on Organic Food," July 24, 2007; accessed June 13, 2012, at http://organic.lovetoknow.com/Lesson_Plan_on_Organic_Food.

40. Casa dei Bambina Montessori, 2012; accessed June 7, 2012, at http://www.santamariapreschool.com.

41. M. Bredngen, B. Wanner, and F. Vitaro, "Verbal Abuse by the Teacher and Child Adjustment from Kindergarten Through Grade 6," *Pediatrics*, 117(5), 2006, 1585–1598.

42. Council of Chief State School Officers, "Addressing the Challenges: A Safe, Supportive, and Healthy School Environment," January 27, 2009; accessed June 6, 2012, at http://www.ccsso.org/projects/School_Health_Project/Addressing_the_Challenges/6498.cfm.

43. Betteye Caldwell, "What Is a Good Kindergarten?" 2010; accessed June 6, 2012, at http://www.fisher-price.com/fp.aspx?st=4081&e=expertadvice&content=57470.

44. Ibid.

45. M. Brendgen, B. Wanner, and F. Vitaro, "Verbal Abuse by the Teacher and Child Adjustment from Kindergarten Through Grade 6," *Pediatrics,* 117(5), May 2006, 1585–1598.

46. L. M. Morrow, *Literacy Development in the Early Years: Helping Children Read and Write,* 5th ed. (Needham, MA: Allyn & Bacon, 2005). Copyright 2005. Reprinted/adapted by permission of Allyn & Bacon.

47. Kansas Parent Information Resource Center, *How to Help Your Child Become a Better Reader: A Parent Guide,* 2008; accessed June 14, 2012, at http://www.kpirc.org/uploads/BetterReaderArranged2color.pdf.

48. Ibid.

49. R. Culham, *The 6 + 1 Traits of Writing: The Complete Guide for the Primary Grades* (Brooklyn, NY: Scholastic, 2005).

50. Contributed by Amanda Bower, former teacher, Cedar Hill, Texas Independent School District.

51. National Council for Social Studies, "About NCSS"; accessed June 7, 2012, at http://www.socialstudies.org/about.

Chapter 10

1. Excerpted and adapted from NAEYC, "NAEYC Standards for Early Childhood Professional Preparation Programs." Position Statement. Washington, DC: NAEYC. Reprinted with permission from the National Association for the Education of Young Children (NAEYC). Copyright © 2009 by NAEYC. Full text of all NAEYC position statements is available at www.naeyc.org/positionstatements.

1. Excerpted and adapted from NAEYC, "NAEYC Standards for Early Childhood Professional Preparation Programs." Position Statement. Washington, DC: NAEYC. Reprinted with permission from the National Association for the Education of Young Children (NAEYC). Copyright © 2009 by NAEYC. Full text of all NAEYC position statements is available at www.naeyc.org/positionstatements.

3. Excerpted and adapted from NAEYC, "NAEYC Standards for Early Childhood Professional Preparation Programs." Position Statement. Washington, DC: NAEYC. Reprinted with permission from the National Association for the Education of Young Children (NAEYC). Copyright © 2009 by NAEYC. Full text of all NAEYC position statements is available at www.naeyc.org/positionstatements.

4. T. W. Briggs, "All-USA Teachers Strive to Give Confidence, Changes," *USA Today,* November 6, 2007; accessed June 29, 2009, at http://www.usatoday.com/news/education/2007-10-17-teacher-team_N.htm?csp=34.

5. Milken Family Foundation, "Milken Educator—Elizabeth Parker"; accessed June 28, 2009, at http://www.mff.org/mea/mea.taf?page=recipient&meaID=22570.

6. T. W. Briggs, "All-USA Teachers Strive to Give Confidence, Changes," *USA Today,* November 6, 2007; accessed June 29, 2009, at http://www.usatoday.com/news/education/2007-10-17-teacher-team_N.htm?csp=34.

7. Milken Family Foundation, "Milken Educator—Yuuko Arikawa"; accessed June 11, 2012, at http://www.mff.org/mea.

8. U.S. Census Bureau, *Newsroom: Facts for Features 2011,* "Back to School: 2011–2012," April 2012; accessed June 11, 2012, at http://www.census.gov/newsroom/releases/archives/facts_for_features_special_editions/cb11-ff15.html.

9. Ibid.

10. U.S. Census Bureau, "Hispanic Americans by the Numbers," Infoplease.com, 2012; accessed June 11, 2012, at http://www.infoplease.com/spot/hhmcensus1.html.

11. Laura Perry and Andrew McConney, "Does the SES of the School Matter? An Examination of Socioeconomic Status and Student Achievement Using PISA 2003," *Teachers College Record,* 2010; accessed June 11, 2012, at http://www.tcrecord.org/Content.asp?Content=15662.

12. Jim Lindsay, "Children's Access to Print Material and Education-Related Outcomes: Findings from a Meta-Analytic Review," *Learning Point Associates,* August 2010; accessed June 11, 2012, at http://www.learningpoint.org.

13. P. L. Ritchie, "Pine Grove Elementary Students Write Cookbook," *St. Petersburg Times,* June 4, 2009; accessed June 5, 2009, from http://www.tampabay.com/news/education/k12/article1006748.ece.

14. United States Census Bureau, "Internet Use in the United States: October 2009," 2009; accessed June 11, 2012, at http://www.census.gov/hhes/computer/publications/2009.html.

15. Office for National Statistics, accessed June 13, 2012, at http://www.ons.gov.uk/ons/rel/rdit2/internet-access---households-and-individuals/2011/stb-internet-access-2011.html.

16. American Academy of Child and Adolescent Psychiatry, "Facts for Families: Obesity in Children and Teens," March 2011; accessed June 11, 2012, at http://aacap.org/cs/root/facts_for_families/obesity_in_children_and_teens.

17. KidsHealth, "Precocious Puberty," 2012; accessed June 11, 2012, at http://kidshealth.org/parent/medical/sexual/precocious.html#.

18. Harvard Health, "Depression in Children and Teenagers," 2011; accessed June 11, 2012, at http://www.health.harvard.edu/newsweek/Depression_in_Children_and_Teenagers.htm.

19. National Institute of Mental Health, "Depression in Children and Adolescents: Factsheet," April 25, 2011; accessed June 11, 2012, at http://www.nimh.nih.gov/health/publications/depression-in-children-and-adolescents/index.shtml.

20. Mental Health in Illinois, "Ideas on Promoting Good Mental Health for Children," 2009; accessed June 11, 2012, at http://www.mentalhealthillinois.org/childrens-health/promoting-childrens-mental-health.

21. National Association of School Psychologists, NASP Resources, "Supporting Children's Mental Health: Tips for Parents and Educators," 2009; accessed June 11, 2012, at http://www.nasponline.org/resources/mentalhealth/mhtips.aspx.

22. Kxan.com news, "E-Textbooks May Soon Be Reality: Traditional Hardbacks Lost in Wave of Future," May 18, 2010; accessed June 11, 2012, at http://www.kxan.com/dpp/news/education/the-web-could-soon-replace-textbooks.

23. Gary Brookings Institution, "Class Size: What Research Says and What It Means for State Policy," May 11, 2011; accessed June 11, 2012, at http://brookings.edu/papers/2011/0511_class_size_whitehurst_chingos.aspx.

24. Ibid.

25. Michigan Department of Education, "Okemos Elementary School Teacher Named Michigan Teacher of the Year," May 14, 2009; accessed June 11, 2012, at http://www.michigan.gov/mde/0,1607,7-140-6530_6526_6551-214772—,00.html.

26. S. Feeney and N. K. Freeman, *Ethics and the Early Childhood Educator: Using the NAEYC Code* (Washington, DC: NAEYC, 2005).

27. Public Schools of North Carolina, Standard Course of Study, "Social Studies: 2006: First Grade Neighborhoods and Communities Around the World"; accessed June 11, 2012, at http://www.dpi.state.nc.us/curriculum/socialstudies/scos/2003–04/021firstgrade.

Chapter 11

1. Excerpted and adapted from NAEYC, "NAEYC Standards for Early Childhood Professional Preparation Programs." Position Statement. Washington, DC: NAEYC. Reprinted with permission from the National Association for the Education of Young Children (NAEYC). Copyright © 2009 by NAEYC. Full text of all NAEYC position statements is available at www.naeyc.org/positionstatements.

2. Excerpted and adapted from NAEYC, "NAEYC Standards for Early Childhood Professional Preparation Programs." Position

Statement. Washington, DC: NAEYC. Reprinted with permission from the National Association for the Education of Young Children (NAEYC). Copyright © 2009 by NAEYC. Full text of all NAEYC position statements is available at www.naeyc.org/positionstatements.

3. Excerpted and adapted from NAEYC, "NAEYC Standards for Early Childhood Professional Preparation Programs." Position Statement. Washington, DC: NAEYC. Reprinted with permission from the National Association for the Education of Young Children (NAEYC). Copyright © 2009 by NAEYC. Full text of all NAEYC position statements is available at www.naeyc.org/positionstatements.

4. NYSUT, "Katie Ferguson; Schenectady Federation of Teachers," April 28, 2012; accessed June 14, 2012, at http://www.nysut.org/cps/rde/xchg/nysut/hs.xsl/ra_17816.htm.

5. Ed.Gov, "IDEA 2004: Building the Legacy"; accessed June 25, 2012, at http://idea.ed.gov./part-c/search/new.

6. Individuals with Disabilities Education Act (IDEA), Public Law 105-17, 1997.

7. Ibid.

8. National Institute for Child Health and Human Development, "Federal Interagency Forum on Child and Family Statistics," July 29, 2010; accessed June 11, 2012, at http://www.nichd.nih.gov/news/releases/chiin99a.cfm.

9. L. Blanton, M. Pugach, and L. Florian, "Preparing General Education Teachers to Improve Outcomes for Students with Disabilities," National Center for Learning Disabilities, 2010; accessed June 25, 2012, at http://www.nationaltechcenter.org/index.php/2011/05/16/preparing-general-education-teachers-to-improve-outcomes-for-students-with-disabilities.

10. The US Technology-Related Assistance for Individuals with Disabilities Act of 1988, Section 3.1, Public Law 100-407, August 9, 1988 (renewed in 1998 in the Clinton Assistive Technology Act), http://section508.gov/docs/AT1998.html#3.

11. U.S. Department of Education: What Works Clearinghouse. *WWC Review of the Report "Enhancing the Effectiveness of Special Education Programming for Children with Attention Deficit Hyperactivity Disorder Using a Daily Report Card"*; accessed July 2, 2012, at http://ies.ed.gov/ncee/wwc.

12. The National Human Genome Research Institute, "Learning about Autism"; accessed June 25, 2012, at http://www.genome.gov/25522099.

13. National Institute of Neurological Disorders and Stroke, "Autism Fact Sheet," updated May 4, 2012; accessed June 28, 2012, at http://www.ninds.nih.gov/disorders/autism/detail_autism.htm.

14. Autism Society of America, *About Autism: Facts and Statistics*; accessed June 18, 2012, at http://www.autism-society.org/about-autism/facts-and-statistics.html.

15. American Psychiatric Association, *Diagnostic and Statistical Manual of Mental Disorders: DSM-IV-TR* (Washington, DC: Author, 2000).

16. Autism Society of America, *About Autism: Facts and Statistics*; accessed June 18, 2012, at http://www.autism-society.org/about-autism/facts-and-statistics.html.

17. Autism Speaks, *Building a Community of Hope, About Autism*, 2007; accessed June 18, 2012, at http://www.autismspeaks.org/docs/Autism_Speaks_Annual_Report_2007.pdf.

18. Ibid.

19. J. J. Woods and A. M. Wetherby, "Early Identification of and Intervention for Infants and Toddlers Who Are at Risk for Autism Spectrum Disorder," *Language, Speech, and Hearing Services in Schools, 34*, 2003, 180–293.

20. S. Mastrangelo, "Play and the Child with Autism Spectrum Disorder: From Possibilities to Practice", *International Journal of Play Therapy, 18*(1), 2009, 13–30.

21. Autism Society of America, *About Autism: Causes*; accessed June 18, 2012, at http://www.autism-society.org/about-autism/causes.

22. The National Human Genome Research Institute, "Learning about Autism"; accessed June 18, 2012, at http://www.genome.gov/25522099.

23. *The International Herald Tribune*, Associated Press, "Gene Clues from Mideast Suggest Autism Occurs When Brain Cannot Learn Properly from Early Life," July 11, 2008; accessed June 10, 2010, at http://www.iht.com/bin/printfriendly.php?id=14407868.

24. K. L. Spittler, "New Evidence Supports Theory of an Environmental Trigger for Autism," *NeuroPsychiatry Reviews*, 2009, 6.

25. The National Human Genome Research Institute, "Learning about Autism"; accessed June 18, 2012, at http://www.genome.gov/25522099.

26. Centers for Disease Control, "Mercury and Vaccines (Thimerosal)," January 1, 2007; accessed July 2, 2012.

27. J. J. Woods and A. M. Wetherby, "Early Identification of and Intervention for Infants and Toddlers Who Are at Risk for Autism Spectrum Disorder," *Language, Speech, and Hearing Services in Schools, 34*, 2003, 180–293.

28. Autism Science Foundation, "Autism Diagnosis," 2012; accessed July 5, 2012, at http://autismsciencefoundation.org/what-is-autism/autism-diagnosis.

29. S. Mastrangelo, "Play and the Child with Autism Spectrum Disorder: From Possibilities to Practice," *International Journal of Play Therapy, 18*(1), 2009, 13–30.

30. T. Wigram and C. Gold, "Music Therapy in the Assessment and Treatment of Autistic Spectrum Disorder: Clinical Application and Research Evidence," *Child Care, Health and Development, 32*(5), 2005, 535–542.

31. Centers for Disease Control, *Attention Deficit/Hyperactivity Disorder: Facts about ADHD*, May 25, 2010; accessed June 10, 2010, at http://www.cdc.gov/ncbddd/adhd/facts.html.

32. Mental Health America, *Fact Sheet: Adult AD/HD in the Work Place*; accessed June 21, 2012, at http://www.mentalhealthamerica.net/go/information/get-info/ad/hd/adult-ad/hd-in-the-workplace/adult-ad/hd-in-the-workplace.

33. Centers for Disease Control, *Attention Deficit/Hyperactivity Disorder: Facts about ADHD*, May 25, 2010; accessed June 21, 2012, at http://www.cdc.gov/ncbddd/adhd/facts.html.

34. Centers for Disease Control and Prevention, "Attention-Deficit/Hyperactivity Disorder (ADHD): Symptoms and Diagnosis," December 12, 2010; accessed June 28, 2012, at http://www.cdc.gov/ncbddd/adhd/diagnosis.html.

35. Ibid.

36. Reprinted with Permission from the *Diagnostic and Statistical Manual of Mental Disorders, Fourth Edition, Text Revision* (Copyright 2000). American Psychiatric Association.

37. HealthyChildren.org, "Understanding ADHD," January 6, 2012; accessed July 2, 2012, at http://www.healthychildren.org/English/health-issues/conditions/adhd/Pages/Understanding-ADHD.aspx.

38. C. Adams, "Girls and ADHD," *Instructor, 116*(6), 2007, 31–35.

39. C. Adams, "Girls and ADHD," 2012; accessed July 5, 2012, at http://www.scholastic.com/browse/article.jsp?id=3746286.

40. Ibid.

41. Ibid.

42. Mental Health America, *Fact Sheet: Adult AD/HD in the Work Place*; accessed June 21, 2012, at http://www.mentalhealthamerica.net/go/information/get-info/ad/hd/adult-ad/hd-in-the-workplace/adult-ad/hd-in-the-workplace.

43. Centers for Disease Control, *Attention Deficit/Hyperactivity Disorder: Facts about ADHD*, May 25, 2010; accessed June 21, 2012, at http://www.cdc.gov/ncbddd/adhd/facts.html.

44. Ibid.

45. Information in this section from the U.S. Department of Education, *Teaching Children with Attention Deficit Hyperactivity Disorder: Instructional Strategies and Practices 2008;* accessed June 21, 2012, at http://www2.ed.gov/rschstat/research/pubs/adhd/adhd-teaching.html.

46. *New York Times*, "Attention Deficit Hyperactivity Disorder (ADHD)," reviewed by Harvey Simon, MD, February 27, 2012; accessed July 2, 2012, at http://health.nytimes.com/health/guides/disease/attention-deficit-hyperactivity-disorder-adhd/medications.html.

47. Ibid.

48. *Pittsburg Post-Gazette*, "Modified PSSA Test in Math Offered for 1st Time," April 18, 2010; accessed June 10, 2010, at http://www.post-gazette.com/pg/10108/1051042-454.stm#ixzz0oUfbWXWV.

49. Jennifer Cheeseman, Day, *Population Projections of the United States by Age, Sex, Race, and Hispanic Origin: 1995 to 2050*, U.S. Bureau of the Census, Current Population Reports, P25-1130, U.S. Government Printing Office, Washington, DC, 1996.

50. Kids Count Data Center, "Children in Immigrant Families (percent)," 2010; accessed July, 2, 2012, at http://datacenter.kidscount.org/data/acrossstates/Rankings.aspx?ind=115.

51. Kids Count Data Center, "Children Who Have Difficulty Speaking English by Children in Immigrant Families (Percent)," March 2010; accessed June 21, 2012, at http://datacenter.kidscount.org/data/acrossstates/Rankings.aspx?ind=128.

52. The Urban Institute, "Immigration Trends," 2010; accessed June 11, 2012, at www.urban.org/uploadedpdf/412203-young-children.pdf.

53. Ibid.

54. The Future of Children, "Immigrant Children and Participation in ECE Programs," May 17, 2011; accessed June 11, 2012, at http://futureofchildren.org/publications/journals/article/index.xml?journalid=74&articleid=541&sectionid=3728.

55. U.S. Census Bureau, Language Use, "American Community Survey Data on Language Use," January 3, 2012; accessed June 11, 2012, at http://www.census.gov/hhes/socdemo/language/data/acs/index.html.

56. The Annie E. Casey Foundation, "Kids Count, Data Snap Shot," 2012; accessed June 11, 2012, at http://www.aecf.org/~/media/Pubs/Initiatives/KIDS%20COUNT/D/DataSnapshotonHighPovertyCommunities/KIDSCOUNTDataSnapshot_HighPovertyCommunities.pdf.

57. R. Linquanti, "Schools Moving Up: WestEd," *Fostering Academic Success for English Language Learners: What Do We Know?*; accessed June 28, 2012, at http://www.wested.org/policy/pubs/fostering.

58. U.S. Department of Commerce, "The Next Four Decades The Older Population in the United States: 2010 to 2050," May 2010; accessed July 5, 2012, at www.census.gov/prod/2010pubs/p25-1138.pdf.

59. Miami–Dade County Public Schools, *Statistical Highlights 2010–2011*; accessed June 11, 2012, at http://drs.dadeschools.net/StatisticalHighlights/SH.asp.

60. E. Jensen, *Teaching with Poverty in Mind*, 2009; accessed June 11, 2012, at http://www.ascd.org/publications/books/109074/chapters/How-Poverty-Affects-Behavior-and-Academic-Performance.aspx.

61. Nation's Report Card, 2011; accessed July 2, 2012, at http://nationsreportcard.gov/reading_2011/nat_g4.asp?subtab_id=Tab3&tab_id=tab1#chart.

62. P. Nyhan, "Immigration and Early Ed: Children in Immigrant Families Falling Behind on Educational Benchmarks," 2012; accessed July 5, 2012, http://thrivebyfivewa.org/2012/07/03/immigration-and-early-ed-children-in-immigrant-families-falling-behind-on-educational-benchmarks.

63. Ibid.

64. M. Carbo, R. Dunn, and K. Dunn, *Teaching Students to Read Through Their Individual Learning Styles* (Boston: Allyn & Bacon, 1991), 2.

65. GreatSchools, "How Important Is Cultural Diversity at Your School?"; accessed June 11, 2012, at http://www.greatschools.org/find-a-school/defining-your-ideal/284-cultural-diversity-at-school.gs?page=all.

Chapter 12

1. Excerpted and adapted from NAEYC, "NAEYC Standards for Early Childhood Professional Preparation Programs." Position Statement. Washington, DC: NAEYC. Reprinted with permission from the National Association for the Education of Young Children (NAEYC). Copyright © 2009 by NAEYC. Full text of all NAEYC position statements is available at www.naeyc.org/positionstatements.

2. Excerpted and adapted from NAEYC, "NAEYC Standards for Early Childhood Professional Preparation Programs." Position Statement. Washington, DC: NAEYC. Reprinted with permission from the National Association for the Education of Young Children (NAEYC). Copyright © 2009 by NAEYC. Full text of all NAEYC position statements is available at www.naeyc.org/positionstatements.

3. W. M. Reinke, J. D. Splett, E. N. Robeson, and C. A. Offutt, "Combining School and Family Interventions for the Prevention and Early Intervention of Disruptive Behavior Problems in Children: A Public Health Perspective," *Psychology in the Schools,* 46(1), January 2009, 33–43; available at http://www3.interscience.wiley.com/cgi-bin/fulltext/121549478/PDFSTART.

4. L. S. Vygotsky, *Mind in Society* (Cambridge, MA: Harvard University Press, 1978), 86.

5. S. Gupta, "Child Rearing in Self Regulation Through Private Speech," February 19, 2008; available at http://www.articles-r-free.com/articledetail.php?artid=17986&catid=162.

6. L. E. Berk and A. Winsler, *Scaffolding Children's Learning: Vygotsky and Early Childhood Education* (Washington, DC: NAEYC, 1995), 45–46.

7. Author unknown, Teaching Expertise, December 2004; accessed June 27, 2012, at http://www.teachingexpertise.com/articles/hydrate-brain-717.

8. B. J. Casey, et al., "Behavioral and Neural Correlates of Delay of Gratification 40 Years Later," *PNAS Early Edition*; accessed June 25, 2012, at http://www.pnas.org/content/early/2011/08/19/1108561108.full.pdf+html.

9. Ibid.

10. H. Kozima, *Children–Robot Interaction: A Pilot Study in Autism Therapy,* National Institute of Information and Communications Technology; accessed June 27, 2012, at http://www.ncbi.nlm.nih.gov/pubmed/17920443.

11. C. Chandler, *Animal-Assisted Therapy in Counseling and School Settings,* ERIC Clearinghouse on Counseling and Student Services, Greensboro, NC, 2001; accessed June 27, 2012, at http://www.ericdigests.org/2002-3/animal.htm.

12. Plano Independent School District, News Archive; accessed June 26, 2012, at http://www.pisd.edu/news/archive/2011-12/character.education.national.awards.shtml.

13. J. Hsueh and H. Yoshikawa, "Working on Nonstandard Schedules and Variable Shifts in Low-Income Families: Associations with Parental Psychological Well-Being, Family Functioning, and Child Well-Being," *Developmental Psychology, 43*(3), 2007, 620–632; accessed June 25, 2012, at http://steinhardt.nyu.edu/scmsAdmin/media/users/jr189/Working_Nonstandard_Schedules_and_Variable_Shifts.pdf.

14. S. Tavernise, "Soaring Poverty Casts Spotlight on 'Lost Decade'," *New York Times,* September 13, 2011; accessed June 25, 2012, at http://www.nytimes.com/2011/09/14/us/14census.html?pagewanted=all.

15. Ibid.

16. E. E. Pinderhughes, K. A. Dodge, J. E. Bates, G. S. Pettit, and A. Zelli, "Discipline Responses, Influences of Parents' Socioeconomic Status, Ethnicity, Beliefs About Parenting, Stress, and Cognitive-Emotional Processes," *Journal of Family Psychology, 14*(3), 2000, 380–400.

17. Ibid.

18. Ibid.

19. Ibid.

Chapter 13

1. Excerpted and adapted from NAEYC, "NAEYC Standards for Early Childhood Professional Preparation Programs." Position Statement. Washington, DC: NAEYC. Reprinted with permission from the National Association for the Education of Young Children (NAEYC). Copyright © 2009 by NAEYC. Full text of all NAEYC position statements is available at www.naeyc.org/positionstatements.

2. Excerpted and adapted from NAEYC, "NAEYC Standards for Early Childhood Professional Preparation Programs." Position Statement. Washington, DC: NAEYC. Reprinted with permission from the National Association for the Education of Young Children (NAEYC). Copyright © 2009 by NAEYC. Full text of all NAEYC position statements is available at www.naeyc.org/positionstatements.

K. Snow, National Association for the Education of Young Children, *Research News You Can Use: Family Engagement and Early Childhood Education*, 2012; accessed July 10, 2012, at http://www.naeyc.org/content/research-news-family-engagement.

4. A. T. Henderson and K. L. Mapp, National Center for Family and Community Connections with Schools, Southwest Educational Development Laboratory, *A New Wave of Evidence: The Impact of School, Family, and Community Connections on Student Achievement,* 2002.

5. W. Bushaw and S. Lopez, "The 42nd Annual Phi Delta Kappa/Gallup Poll of the Public's Attitudes Toward the Public Schools," *Phi Delta Kappan,* September 2010; accessed July 10, 2012, at http://www.gallup.com/poll/142661/phi-delta-kappa-gallup-poll-2010.aspx.

6. A. T. Henderson, V. Johnson, K. L. Mapp, and D. Davies. *Beyond the Bake Sale: The Essential Guide to Family/School Partnerships* (New York: New Press, 2007).

7. H. T. Knopf and K. J. Swick, "Using Our Understanding of Families to Strengthen Family Involvement," *Early Childhood Education Journal, 35*(5), April 2008, 419–427.

8. J. S. Solochek, "Program Empowers Parents to Get More Involved with Children's Lives," *St. Petersburg Times,* April 5, 2009; accessed July 10, 2012, at http://www.tampabay.com/news/education/k12/article989668.ece.

9. U.S. Bureau of Labor Statistics, *Employment Characteristics of Families Summary*, April 26, 2011; accessed July 10, 2012, at http://www.bls.gov/news.release/pdf/famee.pdf.

10. National Association of Child Care Resource and Referral Agencies, "High Quality Child Care Matters," 2012; accessed July 10, 2012, at http://www.naccrra.org/about-child-care/quality-matters; and U.S. Bureau of Labor Statistics, *Employment Characteristics of Families Summary*, 2011; accessed July 10, 2012, at http://www.bls.gov/news.release/famee.nr0.htm.

11. Ibid.

12. U.S. Department of Health and Human Services, "Promoting Responsible Fatherhood," updated 2011; accessed July 10, 2012, at http://fatherhood.hhs.gov/2010Initiative/index.shtml.

13. National Fatherhood Initiative, "Facts on Father Absence," 2010; accessed July 10, 2012, at http://www.fatherhood.org/media/consequences-of-father-absence-statistics#education.

14. TCPalm, *St. Lucie School Digest*. Posting on May 27, 2012; accessed July 11, 2012, at http://www.tcpalm.com/news/2012/may/27/no-headline---tc_sl_school_digest.

15. B. Thatcher, *Colorado Program Helps Dads Become Better Men,* June 16, 2010; accessed July 10, 2012, at http://www.9news.com/seenon9news/article.aspx?storyid=141157&catid=509.

16. N. Roshan, "Dads Enjoy 'DOG' Days at Bellows Spring," June 10, 2010; accessed July 10, 2012, at http://www.explorehoward.com/education/72430/dads-enjoy-dog-days-bellows-spring.

17. Barnes and Noble, *My Fathers Knows the Names of Things,* by Jane Holden, 2010; accessed July 10, 2012, at http://search.barnesandnoble.com/My-Father-Knows-the-Names-of-Things/Jane-Yolen/e/9781416948957.

18. Penguin Group USA, *My Father Is Taller Than a Tree,* 2008; accessed July 10, 2012, at http://us.penguingroup.com/nf/Book/BookDisplay/0,,9780803731738,00.html?strSrchSql=my+father+is+taller+than+a+tree/My_Father_Is_Taller_than_a_Tree_Joseph_Bruchac.

19. Department of Health and Human Services, Centers for Disease Control and Prevention, "Teen Pregnancy: Improving the Lives of Young People and Strengthening Communities by Preventing Teen Pregnancy," 2011; accessed July 10, 2012, at http://www.cdc.gov/chronicdisease/resources/publications/aag/teen-preg.htm.

20. Bureau of Labor Statistics, "Table 4: Families with Own Children: Employment Status of Parents by Age of Youngest Child and Family Type, 2010–11 Annual Averages," April 26, 2012; accessed July 10, 2012, at http://www.bls.gov/news.release/famee.t04.htm.

21. Centers for Disease Control and Prevention, Office of Information Services, updated February, 21, 2012; accessed July 10, 2012, at http://www.cdc.gov/nchs/fastats/births.htm.

22. B. E. Hamilton, J. A. Martin, and S. J. Ventura, "Births: Preliminary Data for 2010," *National Vital Statistics Reports, 56*(7), 2011; accessed July 10, 2012, at www.cdc.gov/nchs/data/nvsr/nvsr60/nvsr60_02.pdf; and Centers for Disease Control and Prevention, "About Teen Pregnancy," March 12, 2012; accessed July 10, 2012, at http://www.cdc.gov/TeenPregnancy/AboutTeenPreg.htm.

23. A. Gelber and A. Isen, *Children's Schooling and Parents' Behavior: Evidence from the Head Start Impact Study,* March 2012; accessed July 11, 2012, at http://www.nber.org/papers/w17704.

24. Ibid.

25. Centers for Disease Control and Prevention, "NCHS Data Brief," April 2012; accessed June 25, 2012, at http://www.cdc.gov/nchs/data/databriefs/db89.htm.

26. *Huffington Post,* "Teen Pregnancy: Mississippi Has the Highest Teen Pregnancy Rate in the U.S.," April 10, 2012; accessed July 10, 2012, at http://www.huffingtonpost.com/2012/04/10/teen-pregnancy-rates_n_1413820.html.

27. Centers for Disease Control and Prevention, "About Teen Pregnancy," updated March 12, 2012; accessed July 10, 2012, at http://www.cdc.gov/TeenPregnancy/AboutTeenPreg.htm.

28. C. Bowers, *Teen Pregnancies End Decade-Long Decline,* January 26, 2010; accessed July 10, 2012, at http://www.cbsnews.com/stories/2010/01/26/eveningnews/main6144496.shtml.

29. A. Dizon, "Seven Local Moms Overcome Stats to Graduate from High School," May 25, 2010; accessed July 10, 2012, at http://lubbockonline.com/education/2010-05-25/seven-local-moms-overcome-stats-graduate-high-school.

30. C. Kieffer, "Dropout Reduction Aim of New Programs," *Tupelo News;* June 7, 2010, at http://nems360.com/view/full_story/7821316/article-Dropout-reduction-aim-of-new-programs?instance=news_special_coverage_right_column.

31. Bureau of Justice Statistics, "Total Correctional Population"; accessed July 10, 2012, at http://bjs.ojp.usdoj.gov/index.cmf?ty=tp&tid=11.

32. Minnesota Fathers and Families Network, *Families with Incarcerated Families Fact Sheet,* 2010; accessed July 10, 2012, at http://www.mnfathers.org/FamiliesOfIncarceratedFACTSHEETfinal.pdf.

33. R. Jervis, "Prison Dads Learn Meaning of 'Father,'" *USA Today,* June, 18, 2010; accessed July 10, 2012, at http://www.usatoday.com/news/nation/2010-06-17-prison-dads_N.htm.

34. Ibid.

35. Personal communication and telephone interview with author, June 22, 2010; maria@getonthebus.us.

36. Ibid.

37. Pew Research Center, "Millenials: Portraits of the Generation Next," February 2010; accessed July 10, 2012, at http://pewsocialtrends.org/assets/pdf/millennials-confident-connected-open-to-change.pdf.

38. Pew Research Center, "The Return of the Multi-generational Family Household," March 8, 2010; accessed July 10, 2012, at http://pewsocialtrends.org/assets/pdf/752-multi-generational-families.pdf.

39. Education Commission of the States, "The Progress of Education Reform," February 2010; accessed July 10, 2012, at http://www.ecs.org/clearinghouse/84/20/8420.pdf.

40. NCCP, *A National Portrait of Chronic Absenteeism in the Early Grades;* accessed July 10, 2012, at http://www.nccp.org/publications/pub_771.html.

41. Generations United, "GrandFacts: Data, Interpretations, and Implications for Caregivers," April 2010; accessed July 10, 2012, at http://www.gu.org/documents/A0/GrandFacts_Fact_Sheet.pdf.

42. S. Plummer, "Future Cowboys," *Tulsa World,* June 11, 2010; accessed July 10, 2012, at http://www.tulsaworld.com/news/article.aspx?subjectid=11&articleid=20100611_11_A11_Veteri115080.

43. J. Klockenga, "Life's a Picnic When You Have a Grandma to Talk To," June 4, 2010; accessed July 10, 2012, at http://www.desmoinesregister.com/article/20100604/NEWS/6040312/1001/NEWS/Life-s-a-picnic-when-you-have-a-grandma-to-talk-to.

44. *Pittsburg Post-Gazette,* "What Happens to Kids Raised by Gay Parents? Research Suggests That They Turn Out About the Same, No Better, No Worse and No More Likely to Be Gay Than Other Kids," June 10, 2007; accessed July 10, 2012, at http://www.post-gazette.com/pg/07161/793042-51.stm#ixzz0qHEotsZP.

45. *CNN,* "Kids of Lesbians Have Fewer Behavioral Problems, Study Suggests," June 7, 2010; accessed July 10, 2012, at http://edition.cnn.com/2010/HEALTH/06/07/lesbian.children.adjustment/index.html.

46. The Gay, Lesbian and Straight Education Network, "LGBT Parents Involved in, Excluded from K–12 Schools; Children Often Harassed," 2008; accessed July 10, 2012, at http://www.glsen.org/cgi-bin/iowa/all/library/record/2271.html?state=research&type=research.

47. Ibid.

48. *Pittsburg Post-Gazette,* "What Happens to Kids Raised by Gay Parents? Research Suggests That They Turn Out About the Same, No Better, No Worse and No More Likely to Be Gay Than Other Kids," June 10, 2007; accessed July 10, 2012, at http://www.post-gazette.com/pg/07161/793042-51.stm#ixzz0qHEotsZP.

49. About.com, "Gay Adoption Statistics Based on U.S. Census 2000, the National Survey of Family Growth (2002), and the Adoption and Foster Care Analysis and Reporting System (2004)"; accessed July 10, 2012, at http://adoption.about.com/od/gaylesbian/f/gayparents.htm.

50. Ibid.

51. U.S. Census Bureau; accessed July 10, 2012, at http://www.census.gov.

52. St. Joseph School District; accessed July 15, 2012, at http://www.sjsd.k12.mo.us/site/default.aspx?PageID=1.

53. The Gay, Lesbian and Straight Education Network, "LGBT Parents Involved in, Excluded from K–12 Schools; Children Often Harassed," 2008; accessed July 10, 2012, at http://www.glsen.org/cgi-bin/iowa/all/library/record/2271.html?state=research&type=research.

54. Ibid.

55. National Military Family Association, "Supporting Children"; accessed July 10, 2012, at http://www.militaryfamily.org/get-info/support-children/.

56. Department of Defense, "Military Personnel Strength Figures," May 31, 2011; accessed July 10, 2012, at https://kb.defense.gov/

app/answers/detail/a_id/253/kw/what%20is%20the%20total%
20number%20of%20people%20in%20the%20US%20armed%
20forces/session/L3RpbWUvMTM0MTk1MDA3OS9zaWQvMVlSdz
lQKms%3D.

57. Department of Defense, "Family Support During Deployment";
accessed July 10, 2012, at http://fhp.osd.mil/deploymentTips.jsp.

58. *Times Observer*, "Youngsville Woman Starts Pennies for Postage to
Help Get Packages to Service Personnel"; accessed July 10, 2012,
at http://www.timesobserver.com/page/content.detail/id/
531862.html.

59. DODEA, "Sure Start: It Takes a Community"; accessed July 10,
2012, at http://www.dodea.edu/instruction/curriculum/ece/
pubs/community/community-portrait.pdf.

60. Enidnews.com, "Program Helps Children of Military Through
Moving"; accessed July 10, 2012, at http://enidnews.com/state/
x1174310405/Program-helps-children-of-military-through-moving.

61. KMBC, "Help Kids in Military Families Cope: Psychiatrist Offers
Tips to Support Children"; accessed July 10, 2012, at http://www
.kmbc.com/military-service/2107168/detail.html.

62. *Military Money*, "Children in Military Families"; accessed July 10,
2012, at http://www.militarymoney.com/home/1101923157.

63. M. McGowan, *Mrs. Marci McGowan's First Grade Website*, 2010;
accessed July 10, 2012, at http://www.mrsmcgowan.com/index
.html.

64. The Teachers' Podcast, "Twitter Used to Develop Second Graders' Writing Skills"; accessed July 10,
2012, at http://teacherspodcast.org/2009/03/31/
ep-36-digital-catchup-and-21st-century-learning-debate.

65. Olathe Unified School District 233, "Students Partner with Parents, Teachers in High-Tech Conferences"; accessed July 10,
2012, at http://www.olatheschools.com/index.php?option=com
_content&task=view&id=1370&Itemid=47.

66. M. Hutchison and B. Ferriter, *Using Blogs and Podcasts in the
Classroom*, sixth grade teachers in Wake County Public School
System, December 4, 2006; accessed July 10, 2012, at http://
digitallyspeaking.pbworks.com/f/Podcasting,+One+Pager.doc.

67. Contributed by Carrie Jostmeyer, first grade teacher, Sparks
Elementary, Frisco ISD, Frisco, Texas.

68. S. Riddell, *Kentucky Teacher*, "More Preschools Collaborating
with Community Partners"; accessed July 11, 2012, at http://
www.kentuckyteacher.org/features/2012/06/more-preschools-
are-collaborating-with-community-partners/.

69. Hills Elementary School Website; accessed July 11, 2012, at
http://www.iowa-city.k12.ia.us/Schools/Hills/Highlights/
HillsHighlights.html.

70. Boston Public Schools, "School Councils," 2012; accessed July 12,
2012, at http://www.bostonpublicschools.org/school-councils.

71. Ibid.

72. Y. Rammohan, *Chicago Tonight*. "New Technology Empowers
CPS Parents"; accessed July 11, 2012, at http://chicagotonight
.wttw.com/2012/06/05/new-technology-empowers-cps-parents.

73. National Civic League, The Campaign for Grade Level Reading;
accessed July 11, 2012, at http://www.allamericacityaward.com.

74. S. Riddell, *Kentucky Teacher*, "Encourage Staff Members to Share
ParentInfo"; accessed July 11, 2012, at http://www.kentuckyteacher
.org/leadership-letter/2012/07/encourage-staff-members-to-share-
parentinfo/.

75. D. Samfield, "When It Comes to Reading, LAW Students Go
Above and Beyond," June 18, 2010; accessed July 10, 2012, at
www.nashobapublishing.com/shirley_news/ci_15325076.

76. "Teacher Visits Hit Home," *Education World,* October 9, 2001
(updated July 14, 2010); accessed July 10, 2012, at http://www
.educationworld.com/a_admin/admin/admin241.shtml.

77. Buder Elementary Schools, PowerPoint presentation; accessed
July 11, 2012, at http://slpses.schoolwires.net//site/Default.aspx?
PageType=6&SiteID=276&SearchString=home%20visits.

78. O. C. Moles, ed., "Personal Contacts," *Reaching All Families: Creating Family-Friendly Schools,* U.S. Department of Education,
Office of Educational Research and Improvement, August 1996
(updated January 8, 2002); available at http://www.ed.gov/pubs/
ReachFam/index.html.

79. *The Herald Sun*, "Business Leaders Get Involved in Durham
Schools," 2010; accessed July 10, 2012, at http://www.heraldsun
.com/view/full_story/3589884/article-Business-leaders-get-
involved-in-Durham-schools.

80. Business Wire, *Project L.E.A.N. Childhood Obesity Prevention
Program Shows Excellent Results at the End of Its Second Year,*
June 13, 2012; accessed July 10, 2012, at http://www.businesswire
.com/news/home/20120613006403/en/Project-L.E.A.N.-
Childhood-Obesity-Prevention-Program-Shows.

81. J. Carey, CUInsight Press Center, *APGFCU Partners with Bay View
Elementary School in North East*; accessed July 10, 2012,
at http://www.cuinsight.com/456/media/news/apgfcu_partners
_with_bay_view_elementary_school_in.html.

GLOSSARY

Accommodation The process of changing old methods and adjusting to new situations.

Active involvement The feature of Piaget's theory of cognitive development stating that children's active hands-on experiences with the physical world provide the foundations for a "minds-on" ability to think and learn.

Adult–child discourse A conversation between an adult/parent and a child.

Advocacy The act of engaging in strategies designed to improve the circumstances of children and families. Advocates move beyond their day-to-day professional responsibilities and work collaboratively to help others.

Alphabetic knowledge (AK) Knowledge of the names and sounds associated with printed letters.

Anecdotal record An informal assessment tool that gives a brief written description of a student's behavior during a single incident.

Antibias curriculum An approach that seeks to provide children with an understanding of social and behavioral problems related to prejudice and to provide them with the knowledge, attitude, and skills needed to combat prejudice.

Applied behavior analysis (ABA) The theory that behavior rewarded is more likely to be repeated than behavior ignored.

Approaches to learning Inclinations, dispositions, and learning styles necessary to interact effectively with the learning environment.

Assessment The process of collecting and recording information about children's development, learning, health, behavior, academic progress, need for special services, and attainment in order to make a variety of educational decisions about children and programs.

Assimilation The taking in of sensory data through experiences and impressions and incorporating them into existing knowledge.

Asthma A chronic inflammatory disorder of the airways.

Atelier A special area or studio in a Reggio Emilia school for creating projects.

Atelierista A Reggio Emilia teacher trained in visual arts who works with teachers and children.

Attachment An enduring emotional tie between a parent/caregiver and an infant that endures over time.

Attention deficit hyperactivity disorder (ADHD) The inability to maintain attention and constrain impulsivity, accompanied by the presence of hyperactivity.

Authentic assessment Assessment conducted through activities that require children to demonstrate what they know and are able to do; also referred to as performance-based assessment.

Autism spectrum disorder A neurological developmental disorder characterized by a deficit in communication and social interactions as well as by the presence of restricted and repetitive behaviors. It is considered a "spectrum" of disorders because different people can have very different symptoms, ranging from mild to severe.

Autonomy An Erikson concept that says as toddlers mature physically and mentally they want to do things by themselves with no outside help.

Balanced approach An approach to literacy in which there is a balance between whole-language methods and phonics instruction.

Basic trust An Erikson concept that involves trust, security, and basic optimism that an infant develops when nurtured and loved.

Behavior guidance A process by which teachers help all children learn to control and direct their behavior and become independent and self-reliant.

Benchmarks Statements that provide a description of student performance expected at specific grade levels, ages, or developmental levels. Benchmarks often are used in conjunction with standards.

Bias-free An environment, classroom setting, or program that is free of prejudicial behaviors.

Bilingual education Education in two languages (e.g., the student's native language and English).

Bipolar disorder A mood disorder involving cycles of depression and mania that are severe and often lead to impaired functioning.

Bonding A relationship between a parent and offspring that usually begins at the time of birth and that establishes the basis for an ongoing mutual attachment.

Bullying To treat abusively or affect by means of force or coercion.

Challenging environment A learning environment that provides achievable and "stretching" experiences for all children.

Checklist A list of behaviors or other traits used in informal assessment to identify children's skills and knowledge.

Child care Comprehensive care and education of young children outside their homes.

Child development The study of how children change over time from birth to age eight.

Child Development Associate (CDA) An individual who has successfully completed the CDA assessment process and has been awarded the CDA credential. CDAs are able to meet the specific needs of children and work with parents and other adults to nurture children's physical, social, emotional, and intellectual growth in a child development framework.

435

Childhood depression A disorder affecting as many as one in thirty-three children that can negatively impact feelings, thoughts, and behavior and can manifest itself with physical symptoms of illness.

Children with disabilities As defined by IDEA, children who need special education and related services because of mental retardation, hearing impairments, speech or language impairments, serious emotional disturbances, orthopedic impairments, autism, traumatic brain injury, other health impairments, or specific learning disabilities.

Chronosystem The environmental influences and events that influence children over their lifetimes, such as living in a technological age.

Circular response Behavior that typically begins to develop in early infancy, in which an infant's own actions cause the infant to react or when another person prompts the infant to try to repeat the original action; similar to a stimulus–response relationship.

Civil behavior In interactions with others, treating them well and, in turn, being treated well.

Classification The ability, developed during the concrete operations stage of cognitive development, to group things together according to their similar characteristics.

Cognitive sensory stimulation The process of providing appropriate sensory stimulation, which, in turn, supports cognitive development.

Cognitive theory Jean Piaget's proposition that children develop intelligence through direct experiences with the physical world. In this sense, learning is an internal (mental) process involving children's adapting new knowledge to what they already know.

Concrete operations Piaget's third stage of operational or logical thought, often referred to as the "hands-on" period of cognitive development because the ability to reason is based on tangible objects and real experiences.

Constructivism Theory that emphasizes the active role of children in developing their understanding and learning.

Constructivist process The continuous mental organizing, structuring, and restructuring of experiences, in relation to schemes of thought, or mental images, that result in cognitive growth.

Content knowledge Knowledge about the subjects (math, science, social studies, art, music, etc.) that teachers plan to teach.

Content standards Standards that are specified by content area and grade.

Critical periods Periods that represent a narrow window of time during which a specific part of the body is most vulnerable to the absence of stimulation or to environmental influences.

Culture A group's way of life, including basic values, beliefs, religion, language, clothing, food, and various practices.

Curriculum The subject matter taught; all of the experiences children have while in school.

Curriculum alignment The process of matching curriculum to the standards and tests that measure student achievement.

Data-driven instruction An approach to teaching in which analysis of assessment data drives the decisions about how to meet the instructional needs of each child.

Developmentally and culturally responsive practice (DCRP) Teaching methods that are sensitive and responsive to children's and families' developmental, cultural, and ethnic backgrounds and needs.

Developmentally appropriate practice (DAP) Teaching methods based on how children grow and develop and on individual and cultural differences.

Differentiated instruction (DI) Instruction that involves planning and teaching in response to the diverse needs of students so that all students within a classroom can learn effectively, regardless of differences in ability.

Dyslexia A learning disability characterized by difficulties in reading, spelling, writing, speaking, or listening, despite at least average intelligence.

Early childhood professional An educator who successfully teaches all children, promotes high personal standards, and continually expands his or her skills and knowledge.

Egocentric Centered on the self; an inability to see events from other people's perspectives.

Embedded instruction An approach to teaching that embeds lessons into naturally occurring classroom activities.

Entitlement programs Programs and services that children and families are entitled to because they meet the eligibility criteria.

Environmental theory A theory of language development stating that while the ability to acquire language might have a biological basis, the content of language is acquired from the child's environment.

Epilepsy A neurological disorder in which electrical discharges in the brain cause a seizure.

Equilibrium A state of balance between the cognitive processes of assimilation and accommodation, allowing children to successfully understand new data.

Ethical conduct Responsible behavior toward students and parents that allows you to be considered a professional.

Event sampling An informal assessment tool that focuses on a particular behavior during a particular event.

Exosystem The environments or settings in which children do not play an active role but which nonetheless influence their development.

Expanding horizons approach or expanding environments approach An approach to teaching social studies in which the student's world is the center of the initial units, with children at each grade level being exposed to a slowly widening environment.

Expressive language A readiness skill that includes the ability to articulate fluently, to communicate needs and ideas with teacher and peers, and to express oneself.

Formal assessment Assessment utilizing standardized tests that have set procedures and instruction for administration and have been normed, thus making it possible to compare a child's score with the scores of children who have already taken the same exam.

Free appropriate public education (FAPE) The requirement under IDEA that children must receive a free education suited to their age, maturity level, condition of disability, achievements, and parental expectations.

Healthy environment A learning environment that provides for children's physical and psychological health, safety, and sense of security.

HighScope educational model A constructivist educational model based on Piaget's cognitive development theory, providing realistic experiences geared to children's current stages of development.

High-stakes testing Using assessment tests to make important and often life-influencing decisions about children, such as whether to admit children into programs or promote them from one grade to the next.

Holophrases One-word sentences that toddlers use to communicate.

Home visitor program A program that involves visitation of children, parents, and other family members in their homes by trained personnel who provide information, training, and support.

Individualized education program (IEP) As required by IDEA, a written instruction plan for a child with a disability, assessing the child's needs and setting clear goals and objectives so that progress can be evaluated.

Individualized family service plan (IFSP) As required by IDEA, a plan created for infants and toddlers with disabilities and their families, specifying what services they will receive to help them reach their specific goals.

Infancy A child's first year of life.

Infant mental health The overall health and well-being of infants and young children in the context of family, school, and community relationships.

Informal assessment Assessment of students' learning, behavior, and development using means other than standardized tests.

Inquiry learning Involvement of children in activities and processes that lead to learning.

Integrated curriculum A curriculum in which one subject area is used to teach another.

Interpretation A three-step process that includes examining the information that has been gathered, organizing and drawing conclusions from that information, and making decisions about teaching based on the conclusions.

Interviewing An informal assessment tool by which observers and researchers obtain information about children by asking questions and engaging them in conversation.

Language experience approach (LEA) A reading instruction method that links oral and written language.

Learned helplessness A condition that can develop when children lose confidence in their abilities and, in effect, learn to feel that they are helpless.

Learning The acquisition of knowledge, behaviors, skills, and attitudes.

Learning centers Areas of the classroom specifically set up to promote student-centered, hands-on, active learning.

Learning disability A disorder in one or more of the basic psychological processes involved in understanding or using spoken or written language, which may manifest itself in an imperfect ability to listen, think, speak, read, write, and spell or to do mathematical calculations.

Learning style The way a child learns—specifically, how the child's environment, emotions, sociological needs, physical characteristics, and psychological inclinations come into play as he or she works to master new or difficult information or skills.

Least restrictive environment (LRE) As part of IDEA, the notion that a child with a disability should have the opportunity to be educated with children who are not disabled, to the greatest extent possible.

Linguistically diverse parents Parents whose English proficiency is minimal and who lack a comprehensive knowledge of the norms and social systems in the United States.

Literacy The ability to read, write, speak, and listen.

Locus of control The source of control over an individual's behavior; the locus may be external (controlled by others) or internal (within oneself). The goal of behavioral guidance is to help children learn that their locus of control is internal, that they are responsible for their own behavior.

Macrosystem The broader culture in which children live (absence or presence of democracy, societal violence, religious freedom, etc.), which influences their development.

Mastery-oriented attributions Personal characteristics that include trying hard, paying attention, determination, and stick-to-itiveness.

Mathematics disorder A learning disability characterized by decided lack of ability to calculate or comprehend mathematical problems.

Maturationist theory A theory of language development stating that language acquisition is innate in all children regardless of culture, and that speech production and other aspects of language will develop as children mature, according to built-in biological schedules.

Mesosystem The links or interactions between microsystems that influence children's development.

Microsystem The various environmental settings in which children spend their time (e.g., children in child care spend about thirty-three hours a week in the microsystem of child care).

Montessori method A system of early childhood education founded on the philosophy, procedures, and materials developed by Maria Montessori. Respect for the child is the cornerstone on which all other Montessori principles rest.

Moral development The process of developing culturally acceptable attitudes and behaviors, based on what society endorses and supports as right and wrong.

Motherese The distinctive way of adapting everyday speech to young children. *See also* parentese.

Multicultural awareness Appreciation for and understanding of people's culture, socioeconomic status, and gender.

Multicultural infusion A situation in which multicultural education permeates the curriculum to influence the way young children and teachers think about diversity issues.

Multiculturalism An approach to education based on the premise that all peoples in the United States should receive proportional attention in the curriculum.

Multiple intelligences Howard Gardner's concept that people can be "smart" in many different ways; those intelligences include verbal/linguistic, musical/rhythmic, mathematical/logical, visual/spatial, bodily/kinesthetic, interpersonal, intrapersonal, and naturalist.

Neural shearing The process of brain connections withering away when they are not used. *See also* pruning.

No Child Left Behind Act A landmark act in education reform designed to improve student achievement and change the culture of America's schools.

Obesity A condition characterized by excessive accumulation and storage of fat in the body.

Object permanence The concept that things out of sight continue to exist; this intellectual milestone typically begins to develop at four to eight months of age.

Observation The intentional, systematic act of looking at the behavior of a child or children in a particular setting, program, or situation; sometimes referred to as kid-watching.

Operation A reversible mental action.

Parent/family involvement A process of helping parents and family members use their abilities to benefit themselves, their children, and the early childhood program.

Parentese The distinctive way of adapting everyday speech to young children. *See also* motherese.

Pedagogical knowledge Knowledge about how to apply instructional practices in order to develop meaningful learning experiences for children.

Performance standards Specific examples of what students should know and do to demonstrate that they have mastered the knowledge and skills stated in content standards.

Pervasive developmental disorders (PDDs) A category of neurological disorders characterized by severe and pervasive impairment in several areas of development.

Philosophy of education A set of beliefs about how children develop and learn and what and how they should be taught.

Phonics instruction A teaching method that emphasizes letter–sound correspondence so children can learn to combine sounds into words.

Phonological awareness (PA) The ability to detect, manipulate, or analyze the auditory aspects of spoken language (including the ability to distinguish or segment words, syllables, or phonemes), independent of meaning.

Phonological memory (PM) The ability to remember spoken information for a short period of time.

Plastic Capable of adapting to conditions, such as the neurons in a child's brain, which are constantly arranging and rearranging connections to form neural pathways.

Play therapy A method that incorporates social experiences and enjoyable interactions into a therapeutic approach to working with children with developmental delays in order to enhance communication skills and other appropriate behavior.

Portfolio A compilation of children's work samples, other artifacts, and teacher observations collected over time.

Poverty The state of a person who lacks a usual or socially acceptable amount of money or material possessions.

Pre-kindergarten A class or program preceding kindergarten for children usually from three to four years old.

Preoperational stage The stage of cognitive development in which young children are not capable of mental representations.

Primary grades Grades one to three.

Private speech An internal conversation between a person and himself or herself. Also called self-discourse.

Professional dispositions The values, commitments, and professional ethics that influence behavior toward students, families, colleagues, and members of the community and affect student learning, motivation, and development as well as the educator's own professional growth.

Program standards Expectations that define the characteristics for quality in early childhood settings, centers, and schools.

Project approach An educational approach that encourages in-depth investigation by an individual student or small group of students, or even by the whole class, of a topic the students want to learn more about.

Pruning The process of brain connections withering away when they are not used. *See also* neural shearing.

Psychosocial development Erik Erikson's theory that cognitive and social development occur simultaneously and cannot be separated.

Rapid automatic naming (RAN) The ability to rapidly name a random sequence, such as a random sequence of letters, digits, colors, or pictures of objects.

Rating scale An informal assessment tool, usually a numeric scale, that contains a list of descriptors for a set of behaviors.

Readiness Being ready to learn; possessing the knowledge, skills, and abilities necessary for learning and for success in school.

Receptive language Language that a person "receives" or understands through spoken, written, or visual communication.

Reflective practice The active process of thinking before teaching, during teaching, and after teaching in order to make decisions about how to plan, assess, and teach.

Reggio Emilia approach An early childhood educational program named for the town in Italy where it originated. The method emphasizes a child's relationships with family, peers, teachers, and the wider community; small-group interaction; schedules set by the child's personal rhythms; and visual arts programs coordinated by a specially trained atelierista.

Research-based programs Programs based on scientific research that demonstrates they can increase student achievement. *See also* scientifically based programs.

Respectful environment A learning environment that shows respect for each individual child and his or her

culture, home language, individual abilities or disabilities, family context, and community.

Response to Intervention/Response to Instruction (RTI) A multitier approach to the early identification and support of students with learning and behavior needs; it evaluates assessment data and employs differentiated instruction, so that students who are struggling can receive more intense intervention.

Responsive relationship The relationship that exists between yourself, children, and their families where you are responsive to their needs and interests.

Reversibility The notion that actions can be reversed. Awareness of reversibility develops during the concrete operations stage of development.

Running record An informal assessment tool that provides a more detailed narrative of a child's behavior, focusing on a sequence of events that occur over a period of time.

Scaffolding Assistance or support of some kind from a teacher, parent, caregiver, or peer to help children complete tasks they cannot complete independently.

Scheme A unit of knowledge that a child develops through experience that defines how things should be.

Scientifically based programs Programs based on scientific research that demonstrates they can increase student achievement. *See also* research-based programs.

Screening The process of identifying the particular physical, social, linguistic, and cognitive needs of children in order to provide appropriate programs and services.

Screening procedures Procedures that give a broad picture of what children know and are able to do, as well as their physical and emotional status.

Self-actualization Abraham Maslow's theory of motivation based on the satisfaction of needs; Maslow maintained that children cannot achieve self-actualization until certain basic needs—including food, shelter, safety, and love—are met.

Self-discourse An internal conversation between a person and himself or herself. Also called private speech.

Self-regulation The ability of preschool children to control their emotions and behaviors, to delay gratification, and to build positive social relations with each other.

Sensitive periods Periods of development during which it is easier to learn something than it is at other times.

Sensorimotor stage The first of Piaget's stages of cognitive development, when children primarily use their senses and motor reflexes to develop intellectually.

Shared reading A teaching method in which the teacher and children read together from a book that is visible to all.

Sight word approach Also called whole-word or look-say, an approach to reading that involves presenting children with whole words so they develop a "sight vocabulary" as opposed to "sounding out" words using phonics.

Social constructivist approach A theory that says children construct or build their behavior as a result of learning from experience and from making decisions that lead to responsible behavior.

Social story A personalized, detailed, and simple script that breaks down behavior and provides rules and directions.

Standards Statements of what pre-K–12 students should know and be able to do.

Standards-based education (SBE) Curriculum, teaching, and testing based on local, state, and national standards.

Supportive environment A learning environment where professionals believe each child can learn and where they help children understand and make meaning of their experiences.

Symbolic language A readiness skill that involves knowing the names of people, places, and things; understanding that words represent concepts.

Symbolic representation The understanding, which develops at about age two, that something else can stand for a mental image; for example, a word can represent a real object or a concept.

Synaptogenesis The formation of connections, or synapses, among neurons; this process of brain development begins before birth and continues until age ten.

Technology The application of tools and information to make products and solve problems. With this definition, technology goes far beyond computers and video games, but the most common use of the term refers to electronic and digital applications.

Telegraphic speech Two-word sentences, such as "Go out" or "All gone," used by toddlers.

Temperament A child's general style of behavior.

Theory A statement of principles and ideas that attempts to explain events and how things happen.

Time sampling An informal assessment tool that records particular events or behaviors during specific, continuous time intervals, such as three or four five-minute periods during the course of a morning.

Title I A federal program designed to improve the basic skills (reading and mathematics) of low-ability children from low-income families.

Toddlerhood The period of a child's life between one and three years of age.

Tourette's syndrome A genetic neuropsychiatric disorder characterized by multiple physical and/or vocal tics.

Traditional assessment Assessment done with standardized tests or teacher-created tests, where students typically select an answer or recall facts, measuring how well children have learned specific information.

Transition A passage from one learning setting, grade, program, or experience to another.

Typically developing Reaching the majority of developmental milestones at the appropriate time and not presenting deficits in social areas.

Unfolding Rousseau's belief that the nature of children—who and what they will be—unfolds as a result of development according to their innate timetables.

Universal design The process of adapting teaching strategies and technology to make the learning environment, the curriculum, and the instruction methods accessible to each young child, regardless of physical limitations or learning disabilities.

Universal preschool The idea that all children and families should have access to public-supported preschools.

Universal public kindergarten The availability of kindergarten to all children.

Whole-language approach Philosophy of literacy development that advocates using all aspects of language—reading, writing, listening, and speaking—to help children become motivated to read and write.

Work sample An example of a child's work that demonstrates what the child knows and is able to do.

Zero reject principle A rule under IDEA that prohibits schools from excluding any student with a disability.

Zone of proximal development (ZPD) The range of tasks that children can perform with help from a more competent partner. Children can perform tasks below their ZPD on their own, but they are not yet able to learn tasks or concepts above their ZPD, even with help.

NAME/AUTHOR INDEX

SUBJECT INDEX